JOURNAL FOR THE STUDY OF THE NEW TESTAMENT
SUPPLEMENT SERIES
138

Sheffield Academic Press

Textual Optimism

A Critique of the United Bible Societies' Greek New Testament

Kent D. Clarke

Journal for the Study of the New Testament
Supplement Series 138

Dedicated to the Memory of Clint Holte, 1972–1994,
a simple man and close friend who taught me that one
can possess peace even in the midst of suffering...

Published by
Sheffield Academic Press Ltd
Mansion House
19 Kingfield Road
Sheffield S11 9AS
England

Typeset by Sheffield Academic Press
and
Printed on acid-free paper in Great Britain
by Bookcraft Ltd
Midsomer Norton, Bath

British Library Cataloguing in Publication Data

A catalogue record for this book is available
from the British Library

ISBN 1-85075-649-X

CONTENTS

ACKNOWLEDGMENTS

It is with some apprehension that I offer this work lest some feel I have been overly pessimistic in my assessment of the United Bible Societies' fourth edition of *The Greek New Testament*. However, let me express at the outset my sincere appreciation for the efforts of the *UBSGNT* Committee, members both past and present. They have without doubt, over the years, continued to produce one of the most useful critical editions of the Greek New Testament available. In many regards the *UBSGNT*[4], which reflects the extent of our modern text-critical methodology, deserves the right to be called the 'Standard Text'. However, the Committee states on page vi of the *UBSGNT*[4] that it is 'always genuinely grateful to readers for their proposals and suggestions'. I have taken this invitation to heart, and, therefore, offer this monograph as constructive criticism to a group of worthy and dedicated scholars.

Although every care has been taken to insure the accuracy of the statistics and calculations included in this work, it is improbable that an analysis of this nature can remain error free. For these shortcomings I alone shoulder the responsibility. Where errors or discrepancies have been found throughout the process of writing and later proofreading, every step has been taken to correct these. On some occasions this has involved painstakingly recalculating over and over again the figures for an entire section. At the same time, I am confident that any remaining oversights have little substantial effect upon the results.

I would like to express my gratitude to some who have helped me in the writing of this study. My mentor and friend, Professor Stanley E. Porter of Roehampton Institute London, was a constant source of support, whose editorial expertise turned the early draft into a publishable work. Professor Craig A. Evans of Trinity Western University, Vancouver, and Dr Larry Perkins of Northwest Baptist Seminary, Vancouver, read the early draft and provided both insightful comments and encouragement. Dr Kevin Bales, from the Sociology Department at Roehampton Institute London, offered oversight and patient assistance

Textual Optimism

in explaining the use and application of the Chi-square to a wary the-ologian, and Dr Eugene A. Nida wrote heartening correspondence on several difficult issues. To Eric Christianson, Doreen Pursglove, and the editors at Sheffield Academic Press, who, among other difficult tasks, labored over a considerable number of detailed charts and inconsistent lists, I would also like to express my gratitude. Finally, I am indebted to my wife, Lauren, for her encouragement, good humor, and wisdom.

CHARTS, TABLES AND LISTS

ABBREVIATIONS

ANRW	*Aufstieg und Niedergang der römischen Welt*
ATR	*Anglican Theological Review*
BETL	Biliotheca ephemeridum theologicarum lovaniensium
BSac	*Bibliotheca Sacra*
BT	*The Bible Translator*
EvQ	*Evangelical Quarterly*
ExpTim	*Expository Times*
FN	*Filología Neotestamentaria*
HTR	*Harvard Theological Review*
JBL	*Journal of Biblical Literature*
JETS	*Journal of the Evangelical Theological Society*
JSNT	*Journal for the Study of the New Testament*
Nestle-Aland	Nestle-Aland Novum Testamentum Graece
Nestle-Aland[26]	Nestle-Aland Novum Testamentum Graece Twenty-sixth Edition
Nestle-Aland[27]	Nestle-Aland Novum Testamentum Graece Twenty-seventh Edition
NovT	*Novum Testamentum*
NovTSup	*Novum Testamentum*, Supplements
NTS	*New Testament Studies*
NTTS	New Testament Tools and Studies
ResQ	*Restoration Quarterly*
SD	Studies and Documents
SJT	*Scottish Journal of Theology*
TLZ	*Theologische Literaturzeitung*
TR	Textus Receptus
TRev	*Theologische Revue*
UBS	United Bible Societies
UBSGNT	United Bible Societies' *Greek New Testament*
UBSGNT[1]	United Bible Societies' *Greek New Testament* First Edition
UBSGNT[2]	United Bible Societies' *Greek New Testament* Second Edition
UBSGNT[3]	United Bible Societies' *Greek New Testament* Third Edition
UBSGNT[3corr.]	United Bible Societies' *Greek New Testament* Third Corrected Edition
UBSGNT[4]	United Bible Societies' *Greek New Testament* Fourth Edition
WH	B.F. Westcott and F.J.A. Hort, *The New Testament in the Original Greek*

INTRODUCTION

Progress in the study of New Testament textual criticism inevitably makes it necessary to bring printed editions of the New Testament up to date at regular intervals. It is therefore not surprising that Nestle's text has undergone twenty-six revisions since 1898. Other texts have similarly been revised, including the United Bible Societies' *The Greek New Testament*, which first appeared in 1966. A second edition came out in 1968 and a third edition, containing a thorough revision of the Greek text and a partial revision of the apparatus, was published in 1975. We are told in the Preface to this edition that a fourth edition is under way in which the patristic and versional evidence in the apparatus will be thoroughly checked. The Greek text of this fourth edition is unlikely to be significantly changed.[1]

This monograph will investigate and compare each edition of the United Bible Societies' *Greek New Testament* (*UBSGNT*), in particular, the most recently published fourth edition.[2] The principal focus of this work will not be the *UBSGNT* text itself, but rather the textual apparatus, the rating of variants, and the changes to that apparatus and ratings within each version. I will seek to show that the *UBSGNT*[4] has introduced a remarkable change to the critical apparatus letter-ratings for a large number of variants, especially as compared to its earlier editions. I will also explore various reasons why these changes have occurred, whether they are justifiable, or whether the editors have been overly optimistic in revising the ratings of many textual variants and/or inconsistent in their standards for variant ratings within the *UBSGNT*[4]. Various statistics and

1. J.K. Elliott, 'The United Bible Societies' Greek New Testament: A Short Examination of the Third Edition', *BT* 30 (1979), p. 135.

2. The United Bible Society has now produced their *Greek New Testament* in five editions (the *UBSGNT*[3corr.], although almost identical to the *UBSGNT*[3], is included as one of these five editions). Hereafter they will be referred to as the *UBSGNT*[1], *UBSGNT*[2], *UBSGNT*[3], *UBSGNT*[3corr.], or the *UBSGNT*[4] according to the specific edition being cited. When a reference is being made to all the editions in general it is listed as the *UBSGNT*.

charts will be utilized in order to demonstrate the unusual degree of modification. Several of the more remarkable upgrades will be examined in specific detail, and the findings will be presented for these variants based upon recognized principles of New Testament textual criticism.

Chapter 1 examines both the history and theory of Westcott and Hort, and details the advancements made in the study of textual criticism since their day. These two areas of discussion directly relate to and act as the wellspring of the *UBSGNT*. They are essential to an understanding of the purpose and rationale behind each *UBSGNT* edition. Other considerations presented in this first chapter include: (1) a discussion concerning the need for a 'new' approach to textual criticism, (2) a brief presentation of each *UBSGNT* edition, and lastly, (3) the relationship of the *UBSGNT* to the Nestle-Aland *Novum Testamentum Graece*.

Chapter 2 provides the 'hard evidence' upon which the monograph is based. Through the use of statistical analysis of data offered in various charts, a critical comparison and evaluation of every variant within each *UBSGNT* edition is undertaken. The progression or digression of each variant rating is clearly revealed. On the basis of these charts and statistics, each variant is able to be evaluated at a glance. Its rating fluctuations, alterations, and appropriateness for study are readily observed. This chapter will also provide a statistical breakdown of each *UBSGNT* edition and the percentage of its *A*, *B*, *C*, and *D* evaluation of evidence letter-ratings. These letter-ratings are also used to create specific categories of variant fluctuation as observed throughout all *UBSGNT* editions together. This provides an even greater insight into the rating modifications. Chapter 2 verifies the thesis of this work and further reveals that there has indeed been an extensive modification to the *UBSGNT*[4] letter-ratings, thus sanctioning a much more certain text. Reasons for this modification are then explored.

Chapter 3 seeks to combine the theory of textual criticism with the 'hard data' gathered from Chapter 2. On the basis of this amalgamation, an evaluation of several of the more remarkable upgrades in the *UBSGNT*[4] are investigated. The results of this investigation are then compared with the *UBSGNT*[4] Editorial Committee's ratings in the text. This allows one to examine the letter-ratings and then to provide a more accurate rating based upon the rational eclectic method of textual criticism. As well as the upgrades being evaluated, it is essential to consider manuscript changes within each edition and for each variant under question. This gives more specific insight into whether the changes have been properly founded upon new manuscript evidence, or if the variant rating is in fact too highly upgraded and based upon inadequate manuscript changes. Through this final chapter one can see with even greater detail and clarity that: (1) the *UBSGNT*[4] Editorial Committee has indeed been too extreme in their ascribing of ratings to variant passages, and (2) they have also been inconsistent in their standards of variant ratings from one edition to the next. The specific variant passages under investigation are Lk. 19.25 and Acts 2.44.

Chapter 1

THE HISTORY OF THE UNITED BIBLE SOCIETIES' GREEK NEW TESTAMENT

1. *The Textual Tradition behind the UBSGNT*

Westcott and Hort and their History[1]
They have been hailed with honor:

> One who works in the textual criticism of the New Testament today is like a traveler in a far country where all the landmarks were made of clay and the rains were heavy. The old maps and road-guides are useless, for the fixed points have either vanished or been transformed. Those fixed points were erected by the epoch-making work of Westcott and Hort.[2]

And they have been scorned with contempt:

> Modern textual criticism is psychologically 'addicted' to Westcott and Hort. Westcott and Hort, in turn, were rationalists in their approach to the textual problem in the New Testament and employed techniques within which rationalism and every other kind of bias are free to operate. The result of it all is a methodological quagmire where objective controls on the conclusions of critics are nearly nonexistent. It goes without saying that no Bible-believing Christian who is willing to extend the implications of his faith to textual matters can have the slightest grounds for confidence in contemporary critical texts.[3]

Regardless of how they have been viewed, F.J.A. Hort and B.F. Westcott, along with perhaps C. von Tischendorf, have arguably been the most

---

1. In preparing this 'history' dealing with Westcott and Hort, two sources have been especially helpful: F. Pack, 'One Hundred Years Since Westcott and Hort: 1881–1981', *ResQ* 26 (1983), pp. 65-79; and G.A. Patrick, '1881–1981: The Centenary of the Westcott and Hort Text', *ExpTim* 92 (1981), pp. 359-64.

2. E.C. Colwell, 'The Complex Character of the Later Byzantine Text of the Gospels', *JBL* 54 (1935), p. 211.

3. Z.C. Hodges, 'Rationalism and Contemporary New Testament Textual Criticism', *BSac* 128 (1971), p. 35.

influential scholars in New Testament textual studies. Hort explains why he and Westcott began the work that would eventually shape the discipline of textual criticism from their day until the present:

> These facts justify, we think, another attempt to determine the original words of the Apostles and writers of the New Testament. In the spring of 1853 we were led by the perplexities of reading encountered in our own study of Scripture to project the construction of a text such as is now published. At that time a student aware of the untrustworthiness of the 'Received' texts had no other guides than Lachmann's text and the second of the four widely different texts of Tischendorf. Finding it impossible to assure ourselves that either editor placed before us such an approximation to the apostolic words as we could accept with reasonable satisfaction, we agreed to commence at once the formation of a manual text for our own use, hoping at the same time that it might be of service to others.[4]

Who were these men whose names will long be remembered for the overthrow of the 'Received' text, or the Textus Receptus?[5] In order that they might prepare for ministry in the Church of England, both men attended Cambridge University. It was here at Trinity College that their lifelong friendship began to form. However, as young scholars, each moved on to other endeavors. Westcott (1825–1901) taught at the distinguished Harrow public school and was then chosen to serve at Peterborough Cathedral in eastern England. He later became Regius Professor of Divinity at Cambridge, and, in 1890, was appointed Bishop of Durham. Hort (1828–1892) spent thirteen years as a parish priest in rural Hertfordshire. He too would later return to teach at Cambridge as a Fellow of Trinity College and finally received the position of Lady Margaret Professor.

While teaching at Cambridge, these two, along with close friend J.B. Lightfoot, would form the Cambridge Triumvirate (as they came to

---

4. B.F. Westcott and F.J.A. Hort, *Introduction to the New Testament in the Original Greek* (Peabody, MA: Hendrickson, 1988), p. 16. Reprinted from the edition originally published by Harper and Brothers, New York, 1882.

5. Two brothers from the Elzevir family of Holland published seven editions of the Greek New Testament between 1624 and 1678. Their text relied heavily upon Erasmus's text. It was these two brothers who coined the phrase 'Textus Receptus', or 'Received Text', which was later used to refer to the hastily produced edition of Erasmus and all the followers who adopted his type of text. The Elzevir brothers in their second edition, published in 1633, stated optimistically 'Textum ergo habes nunc ab omnibus receptum' (You have therefore the *text received* by all, in which we give nothing altered or corrupt); thus the name 'Textus Receptus'.

be known).[6] Together, they would produce a remarkable series of New Testament commentaries, and would also labor on the Revised Version of the New Testament. However, neither of these two endeavors would overturn the scholarly community of their day as did their work in textual criticism.

When their work on the text of the Greek New Testament began in 1853, Westcott was at Harrow, and Hort at Trinity. Both felt their task would last only two or three years. In fact, it continued on for almost three decades. Correspondence carried on between the two men from 1853 until 1870. They periodically met together to discuss their research. Then, when together at Cambridge from 1870, they worked untiringly to finish their project. As B.M. Metzger notes, the year 1881 marked the publication of the most noteworthy critical edition of the Greek New Testament ever produced by British scholarship.[7] After working about twenty-eight years on this edition (1853–1881) Westcott and Hort issued two volumes entitled *The New Testament in the Original Greek*. The first volume came out on 12 May 1881 and contained the Greek text. The second volume was released on 4 September and included an introduction written by Hort, in which he detailed the method Westcott and he had followed in arriving at their Greek text. An appendix containing a very detailed examination of a great number of variants and notes on selected readings was also included in this second volume (with 425 of these notes containing a discussion regarding the choice of text made by Westcott and Hort). E.C. Colwell comments on this Greek edition and particularly the contributions of Hort:

> In that day he presented a carefully reasoned account of textual criticism that was comprehensive in its discussion of method, in its reconstruction of the history of the manuscript tradition, and in its appraisal of text-types. He did not try to be comprehensive in his discussion of the *materials* of textual criticism. He published no catalogue of manuscripts. He cited no manuscript evidence in a critical apparatus. But, having studied the

6. Pack states that 'Westcott, Hort, and J.B. Lightfoot were men of very congenial mind, who worked together in support and help of one another'. See Pack, 'One Hundred Years', p. 66. For an excellent discussion concerning Lightfoot, Westcott, and Hort, see S. Neill and T. Wright, *The Interpretation of the New Testament: 1861–1986* (Oxford/New York: Oxford University Press, 2nd edn, 1988), pp. 35-40, 74-81, and 92-103.

7. B.M. Metzger, *The Text of the New Testament: Its Transmission, Corruption, and Restoration* (New York/Oxford: Oxford University Press, 3rd edn, 1992), p. 129.

evidence that others had accumulated, he applied to its interpretation the powers of a great intellect, and, with the help of his collaborator, produced the best edition of the Greek New Testament that we possess.[8]

Various authors comment on the personality and outlook of both men. Hort was a trained scientist, a keen botanist, a geologist, and thought to be a perfectionist. The detail of textual work appealed more to him than to Westcott. It is said that Hort was the bolder of the two men and also the more open-minded. He believed strongly that the Christian was a defender of unpopular causes and issues and that one must stand up for these despite opposition. These traits would explain why some writers note that Hort was one of the first theologians to support Charles Darwin and the theory of evolution.[9] It was Hort who believed that he and Westcott must pursue their textual revision no matter what opposition confronted them. Although Westcott often helped his friend to keep a sense of proportion in their work, as time went on, it was Westcott who usually needed to be encouraged. Undoubtedly, Westcott found the task of textual criticism tedious and wearisome. Revealing is an oft-quoted letter dated 7 May 1862 (almost twenty years before the completion of the project) from Westcott to Hort, expressing real doubts as to the value of their work, and Westcott's growing impatience in the minute detail it required:

> Generally, indeed, I feel very great repugnance to the whole work of revision. I do not see my way to a positive result nearly so clearly as I once did. Perhaps I think that the result of labor is wholly unequal to the cost, and indeed too often worthless. It is impossible to treat the Text mechanically, and equally impossible to enter as one could wish into the subtle points of interpretation which often arise. I cannot express to you the positive dislike—I want a stronger term—with which I took on all details of spelling and breathing and form. How you will despise me! but I make the frank confession nevertheless, and am quite prepared to abide by it.[10]

In reply, Hort confided in Westcott that he, too, had off-days. He then went on to encourage his friend in the value of their project: 'The work

---

8.   E.C. Colwell, 'Hort Redivivus: A Plea and a Program', in his *Studies in Methodology in Textual Criticism of the New Testament* (NTTS; Leiden: Brill, 1969), p. 148.

9.   See Patrick, '1881–1981', p. 362.

10.   A. Westcott, *Life and Letters of Brooke Foss Westcott* (London: Macmillan, 1903), I, p. 281. For this same citation see, among others, R.L. Omanson, 'A Perspective on the Study of the New Testament Text', *BT* 34 (1983), p. 110.

has to be done, and never can be done satisfactorily without vast labor, a fact of which hardly anybody in Europe except ourselves seems conscious... It would, I think, be utterly unpardonable for us to give up our task...'[11]

In 1869, another exchange of views took place between the two men. This time it was regarding the 'Introduction' and 'Appendix' to their work. While Westcott urged brevity in the Introduction, feeling that few would read it, Hort, on the other hand, stressed the need for detail in their explanation. Hort claimed that even if only a few read it, it was important that readers be instructed. Later, Westcott asked Hort to do the Appendix as well. He expressed the wish that this, too, should be much briefer than Hort suggested, and claimed that he was not prepared to do the work himself, especially on such a large scale.[12]

Another aspect that Westcott and Hort faced as they continued in their endeavors was the wall of antagonism and hostility with which they were confronted:

> The forceful attack upon their work, and upon the Revised Version which relied considerably on their work, by Dean Burgon and others in the years 1881–3 is a reminder of the reverence accorded to the Textus Receptus by a large number of Scholars at that time. Westcott and Hort were challenging the orthodoxy of their day. They were aware of critical and prejudiced eyes upon them as they progressed on their project and we should not underestimate the courage it required to see the work through.[13]

Indeed, in one further letter to a friend, dated November 1864, Hort explains: 'I do not know that I am greatly alarmed at the charge of heresy about the text personally. Nobody in their senses likes it, I suppose; but I hardly remember when I have felt myself anything else but a

11. A.F. Hort, *Life and Letters of Fenton John Anthony Hort* (London: Macmillan, 1896), I, p. 455.

12. Contained in unpublished letters at Cambridge University Library, CUL Add MS 6597 (June, July, 1869). Also cited by Patrick, '1881–1981', pp. 362-63.

13. Patrick, '1881–1981', p. 363. Metzger describes John W. Burgon (1813–1888), Dean of Chichester, as '"a High-churchman of the old school" who became notorious as "a leading champion of lost causes and impossible beliefs; but the vehemence of his advocacy somewhat impaired its effects". His conservatism can be gauged from a sermon he preached at Oxford in 1884 in which he denounced the higher education of "young women as young men" as "a thing inexpedient and immodest"; the occasion was the admission of women to university examinations!' Metzger, *The Text of the New Testament*, p. 135.

predestined heretic in the eyes of others'.[14] Even close companion Lightfoot wrote to Hort in August 1870, apparently concerned with the radical nature of Hort's and Westcott's proposals. In this letter, Lightfoot requested of Hort that he include some type of reassuring paragraph that would downplay the changes they were making in the text. Hort's response was significant: 'My own impression is that it is not possible to write such a reassuring paragraph as you propose without danger of mis-apprehension'.[15] He went on to affirm that in no way could their text be regarded as a conservative revision of the Textus Receptus. Hort was unwilling to apologize for the radical nature of his and Westcott's work—even to a close friend.

In the midst of all this debate, however, Westcott and Hort found their Greek text, as well as their methodology, gaining respect and prestige among scholars. Thus, after thirty years of labor, a new era was marked by the toppling of the Textus Receptus. Their epoch-making book concludes with these words:

> It only remains to express an earnest hope that whatever labor we have been allowed to contribute towards the ascertainment of the truth of the letter may also be allowed, in ways which must for the most part be invisible to ourselves, to contribute towards strengthening, correcting, and extending human apprehension of the larger truth of the Spirit. Others assuredly in due time will prosecute the task with better resources of knowledge and skill, and amend the faults and defects of our processes and results. To be faithful to such light as could be enjoyed in our own day was the utmost that we could desire. How far we have fallen short of the standard, we are well aware: yet we are bold to say that none of the shortcomings are due to lack of anxious and watchful sincerity. An implicit confidence in all truth, a keen sense of its variety, and a deliberate dread of shutting out truth as yet unknown are no security against some of the wandering lights that are apt to beguile a critic: but, in so far as they are obeyed, they at least quenched every inclination to guide criticism into delivering such testimony as may be to the supposed advantage of truth already inherited or acquired. Critics of the Bible, if they have been taught by the Bible, are unable to forget that the duty of guileless workmanship is never superseded by any other. From Him who is at once the supreme Fountain of truth and the all-wise Lord of its uses they have received both

14. Contained in unpublished letters at Cambridge University Library, CUL Add MS 6597 (June, July, 1869). Also cited by Patrick, '1881–1981', p. 363; and Omanson, 'A Perspective', p. 110.

15. In the Lightfoot Correspondence, Chapter Library, Durham. Also cited by Patrick, '1881–1981', p. 363.

the materials of knowledge and the means by which they are wrought into knowledge: into His hands, and His alone, when the working is over, must they render back that which they have first and last received.

ΕΞ ΑΥΤΟΥ ΚΑΙ ΔΙ ΑΥΤΟΥ ΚΑΙ ΕΙΣ ΑΥΤΟΝ ΤΑ ΠΑΝΤΑ.
ΑΥΤΩ Η ΔΟΞΑ ΕΙΣ ΤΟΥΣ ΑΙΩΝΑΣ.
ΑΜΗΝ.[16]

Westcott and Hort and their Theory

The work of Lachmann, Tischendorf, and their predecessors set the stage for an epochal event in the history of New Testament textual criticism, the publication in 1881 of *The New Testament In The Original Greek*, by B.F. Westcott and F.J.A. Hort. They contributed, in addition to a new edition of the Greek text, a fundamental statement of methodological principles upon which it was based and a reconstruction of the history of the text. While new discoveries (especially the papyri) have led contemporary textual critics to lay aside Westcott and Hort's historical reconstruction, their methodology was so sound and insightful that these same discoveries have essentially confirmed their edition of the text. So significant was their work that whereas it overshadows all previous efforts to recover the original text, almost all fundamental progress since then has in some way been built upon or in relation to their foundation.[17]

It would be erroneous to assume that Westcott and Hort acted independently of others in the establishment of their new methodology and subsequent Greek text. Both previous and contemporary scholars influenced Westcott and Hort, making their insights possible and work conceivable. Earlier, the German scholar J.J. Griesbach had published his Greek Testament, including a great mass of evidence from the ancient versions and Church Fathers. In 1831, K. Lachmann, a German classical scholar, brought out the first edition that rejected the Textus Receptus. Tischendorf, the greatest discoverer and student of ancient biblical manuscripts in the nineteenth century, was concurrently carrying on his work. And the English scholar, S.P. Tregelles, tirelessly traveled and collated manuscripts, correcting old errors and publishing his Greek Testament consisting of six parts, between 1857 and 1872. As Metzger comments, men such as these formed an essential link to the efforts of Westcott and Hort:

16. Westcott and Hort, *Introduction*, pp. 323-24. Rom. 11.36: 'From Him and through Him and to Him are all things. To Him be the glory forever. Amen.'
17. M.W. Holmes, 'Textual Criticism', in D.A. Black and D.S. Dockery (eds.), *New Testament Criticism and Interpretation* (Grand Rapids: Zondervan, 1991), p. 111.

> Unlike earlier editors, neither Westcott nor Hort was concerned to collate
> manuscripts, nor did they provide a critical apparatus. Rather, utilizing
> previous collections of variant readings, they refined the critical method-
> ology developed by Griesbach, Lachmann, and others, and applied it rig-
> orously, but with discrimination, to the witnesses to the text of the New
> Testament.[18]

In the classic 'Introduction' of Westcott and Hort's work, Hort set out
the theories upon which their Greek text is based. Patrick calls the introduction a 'masterpiece of English prose, concise, lucid, and unemo-
tional'.[19] S. Neill states that the Introduction was 'written in a cool,
judicious, perfectly lucid prose; so orderly, so closely connected, so
unadorned, so concentrated, that it is almost impossible to abridge or
summarize them, and almost any passage could be quoted in illustration
of the tone and method of the whole'.[20] Hort isolates four methods of
determining the correct variant reading when there are several alternatives available. He introduces the minor methods first, and then turns to
the 'higher methods' as he calls them. The first of these minor methods
is *Internal Evidence of Readings*:

> The most rudimentary form of criticism consists in dealing with each
> variation independently, and adopting at once in each case out of two or
> more variants that which looks most probable. The evidence here taken
> into account is commonly called 'Internal Evidence'... more precisely
> 'Internal Evidence of Readings'. Internal Evidence of Readings is of two
> kinds, which cannot be too sharply distinguished from each other; appeal-
> ing respectively to Intrinsic Probability, having reference to the author,
> and what may be called Transcriptional Probability, having reference to
> the copyists. In appealing to the first, we ask what an author is likely to
> have written: in appealing to the second, we ask what copyists are likely
> to have made him seem to write.[21]

Intrinsic Probability takes into consideration the author and such things
as his grammatical usage and vocabulary, his writing style, his theology,
and both the immediate and larger contexts of his writing. *Transcriptional Probability* focuses upon the scribe or copyist and considers
aspects such as the reading that best explains the rise of the others,
clerical or mechanical corruption arising from scribal carelessness or
deception of the eye or ear, and mental factors occasioning error.

18. Metzger, *The Text of the New Testament*, p. 129.
19. Patrick, '1881–1981', p. 360.
20. Neill and Wright, *Interpretation*, p. 77.
21. Westcott and Hort, *Introduction*, pp. 19-20.

Transcriptional Probability often points to the more difficult or shorter reading as authentic, for, as Hort states: 'Mere blunders apart, no motive can be thought of which could lead a scribe to introduce consciously a worse reading in place of a better'.[22] It is when both Intrinsic and Transcriptional Probabilities are in agreement that '[I]nternal Evidence of Readings attains the highest degree of certainty which its nature admits...'.[23] However, this agreement is not always the case: 'Where one reading (a) appears intrinsically preferable, and its excellence is of a kind that we might expect to be recognized by scribes, while its rival (b) shews no characteristic likely to be attractive to them, Intrinsic and Transcriptional Probability are practically in conflict'.[24] In view of the evident difficulty, Westcott and Hort supplemented this first method with a second.

Hort terms his and Westcott's second principle *Internal Evidence of Documents*. Here the emphasis is placed upon the actual individual documents themselves, rather than individual readings. To enhance and verify the decisions made in conjunction with the Internal Evidence of Readings, the text critic must look upon the comparative value of the documents holding each variant reading. Therefore, one asks which entire document is more credible and trustworthy, rather than evaluating one individual reading after another. As Hort states, one of the most valuable means of determining manuscript reliability lies in the determining of manuscript age:

> The most prominent fact known about a manuscript is its date, sometimes fixed to a year by a note from the scribe's hand, oftener determined within certain limits by paleographical or other indirect indications, sometimes learned from external facts or records. Relative date... affords a valuable presumption as to relative freedom from corruption...[25]

Hort goes on to summarize Internal Evidence of Documents:

> Where then one of the documents is found habitually to contain these morally certain or at least strongly preferred readings, and the other habitually to contain their rejected rivals, we can have no doubt, first, that the text of the first has been transmitted in comparative purity, and that the text of the second has suffered comparatively large corruption; and next, that the superiority of the first must be as great in the variations in which

22. Westcott and Hort, *Introduction*, p. 22.
23. Westcott and Hort, *Introduction*, p. 29.
24. Westcott and Hort, *Introduction*, p. 29.
25. Westcott and Hort, *Introduction*, p. 31.

Internal Evidence of Readings has furnished no decisive criterion as in those which have enabled us to form a comparative appreciation of the two texts. By this cautious advance from the known to the unknown we are enabled to deal confidently with a great mass of those remaining variations, open variations, so to speak, the confidence being materially increased when, as usually happens, the document thus found to have the better text is also the older.[26]

Again, as Hort expresses it: 'KNOWLEDGE OF DOCUMENTS SHOULD PRECEDE FINAL JUDGMENT UPON READINGS'.[27]

Hort recognizes weaknesses and limitations within this second method as well. For example, what does one do if two trustworthy manuscripts conflict, or if each document supports an opposing reading? In the light of these questions, Hort proposes that one must investigate not only individual manuscripts, but possible relationships of genealogy that might exist between manuscripts. This leads to his and Westcott's third method called *Genealogical Evidence*:[28]

The first great step in rising above the uncertainties of Internal Evidence of Readings was taken by ceasing to treat Readings independently of each other, and examining them connectedly in series, each series being furnished by one of the several Documents in which they are found. The second great step, at which we have now arrived, consists in ceasing to treat Documents independently of each other, and examining them connectedly as parts of a single whole in virtue of their historical relationships.[29]

In explaining Genealogical Evidence, Hort states that documents are not independent, but are in fact closely related to each other like a family history or family tree:

---

26. Westcott and Hort, *Introduction*, pp. 32-33.

27. Westcott and Hort, *Introduction*, p. 31 (small caps appear in original).

28. The proposal of the 'Genealogical Evidence' theory by Westcott and Hort further shows their reliance upon the work of other individuals. An earlier form of this theory was developed as the basis for preparing a text in the editing of classical works, rather than biblical works. Three German scholars, F. Wolf, I. Bekker, and K. Lachmann, were influential in developing this early version of Westcott and Hort's theory. In turn, Westcott and Hort have been criticized for basing their theory upon methodology that was first meant for application upon the 'far from divinely inspired classical works'. For criticism of this nature, see the articles by Hodges, 'Rationalism', pp. 29-30; and *idem*, 'Modern Textual Criticism and the Majority Text: A Response', *JETS* 21 (1978), p. 145.

29. Westcott and Hort, *Introduction*, p. 39.

> [B]y the nature of the case they are all fragments, usually casual and scattered fragments, of a genealogical tree of transmission, sometimes of vast extent and intricacy. The more exactly we are able to trace the chief ramifications of the tree, and to determine the places of the several documents among the branches, the more secure will be the foundations laid for a criticism capable of distinguishing the original text from its successive corruptions. It may be laid down then emphatically, as a second principle, that ALL TRUSTWORTHY RESTORATION OF CORRUPTED TEXTS IS FOUNDED ON THE STUDY OF THEIR HISTORY, that is, of the relations of descent or affinity which connect the several documents.[30]

Hort then gives an illustration of ten manuscripts where nine agree against one. The natural tendency is to take the numerically dominant manuscripts over the odd one out. If, however, it is found that the nine have a common original, then the numerical dominance is no longer important. Both groups of manuscripts have equal validity in attesting to the early autographs, regardless of number. It is the presence of 'mixed' or 'conflate' readings within manuscripts that serve as the most valuable means for determining genealogy. 'Conflate' readings are readings that have derived from a combination of other readings that existed previously in separate manuscripts. Hort explains:

> The clearest evidence for tracing the antecedent factors of mixture in texts is afforded by readings which are themselves mixed or, as they are sometimes called, 'conflate', that is, not simple substitutions of the reading of one document for that of another, but combinations of the readings of both documents into a composite whole, sometimes by mere addition with or without a conjunction, sometimes with more or less of fusion. Where we find a variation with three variants, two of them simple alternatives to each other, and the third a combination of the other two, there is usually a strong presumption that the third is the latest and due to mixture, not the third the earliest and the other two due to two independent impulses of simplification.[31]

It is Genealogical Evidence that Westcott and Hort deem most important of all in determining the correct reading. They claim that it is unwise to reject any reading that is clearly supported by it.

The fourth and final method introduced by Westcott and Hort is entitled *Internal Evidence of Groups*. This technique lies between Internal Evidence of Documents and Genealogical Evidence. We have already seen the importance of determining the general traits of a given

---

30. Westcott and Hort, *Introduction*, pp. 39-40.
31. Westcott and Hort, *Introduction*, p. 49.

manuscript. Again, this is accomplished by observing how often that manuscript supports or rejects readings that have already been evaluated individually on the basis of the first method presented—Internal Probability. So too, it is necessary to understand the general traits of a given group of manuscripts in order that they may be compared with other groups. Hort elucidates on the entire principle:

> We have reserved for this place the notice of another critical resource which is in some sense intermediate between Internal Evidence of Documents and Genealogical Evidence, but which in order of discovery would naturally come last... Just as we can generalize the characteristics of any given MS by noting successively what readings it supports and rejects, (each reading having previously been the subject of a tentative estimate of Internal Evidence of Readings, Intrinsic and Transcriptional) and by classifying the results, so we can generalize the characteristics of any given group of documents by similar observations on the readings which it supports and rejects, giving special attention to those readings in which it stands absolutely or virtually alone.[32]

Hort continues to explain that the validity of this final method 'depends on the genealogical principle that community of reading implies community of origin',[33] or, to simplify the statement, if any given group of manuscripts displays a succession of readings, a common ancestor must lie behind all the manuscripts of that group. Generalizations that result in an exploration of Internal Evidence of Groups assist the critic in making decisions in instances where mixture within manuscripts makes it difficult to calculate the genealogical tree.

As Westcott and Hort applied these four methods to the New Testament text, they identified four principal text-types. The first was called the *Syrian* or *α Text* (also called the 'Byzantine', 'Koine', 'Antiochian', or 'Ecclesiastical' text).[34] This text, which is seen in its most recent form as the Textus Receptus, is the latest of the four text-types. Two factors in

32. Westcott and Hort, *Introduction*, p. 60.
33. Westcott and Hort, *Introduction*, p. 60.
34. Several of the names for this text-type come from other textual critics such as H. von Soden (Koine), K. Lake (Ecclesiastical), and J.H. Ropes (Antiochian). See von Soden's *Die Schriften des Neuen Testaments in ihrer ältesten erreichbaren Textgestalt* (Göttingen: Vandenhoeck & Ruprecht; vol. I, 1902–10; vol. II, 1913); Lake's *The Text of the New Testament* (ed. Silva New; London: Rivingtons, 6th rev. edn, 1928); and lastly Ropes's *The Text of Acts* in F.J. Foakes, F. Jackson and K. Lake (eds.), *The Beginnings of Christianity: Part I, The Acts of the Apostles* (5 vols.; London: Macmillan, 1926), III.

particular indicate that this text is furthest removed from the original autographs, and, therefore, the least valuable of the four: (1) it is absent from any quotations from Church Fathers prior to 350 CE; (2) it has a large number of conflate readings (again, these are readings that are derived from a combination of other readings that existed previously in separate manuscripts).[35] Hort proposed that this text was the result of a deliberate recension of the three earlier texts made by one or more editors desiring to produce a smooth, understandable, and complete text. Hort comments on the Syrian text:

> To state in few words the results of examination of the whole body of Syrian readings, distinctive and non-distinctive, the authors of the Syrian

---

35. The use of the phrases 'original autographs' or 'original manuscripts' throughout this monograph needs to be clarified. It has been stated that the primary goal of textual criticism is to recover a text as close to the original autographs as possible. Westcott and Hort clearly defined their task in a similar manner by stating that the goal of their Introduction constituted '... an attempt to present exactly the original words of the New Testament, so far as they can now be determined from surviving documents': Westcott and Hort, *Introduction*, p. 1. However, statements such as this may possibly oversimplify the matter. More recent work by scholars suggests that there is strong evidence revealing a mixture and intermingling of both written and oral traditions within the early church. Some would even assert, at least within the Gospel traditions, that there never was only one original autograph, but rather a number of traditions, both written and oral, that competed for the position of prominence throughout this early period. See, for example, N.A. Dahl, 'The Passion Narrative in Matthew', in his *Jesus in the Memory of the Early Church* (Minneapolis, MN: Augsburg, 1976), pp. 37-51. For the Pauline epistles, a number of scholars have claimed that all our extant manuscript evidence bears witness to these works in their later collected form of around 100 CE, and not in their earlier, pre-canonized and pre-collected form. See works such as G. Zuntz, *The Text of the Epistles: A Disquisition upon the Corpus Paulinum* (Schweich Lectures, 1946; London: British Academy, 1953), pp. 278-79. Finally, in view of what has already been discussed, the more recent discoveries of the Bodmer and Beatty papyri indicate: (1) that the Egyptian text-type of the great fourth-century uncials dates back to at least 200 CE, (2) that the Western text-type holds more value than first ascribed to it by Westcott and Hort, and (3) that the Byzantine text is represented by readings dating back as early as the second and third century. Because of these points, some textual critics claim it is difficult, if not impossible (1) to construct an adequate history of the New Testament text prior to 200 CE, and (2) to reconstruct the text of the original autographs based on a 'neutral' text. Instead, for some scholars, the goal becomes the reconstruction of the best received text of the apostolic age or somewhat later. It is with this discussion and ongoing debate in mind that the term 'original autographs', and similar terms, are used throughout this work.

text had before them documents representing at least three earlier forms of text, Western, Alexandrian, and a third. Where they found variation, they followed different procedures in different places. Sometimes they transcribed unchanged the reading of one of the earlier texts, now of this, now of that. Sometimes they in like manner adopted exclusively one of the readings, but modified its form. Sometimes they combined the readings of more than one text in various ways, pruning or modifying them if necessary. Lastly, they introduced many changes of their own where, so far as appears, there was no previous variation.[36]

Hort claimed that this recension took place in Antioch, the capital of Syria (thus the name 'Syrian') in the latter part of the fourth century. The text was then carried to Constantinople where it circulated throughout the entire Byzantine empire.[37] The Syrian text is best illustrated in manuscripts such as Codex Alexandrinus (A02), the later uncial manuscripts, and a large number of minuscules. Hort's classic description of the Syrian text is to the point:

The qualities which the authors of the Syrian text seem to have most desired to impress on it are lucidity and completeness. They were evidently anxious to remove all stumbling-blocks out of the way of the ordinary reader, so far as this could be done without recourse to violent measures. They were apparently equally desirous that he should have the benefit of instructive matter contained in all the existing texts, provided it did not confuse the context or introduce seeming contradictions. New omissions accordingly are rare, and where they occur are usually found to contribute to apparent simplicity. New interpolations on the other hand are abundant, most of them being due to harmonistic or other assimilation, fortunately capricious and incomplete. Both in matter and in diction the Syrian text is conspicuously a full text. It delights in pronouns, conjunctions, and expletives and supplied links of all kinds, as well as in more considerable additions. As distinguished from the bold vigor of the 'Western' scribes, and the refined scholarship of the Alexandrians, the spirit of its own corrections is at once sensible and feeble. Entirely blameless on either literary or religious grounds as regards vulgarized or unworthy diction, yet shewing no marks of either critical or spiritual insight, it presents the New Testament in a form smooth and attractive, but appreciably impoverished in sense and force, more fitted for cursory perusal or recitation than for repeated and diligent study.[38]

36. Westcott and Hort, *Introduction*, pp. 116-17.
37. Westcott and Hort, *Introduction*, pp. 135-46.
38. Westcott and Hort, *Introduction*, pp. 134-35.

In the light of the above observations, Westcott and Hort considered the Syrian text the least valuable text for determining the words of the original autographs. Hort states that 'all distinctively Syrian readings may be set aside at once as certainly originating after the middle of the third century, and therefore, as far as transmission is concerned, corruptions of the apostolic text'.[39]

The second text-type proposed by Westcott and Hort was termed the *Western* or *δ Text*. This text came into existence much earlier than the Syrian text, perhaps around the middle of the second century. It was first used by the Syriac-speaking church around Edessa, but was later brought to the West where it is preserved in manuscripts like Codex Bezae (D05), Codex Claromontanus (D06), the Old Latin versions, the Curetonian Syriac, and various Latin Fathers such as Cyprian, Hippolytus, Irenaeus, Justin, Marcion, Tatian, and Tertullian. Its most prominent characteristics are paraphrase and additions. Despite its early origin, Westcott and Hort had a low regard for this text-type due to its tendency towards paraphrase, additions, and harmonization of divergent passages. Because both men agreed that the shorter text was usually closer to the original, they regarded the expanded Western readings with suspicion. Only nine passages from the Western text were considered to follow more closely the original documents above any other text-type. This was due to their shorter readings (Mt. 27.49; Lk. 22.19-20; 24.3, 6, 12, 36, 40, 51, and 52).[40] Westcott and Hort called these readings 'Western Non-Interpolations' meaning that 'the original record has here, to the best of our belief, suffered interpolation in all the extant Non-Western texts'.[41] Various other similar passages in the Gospels, although acting, in the words of Hort, as 'an intermediate class of Western omissions' were not to be ruled out.[42] Again, Hort comments upon the intricate characteristics of the Western text:

> The chief and most constant characteristic of the Western readings is a love of paraphrase. Words, clauses, and even whole sentences were changed, omitted, and inserted with astonishing freedom, wherever it

39. Westcott and Hort, *Introduction*, p. 117.
40. Westcott and Hort, *Introduction*, pp. 175-76. For more clarification on these Western non-interpolations, see the discussion which follows under the Neutral Text-Type.
41. Westcott and Hort, *Introduction*, p. 175.
42. For further discussion of these Western readings, see Westcott and Hort, *Introduction*, p. 176.

seemed that the meaning could be brought out with greater force and definiteness. They often exhibit a certain rapid vigor and fluency which can hardly be called a rebellion against the calm and reticent strength of the apostolic speech, for it is deeply influenced by it, but which, not less than a tamer spirit of textual correction, is apt to ignore pregnancy and balance of sense, and especially those meanings which are conveyed by exceptional choice or collocation of words... Another equally important characteristic is a disposition to enrich the text at the cost of its purity by alterations or additions taken from traditional and perhaps from apocryphal or other non-biblical sources... Besides these two marked characteristics, the Western readings exhibit the ordinary tendencies of scribes whose changes are not limited to wholly or partially mechanical corruptions... the insertion and multiplication of genitive pronouns, but occasionally their suppression where they appeared cumbrous; the insertion of objects, genitive, dative, or accusative, after verbs used absolutely; the insertion of conjunctions in sentences which had none, but occasionally their excision where their force was not perceived and the form of the sentence or context seemed to commend abruptness; free interchange of conjunctions; free interchange of the formulae introductory to spoken words; free interchange of participle and finite verb with two finite verbs connected by a conjunction; substitution of compound verbs for simple as a rule, but conversely where the compound verb of the true text was difficult or unusual; and substitution of aorists for imperfects as a rule, but with a few examples of the converse, in which either a misunderstanding of the context or an outbreak of untimely vigor has introduced the imperfect... Another impulse of scribes abundantly exemplified in Western readings is the fondness for assimilation. In its most obvious form it is merely local, abolishing diversities of diction where the same subject matter recurs as part of two or more neighboring clauses or verses, or correcting apparent defects of symmetry. But its most dangerous work is 'harmonistic' corruption, that is, the partial or total obliteration of differences in passages otherwise more or less resembling each other. Sometimes the assimilation is between single sentences that happen to have some matter in common; more usually however between parallel passages of greater length, such especially as have in some sense a common origin.[43]

The third text-type proposed by Westcott and Hort was named the *Neutral* or *β Text*. It is this text that both men felt was closest to the original autographs and was most free from error. They believed that this Neutral text had been transmitted practically without editorial revision. The use of the term 'Neutral' reflects Westcott and Hort's view

---

43. Westcott and Hort, *Introduction*, pp. 122-25.

that this text-type was relatively free from the bias of later scribes and had little corruption, conflation, or mixture from other texts. This text that originated in Egypt is best represented by two of the oldest and most prominent manuscripts known today, Codex Vaticanus (B03), and Codex Sinaiticus (‭א‬01). Although not as significant, a number of other mainly Egyptian manuscripts are also included in this text-type. Where Codex Vaticanus and Codex Sinaiticus agree on a reading, it is regarded by Westcott and Hort as almost conclusive evidence for its authentic representation of the original autographs. They conclude:

> [I]t is our belief (1) that readings of ‭א‬B should be accepted as the true readings until strong internal evidence is found to the contrary, and (2) that no readings of ‭א‬B can safely be rejected absolutely, though it is sometimes right to place them only on an alternative footing, especially where they receive no support from Versions or Fathers.[44]

It should, however, be noted that for the Western non-interpolations Westcott and Hort ascribed significantly more weight to the passages containing these readings, over against the readings of the Neutral text. In these instances, the Western text, which usually contains the longer and more complete reading, is instead shorter and resembles more closely the kinds of readings usually found in the Neutral text. However, the Neutral text of these passages has evidently been edited and lengthened. Therefore, in these passages Westcott and Hort rejected the ‭א‬01/B03 readings and followed, instead, these Western non-interpolations.

The fourth and final text-type of Westcott and Hort was called the *Alexandrian* or *γ Text*. This text, originating in Alexandria, is best preserved in Codex Ephraemi (C04), Codex Regius (L019), Codex 33, the Coptic versions, and Alexandrian Fathers such as Clement, Origen, Dionysius, Didymus, and Cyril. Although manuscripts that fall under this text-type are similar to Codex Vaticanus and Codex Sinaiticus, they have often been modified by editors to resemble more closely the Syrian text. Westcott and Hort called this text-type a fourth-century 'recension', meaning that it had been copied and changed from manuscripts such as those used to establish the Neutral text. Being that these Alexandrian manuscripts came from a Greek literary center, much of their alteration included matters of syntax and stylistic polish. Westcott and Hort comment on the Alexandrian text:

---

44. Westcott and Hort, *Introduction*, p. 225.

On grounds of Intrinsic and Transcriptional Probability alike, the readings
which we call Alexandrian are certainly as a rule derived from the other
Non-Western Pre-Syrian readings [i.e. the Neutral text], and not *vice-versa*. The only documentary authorities attesting them with any approach
to constancy, and capable of being assigned to a definite locality, are
quotations by Origen, Cyril of Alexandria, and occasionally other
Alexandrian Fathers, and the two principal Egyptian Versions, especially
that of Lower Egypt [i.e. the Bohairic]. These facts, taken together, shew
that the readings in question belong to a partially degenerate form of the
Non-Western Pre-Syrian text, apparently limited in its early range, and
apparently originating in Alexandria. It cannot be later in date than the
opening years of the third century, and may possibly be much earlier...
The changes made have usually more to do with language than matter, and
are marked by an effort after correctness of phrase. They are evidently the
work of careful and leisurely hands, and not seldom display a delicate
philological tact which unavoidably lends them at first sight a deceptive
appearance of originality.[45]

In concluding this presentation of Westcott and Hort's method, one can
now summarize the major guidelines that they adhered to:

1. The older readings, manuscripts, and groups of documents are
   more likely to contain the original text.
2. The shorter readings are more likely to contain the original
   text.
3. The more difficult readings (i.e. the least smooth) are more
   likely to contain the original text.
4. The reading that best explains the existence of other readings is
   more likely to contain the original text.
5. The quality of manuscript support for a reading, rather than the
   numerical support of a reading, is to be considered in determining the original text.
6. Weight should be given to manuscripts that continually contain
   the preferred readings, rather than manuscripts that often show
   mixture or conflation.
7. Conflated or mixed readings are likely to be later in date than
   manuscripts that do not have conflated or mixed readings.
8. Western non-interpolations should be accepted above any other
   readings in establishing the original text.
9. Readings not found in Neutral, Alexandrian, or Western texts
   are most likely Syrian in nature.

45. Westcott and Hort, *Introduction*, pp. 130-32.

10. Any Western or Alexandrian reading that is not supported by the Neutral text is to be rejected.

In essence, Westcott and Hort proposed that the main manuscripts to be trusted were representatives of the uncorrupted Neutral text, more specifically Codex Vaticanus, and to some degree Codex Sinaiticus, especially when the two were in agreement. The Syrian text, they believed, was the latest and most inferior of all text-types. The Alexandrian, although resembling the Neutral text, was a later modification of this text which often resembled the Syrian text. The Western text, although containing a small number of original readings (Western non-interpolations), illustrated a significant departure, with its paraphrases and additions, from the Neutral text. The application of these methods by Westcott and Hort resulted in the eventual collapse of the Textus Receptus and the Syrian (also called Byzantine) text that it represented. Defenders of this text could not explain issues such as its late age, its number of conflated and mixed readings, the editing process of scribes producing a smoother text, and its apparent development from other texts. The Syrian text simply could not explain the rise of other readings. As Patrick has stated:

> *The New Testament In The Original Greek* opened a new epoch in textual studies. Building upon the work of continental scholars before them, Westcott and Hort for the first time established the study of the text of the Greek NT on clear scientific principles. In doing so they set the pattern for all future textual study of the NT. Things could never again be the same.[46]

Advances since Westcott and Hort

> The past hundred years have seen many new discoveries and developments in the textual criticism of the New Testament. The result is a substantial modification of the picture painted by Westcott and Hort, a muddying of their clear stream.[47]

Although the methodological presuppositions of Westcott and Hort have been, to some degree, modified and revised throughout this century, without doubt, the greatest advancement in New Testament textual criticism since their day lies in the realm of new manuscript discoveries. The most important to consider are over 90 papyri (Westcott and Hort did

46. Patrick, '1881–1981', pp. 359-60.
47. Patrick, '1881–1981', p. 361.

not even mention the papyrus manuscripts), over 290 uncials (Westcott and Hort apparently used about 45), over 2800 minuscules (again, Westcott and Hort used only about 150), and almost 2300 lectionary manuscripts.[48] Versional manuscripts and Patristic quotations are well into the tens of thousands.[49] Indeed, E.J. Epp rightly states:

> We have, therefore, a genuine embarrassment of riches in the quantity of MSS that we possess, and this accounts, on the one hand, for the optimism in the discipline and for the promise of solid results, but also, on the other hand, for the extreme complexity in the study of the NT text.[50]

Of these new discoveries, it is the papyri that hold the greatest attention of scholars. The most significant papyri finds since Westcott and Hort can be traced back largely to the third/fourth centuries. Included are the Chester Beatty manuscripts ($\mathfrak{P}^{45}$, $\mathfrak{P}^{46}$, $\mathfrak{P}^{47}$), which were recovered in 1930–31, and a number of the Bodmer manuscripts ($\mathfrak{P}^{66}$, $\mathfrak{P}^{72}$, $\mathfrak{P}^{75}$), beginning in 1956. Since the discovery of these precious new papyri, Westcott and Hort's theories, as well as the entire field of textual criticism, have needed to be re-examined. Some of the more prominent areas of recent and current discussion deal with the following aspects.

First, there has been a dissatisfaction with the results of Westcott and Hort's genealogical method. Advocates and adversaries alike have commented that Westcott and Hort did not actually practically apply the genealogical method to the manuscripts of the New Testament. Instead,

48. K. and B. Aland, *The Text of the New Testament* (Grand Rapids: Eerdmans, rev. edn, 1989), pp. 96-102, 103, 128, and 163 respectively. The terms 'minuscule' and 'cursive' are often used interchangeably. However, there is clear evidence showing that cursives were a less formal character than the minuscules, which derived from the cursive hand. That there is a distinct difference between the two is clear when one compares the cursive marginal notes that are often written in New Testament minuscule manuscripts. For this point, see J. Harold Greenlee, *Introduction to New Testament Textual Criticism* (Peabody, MA: Hendrickson, rev. edn, 1995), p. 19 n. 3.

49. Metzger states that the staunch defender of the Textus Receptus, Dean J.W. Burgon, with the help of his assistants, catalogued over 86,439 Patristic quotations. Metzger also states that there are at least 30,000 quotations made by Augustine alone. See B.M. Metzger, 'Patristic Evidence and the Textual Criticism of the New Testament', *NTS* 18 (1972), p. 383.

50. E.J. Epp, 'Decision Point in Past, Present, and Future New Testament Textual Criticism', in E.J. Epp and G.D. Fee, *Studies in the Theory and Method of New Testament Textual Criticism* (SD 45; Grand Rapids: Eerdmans, 1993), p. 31. This excellent volume consists of a collection of previously published essays.

they state that rather than breaking down all the manuscripts into their respective families or groups, Westcott and Hort used the genealogical method to oust the Syrian/Byzantine text and then they fell backwards onto internal evidence to show the superiority of the older manuscripts. Some scholars state that this was in fact an unsupported hypothesis.[51] On the other hand, some textual critics assert that the genealogical method must exist, even if we have not or cannot trace these families or groups in the New Testament manuscripts. In the light of this, these scholars conclude that the principle of weighing manuscripts rather than simply counting manuscripts is still valid.[52]

Secondly, the new papyri discoveries have apparently shown that an early form of Syrian/Byzantine readings, *not* Syrian/Byzantine text-types, existed prior to the fourth century, and perhaps as early as the second century.[53] Westcott and Hort stated that there were no Syrian readings, and therefore no Syrian text-type, before the fourth century

51. See Hodges, 'Rationalism', pp. 27-35 and especially pp. 33-34; W.N. Pickering, *The Identity of the New Testament Text* (Nashville: Thomas Nelson, 1977), especially chs. 3-4; G.D. Fee, 'Rigorous or Reasoned Eclecticism—Which?', in Epp and Fee, *Studies in the Theory*, p. 126; E.J. Epp, 'The Eclectic Method in New Testament Textual Criticism: Solution or Symptom?', in Epp and Fee, *Studies in the Theory*, p. 159; and K. and B. Aland, *The Text of the New Testament*, p. 18.

52. For a discussion concerning the genealogical method and the local-genealogical method, see works such as B.M. Metzger, *A Textual Commentary on the Greek New Testament* (London/New York: United Bible Societies, 2nd edn, 1994 [1971; corrected edn, 1975]), p. 12*; G.D. Fee, 'On the Types, Classification, and Presentation of Textual Variation', in Epp and Fee, *Studies in the Theory*, pp. 67-68; Epp, 'The Eclectic Method', pp. 143 n. 4; G.D. Fee, 'The Majority Text and the Original Text of the New Testament', in Epp and Fee, *Studies in the Theory*, pp. 190-93; G.D. Fee, 'Codex Sinaiticus in the Gospel of John: A Contribution to the Methodology in Establishing Textual Relationships', in Epp and Fee, *Studies in the Theory*, pp. 224-27; G.D. Fee, 'P75, P66, and Origen: The Myth of Early Textual Recension in Alexandria', in Epp and Fee, *Studies in the Theory*, pp. 272-73; D.A. Carson, *The King James Version Debate* (Grand Rapids: Baker, 1979), pp. 108-10, esp. 109; and K. and B. Aland, *The Text of the New Testament*, p. 34. For an excellent discussion concerning text-types, and retrospectively, genealogical relationships, as seen in the early New Testament witnesses, especially the papyri, see E.J. Epp, 'The Significance of the Papyri for Determining the Nature of the New Testament Text in the Second Century: A Dynamic View of Textual Transmission', in Epp and Fee, *Studies in the Theory*, pp. 274-97.

53. See G.D. Fee, 'Textual Criticism of the New Testament', in Epp and Fee, *Studies in the Theory*, pp. 8, 12; and Omanson, 'A Perspective', p. 115.

($\mathfrak{P}^{66}$, the highly erratic papyrus dated about 200 CE, contains Syrian/Byzantine-type readings).

Thirdly, papyrus manuscripts have revealed that the Alexandrian text is not, as Westcott and Hort proposed, a fourth-century recension developing in Egypt. Instead, it is a text-type that closely resembles Codex Vaticanus (B03) and existed as early as the second century, thus supporting Westcott and Hort's conclusion concerning the antiquity of the Alexandrian texts.[54]

Fourthly, these early papyri do not prove that the Alexandrian text is the original text, but they do show that Westcott and Hort were correct in viewing Codex Vaticanus (B03) as an early manuscript that represented a relatively pure transmission from a very old text form.[55]

Fiftly, when various papyri have been examined (such as $\mathfrak{P}^{45}$, $\mathfrak{P}^{46}$, $\mathfrak{P}^{66}$, $\mathfrak{P}^{75}$), it has been found that they do not precisely fit into any of the four text-types proposed by Westcott and Hort.[56] To attempt to place them into text-types, therefore, is illogical due to the very fact that they generally precede the date of the most prominent manuscripts used to determine each text-type.

Although a number of the above points reveal, at least to a small extent, some amount of modification to Westcott and Hort's theories, there is perhaps one area in particular where deviation is more noticeably seen. Crucial to Westcott and Hort's methodology was the concept of text-types, these being the Syrian, Western, Alexandrian, and Neutral. At present, in the wake of contentions regarding (1) the genealogical method, (2) early second-century Syrian/Byzantine readings, (3) the newly recognized importance of the Alexandrian text, and (4) the lack of text-types that allow newly discovered papyri to be categorized, there has been a significant questioning and reconsideration concerning the validity of text-types (at least text-types during the first two centuries of New Testament textual transmission). Epp comments on what he terms the 'struggle over the text-type':

> Perhaps the word 'struggle' is too strong, yet there is a continuing and
> genuine disagreement, if not contention, as to whether or not 'text-types'

54. See Fee, 'Textual Criticism', p. 7; 'Decision Points', p. 42; Epp, 'Significance of the Papyri', p. 290; and Omanson, 'A Perspective', p. 115.

55. See Fee, 'Textual Criticism', p. 7; 'Decision Points', p. 42; and Omanson, 'A Perspective', p. 115.

56. See Epp, 'Decision Points', p. 37; 'Significance of the Papyri', p. 283; and Patrick, '1881–1981', pp. 361.

existed in the earliest centuries of the transmission of the NT text. That question in itself may not seem to involve a significant issue, but the answer to it does affect rather directly the obviously important issue of whether or not—and if so, how—we can trace the history of the earliest NT text, which—in turn—is related directly to the ultimate goal of recovering the original text. The validity of these steps is, at any rate, the conviction of many of us, with the result that the question of early text-types deserves close attention... Yet it is clear enough that the study of the early and extensive papyri constitutes the turning point from confidence to skepticism about early text-types.[57]

Aland also reveals the degree of disparagement regarding text-types when he makes a rather extreme assertion regarding the formation of the Alexandrian text (Egyptian), and the Antiochian text (Byzantine):

These are, it seems to me, the only text-types which may be regarded as certain, and that only since the fourth century. Everything else is extremely doubtful. It is impossible to fit the papyri, from the time prior to the fourth century, into these two text-types, to say nothing of trying to fit them into other types, as frequently happens. The simple fact that all these papyri, with their various distinctive characteristics, did exist side by side, in the same ecclesiastical province, that is, in Egypt, where they were found, is the best argument against the existence of any text-types, including the Alexandrian [Egyptian] and the Antiochian [Byzantine].[58]

It should be noted, however, that the present scholarly concern over text-types is not a new issue within the discipline of textual criticism. In fact, this debate has been ongoing for years, and has been discussed by individuals such as F.C. Burkitt, who, in 1899, challenged Westcott and Hort's view of the Western text.[59] In 1908, K. Lake presented the view

57. Epp, 'Decision Points', pp. 37-38.

58. K. Aland, 'The Significance of the Papyri for Progress in New Testament Research', in J.P. Hyatt (ed.), *The Bible in Modern Scholarship: Papers Read at the 100th Meeting of the Society for Biblical Literature, December 28-30, 1964* (Nashville/New York: Abingdon, 1965), pp. 336-37. The Alands consider the Egyptian text to be an offshoot of the Alexandrian text-type. As years passed, the Alexandrian text became corrupted by the Koine (or Byzantine) influence. Eventually the Alexandrian text produced the Egyptian text. The circulation of this text became increasingly limited because of the growing popularity of the Coptic versions. See K. and B. Aland, *The Text of the New Testament*, pp. 56, 70-71. For further statements by the Alands regarding some contemporary problems with text-types, see this same volume, p. 332. A more balanced discussion concerning the matter of text-types can be found in Epp, 'Significance of the Papyri', pp. 274-79.

59. See F.C. Burkitt's *Introduction* to P.M. Barnard's *The Biblical Text of*

that the Neutral text was perhaps more corrupt, while the Western text more authentic, than Westcott and Hort had first thought.[60] A.C. Clark, in 1914, proposed that the Western text, complete with its longer readings, was the original text, while the Neutral text was a recension of it.[61] And again in 1926, J.H. Ropes re-affirmed the original position of Westcott and Hort.[62] Just prior to Ropes, in 1924, B.H. Streeter asserted that another text-type existed alongside those given by Westcott and Hort. He claimed that this text originated in Caesarea of Palestine, perhaps under the influence of Origen. Thus was born the *Caesarean text-type*, with its main witnesses being Θ, fam. 1, fam. 13, and several other manuscripts.[63]

At the present time, scholars tend to lean towards four text-types, based somewhat upon Westcott and Hort, as well as subsequent scholarship. The first is called the *Alexandrian* text, and consists of a combining of Westcott and Hort's Neutral and Alexandrian texts. Its major witnesses would include Codex Vaticanus (B03), Codex Sinaiticus (א01), $\mathfrak{P}^{66}$, $\mathfrak{P}^{75}$, and the Sahidic and Bohairic versions. The second is the *Western* text. However, whereas Westcott and Hort rejected all readings except Western non-interpolations, more recently scholars have pushed aside these non-interpolations and have accepted some of the Western text readings. Witnesses to this text-type would include Codex Bezae (D05), Codex Claromontanus (D06), portions of Codex Washingtonianus (W032), $\mathfrak{P}^{38}$, $\mathfrak{P}^{48}$, and various Old Latin versions. The third text-type is,

Clement of Alexandria in the Four Gospels and the Acts of the Apostles, in J.A. Robinson (ed.), *Texts and Studies* (Cambridge: Cambridge University Press, 1899), V, p. xviii. Further aspects of this ongoing debate are nicely summarized by D. Parker in 'The Development of Textual Criticism since B.H. Streeter', *NTS* 24 (1977), pp. 149-62.

60. Lake, *The Text of the New Testament*, p. 70.

61. A.C. Clark, *The Primitive Text of the Gospels and Acts* (Oxford: Oxford University Press, 1918), pp. vi-vii, 19-20, and 106-12.

62. Ropes, *The Text of Acts*, pp. vii-xii.

63. B.H. Streeter, *The Four Gospels: A Study of Origins, Treating of the Manuscript Tradition, Sources, Authorship, and Dates* (London: Macmillan, 1924), pp. 77-108. Subsequent study by individuals such as K. Lake, R.P. Blake, and S. New has revealed that this text-type probably originated in Egypt rather than Caesarea, but was carried by Origen to Caesarea and from here it continued to spread. See K. Lake and R.P. Blake, 'The Text of the Gospels and the Koridethi Codex', *HTR* 16 (1923), pp. 267-86; and K. Lake, R.P. Blake, and S. New, 'The Caesarean Text of the Gospel of Mark', *HTR* 21 (1928), pp. 207-404.

for the most part, the familiar Syrian text of Westcott and Hort. But today, it is more commonly referred to as the *Byzantine* text. Major witnesses to this text-type are the Gospel portions of Codex Alexandrinus (A02), the later uncial manuscripts, and the majority of minuscule manuscripts. The fourth is called the *Caesarean* text, which was first proposed by Streeter. However, this text-type has suffered at the hands of its recent critics and currently its status as an integral text-type is disintegrating.[64] Its primary representatives include Codex Coridethianus (Θ038), and the Armenian and Georgian versions. Again, the dilemma of the Caesarean text reveals the faltering nature of text-types in general.

In the light of past and present dissatisfaction over, among other factors, Westcott and Hort's use of genealogical methodology, as incorporated to determine text-types and provide external evidence, and their oft-disputed assumption that the original New Testament text had survived relatively error free in their so-called Neutral (Egyptian or Alexandrian) text-type, experts have sought a new approach and solution to the textual problem of the New Testament. Rather than adhering to the classical method of Westcott and Hort, a method that relied heavily upon these genealogical relationships and principles, scholars have gradually concluded that no one manuscript or group of manuscripts has preserved the original, unaltered autographs. Therefore, the modern textual critic must explore all traditions and criteria rather than conclude that one particular type of reading, manuscript, family of manuscripts, or text-type holds the answer to the problem of the New Testament text. The words of A.F.J. Klijn seem to represent the current opinion of the present situation: 'The discovery of the original text will not be in a MS or in a text. We shall have to hammer out the text of the original NT reading by reading, discussing every possibility.'[65] Statements such as this clearly show that since the era of Westcott and Hort, the discipline of textual criticism has been influenced, to some extent, by new discoveries and developments. The need to 'hammer out the text of the original New Testament reading by reading' has in turn given rise to what some scholars term the 'eclectic approach'.

---

64. J.N. Birdsall correctly summarizes recent scholarly thought regarding the Caesarean text-type: 'The Caesarean Text is not a text-type, but at least two...'; J.N. Birdsall, 'The Recent History of New Testament Textual Criticism', *ANRW* II.26.1 (1992), p. 176.

65. A.F.J. Klijn, *A Survey of the Researches into the Western Text of the Gospels and Acts* (Utrecht: Kemink, 1949), p. 171.

If one accepts that (1) the complete original text is not to be found in one single, reliable witness, (2) the ancient readings cannot always be followed solely because of their antiquity, and (3) the original text of the New Testament is to be chosen variant by variant, then a reliance upon one of four prominent methods must ensue. The first three methods— Reasoned Eclecticism, Rigorous Eclecticism, and the Historical-Documentary method—are distinctively eclectic. The final method, the Majority Text approach, is not distinctively eclectic.

By using the term 'eclectic' or 'eclecticism', and by adhering to the eclectic method, one means that the 'original' text of the New Testament is to be chosen variant by variant, using all the principles of critical judgment without regarding one manuscript or text-type as necessarily preserving that 'original'.[66] There is, however, at least one inherent difficulty in defining 'eclecticism'. To some textual critics, eclecticism means an equal assessment of both internal evidence (factors relating to the original author and to the later scribe) and external evidence (factors relating to the manuscripts). This approach is called *Rational* or *Reasoned Eclecticism*. For others it means a use of internal considerations alone. This approach is known as *Rigorous, Thorough Going, Radical*, or *Consistent Eclecticism*. Generally, the level of a textual critic's dependence upon external evidence determines the type of eclecticism that he or she employs in solving textual difficulties. Some textual scholars would even go to the extreme and claim that the original reading may appear in one single medieval manuscript even when all of that manuscript's relatives do not have the reading. As R.V.G. Tasker notes:

> It is in consequence generally accepted today that there is no single witness, or group of witnesses, which can be regarded as always reliable— much less, infallible; that all 'rule-of-thumb' methods of dealing with the evidence must be eschewed; that ancient readings cannot always be followed solely because of their antiquity; and that the possibility must be left open that in some cases the true reading may have been preserved in only a few witnesses—or even in a single, relatively late, witness.[67]

66. Fee, 'Textual Criticism', p. 15.

67. R.V.G. Tasker, *The Greek New Testament* (Oxford/Cambridge: Oxford University Press/Cambridge University Press, 1964), p. viii. For further statements of this nature, see J.K. Elliott, 'Keeping up with Recent Studies XV: New Testament Textual Criticism', *ExpTim* 99 (1987), p. 43; and *idem*, 'Can We Recover the Original Text of the New Testament: An Examination of the Rôle of Thoroughgoing Eclecticism', in his *Essays and Studies in New Testament Textual Criticism* (FN 3; Cordoba: Ediciones El Almendro, 1992), p. 28.

It is the eclectic approach, and more specifically the rational eclectic approach, that the *UBSGNT*, and for that matter many other Greek New Testament critical editions, have been based upon. For as Metzger declares, the editors of the *UBSGNT*[3] worked with the principle that 'each set of variants be evaluated in the light of the fullest consideration of both external evidence and internal probabilities'.[68] We now turn to a discussion of reasoned eclecticism, rigorous eclecticism, the historical-documentary method, and the majority text method.

Reasoned Eclecticism
It is the reasoned eclectic approach that holds the most favorable position among New Testament textual scholars. This method is also called rational, moderate, and genuine eclecticism. The primary consideration that stands behind a reasoned eclectic approach to the New Testament text is that *the variant most likely to be original is the one that best explains and accounts for the existence of the others*. To state this in different terms, when one is confronted with several differing variants, the original variant is most likely to be that which explains, in consideration of both *external* and *internal* evidence, the existence of the other variants. Reasoned eclecticism cannot function apart from considering both external and internal evidence because *reconstructing the history of the textual variant is a prerequisite to reaching a judgment about that variant*. It is external evidence that aids the scholar in reconstructing the textual history. Only the variant that can best account for all the evidence, external and internal criteria alike, has serious claims to being the original. Reasoned eclecticism recognizes that no single criterion or invariable combination of criteria will resolve all cases of textual variation; therefore, it attempts to apply evenly and without prejudice any and all criteria—external and internal—appropriate to a given case, arriving at an answer based upon the relative probabilities among those applicable criteria.[69] Keeping in mind the above principles, we now focus our attention upon the two criteria of judgment underlying the reasoned eclectic method—external evidence and internal evidence.[70]

68. Metzger, *A Textual Commentary*, 1971, p. xxxi; 1994, p. 16*.

69. Epp, 'Decision Points', pp. 35-36.

70. For a presentation of the following principles consult the standard handbooks dealing with textual criticism such as Metzger, *The Text of the New Testament*; K. and B. Aland, *The Text of the New Testament*; Greenlee, *Textual Criticism*; and L. Vaganay and C.B. Amphoux, *An Introduction to New Testament Textual Criticism* (Cambridge/New York: Cambridge University Press, 2nd edn, 1991).

External evidence. External evidence is concerned with factors relating to the manuscripts and other witnesses. There are four considerations inherent to external evidence: (1) *The relative date and character of the witnesses*—generally, the earlier manuscripts are more likely to be free from errors of repeated copying. Do the earlier manuscripts support one variant more than others? Are some variants without any early support? Or do all the readings have early support?

(2) *The geographic distribution of the witnesses that support a variant*—in general, the broader the geographical distribution of the supporting witnesses for a given variant, the greater the likelihood that the variant may be original. However, one must be certain that geographically remote witnesses are really independent of one another.[71]

(3) *The genealogical relationships among texts and families of manuscripts*—one must determine if the manuscripts supporting a variant reflect the readings present in numerous text-types or represent one single text-type. If the latter case is true, it may be that a variant represents a sole peculiarity of that one text-type. However, if in a given sentence reading x is supported by 20 manuscripts while reading y is supported by only one manuscript, the numerical support favoring reading x counts for nothing if all 20 manuscripts are discovered to be copies made from a single, no longer existing manuscript, whose scribe first introduced that particular variant reading. In this case, the comparison must be made between the one manuscript containing reading y and the single ancestor of the 20 manuscripts containing reading x.[72]

(4) *The relative quality of the witnesses*—manuscripts are to be weighed rather than counted. Bearing in mind the principle of the previous paragraph, those manuscripts which are found to be more trustworthy in obvious instances of variation should be accorded this predominant position in less obvious instances of variation. However, this should not be held as a constant mechanical principle, but instead, should be a consideration when evaluating the entire spectrum of evidence.

Internal evidence. Internal evidence is of two kinds. It is concerned with *transcriptional* probabilities (factors relating to the habits, mistakes, and tendencies of scribes), as well as *intrinsic* probabilities (the style and thought of the author).

71. Metzger, *A Textual Commentary*, 1971, p. xxv; 1994, p. 12*.
72. Metzger, *A Textual Commentary*, 1971, p. xxvi; 1994, p. 12*.

(1) *Transcriptional probabilities*—this involves the consideration that readings may have resulted due to slips, errors, alterations, or harmonizations of other passages made by the scribe as he copied his manuscript from an exemplar. In the light of these scribal tendencies, two major points should be considered: the more difficult reading is to be preferred, and the shorter reading is to be preferred. To be considered here are the various types of unintentional and intentional alterations that scribes would make to the text. These are essential to a consideration of transcriptional probabilities.[73]

(2) *Intrinsic probabilities*—the primary aim here is to consider the variant readings on the basis of what the author was most likely to have written. Aspects that one might investigate would include the author's vocabulary usage, writing style, flow of thought and logic, ideational congruence, theological perspectives and teachings, and possible use of traditional material. All these considerations must be evaluated in the immediate context of the variant passage and in the greater context of the entire book and other works by the particular author. In the Gospels, further considerations would also include the possible Aramaic or Greek background of the teachings of Jesus, the Markan priority of the Gospels, and the influence of the Christian community upon the formulation and transmission of the passage in question.[74]

Fee explains one final consideration pertaining to the relationship between external and internal evidence, and thus to the entire reasoned eclectic approach:

> While... we may grant that not all of the principles of textual criticism are applicable to each variant, contemporary critics generally agree that questions of internal evidence should usually be asked first and that the weight of the manuscript evidence should be applied secondarily. What becomes obvious, however, is that on the grounds of internal evidence certain MSS tend to support the 'original' text more often than others and that those MSS are the early Egyptian [Alexandrian]. Therefore, when internal evidence cannot decide, the safest guide is to go with the 'best' MS.[75]

---

73. See the standard handbooks such as Metzger, *The Text of the New Testament*, pp. 209-10; Greenlee, *Textual Criticism*, pp. 55-61, 111-116; and Vaganay and Amphoux, *An Introduction*, pp. 79-81.

74. See Metzger, *A Textual Commentary*, 1971, p. xxviii; 1994, pp. 13*-14*.

75. Fee, 'Textual Criticism', pp. 15-16.

Although the reasoned eclectic approach holds the most favorable position among New Testament textual scholars,[76] one must not conclude that it is without difficulties or that it is the final word in critical methodologies. For as Clark stated, as early as the mid-1950s, reasoned eclecticism is perhaps a temporary interlude:

> The eclectic method is openly embraced in our day. Indeed, it is the only procedure available to us at this stage, but it is very important to recognize that it is a secondary and tentative method. It is not a new method nor a permanent one; it does not supplant the more thorough procedure of Westcott and Hort but only supplants it temporarily. The eclectic method cannot by itself create a text to displace Westcott-Hort and its offspring. It is suitable only for exploration and experimentation. From it may one day come the insight about which a multitude of itemized researches may gather and find unity and meaning. The eclectic method, by its very nature, belongs to a day like ours in which we know only that the traditional theory of the text is faulty but cannot yet see clearly to correct the fault. While, therefore, we are indebted to 'the eclectics' for their scholarly judgments, we should not expect thus to be provided with an improved critical text. Paradoxically, the eclectic method as applied today presupposes the general correctness of our traditional textual theory.[77]

Birdsall also comments upon the temporary predominance of reasoned eclecticism:

> Although for the present we must utilize these diverse criteria and establish a text by an eclectic method, it is impossible to stifle the hope that, at some future time, we shall find our methods and our resultant text justified by manuscript discoveries and by the classical methods... which Hort exemplified so brilliantly in his work.[78]

---

76. See such statements made by Epp, 'Decision Points', pp. 36, 40

77. K.W. Clark, 'The Effect of Recent Textual Criticism upon New Testament Studies', in W.D. Davies and D. Daube (eds.), *The Background of the New Testament and its Eschatology* (Cambridge: Cambridge University Press, 1964), pp. 37-38. One is able to state, as Clark does, that eclecticism 'is not a new method', in that individuals such as Bengel (1725), Griesbach (1796), and Lachmann (1842) recognized the importance of evaluating both internal and external evidence when weighing textual matters. Thus, reasoned eclecticism, in its broadest meaning, had its early precursors. For more clarification of this point, see Epp, 'The Eclectic Method', p. 142.

78. J.N. Birdsall, 'The Text of the Fourth Gospel: Some Current Questions', *EvQ* (1957), p. 199.

Rigorous Eclecticism

This method is similarly known as thoroughgoing, radical, or consistent eclecticism. Rigorous eclecticism is a more recent method of textual criticism and has been endorsed and practiced in particular by two British scholars, the late G.D. Kilpatrick and his student J.K. Elliott.[79] Eclecticism of this nature examines all the variant readings available for any one variant unit and then selects the reading that best explains aspects of internal criteria alone. In other words, the variant that is selected as the original reading should be the one that best fits into the context of the passage, and the author's style, vocabulary or theology (all intrinsic probabilities), while at the same time falling in line with scribal habits, including the tendency to conform to a Koine or Attic Greek style, Semitic forms of expression, parallel passages, Old Testament passages, and liturgical forms and uses (all transcriptional probabilities). Little regard, if any, is given to characteristics of external evidence. Elliott explains this emphasis upon internal evidence alone:

> By contrast I think it is perfectly feasible to try to reconstruct the original text by applying *only* internal criteria. This method has been dubbed radical or thoroughgoing eclecticism. According to this method (which I support and which I try to apply) the manuscripts are of importance primarily as bearers of readings. As I have already indicated, no one manuscript has the monopoly of original readings. On the other hand, it is unlikely that the original text has not survived *somewhere* in our known manuscripts even if this may occasionally turn out to be a representative of the late, [B]yzantine, type of text.[80]

Elliott goes on to explain that 'the number or age of the manuscripts supporting the readings are of little significance'.[81] Therefore, as Colwell explains, a rigorous eclectic critic uses the term 'eclectic' in the following manner:

> By 'eclectic' they mean in fact free choice among readings. This choice in many cases is made solely on the basis of intrinsic probability. The editor chooses that reading which commends itself to him as fitting the context,

79. For representative collections of these two scholars' work, see J.K. Elliott (ed.), *The Principles and Practice of New Testament Textual Criticism: Collected Essays of G.D. Kilpatrick* (BETL 96; Leuven: Leuven University Press/Peeters, 1990); and Elliott, *Essays and Studies in New Testament Textual Criticism*. For a refutation of the method supported by Kilpatrick and Elliott, see, among other works, Fee, 'Rigorous or Reasoned', pp. 124-40.

80. Elliott, 'Recent Studies', p. 43.

81. Elliott, 'Recent Studies', p. 43.

whether in style, or idea, or contextual reference. Such an editor relegates the manuscripts to the role of the supplier of readings. The weight of the manuscript is ignored. Its place in the manuscript tradition is not considered.[82]

The fact that many of the papyri and uncials come from a very early period of textual transmission does not lend to them any special consideration, authority, character, or value. Rigorous eclectic scholars search the prominent early manuscripts and the later Byzantine manuscripts alike, looking for the original text without any distinguished regard for the older witnesses. Whereas in reasoned eclecticism the shorter reading is to be preferred, rigorous eclecticism emphasizes a preference for the longer reading by explaining that the shortening of a text is often due to the careless copying of a scribe especially when paleographical peculiarities can be demonstrated to have aided optical illusions. Although practitioners of rigorous eclecticism admit that the lengthening of a text undoubtedly occurred when scribes deliberately included explanatory glosses and additional material from the exemplar, the more reliable explanation, they claim, is that the longer reading is more likely to be the original.[83]

Rigorous eclecticism has come up against some tough opposition, and, as with reasoned eclecticism, this method too has its limitations, perhaps even more than reasoned eclecticism. Although most scholars would agree that no single manuscript or group of manuscripts can always be regarded as reliable, few would admit that because no manuscripts have escaped corruption, all are virtually equally corrupt, which this method seems to imply. Some scholars note that rigorous eclecticism rests upon this theory of textual corruption and transmission, and ends up being unhistorical in its approach.[84] In fact, studies have revealed that some manuscripts do preserve the original text more faithfully than others.[85] Another criticism of radical eclecticism is its subjectivity. Some would argue that textual judgments are left too much to the fancy of the individual scholar. Readings are accepted that often have only a minimal

82. Colwell, 'Hort Redivivus', p. 154.

83. See Elliott, 'Recent Studies', pp. 43-44.

84. See Fee, 'Rigorous or Reasoned', p. 127; and Omanson, 'A Perspective', p. 119.

85. See Zuntz, *The Text of the Epistles*, esp. pp. 212-13; and G.D. Fee, *Papyrus Bodmer II (P66): Its Textual Relationships and Scribal Characteristics* (SD 34; Salt Lake City, UT: University of Utah Press, 1968), pp. 36-56.

amount of external manuscript support because they appeal to the judgment of the critic.[86] Therefore, it might be said that '[A]lthough considerations of the literary usage of a New Testament author [i.e. internal evidence] will be of considerable value to the textual critic, it must not be made the primary criterion in the evaluation of variant readings to the virtual neglect of external evidence'.[87] In arriving at decisions concerning variant readings, most textual scholars believe that one must utilize all the various methods that might provide insight into a solution regarding the original text. External evidence cannot be overlooked. Neglecting this criterion means to do away with half the tools of use to the textual critic. Taking into account these previous arguments it would be practicable to conclude that the eclectic method:

> ... should be always connected with a careful study and evaluation of the manuscript tradition. This study may reveal that there is a certain favorable presumption on the trustworthiness of certain manuscripts because they were transmitted in a situation which was not influenced by the trend of stylistic emendation which was felt in other places and times.[88]

Historical-Documentary Method
This method, initially advocated by individuals such as E.C. Colwell and K.W. Clark, seeks to reconstruct the history of the New Testament text by examining our extant manuscripts and re-establishing the lines of transmission from these witnesses to the earliest stages of writing, thereby allowing one to choose the reading that comes closest to the original autographs. This method is based upon the theory that we should be able to organize all our existing manuscripts into groups or clusters, each representing a distinct text-type. These distinct text-types are then evaluated with the purpose of determining the specific clusters of manuscripts, or ideally the one lone cluster that represents the earliest known group out of all those examined. With the earliest group determined, all other groups can be subsequently categorized by their later chronological succession. This method further attempts to reconstruct the line of textual transmission that has resulted in the production of all our known manuscripts, thereby seeing each witness as a possible branch extending forth with other branches from the 'main trunk' of

86. Fee, 'Rigorous or Reasoned', pp. 136-38.
87. Metzger, *The Text of the New Testament*, pp. 178-79.
88. C.M. Martini, 'Eclecticism and Atticism in the Textual Criticism of the Greek New Testament', in M. Black and W.A. Smalley (eds.), *On Language, Culture, and Religion: In Honor of Eugene A. Nida* (The Hague/Paris: Mouton, 1974), p. 155.

the earliest texts. If this textual tree with its network of manuscript branches and witness off-shoots can be reconstructed, then one will be able to identify not only the earliest points of departure from the trunk, but the actual trunk (those manuscripts closest to the originals) and roots of the tree itself (the autographs).

Therefore, theoretically, when confronted by a textual variant posing different readings, the reading that comes from the earliest cluster would be the one chosen. Clearly this method emphasizes external evidence such as age and place of origin (hence it is also called external or documentary textual criticism), and is, in comparison to rigorous eclecticism and internal evidence, at the opposite end of the methodological spectrum (with reasoned eclecticism falling somewhere in between). As one can recognize, this method has close similarities with Westcott and Hort's theory of genealogical evidence. In respect to the emphasis upon manuscript age in the historical-documentary method, one can understand how the early papyri and uncials play a vital role in this theory. The textual tree can now be reconstructed back to a point of no more than 150–200 years after the date of writing of the originals.

As with the prior two methods, there are difficulties in the historical-documentary approach. Whereas radical eclecticism overemphasizes internal evidence, this method errs in its overemphasis on external evidence, especially manuscript age. Again the debate over text-types and mixture in manuscripts, as discussed earlier, erects some problematic hurdles for this method, just as it did for Westcott and Hort's genealogical method. As Epp states regarding the genealogical method, and as is evident to some extent in the historical-documentary method, a 'strict genealogical method has never been feasible in NT textual criticism, for there is too much textual mixture in the complex array of MSS'.[89] And lastly, although this method is ideal and the most preferred, however not the most practiced, it falls short in that the numerical lack of early manuscripts renders the approach overly reliant upon only those early manuscripts that are presently known. If there were a greater number of these early witnesses, this method would provide a much larger body of information.

Majority Text Method

As earlier explained, individuals such as J.W. Burgon were adamantly opposed to the theories of Westcott and Hort. Instead, men such as

89. Epp, 'Decision Points', p. 33.

Burgon ceaselessly defended the Textus Receptus. While some scholars still accept the readings present in the Textus Receptus, most serious scholarly support of this text has now ceased.[90]

The method under discussion, the majority text approach, although not defending the Textus Receptus specifically, supports the Byzantine texts that gave rise to the Textus Receptus. This method rejects the prominent view stating that the later Byzantine manuscripts are inferior. Instead, those holding this approach would claim that these manuscripts are a purer form of the text. The majority text view is based upon the following principle: *the original reading of any particular passage is to be found in a majority of the manuscripts*. It seeks to prove that the supposed 'Byzantine' witnesses should be taken as essentially independent witnesses.

The majority text method strives to eliminate any appeal to internal evidence, and replaces this with the opinion that any textual variant that is supported by the majority of manuscripts should be determined as the original. In other words, this approach rejects the previous premise stated under reasoned eclecticism that 'manuscripts should be weighed not counted', because ten thousand copies of a mistake do not make it any less of a mistake.[91] The majority text method, along with rigorous eclecticism, fails to examine the history of the text. Although the majority text method does present some interesting considerations, it is plainly disregarded by the large bulk of textual critics.

Regardless of the changes since Westcott and Hort, one thing is certain— we cannot take for granted or underestimate the immense impact these two men have had upon modern textual criticism. Metzger notes that:

90. However, a number of works written in the past few decades continue to support both the Textus Receptus and the King James Version that extends from it. See such works as E.F. Hills, *The King James Defended! A Space-Age Defense of the Historic Christian Faith* (Des Moines, IA: Christian Research Press, 3rd rev. edn, 1978); D.O. Fuller, *Which Bible?* (Grand Rapids: Grand Rapids International Publications, 5th edn, 1975); H.A. Sturz, *The Byzantine Text-Type and New Testament Textual Criticism* (Nashville/Camden/New York: Thomas Nelson, 1984); Pickering, *Identity of the New Testament*; and the Greek New Testament edition by Z.C. Hodges and A.L. Farstad (eds.), *The Greek New Testament according to the Majority Text* (Nashville/Camden/New York: Thomas Nelson, 1982). These works are not seriously regarded by most textual critics. For a rebuttal of the majority text method, see Fee, 'The Majority Text', pp. 183-208.

91. Holmes, 'Textual Criticism', p. 113.

> [T]he overwhelming consensus of scholarly opinion recognizes that their
> [Westcott and Hort's] critical edition was truly epoch-making. They pre-
> sented what is doubtless the oldest and purest text that could be attained
> with the means of information available in their day. Though the discov-
> ery of additional manuscripts has required the realignment of certain
> groups of witnesses, the general validity of their critical principles and
> procedures is widely acknowledged by textual scholars today.[92]

Westcott and Hort have truly served as the foundation for the study of
New Testament textual criticism. Whether or not current textual criticism
continues to be built upon the same footings, one cannot dismiss that
these two men began construction upon what has become a huge edifice.

> Though a hundred years have passed, it is still prudent to keep in mind the
> two—and the only two—principles that Hort printed in large type in his
> chapter on method: 'Knowledge of documents should precede final judg-
> ment upon readings' and 'All trustworthy restoration of corrupted texts is
> founded on the study of their history.'[93]

2. *The Editions of the UBSGNT*

Westcott and Hort and the Foundation of the UBSGNT Text

> Hort's statement is definitive; his principles have been so generally
> accepted that few students trouble to read the original work in which they
> were first set forth. The canons of criticism established by Hort have
> passed into every manual on the subject, and into every Introduction to the
> New Testament, often without acknowledgment. No sane scholar would
> ever think today of tackling the work of textual criticism on any principles
> other than these; but he may be unaware of the direction in which his main
> indebtedness lies.[94]

Despite the modifications made to Westcott and Hort's methodology by
subsequent scholarship, namely in matters dealing with the criticism of
their genealogical principle and the ongoing discussion concerning text-
types, countless scholars have attested to the fact that 'Almost every
modern translation of the New Testament reflects the influence of the

---

92. Metzger, *The Text of the New Testament*, p. 137.

93. Fee, 'Decision Points', p. 39.

94. Neill and Wright, *Interpretation*, p. 77. In a footnote to this statement, the
authors add that 'Naturally there is progress in this field as in every other. Notable
introductions to the study of textual criticism have been written in later times... But
every one of these is based ultimately on the principles which Hort so lucidly laid
down.'

Westcott-Hort Testament. And it has to be said that very little progress has been made in the field of the history of the text and the theory of textual criticism since Westcott-Hort.'[95] Pack supports this statement, which he made in 1983, by pointing out that ten major editions had been issued since 1881, all profoundly influenced by Westcott-Hort.[96] Fee echoes these sentiments when he states:

> [A]ll subsequent critical texts look far more like WH than like the TR or the Western MSS. Therefore, it is fair to say that, whether intentionally or not, the mainstream of NT textual criticism since Westcott and Hort has moved toward modifying and advancing their work.[97]

K.W. Clark likewise affirms the above points: 'All the critical editions since 1881 are basically the same as Westcott and Hort. All are founded on the same Egyptian recension, and generally reflect the same assumptions of

---

95. Pack, 'One Hundred Years', p. 68. Although modifications have been made to Westcott and Hort's genealogical principles and their designation of text-types, one must not be overly eager to disregard their work in these two areas. Neill and Wright correctly point out that 'We now know that the text represented in Sinaiticus and Vaticanus is also the result of a revision, a very scholarly and sober revision indeed, but still a revision, and we see that Hort's dream of an uncorrupted and unadulterated text is one of those illusions from which he himself had not yet been set free. Yet, Hort was, after all, not so far astray. B is by far the greatest and the best of all the manuscripts of the New Testament that have come down to us.' Neill and Wright, *Interpretation*, p. 79. In regard to Westcott and Hort's view of the Neutral and Western text-types, Epp states that, 'Yet, nearly a century later we still affirm the general superiority of the Neutral text-type and the generally secondary character of the Western, and we do so largely on the same grounds as did Hort: a similar picture of the early history of the text and a similar subjective judgment about the respective quality of the two early text-groups'. E.J. Epp, 'The Twentieth-Century Interlude in New Testament Textual Criticism', in Epp and Fee, *Studies in the Theory*, p. 89.

96. Pack, 'One Hundred Years', p. 70. These editions specifically referred to are Weymouth (1886); B. Weiss (1894–1900); Nestle and now Nestle–Aland (1898–1993); The British and Foreign Bible Society Testaments (1904, 1958); A. Souter (1910–1947); H. von Soden (1902–1910); texts edited by three Catholic scholars, H.J. Vogels (1920), A. Merk (1933), and J.M. Bover (1943); and the *UBSGNT* (1966–1993). For this same point, see Epp, 'The Twentieth-Century', pp. 84-85. The critical edition prepared by Hodges and Farstad, *The Greek New Testament according to the Majority Text*, is an exception. Not only does this edition deny the principles of Westcott and Hort, it also disregards much contemporary text-critical methodology.

97. Fee, 'Textual Criticism', p. 12.

transmission.'[98] Again Clark comments, although somewhat antago-
nistically, upon the results of a study conducted by eight students at
Duke University in which Westcott and Hort's edition was compared to
an extensive number of other critical texts. He concludes:

> Since 1881 twenty-five editors have issued about seventy-five editions of
> the Greek New Testament. The collation of these many 'critical' texts
> consistently exposes the fact that each of them is basically a repetition of
> the Westcott-Hort text of which we may be permitted to declare with truth:
> 'You now have the text which is accepted by all.' Indeed, we have con-
> tinued for eighty-five years to live in the era of Westcott and Hort, our
> *textus receptus*.[99]

Epp, while acknowledging modern textual criticism's reliance upon
Westcott and Hort, provides a noteworthy and straightforward explanation as to why this is the case:

> One response to the fact that our popular critical texts are still so close to
> that of WH might be that the kind of text arrived at by them and supported
> so widely by subsequent criticism is in fact and without question the best
> attainable NT text; yet every textual critic knows that this similarity of text
> indicates, rather, that we have made little progress in textual *theory* since
> Westcott-Hort; that we simply do not know how to make a definitive
> determination as to what the best text is; that we do not have a clear picture
> of the transmission and alteration of the text in the first few centuries; and,
> accordingly, that the Westcott-Hort kind of text has maintained its domi-
> nant position largely by default.[100]

In 1981, Patrick specifically stated that Westcott and Hort's continuing
influence 'is seen most recently in the text of the NEB and in the United
Bible Societies' edition of 1966'.[101] Specifically stated in the preface of
the *UBSGNT*[1] is the attestation that Westcott and Hort's Greek New
Testament was used as the basis for a comparison with other various

---

98. K.W. Clark, 'Today's Problems with the Critical Text of the New
Testament', in J.C. Rylaarsdam (ed.), *Transitions in Biblical Scholarship* (Essays in
Divinity 6; Chicago/London: University of Chicago Press, 1968), p. 159.

99. Clark, 'Today's Problems', pp. 160. See statements of a similar nature made
by Clark in 'Recent Textual Criticism', in Davies and Daube, *Background of the
New Testament*, p. 36.

100. Epp, 'The Twentieth-Century', p. 87. See this entire chapter, pp. 83-108, for
an excellent summary discussing modern textual criticism's reliance upon Westcott
and Hort.

101. Patrick, '1881–1981', pp. 361-62.

editions to determine relevant variants.[102] To add further, Metzger, in his *Textual Commentary* upon the *UBSGNT*, states once more that Westcott and Hort's text 'was taken as the basis for the present United Bible Societies' edition'.[103] M. Black, another member of the *UBSGNT* editorial committee, comments upon Westcott and Hort's influence in the *UBSGNT*[1], *UBSGNT*[2], and *UBSGNT*[3]:

> It is certainly true, as L.W. Hurtado pointed out, that in this UBS text 'Hort's general views are coming back into greater favor than at some times in the past'. The *new* external evidence, in particular that of the Papyri, has led to the vindication of the superiority of the B-א textual tradition, so that it is not surprising that UBS 1, 2, 3 reflect, by and large, fundamentally the Westcott-Hort text-type. But this does not mean that Westcott-Hort has been followed blindly, where the internal and exegetical evidence goes against them; or that full account has not been taken of internal evidence of exegesis and author's style, etc. The truth is that the Hortian type of text is the best available and accessible form of the ancient text of the New Testament. To depart from it and produce an eclectic text may well end in the fabrication of a mosaic of arbitrary readings...[104]

And finally, J.K. Elliott, who has written perhaps some of the most detailed articles dealing with the *UBSGNT*, in an article discussing the *UBSGNT*[3], comes to this same prognosis: '[T]he general verdict of UBS 3rd edn is that its text is closer to Westcott and Hort's text. It is in many ways a "safer" text than the first and second UBS editions insofar as many more of the readings of Codex Vaticanus and Codex Sinaiticus appear in UBS 3rd edn.'[105] The previous assertions and judgments

102. UBSGNT[1], p. v.

103. Metzger, *A Textual Commentary*, 1971, p. xxiii; 1994, p. 10*.

104. M. Black, 'The United Bible Societies' Greek New Testament Evaluated—A Reply', *BT* 28 (1977), p. 120. For the reference to L.W. Hurtado, see his review of Metzger's *Textual Commentary*, *JBL* 92 (1973), pp. 621-22. See also the review article by Moir entitled 'The Bible Societies' Greek New Testament' in *NTS* 14 (1967), pp. 136-43. This latter article, which reviews the *UBSGNT*[1], also emphasizes Westcott and Hort's clear influence upon the United Bible Societies' first edition of the Greek New Testament.

105. J.K. Elliott, 'The United Bible Societies' Greek New Testament: A Short Examination of the Third Edition', *BT* 30 (1979), p. 138. In an earlier article, Elliott also points out that 'Despite the alleged aim of producing an eclectic text, one of the United Bible Societies' spokesmen, R.P. Markham, and one of the text editors, Matthew Black, were already on record in 1966 writing that the UBS text was basically to be Westcott and Hort revised': J.K. Elliott, 'The United Bible Societies' Textual Commentary Evaluated', *NovT* 17 (1975), p. 132. As Elliott points out,

strongly reveal the continuing influence of Westcott and Hort's Greek New Testament upon, not only the various *UBSGNT* editions, but many other critical editions as well.[106] In consideration of this, it is appropriate to evaluate the development of the individual *UBSGNT* editions with reference to their partner text, the Nestle-Aland *Novum Testamentum Graece.*

The First Edition of the UBSGNT (UBSGNT[1])

Work began on the United Bible Societies' first edition of the Greek New Testament in 1955. The editorial committee consisted of Kurt Aland (University of Münster, West Germany), Matthew Black (St Mary's

---

Markham does state that 'In preparing this new edition, the committee based its work on the Westcott-Hort text since it was the pinnacle of 19th century textual criticism and has never really been superseded': R.P. Markham, 'The Bible Societies' Greek Testament: The End of a Decade or Beginning of an Era', *BT* 17 (1966), p. 109. Black states that 'The resultant text is not a revolutionary departure, but substantially the Westcott/Hort type of text': M. Black, 'The Greek New Testament', *SJT* 19 (1966), p. 487.

106. One point of exception should be added. It is interesting to note the Alands' statement, directly in contrast to the above remarks made by their fellow *UBSGNT* committee members, concerning Westcott and Hort, and the *UBSGNT*[3]: '[T]he editorial committee (or more precisely its majority) decided to abandon the theories of Westcott-Hort and the "Western non-interpolations"': K. and B. Aland, *The Text of the New Testament,* p. 33. Being that the text of the *UBSGNT*[4] remains essentially that of the *UBSGNT*[3] and *UBSGNT*[3corr.] (see p. 1* in *UBSGNT*[3], and p. x in *UBSGNT*[3corr.] where only punctuation of the text is said to be modified), one can assume with some degree of certainty that the *UBSGNT*[4] text is influenced by Westcott-Hort to the same extent as its similar *UBSGNT*[3] text. Clearly there is a discrepancy of opinion between the Alands and their fellow committee members. Despite the assertions made by other *UBSGNT* editorial members pertaining to Westcott and Hort, it appears evident that the Alands strongly wish to dissociate their work from that of Westcott and Hort. See further statements to this effect made by Birdsall who likewise asserts that, 'The Alands on the other hand seem possessed by an intense antagonism to Westcott and Hort, and a desire to emphasize the total difference between themselves and these past scholars': Birdsall, 'The Recent History', p. 176. Epp also notices the Alands' antagonism in regard to Westcott and Hort, however in relation to the Nestle-Aland editions. See E.J. Epp, 'New Testament Textual Criticism Past, Present, and Future: Reflections on the Alands' *Text of the New Testament*', *HTR* 82 (1989), pp. 221-22, esp. note 21. For a discussion regarding specific textual disagreements between *UBSGNT* committee members and the use of dissentient notes in Metzger's 1971 *Textual Commentary*, see Elliott, 'Textual Commentary', pp. 132-36.

College, University of St Andrews, Scotland), Bruce M. Metzger (Princeton Theological Seminary), Allen Wikgren (University of Chicago), and, in the first four years of the endeavor, Arthur Vööbus (Chicago Lutheran Theological Seminary). This effort marked the involvement of five Bible societies who desired to: (1) produce an edition of the Greek New Testament that reflected twentieth-century textual scholarship, (2) make use of the ever-increasing number of new manuscripts (more specifically the Bodmer papyri), and (3) provide Bible translators and missionaries with a Greek New Testament that would assist them in their task. This ecumenical cooperation between international and inter-denominational organizations initially involved the American Bible Society, the National Bible Society of Scotland, and the Württemberg Bible Society. They were later joined by the British and Foreign Bible Society, and the Netherlands Bible Society. These five groups were officially called the United Bible Societies, and functioned under the influence and guidance of the linguist and translation-theorist Eugene A. Nida. Also involved in the project was the Institute for New Testament Textual Research at Münster, the Greek Lectionary Project at Chicago, and an advisory board of 43 scholars. As a result of efforts by these people and groups, in May 1966, the United Bible Societies' first Greek New Testament was published.

The primary aim of this first edition and, consequently, its subsequent editions was to provide translators with the nearest text to the autographs believed to be available at present. On p. vii of the *UBSGNT*[1], the editors write:

> Since this edition is intended primarily for translators it is not to be regarded as in competition with other modern editions, e.g. the continuing Nestle-Aland editions, which provide a more restricted selection of data from witnesses on a much wider range of variant readings.

One can conclude from this quotation that the edition is intended primarily for translators. It is also apparent that the *UBSGNT* records fewer variants, although these variants have much fuller manuscript citations than compared to the Nestle-Aland editions. The main critical apparatus of the *UBSGNT*[1] cites approximately 1400 passages, whereas the Nestle-Aland *Novum Testamentum Graece* cites closer to 10,000. This averages out to 1.6 variants per page in the *UBSGNT*[1], and 20 variants per page in the Nestle-Aland editions.

As I.A. Moir indicates, the *UBSGNT*[1] holds to the historical and traditional standards of textual criticism: 'It is clear that even in those places where the editors have detected uncertainty as to the reading by publishing the apparatus, their discussions have not led them to any radical departures from the lines which have established themselves in the past century.'[107] Westcott and Hort's text is closely supported, while its views are upheld. Again, Moir states: 'Even if recent discoveries have tended to vindicate WH views to some extent and even if there is no slavish following of WH, it is still of interest to note that in Mark some two-thirds of the C and D readings adopted in the text are already those of WH'.[108]

In comparison with other Greek editions of its day, the *UBSGNT*[1] has several distinct features: (1) for the first time in the history of Christendom, an edition of the Greek New Testament was produced by an international committee; (2) there was an extensive inclusion and citation of readings as they appeared in many known manuscripts, versions, and Patristic authors not previously cited in other Greek editions; (3) somewhat similar to Bengel's 1734 Greek edition, the *UBSGNT* editors included a letter-rating system that indicated the committee's judgment on the certainty of the ascribed reading selected in the *UBSGNT* text; and (4) a special apparatus provided information concerning more than six hundred differences in punctuation. Since the early Greek manuscripts of the New Testament contain very little punctuation, editors must supply them, and in these six hundred references a systematic attempt was made to provide meaningful alternative punctuation.

Upon publication of the *UBSGNT*[1], several future intentions were already made known to the wider academic community. These included plans for Metzger to begin production of his supplemental textual commentary and the ensuing development of a common text between forthcoming *UBSGNT* and Nestle-Aland editions. We finally note several of the more technical aspects that were present in the *UBSGNT*[1], such as its eleven-point Porson font, verse divisions based on the Nestle-Aland[25] (with a few exceptions, these divisions are identical to those first introduced by Stephanus in his 1551 edition of the Greek New Testament), and its incredibly low price of US $1.39. The *UBSGNT* is also the first critical Greek text to be typeset in the United States. It was composed by the firm of Maurice Jacobs, Inc., of Philadelphia, and was printed by the Württemberg Bible Society of Stuttgart, West Germany. Moir summarizes the situation regarding the *UBSGNT*[1]:

107. Moir, 'Greek New Testament', p. 141.
108. Moir, 'Greek New Testament', p. 141.

The preface to UGT [*UBSGNT*] contains the promise that 'it is the intention of the Committee from time to time to revise its work in order to take into account new discoveries and fresh evidence... This edition of the Greek New Testament is in no sense final, but merely representative of a significant stage in New Testament Studies.' In that case the Committee or its successor must already be kept in being and be active. This kind of work cannot be done in a day. It is essential therefore that cumulative supplementation giving place to a full revision within twenty years must be written into the plan of work to preserve both it and the translation world from stagnation. We accept then that the volume carries with it the seeds of its own destruction and can only hope that in due course it will give place to an even nobler phoenix.[109]

The Second Edition of the UBSGNT (UBSGNT^2)

The second edition of the *United Bible Societies' Greek New Testament* was published in 1968. However, at the time of publication of this second edition it was apparent from statements made in it, and also statements made in the earlier *UBSGNT^1*, that it was not to be the last edition. The *UBSGNT^2* added to the editorial committee Carlo M. Martini, of the Pontifical Biblical Institute in Rome. The Pontifical Biblical Institute was also included in the project, along with the previously mentioned Bible societies. Although the Institute for New Testament Textual Research at Münster is mentioned in the *UBSGNT^1*, in the *UBSGNT^2* it received official recognition by being mentioned upon the title page.

The major changes that occurred within the *UBSGNT^2* included the correction of typographical errors, forty-five alterations in the evaluation of evidence letter-ratings (A, B, C, D), five modifications of the text or punctuation, and eleven changes involving bracketed text. Single bracket text '[ ]' denoted words which were regarded as having 'dubious textual validity'. Double brackets '[[ ]]' were used to enclose passages that were regarded as later additions to the text, but had been retained due to their evident antiquity and textual tradition.

The two years that elapsed between the use of the *UBSGNT^1* and the *UBSGNT^2* revealed scholars' general thoughts on the escalating popularity of the *UBSGNT* tradition. As Elliott states:

> Worldwide interest has been expressed in this text and it is now frequently quoted and referred to. The editors have claimed that it is not their intention

109. Moir, 'Greek New Testament', p. 139. See also p. vii of the preface to the *UBSGNT^1*; and R.P. Markham and E.A. Nida, *An Introduction to the Bible Societies' Greek New Testament* (New York: United Bible Societies, 1969), p. 26.

to supersede other modern editions. However, some reviewers seemed to
welcome it as the leading Greek New Testament.[110]

Elliott goes on to cite several further opinions pertaining to the
UBSGNT. One reviewer in *The Expository Times* claimed that the new
edition (already referring to the growing popularity of the *UBSGNT*[1])
has 'much to commend it, and it is probable that it will soon be widely
accepted as the standard text for use by students of the New
Testament'.[111] Moir likewise draws attention to this standardization of
the *UBSGNT* and claims that 'With its non-local origins and wide spon-
sorship, it would seem that UGT [*UBSGNT*] is on the way to being the
first candidate for this position [of standardization] as far as the New
Testament is concerned.'[112] And finally, Haufe echoes these above sentiments when he asserts that quite obviously this new edition (the
UBSGNT) serves not essentially as a text-critical study but as a collaboration of a more quasi-ecumenical standard text.[113]

Clearly, articles and individual comments revealed that the *UBSGNT*
had won over many readers due to its full citation of manuscripts for
each variant, its clear, concise presentation of data in the critical apparatus, its letter-rating system for evaluating evidence, and its full, lucid
Introduction. On the other hand, it was criticized for such things as its
limited number of variants in comparison to Nestle-Aland's 10,000 citations, its inconsistency of the punctuation apparatus, its confusing and
selective use of bracketed text, and its heavy reliance upon Westcott and
Hort, and Codices Vaticanus (B03), Sinaiticus (ℵ01), and Alexandrinus
(A02).[114]

110. J.K. Elliott, 'The United Bible Societies' Greek New Testament: An
Evaluation', *NovT* 15 (1973), p. 278.

111. Author not cited, 'Notes of Recent Exposition', *ExpTim* 77 (1966), p. 353.

112. Moir, 'Greek New Testament', p. 138.

113. G. Haufe, 'Neues Testament: The Greek New Testament; *TLZ* 92 (1967),
column 513: 'Ganz offensichtlich soll die neue Ausgabe nicht eigentlich der text-
kritischen Forschung, sondern der Festlegung eines quasi ökumenischen
Standardtextes dienen'.

114. For these various points see review articles such as those by Elliott, 'An
Evaluation', pp. 278-300; *idem*, 'The Third Edition of the United Bible Societies'
Greek New Testament', *NovT* 20 (1978), p. 243; and J.M. Ross, 'The United Bible
Societies' Greek New Testament', *JBL* 95 (1976), pp. 112-21. For a refutation of
the criticism that the *UBSGNT* relies too heavily upon Codex Vaticanus and Codex
Sinaiticus, see E.G. Edwards, 'On Using the Textual Apparatus of the UBS Greek
New Testament', *BT* 28 (1977), pp. 141-42.

The Third Edition of the UBSGNT (UBSGNT³)

The third edition of the *United Bible Societies' Greek New Testament* was published in 1975. It contained a more thorough revision of the Greek Text. More than 500 changes were introduced into the *UBSGNT*³, the majority of these involving the addition of brackets and bracketed text. Many of these changes were brought about in order to bring future *UBSGNT* and Nestle-Aland texts into agreement and commonality, thus enabling the establishment of one single text between the two. However, this mutual editing was not to change the individual goals of each edition.

Numerous minor errors in the previous text and apparatus were also corrected, as well as several alterations in the evaluation of evidence letter-ratings. Modifications to the punctuation apparatus took place as well, but these consisted of negligible adjustments and corrections. The standards for the inclusion of Old Testament quotations were also made more rigid by the elimination of highlighting of all allusions or literary echoes. This resulted in fewer explicitly recorded Old Testament references. In the Introduction of the *UBSGNT*³ more witnesses were added to the lists of manuscripts, yet only a few of these new additions were actually cited in the critical apparatus in support of variants (only about 50 of the 250 newly listed manuscripts appear in the critical apparatus). No new sets of variant units were added in the *UBSGNT*³, although some minor modifications were made to a small and select number of individual variant options contained within their broader variant units.[115] Due to the numerous corrections in the *UBSGNT*³, it tended to be more reliable, and had a higher degree of accuracy when compared to the previous *UBSGNT* editions.

Upon the publication of the *UBSGNT*³, criticism was once again raised in regard to bracketed text. It seemed that the use of these brackets still remained confusing to most. In the previous editions, bracketed text denoted words, or parts of words, whose presence in the original autographs was disputed. However, in the *UBSGNT*², the brackets were also used to enclose words whose position in the text was of question.

---

115. In the *UBSGNT*, the term 'variant unit' is used simply to designate any particular biblical passage and its given variant options or readings where a textual choice must be made. For a detailed discussion and further clarification of this mistakenly 'simple' term, along with other foundational definitions used by textual critics, see Epp, 'Toward the Clarification of the Term "Textual Variant"', in Epp and Fee, *Studies in the Theory*, pp. 47-61; and Fee, 'On the Types', pp. 62-79.

Other changes such as the substitution of one word for another of a previous edition, alterations in the tense, mood, voice and person of a verb, and punctuation and orthographic modifications caused questioning among textual scholars.[116]

Elliott describes perhaps the most significant alteration that occurred in the *UBSGNT*[3]:

> UBS 3rd edn is presented as a less confident text. The editors have occasionally downgraded the printed text where variants are shown by reducing the rating. A former 'C' rating now sometimes appears as 'D', and occasionally an 'A' in UBS 2nd edn now appears as 'B' or a 'B' as 'C'. Irrational as this rating system is in its application and unnecessary as it appears to many critics, it is significant for revealing to us the editors' increasing (and understandable) diffidence in printing many variants as the original text.[117]

The general scholarly consensus placed the *UBSGNT*[3] closer than previous *UBSGNT* editions to the text presented by Westcott and Hort.[118] Again, Elliott states that the *UBSGNT*[3] is a 'safer' text compared to the *UBSGNT*[1] and the *UBSGNT*[2], because many more of the readings are supported by Codex Vaticanus and Codex Sinaiticus. Several other changes that took place in this edition included the lengthening of the bibliography over previous editions, the pericope in John 7.53–8.11 being taken from the end of the Gospel and placed in its traditional location,[119] and allusions to a fourth edition being expressed. The *UBSGNT*[3] also states that this future fourth edition will include a thorough revision of its textual apparatus with special emphasis upon evidence from ancient versions, the Diatessaron, and the Church Fathers.

The Third Corrected Edition of the UBSGNT (UBSGNT[3corr.])
The United Bible Societies' Third Corrected Edition was published in 1983. Due to fresh collations of manuscript evidence present in the Nestle-Aland[26], the citation of evidence in the *UBSGNT*[3] was corrected.

---

116. For these various points, see review articles such as those by Elliott, 'The Third Edition', pp. 255-67; and *idem*, 'A Short Examination', pp. 136-37.

117. Elliott, 'A Short Examination', p. 137.

118. See the various comments and references to this effect in nn. 101-108, and esp. n. 105 of this chapter.

119. Metzger notes that in the *UBSGNT*[3corr.] the ascribing of an *A* rating to this passage concerning the pericope of the adulteress is incorrectly applied to the inclusion of this variant into the New Testament text, instead of to its absence. See Metzger, *The Text of the New Testament*, p. 280.

This was done to conform to the Nestle-Aland textual apparatus (the modifications in the *UBSGNT*[3] were designed to bring mutuality between the Nestle-Aland text rather than the apparatus). The punctuation apparatus was also altered to conform to Nestle-Aland[26]. Over half of the total number of pages in this corrected *UBSGNT* edition had at least one alteration.

In the *UBSGNT*[3], Old Testament allusions and verbal parallels were no longer explicitly recorded, whereas in the *UBSGNT*[3corr.] they were provided in list form at the back of the volume. The actual text, variant units, and letter-ratings were not changed and remained identical to the *UBSGNT*[3]. The *UBSGNT*[3corr.] was to act as an interim text between the *UBSGNT*[3] and the *UBSGNT*[4].

The Fourth Edition of the UBSGNT (UBSGNT[4])

The most recent edition of the *UBSGNT* was published in 1993. Jan deWaard replaced Eugene Nida in representing the entire committee and the United Bible Societies. In replacement of the retiring Black and Wikgren, Barbara Aland and Johannes Karavidopoulos were added to the editorial committee. If the third edition was characterized by Elliott as a more certain and safer text, then the *UBSGNT*[4] surpassed it to a radical degree.[120] Changes to this edition consisted of: (1) a thorough revision of its textual apparatus rather than continuing to cite variants drawn from secondary (and often inaccurate) sources, and (2) an extensive review and new selection of variant units (keeping in mind that all four previous *UBSGNT* editions had very similar, and almost identical, variant passages cited in the textual apparatus). The intention was to provide an apparatus where the most important international translations of the New Testament were represented, and their notes regarding textual variants, or even differences in translation and interpretation, were recorded. Other more significant variants were also included. This resulted in the elimination of a large number of variant units where readings were thought to be of minor significance for translators and other readers or were only concerned with the smallest textual variations, and the inclusion of others having a greater importance for the reader's understanding of the history of the text and exegesis. Based upon these somewhat vaguely stated considerations, 284 new variants were

---

120. For this reference to a 'safer' text, see once again n. 105.

included, while 273 variants previously listed in other editions were removed.[121]

A redefinition of the various letter-rating levels (*A*, *B*, *C*, *D*) in the evaluation of evidence also occurred. This redefinition modified their relative degrees of certainty. Therefore, all 1437 sets of variants cited in the apparatus were reconsidered as to their letter-rating. In consideration of the new definitions, a 3-level, rather than a 4-level classification, would seem more appropriate as *D* letter-ratings are essentially non-existent in the *UBSGNT*[4].[122]

The punctuation apparatus, now referred to as 'The Discourse Segmentation Apparatus', was also revised in order to be of greater usefulness for translators. It no longer indicates all the punctuation marks found in representative modern translations. Instead, only major and minor divisions that influence the interpretation of the text as well as sentence and paragraph structure are considered, thus revealing a more selective incorporation of data into the apparatus. Minor differences such as stylistic considerations, rather than semantic considerations, have been omitted. It was also felt that the punctuation apparatus of the earlier *UBSGNT* editions, while useful, needed to be further revised because it was inadequate in that it did not take into account discourse segmentation above the clause and sentence level.[123] The number of Greek texts and modern translations used for comparison is greater, while abbreviations have been employed to identify particular segments (such as 'MS' for major section, and 'SP' for sub-paragraph).[124] Aside from punctuation, the text itself remains unchanged from the *UBSGNT*[3] and the *UBSGNT*[3corr.], and is the same as the Nestle-Aland[26,27].[125]

---

121. Chapter 2, Section 2 will present an evaluation of this aspect of the *UBSGNT*[4] revisions.

122. This entire facet of the textual apparatus will be discussed in Chapter 2.

123. For this point, see H.P. Scanlin, 'Review Symposium of GNT[4]', *BT* 45 (1994), p. 349.

124. For these points, see pp. 39*-45* of the *UBSGNT*[4] and M. Silva, 'Review Symposium of GNT[4]', *BT* 45 (1994), pp. 349-50. For further discussion regarding the new *UBSGNT*[4] Discourse Segmentation Apparatus, see J.K. Elliott, 'The New Testament in Greek: Two New Editions', *TLZ* 119 (1994), p. 493; and *idem*, 'The Fourth Edition of the United Bible Societies' Greek New Testament', *TRev* 90 (1994), cols. 9-10.

125. With all the changes in variants, it seems likely that the text of the *UBSGNT*[4] would differ from that of the *UBSGNT*[3] and *UBSGNT*[3corr.]. Yet this is not the case. The only modification comes in the inclusion or exclusion of variants that were

The underlying principles of this most recent edition were established by the committee in 1981. At that time decisions regarding eliminations and inclusions in the apparatus of variant readings, reconsideration of the letter-ratings, and guidelines for witnesses to be included in the apparatus were discussed and established. Careful consideration was given to the selection of individual witnesses within each group of manuscripts. This was done in order to reflect the character of the textual tradition and to exclude elements of uncertainty. Manuscripts were recollated and checked from photocopies or films, and versions from the standard editions of the texts or manuscripts. This new selection of manuscripts was based upon verifiable tests of the entire Greek manuscript tradition conducted at the Institute for New Testament Textual Research at Münster.

The use of single brackets within the Greek text was again modified to show that the enclosed word, words, or parts of words may be regarded as the original text. However, present textual scholarship cannot prove this with complete certainty. All such passages have been accorded a *C* letter-rating in the critical apparatus. If the variant is of minor grammatical significance with no appreciable bearing upon translation, it is not noted in the apparatus. However, the number of these bracketed passages has been considerably increased in the *UBSGNT*[4]. The explanation and use of double brackets remains consistent.[126]

Three concluding remarks should be made. The number of passages

previously consulted in order to establish the text of earlier editions. Although a large number of variants have been dropped in the *UBSGNT*[4], the text represented by these excluded variants has not changed from the *UBSGNT*[3] and *UBSGNT*[3corr.] where these variants were included. In other words, the *UBSGNT*[4] text continues to represent the choices made for variants in the *UBSGNT*[3] and *UBSGNT*[3corr.] regardless of these variants having been excluded in the *UBSGNT*[4]. Likewise, the addition of new variants into the *UBSGNT*[4] has not altered the text. Instead, variants which were earlier examined to determine the text for previous editions, although not included in the apparatus of these particular editions, have now been newly included in the *UBSGNT*[4]. The text represented by a particular variant may be included in the *UBSGNT* editions even though the variant itself is not included in the critical apparatus. See Chapter 2, Section 2 for further clarification of this point.

126. Compare the much revised statement regarding bracketed text, located on p. 2* of the *UBSGNT*[4], with statements made regarding bracketed text in earlier *UBSGNT* editions such as p. xii of the *UBSGNT*[3corr.]. Silva rightly points out that although we are now informed that all such bracketed passages receive a *C* rating, we are still not told how they differ in degree of certainty from other *C* rated passages that are not bracketed. See Silva, 'Symposium', p. 351. For a brief discussion of bracketed text in the *UBSGNT*[4], see Elliott, 'The Fourth Edition', col. 12.

within the textual apparatus (1438) remains similar to previous editions. There is a change in font that most reviewers seem to dislike. Because the font is lighter and somewhat italicized, it is more difficult to read than the font of previous editions. Lastly, similar to the very first *UBSGNT* edition, the methodology of Westcott and Hort remains the underlying foundation of this most recent edition.[127]

A Brief Comparison of the UBSGNT and the Nestle-Aland Editions[128]
The above discussion concerning the various editions of the *UBSGNT* clearly reveals the impact of the Nestle-Aland versions upon the *UBSGNT*, especially the later editions. In consideration of this, a brief discussion and history of the Nestle-Aland text is appropriate.

Eberhard Nestle (1851–1913) published his first edition of the *Novum Testamentum Graece* in 1898, under the auspices of the Württemberg Bible Society in Stuttgart, Germany. What Nestle did was to establish a majority consensus text based upon three editions. He compared the texts of Tischendorf and of Westcott and Hort. When these two did not agree, he consulted a third text (he first used Richard Francis Weymouth's second edition published in 1892, and after 1901, he used Bernhard Weiss's 1894–1900 edition).[129] Thus whenever a consensus of two texts was established, that was the text Nestle accepted. The reading of the third differing text was included in an apparatus, and, therefore, the reader was able to reconstruct the texts of each of the editions used by Nestle. As Aland states, 'this purely mechanical system of a majority text summarized the results of nineteenth-century textual scholarship'.[130]

1927 marked the publication of the thirteenth edition of the Nestle text. Eberhard Nestle's son, Erwin Nestle (1883–1972), was responsible for this most recent and important edition. Under Erwin Nestle's revisions, the thirteenth edition threw off its primitive format of 1898 and

---

127. See S. Wong's review of the *UBSGNT*[4] in *Jian Dao* 1 (1994), pp. 121-22; and Metzger, *A Textual Commentary*, 1994, p. 10*.
128. For this final section of Chapter 1, I have relied heavily upon K. Aland's own evaluation and critique of his work upon the *UBSGNT* and the Nestle-Aland editions. Much of this information has been gathered from K. and B. Aland, *The Text of the New Testament*, pp. 11-47. For specific comparisons of the *UBSGNT*[4] and Nestle-Aland[27], see Elliott 'Two New Editions', pp. 493-96; *idem*, 'The Fourth Edition', cols. 9-20; and *idem*, 'The Twentyseventh Edition of Nestle-Aland's Novum Testamentum Graece', *TRev* 90 (1994), cols. 19-24.
129. K. and B. Aland, *The Text of the New Testament*, p. 19.
130. K. and B. Aland, *The Text of the New Testament*, p. 20.

became the scholarly manual so desired by German New Testament scholars of the day. The revisions included a true critical apparatus based on actual manuscripts, versions, and Patristic writers. The readings of von Soden's text were also added to the apparatus.

Kurt Aland became involved with the work around 1950. His name was first mentioned as an associate in the 21st edition of 1952, and in the 22nd edition his name was recorded on the title page. Aland's first task was to verify the data in the Nestle edition, and at the same time to re-examine the text in preparation for a new edition.

In 1955, under the direction of the Translations Secretary, Eugene Nida, of the American Bible Society, a committee of international scholars was established, and was given the task of producing a Greek New Testament that specifically met the needs of Bible translators. Aland was one of the scholars invited to take part in this committee. However, with the full understanding of his colleagues, he continued to work on the new Nestle editions. Thus, Aland commenced work on two somewhat competing volumes. As both endeavors progressed, Aland continually influenced, and was influenced by, the committee. On the basis of the various suggestions and discussions that ensued as the various editions progressed and were revised, both became increasingly similar. Therefore, by the publication of the *UBSGNT*[3] (1975) and the Nestle-Aland[26] (1979), a majority of the differences had been removed and one common text existed. In the preface to the *UBSGNT*[3] (pp. viii-ix), the following statement is made concerning the two texts:

> In a series of meetings the Committee... undertook a thorough review of the text of the First Edition by carefully considering not only a number of suggestions made by specialists in the field of New Testament studies, but also numerous recommendations resulting from the experience of the members of the Committee as they worked with the text of the First Edition. The greater part of these suggestions for further modification came from Kurt Aland, who had been making a detailed analysis of changes proposed for the 26th edition of the Nestle-Aland text. A number of these were textual alterations which had not been previously discussed by the Committee in their work on the First Edition. As a result of the Committee's discussions, more than five hundred changes have been introduced into this Third Edition. The Committee, sponsored by the United Bible Societies, has thus been able to establish a single text for the Third Edition Greek New Testament and for the 26th edition of the Nestle-Aland text. That this step marks a significant advance will be obvious to all who work with the Greek text of the New Testament. At the same time the goals of both publications remain unchanged. The 26th

edition of the Nestle-Aland text will develop even further in the direction of [a] handy sized scientific edition through an extension and improvement of the critical apparatus, and this Greek New Testament [*UBSGNT*³] will continue to cite more extensive evidence for a more select number of variants. Though the arrangement and format of the two publications will be different, the texts will be the same, and both will be published under the editorship of the Committee.

One final quotation, located on p. 1* of the *UBSGNT*⁴ Introduction, reveals the following information concerning this common text:

> This edition reproduces the Greek text of the Third Edition (corrected) without change. Its text remains identical with that of Nestle-Aland in its 26th edition, and also in its 27th edition which is in the final stages of preparation and offers the same text unchanged.

In this way, the *UBSGNT* and the Nestle-Aland *Novum Testamentum Graece*, originally two quite independent editions, approached a close degree of unity with regard to their text, or as Aland states, 'more precisely, their wording'.[131] However, there remain some differences between both texts in orthography, punctuation, paragraphing, and general format. The following table concisely lists some of the differences between the two editions.

Differences between the UBSGNT and the Nestle-Aland Editions

UBSGNT	Nestle-Aland
• Originated in 1966.	• Originated in 1898.
• Lists a lower number of variants (1400 = 1.6/page).	• Lists a higher number of variants (10,000 = 20/page).
• Lists almost completely full manuscript citations for each variant option.	• Lists briefly only major manuscripts necessary to represent the variant option and make decisions regarding text.
• Divided into standard pericopes.	• Not divided so much into pericopes, but tends to replace these with original structural divisions of the text.
• Lacks both Eusebian canon numbers and chapter divisions.[132]	• Records Eusebian canon numbers and chapter divisions traditional in Greek New Testament manuscripts.

131. K. and B. Aland, *The Text of the New Testament*, p. 33.
132. Eusebius of Caesarea developed a brilliant method that assisted one to locate

UBSGNT	Nestle-Aland
• Includes a punctuation apparatus.	• Does not include a punctuation apparatus.
• Intended primarily for translators and New Testament students.	• Intended exclusively as a scientific pocket edition for use in universities and by New Testament specialists.
• Limited reference to parallel passages.	• More extensive reference to parallel passages.
• Special purposes of *UBSGNT* make inclusion of historical editions neither expected nor desirable.	• Lists all textual differences between editions from Tischendorf to the present Nestle-Aland edition in an appendix providing a survey of the New Testament text over the last century.
• Evaluates evidence with *A, B, C, D*, letter-ratings.	• Contains no explicit evaluation of evidence.
• Punctuation of text in earlier editions tended to follow English usage but *UBSGNT*[3corr.] adopts Nestle-Aland punctuation.	• Punctuation of text tends to follow Greek usage.
• **Bold face** identifies Old Testament quotations	• *Italics* identify Old Testament quotations.
• Includes section headings.	• Does not include section headings.
• Some review comments indicate that the *UBSGNT* text acted as the standard of comparison over the Nestle-Aland text.[133]	• Nestle-Aland text seems to change more to reflect *UBSGNT* rather than vice-versa.

parallel passages in the Gospels. This method was found to be very useful to scribes and readers alike and, therefore, is recorded in many Greek Gospel manuscripts and versions.

133. It is often stated that the Nestle-Aland[26] edition adopted the text of the *UBSGNT*. Aland states that this misconstrues the facts, and indicates that the late publication of the Nestle-Aland text was due to the amount of time required for preparing its critical apparatus. See K. and B. Aland, *The Text of the New Testament*, p. 33, note 59.

Chapter 2

A STATISTICAL PRESENTATION OF THE *UBSGNT*

In this chapter attention is now directed toward a detailed examination of the actual *UBSGNT* editions, with special reference to the *UBSGNT*[4]. The first task at hand is to reveal that there has been a great deal of change introduced to the *UBSGNT*[4] critical apparatus letter-ratings. The second goal is to explore various reasons why these remarkable changes might have occurred and if they are justifiable. Once this is determined, judgment can be made as to whether or not the editors have been too extreme in revising the ratings of textual variants, and/or inconsistent in their standards of variant ratings within the *UBSGNT*[4]. Prior to beginning this examination, a brief discussion outlining the use of the critical apparatus and variant letter-ratings will be presented. Familiarity of the critical apparatus and variant letter-ratings used within the *UBSGNT* is essential to understanding this second chapter.

The study and process of textual criticism is best displayed in Greek editions of the New Testament through the use of a *critical* or *textual apparatus*. These apparatuses vary in form throughout the numerous Greek New Testament editions. However, they generally serve the same function, which is to provide information about different readings that are found in manuscripts and early translations, and, by means of the apparatus, supply the reader with the material necessary to make decisions concerning the text, its integrity, and its modification by manuscript transmission.[1] Elliott notes one further use of a textual apparatus:

> The apparatus often serves an editor as a useful safety valve. On many of those occasions when he is uncertain which variant to print as the original, an editor can enable his readers to share his dilemma by reproducing the evidence in the apparatus. Those readings designated by the grading letter D in the UBS text may be seen in this way.[2]

1.   See K. Junack, 'The Reliability of the New Testament Text from the Perspective of Textual Criticism', *BT* 29 (1978), p. 130.
2.   Elliott, 'Recent Studies', p. 41.

Particular textual apparatuses are usually explained in the introduction to the Greek edition in which they appear. Here, the reader can find an explanation as to how the apparatus functions, how the manuscripts are listed, and how to use any special features or footnoting procedures. The textual apparatus of obvious concern in this monograph is the one present in each of the *UBSGNT* editions, and again, especially that of the *UBSGNT*[4].

The *UBSGNT* notes textual variants by placing a small superscript number in the main body of text and at the end of the text in question. Mt. 17.26, as recorded in the *UBSGNT*[4], will serve as an illustration. At the beginning of this passage the following can be observed: 'εἰπόντος δέ[6]...'. One should take note of the superscript number '6'. The number is used to indicate a textual variant at this point in the text. This specific number shows the reader that this is the sixth variant in Matthew 17. The same superscript number is found in the textual apparatus located directly under the text. Following this number in the apparatus, we find the verse reference in bold print. In this case it is verse **26**. Again, this records the particular verse containing the textual variant. After the verse reference there is a letter placed in braces {B}. This letter is a special feature common only to the *UBSGNT* textual apparatus.[3] It is called an 'Evaluation of Evidence Letter-Rating'. By the use of this letter, the editors of the *UBSGNT*[4] provide the reader with the following information (see page 3* of the fourth edition for these specific categories):

- The braced letter {A} indicates that the text is certain.
- The braced letter {B} indicates that the text is almost certain.
- The braced letter {C} indicates that the editors had difficulty in deciding which variant to place in the text.
- The braced letter {D} indicates that the editors had great difficulty arriving at a decision.

Taking these delineations into account, one can see that the editors find this text of Mt. 17.26 to be almost certain. Following the braced letter {B}, the Greek words εἰπόντος δέ occur. This indicates that all the

---

3.   Although this evaluation of evidence is common only to the *UBSGNT*, J.A. Bengel, in his New Testament Greek edition of 1734, utilized the same method to designate readings as superior to, equal to, or inferior to the readings printed in his text. See J.A. Bengel, *Novum Testamentum Graecum* (Tübingen: George Cottae, 1734). For further discussion, see Junack, 'Reliability', p. 1 and Metzger, *A Textual Commentary*, 1971, p. xxviii n. 10; and 1994, p. 14* n.

manuscripts following these words have this particular reading as their text. Following these two Greek words, we are provided with a list of the particular manuscripts. The manuscripts are listed in the following order: papyri, uncials, minuscules, lectionaries, ancient versions, Greek Church Fathers, and lastly, Latin Church Fathers. Often special characters such as brackets ( ), asterisks *, superscript numerals $^{1/2}$, and superscript letters ^{mss} are recorded with the manuscripts. These characters provide additional information pertaining to those manuscripts cited. A master list of symbols and abbreviations, located on pages 47*-52* of the *UBSGNT*[4], explains each of these. A double slash '//' follows the first group of manuscripts cited or listed. This symbol indicates the end of the first variant and the start of the next variant. Therefore, in Mt. 17.26 one can see six distinct variants for this passage alone. These variants are:

i.   εἰπόντος δέ //
ii.   εἰπόντος δὲ τοῦ Πέτρου //
iii. λέγει αὐτῷ ὁ Πέτρος //
iv.   λέγει αὐτῷ //
v.   ὁ δὲ ἔφη, Ἀπὸ τῶν ἀλλοτρίων. εἰπόντος δέ //
vi.   λέγει αὐτῷ ὁ Πέτρος, Ἀπὸ τῶν ἀλλοτρίων. εἰπόντος δὲ αὐτοῦ //

All six of these readings or variants together are called a *variant unit*. The *UBSGNT* always places the first variant occurring in a variant unit into the main body of the text. Therefore, the first variant εἰπόντος δέ is the variant included in the text and also the variant given the {B} rating. Each variant listed in a variant unit follows the same format as just described (i.e. double slash //, followed by the particular variant reading in the Greek text and manuscript witnesses in the order of papyri, uncials, minuscules, lectionaries, ancient versions, Greek Church Fathers, and lastly, Latin Church Fathers).

Several further points pertaining to the *A*, *B*, *C*, and *D* Evaluation of Evidence Letter-Ratings should be mentioned. This method of rating the text has received mixed reviews. Omanson indicates some further positive reasons for the inclusion of these letter-ratings: 'The purpose of this rating system is to help translators scattered around the world to have some idea of when they may more safely depart from the UBS text and when they should stay with it'.[4] However, as J.M. Ross states, and as

4.   Omanson, 'A Perspective', p. 122.

will be explored below, this lettering system has been judged by some as inadequate:

> The attempt to indicate by the letters A B C and D the judgment of the editors as to the probability of the printed text represents an important advance on all previous editions, but these markings do not turn out in practice to be as useful as they promised to be at first sight. The scale of four grades from A to D is over-subtle.[5]

We now turn to the investigation of the actual *UBSGNT* editions. The statistics, charts, and explanations that follow can be categorized into four main sections. The first section presents the type or level of variant letter-ratings (*A*, *B*, *C*, or *D*) and the number of variant letter-ratings that appear throughout each edition of the *UBSGNT* and each biblical book. This is followed by an analysis of the letter-ratings using a statistical tool called a Chi-square. Finally, this first section provides a summary of all the biblical books, revealing the successive modifications made to these ratings and, consequently, enabling one to observe the ascending, descending, or static level of variant letter-ratings as they occur in each biblical book and each *UBSGNT* edition. The second section elaborates further on the information gleaned from the first section by providing statistics that more accurately reflect the exact nature and type of modifications made to the *UBSGNT*[4] letter-ratings. A second Chi-square statistic is used here as well. The third section develops categories and trends based on the type of rating changes made throughout all the *UBSGNT* editions together. A comparison of the number of times these categories appear in each biblical book, and a presentation of these categories as grand totals, completes this section. The fourth and final section of this second chapter begins to explore answers to the all-important question—why have these changes occurred? Here, variants are dealt with in a more specific manner. Detailed manuscript evidence and citations are charted as they occur in selected variant passages within portions of the *UBSGNT*[4]; percentage statistics are provided in order to exhibit primary manuscripts and their groupings in reference to the letter-ratings given for variants; and a discussion concerning the various levels of letter-rating and how they are defined in each *UBSGNT* edition constitutes the last area of investigation. Each section is based upon data that are too detailed to present in the main body of this chapter. Therefore, they have been included in the final appendices. These

---

5.   Ross, 'The United Bible', p. 117.

appendices can be consulted for additional information that is often more detailed and more precise than that given in the content of this chapter. The following section, containing various statistics and charts, begins with a thorough explanation. When appropriate, specific examples are used within each section in order to furnish further clarification. A concluding summary follows each of the four sections and serves to represent the overall thrust of the statistical survey.

1. *Analysis of Variant Letter-Ratings (A, B, C, D) within Each UBSGNT Edition and within Each Biblical Book*

The information provided here is designed to reveal that the *UBSGNT*[4] has introduced an extensive change to the critical apparatus letter-ratings for many variants, especially when seen in the light of earlier editions. The data represent an analysis based upon the charts of Appendix I and Appendix II. This first section of Chapter 2 is divided into a number of further areas of investigation. The first area, consisting of two charts, focuses predominantly upon letter-rating correlations and statistics. The second area, consisting of one chart, makes use of the Chi-square statistic, while the third area presents each book in its normal canonical order and provides a summarizing paragraph detailing the specific trend of each book.

Charts 1 and 2 are relatively simple to understand. In the first chart, each *UBSGNT* edition is listed as a vertical column. Under each edition the four possible variant ratings (*A, B, C, D*) are given; also listed are the totals (*Tot.*), which record the *total number of letter-rated variants* that occur in each particular book and edition, (*A* + *B* + *C* + *D* = *Tot.*). Each biblical book is listed as one horizontal row. The numbers appearing under each letter-rating and in line with each book represent the number of times a particular rating occurs within a given book and given edition. The horizontal row, entitled '*Overall Totals*', performs two tasks: (1) it tallies the total number of times each specific letter-rating (*A, B, C,* or *D*) occurs in each edition, and (2) it tallies the total number of all letter-rated variants present in each edition.[6] The final horizontal row, entitled

---

6. The '*Overall Totals*' figures are based upon variants that have a letter-rating. Variants without the *A, B, C,* or *D* letter-rating are not calculated. This is one explanation for the difference between these totals and other totals given for *UBSGNT* editions. Section 3, notes 39-42, also provides further explanation concerning a number of these discrepancies.

'*Overall Percentage*', simply breaks down the '*Overall Totals*' row into percentages. For example, in the *UBSGNT*[1] there is an overall total of 136 *A* rated variants, therefore constituting 9 percent of all rated variants in this edition (136 ÷ 1446 = 9.4%). There is an overall total of 486 *B* rated variants, therefore constituting 34 percent of all rated variants in this edition (486 ÷ 1446 = 33.6%), etc. The second chart is similar to the first, except that it changes all figures into percentages. Percentage statistics are calculated by dividing the number of times any one variant rating occurs by the number of total variants in each particular book and edition, again represented by the total column (*Tot.*). In other words, the total column indicates the total number of rated variants that the percentage figures are based upon. The percentage calculations display each variant rating (*A*, *B*, *C*, or *D*) in relationship to the other three ratings.[7]

Using the Gospel of Matthew as an example, one can better comprehend how both charts function. In the *UBSGNT*[1] the *A* letter-rating occurs 8 times (Chart 1) making up only 4 percent of the total number of rated variants (8 ÷ 185 = 4.3%; Chart 2). *B* occurs 76 times in the first edition (Chart 1) amounting to 41 percent of the total number of variants (76 ÷ 185 = 41%; Chart 2). *C* occurs 93 times (Chart 1), constituting 50 percent of the total number of variants (93 ÷ 185 = 50.2%; Chart 2). *D* occurs 8 times (Chart 1) amounting to 4 percent of the total number of variants (8 ÷ 185 = 4.3%; Chart 2). The total number of variants listed in the total column is 185 (8[*A*]+76[*B*] + 93[*C*] + 8[*D*] = 185 total variants). The *UBSGNT*[1] is then followed by the other editions. By examining each *UBSGNT* edition in relationship to the others, one is clearly able to evaluate the changes that result in the Gospel of Matthew and subsequent books.

---

7.   The percentage calculations are rounded off to the nearest whole number based upon the first decimal figure.

Analysis of Variant Letter-Ratings (A, B, C, D) within Each UBSGNT Edition and within Each Biblical Book—Chart 1

Biblical Book	1st Edition Variants (UBSGNT¹)					2nd Edition Variants (UBSGNT²)					3rd Edition Variants (UBSGNT³)					3rd Corrected Edition Variants (UBSGNT³corr.)					4th Edition Variants (UBSGNT⁴)				
	A	B	C	D	Tot.	A	B	C	D	Tot.	A	B	C	D	Tot.	A	B	C	D	Tot.	A	B	C	D	Tot.
Matthew	8	76	93	8	185	9	75	91	10	185	9	69	94	13	185	9	69	94	13	185	34	73	53	1	161
Mark	49	54	59	8	170	43	59	60	8	170	40	59	57	14	170	40	59	57	14	170	46	50	45	1	142
Luke	7	47	97	26	177	7	47	97	26	177	7	45	100	25	177	7	45	100	25	177	45	78	44	0	167
John	30	57	76	9	172	27	58	78	9	172	27	55	78	12	172	27	55	78	12	172[8]	46	65	42	1	154
Acts	10	76	87	19	192	11	77	84	20	192	11	76	84	21	192	11	76	83	21	191[8]	74	81	42	1	198
Romans	12	35	42	2	91	12	34	42	3	91	11	32	42	6	91	11	32	42	6	91	41	21	22	1	85
1 Corinthians	7	16	30	6	59	8	14	31	6	59	8	14	30	7	59	8	14	30	7	59	23	22	14	1	60
2 Corinthians	0	9	19	6	34	0	6	23	5	34	0	6	22	6	34	0	6	22	6	34	12	18	10	0	40
Galatians	1	12	5	4	22	1	12	5	4	22	1	11	5	5	22	1	11	5	5	22	16	3	9	0	28
Ephesians	0	12	8	3	23	0	11	9	3	23	0	11	9	3	23	0	11	9	3	23	15	12	8	0	35
Philippians	0	8	7	1	16	0	8	7	1	16	0	9	6	1	16	0	9	6	1	16	10	7	4	0	21
Colossians	1	5	11	5	22	1	5	11	5	22	1	5	11	5	22	1	5	11	5	22	8	12	8	0	28
1 Thessalonians	2	5	4	0	11	2	5	4	0	11	2	4	5	0	11	2	4	5	0	11	9	3	3	0	15
2 Thessalonians	0	2	7	0	9	0	2	7	0	9	0	2	7	0	9	0	2	7	0	9	3	3	2	0	8
1 Timothy	2	5	4	0	11	2	5	4	0	11	2	5	4	0	11	2	5	4	0	11	15	2	2	0	19
2 Timothy	0	2	6	0	8	0	2	6	0	8	0	2	6	0	8	0	2	6	0	8	2	5	1	0	8
Titus	0	2	2	0	4	0	2	2	0	4	0	2	2	0	4	0	2	2	0	4	2	1	1	0	4
Philemon	0	2	2	0	4	0	2	2	0	4	0	2	2	0	4	0	2	2	0	4	2	3	0	0	5
Hebrews	2	11	20	5	38	2	12	19	5	38	2	12	19	5	38	2	12	19	5	38	20	12	12	0	44
James	1	6	7	4	18	1	7	6	4	18	1	7	7	3	18	1	7	7	3	18	7	12	4	0	23
1 Peter	1	9	16	2	28	1	10	15	2	28	1	10	14	2	27	1	10	14	2	27	20	9	8	0	37
2 Peter	0	4	10	6	20	0	4	10	6	20	0	4	10	6	20	0	4	10	6	20	8	8	7	1	24
1 John	2	11	10	2	25	2	12	9	2	25	2	12	8	3	25	2	12	8	3	25	19	8	5	0	32
2 John	0	3	3	0	6	0	4	2	0	6	0	4	2	0	6	0	4	2	0	6	4	2	0	0	6
3 John	0	1	2	0	3	0	1	2	0	3	0	1	2	0	3	0	1	2	0	3	1	1	0	0	2
Jude	0	2	3	1	6	0	2	3	1	6	0	2	3	1	6	0	2	3	1	6	9	0	0	0	13
Revelation	1	14	72	5	92	1	14	72	5	92	1	14	71	6	92	1	14	71	6	92	23	30	18	1	72
Overall Totals	136	486	702	122	1446	130	490	701	125	1446	126	475	700	144	1445	126	475	699	144	1444	514	541	367	9	1431
Overall Percent	9	34	49	8	100	9	34	48	9	100	9	33	48	10	100	9	33	48	10	100	36	38	26	1	101

8. Here in the *UBSGNT*³corr., the letter-rating for the first variant at Acts 5.32 is mistakenly left out of the edition. This variant should most likely be regarded as a *C* rated passage. All percentage figures have been either rounded up, or rounded down to the nearest whole number. This is based upon the numerical value of the first decimal place.

Analysis of Variant Letter-Ratings (A, B, C, D) within Each UBSGNT Edition
and within Each Biblical Book Viewed as Percentages[9] —Chart 2

Biblical Book	1st Edition Variants (UBSGNT[1])					2nd Edition Variants (UBSGNT[2])					3rd Edition Variants (UBSGNT[3])					3rd Corrected Edition Variants (UBSGNT[3corr.])					4th Edition Variants (UBSGNT[4])				
	A	B	C	D	Tot.	A	B	C	D	Tot.	A	B	C	D	Tot.	A	B	C	D	Tot.	A	B	C	D	Tot.
Matthew	4%	41%	50%	4%	185	5%	41%	49%	5%	185	5%	37%	51%	7%	185	5%	37%	51%	7%	185	21%	45%	33%	1%	161
Mark	29%	32%	35%	5%	170	25%	35%	35%	5%	170	24%	35%	34%	8%	170	24%	35%	34%	8%	170	32%	35%	32%	1%	142
Luke	4%	27%	55%	15%	177	4%	27%	55%	15%	177	4%	25%	56%	14%	177	4%	25%	56%	14%	177	27%	47%	26%	0%	167
John	17%	33%	44%	5%	172	16%	34%	45%	5%	172	16%	32%	45%	7%	172	16%	32%	45%	7%	172	30%	42%	27%	1%	154
Acts	5%	40%	45%	10%	192	6%	40%	44%	10%	192	6%	40%	44%	11%	192	6%	40%	44%	11%	191	37%	41%	21%	1%	198
Romans	13%	39%	46%	2%	91	13%	37%	46%	3%	91	11%	32%	42%	6%	91	11%	32%	42%	6%	91	48%	25%	26%	1%	85
1 Corinthians	12%	27%	51%	10%	59	14%	24%	53%	10%	59	14%	24%	51%	12%	59	14%	24%	51%	12%	59	38%	37%	23%	2%	60
2 Corinthians	0%	26%	56%	18%	34	0%	18%	68%	15%	34	0%	18%	65%	18%	34	0%	18%	65%	18%	34	30%	45%	25%	0%	40
Galatians	5%	55%	23%	18%	22	5%	55%	23%	18%	22	5%	50%	23%	23%	22	5%	50%	23%	23%	22	57%	11%	32%	0%	28
Ephesians	0%	52%	35%	13%	23	0%	48%	39%	13%	23	0%	48%	39%	13%	23	0%	48%	39%	13%	23	43%	34%	23%	0%	35
Philippians	0%	50%	44%	6%	16	0%	50%	44%	6%	16	0%	56%	38%	6%	16	0%	56%	38%	6%	16	48%	33%	19%	0%	21
Colossians	5%	23%	50%	23%	22	5%	23%	50%	23%	22	5%	23%	50%	23%	22	5%	23%	50%	23%	22	29%	43%	29%	0%	28
1 Thessalonians	18%	45%	36%	0%	11	18%	45%	36%	0%	11	18%	36%	45%	0%	11	18%	36%	45%	0%	11	60%	20%	20%	0%	15
2 Thessalonians	0%	22%	78%	0%	9	0%	22%	78%	0%	9	0%	22%	78%	0%	9	0%	22%	78%	0%	9	38%	38%	25%	0%	8
1 Timothy	18%	45%	36%	0%	11	18%	45%	36%	0%	11	18%	45%	36%	0%	11	18%	45%	36%	0%	11	79%	11%	11%	0%	19
2 Timothy	0%	25%	75%	0%	8	0%	25%	75%	0%	8	0%	25%	75%	0%	8	0%	25%	75%	0%	8	25%	63%	13%	0%	8
Titus	0%	50%	50%	0%	4	0%	50%	50%	0%	4	0%	50%	50%	0%	4	0%	50%	50%	0%	4	50%	25%	25%	0%	4
Philemon	0%	50%	50%	0%	4	0%	50%	50%	0%	4	0%	50%	50%	0%	4	0%	50%	50%	0%	4	40%	60%	0%	0%	5
Hebrews	5%	29%	53%	13%	38	5%	32%	50%	13%	38	5%	32%	50%	13%	38	5%	32%	50%	13%	38	45%	27%	27%	0%	44
James	6%	33%	39%	22%	18	6%	39%	33%	22%	18	6%	39%	39%	17%	18	6%	39%	39%	17%	18	30%	52%	17%	0%	23
1 Peter	4%	32%	57%	7%	28	4%	36%	54%	7%	28	4%	37%	52%	7%	27	4%	37%	52%	7%	27	54%	24%	22%	0%	37
2 Peter	0%	20%	50%	30%	20	0%	20%	50%	30%	20	0%	20%	50%	30%	20	0%	20%	50%	30%	20	33%	33%	29%	4%	24
1 John	8%	44%	40%	8%	25	8%	48%	36%	8%	25	8%	48%	32%	12%	25	8%	48%	32%	12%	25	59%	25%	16%	0%	32
2 John	0%	50%	50%	0%	6	0%	67%	33%	0%	6	0%	67%	33%	0%	6	0%	67%	33%	0%	6	67%	33%	0%	0%	6
3 John	0%	33%	67%	0%	3	0%	33%	67%	0%	3	0%	33%	67%	0%	3	0%	33%	67%	0%	3	50%	50%	0%	0%	2
Jude	0%	33%	50%	17%	6	0%	33%	50%	17%	6	0%	33%	50%	17%	6	0%	33%	50%	17%	6	69%	0%	23%	8%	13
Revelation	1%	15%	78%	5%	92	1%	15%	78%	5%	92	1%	15%	77%	7%	92	1%	15%	77%	7%	92	32%	42%	25%	1%	72

9. Again, all percentage figures have been either rounded up, or rounded down to the nearest whole number. This is based upon the numerical value of the first decimal place.

Chi-Square (χ^2) Statistics

In many types of survey or research, as in this analysis of the *UBSGNT* letter-ratings, one may be interested in knowing whether scores have fallen in equal numbers into several categories (after allowing for the effects of mere chance). The Chi-square (χ^2) statistic, which takes its name from the Greek letter Chi, can be used to reveal whether or not there is a fluctuation, discrepancy, or independence between observed numbers (also called frequencies) within various categories, and whether or not this fluctuation, discrepancy, or independence has occurred by chance. In other words, the Chi-square will measure whether there is a significant degree of fluctuation in the specific *A*, *B*, *C*, and *D* letter-rating totals within the *UBSGNT* editions, and whether this has occurred by mere chance. Although a brief examination of the previous chart reveals that there is a considerable fluctuation in the *UBSGNT* letter-ratings, the Chi-square statistic provides a more accurate and mechanical means of verifying this conclusion. Based upon the figures recorded in the previous chart, the following Chi-square table has been developed.[10]

The specific Chi-square test used here is called a Complex Chi-square because the table contains more than four cells. More specifically, it can be called a 4 × 5 Contingency Table consisting of twenty cells (also termed Cross Tabulation or Cross Classification Tables). The goal of such a table is to examine the relationship between the row and column variables (also called a measurement of association). The Chi-square statistic works by taking each of the *obtained* or *observed frequencies* in the cells (the non-italicized actual figures recorded for letter-ratings in the *UBSGNT* editions) and comparing these with each of the *expected frequencies* (the italicized figures one would expect to see based to some extent on the law of averages or patterns of distribution as revealed in

10. This section will only briefly explain how the Chi-square statistic functions. For a more thorough presentation of this tool, one should consult Frances Clegg's work entitled *Simple Statistics* (Cambridge: Cambridge University Press, 1991), pp. 91-101, and 173-79. Other helpful works on Chi-square statistics, although varying in degrees of technicality, include R.L.D. Wright, *Understanding Statistics* (New York: Harcourt Brace Jovanovich, 1976), pp. 429-35; C. Morris, *Quantitative Approaches in Business Studies* (London: Pitman Publishing, 3rd edn, 1993), pp. 205-10; and B.H. Erickson and T.A. Nosanchuck, *Understanding Data* (Philadelphia: Open University Press, 1985), pp. 247-63.

Chi-Square (χ^2) Statistics for Variant Letter-Ratings (A, B, C, D)
within Each UBSGNT Edition

	Col. 1 UBSGNT[1]	Col. 2 UBSGNT[2]	Col. 3 UBSGNT[3]	Col. 4 UBSGNT[3corr.]	Col. 5 UBSGNT[4]	Row Total
Row 1 A Rating	136 *206.915*	130 *206.915*	126 *206.772*	126 *206.628*	514 *204.768*	1032
Row 2 B Rating	486 *494.631*	490 *494.631*	475 *494.289*	475 *493.947*	541 *489.500*	2467
Row 3 C Rating	702 *635.381*	701 *635.381*	700 *634.942*	699 *634.503*	367 *628.790*	3169
Row 4 D Rating	122 *109.071*	125 *109.071*	144 *108.996*	144 *108.920*	9 *107.940*	544
Column Total	1446	1446	1445	1444	1431	Grand Total 7212

Non-italicized Figures = Observed Frequencies $\chi^2 = 843.048$
Italicized Figures = Expected Frequencies $df = 12$

previous categories; or in this case, as revealed in previous *UBSGNT* editions).[11] To obtain the values which will be added together to get the χ^2 figure, the difference between the observed and expected frequencies is found by subtracting the smaller figure from the larger figure for every cell in the table. The greater the differences are, the more the distributions vary from each other. This number is then squared, and the value divided by the expected frequency for that particular cell.[12] Once all figures in each cell have been calculated in this manner, they are added

11. The expected frequency figures are calculated by taking the Row Total and Column Total that intersect at each given cell, multiplying these two numbers together, and then dividing this figure by the Grand Total figure. For example, the expected frequency figure provided at the Row 1 and Col. 1 intersection (206.915) is calculated by multiplying 1032 by 1446. This figure (1,492,272) is then divided by the grand total figure (7212) with the expected frequency coming to 206.915. The expected frequency figure provided at the Row 3 and Col. 4 intersection (634.503) is calculated by multiplying 3169 by 1444. This figure (4,576,036) is then divided by the grand total figure (7212) with the expected frequency coming to 634.503.

12. For example, the difference between the figures recorded in Row 1 and Col. 1 is 70.915. This is obtained by subtracting 136 from 206.915. This figure is then squared ($70.915^2 = 5028.937$) and divided by the expected frequency for Row 1 and Col. 1 ($5028.937 \div 206.915 = 24.304$). The difference between the figures recorded in Row 2 and Col. 1 is 8.631. This is obtained by subtracting 486 from 494.631. This figure is then squared ($8.631^2 = 74.494$) and divided by the expected frequency for Row 1 and Col. 1 ($74.494 \div 494.631 = 0.150$).

together to obtain the χ^2 value.[13] The Chi-square (χ^2) value for the above table is 843.048. Once again, the larger this value is, the more likely the distributions are to differ. However, the degree of difference required before the distributions can be considered *really* different must be determined through the employment of what is called the 'Test of Statistical Significance and Difference'. First, the Degrees of Freedom (*df*) value must be calculated. This figure is determined by multiplying the number of rows in a given table minus 1 by the number of columns minus 1.[14] Second, using the *df* figure (12), one must now refer to what is called a 'Critical Values for Chi-square Table' in order to see if there is a significant difference between the actual obtained frequencies and the expected frequencies. An excerpt from a Critical Values for Chi-square Table follows. The probability value at the top of each column refers to the likelihood of the values of Chi-square (χ^2) listed below being reached or exceeded merely by chance. The far left-hand column records the *df* figure.[15]

Critical Values of Chi-square (χ^2)

df	Level of Significance and Probability Values			
	0.1	0.05	0.01	0.001
1	2.706	3.841	6.635	10.83
2	4.605	5.991	9.210	13.82
3	6.251	7.815	11.34	16.27
4	7.779	9.488	13.28	18.47
5	9.236	11.07	15.09	20.52
6	10.64	12.59	16.81	22.46
7	12.02	14.07	18.48	24.32
8	13.36	15.51	20.09	26.12
9	14.68	16.92	21.67	27.88
10	15.99	18.31	23.21	29.59

13. The actual formula for the Chi-square calculation is $\chi^2 = \Sigma\,(O - E)^2 \div E$. In this equation, E = the expected frequencies, O = the observed frequencies, and Σ = the sum of.

14. Therefore, the *df* = (Rows – 1)(Columns – 1). According to our table, the *df* = 12: (4–1)(5–1) = 3 x 4 = 12. The *df* figure actually refers to how many items in a table one needs to know before the remainder are fixed, or, the number of categories in which frequencies of scores are merely the dependent variable.

15. This is similar to other statistical tests where a specific chart or table often provides the mean figures upon which a comparison of data occurs. A Critical Values for Chi-square Table can be found in most text-books dealing with statistics. The following table is taken from Clegg, *Simple Statistics*, p. 175. For a more detailed table see Erickson and Nosanchuk, *Understanding Data*, p. 382.

	Level of Significance and Probability Values			
df	0.1	0.05	0.01	0.001
11	17.28	19.68	24.73	31.26
12	18.55	21.03	26.22	32.91
13	19.81	22.36	27.69	34.53

When the appropriate *df* figure (12) is located in the left-hand margin of the above table, the probability values, reading horizontally from the *df* column, are found to be 18.55, 21.03, 26.22, and 32.91. Therefore, when the *df* = 12 the value of Chi-square (χ^2) must be equal to or greater than 18.55, 21.03, 26.22, or 32.91 in order for one to conclude that there is a significant divergence or fluctuation in the observed frequencies. The Chi-square value from the first table ($\chi^2 = 843.048$) exceeds these figures by a considerable degree (as is often the case when using the Chi-square statistic), therefore, one may conclude that the ratio of letter-rated variants in the five *UBSGNT* editions varies substantially and that the specific letter-rating categories for the *UBSGNT* were not being treated in a similar fashion from edition to edition. In other words, the Chi-square statistic has revealed a significant degree of fluctuation in the specific *A*, *B*, *C*, and *D* letter-rating totals within the *UBSGNT* editions, and because of the extent of variation observed, this has not occurred by mere chance.

One must, however, be cautious in the interpretation of what constitutes 'significant' results. Unfortunately, even if one knows, from the calculated value of χ^2, that the letter-rating distributions differ from each other, the Chi-square test tells us nothing about where precisely in the table the crucial differences are to be found or why these differences exist. Although 'eye-balling' where the biggest discrepancies occur between the observed and expected frequencies reveals clues as to where divergent distributions lie, the data should be consulted directly in order to make firm conclusions. The test only tells us that the letter-rating numbers come from distributions having different shapes or totals. One has to decide how the shapes differ, and where the most substantial discrepancies lie by inspection of the actual data.

Book Summaries
Matthew summary. In the Gospel of Matthew the greatest change takes place in the *UBSGNT*[4]. Only minor deviations arise in the other editions. The *UBSGNT*[1] and *UBSGNT*[2] are congruent. The *UBSGNT*[3] and *UBSGNT*[3corr.] are identical.[16] In the *UBSGNT*[4], *A* variants increase a

---

16. As explained in Chapter 1, p. 63, and n. 125, this is due to the corrective nature of the *UBSGNT*[3corr.], whereby the editors sought to bring closer correlation

dramatic 16 percent (from approximately 9 in all earlier editions to 34 in the *UBSGNT*[4]).[17] *B* variants remain similar in all editions (the first four editions remain between 69-76, while the *UBSGNT*[4] contains 73). *C* variants drop considerably from an average of 50 percent to 33 percent (from between 91-94 in the four earlier editions to 53 in the *UBSGNT*[4]). Proportionately, *D* variants fall much lower as well (between 8-13 in all earlier editions to only 1 in the *UBSGNT*[4]). The overall number of total variants declines from 185 in each of the four earlier *UBSGNT* editions to 161 in the *UBSGNT*[4]. The Gospel of Matthew reveals substantial variant letter-rating fluctuation in the *UBSGNT*[4], especially corresponding to *A*, *C*, and *D* letter-ratings.

Mark summary. In Mark we see a lower degree of variation since all five *UBSGNT* editions remain relatively constant. The greatest alteration lies in the drop of *D* ratings in the *UBSGNT*[4] (the *UBSGNT*[1] and *UBSGNT*[2] each contain 8, the *UBSGNT*[3] and *UBSGNT*[3corr.] each contain 14, while the *UBSGNT*[4] drops down to 1 *D* rated variant). *A*, *B*, and *C* ratings fluctuate to some extent, but generally remain similar in all editions. Other than a drop in the total number of variants (falling from 170 in each of the four earlier editions to 142 in the *UBSGNT*[4]), and the falling *D* ratings in the *UBSGNT*[4], there is no contestable change in the Gospel of Mark.

Luke summary. The first four editions remain remarkably harmonious. However, in the *UBSGNT*[4] we observe incredible divergence. *A* ratings increase greatly from 4 percent (7 *A* ratings in each of the four earlier editions) to 27 percent (45 *A* ratings in the *UBSGNT*[4]). *B* ratings increase to a large degree as well (between 45-47 in the first four editions climbing to 78 in the *UBSGNT*[4]). *C* ratings take a dramatic drop from 56 percent down to 26 percent (from an average of 99 in the first four editions down to 44 in the *UBSGNT*[4]). But perhaps the greatest movement occurs in the *D* rated variants, dropping from about 14 percent (from an average of 26 in each of the four earlier editions) down to 0 percent in the *UBSGNT*[4]. Once again the total number of variants falls

between the Nestle-Aland[26] edition and further *UBSGNT* editions. The changes that were made to bring about this closer resemblance had very little focus upon variant letter-ratings as the Nestle-Aland editions do not make use of these ratings.

17. As in Charts 1 and 2, all numbers representing averaged figures have been either rounded up, or rounded down to the nearest whole number. This is based upon the numerical value of the first decimal place.

(from 177 in each of the four earlier editions to 167 in the *UBSGNT*[4]). Luke is a noteworthy example of extensive change.

John summary. The *UBSGNT*[1] to the *UBSGNT*[3corr.] are again consistent. The *UBSGNT*[4] continues in its unsteady trend. *A* ratings increase significantly (from an average of 28 in the first four editions to 46 in the *UBSGNT*[4]), *C* ratings dwindle much lower (from an average of 78 in the four earlier editions to 42 in the *UBSGNT*[4]), and *D* ratings are almost non-existent, falling from about 7 percent to 1 percent (the *UBSGNT*[1] and the *UBSGNT*[2] contain 9 *D* rated variants each, the *UBSGNT*[3] and the *UBSGNT*[3corr.] contain 12 *D* rated variants each, while the *UBSGNT*[4] contains only 1). The total number of variants slides downward by 18 (falling from 172 in each of the four earlier editions to 154 in the *UBSGNT*[4]).

Acts summary. Acts shows remarkable variance in the *UBSGNT*[4]. The previous editions are consistent. *A* variants increase from about 6 percent in the earlier *UBSGNT* editions to 37 percent in the *UBSGNT*[4] (from an average of 11 in the four earlier editions to 74 in the *UBSGNT*[4]). *C* variants decrease in half from approximately 44 percent down to 21 percent (from an average of 85 in the first four editions to 42 in the *UBSGNT*[4]). *D* variants decline from around 10 percent to 1 percent (from an average of 20 in the four earlier editions to 1 in the *UBSGNT*[4]). *B* variants are similar in all five editions. However, one change is contrary to the previous books examined; the total number of variants expands from 192 in the first four editions to 198 in the *UBSGNT*[4].

Romans summary. Although there is noticeable change among the first four editions, the *UBSGNT*[4] shows the greatest deviation. The *UBSGNT*[1] and *UBSGNT*[2] are alike in nature. The *UBSGNT*[3] and *UBSGNT*[3corr.] show a moderate increase in *D* ratings (the first two editions have 2 and 3 *D* ratings respectively, while the *UBSGNT*[3] and *UBSGNT*[3corr.] each have 6). The *UBSGNT*[4] again follows a consistent pattern of increasing *A* ratings (rising from an average of 12 in the first four editions to 41 in the *UBSGNT*[4]), decreasing *C* ratings (falling from 42 in each of the four earlier editions to 22 in the *UBSGNT*[4]), and almost non-existent *D* ratings (only 1 in the *UBSGNT*[4], whereas the four earlier editions average 4 *D* ratings each). The total number of variants decreases from 91 in each of the first four editions to 85 in the *UBSGNT*[4].

1 Corinthians summary. 1 Corinthians continues the trend in which the *UBSGNT*[1] to the *UBSGNT*[3corr.] remain closely consistent, but the *A* ratings of the *UBSGNT*[4] increase considerably from an average of 13 percent to 38 percent (an average of 8 *A* ratings are in each of the first four editions, while 23 *A* ratings are recorded in the *UBSGNT*[4]). There is also a significant fluctuation in the *B* ratings, increasing from approximately 25 percent to 37 percent (there is an average of 15 *B* ratings in the first four editions, however, this rises to 22 in the *UBSGNT*[4]). The *C* ratings decrease by over half in the *UBSGNT*[4], falling from about 51 percent (an average of 30 *C* ratings in the first four editions) down to 23 percent (14 *C* ratings in this latest edition). The *D* ratings decrease from approximately 11 percent (an average of 7 in the first four editions) to 2 percent (only 1 in the *UBSGNT*[4]). The total number of variants increases only slightly in the *UBSGNT*[4] (from 59 in each of the first four editions to 60 in the *UBSGNT*[4]).

2 Corinthians summary. Proportionately, 2 Corinthians may well be one of the books showing the greatest amount of modification in the *UBSGNT*[4]. The *UBSGNT*[2], *UBSGNT*[3], and the *UBSGNT*[3corr.] remain similar, but these editions do show a noticeable degree of change from the *UBSGNT*[1]. However, it is the *UBSGNT*[4] that reveals the most drastic shift. *A* rated variants increase from a consistent 0 percent in all previous editions to a remarkable 30 percent in the *UBSGNT*[4] (12 *A* rated variants). *B* rated variants jump from an average of 20 percent to 45 percent (there are 9 *B* rated variants in the *UBSGNT*[1], 6 *B* rated passages in the *UBSGNT*[2] to the *UBSGNT*[3corr.], and 18 *B* rated passages in the *UBSGNT*[4]). *C* rated variants plunge from around 64 percent (constituting an average of 22 *C* ratings in the first four *UBSGNT* editions) to 25 percent (constituting only 10 *C* rated passages in the *UBSGNT*[4]). *D* rated variants fall from an average of 6 (17%) in each earlier edition to 0 in the *UBSGNT*[4]. Consistent with the book of Acts and 1 Corinthians, 2 Corinthians experiences increase, rather than decrease, in the total number of variants (rising from 34 in each of the earlier editions to 40 in the *UBSGNT*[4]).

Galatians summary. In Galatians there is no substantial alteration within the first four *UBSGNT* editions. Again, the *UBSGNT*[4] deviates significantly. *A* rated passages increase from a consistent 5 percent to an incredible 57 percent (from 1 *A* rating in each of the first four editions to 16 in the *UBSGNT*[4]). *B* rated passages decline from an average of 53 percent (approximately 12 *B* rated passages in each of the first four editions) to 11 percent (3 *B* rated passages in the *UBSGNT*[4]). *C* rated variants do not follow their usual norm of decrease, but instead increase from a consistent 23 percent (5 *C* rated variants in each of the earlier editions) to 32 percent (9 *C* rated variants in the *UBSGNT*[4]), thus constituting a rise of 9 percent. *D* rated variants fall from approximately 20 percent (an average of 5 in each of the earlier editions) to 0 percent in the *UBSGNT*[4]. The total number of variants increases from 22 in each of the earlier editions to 28 in the *UBSGNT*[4].

Ephesians summary. Another of the major changes in variants takes place in Ephesians, where *A* ratings leap from a constant 0 percent in all prior *UBSGNT* editions, to an incredible 43 percent (15 *A* rated variants) in the *UBSGNT*[4]. *B* and *C* ratings remain uniform in all five *UBSGNT* editions. *D* ratings decline to 0 percent in the *UBSGNT*[4] (from 3 consistent *D* ratings in the first four editions to 0 in the *UBSGNT*[4]). The total number of variants increases remarkably from 23 in each of the four earlier editions to 35 in the *UBSGNT*[4], obviously accounting somewhat for the rise in *A* rated passages.

Philippians summary. A consistent pattern emerges, with congruence between the *UBSGNT*[1], *UBSGNT*[2], *UBSGNT*[3], and *UBSGNT*[3corr.], and variation in the *UBSGNT*[4]. Contrary to Ephesians, the small rise in total number of variants (from 16 in each of the earlier editions to 21 in the *UBSGNT*[4]) does not give excuse for the large number of *A* ratings in Philippians. *A* rated passages rise from 0 percent in all previous editions to 48 percent (10 *A* rated passages) in the *UBSGNT*[4]. The other letter-ratings reveal only minor modification.

Colossians summary. Although identical percentages appear in the *UBSGNT*[1] to the *UBSGNT*[3corr.], the *UBSGNT*[4] again displays substantial variation. *A* ratings increase from 5 percent to 29 percent (there is 1 *A* rating in each of the first four editions, while there are 8 in the *UBSGNT*[4]). *B* ratings climb from 23 percent to 43 percent (there are 5 *B* ratings in each of the first four editions and 12 in the *UBSGNT*[4]). *C* ratings slide from 50 percent to 29 percent (dropping from 11 in each of the earlier editions to 8 in the *UBSGNT*[4]). *D* ratings fall to 0 percent in the *UBSGNT*[4] from a previous 23 percent (5 *D* ratings) in each of the first four editions. The total number of variants increases by 6 (there are 22 in each of the earlier editions and 28 in the *UBSGNT*[4]).

1 Thessalonians summary. Little variation occurs in the first four editions. The greatest change is seen in the higher percentage of *A* rated variants in the *UBSGNT*[4], rising from 18 percent (2 *A* ratings in each of the first four editions) to 60 percent (9 *A* ratings in the *UBSGNT*[4]). *B* and *C* variants remain comparable while *D* variants hold at a constant 0 percent in all editions. There is also a rise of four in the total number of variants (climbing from 11 in the earlier editions to 15 in the *UBSGNT*[4]).

2 Thessalonians summary. In 2 Thessalonians, the first four *UBSGNT* editions remain identical. However, the *UBSGNT*[4] continues to reveal fluctuation. The most visible change is seen in *A* rated variants, increasing from 0 percent in all previous editions to 38 percent in the *UBSGNT*[4] (3 *A* rated variants), and in *C* rated passages, decreasing from 78 percent (7 *C* rated passages in each earlier edition) to 25 percent (2 *C* rated passages in the *UBSGNT*[4]). This book shows a minor decline in its total number of variants, from 9 in the first four editions to 8 in the *UBSGNT*[4].

1 Timothy summary. As in 2 Thessalonians, this book sees no statistical variation until the *UBSGNT*[4]. Again *A* ratings rapidly climb from 18 percent to 79 percent (the first four editions each contain 2, while the *UBSGNT*[4] records 15). *B* ratings fall to 11 percent from an initial 45 percent (the four earlier editions have 5 each, while the *UBSGNT*[4] has 2). *C* ratings fall from 36 percent (4 in each of the four earlier editions) to 11 percent (2 in the *UBSGNT*[4]). *D* ratings remain at a consistent 0 percent in all five editions. There is an increase within the *UBSGNT*[4] from 11 variants in each of the first four editions to 19 variants in total.

2 Timothy summary. The *UBSGNT*[4] is the only edition that introduces change to the variant ratings in 2 Timothy. *A* ratings increase from 0 in all earlier editions to 2 (25%) in the *UBSGNT*[4]. *B* ratings increase from 2 (25%) in each of the four earlier editions to 5 (63%) in the *UBSGNT*[4]. However, *C* ratings decrease from 6 (75%) in each of the first four editions to 1 (13%) in the *UBSGNT*[4]. *D* ratings remain constant at 0 percent, and the total number of variants remains identical at 8 in all *UBSGNT* editions.

Titus summary. The *UBSGNT*[1] to the *UBSGNT*[3corr.] does not vary. *A* and *D* rated variants remain at 0 percent in these first four editions. *B* and *C* rated variants also remain constant, holding at 50 percent (2 *B* rated variants and 2 *C* rated variants) in these first four editions. Although there are only four total variants in each of the five editions, proportionately there exists consistent alteration. In the *UBSGNT*[4] *A* ratings increase from 0 percent in the first four editions to 50 percent (2 *A* rated variants). Both *B* and *C* ratings fall from 50 percent (2) in the first four editions to 25 percent (1) in the *UBSGNT*[4].

Philemon summary. As in many of the smaller books, there is proportional change in Philemon as well. The first four editions remain constant, whereas the *UBSGNT*[4] introduces changes. *A* ratings rise from 0 percent in the earlier editions to 40 percent (2 *A* rated variants) in the *UBSGNT*[4]. *B* ratings also rise from 50 percent (2 *B* rated variants) in each of the first four editions to 60 percent (3 *B* rated variants) in the *UBSGNT*[4]. *C* ratings fall from 50 percent (2 *C* rated variants in each of the first four editions) to 0 percent in the *UBSGNT*[4]. *D* ratings hold at 0 percent in all five editions. The total number of variants increases from 4 each in the earlier editions to 5 in the *UBSGNT*[4].

Hebrews summary. In Hebrews, the total number of variants increases from 38 in each of the first four editions to 44 in the *UBSGNT*[4]. There is strict congruence among the *UBSGNT*[1], *UBSGNT*[2], *UBSGNT*[3], and the *UBSGNT*[3corr.]. In the *UBSGNT*[4] *A* rated variants rise to 20 (45%) from 2 (5%) in each of the first four editions. *B* rated passages undergo little change. *C* ratings fall from approximately 50 percent (20 *C* rated variants) in the first four editions to 27 percent (12 *C* rated variants) in the *UBSGNT*[4]. *D* ratings also decline from 13 percent (5 *D* ratings) in each of the first four editions to 0 percent in the *UBSGNT*[4].

James summary. The first four *UBSGNT* editions are characterized by their similarity, while the *UBSGNT*[4] is characterized by an upgrade of ratings. *A* variants rise from 1 (6%) in each of the first four editions to 7 (30%) in the *UBSGNT*[4]. *B* variants also rise from an average of 7 (approximately 38%) in the first four editions to 12 (52%) in the *UBSGNT*[4]. *C* variants are comparable in all editions. An average of 4 *D* rated variants (approximately 20%) in each of the first four editions drops to 0 in the *UBSGNT*[4]. The total number of variants increases from 18 in each of the first four editions to 23 in the *UBSGNT*[4].

1 Peter summary. 1 Peter reveals continued *UBSGNT*[4] divergence. *A* ratings increase from 1 in each of the four earliest editions to 20 in the

$UBSGNT^4$ (from 4% in the first four editions to 54% in the $UBSGNT^4$).
B ratings remain similar in all five editions. *C* ratings decrease from an
average of 15 in each of the first four editions to 8 in the $UBSGNT^4$
(from approximately 54% in the first four editions to 22% in the
$UBSGNT^4$). *D* ratings drop from 2 (7%) in each of the first four editions
to none in the $UBSGNT^4$. The total number of variants increases from an
average of 28 in each of the four earliest editions to 37 in the $UBSGNT^4$.

2 Peter summary. There is no divergence in the $UBSGNT^1$ to the
$UBSGNT^{3\text{corr.}}$, but in the $UBSGNT^4$ *A* rated variants climb from 0 percent in all earlier editions to 33 percent (8 *A* rated variants in the
$UBSGNT^4$). *B* rated variants also increase from 20 percent to 33 percent
(4 *B* rated variants in each of the first four editions to 8 in the
$UBSGNT^4$). *C* ratings fall from 10 (50%) in each of the first four editions to 7 (29%) in the $UBSGNT^4$. *D* ratings likewise fall from 6 (30%)
in each of the first four editions to 1 (4%) in the $UBSGNT^4$. The total
number of variants grows from 20 in each of the first four editions to 24
in the $UBSGNT^4$.

1 John summary. Although there is minor deviation in the first four
UBSGNT editions, the $UBSGNT^4$ exhibits clear divergence. *A* ratings
are upgraded drastically from a constant 8 percent (2 *A* rated variants)
in each of the first four editions to 59 percent (19 *A* rated variants) in
the $UBSGNT^4$. *B* ratings drop from an average of 12 (approximately
47%) in each of the first four editions to 8 (25%) in the $UBSGNT^4$.
C ratings fall from an average of 9 (approximately 35%) in the first four
editions to 5 (16%) in the $UBSGNT^4$. *D* ratings are downgraded to
0 percent in the $UBSGNT^4$ from an average of 10 percent (about 3) in
each of the first four editions. The total number of variants increases
from 25 in each of the four earliest editions to 32 in the $UBSGNT^4$.

2 John summary. In 2 John there is a small change from the $UBSGNT^1$
to the $UBSGNT^2$, $UBSGNT^3$, and $UBSGNT^{3\text{corr.}}$. However, this change
is minor when compared to the modifications in the $UBSGNT^4$. *A* ratings increase from 0 in all previous editions to 4 in the $UBSGNT^4$
(climbing from 0% to 67%). *B* ratings decline from an average of four
in each of the earlier editions to 2 in the $UBSGNT^4$ (falling from an
average of 63% to 33%). *C* ratings drop from an average of 2 in each of
the first four editions to none in the $UBSGNT^4$ (falling from an average
of 37% to 0%). *D* ratings and the total number of variants remain consistent in all five editions, holding at 0 percent and 6 respectively.

3 John summary. The number of variants in 3 John is limited. Nevertheless, the *UBSGNT*[4] deviates from earlier editions. *A* variants ascend in number, from none in the first four editions to 1 (50%) in the *UBSGNT*[4]. *B* variants are constant in all five editions (remaining at 1). *C* ratings fall from 2 (67%) in all earlier editions to none in the *UBSGNT*[4]). *D* rated passages also remain at a consistent 0 percent in all editions. The total number of variants declines from 3 in each of the first four editions to 2 in the *UBSGNT*[4].

Jude summary. The first four editions of the *UBSGNT* remain static. Following the prevalent trend, the *UBSGNT*[4] introduces abrupt fluctuations. The greatest alterations occur in the *A* ratings statistic, increasing from 0 percent in each of the first four editions to 69 percent (9) in the *UBSGNT*[4]. *B* ratings fall from 33 percent (2) in each of the four earliest editions to 0 percent in the *UBSGNT*[4]. *C* ratings and *D* ratings are identical in all five editions (remaining at 3 and 1 respectively). The total number of variants more than doubles from a consistent 6 in each of the previous editions to 13 in the *UBSGNT*[4].

Revelation summary. In Revelation *A* rated variants soar from 1 percent to 32 percent (rising from 1 in each of the first four editions to 23 in the *UBSGNT*[4]). Likewise, *B* rated variants climb from 15 percent to 42 percent (more than doubling from 14 in each of the first four editions to 30 in the *UBSGNT*[4]). *C* rated variants fall from about 78 percent to 25 percent (dropping from an average of 72 in each of the four earlier editions to 18 in the *UBSGNT*[4]). And finally, *D* variants decline from an average of 6 percent (approximately 6 in each of the first four editions) to 1 percent (1 in the *UBSGNT*[4]). There is also a significant fall in the number of total variants (declining from 92 in each of the first four editions to 72 in the *UBSGNT*[4]) thus eliminating the increased number of variants as an explanation for the increased *A* rated passages.

Concluding Summary

This first section of Chapter 2 introduces overwhelming proof that the *UBSGNT*[4] has introduced a radical change to the critical apparatus letter-ratings for many variants. Charts 1 and 2, as well as the Chi-square statistics, provide an overall sense of the changes that occur in each *UBSGNT* edition. By comparing each edition, one cannot help but notice the divergence seen in the *UBSGNT*[4]. Of even greater value, and clearly more revealing, are the *Overall Totals* and the *Overall Percentage* columns recorded in Chart 1. These totals reveal the true nature, and the astonishing extent of fluctuation that takes place, again particularly in the *UBSGNT*[4]. Several prominent trends have been revealed in this analysis.

In comparing the various variant letter-ratings seen in the *UBSGNT* editions, one becomes aware of close relationships that exist between several of these editions. The *UBSGNT*[1] and *UBSGNT*[2] often resemble each other. This is understandable since they are the first two works in a progressive series produced by the United Bible Societies. The *UBSGNT*[3] and the *UBSGNT*[3corr.] are virtually identical.[18] However, the *UBSGNT*[3] and the *UBSGNT*[3corr.] show only a moderate degree of change from the *UBSGNT*[1] and the *UBSGNT*[2]. Although the *UBSGNT*[1] to the *UBSGNT*[3corr.] utilize a majority of the same variants, the *UBSGNT*[4] eliminates a substantial number of these and replaces them with totally new variants. Some may remark that it is the addition of these new variants in the *UBSGNT*[4] that gives rise to the escalating number of *A* or *B* rated passages, and to some extent this is true.[19] But even taking this into consideration, as will be the specific aim in the next section, one cannot dismiss the fact that the newly added variants placed within the *UBSGNT*[4] constitute only a minority percentage of the actual fluctuations that occur in this edition (particularly in *A* and *B* rated variants). In other words, newly added *A* rated variants in the *UBSGNT*[4] can only account for a small percentage of the overall *A* rating increases that take place from earlier *UBSGNT* editions to the *UBSGNT*[4]. Even if one were to accept these new *A* variant additions as an excuse for the increase in *A* variant ratings, many of the older variants from previous editions do experience exceptional letter-rating increases. Consequently, there is still an astonishing upgrade in the *UBSGNT*[4] and, therefore, a newly proposed quality of text. As has been revealed in the above analysis, there is a strong tendency for each biblical book (excluding Mark) to move towards an increasing degree of certainty regarding debated readings, and thus, an overall upgrade in the quality of text. These *UBSGNT*[4] modifications progress at an inconsistent rate and are incongruent with those alterations made throughout the *UBSGNT*[2], *UBSGNT*[3], and the

18. Once again, this is due to the corrective nature of the *UBSGNT*[3corr.], whereby the editors sought to bring closer correlation between the Nestle-Aland[26] edition and further *UBSGNT* editions. The changes that were made to bring about this closer resemblance had very little focus upon variant letter-ratings.

19. There are several biblical books that may indicate this type of conclusion: Ephesians, 1 Timothy, 1 Peter, 1 John, and Jude are perhaps the more obvious ones.

$UBSGNT^{3corr.}$. As a result, the $UBSGNT^4$ apparently insinuates that the text is much more incontestable (*A* ratings denote a positive degree of certainty) and much more reliable than the text of the earlier editions. Among each of the $UBSGNT^1$, $UBSGNT^2$, $UBSGNT^3$, and the $UBSGNT^{3corr.}$, there is an average of 130 *A* rated variants. These 130 *A* rated variants in each of the first four editions make up approximately 9 percent of all the letter-rated variants in total. The $UBSGNT^4$ increases this number to 514 *A* rated passages, thereby constituting 36 percent of all letter-rated variants in this edition. This is an increase of 384 *A* rated variants in the $UBSGNT^4$. There is an average of 482 *B* rated variants (approximately 34% of all letter-rated variants) in each of the first four editions, but again, in the $UBSGNT^4$ we see this rise to 541 (or 38% of all letter-rated variants). This is an increase of 59 *B* rated passages in the $UBSGNT^4$. There is an average of 701 *C* rated passages in each of the four earlier editions (constituting about 48% of all letter-rated variants). *C* rated variants drop by 334 in the $UBSGNT^4$, to a greatly reduced total of 367 *C* rated variants (making up only 26% of all letter-rated variants). Finally, *D* rated passages abruptly descend from an average of 134 in each of the first four editions (making up about 9% of all letter-rated variants) to only 9 in the $UBSGNT^4$ (constituting 1% of all letter-rated variants).[20] This is a decrease of 125 *D* rated variants in the $UBSGNT^4$. Because of the drop in *D* rated passages, perhaps one should question the entire relevance of this *D* category in the $UBSGNT^4$. In effect, the United Bible Societies' evaluation of evidence drops from a four-point system in previous *UBSGNT* editions to a three-point system in the $UBSGNT^4$.

One should also keep in mind that all these modifications occur as the overall number of variants drops slightly in the latest edition (falling from an average of 1445 total letter-rated variants in each of the first four *UBSGNT* editions to 1431 in the $UBSGNT^4$). There can be no doubt that there is a considerable upgrade in the perceived quality of the text as seen by the $UBSGNT^4$ editorial committee. This is substantiated by the rising number of *A* and *B* variants, and the declining number of *C* and *D* variants.

---

20. These nine *D* rated passages are Mt. 23.26; Mk 7.9; Jn 10.29; Acts 16.12; Rom. 14.19; 1 Cor. 7.34; 2 Pet. 3.10; Jude 5; and Rev. 18.3.

2. *Variants that Have Been Newly Added or Dropped from the UBSGNT⁴*

The statistics recorded in this section are important to the examination of upgrading variant letter-ratings because they more accurately reflect the exact nature and type of modifications made to the *UBSGNT*⁴ ratings. Two categories will be presented in this section: (1) the number of new variants added to the *UBSGNT*⁴, and (2) the number of variants dropped out of the *UBSGNT*⁴. Each category is based upon a complete list. The first list records the total number of variants that have been dropped out of the *UBSGNT*⁴. Both lists have been placed at the end of this section.

With the addition and omission of many variants, along with the other modifications made to the *UBSGNT*⁴, it seems unlikely that the text of this last edition would remain the same as the text of the *UBSGNT*³ and *UBSGNT*³ᶜᵒʳʳ·. Nevertheless, it remains exactly the same. Although a large number of variants have been dropped from the *UBSGNT*⁴, its text still represents the previous choices made for each of these excluded variants (i.e. those variants that were included in earlier editions but have now been removed from comment by the *UBSGNT*⁴). Likewise, the addition of new variants into the *UBSGNT*⁴ has not altered the text. Instead, variants used to determine the text of earlier editions, although not included in the apparatus of those editions at that time, were newly added to the *UBSGNT*⁴. These variants represent the choices made in the text for previous editions. In other words, a particular variant may be included in the text of the *UBSGNT* editions even though the variant itself is not represented in the critical apparatus. Metzger provides further clarification and support for these points:

> [P]lans had already been made for the fourth edition of the United Bible Societies' *Greek New Testament*. In 1981 at a meeting of the five members of the Editorial Committee (the places that had been left vacant by the retirement of Matthew Black and Allen Wikgren were taken by Barbara Aland and John Karavidopoulos of Salonica) decisions were taken to introduce into the apparatus a certain number of additional sets of variant readings for passages of exegetical importance. Furthermore, *though no change was voted to alter the wording of the Scripture text* [italics added], it was agreed that in some cases a modification needed to be made in the assignment of the categories of A, B, C, and D relating to the degree of certainty of readings adopted as the text. In a number of instances a C evaluation was raised to the level of B, and, in a smaller number of

instances, a B evaluation was raised to A. It is expected that the fourth edition, embodying these changes, will become available at the close of 1992.[21]

Although Metzger dramatically understates the re-distribution of *UBSGNT*[4] variant letter-ratings, this quotation unmistakably reveals that the text itself has not changed from that of the previous *UBSGNT*[3] and *UBSGNT*[3corr.] editions. Again, this is confirmed by the following remark on p. 1* of the *UBSGNT*[4] Introduction:

> This edition reproduces the Greek text of the Third Edition (corrected) without change. Its text remains identical with that of Nestle-Aland in its 26th edition, and also in its 27th edition which is in the final stages of preparation and offers the same text unchanged.[22]

Considering the addition and deletion of numerous variants into, or out of, the *UBSGNT*[4], one might expect the editorial committee to reveal the criteria used by them in the determination of which variants were added and which variants were removed from the critical apparatus. However, there is no such set of criteria presented by the committee. Other than the vague statements that follow, the reader is left with no detailed explanation regarding these modifications.[23]

On p. xi of both the *UBSGNT*[1] and the *UBSGNT*[2], as well as on p. xiii of both the *UBSGNT*[3] and the *UBSGNT*[3corr.], the following statement is made: 'The apparently large number of C decisions is due to the circumstance that many readings in the A and B classes have had no variants included in the apparatus, because they were not important for the purposes of this edition'.[24]

---

21. Metzger, *The Text of the New Testament*, p. 281.

22. For further confirmation of this point, see Silva, 'Symposium', p. 349; Elliott, 'Two New Editions', p. 493; *idem*, 'The Fourth Edition', cols. 10-11; *idem*, 'The Twentyseventh Edition', col. 19; and the Nestle-Aland[27], pp. 45*-46*.

23. This vagueness in explaining the methodological principles underlying the *UBSGNT* editions, and particularly the *UBSGNT*[4], will be further discussed in Chapter 3.

24. It is interesting to note that this paragraph is no longer included in the *UBSGNT*[4]. However, it is hoped that the new addition of A and B ratings into the *UBSGNT*[4] are at least 'important for the purposes' of this latest edition. Perhaps it should be asked if these new A and B variant additions are the same as those that were left out of the previous four editions and regarded as 'less important'. If this is the case, which it seems to be, the *UBSGNT* committee have apparently contradicted themselves and their previous statements concerning these particular variants. Those A and B rated variants that were left out of the earlier *UBSGNT* editions because

On p. v of the Preface to the *UBSGNT*[4] the following statement is made:

> The GNT continues to offer 'more extensive evidence for a more select number of variants' (Preface to the Third Edition, p. xi), but the selection of passages for the apparatus was thoroughly reviewed by the Committee. This resulted in eliminating from the apparatus a large number of variant units where the readings were of minor significance, concerned only with the minutest textual variations, and including others having a greater importance for the reader's understanding of the history of the text and exegesis.

On p. vi of the Preface to the *UBSGNT*[4], another statement is made concerning the addition and deletion of variants:

> The principles underlying the present revision were established at a long working session of the Committee in 1981 for which detailed preparations had been made. At that time the decisions were made for eliminations and inclusions in the apparatus of variant readings, and also for reconsidering the evaluation of readings. The guidelines for witnesses to be included in the apparatus were also thoroughly discussed and established.

On p. 2* of the *UBSGNT*[4] Introduction, these words are recorded:

> The selection of passages for the apparatus has undergone considerable revision since the Third Edition (corrected). The intention was to provide an apparatus where the most important international translations of the New Testament show notes referring to textual variants or even have differences in their translations or interpretations. Other groups of variants have also been included when for various reasons they are significant and worthy of consideration.

And finally, as Metzger explains in the quotation above, these alterations were made on the basis of 'exegetical importance'.[25] One must turn outside of the *UBSGNT*[4] and the vague explanations of the editorial committee in order to find greater clarification regarding the criteria for assessing the addition and deletion of variants. H.P. Scanlin more clearly points out that:

> After decades of use by those engaged in Bible translation, it was decided that the Fourth Edition should incorporate changes in the apparatus to enhance its usefulness for translators. About 15 translations in several

they were 'less important', are now included in the *UBSGNT*[4] and, as will be seen shortly, seem to be regarded as 'more important'.

25. See n. 21 above.

major languages were carefully checked to see where these translators
made text-critical decisions that affected their translation. The Editorial
Committee then carefully reviewed both the existing items in the apparatus
and the additional items that could be useful to translators to determine
which items could be removed from the textual apparatus and which
should be added.[26]

M. Silva provides even greater clarity as he explains the reasoning
behind the addition and deletion of variants in the *UBSGNT*[4]:

> Many of these changes seem reasonable because the grounds for the deci-
> sions are fairly obvious. For example, eight of the new items involve the
> divine names, particularly the variation Jesus Christ/Christ Jesus; differ-
> ences of this type do not really affect the meaning, but clearly they do
> affect the translation, and so they would be significant for many users of
> the edition. Conversely, many of the deletions are variants that would not
> affect the translation, such as *en tō nomō* versus the simple dative *tō nomō*
> in Rom 7.23. It was also wise, in my opinion, to delete such variations as
> acute versus circumflex accent on the verb *krinei* at 1 Cor 5.13; though the
> difference is substantial (present/future tense), the markings on some
> manuscripts reflect a scribal interpretation and not a textual variation as
> such. But then why was the variation of *oidamen* versus *oida men* added
> at Rom 7.14? Word divisions in the manuscripts are not to be regarded as
> witnessing to the form of the original text. (For a similar reason, I ques-
> tion the inclusion of the syntactical problem at Jn 1.3-4 in the textual appa-
> ratus. To avoid confusion of categories, it would be better to include that
> kind of information in the discourse segmentation apparatus.)[27]

Although Silva states that 'many of these changes seem reasonable', he
later adds that 'Unfortunately, there are plenty of instances where the
reason for including or excluding a variation unit is not at all obvious'.[28]

---

26. Scanlin, 'Symposium', p. 349.
27. Silva, 'Symposium', p. 350.
28. Silva, 'Symposium', p. 350. Elliott also notes that 'Although we have been
told in each edition that its selection was carefully chosen to reflect variants of relevance to translators, obviously the slightly revamped committee responsible for
UBS4 disagreed with the earlier choice [in view of the 284 (285) newly added variants placed into the *UBSGNT*[4]]. B.M. Metzger, a committee member, in the companion volume to UBS3, *A Textual Commentary on the Greek New Testament* was
himself dissatisfied with the original selection and therefore added a further 600 variants for discussion.' Elliott may be a little pessimistic here as Metzger claims, without a hint of dissatisfaction, that the committee together suggested the inclusion of at
least a number of extra variants. See Metzger, *A Textual Commentary*, 1971, pp. v-
vi. Regardless, Elliott aptly continues, 'The conclusion to be drawn is the obvious

Therefore, in view of these above quotations, it appears that the addition of new variants and the removal of old variants occurs primarily on the basis of: (1) their significance, or insignificance, for providing the reader with an understanding of the history of the text; (2) their significance, or insignificance, for reflecting the most important translational difficulties; and (3) their significance, or insignificance, in representing exegetical aspects and considerations.

As was seen in Section 1 of this chapter, and as we will continue to see in this section, a considerable number of new letter-rated variants have been added to the $UBSGNT^4$ text (predominantly A ratings). However, when it is noted that a large number of these new variants have A ratings, while a considerably smaller number have C ratings, one must question if this pattern accurately reflects the above premises. Perhaps in some instances it would seem more important, in the light of textual history, translational considerations, and exegesis, to include those variants where there is a greater degree of uncertainty regarding the correct reading of the text (i.e. C ratings) rather than including in the critical apparatus those variants where textual decisions can be made with certitude and confidence (i.e. A ratings).

One further point regarding the addition and deletion of variants from the $UBSGNT^4$ should be mentioned. Taking into account the identical text shared between the $UBSGNT^4$ and the Nestle-Aland[26,27], an examination was briefly made to ascertain whether the Nestle-Aland text and apparatus had influenced the change in variants within the $UBSGNT^4$. In evaluating several of the Gospels, it was found that all the $UBSGNT^4$ variants, whether newly added or deleted, were also contained in the Nestle-Aland apparatus. Therefore, no sound decision regarding Nestle-Aland influence could be made. Because the Nestle-Aland text cites over 10,000 variants, while the $UBSGNT^4$ cites only about 1400, it is understandable that all the $UBSGNT^4$ variants might be included in the much more extensive Nestle-Aland apparatus.

---

one that it is a thankless and delusive task to try and restrict the number of variants too narrowly or to try to define which 1400 or so variants are "of interest to the translator"'. See Elliott, 'Two New Editions', pp. 493-94. See also *idem*, 'The Fourth Edition', cols. 11-12, where Elliott states that 'In any selection [of variants for an apparatus] it is difficult to get it right. But what is clear is that the new edition [$UBSGNT^4$] has striven to produce a better selection of variant units.'

Number of New Variants Added to the UBSGNT[4]

This category records the number of new letter-rated variants (i.e. variants that have an *A*, *B*, *C*, or *D* letter-rating) that have been added to the *UBSGNT*[4]. These statistics are significant because, rather than simply counting the number of ratings present in each edition (as was done in Section 1), they more accurately reflect the modifications made to the actual *UBSGNT*[4] letter-ratings. This is done by distinguishing between those variants and their respective letter-ratings that have been newly added into the *UBSGNT*[4] and those variants, with fluctuating or consistent ratings, that have been included in earlier *UBSGNT* editions as well as the *UBSGNT*[4]. The question that must be asked here is this—out of the total number of specific *A*, *B*, *C*, and *D* letter-ratings that occur in the *UBSGNT*[4] (i.e. $A = 514$, $B = 541$, $C = 367$, and $D = 9$), how many are old variants with a previous history in earlier *UBSGNT* editions that have also been included in the *UBSGNT*[4], and how many are new variants added to the *UBSGNT*[4] that have never before been cited in a previous *UBSGNT* edition? The simple calculation used here is: (Total number of *A*, *B*, *C*, or *D* rated variants in *UBSGNT*[4]) minus (Total number of old *A*, *B*, *C*, or *D* rated variants with a previous history in earlier *UBSGNT* editions that have also been included in the *UBSGNT*[4])[29] = (Total number of new *A*, *B*, *C*, or *D* rated variants newly added to the *UBSGNT*[4] that have never before been cited in a previous *UBSGNT* edition).[30] The calculations for each specific letter-rating follow.

29. This category records the total number of old variants with a previous history in earlier *UBSGNT* editions that have also been included into the *UBSGNT*[4]. The 'previous history' of each variant and each specific group of letter-rated variants (*A*, *B*, *C*, and *D*) is not specifically noted. However, any variant included in this category may have been upgraded, downgraded, or remained consistent when it was placed into the *UBSGNT*[4] apparatus. Based upon the figures and charts of Chapter 2, Section 1, it would seem as though a large number of these old variants with previous histories were clearly upgraded to *A* rated variants.

30. Again, the complete figures for this discussion are recorded in the two lists located at the end of this section. The exact total figures for 'New Variants Added to the *UBSGNT*[4]' are recorded on pp. 106-107, while the exact total figures for 'Number of Variants Dropped Out of the *UBSGNT*[4]' are recorded on pp. 108-109.

Textual Optimism

Summary Comparing Total Number of New Variants Added to UBSGNT[4]

Variant Letter-Ratings	Total Number of Variants in UBSGNT[4]	Total Number of Old Variants Included in UBSGNT[4]	Total Number of New Variants Added to UBSGNT[4]
A	514 (36%)	346 (30%)	168 (59%)
B	541 (38%)	479 (42%)	62 (22%)
C	367 (26%)	312 (27%)	55 (19%)
D	9 (1%)	9 (1%)	0 (0%)
Totals	1431	1146	285

When one examines and compares the column 'Total Number of Old Variants Included in the *UBSGNT*[4]' with the total number of variants listed in the *UBSGNT*[3] and *UBSGNT*[3corr.], as seen in the following chart, some interesting insights can be observed. When comparing the totals of earlier *UBSGNT* editions and the *UBSGNT*[4] totals, one should use the category 'Total Number of Old Variants Included in the *UBSGNT*[4]' instead of the category 'Total Number of Variants in the *UBSGNT*[4]'.

Summary Comparing the Change of Figures in the UBSGNT[4]

Variant Letter-Ratings	Total Number of Variants in UBSGNT[3/3corr.]	Total Number of Old Variants Included in UBSGNT[4]	Change of Figures in the UBSGNT[4]
A	126 (9%)	346 (30%)	+220
B	475 (33%)	479 (42%)	+4
C	699[31] (48%)	312 (27%)	−387
D	144 (10%)	9 (1%)	−135
Totals	1444	1146	N/A

This is due to the biased and slanted figures present in the category 'Total Number of Variants in the *UBSGNT*[4]'. This category includes the number of *newly added* variants and their respective letter-ratings into its totals, therefore increasing the number of each specific letter-rating in the *UBSGNT*[4]. However, when one makes use of the category entitled 'Total Number of Old Variants Included in the *UBSGNT*[4]', these newly added variant figures are eliminated, thereby leaving only those variants with letter-ratings that existed in prior *UBSGNT* editions. The figures

---

31. The figure 699 has been recorded here for the *UBSGNT*[3corr.], whereas the *UBSGNT*[3] records 700. Again, this discrepancy is due to a missing variant letter-rating, likely a C rating, at Acts 5.32 in the *UBSGNT*[3corr.].

present in the category entitled 'Total Number of Variants in the *UBSGNT*[4]' record all variants with letter-ratings, regardless of whether they are new additions (which obviously could not be modified in previous editions) or old variants from earlier editions (which could be modified). Even though the figures for 'newly added variants' have been eliminated from the *UBSGNT*[4] totals (thus making our calculations more accurate than those presented in Section 1), it is clear that the number of *A* rated variants or *A* letter-ratings still experiences a very large increase from the *UBSGNT*[3] and *UBSGNT*[3corr.] totals to the *UBSGNT*[4] totals as represented by the category 'Total Number of Old Variants Included in the *UBSGNT*[4]'. One can also observe that the number of *B* rated variants or *B* letter-ratings remains similar between the editions, while, as again was revealed in Section 1 of this chapter, the *C* and *D* rated variants or letter-ratings fall extensively. This second section of inquiry continues to support the conclusions reached in the previous section: (1) *A* ratings greatly increase in the *UBSGNT*[4]; (2) *B* ratings increase slightly, but overall they experience a general consistency; (3) *C* ratings drop extensively; (4) *D* ratings fall to almost non-existent levels; and, lastly and most noteworthy (5) based upon the increase of *A* and *B* letter-ratings, and the decrease of *C* and *D* letter-ratings, there is an extensive improvement and increased confidence in the overall quality and certainty of the *UBSGNT*[4] text.[32] Despite the elimination of the additional 285 newly added variants to the *UBSGNT*[4], therefore lowering the *UBSGNT*[4] numerical totals calculated for this section (1146) as compared to the earlier editions (1444 in the *UBSGNT*[3corr.] and 1445 in the *UBSGNT*[3]), the *UBSGNT*[4] has introduced an extensive change to the letter-ratings of the critical apparatus for a large number of variants.

As in Chapter 2, Section 1, the Chi-square statistic is again used to verify these conclusions. However, this second Chi-square differs from

---

32. If one also takes into consideration the specific type and total number of new variants added to the *UBSGNT*[4], it becomes possible to see, from a slightly different angle, an improved and more confident *UBSGNT*[4] text. The total number of new *A* variants that are added (168) exceeds the combined total of *B* (62), *C* (55), and *D* (0) variants (117). When newly added *A* and *B* rated variants are compared to newly added *C* and *D* rated variants, this point is once again confirmed. Again, one might ask if it would not, at least in some instances, be more important, both in light of textual history and especially exegesis, to include the uncertain *C* and *D* rated variants into the critical apparatus instead of the more certain *A* and *B* rated variants.

the first in that, similar to this entire section, all newly added variants, and therefore, their letter-ratings, are eliminated from the total number of *A*, *B*, *C*, and *D* rated variants recorded in the *UBSGNT*[4]. The Chi-square works perfectly in this instance because unequal sample sizes, such as the differing number of variants in each *UBSGNT* edition, pose no problems for the calculations this tool provides. Excluding those variants newly added into the *UBSGNT*[4], the following Chi-square table has been prepared.

Chi-Square (χ^2) Statistics for Variant Letter-Ratings (A, B, C, D) within Each UBSGNT Edition excluding New Variants in UBSGNT[4]

	Col. 1 *UBSGNT*[1]	Col. 2 *UBSGNT*[2]	Col. 3 *UBSGNT*[3]	Col. 4 *UBSGNT*[3corr.]	Col. 5 *UBSGNT*[4]	*Row Total*
Row 1 *A Rating*	136 *180.358*	130 *180.358*	126 *180.233*	126 *180.109*	346 *142.939*	864
Row 2 *B Rating*	486 *502.039*	490 *502.039*	475 *501.692*	475 *501.345*	479 *397.882*	2405
Row 3 *C Rating*	702 *650.042*	701 *650.042*	700 *649.592*	699 *649.143*	312 *515.178*	3114
Row 4 *D Rating*	122 *113.559*	125 *113.559*	144 *113.480*	144 *113.402*	9 *89.999*	544
Column Total	1446	1446	1445	1444	1146	*Grand Total* 6927

Non-italicized Figures = Observed Frequencies
Italicized Figures = Expected Frequencies

$\chi^2 = 553.312$
$df = 12$

With the elimination of newly added variants from the *UBSGNT*[4], the figures in this second Chi-square change from those given in the first Chi-square. However, the same procedure is used to analyze the data. Whereas the χ^2 figure for the first table was 843.048, the calculation for χ^2 comes to 553.312 in this second table. Although the Chi-square figure is lower in this second table, which can be attributed to the elimination of newly added variants in the *UBSGNT*[4], this number still greatly exceeds the probability values of 18.55, 21.03, 26.22, and 32.91 when the Degrees of Freedom (*df*) = 12 (as the number of rows and columns in this second table has not changed). Therefore, one is able to determine that there is a significant degree of fluctuation in the specific *A*, *B*, *C*, and *D* letter-rating totals within the *UBSGNT* editions. Despite the elimination of the additional 285 newly added variants to the *UBSGNT*[4], therefore lowering the *UBSGNT*[4] numerical totals calculated for this section (1146), the earlier conclusion, that the ratio of letter-rated variants in the five *UBSGNT* editions varies substantially and that the specific letter-rating categories for the *UBSGNT* were not being treated in a similar fashion from edition to edition, can be sustained. The Chi-square statistic continues to support the fact that a highly significant degree of fluctuation in the specific A, B, C, and D letter-rating totals within the *UBSGNT* editions has occurred, and because of the extent of divergence, this could not have taken place by chance.

Number of Variants Dropped Out of the UBSGNT[4]

An obvious question to ask concerning variants that have been dropped out of the *UBSGNT*[4] is, For what reasons have these variants not been included in this latest *UBSGNT* edition? As already presented, the answer to this question is not to be found explicitly stated in the *UBSGNT*[4]. Some might deduce that A rated variants, because of their considered certainty in establishing the New Testament text, are no longer needed in the apparatus. Based upon the large number of A rated variants that have been retained and even added to the *UBSGNT*[4], however, this explanation does not seem to ring true. It seems more likely that variants were dropped from the *UBSGNT*[4] for any one of the following reasons: (1) they were thought to be of little significance for providing the reader with an understanding of the history of the text, (2) they were not thought to reflect the most important international translations, and (3) their exegetical importance was thought to be limited.

In spite of the fact that these variants were not included in the *UBSGNT*[4], their exclusion provides us with an important insight into the *UBSGNT*[4] as a whole. A total of 300 variants were not included in this last edition's textual apparatus. Of the 300 variants dropped out of the *UBSGNT*[4], 23 (almost 8%) were A rated variants, 99 (33%) were B rated variants, 162 (54%) were C rated variants, and lastly, 16 (about 5%) of the faltering D rated variants were removed from the *UBSGNT*[4]. It is apparent that the A rated variants are preserved in the *UBSGNT*[4], while the C rated variants are eliminated.

When a comparison is made between the particular type and number of variants dropped from the *UBSGNT*[4] and the type and number of variants added to the *UBSGNT*[4], there is a direct correlation. It would appear as though the editorial committee altered the letter-rated variants in order that the perceived quality of text present in this latest edition might reflect an overall upgrade and new optimism. The result of this upgrade affects the perceived quality of text, which is now granted a much higher degree of certainty than is found in any of the earlier *UBSGNT* editions. According to its textual apparatus, the $UBSGNT^4$ by far outweighs the quality and degree of certainty of the previous four *UBSGNT* editions. There exists a direct relationship between the addition and omission of letter-rated variants in this latest *UBSGNT* edition. Those variants that denote a higher degree of certainty (i.e. *A* and *B* ratings) have more representation in the $UBSGNT^4$ text, while those that denote a lower degree of certainty (i.e. *C* and *D* ratings) have less representation. As well, those variants that denote a higher degree of certainty are preserved in the $UBSGNT^4$ text, while those that denote a lower degree of certainty are more readily omitted. The following chart provides the exact figures:

Summary Comparing Variants Added and Variants Dropped from the $UBSGNT^4$

Variant Letter-Ratings	Number of Variants Dropped in the $UBSGNT^4$	Number of New Variants Added to the $UBSGNT^4$
A	23 (8%)	168 (59%)
B	99 (33%)	62 (22%)
C	162 (54%)	55 (19%)
D	16 (5%)	0 (0%)
Totals	300	285

Lists of Variants Added and Dropped Out of the $UBSGNT^4$

The following lists record every variant that is either added or dropped out of the $UBSGNT^4$ edition. Occasionally a variant reference will include a superscript number after its citation. This number corresponds to the reference listings in Appendix I, not with the reference listings of the $UBSGNT^4$. For example, in the first list, the first added variant is Mt. 11.2^2. The superscript numeral '2' indicates that there are at least two variants located in Mt. 11.2, and that the specific variant being referred to here is the second reference. By locating this second reference in the charts of Appendix I, one can observe a slash mark '/' for all editions prior to the $UBSGNT^4$, indicating that this variant was not present in any previous *UBSGNT* edition. However, in the $UBSGNT^4$ a *B* letter-rating is recorded, thus designating the new addition of this second reference.

New Variants Added to the UBSGNT[4]

Matthew
- 11.2² (B)
- 11.27 (A)
- 16.20 (B)
- 16.27 (B)
- 17.2 (A)
- 17.4 (B)
- 18.19 (C)
- 19.20 (A)
- 19.24 (A)
- 20.10 (C)
- 20.16 (A)
- 20.22 (A)
- 20.23 (C)
- 20.31 (C)
- 23.9 (B)
- 23.23 (C)
- 23.25 (A)
- 24.7 (B)
- 24.38 (C)
- 24.42 (B)
- 25.13 (A)
- 27.9 (A)
- 27.35 (A)
- 28.8 (B)
- 28.11 (B)
- 28.15 (C)

A = 10 added
B = 9 added
C = 7 added
D = 0 added
= 26 TOTAL

Mark
- 1.6 (A)
- 4.15 (C)
- 4.28 (C)
- 6.3 (B)
- 6.45 (A)
- 6.51¹ (C)
- 9.14 (B)
- 10.13 (A)
- 10.21 (A)
- 10.25 (A)
- 10.31 (C)
- 10.36 (C)
- 12.26 (C)
- 12.34 (C)
- 14.65¹ (A)
- 16.2 (A)
- 16.8 (A)

A = 8 added
B = 2 added
C = 7 added
D = 0 added
= 17 TOTAL

Luke
- 4.18 (A)
- 5.39 (C)
- 6.4 (A)

- 7.32 (B)
- 7.35 (B)
- 7.45 (A)
- 9.10 (B)
- 9.49 (B)
- 9.62¹ (C)
- 13.35¹ (B)
- 15.1 (A)
- 16.21² (A)
- 16.22-23 (A)
- 17.3 (A)
- 18.25 (A)
- 20.34 (A)
- 20.36 (B)
- 22.31 (B)
- 24.17 (B)

A = 9 added
B = 8 added
C = 2 added
D = 0 added
= 19 TOTAL

John
- 1.13² (A)
- 1.19 (C)
- 2.12¹ (C)
- 2.24 (C)
- 3.34 (B)
- 4.3 (A)
- 4.5 (A)
- 4.35-36 (B)
- 7.52 (B)
- 9.38-39 (B)
- 10.19 (B)
- 10.39 (C)
- 11.21 (A)
- 16.16 (A)
- 16.18 (C)
- 16.23¹ (B)
- 17.14 (A)
- 17.23 (A)
- 19.16 (B)
- 19.24 (C)
- 20.19 (A)
- 20.21 (C)
- 21.15 (B)
- 21.16 (B)
- 21.17 (B)
- 21.23 (C)
- 8.6 (A)
- 8.7¹ (A)
- 8.7² (A)

A = 11 added
B = 10 added
C = 8 added
D = 0 added
= 29 TOTAL

Acts
- 1.2 (A)
- 1.23 (A)

- 3.14 (A)
- 5.17 (A)
- 5.29 (A)
- 5.39 (A)
- 8.5 (C)
- 8.24 (A)
- 8.39 (A)
- 9.29 (A)
- 10.37 (B)
- 11.2 (A)
- 11.17¹ (A)
- 11.17² (A)
- 11.22 (C)
- 11.28 (A)
- 12.10 (A)
- 12.23 (A)
- 13.25 (B)
- 13.27 (A)
- 13.43¹ (A)
- 13.43² (A)
- 14.25 (B)
- 15.2 (A)
- 15.6 (A)
- 15.7¹ (A)
- 15.12 (A)
- 15.17-18 (B)
- 15.40 (B)
- 15.41 (A)
- 16.7 (A)
- 16.11 (B)
- 16.35¹ (A)
- 16.35² (B)
- 16.39 (A)
- 17.4¹ (B)
- 17.31 (A)
- 18.8 (A)
- 19.1 (A)
- 19.28 (A)
- 21.16-17 (A)
- 23.29 (A)
- 24.27 (A)
- 27.35 (A)
- 28.19 (A)
- 28.31 (A)

A = 37 added
B = 7 added
C = 2 added
D = 0 added
= 46 TOTAL

Romans
- 1.1 (B)
- 1.31 (A)
- 2.16 (C)
- 4.15 (B)
- 6.4 (A)
- 6.8 (A)
- 7.14 (A)
- 7.20 (C)
- 7.22 (A)
- 8.34¹ (C)
- 8.38 (A)

- 11.25 (C)
- 13.12 (A)
- 15.24 (A)

A = 8 added
B = 2 added
C = 4 added
D = 0 added
= 14 TOTAL

1 Corinthians
- 1.1 (B)
- 2.16 (B)
- 3.2 (A)
- 3.5 (A)
- 4.17² (C)
- 6.14 (B)
- 7.40 (A)
- 9.22 (A)
- 11.15 (C)
- 11.24¹ (A)
- 13.4 (C)
- 13.5 (A)

A = 6 added
B = 3 added
C = 3 added
D = 0 added
= 12 TOTAL

2 Corinthians
- 3.3 (A)
- 5.3 (C)
- 8.9 (B)
- 8.19² (C)
- 9.4² (B)
- 11.17 (A)
- 11.21 (B)
- 12.9 (A)
- 12.19 (A)
- 13.4² (A)

A = 5 added
B = 3 added
C = 2 added
D = 0 added
= 10 TOTAL

Galatians
- 1.11 (C)
- 3.19 (A)
- 3.28 (A)
- 5.23 (A)
- 5.24 (C)
- 6.10 (A)
- 6.15 (A)

A = 5 added
B = 0 added
C = 2 added
D = 0 added
= 7 TOTAL

New Variants Added to the UBSGNT[4]—Continued

Ephesians
- 1.6 (A)
- 1.18 (C)
- 2.5[2] (A)
- 3.1 (C)
- 3.13 (A)
- 3.20 (A)
- 4.6 (A)
- 4.9 (C)
- 4.19 (A)
- 4.29 (A)
- 5.14 (A)
- 6.20 (C)
- 6.24 (C)

A = 9 added
B = 0 added
C = 4 added
D = 0 added
= 13 TOTAL

Philippians
- 2.9 (B)
- 2.11[1] (C)
- 2.11[2] (A)
- 3.12[2] (C)
- 3.15 (A)
- 4.7 (A)
- 4.8 (A)
- 4.13 (A)
- 4.19 (B)

A = 5 added
B = 2 added
C = 2 added
D = 0 added
= 9 TOTAL

Colossians
- 1.12[2] (B)
- 1.14 (A)
- 2.7[1] (A)
- 2.13[2] (A)
- 3.21 (B)
- 4.3 (A)
- 4.12 (C)

A = 4 added
B = 2 added
C = 1 added
D = 0 added
= 7 TOTAL

1 Thessalonians
- 1.5 (A)
- 2.16 (A)
- 4.1 (A)
- 4.11 (C)
- 4.17 (A)

A = 4 added
B = 0 added
C = 1 added

D = 0 added
= 5 TOTAL

2 Thessalonians
- 0 NO CHANGE

1 Timothy
- 1.1 (A)
- 1.4[1] (B)
- 1.4[2] (A)
- 1.17 (A)
- 2.1 (A)
- 5.18 (A)
- 6.9 (A)
- 6.13 (C)
- 6.19 (A)

A = 7 added
B = 1 added
C = 1 added
D = 0 added
= 9 TOTAL

2 Timothy
- 3.14 (B)
- 4.22[1] (B)

A = 0 added
B = 2 added
C = 0 added
D = 0 added
= 2 TOTAL

Titus
- 0 NO CHANGE

Philemon
- 1.2 (A)

A = 1 added
B = 0 added
C = 0 added
D = 0 added
= 1 TOTAL

Hebrews
- 1.12[1] (A)
- 2.8 (C)
- 4.3[2] (C)
- 7.21 (A)
- 9.1 (C)
- 9.14[1] (A)
- 9.17 (A)
- 11.1 (A)
- 11.23 (A)

A = 6 added
B = 0 added
C = 3 added
D = 0 added
= 9 TOTAL

James
- 2.25 (A)
- 3.8 (B)
- 3.9 (A)
- 4.12 (C)
- 5.4 (A)
- 5.14 (A)

A = 4 added
B = 1 added
C = 1 added
D = 0 added
= 6 TOTAL

1 Peter
- 1.9 (C)
- 2.19[1] (B)
- 2.12[2] (B)
- 2.25 (B)
- 3.1 (C)
- 3.7 (B)
- 3.8 (A)
- 3.14 (A)
- 5.3 (A)
- 5.6 (A)
- 5.10[1] (A)
- 5.13 (A)
- 5.14[1] (A)

A = 7 added
B = 4 added
C = 2 added
D = 0 added
= 13 TOTAL

2 Peter
- 1.2 (A)
- 1.4 (B)
- 1.5 (B)
- 2.13[2] (A)
- 2.14 (A)

A = 3 added
B = 2 added
C = 0 added
D = 0 added
= 5 TOTAL

1 John
- 2.4 (A)
- 2.6 (C)
- 2.14 (A)
- 2.18 (B)
- 3.19[2] (A)
- 4.10 (B)
- 5.17 (A)
- 5.18[1] (A)

A = 5 added
B = 2 added
C = 1 added
D = 0 added
= 8 TOTAL

2 John
- 0 NO CHANGE

3 John
- 0 NO CHANGE

Jude
- 1.1[1] (A)
- 1.4[1] (A)
- 1.4[2] (A)
- 1.8 (A)
- 1.12 (A)
- 1.19 (A)
- 1.25 (A)

A = 7 added
B = 0 added
C = 0 added
D = 0 added
= 7 TOTAL

Revelation
- 2.7 (A)
- 4.11 (A)
- 5.10[1] (A)
- 6.3-4 (B)
- 11.1 (A)
- 11.12 (B)
- 14.1 (A)
- 16.17 (A)
- 18.2 (C)
- 18.12 (A)
- 21.12 (C)

A = 7 added
B = 2 added
C = 2 added
D = 0 added
= 11 TOTAL

Total Number of Variants Added to UBSGNT[4]
A = 168
B = 62
C = 55
D = 0
= 285 TOTAL

Variants Dropped from the UBSGNT[4]

Matthew
- 3.12 (C)
- 4.23 (C)
- 5.13 (C)
- 5.25 (B)
- 5.37 (B)
- 7.18 (B)
- 8.8 (C)
- 8.9 (B)
- 8.12 (C)
- 8.13 (B)
- 8.23 (C)
- 9.26 (B)
- 10.4 (B)
- 10.37 (B)
- 10.42 (C)
- 11.2[1] (C)
- 12.30 (A)
- 12.31 (B)
- 13.40 (C)
- 13.44 (C)
- 14.3[1] (C)
- 14.22[1] (C)
- 14.22[2] (B)
- 14.27 (D)
- 15.26 (C)
- 15.36 (B)
- 15.38 (D)
- 16.5 (A)
- 16.8 (C)
- 16.21 (C)
- 17.10 (C)
- 17.15 (B-C)
- 18.7 (C)
- 18.21 (C)
- 18.34 (C)
- 19.3[1] (C)
- 19.3[2] (C)
- 19.22 (C)
- 19.25 (B)
- 20.17[1] (C)
- 20.17[3] (B)
- 25.17 (B)
- 25.41 (B)
- 26.14 (B)
- 26.61 (C)
- 26.63 (C)
- 27.5 (D)
- 27.43 (C)
- 27.64 (A)
- 28.7 (C)
- 28.17 (C)

A = 3 dropped
B = 16 dropped
C = 29 dropped
D = 3 dropped
= 51 TOTAL

Mark
- 1.8[2] (A)
- 1.21 (C)
- 1.39[2] (B)
- 2.10 (B)
- 2.26 (A)
- 3.8[1] (B)
- 3.19 (B)
- 3.29[1] (A-B)
- 4.16 (B)
- 5.21[2] (C-D)
- 5.27 (C)
- 5.42 (D)
- 6.2[1] (A)
- 6.39 (B)
- 6.50 (B)
- 7.6 (B)
- 7.35[2] (B)
- 7.37 (C)
- 8.13 (C)
- 8.15[1] (C)
- 8.16[1] (C)
- 8.16[2] (C)
- 8.17 (B)
- 8.35 (C)
- 9.34 (B)
- 9.43[1] (A-B)
- 10.14 (C)
- 10.46 (C)
- 10.47 (A)
- 11.31 (C)
- 11.32 (B)
- 12.40 (A)
- 13.22 (B)
- 14.4 (C)
- 14.10 (B)
- 14.20 (B)
- 14.30 (B)
- 14.52 (C)
- 14.60 (A-B)
- 15.1 (B)
- 15.10 (B)
- 15.25 (A)
- 15.39[1] (B)
- 16.9 (A)
- 16.14 (A)

A = 8 dropped
B = 22 dropped
C = 13 dropped
D = 2 dropped
= 45 TOTAL

Luke
- 1.17 (A)
- 1.37 (B)
- 1.68 (B)
- 1.70 (B)
- 2.15 (D)
- 2.22 (C)
- 3.9 (C)
- 6.1[2] (B)
- 6.2 (B)
- 6.16 (C)
- 6.26 (C)
- 6.38 (C)
- 6.42 (C)

- 7.28[1] (C)
- 7.42 (C)
- 8.5 (B)
- 8.27 (C)
- 9.62[3] (C)
- 10.1[1] (C)
- 12.1 (C)
- 12.11 (C)
- 12.20 (D)
- 16.14 (C)
- 17.23 (C)
- 20.20 (C)
- 20.26 (C)
- 21.6 (C)
- 22.52 (C)
- 24.9 (D)

A = 1 dropped
B = 6 dropped
C = 19 dropped
D = 3 dropped
= 29 TOTAL

John
- 1.15 (A)
- 2.12[2] (B)
- 3.5 (A)
- 3.20 (C)
- 3.28 (C)
- 4.25 (A)
- 5.2[1] (B)
- 5.4[6] (B)
- 5.4[7] (B)
- 5.4[8] (B)
- 5.4[9] (A)
- 5.4[10] (C)
- 5.9 (B)
- 6.42[1] (B)
- 6.42[2] (C)
- 6.55 (C)
- 6.71 (C)
- 7.4 (C)
- 7.12 (D)
- 7.31 (B)
- 8.16[1] (B)
- 8.38[3] (C)
- 8.53 (C)
- 9.4[2] (C-D)
- 9.6 (B)
- 9.11 (C)
- 9.28 (C)
- 9.36 (C)
- 10.29[2] (C)
- 10.32 (C)
- 10.34 (B)
- 11.19 (B)
- 11.45 (B)
- 12.4 (C)
- 12.12 (C)
- 13.24 (B)
- 13.26[3] (C)
- 16.3 (C)
- 18.16 (C)

- 20.11 (C)
- 20.16 (B)
- 20.17 (C)
- 21.18 (C)
- 8.2 (B)
- 8.3 (C)
- 8.4 (A)
- 8.8 (A)

A = 6 dropped
B = 16 dropped
C = 23 dropped
D = 2 dropped
= 47 TOTAL

Acts
- 1.9 (B)
- 1.18 (A)
- 1.26 (A)
- 2.7 (B)
- 3.13 (C)
- 5.32 (B)
- 5.37 (C)
- 6.9 (B)
- 7.32 (C)
- 9.4 (A)
- 9.5-6 (A)
- 10.17 (C)
- 10.33[1] (C)
- 11.9 (C)
- 12.18 (C)
- 13.14 (B)
- 14.18 (C-B)
- 14.19[1] (C)
- 14.19[2] (C)
- 15.7[2] (B)
- 15.18 (C)
- 15.23[1] (B)
- 17.14 (B)
- 17.27[2] (C)
- 17.30 (C)
- 18.19 (C)
- 18.21-22 (B)
- 19.2 (B)
- 20.5 (C)
- 20.13 (B-C)
- 21.20 (B)
- 21.23 (D)
- 22.13 (C)
- 23.20 (C)
- 23.28 (C)
- 24.15 (B-A)
- 25.13 (B)
- 27.27 (D)
- 27.34 (B)
- 28.14 (C)

A = 5 dropped
B = 14 dropped
C = 19 dropped
D = 2 dropped
= 40 TOTAL

Variants Dropped from the UBSGNT[4]—*Continued*

Romans
- 1.7[2] (B)
- 2.2 (B)
- 3.9 (B)
- 3.26 (C)
- 5.12 (C)
- 5.17 (B)
- 6.16 (C)
- 7.6 (B)
- 7.23 (B)
- 8.11 (D)
- 8.34[2] (C)
- 10.5[1] (C)
- 10.5[2] (C)
- 10.9 (B)
- 11.16 (B)
- 13.5 (B)
- 14.16 (C)
- 15.23 (B)
- 16.7[2] (C)
- 16.27[1] (C)

A = 0 dropped
B = 10 dropped
C = 9 dropped
D = 1 dropped
= 20 TOTAL

1 Corinthians
- 2.14 (B-C)
- 3.10 (C)
- 4.17[1] (C)
- 5.13 (C)
- 7.13 (D)
- 8.2 (B)
- 8.3[2] (C)
- 10.10 (C)
- 14.19 (C-B)
- 14.37 (C)
- 14.39 (D)

A = 0 dropped
B = 2 dropped
C = 7 dropped
D = 2 dropped
= 11 TOTAL

2 Corinthians
- 2.7 (C)
- 8.19[1] (D)
- 9.12 (B)
- 12.10 (C)

A = 0 dropped
B = 1 dropped
C = 2 dropped
D = 1 dropped
= 4 TOTAL

Galatians
- 6.13 (C)

A = 0 dropped

B = 0 dropped
C = 1 dropped
D = 0 dropped
= 1 TOTAL

Ephesians
- 5.20 (C)

A = 0 dropped
B = 0 dropped
C = 1 dropped
D = 0 dropped
= 1 TOTAL

Philippians
- 2.2 (B)
- 2.4 (B)
- 3.12[1] (B)
- 3.21 (B)

A = 0 dropped
B = 4 dropped
C = 0 dropped
D = 0 dropped
= 4 TOTAL

Colossians
- 2.12 (C)

A = 0 dropped
B = 0 dropped
C = 1 dropped
D = 0 dropped
= 1 TOTAL

1 Thessalonians
- 5.21 (C)

A = 0 dropped
B = 0 dropped
C = 1 dropped
D = 0 dropped
= 1 TOTAL

2 Thessalonians
- 2.8[2] (C)

A = 0 dropped
B = 0 dropped
C = 1 dropped
D = 0 dropped
= 1 TOTAL

1 Timothy
- 1.12 (B)

A = 0 dropped
B = 1 dropped
C = 0 dropped
D = 0 dropped
= 1 TOTAL

2 Timothy
- 2.22 (C)
- 4.8 (C)

A = 0 dropped
B = 0 dropped
C = 2 dropped
D = 0 dropped
= 2 TOTAL

Titus
- 0 NO CHANGE

Philemon
- 0 NO CHANGE

Hebrews
- 11.4[1] (C)
- 11.4[2] (C)
- 13.21[2] (C)

A = 0 dropped
B = 0 dropped
C = 3 dropped
D = 0 dropped
= 3 TOTAL

James
- 1.27 (B)

A = 0 dropped
B = 1 dropped
C = 0 dropped
D = 0 dropped
= 1 TOTAL

1 Peter
- 4.1[2] (B)
- 4.3 (B)
- 5.14[3] (C)

A = 0 dropped
B = 2 dropped
C = 1 dropped
D = 0 dropped
= 3 TOTAL

2 Peter
- 2.21 (C)

A = 0 dropped
B = 0 dropped
C = 1 dropped
D = 0 dropped
= 1 TOTAL

1 John
- 2.17 (C-B)

A = 0 dropped
B = 1 dropped
C = 0 dropped
D = 0 dropped

= 1 TOTAL

2 John
- 0 NO CHANGE

3 John
- 1.3 (C)

A = 0 dropped
B = 0 dropped
C = 1 dropped
D = 0 dropped
= 1 TOTAL

Jude
- 0 NO CHANGE

Revelation
- 2.2 (C)
- 2.10[1] (C)
- 2.10[2] (C)
- 2.13[1] (C)
- 2.13[2] (C)
- 2.23 (B)
- 3.2 (C)
- 4.7 (C)
- 5.1 (B)
- 5.4 (C)
- 6.3 (C)
- 6.4 (C)
- 6.8[2] (C)
- 6.11 (C)
- 6.12 (B)
- 7.12 (C)
- 8.8 (C)
- 9.7 (C)
- 9.20 (C)
- 9.21 (C)
- 10.7 (C)
- 11.19 (C)
- 13.8 (C)
- 14.5 (C)
- 14.19 (C)
- 15.4 (C)
- 16.18 (C)
- 18.8 (C)
- 18.11 (C)
- 21.5 (C)
- 22.21[3] (C)

A = 0 dropped
B = 3 dropped
C = 28 dropped
D = 0 dropped
= 31 TOTAL

**Total Number Variants
Dropped in *UBSGNT*[4]**
A = 23
B = 99
C = 162
D = 16
= 300 TOTAL

The list that follows represents the extent of variants added to or removed from any of the *UBSGNT* editions prior to the *UBSGNT*[4]. When compared with the previous two lists based upon the *UBSGNT*[4], this final list clearly reveals that there is a much lower degree of variant addition and omission in the first four *UBSGNT* editions. It appears that all editions prior to the *UBSGNT*[4] make use of an almost standard set of variants to represent their texts, while the *UBSGNT*[4] greatly modifies this.[31]

Variants Added or Dropped in Editions Prior to the UBSGNT[4]

Luke 9.55	Dropped after *UBSGNT*[1]: *C*—(consistent *C*)
Luke 9.55-56	Added into *UBSGNT*[2] and on: *C—A UBSGNT*[4]— (2 step upgrade)
Luke 22.42	Dropped after *UBSGNT*[2]: *C*—(consistent *C*)
Luke 22.43-44	Added into *UBSGNT*[3] and on: *C—A UBSGNT*[4]— (2 step upgrade)
Luke 24.53[3]	In *UBSGNT*[3] and *UBSGNT*[3corr.]: no rating
John 18.13	Dropped out of *UBSGNT*[4]: no previous rating
John 21.24	Dropped after *UBSGNT*[2]: no previous rating
John 21.25	Added into *UBSGNT*[3] and on: no rating
1 Peter 3.18[2]	Dropped after *UBSGNT*[2]: *C*—(consistent *C*)

Concluding Summary

This second section of Chapter 2 has provided incontestable support and clear verification of the conclusions arrived at in Section 1 of this same chapter. Both sections uphold the following: (1) *A* rated variants show a large degree of increase in the *UBSGNT*[4]; (2) *B* ratings increase slightly, but overall remain fairly consistent in number; (3) *C* ratings drop extensively in the *UBSGNT*[4]; (4) *D* ratings fall to almost non-existent levels, and thereby partially constitute an unnecessary classification in the United Bible Societies' evaluation of evidence letter-ratings; and (5) based upon the increase and preservation of *A* and *B* letter-ratings, and the decrease and elimination of *C* and *D* letter-ratings, the *UBSGNT* editorial committee clearly insinuates that the text of the *UBSGNT*[4] is much more incontestable, much more reliable, and much more certain than the text present in the earlier editions of the *UBSGNT*. It is apparent that a revolutionary change has been introduced into the critical apparatus letter-ratings for a large number of variants contained in the *UBSGNT*[4].

31. All bracketed statements such as '(consistent *C*)' or '(2 step upgrade)' refer to specific categories that are developed and further explained in Section 3 of this chapter.

3. *Analysis of Variant Letter-Ratings (A, B, C, D) as Compared throughout All UBSGNT Editions and within Each Biblical Book*

In the first section of Chapter 2, an analysis was made based upon variant ratings as they appeared in each particular edition and each particular book. This third section places the previous data into the context of totals as seen, once again, in each book. However, at this point a comparison is made of the variant ratings as they occur throughout all the *UBSGNT* editions and within each biblical book. By developing various categories of fluctuation and change, one is able to comprehend the type of manipulations that have taken place in each specific book. It should be noted that this analysis shows general trends rather than specific changes in each edition. In other words, each variant is examined and the general trend of rating fluctuation within a variant is discovered. The variant in Mt. 9.8 serves as an example. In the *UBSGNT*[1] there is a *B* rating. In the *UBSGNT*[2] there is a *B* rating. In the *UBSGNT*[3] there is a *B* rating. In the *UBSGNT*[3corr.] there is, again, a *B* rating. And in the *UBSGNT*[4], this *B* rating is changed to an *A* rating. Therefore, rather than list all five specific letter grades, one can deduce that Mt. 9.8, climbing from a *B* rating to an *A* rating, exhibits a general trend of one step increase throughout all five editions. To observe the exact alterations Appendix I can be consulted, as this section is based upon the charts in that appendix, and also the statistics of Appendix III. The following categories of fluctuation have been developed to aid analysis:

- *Number of Variants with Ratings Improving One Step*: this category simply indicates passages that have shown an overall increase of one letter-rating throughout all *UBSGNT* editions. Therefore, the only possibilities that exist are *D* to *C* rating changes, *C* to *B* rating changes, and *B* to *A* rating changes.

- *Number of Variants with Ratings Improving Two Steps*: this category indicates variant ratings that have improved two letter-grades throughout all *UBSGNT* editions. The two possibilities here are *D* to *B* rating changes and *C* to *A* rating changes.

- *Number of Variants with Ratings Improving Three Steps*: this final category showing improving trends deals with variants that have jumped three letter-grades throughout all *UBSGNT* editions. There is only one possibility, *D* ratings that have been upgraded to *A* ratings.

- *Number of Variants with Ratings Decreasing One Step*: the next three categories are the converse of the previous three. This specific category represents variant ratings that have decreased by one letter. The three possibilities that exist here are *A* to *B* rating changes, *B* to *C* rating changes, and *C* to *D* rating changes.

- *Number of Variants with Ratings Decreasing Two Steps*: this classification records variants that decrease by two letter grades. There are two options: *A* to *C* rating changes, and *B* to *D* rating changes. There are actually no *UBSGNT* variants that decrease by two steps. However, this information was not known at the onset of the investigation. For the sake of completeness this category has been retained within the following evaluation.

- *Number of Variants with Ratings Decreasing Three Steps*: this final decreasing category depicts variant ratings that fall three letter grades in total. There is only one option, *A* rated variants that fall to *D* rated variants. As in the above category, there are no *UBSGNT* variants that characterize this group. It, too, has been included for the same reason as mentioned above.

- *Number of Variants with Consistent Ratings throughout All Occurring Editions*: the definitive word that explains this category is 'consistent'. In order for a variant to be recorded here, it must maintain the same rating in *all UBSGNT* editions in which it occurs. This does not necessarily mean that the consistent variant rating must exist in all five editions. It must only remain constant throughout all the editions in which it is listed. Each of the four letter ratings (*A*, *B*, *C*, and *D*) are represented.[34]

- *Number of Variants with Fluctuating Ratings*: a fluctuating variant is a variant that consists of three or more letter-ratings that could be defined as non-sequential, non-successive, non-consecutive, or random in nature. The following two groups of letter-ratings would be considered fluctuating variants: *C-D-C*; *B-D-C*. The next two groups would not be categorized as fluctuating variants due to their consecutive nature: *D-C-B*; *A-B-C*. Instead, the first group of letters in this last example would be categorized as a variant improving two steps, and the second group would be recorded as a variant decreasing by two steps. Fluctuating variants are a unique class of

34. For a further example of this category, consult n. 41 below.

ratings (due to this uniqueness, a complete list of all the fluctuating variants within the *UBSGNT* editions has been included near the end of this section). Often there is astonishing oscillation within variant letter-ratings. At times it appears that the *UBSGNT* editorial committee contradicts previous decisions. One particular example of astonishing fluctuation can be seen in Jas 4.14. Here the variant is changed from a *D* rating to a *C* rating, back to a *D* rating, and then finally, again to a *C* rating. At the least, the committee had an extremely difficult time coming to a point of unanimity as they edited the various editions. In fact, numerous fluctuating variants are also recorded as exceptional variants (to be discussed later) because of their peculiar nature.

- *Number of New Variants Added to the UBSGNT*[4]: based upon the discussion and statistics of Section 2, this category simply records the number of new letter-rated variants (i.e. variants that have an *A*, *B*, *C*, or *D* letter-rating) that have been added to the *UBSGNT*[4]. This statistic is important because it more accurately reflects the modifications made to the *UBSGNT*[4] letter-ratings. This is done by detailing those variant ratings that have not actually been changed, but instead, have been newly added into the apparatus of the *UBSGNT*[4]. The addition of ratings occurs because a new variant, along with its letter-rating, has been freshly included into the *UBSGNT*[4] apparatus. See the previous section (Section 2) entitled 'Variants that Have Been Newly Added or Dropped Out of the *UBSGNT*[4]', and more specifically the discussion concerning 'Number of New Variants Added to the *UBSGNT*[4]'.

- *Number of Variants Dropped Out of the UBSGNT*[4]: based upon the discussion and statistics of Section 2, this category contains letter-rated variants that have been withdrawn from the *UBSGNT*[4]. The passages that are recorded in this category are not included in the following 'Total Number of Variants Cited' category.[35] For a

35. There are only two reasons why a variant would not appear in all five *UBSGNT* editions: (1) it is a new variant that has been added at some point (almost always into the *UBSGNT*[4]. See the final small chart pertaining to added and dropped variants in editions other than the *UBSGNT*[4] located in Section 2 of this chapter), or (2) it is an old variant that has been dropped. Therefore, if a variant does not occur in all five editions it is placed in the category of either 'Number of New Variants Added to the *UBSGNT*[4]', or 'Number of Old Variants Dropped Out of the *UBSGNT*[4]'. If

brief explanation and list of these passages see the preceding section (Section 2) entitled 'Variants that Have Been Newly Added or Dropped Out of the *UBSGNT*[4]', and more specifically the discussion concerning 'Number of Variants Dropped Out of the *UBSGNT*[4]'.

- *Total Number of Variants Cited*: this final category simply adds all the other categories together (excluding the 'Number of Variants Dropped Out of the *UBSGNT*[4]' due to reasons explained in n. 35). The figures recorded here express the number of total variants cited in the particular book throughout all *UBSGNT* editions. This total includes all new additions and omissions as well.

In Appendix III, if a variant does not characterize or fit into a specific category, or when it is uncertain where the variant should be included, it is listed by its biblical reference and placed in the most appropriate category. For example, Lk. 9.55 only occurs as a *C* rated variant in the *UBSGNT*[1]. Therefore, it is specifically listed under the category 'Number of Variants with Consistent Ratings throughout All Occurring Editions', although it only appears in one edition (this variant is also included in the category 'Number of Variants Dropped Out of the

the variant is included in the 'Number of Old Variants Dropped Out of the *UBSGNT*[4]', it is again recorded in the category in which it would most appropriately fit (this is often the 'Consistent Variant' statistic). Therefore, the totals for the category 'Number of Old Variants Dropped Out of the *UBSGNT*[4]' are not included in the category 'Total Number of Variants Cited', because these variants would then be counted twice. Two examples should help explain this point. Because the variant at Mt. 3.12 is removed from the *UBSGNT*[4], it is placed in the category 'Number of Old Variants Dropped Out of the *UBSGNT*[4]'. This variant also receives a consistent *C* rating in the four previous editions, and is added to the category 'Number of Consistent Ratings throughout All Occurring Editions'. Bearing this in mind, the totals for the category 'Number of Old Variants Dropped Out of the *UBSGNT*[4]' are not included in the final category 'Total Number of Variants Cited', because then Mt. 3.12 would be counted twice. In other words, each old variant that has been dropped from the *UBSGNT*[4] is also recorded in one other applicable category, therefore, it is not necessary to include the 'Number of Old Variants Dropped Out of the *UBSGNT*[4]' into the total number of variants cited as they would all be counted twice. Mt. 16.20 is only present in the *UBSGNT*[4] and is, therefore, placed in the category 'Number of New Variants Added to the *UBSGNT*[4]'. This category is included in the 'Total Number of Variants Cited' statistic because it has no previous history that can be used for delineation.

UBSGNT[4]', but is placed into the above-mentioned category according to the explanation provided in n. 35). Another variant occurring in Lk. 9.55-56 is not present in the *UBSGNT*[1], but climbs from a *C* rating to an *A* rating in the four later editions. Consequently, it is specifically recorded in the category 'Number of Variants with Ratings Improving Two Steps'. This specific recording of variants is not possible in these charts, therefore, Appendix III can be referred to for these details.

Each category discussed above is represented in the following chart by a vertical column. When appropriate, the specific letter-rating possibilities are listed directly beneath the category heading. For example, under the category heading 'Number of Variants with Ratings Improving One Step', the three rating possibilities occur (these being *D-C*, *C-B*, and *B-A* increases). As in the charts of Section 1, each biblical book is designated a horizontal row. By moving across the chart horizontally from left to right, the reader can determine the number of passages that characterize any given category.[36] The final horizontal row of this chart records the grand total figures of each column, and in many cases, the figures for each rating possibility within any given category. This total is calculated by simply adding together the numbers present in each vertical column.

---

36. One should keep in mind that these numbers do not represent individual letter-ratings as in the other charts. Instead, these numbers denote the fluctuating trend of each variant's various letter-ratings as they occur successively in all the *UBSGNT* editions together and within each biblical book. Again, these figures are based solely upon letter-rated passages.

Analysis of Variant Letter-Ratings (A, B, C, D) as Compared throughout All Editions and within Each Particular Book—Chart 3

Biblical Book	Number of Variants with Ratings Improving One Step			Number of Variants with Ratings Improving Two Steps		Number of Variants with Ratings Improving Three Steps	Number of Variants with Ratings Decreasing One Step			Number of Variants with Ratings Decreasing Two Steps		Number of Variants with Ratings Decreasing Three Steps
	D-C	C-B	B-A	D-B	C-A	D-A	A-B	B-C	C-D	A-C	B-D	A-D
Matthew	4	24	19	0	1	0	1	3	0	0	0	0
Mark	6	15	6	1	9	0	10	4	2	0	0	0
Luke	13	40	20	9	9	1	2	0	0	0	0	0
John	6	23	9	1	5	0	2	3	0	0	0	0
Acts	11	34	24	4	6	1	0	1	1	0	0	0
Romans	0	12	16	0	5	0	0	1	0	0	0	0
1 Corinthians	3	13	7	0	3	0	0	1	0	0	0	0
2 Corinthians	2	11	4	3	0	0	0	0	0	0	0	0
Galatians	4	2	10	0	0	0	0	0	0	0	0	0
Ephesians	1	4	6	2	0	0	0	0	0	0	0	0
Philippians	1	4	4	1	1	0	0	0	0	0	0	0
Colossians	5	8	3	0	0	0	0	0	0	0	0	0
1 Thessalonians	0	2	3	0	0	0	0	1	0	0	0	0
2 Thessalonians	0	3	2	0	1	0	0	0	0	0	0	0
1 Timothy	0	1	4	0	2	0	0	0	0	0	0	0
2 Timothy	0	3	2	0	0	0	0	0	0	0	0	0
Titus	0	1	2	0	0	0	0	0	0	0	0	0
Philemon	0	2	1	0	0	0	0	0	0	0	0	0
Hebrews	4	10	10	1	2	0	0	0	0	0	0	0
James	1	4	0	2	2	0	0	0	0	0	0	0
1 Peter	1	4	7	1	5	0	0	0	0	0	0	0
2 Peter	3	4	4	2	1	0	0	0	0	0	0	0
1 John	1	5	10	1	2	0	0	0	0	0	0	0
2 John	0	2	3	0	1	0	0	0	0	0	0	0
3 John	0	1	1	0	0	0	0	0	0	0	0	0
Jude	0	0	2	0	0	0	0	0	0	0	0	0
Revelation	3	26	10	1	5	0	0	0	0	0	0	0
Grand Totals	68	258	189	29	52	2	13	14	3	0	0	0

Biblical Book[37]	Number of Variants with Consistent Ratings throughout All Occurring Editions				Number of Variants with Fluctuating Ratings	Number of New Variants Added to the UBSGNT4				Number of Variants Dropped Out of the UBSGNT4				Total Number of Variants Referenced
	A	B	C	D		A	B	C	D	A	B	C	D	
Matthew	7	49	63	4	10	10	9	7	0	3	16	29	3	211
Mark	39	44	36	1	5	8	2	7	0	8	22	13	2	187
Luke	7	25	50	3	2	9	8	2	0	1	6	19	3	198
John	27	44	46	2	3	11	10	8	0	6	16	23	2	201
Acts	10	49	46	3	3	37	7	2	0	5	14	19	2	238
Romans	11	15	23	2	6	8	2	4	0	0	10	9	1	105
1 Corinthians	7	6	13	3	2	6	3	3	0	0	2	7	2	70
2 Corinthians	0	2	7	1	4	5	3	2	0	0	1	2	1	44
Galatians	1	1	3	0	1	5	0	2	0	0	0	1	0	29
Ephesians	0	5	3	0	2	9	0	4	0	0	0	1	0	36
Philippians	0	4	2	0	0	5	2	2	0	0	4	0	0	25
Colossians	1	2	3	0	0	4	2	1	0	0	0	1	0	29
1 Thessalonians	2	1	2	0	0	4	0	1	0	0	0	0	0	16
2 Thessalonians	0	0	3	0	0	0	0	0	0	0	0	1	0	9
1 Timothy	2	0	1	0	0	7	1	1	0	0	1	0	0	20
2 Timothy	0	0	3	0	0	0	2	0	0	0	0	2	0	10
Titus	0	0	1	0	0	0	0	0	0	0	0	0	0	4
Philemon	0	1	0	0	0	1	0	0	0	0	0	0	0	5
Hebrews	2	1	7	0	1	6	0	3	0	0	0	3	0	47
James	1	5	0	0	3	4	1	1	0	0	1	0	0	24
1 Peter	1	2	6	0	0	7	4	2	0	0	2	1	0	40
2 Peter	0	0	4	1	1	3	2	0	0	0	0	0	0	25
1 John	2	1	2	0	1	5	2	1	0	0	1	0	0	33
2 John	0	0	0	0	0	0	0	0	0	0	0	0	0	6
3 John	0	0	1	0	0	0	0	0	0	0	0	1	0	3
Jude	0	0	3	1	0	7	0	0	0	0	0	0	0	13
Revelation	1	4	40	1	1	7	2	2	0	0	3	28	0	103
Grand Totals[37]	121	262	368	22	45	168	62	55	0	23	99	162	16	1731
							Total = 285[38]				Total = 300 (UBS4 states 273)[39]			(1437 or 1438 in the UBSGNT4)[40]

Notes to Chart 3

37.   If any figure in this chart shows a discrepancy with the *UBSGNT* Committee's figures, it is footnoted and discussed. All figures were checked at least three times when a discrepancy was revealed. This often involved recalculating the statistics of an entire section. The following explanations also provide insight into the discrepancies existing in these figures: (1) in defining their numerical additions and deletions, the *UBSGNT* committee has used the term 'passages' (see p. 2* of the *UBSGNT*[4] Introduction). Discrepancies may result because this term denotes an actual biblical passage that may include more than one variant; (2) this chapter provides statistics only for passages that have been ascribed a letter-rating. If a variant has not been given this rating, it will not appear in these charts or the statistics.

38.   When the four totals recorded in this category (168, 62, 55, 0) are added together, the calculation comes to 285 new variants added to the *UBSGNT*[4] (i.e. 168 [A] + 62 [B] + 55 [C] + 0 [D] = 285). On p. 2* of the *UBSGNT*[4] Introduction, 284 new passages are said to be added. The statistical differences between this chart and the totals given in the *UBSGNT*[4] are negligible. However, although the discrepancy here is minor, one can consult the list of 'New Variants Added to the *UBSGNT*[4]', in Section B of this chapter, in order to examine the exact passages included in this tally.

39.   On p. 2* of the *UBSGNT*[4], we are told that 273 'passages' were removed. Again, the first point in n. 37 above may account for some, if not all, of the discrepancy here. However, one may wish to consult the list entitled 'Variants Dropped Out of the *UBSGNT*[4]', in Section B of this chapter, in order to examine the actual 300 omitted variants.

40.   On p. v of the preface to the *UBSGNT*[4], the total number of variants given is 1437. Again, on p. 2* of the Introduction, 1438 passages are said to be the scope of the apparatus. It is uncertain whether the term 'passage' refers to individual variants or to actual biblical passages where variants occur. Regardless, the reason for this minor discrepancy within the *UBSGNT*[4] is not explained and is, therefore, uncertain. However, the figure given here in Chart 3 is 1731 total variants cited. It should be kept in mind that the number here indicates all variants examined within all editions, not just the *UBSGNT*[4]. This includes variants that may have only occurred in one edition and were later removed. Therefore, in all the *UBSGNT* editions combined, a total of 1731 letter-rated passages have been dealt with (this figure does not include unrated passages which provide little information for this chapter). In Section 1 of this chapter, the total number of variants recorded in the *UBSGNT*[4] comes to 1431 (514 [A] + 541 [B] + 367 [C] + 9 [D] = 1431). As recorded immediately above, the *UBSGNT*[4] committee claims there are either 1437 or 1438 variant passages. The discrepancy here (between 1431 or 1437-38 variant passages) may well be due to any number of the above explanations, yet it should be noted that this difference is negligible and has no sizable effect whatsoever upon the conclusions of this monograph.

By focusing attention upon the grand total figures calculated in this chart, we can evaluate what categories occur most frequently, and what specific trends develop throughout the *UBSGNT* editions. Although this chart does not add further conclusive evidence to the discussion regarding individual ratings, along with Section 2 it does detail more precisely the specific type of rating fluctuations.

The first category documents one-step improvement. *C-B* variant increases are most common (258). This is followed by *B-A* variant increases (189). And occurring to a much lower extent are *D-C* variant increases (68). The second category records two-step increase, and is characterized by a greater number of *C-A* rating improvements (52) over *D-B* improvements (29). The third category of increase details three-step *D-A* variant fluctuations. Although there are only two variants that fall under this category (Lk. 19.25 and Acts 2.44 both undergo this three-step *D-A* increase), the extensive nature of upgrading that occurs in these passages warrants closer examination. This will take place in Chapter 3 (see also the 'Exceptional Variant List' near the end of this section for passages that experience further exceptional change).

Categories of decrease show different results. For one-step decreases, *B-C* and *A-B* variant digression is similar (14 and 13 respectively), while *C-D* changes lag behind (3). But one cannot help noticing the difference between improving variants (68 + 258 + 189 + 29 + 52 + 2 = 598) and decreasing variants (13 + 14 + 3 = 30). There is a vast gap that separates the totals of these two groups (598 − 30 = 568). Once again, this points to an overall upgrade in the *UBSGNT*[4] text. Neither two-step nor three-step decreases occur in the *UBSGNT* editions.

The category, 'Number of Variants with Consistent Ratings...', reveals some interesting figures. Leading this field by far are consistent *C* variants ($A = 121$, $B = 262$, $C = 368$, $D = 22$). Within Section A above, we saw a dramatic drop in *C* rated passages within the *UBSGNT*[4]. Yet when the number of consistent *C* variants seen throughout all editions (368) is compared to the total number of *C* variants in the *UBSGNT*[4] (367), one may conclude that many *C* rated passages left in the *UBSGNT*[4] remain as variants that have held their consistency throughout all editions (these can be called 'natural *C* variants').[41]

---

41. A consistent variant does not have to occur in all five *UBSGNT* editions. As long as a letter-rated passage remains constant in its ratings throughout all editions within which it is recorded, that passage can be categorized as a consistent variant. Therefore, a variant that appears in only two editions, but has a *C* rating in both,

Fluctuating variants have already been explained above. Suffice it to say that there are 45 fluctuating variants in total. A detailed list documenting the general trends of fluctuation within each of these variants follows below. Another category of interesting statistics focuses upon new variant additions. As seen in the previous section, this grouping argues that there has been an overall upgrade in the quality of the *UBSGNT* text (keeping in mind that most of these additions occur in the *UBSGNT*[4]). The category 'Number of New Variants Added' consists overwhelmingly of *A* rated variants (168), followed by *B* rated variants (62), *C* rated variants (55), and lastly, *D* rated variants (0). The number of new *A* and *B* ratings (230) compared to the number of new *C* and *D* ratings (55) shows considerable support of an improving textual tradition within the *UBSGNT* editions, especially the *UBSGNT*[4].

By comparing the number and type of variants dropped out of the *UBSGNT*[4] ($A = 23$, $B = 99$, $C = 162$, $D = 16$, total = 300) with the number of variants added to the *UBSGNT*[4] ($A = 168$, $B = 62$, $C = 55$, $D = 0$, total = 285), although one notices that there have been slightly more variants dropped than added, the more important trend to observe concerns the increasing *UBSGNT*[4] textual certainty. This is seen by the higher preservation of *A* rated variants and the greater omission of *C* rated variants. The final category simply records the total number of variants cited (1731).

Chart 3 provides valuable information in the development of two further classifications. Each of the two areas appears as a list. The first list, of which much has already been said, presents fluctuating variants. One can consult the previous discussion and category explanations to complement this following inventory. The second list presents exceptional variants. A definition of this category begins directly after the Fluctuating Variant List.

would be considered consistent. Several of the consistent *C* variants recorded in this total (368) are not present as variants in the *UBSGNT*[4], but instead existed in other editions. However, a large number of consistent *C* variants do carry on into the *UBSGNT*[4]. In the light of this, when we see a *C* rating in this last edition, it is often a consistent variant.

Fluctuating Variants[42]

Matthew (10)
- 5.11 (C-D-C)
- 5.32 (B-C-B)
- 6.15 (C-D-C)
- 11.9 (B-C-B)
- 11.23 (C-D-C)
- 16.2-3 (C-D-C)
- 19.9a (B-C-B)
- 19.9b (B-C-B)
- 20.30 (C-D-C)
- 23.38 (B-C-B)

Mark (5)
- 1.41 (C-D-B)
- 5.21 (B-D-C)
- 6.20 (C-D-C)
- 6.23 (C-D-C)
- 10.7 (C-D-C)

Luke (2)
- 11.11 (B-C-B)
- 22.17-20 (B-C-B)

John (3)
- 3.13 (A-C-B)
- 7.10 (B-D-C)
- 9.4 (C-D-C)

Acts (3)
- 2.16 (C-D-B)
- 3.6 (B-D-C)
- 4.6 (B-C-A)

Romans (6)
- 3.25 (B-D-C)
- 5.6 (C-D-C)
- 8.2 (C-D-B)
- 9.4 (B-C-B)
- 11.31 (B-D-C)
- 15.33 (A-B-A)

1 Corinthians (2)
- 1.14 (B-D-C)
- 10.9 (B-C-B)

2 Corinthians (4)
- 3.2 (B-C-A)
- 7.8 (C-D-C)
- 12.1a (B-C-A)
- 12.1b (B-C-A)

Galatians (1)
- 1.15 (B-D-C)

Ephesians (2)
- 4.28 (C-D-C)
- 5.19 (B-C-B)

Philippians (0)

Colossians (0)

1 Thessalonians (0)

2 Thessalonians (0)

1 Timothy (0)

2 Timothy (0)

Titus (0)

Philemon (0)

Hebrews (1)
- 3.2 (C-D-C)

James (3)
- 1.17 (B-C-B)
- 3.3 (C-D-C)
- 4.14 (D-C-D-C)

1 Peter (0)

2 Peter (1)
- 2.11 (C-D-C)

1 John (1)
- 3.19 (C-D-C)

2 John (0)

3 John (0)

Jude (0)

Revelation (1)
- 13.15 (C-D-C)

Total Fluctuating
Variants = 45

Exceptional Variant List

An exceptional variant is defined by the following parameters: (1) the variant contains a rating that increases or decreases by at least two letter grades, (2) the variant contains irregular fluctuating ratings involving at least three differing letters, or (3) the variant consists of fluctuating ratings that repeatedly contradict previous editorial decisions made in earlier editions.[43] The subsequent list of 98 exceptional variants is significant in that it presents the passages that experience the greatest modification

42. This list shows general trends rather than exact changes as seen throughout each edition. Instead of recording all five ratings given in each *UBSGNT* edition, this list represents the basic movement of the variant.

43. Once again, there are no variants in the *UBSGNT* editions that decrease by two or more letter-ratings. But for the sake of inclusiveness these categories have been retained. The following ratings would not be considered exceptional because they do not increase by at least two letter grades or contain three differing letters: *B-A-B*; *C-C-B*. The next two examples would be considered exceptional because they do contain either three differing letters or an increase of at least two letter grades: *D-C-B*; *C-A*. The following fluctuating variants are also considered exceptional because they possess either three differing letters or repeatedly contradict previous variant ratings: *B-D-C*; *D-C-D-C*.

and alteration within the *UBSGNT* tradition. This list acts as the basis for determining the two most notable passages of exception that will be dealt with in Chapter 3 (these being Lk. 19.25 and Acts 2.44). Occasionally a variant reference will include a superscript number after its citation. This number corresponds to the reference listings in Appendix I, not to the reference listings of the *UBSGNT*[4]. For example, the first variant in the list is Mt. 14.3^2. The superscript numeral '2' indicates that there are at least two variants located in Mt. 14.3, and that the specific variant being referred to here is the second reference.

Exceptional Variants[44]

Matthew (1)
- 14.3^2 (C-B-A)

Mark (4)
- 1.41 (C-D-B)
- 5.21^1 (B-D-C)
- 10.19 (C-A)
- 13.33 (D-C-B)

Luke (19)
- 6.4^1 (C-A)
- 6.10 (C-A)
- 7.10 (C-A)
- 7.39 (C-A)
- 9.55-56 (C-A)
- 12.27 (D-B)
- 19.25 (D-C-A)
- 22.43-44 (C-A)
- 22.62 (C-A)
- 23.15 (C-A)
- 23.34 (C-A)
- 24.3 (D-B)
- 24.6 (D-B)
- 24.12 (D-B)
- 24.36 (D-B)
- 24.40 (D-B)
- 24.47^1 (D-B)
- 24.51 (D-B)
- 24.52 (D-B)

John (8)
- 3.13 (A-C-B)
- 4.9 (C-A)
- 7.10 (B-D-C)
- 8.16^2 (C-A)
- 8.34 (C-A)
- 12.8 (C-A)
- 12.32 (D-B)
- 13.37 (C-A)

Acts (14)
- 1.11 (C-A)
- 2.16 (C-D-B)
- 2.18^1 (C-A)
- 2.44 (D-A)
- 3.6 (B-D-C)
- 4.6 (B-C-A)
- 10.30 (D-B)
- 13.33^2 (D-B)
- 17.26 (D-B)
- 17.27^1 (C-A)
- 17.28 (C-A)
- 21.1 (C-A)
- 22.26 (C-B-A)
- 24.6-8 (D-B)

Romans (8)
- 3.25 (B-D-C)
- 5.1 (C-A)
- 8.2 (C-D-B)
- 8.21 (C-A)
- 8.23 (C-A)
- 11.31 (B-D-C)
- 13.1 (C-A)
- 16.27^2 (C-A)

1 Corinthians (4)
- 1.13 (C-B-A)
- 1.14 (B-D-C)
- 11.29^1 (C-A)
- 11.29^2 (C-A)

2 Corinthians (6)
- 1.10^1 (D-B)
- 1.12 (D-B)
- 3.2 (B-C-A)
- 12.1^1 (B-C-A)
- 12.1^2 (B-C-A)
- 12.7^2 (D-C-B)

Galatians (1)
- 1.15 (B-D-C)

Ephesians (2)
- 5.22 (D-C-B)
- 6.12 (D-B)

Philippians (2)
- 1.11 (C-B-A)
- 1.14 (D-B)

Colossians (0)

1 Thessalonians (0)

2 Thessalonians (1)
- 3.18 (C-A)

1 Timothy (2)
- 6.7 (C-A)
- 6.21 (C-A)

2 Timothy (0)

Titus (0)

Philemon (0)

Hebrews (3)
- 12.18 (D-C-B)
- 13.21^3 (C-B-A)
- 13.25 (C-A)

James (5)
- 1.3 (C-B-A)
- 1.12 (C-B-A)
- 4.14^1 (D-C-B)
- 4.14^3 (D-C-D-C)
- 5.20^1 (D-C-B)

1 Peter (6)
- 1.7 (C-B-A)
- 1.22^1 (C-A)
- 3.18^1 (D-B)
- 3.21 (C-A)
- 5.11^2 (C-A)
- 5.14^2 (C-A)

2 Peter (2)
- 1.3 (D-B)
- 2.13^3 (D-C-B)

1 John (3)
- 2.20 (D-B)
- 3.5 (D-B)
- 3.14 (C-A)

2 John (1)
- 1.3 (C-B-A)

3 John (0)

Jude (0)

Revelation (6)
- 5.9 (C-A)
- 5.10^2 (C-A)
- 6.17 (C-A)
- 13.17 (C-A)
- 20.9 (C-A)
- 21.3^1 (D-B)

Total Exceptional
Variants = 98

44. This list shows general trends, not the exact changes as seen throughout each *UBSGNT* edition. Rather than recording all five ratings given in each *UBSGNT* edition, this list represents the basic movement of the variant.

Concluding Summary

Although this third section of Chapter 2 still leaves one unable to make judgments pertaining to the legitimacy or inconsistency of the editorial changes made in the *UBSGNT*⁴, a closer examination of the evidence, based upon various categories of letter-rating fluctuation, has more precisely revealed the nature of these alterations. First, there are a greater number of variants with improving or upgraded letter-ratings (598) over against variants with decreasing or downgraded letter-ratings (30) in the *UBSGNT*⁴. Secondly, there are a greater number of new *A* rated variants added to the *UBSGNT*⁴ (168) than any other group of newly added letter-rated variants ($B = 62$, $C = 55$, $D = 0$). Along these same lines, the total number of new *A* and *B* letter-rated variants (230) far exceeds the total number of new *C* and *D* letter-rated variants (55) added to the *UBSGNT*⁴. Thirdly, there are more *C* rated variants removed from the *UBSGNT*⁴ textual apparatus (162) than any of the three other letter-rating groups, or even the combined total of these three groups ($A = 23$, $B = 99$, $D = 16$, Total = 138). This reveals that a greater number of *A* rated variants, rather than *C* rated variants, are preserved within the *UBSGNT*⁴. These three factors continue to confirm, along with the previous sections of this chapter, that there has been an extensive upgrade in the quality of text presented in the *UBSGNT*⁴. Silva, evaluating the letter-rating upgrades for Romans to Galatians as recorded in the *UBSGNT*³ and the *UBSGNT*⁴, comes to the same conclusion. He states emphatically:

> [T]he rating for most passages has been raised. For Romans through Galatians, 19 passages were already given an A in the third edition and thus could not be raised. Out of the remaining 152 passages (206 minus 19 As minus 35 deletions), a full 105 are given a higher evaluation, that is, 69 percent. Specifically, 15 were raised from D to C, 41 from C to B, and 37 from B to A; and, as if that were not enough, 2 passages were raised from D to B, and a full 10 from C to A! Out of the 43 variation units added to the fourth edition, no fewer than 24 are given an A. How radically different is the resulting complexion of the material can be seen by comparing the totals from the third and fourth editions: Third Fourth A 20 93 B 62 64 C 99 55 D 25 2...[45]

---

45. Silva, 'Symposium', p. 352. Although Silva's figures reveal a marginal discrepancy from, those calculated in this chapter, his main emphasis is more than clear—there has been a radical upgrade of the *UBSGNT*⁴ letter-ratings.

4. *Various Possible Reasons for the Rating Changes from Previous UBSGNT Editions to the UBSGNT*[4]

Progress within textual criticism is often painstakingly slow. In fact, some modern textual critics feel that the discipline is at a methodological interlude 'between the grand achievement of Westcott-Hort and whatever significant second act is to follow'.[46] Although much of textual criticism's present lack of forward momentum stems directly from the nature of the work at hand, perhaps another contributing factor is the discipline's binding ties to past tradition. Epp comments upon this very point:

> Though textual criticism has shown itself to be—by its very nature—a highly conservative discipline, an overly cautious attitude when exploring theoretical issues will forestall the progress so urgently required in the field. We need to open some new windows, and—if possible—a few doors as well![47]

It would appear that the *UBSGNT*[4] editorial committee took a similar type of maxim to heart. Whereas the previous discussion reveals clear evidence that the quality of text has been greatly upgraded in the *UBSGNT*[4], this final section of Chapter 2 investigates the validity of these modifications and explores a number of possible reasons for the apparent upgrade. Are changes within the *UBSGNT*[4] justified? Has the *UBSGNT* editorial committee based their alterations on valid and verifiable evidence? On the other hand, does a closer examination of this latest *UBSGNT* edition disclose an unfounded letter-rating upgrade that may, based upon the presented quality and certainty of the *UBSGNT*[4], instill a false sense of security in the text?

A substantial amount of criticism has been leveled at the variant letter-rating fluctuations seen among the *UBSGNT* editions. Concerning the first four editions, J.M. Ross states:

> Of course, every student of the NT has his own views on the probabilities of readings, but perhaps an impression may be recorded here—which remains in many instances in spite of the explanations in the committee's [Metzger's] Commentary—that often the editors have attached a high degree of probability (evaluation B or even A) to readings which others would consider much more doubtful or would even reject altogether.[48]

---

46. Epp, 'The Twentieth-Century', p. 84.
47. Epp, 'Significance of the Papyri', p. 286.
48. Ross, 'The United Bible', p. 118. Ross goes on to point out a number of

C.M. Martini, an editor of the *UBSGNT* since its second edition, attempts to justify the minor rating changes that take place in the *UBSGNT*[3] from the *UBSGNT*[2] (extremely minor when compared to the *UBSGNT*[4]). He states that changes in the ratings should not cause astonishment because:

> [I]t derives from the very nature of New Testament textual criticism, which, in many cases, has to deal with almost equally balanced arguments in favor of one variant or another. In these cases, more careful consideration of the external evidence, light thrown by a new papyrus or further study of the stylistic peculiarities of an author can lead one to choose as more probable a different reading from the one previously chosen.[49]

Although this type of response *may* hold credibility for the moderate number of changes made to the earlier *UBSGNT* editions, it is hardly acceptable when defending the extensive upgrades in the *UBSGNT*[4], where ratings are increasing two and even three steps. These modifications are not what one would call 'equally balanced arguments' that can simply be decided by 'more careful consideration'. As Elliott critically concludes, immediately after citing Martini's quotation, 'While applauding the editorial board for their flexibility in building up the text, we repeat our original criticism that the rating system is of little value to the translators or students for whom this text is aimed'.[50] Elliott states further, 'it is not usually apparent why this letter has been changed, even though *the text [UBSGNT*[3]*] remains identical* with UBS[2]'.[51] Any explanation supporting the *UBSGNT*[4] letter-rating upgrades will have to be established upon a much firmer foundation. The matter is, simply put, not as elementary in the *UBSGNT*[4]. Pertaining directly to the *UBSGNT*[4], perhaps the loudest voice to speak out against the letter-rating fluctuations and the entire system as a whole, is, once again, Elliott. He states:

> The bizarre and often criticized system of allocating rating letters to each variation unit has been preserved... The new editorial team voted on all the variation units and not merely on the ones new in this edition. As a

specific variants in the *UBSGNT*[2] where the letter-ratings may be too highly ascribed. A few of his numerous examples are Mt. 1.16, 25; 6.28; 10.3; 23.14; and 27.49.

49. C.M. Martini, review of *Studies in New Testament and Early Christian Literature: Essays in Honor of Allen P. Wikgren* in *BT* 25 (1974), pp. 150-52. It should also be noted that there have been no significant new papyri finds that throw light upon the *UBSGNT*[3] or following editions.

50. Elliott, 'The Third Edition', p. 270.

51. Elliott, 'The Third Edition', p. 270.

result many of the rating letters in UBS[3a] have changed, thereby confirming our already formed opinion about the arbitrariness of the whole
procedure... Taking Matthew's gospel as an example we have some B
readings in UBS[3a] transformed with a wave of the magician's wand into
an A reading... readings transmogrified from C-B... Upgrading from D-
C... At Mark 1.41 we can witness a spectacular leap from D-B without
any real change in the attestation... These rating letters are an unnecessary intrusion. It seems unlikely that a translator (or student), able to read
the critical apparatus would base his judgment on the arbitrary and fluctuating rating letters.[52]

Elsewhere, Elliott adds fuel to the fire by making the following comments:

Such guidance [i.e. that given by the letter-ratings] may seem to be helpful
to non-experts, but the fluctuations in the letters attached to the same variant over the different editions is more likely to confuse the user than
help... I doubt if a translator should set much store by the imprecise and
fluctuating system to help him decide on the reliability of the printed text.
If I were a free agent, able to part company with the UBS/NA text for my
translation, I doubt if the editors' volatile voting for A, B, C, or D would
sway my interpretation of the *apparatus* at that point.[53]

The United Bible Society provides various reasons for a variety of
changes they have made to the *UBSGNT*[4]. For example, the committee
explains that the actual text of the *UBSGNT*[3corr.] and *UBSGNT*[4] has
been modified in order to establish a single, shared text with Nestle-
Aland in its 26th and 27th editions (see p. 1* of the *UBSGNT*[4]). Changes
to the citation of manuscripts, as well as the punctuation apparatus of
the *UBSGNT*[4] are also explained in similar fashion (see p. vi of the
UBSGNT[4]). The Bible Society's use of bracketed text, and the designation of such texts with a *C* letter-rating, are again clarified (see p. 2*
of the Introduction to the *UBSGNT*[4]). And one final example, elucida-
tion is also given, although somewhat vaguely, regarding the removal
and inclusion of variant passages (see pp. v and 2* of the Introduction to
the *UBSGNT*[4]). These kinds of modification are not strongly questioned,
perhaps because they are usually well documented. But what clarification, if any, is given to vindicate the comprehensive revisions of variant
letter-ratings? In order to formulate an opinion regarding this issue, one
must explore several possible explanations that attempt to justify the
upgrading of these variant letter-ratings.

52. Elliott, 'The Fourth Edition', cols. 18-19.
53. Elliott, 'Two New Editions', p. 495. On p. 496 of this same article, Elliott
alludes to the letter-ratings as a 'patronizing spoon-feeding'.

A Redefining of the Letter-Rating Levels

The first possible justification deals with the definitions of the various ratings themselves. Have the *A*, *B*, *C*, and *D* variant rating levels been newly defined in the *UBSGNT*[4]? Or have they remained the same throughout all five *UBSGNT* editions? This is a question that the *UBSGNT* editorial committee addresses. On page v of the preface to the fourth edition, the following statement is made: '[T]he Committee also redefined the various levels in the evaluation of evidence on the basis of their relative degrees of certainty. Thus the evaluation of all the 1437 sets of variants cited in the apparatus have been completely reconsidered.' Again, on page vi of this same section, one further statement provides a small amount of illumination pertaining to a redefinition of the various letter-ratings: 'At that time [1981 at a meeting of the committee] the decisions were made for eliminations and inclusions in the apparatus of variant readings, and also for reconsidering the evaluation of readings'.

A closer look at these newly fashioned demarcations reveals the extent of variation that occurs between the first four *UBSGNT* editions and the *UBSGNT*[4]. The definitions for the *A*, *B*, *C*, and *D* letter-ratings are identical in the *UBSGNT*[1] to the *UBSGNT*[3corr].[54] They are defined as follows:

- the letter *A* signifies that the text is virtually certain
- the letter *B* indicates that there is some degree of doubt
- the letter *C* means that there is a considerable degree of doubt whether the text or the apparatus contains the superior reading
- the letter *D* shows that there is a very high degree of doubt concerning the reading selected for the text

When the same section of the *UBSGNT*[4] is explored, we find the ensuing new delineations:[55]

- the letter *A* indicates that the text is certain
- the letter *B* indicates that the text is almost certain
- the letter *C*, however, indicates that the Committee had difficulty in deciding which variant to place in the text
- the letter *D*, which occurs only rarely, indicates that the Committee had great difficulty in arriving at a decision

---

54. See pp. x-xi of the *UBSGNT*[1] and *UBSGNT*[2], and pp. xii-xiii of the *UBSGNT*[3] and *UBSGNT*[3corr].

55. See p. 3* of the *UBSGNT*[4].

Although it is obvious that there has been a redefinition of the letter-rating classifications used in the *UBSGNT*⁴, the two short statements above constitute the only specific references made regarding this change.[56] One searches in vain for an explanation as to why this redefinition has occurred and how exactly it affects the committee's reconsideration of cited variants. The purpose for this redefinition of the various levels in the evaluation of evidence letter-ratings within the *UBSGNT*⁴ needs to be greatly clarified and improved, especially since this redefinition introduces such a radical departure from the quality of text presented in previous *UBSGNT* editions.

Despite the *UBSGNT* editorial committee's failure to provide adequate documentation detailing the modification made to the *A, B, C,* and *D* letter-ratings, it is clear that some type of redefinition has occurred. But again, one must ask whether these new standards allow for and elucidate the bold upgrading that takes place among variant letter-ratings within the *UBSGNT*⁴. There are two lines of argument to pursue in order to answer this question. The first deals with the definition of terms. By examining both descriptions of the letter-ratings, it could be asserted that there has not been enough of a *substantial* modification made between the two standards. *A* ratings have been redefined as 'certain' from the previous 'virtually certain'. Does this change even qualify as a 'redefinition'? It could be argued here that this new standard is a matter of precision, or perhaps a type of word play. How one defines the word *virtually* is all-important. By using this word, does one mean to express certainty, or almost certainty?[57] It is important to

56. On p. 45 of the Alands' book *The Text of the New Testament*, one also finds the following statement: 'The only question is whether the editors have not been too cautious in applying the classifications, so that a B should often be replaced by an A, a C by a B, and a D by a C (a thorough reexamination has led to a revision of these for the fourth edition of *GNT*)'. It is this 'thorough reexamination' that is now in question within this section. However, if the *UBSGNT* editors felt they were too conservative in ascribing letter-ratings to the variants, this is not mentioned anywhere in any *UBSGNT* edition. It would seem that they stuck closely to their letter-rating classifications, and so they should, once these were established. Regardless, it is not mere conservatism extending from the previous *UBSGNT* editions that gives excuse to the major alterations in the *UBSGNT*⁴. Even the Alands negate this excuse when they claim there is a revision of these letter-ratings. Therefore, the *UBSGNT*⁴ revision alone acts as the basis for evaluation.

57. A humorous illustration might help here. I cannot help but think of the 'Cascade' dish-washing detergent. This product is renowned for its advertising

understand the use of this word in the earlier *UBSGNT* editions, so as to clarify the degree of certainty and redefinition expressed in the *UBSGNT*[4]. If it is assumed that the word 'virtually' is to denote 'almost certainty', then one may still be faced with only a small margin of increase in the new *A* rating standard present within the final *UBSGNT* edition. Regardless of whether this can be called a redefinition or not, this ambiguity needs to be clarified.

B ratings change from 'some degree of doubt' to 'almost certain'. Have *B* ratings now fulfilled the role of 'virtual certainty' expressed in the old definition for *A* ratings? Or, in other words, have *B* ratings been bumped up one step from their previous delineation? Is the more pessimistic term, 'some degree of doubt', the equivalent of the more optimistic phrase 'almost certain'? Although this may be the case, there is, once again, some apparent ambiguity.

C ratings previously indicated that 'there is a considerable degree of doubt whether the text or the apparatus contains the superior reading'. They now reveal that 'the Committee had difficulty in deciding which variant to place in the text'. Whereas *D* ratings once attested to 'a very high degree of doubt concerning the readings selected for the text', their new limits express that 'the Committee had great difficulty in arriving at a decision'. One could again dispute whether *C* and *D* ratings have actually changed at all. Instead, it could be argued that the new definitions for *C* and *D* ratings have simply been expressed in a more optimistic manner.

In the *UBSGNT*[4], the committee redefines the *A*, *B*, *C*, and *D* levels on the basis of their 'relative degrees of certainty'. However, in the *UBSGNT*[1] to the *UBSGNT*[3corr.], these same letter-ratings were defined on the basis of their 'degree of doubt'. Perhaps a further illustration will clarify the point. Two people enter a room together and are instructed to explain what they see. Situated on a table in the middle of the room is a glass of water. The first person describes the vessel as being 'half full', while the second person states that it is 'half empty'. Who is correct? Obviously both are right. Although each chooses to explain what they see with opposite descriptions, perhaps one being more optimistic and

---

phrase, 'Gets your dishes *virtually* spotless or your money back'. The bottom line is, does this detergent clean my dishes or not? Are they spotless or almost spotless? As is clear, there could be a sense of deception, or a hidden agenda behind the use of this word. What does the United Bible Society mean by their use of the word 'virtually'?

the other more pessimistic, each is describing the same thing. There is no real difference in what each statement concludes. One's perspective is the determining factor. Could this be the type of 'redefinition' that has taken place in the *UBSGNT*[4] (admittedly pertaining more so to *B*, *C*, and *D* ratings)? Perhaps this 'redefinition' would be better categorized as a restatement based upon perspective. Regardless, these new standards, when compared to the old, are too ambiguous to be useful. Conceivably, more precise wording, a greater detailed redefining of the various letter-rating levels, and an enhanced degree of separation from the old delineations would alleviate this problem. However, as it now stands in the *UBSGNT*[4], this redefinition is over-subtle and renders the new categories for *A*, *B*, *C*, and *D* letter-ratings too ambiguous. Silva, in his review of the *UBSGNT*[4], notes a further element of ambiguity relating to the newly defined letter-ratings:

> Perhaps the most obvious revision of this work is in the set of ratings used to evaluate textual problems. The very description of these ratings is different... The language used in this edition to describe C and D ratings is a little more helpful than was the case before, but a certain ambiguity remains. The expression 'the Committee had [great] difficulty' could refer to a subjective sense of doubt shared by all the members, but it could also refer to the objective fact that there was no agreement among them (even though they may have felt very sure about their vote!). Perhaps this is splitting hairs, and one could argue that the result is the same, but I for one would like to know. For example, if in my judgment a reading is 'almost certain' (therefore B), but the committee gives it a C, should I temper my judgment? I should if all the members feel uncertain, but not if the decision was really based on the strong, but perhaps idiosyncratic, protests of only one member.[58]

It should likely be conceded that the various levels in the evaluation of evidence have actually been redefined one step higher.[59] In other words, by evaluating the two sets of standards presented earlier, one could conclude that the *UBSGNT*[4] redefinitions have increased in their degree of certainty, rather than declined in their degree of certainty. Thus, *A* ratings have increased in their level of confidence from 'almost

---

58. Silva, 'Symposium', p. 352.

59. To be true to the issue, it appears that Silva finds less ambiguity in the redefinition and actual wording of the evaluation of evidence letter-ratings. He concludes, at least for *A* and *B* letter-ratings, that '[T]he description for A and B ratings is a good bit more positive than in the previous edition'. See Silva, 'Symposium', p. 352.

(virtually) certain' to 'certain', while *B* ratings have increased from a less confident 'some degree of doubt' to a more confident 'almost certain', and so on. If we conclude that each letter-rating has been redefined, therefore making the new definitions more assured in their degree of certainty, the logical result is that it would be harder for a variant in the first four *UBSGNT* editions to achieve this newly heightened certitude in the *UBSGNT*[4]. Standards that have been made more assured (or more difficult to achieve, based on their higher degree of certainty) should give way to a smaller number of variants in them. It should be harder for variants to maintain their letter-rating as prescribed in the earlier *UBSGNT* editions, given that the new *UBSGNT*[4] delineations make it more difficult to attain these standards. However, not only do many of these variants maintain their old letter-rating, a large number of them actually move upward to a new letter grade—one that has been freshly defined with higher demarcations. If the letter-grade definitions were to decline in their degree of certainty, then many variants could logically be upgraded. But these definitions do not indicate a decline. Instead, or so it appears, they become more rigid and certain. The trend of upgrading variants in the *UBSGNT*[4] in fact reverses this logic. There is an increase in the number of *A* and *B* rated passages, but also a decrease in the number of *C* and *D* rated passages. With the strengthened standards in the *UBSGNT*[4], one would think that these trends might be reversed. It should be more difficult for an *A* or *B* rated variant, present in the *UBSGNT*[1] or the *UBSGNT*[3corr.], to maintain its *A* or *B* rating in the *UBSGNT*[4]. In order for an *A* variant of past editions to remain an *A* variant in the *UBSGNT*[4], it can no longer be 'almost (virtually) certain'. It must now be 'certain'. In order for a *B* variant of past editions to remain a *B* variant in the *UBSGNT*[4], it can no longer indicate 'some degree of doubt'. It must now indicate 'almost certainty'. Granted, there has been an immense upgrade. Yet, this upgrade cannot be adequately accounted for on the basis of the letter-rating redefinitions within the *UBSGNT*[4].

The Addition of New Manuscripts Adding Further Information
The most logical explanation of the upgrades in the *UBSGNT*[4] would be new manuscript evidence. Have there in fact been new manuscripts cited within the variants themselves, thus indicating more certainty in, or shedding further light on the establishment of the more probable text? Page x of the *UBSGNT*[3] states that the forthcoming *UBSGNT*[4] 'will

have a completely new treatment of textual data'. By examining and comparing all five editions and the variants and manuscripts cited in them, one can conclude that within the *UBSGNT*[4] there has been a marginal rearranging of the manuscripts cited as witnesses for variants. This has most often included the removal of various manuscripts, and the new inclusion of already known manuscripts not previously cited in the *UBSGNT* editions. To a large extent, manuscripts that have been added or removed are not those witnesses of higher quality used for determining the correct reading, but are witnesses that better represent the overall manuscript tradition and textual history.[60] Again, this is a marginal rearranging. The addition of these various witnesses has not necessarily brought new insight or fresh proof into the evaluation of variants, and hence the determining of a more likely reading. Therefore, the manuscripts themselves do not give rise to the extent of upgrading that occurs in the *UBSGNT*[4]. To explain further, there have been no significant new manuscripts found, and no recent enlightening information regarding a previously known manuscript that would allow for a *C* rated passage to be changed to an *A* rated passage (this would include the papyri as well). Again, Silva, speculating on the reason for the extensive *UBSGNT*[4] upgrade, affirms the above points and more when he rightly states:

> Since the manuscript evidence is not substantially different from what it was a decade ago [apparently referring to *UBSGNT*[3corr.]], do these changes mean that the committee members have used different principles, or that they have implemented the principles differently, or that they have become more certain of their decisions, or merely that they are concerned that users of the earlier editions might have misunderstood the relatively few instances of A ratings? No explanation is given...[61]

On page x of the *UBSGNT*[3], this statement is made:

> Plans are already underway for a Fourth Edition of the Greek New Testament, which will contain a correspondingly thorough revision of the textual apparatus, with special emphasis upon evidence from the ancient versions, the Diatessaron, and the Church Fathers. In addition, the evidence from Greek manuscripts will be carefully controlled by direct comparison with manuscript readings. This will apply particularly to the evidence which could not be so treated in previous editions.

---

60. Although on a limited scale, this will be clearly revealed in the discussion of Lk. 19.25 and Acts 2.44 in Chapter 3.

61. Silva, 'Symposium', pp. 352-53.

On page 1* of the *UBSGNT*[4], now a reality rather than simply alluded to as in the above quotation, we find further explanation regarding the revision of the textual or critical apparatus:

> The present fourth edition of *The Greek New Testament* contains as planned a thorough revision of its critical apparatus. All the data have been repeatedly collated and double-checked: the manuscripts from photocopies or films, and the oriental versions from standard editions of the texts or of manuscripts.

Each of these quotations makes statements regarding revisions of known manuscripts, not distinctly the addition of new manuscripts. With regard to a 'special emphasis upon evidence from the ancient versions, the Diatessaron, and the Church Fathers', Metzger, one of the editors on the *UBSGNT* committee throughout all five editions, states a principle still held by the large majority of today's textual critics:

> In choosing among variant readings of any given passage of the New Testament, most scholars have followed the traditional and time-honored procedure of beginning with the Greek manuscripts themselves, and then supplementing their testimony by consulting the early versions and the patristic quotations... a majority of modern textual scholars consider patristic evidence, so long as it stands alone, to count for almost nothing in ascertaining the original text... Accordingly, it is only when patristic evidence coincides with the evidence of the Greek manuscripts, or with some unmistakable indication in the early versions, that any stress can be laid upon it. But whenever this is the case, it rises at once into great importance.[62]

Metzger goes on to discuss several individuals who oppose this time-honored method of evaluation, only to state that in his view he believes them to be incorrect. In the concluding section of this article, Metzger states:

> [W]e have found no reason to abandon the view that, in the nature of the case, it is the Greek manuscripts which provide direct evidence for the text of the New Testament, whereas the versions and patristic quotations pro- vide indirect evidence... the indirect testimony of versions and Fathers is of the greatest value when it is found to corroborate the direct testimony of the Greek manuscripts.[63]

---

62. B.M. Metzger, 'Patristic Evidence and the Textual Criticism of the New Testament', *NTS* 18 (1972), pp. 385-86.
63. Metzger, 'Patristic', p. 395.

Like Metzger, K. Aland apparently agrees when he states rule five of his 'Twelve Basic Rules for Textual Criticism':

> The primary authority for a critical textual decision lies with the Greek manuscript tradition, with the versions and Fathers serving no more than a supplementary and corroborative function, particularly in passages where their underlying Greek text cannot be reconstructed with absolute certainty.[64]

If use of the ancient versions and the Church Fathers is the basis of the extensive *UBSGNT*[4] letter upgrades, clearly contrary to statements by Metzger and Aland, this needs to be explained, and the reasons for this new methodology should be described. It is, however, highly doubtful that this is the case. Therefore, if the addition of new manuscript evidence is the reason for upgraded letter-ratings in the *UBSGNT*[4], which again seems unlikely, the Greek manuscripts alone are to be used in order to give an accounting of the *UBSGNT*[4] modifications.

The situation is further complicated by a statement found on page v of the *UBSGNT*[4], quoting the *UBSGNT*[3]: 'The GNT continues to offer "more extensive evidence for a more select number of variants" (Preface to the Third Edition, p. xi)'. This small excerpt from the *UBSGNT*[3] quoted in, and again applied to, the *UBSGNT*[4] raises some larger questions. Does it qualify both the *UBSGNT*[3] and the *UBSGNT*[4] as basically offering the same 'more extensive evidence'? Or are we to assume that the *UBSGNT*[4] carries on from where the *UBSGNT*[3] left off, and therefore adds further 'extensive evidence' not previously contained in the *UBSGNT*[3]?[65] Despite the ambiguity, the latter is most likely the case. However, does this more extensive evidence really add that much additional information to the *UBSGNT*[4], especially considering that it existed in some preliminary form within the *UBSGNT*[3]? And does it justify the radical letter-rating changes made in the *UBSGNT*[4]? One would think not, especially since the *UBSGNT*[3] and *UBSGNT*[4] make use of the same primary manuscripts to witness to their respective textual variants. The only modification between these two editions tends to be

---

64. K. and B. Aland, *The Text of the New Testament*, p. 280.

65. It should be pointed out that the *UBSGNT* editorial committee use the phrase 'more extensive evidence for a more select number of variants' in order to contrast the *UBSGNT* from the Nestle-Aland editions. The latter edition offers a greater number of variants in its textual apparatus but far fewer manuscripts are cited in support of each variant. This phrase is not specifically used to provide support for upgraded letter-ratings.

the removal of one manuscript and its replacement by another of equal quality and weight within the *UBSGNT*[4]. This is done not to provide greater evidence for determining the certainty of a given reading, but instead to round out the history of the particular variant and the textual tradition.

One final detail needs to be mentioned. An argument of omission exists here in the *UBSGNT*[4]. The *UBSGNT* editors state that the letter-ratings or evaluations of all 1437 variants have been completely reconsidered in the light of the redefinition of the various levels in the evaluation of evidence (once again, see p. v in the *UBSGNT*[4]), not on the basis of new manuscript discoveries or new insight into previously known manuscripts.[66] And already, we have discussed the short-comings in this redefinition of the various levels in the evaluation of evidence. If, in fact, new manuscript discoveries or new information pertaining to old manuscripts were the basis of the *UBSGNT*[4] letter-rating upgrades, which would be a perfect justification for these upgrades, this has been kept from general scholarly knowledge. But the fact that the *UBSGNT* editors do not indicate such a knowledge reveals that it is not the reason for the highly increased quality of text present in the *UBSGNT*[4].[67]

Manuscript Groupings that Affect the Letter-Ratings

> The Committee sought to arrive at a text that did not mechanically reflect the readings of any single MS. or pair of MSS. or group of MSS... It is true, however, that if one looks at the footnotes and observes whether readings supported by Aleph and/or B are preferred or rejected, to a very large degree they are preferred, not rejected. In fact, there are few texts on

66. Although Silva asserts that 'No explanation is given' for the *UBSGNT*[4] upgrade (see once again Silva, 'Symposium', p. 352, and n. 61 in this chapter), this is not completely true. The *UBSGNT* committee do claim that their redefinition of the various levels for letter-ratings brought about the reconsideration of the evaluations of all 1437 sets of variants cited in the *UBSGNT*[4] apparatus (see p. v of the *UBSGNT*[4]).

67. Elliott points out that although the *UBSGNT*[4] committee add a significant number of new witnesses to the manuscript lists in the Introduction, many of these are rarely or never cited in the critical apparatus. Using the papyri as an example, Elliott points out that 'Despite the apparent intention that all the papyri are to be found in an apparatus I have located only 60 of these 94, in other words over one third are absent'. He also reveals that the same problem occurs with the uncials and concludes, 'Why list an MS. if a reader is not going to encounter it in the apparatus?' See Elliott, 'The Fourth Edition', cols. 13-14.

which Aleph and B agree that do not end up to be the preferred reading; and also there are few preferred readings that do not have the support of either Aleph or B or one of their corrected forms, so to speak.[68]

E.G. Edwards, referring to the *UBSGNT*[3], explains in the above quotation that manuscript groups played a role in the establishment of the preferred reading. Likewise, Z.C. Hodges, by no means a supporter of the eclectic type of text presented in the *UBSGNT*, recognized particular manuscript groupings that occurred in the textual apparatus of editions as early as the *UBSGNT*[1]. He states that:

> The recent Bible societies text [*UBSGNT*[1]], edited by Kurt Aland, Matthew Black, Bruce M. Metzger and Allen Wikgren, does not often reject readings supported by both $\mathfrak{P}^{75}$ and B. Small wonder that it can thus be regarded as a near relative of these two manuscripts which go back to a common ancestor.[69]

The primary thrust of this section is to determine if there is a certain group of manuscripts that tend to influence the letter-ratings within variants. Or, to ask the question differently, what type of manuscripts have a high degree of occurrence, or are regularly cited within the given letter-ratings? Are there special manuscript groupings that determine what kind of letter-rating a variant will receive? What type of manuscript is important to the *UBSGNT* editors in their designation of *A*, *B*, *C*, and *D* letter-ratings?

In order to answer these questions, five charts have been prepared based upon the data presented in Appendix IV and Appendix V. These charts are selective in the variants they evaluate. Five biblical books have been chosen to represent these high percentage manuscript groupings present in the *UBSGNT*[4]. These books are Luke (representing the Gospels), Acts, Romans (representing the Pauline Epistles), 1 Peter (representing the Catholic or General Epistles), and Revelation. Every variant present in the first eight chapters of each book has been evaluated (except 1 Peter, consisting of only five chapters, where the entire book is evaluated).

Obviously, there are some limitations inherent to this type of statistical survey. Some may feel that this is simply counting manuscripts, which, in fact, it is. However, this counting of manuscripts is performed in order

---

68. Edwards, 'Textual Apparatus', p. 141.

69. Z.C. Hodges, 'The Greek Text of the King James Version', *BSac* 125 (1968), p. 337 n. 7.

to determine what witnesses are deemed important to the *UBSGNT* text and its editors, and to ascertain if the ascribing of letter-ratings is based to any significant degree upon logical, calculated manuscript groupings. These figures should not be used to determine which variant options and manuscripts are closer to the original reading. Instead, this is the task of both internal and external evidence, not of a statistical counting of manuscripts. Obviously, an evaluation of more variant passages (and ideally all variant passages) within the *UBSGNT*[4] would reveal stricter manuscript presence (or, an evaluation of more *UBSGNT*[4] variants would result in lower percentage rates of occurrence and citation). Therefore, these charts do not reveal concrete conclusions, but only general trends of high percentage manuscript presence. On some occasions, manuscripts that are considered important in the establishment of the original text do not appear in these charts (one particular example is $\mathfrak{P}^{75}$). This is usually due to the limited focus of the sample or the fragmentary nature of a given manuscript. As stated above, the charts only refer to selected portions of the *UBSGNT*[4], and a given manuscript may not contain the particular chapters analyzed in these charts (this is especially true of the fragmentary papyri manuscripts). Therefore, a particular manuscript may not be used as a witness to a high enough frequency within the variants selected and, in the light of this, it has a low percentage of occurrence and citation, even though it may be an important manuscript. In any case, these charts do record manuscripts that occur and are cited to a high degree within the *UBSGNT*[4] variants. One is able to say of these charts, 'these are the manuscripts that will appear in a large number of *A* rated passages within the book of Luke', or, 'these are the manuscripts that will often be cited in *B* rated variants within the book of Acts', etc. This type of investigation has, in fact, been done by other individuals working on the *UBSGNT*. For example, Moir makes use of a similar method to analyze the manuscript evidence in the book of Luke as recorded in the *UBSGNT*[1]. He provides the following table:[70]

Variants listed in Luke apparatus	181
The printed text supported by B	141
ℵ	113
$\mathfrak{P}^{75}$	98
Θ	59
D	33

70. Moir, 'Greek New Testament', p. 141.

Based upon the figures of this table, Moir develops a high occurrence manuscript grouping. With this grouping in mind he concludes:

> These figures make clear that the text presented [*UBSGNT*[1]] is a near relative of Codex Vaticanus and of its new ally $\mathfrak{P}$[75]. The evidence shows that this type of text has been carefully copied over a long period in the early history of transmission and it may well serve as basic until such time as sufficient evidence is forthcoming to support the claims of any rival.[71]

Each of the following charts contains *A*, *B*, and *C* rated variants (again, there are only nine *D* rated passages in the *UBSGNT*[4], none of which occur in the selected test groups). However, the primary focus is upon variants that receive either an *A* or a *B* rating. There are two reasons for preferring *A* and *B* rated variants. First, variants with the *A* or *B* letter-ratings reflect, due to their higher degrees of certainty, a more 'ideal' group of manuscript witnesses; whereas *C* or *D* letter-rated variants reflect, due to their lower degrees of certainty, a less than 'ideal' group of manuscript witnesses. On the basis of external evidence alone, a variant is often accorded a *C* or *D* letter-rating because its reading is not attested by the more influential manuscripts or manuscript groupings. When a *C* or *D* rated variant does contain the more influential manuscripts and manuscript groupings, one can assume that the *UBSGNT* committee employed internal evidence in the allocation of a letter-rating for that given variant. For the most part, however, there is a clear distinction between the type and number of manuscripts cited in *A* and *B* rated variants as opposed to *C* and *D* rated variants. *A* and *B* rated variants tend to include a greater number and particular grouping of the more influential manuscripts. On the other hand, *C* and *D* rated variants, although at times containing some of the more important manuscripts, do not include as great a number nor the particular groupings of these influential manuscripts as do *A* and *B* rated variants. The second reason for preferring the more certain letter-rated variants in the formulation of high percentage manuscript groupings is the simple fact that there are a greater number of *A* and *B* rated variants than *C* and *D* rated variants. Therefore, because these high percentage manuscript groupings are based upon a greater number of variants, it can be assumed that these groups are more clearly defined and delineated.

Under the heading '*Mss*' (denoting 'Manuscripts'), a list of the 'high percentage of citation' witnesses is given. Under the heading '*Type/Ct.*',

---

71. Moir, 'Greek New Testament', p. 141. For further verification of Moir's point here, see Black's quotation in Chapter 1 n. 104.

the 'Type' of Greek manuscript or citation and, when appropriate, the 'Category' to which it belongs are recorded.[72] And lastly, the '*Percent*' heading lists the percentage of variants in which the manuscript appears in the particular book, chapters, and letter-ratings. Only manuscripts that are listed at least 70 percent of the time in a given book are recorded in these charts. However, Appendix V records manuscripts that are cited from 1 percent to 100 percent in a given book and given chapters.

Several examples illustrate the use of these charts. In the first eight chapters of Luke, Codex Vaticanus (B03), a category I uncial, is cited in 100 percent of the *A* rated variants, and Codex Freerianus (W032), a category III uncial, is also cited in 100 percent of the *A* rated variants.

---

72. These five categories are presented in K. and B. Aland, *The Text of the New Testament*, pp. 106, 159, 332-337, and in the *UBSGNT*[4], pp. 4*-5*. The categories are used in this section in order to provide some differentiation among the levels of significance within the manuscripts. For sake of ease to the reader, these categories are as follows: *Category I*: manuscripts of a very special quality which should always be considered in establishing the original text; *Category II*: manuscripts of a special quality, but distinguished from manuscripts of Category I by the presence of alien influences, and yet important for establishing the original text; *Category III*: manuscripts of a distinctive character with an independent text, usually important for establishing the original text, but particularly important for the history of the text; *Category IV*: manuscripts of the D text; *Category V*: manuscripts with a purely or predominantly Byzantine text. Each manuscript is assigned to one of these five categories, on the basis of the number and types of readings that manuscript contains. The Alands divide the different reading types into four classes, represented by the four superscript figures 1, 2, S, and 1/2 (or 1/). Class 1 readings represent the Majority text (including the Byzantine text); Class 2 readings represent the ancient text (presumably the original text) and those readings that correspond to the *UBSGNT* and Nestle-Aland editions; Class S represents special or peculiar readings that do not fall under Classes 1 and 2; and Class 1/2 represents readings in which the ancient text and the Majority text are in agreement (sometimes abbreviated as 1/). By using ℵ01 as an example, one can see how these four classes work in the Alands' *The Text of the New Testament*. In examining the book of Acts in Codex Sinaiticus (ℵ01), 121 test readings were used. Of these 121 readings, 11 were Class 1, 24 were Class 1/2, 68 were Class 2, and 18 were Class S. Therefore, on p. 107 of the Alands' text, these figures are recorded for the book of Acts within Codex Sinaiticus (ℵ01) in the following manner: Acts 11^1 $24^{1/2}$ 68^2 18^S. One can clearly see the strong majority of ancient readings (Class 2) as opposed to the other reading types (Classes 1, 1/2, and S). The important statistics for a manuscript are its total number of readings in each of the respective classes of readings. Again, these totals are the basis for assigning a manuscript's category rating. See the Alands' *The Text of the New Testament*, p. 333.

Codex Sinaiticus ($\aleph$01), another category I uncial, is cited in 94 percent of the *A* rated variants in the first eight chapters of Luke, and Codex Regius (L019), a category II uncial, is cited in 89 percent of the *A* rated variants. The Sahidic Coptic version (cop^{sa}) is also cited in 89 percent of the *A* rated variants contained in the first eight chapters of Luke. Manuscript 579, a category II minuscule, is cited in 78 percent of the *A* rated variants in the first eight chapters of Luke, and Manuscript 1241, a category III minuscule, is cited in 72 percent of the *A* rated variants. And finally, the Bohairic Coptic version (cop^{bo}) is also cited in 72 percent of the *A* rated variants contained in the first eight chapters of Luke. One might now take into account the category classifications in order to determine which manuscripts hold the greatest authority.

What we now have is a list of manuscripts that are cited, to a very high degree, in *A* rated variants in the *UBSGNT*[4] and within the first eight chapters of Luke. If one now uses these manuscripts as a base group and begins a search of other *A* rated passages in Luke, it will be revealed that a majority of these manuscripts are also cited in these other variants. Consequently, although obviously to a lesser degree, these same manuscripts are regularly cited within the Gospel of Luke as it appears in the earlier *UBSGNT* editions as well. It seems that if the edition is more recent there is a higher likelihood of these same manuscript groupings occurring, especially category I and category II manuscripts. This would appear to be natural. Perhaps not all manuscripts are cited, but to a large extent most will be included. Based on this test group, we have now successfully determined that there exists within *A* rated variants and in the Gospel of Luke a manuscript grouping consisting of these following witnesses: Category I (B03, $\aleph$01), Category II (L019, 579), Category III (W032, 1241), and versional witnesses (cop^{sa}, cop^{bo}). We can also conclude that very often variants with these citations are determined by the *UBSGNT* committee to be *A* rated passages. It must be kept in mind that this is based upon a counting of manuscripts. Very little internal or external evidence has been specifically regarded, other than that already inherently ascribed to each variant by the *UBSGNT* committee. And it is hoped that the *UBSGNT* committee has considered this type of information in ascribing letter-ratings to the variants. Regardless, these charts still measure general trends and manuscript groupings that are regularly cited. By duplicating this type of above example in each of the following charts, the reader is able to determine the relative manuscript clusters contained in each test group.

High Percentage Manuscript Groupings in Luke 1–8

A Rated Variants (18 Possible Total)			B Rated Variants (26 Possible Total)			C Rated Variants (7 Possible Total)		
Mss	Type/Ct.	Percent	Mss	Type/Ct.	Percent	Mss	Type/Ct.	Percent
B03	unc. (I)	100%	B03	unc. (I)	96%	L019	unc. (II)	71%
W032	unc. (III)	100%	ℵ01	unc. (I)	77%	cop^{bo}	coptic	71%
ℵ01	unc. (I)	94%	cop^{sa}	coptic	73%			
L019	unc. (II)	89%						
cop^{sa}	coptic	89%						
579	min. (II)	78%						
1241	min. (III)	72%						
cop^{bo}	coptic	72%						

High Percentage Manuscript Groupings in Acts 1–8

A Rated Variants (21 Possible Total)			B Rated Variants (20 Possible Total)			C Rated Variants (12 Possible Total)		
Mss	Type/Ct.	Percent	Mss	Type/Ct.	Percent	Mss	Type/Ct.	Percent
ℵ01	unc. (I)	100%	A02	unc. (I)	85%	945	min. (III)	75%
A02	unc. (I)	100%	B03	unc. (I)	85%	1739	min. (II)	75%
1175	min. (I)	100%	ℵ01	unc. (I)	80%	arm	armenian	75%
B03	unc. (I)	95%	cop^{sa}	coptic	75%			
𝔓⁷⁴	pap. (I)	90%	1175	min. (I)	70%			
181	min. (III)	90%	it^{dem}	old latin	70%			
it^{ph}	old latin	90%	vg	vulgate	70%			
it^{ro}	old latin	90%	cop^{bo}	coptic	70%			
Ψ044	unc. (III)	86%						
1409	min. (II)	86%						
2344	min. (III)	86%						
it^c	old latin	86%						
it^{dem}	old latin	86%						
cop^{sa}	coptic	86%						
arm	armenian	86%						
geo	georgian	86%						
33	min. (I)	81%						
307	min. (III)	81%						
453	min. (III)	81%						
614	min. (III)	81%						
945	min. (III)	81%						
1678	min. (III)	81%						
1739	min. (II)	81%						
vg	vulgate	81%						
cop^{bo}	coptic	81%						
Chrys.	gk father	81%						
36a	min. (II)	76%						
610	min. (III)	76%						
1891	min. (II)	76%						
it^{w(a)}	old latin	76%						
syr^h	syriac	76%						
eth	ethiopic	76%						
81	min. (II)	74%						
C04	unc. (II)	71%						
E08	unc. (II)	71%						
it^{ar}	old latin	71%						

High Percentage Manuscript Groupings in Romans 1–8

A Rated Variants (16 Possible Total)			*B Rated Variants* (14 Possible Total)			*C Rated Variants* (12 Possible Total)		
Mss	*Type/Ct.*	*Percent*	*Mss*	*Type/Ct.*	*Percent*	*Mss*	*Type/Ct.*	*Percent*
1739	min. (I)	100%	ℵ01	unc. (I)	86%	424ᶜ	min. (III)	92%
B03	unc. (I)	88%	copᵇᵒ	coptic	86%	ℵ01	unc. (I)	83%
6	min. (III)	88%	81	min. (II)	79%	81	min. (II)	83%
1881	min. (II)	88%	1506	min. (II)	79%			
Origen	gk father	88%	Augus.	lt father	79%			
D06	unc. (II)	81%	arm	armenian	71%			
424ᶜ	min. (III)	81%						
1319	min. (III)	81%						
1506	min. (II)	81%						
1573	min. (III)	81%						
copˢᵃ	coptic	81%						
Augus.	lt father	81%						
ℵ01	unc. (I)	75%						
A02	unc. (I)	75%						
256	min. (II)	75%						
263	min. (III)	75%						
1852	min. (III)	75%						
2127	min. (II)	75%						
2200	min. (III)	75%						
itᵈ	old latin	75%						
copᵇᵒ	coptic	75%						
eth	ethiopic	75%						

High Percentage Manuscript Groupings in 1 Peter

A Rated Variants (20 Possible Total)			*B Rated Variants* (9 Possible Total)			*C Rated Variants* (12 Possible Total)		
Mss	*Type/Ct.*	*Percent*	*Mss*	*Type/Ct.*	*Percent*	*Mss*	*Type/Ct.*	*Percent*
B03	unc. (I)	90%	B03	unc. (I)	89%	1241	min. (I)	100%
1739	min. (I)	85%				1243	min. (I)	100%
𝔓⁷²	pap. (I)	75%				1739	min. (I)	88%
Ψ044	unc. (II)	75%				1881	min. (II)	88%
copˢᵃ	coptic	75%				ℵ01	unc. (I)	75%
322	min. (II)	70%				[K018]	unc. (V)	75%
323	min. (II)	70%				[L020]	unc. (V)	75%
945	min. (III)	70%				[P024]	unc. (V)	75%
1881	min. (II)	70%				Ψ044	unc. (II)	75%
geo	georgian	70%				81	min. (II)	75%
						322	min. (II)	75%
						323	min. (II)	75%
						1175	min. (I)	75%
						1292	min. (II)	75%
						1611	min. (III)	75%
						1852	min. (II)	75%
						2138	min. (III)	75%
						2298	min. (II)	75%
						2464	min. (II)	75%
						copᵇᵒ	coptic	75%

High Percentage Manuscript Groupings in Revelation 1–8

A Rated Variants (10 Possible Total)			B Rated Variants (10 Possible Total)			C Rated Variants (3 Possible Total)		
Mss	Type/Ct.	Percent	Mss	Type/Ct.	Percent	Mss	Type/Ct.	Percent
ℵ01	unc. (I)	90%	cop^bo	coptic	100%			
2053	min. (I)	70%	arm	armenian	100%			
			C04	unc. (II)	90%			
			1611	min. (II)	90%			
			cop^sa	coptic	90%			
			A02	unc. (I)	80%			
			1006	min. (II)	80%			
			2053	min. (I)	80%			
			Andrew of Caesar.	gk father	80%			
			P025	unc. (V)	70%			
			1841	min. (II)	70%			

The preceding five charts reveal that, based on the above selected passages and variants, there are manuscript groupings that tend to have an influence on the prescribing of variant letter-ratings. These manuscripts that are often cited throughout the entire *UBSGNT* tradition give some type of description as to what witnesses are considered important to the *UBSGNT* editors. In the opening of this section, the following questions concerning the bold upgrades introduced in the *UBSGNT*[4] were asked: Are these changes within this latest edition justified, or are they, as first glance would lead one to believe, an unfounded upgrading in the quality of text presented? Have the *UBSGNT* editors based their alterations on tangible evidence, or have we simply been given a false sense of security in the *UBSGNT*? It can be concluded that, indeed, letter-ratings in the *UBSGNT*[4] are based, at least to some extent, on consistent and logical patterns of manuscript groupings. It would appear that these upgrades have not been randomly introduced to instill a false sense of security in the *UBSGNT*, but are, in fact, based upon some type of tangible evidence (however, this evidence tends to be predominantly external evidence alone). However, the exact nature and reasoning behind these upgradings is still in question. Although we have seen to some extent verifiable manuscript groupings in the *UBSGNT*[4], for the most part these same clusters or manuscript groupings are evident in the earlier *UBSGNT* editions as well. Because traces of these witness groupings appear in all editions, would it not follow that the *UBSGNT*[4] modifications should progress at a more moderate rate? One can account for some level of enhancement to the *UBSGNT*[4] variant letter-ratings perhaps based on the more defined and circumscribed manuscript groupings present in this edition. However, do these witness clusters or groupings change to a large enough extent in the *UBSGNT*[4] to warrant the type of upgrading that results? Although a partial constituent of letter-rating fluctuations in the *UBSGNT*[4] may be attributed to this assemblage of witnesses and their moderate change from edition to edition, the large degree of modification is not justified. Once again, one should keep in mind that the *UBSGNT* committee specified that the *UBSGNT*[4] modifications took place in the light of a redefining of the various levels of certainty in the evaluation of evidence letter-ratings, not on the basis of high percentage manuscript groupings. Although these manuscript groups do reveal, to some extent, that the *UBSGNT*[4] upgrades follow some type of logical and consistent pattern, another explanation must be sought for the bold upgrades that occur in this *UBSGNT* edition.

A New Consensus Concerning an Old Group of Manuscripts

Perhaps these modifications are founded upon a new consensus among scholars concerning the authority, importance, and merit of older, previously known manuscripts. The ancient papyri would seem to provide the basis for this 'new consensus'. To be sure, it is no secret that at least one member of the *UBSGNT* committee places a great deal of importance and stress upon the ancient papyri.[73] As seen in the previous discussion regarding high percentage manuscript groupings, the papyri do, on occasion, play a significant role in the ascribing of variant letter-ratings. Examples of this are seen where $\mathfrak{P}^{74}$ is cited in 90 percent of *A* rated

---

73. Perhaps the most vocal advocate for a strong reliance upon the papyri has been K. Aland. Epp states that Aland affords the earliest papyri 'extraordinary status' and 'not only affirms their "automatic significance" as textual witnesses', but 'makes the astounding claim that in the forty papyri (and uncials) prior to about AD 300 the early history of the NT text "can be studied in the original," and that all other efforts to get a glimpse of the early text "must remain reconstructed theories"'. See Epp, 'Decision Points', p. 42. Elliott, in a recent article, similarly notes the Alands' bias for the papyri manuscripts. He states, 'All the papyri fragments regardless of age are now given the status of constant witnesses, and many of their singular readings are recorded. This reflects the importance the Alands attach to this category of witness, although they recognize one must not be mesmerized by the writing material alone.' Elliott, 'The Twentyseventh Edition', col. 21. See also n. 83 below and its corresponding quotation. For an excellent assessment of the current trends in New Testament textual criticism in the light of the papyri, see once more Epp, 'Decision Points', pp. 42-44; and *idem*, 'Significance of the Papyri', pp. 274-97.

variants within the first eight chapters of Acts, and where $\mathfrak{P}^{72}$ is cited in 75 percent of *A* rated variants within 1 Peter. It needs to be noted, however, that the limited selection of passages in determining the high percentage manuscript groupings (generally the first eight chapters of a particular book) and the fragmentary nature of the papyri themselves often result in their exclusion from the group of witnesses recorded in the high percentage manuscript clusters. In order to remedy this problem a detailed investigation has been undertaken in order to evaluate more accurately the role the papyri play in the ascribing of letter-ratings. Appendix VI forms the basis of this investigation where the books of Luke and Acts in their entirety, and the list of exceptional variants (as given in Section 3 of this chapter), are examined so as to determine the possible influence of the papyri upon the allocation of variant letter-ratings within the *UBSGNT*[4].

A number of important findings can be summarized from the data provided in Appendix VI. First, on the basis of their high attestation within the books of Luke and Acts, a number of specific papyri stand out. Of the 167 variants listed in the Gospel of Luke, $\mathfrak{P}^{75}$ is cited as a witness in 96 (57%) of these. This papyrus occurs in 25 (56%) of the 45 *A* rated variants, in 55 (71%) of the 78 *B* rated variants, and in 16 (36%) of the 44 *C* rated variants. In comparison to other letter-ratings, $\mathfrak{P}^{75}$ is cited as a witness in *A* rated variants 26 percent of the time, as a witness in *B* rated variants 57 percent of the time, and as a witness in *C* rated variants 17 percent of the time. Of the 198 variants listed in the book of Acts, $\mathfrak{P}^{74}$ is cited as a witness in 140 (71%) of these. This papyrus occurs in 66 (89%) of the 74 *A* rated variants, in 59 (73%) of the 81 *B* rated variants, and in 15 (36%) of the 42 *C* rated variants. In relationship to the other letter-ratings, $\mathfrak{P}^{74}$ is cited as a witness in *A* rated variants 47 percent of the time, as a witness in *B* rated variants 42 percent of the time, and as a witness in *C* rated variants 11 percent of the time. One can conclude from these statistics that $\mathfrak{P}^{75}$ in Luke, and especially $\mathfrak{P}^{74}$ in Acts, are seen as important manuscripts by the *UBSGNT* committee. The figures presented here make clear that the text of Luke follows, to a significant degree (57% of the time) the readings attested in $\mathfrak{P}^{75}$, while the text of Acts follows to a larger degree (71% of the time) the readings attested in $\mathfrak{P}^{74}$. Perhaps of more importance is the fact that 56 percent of *A* rated variants and 71 percent of *B* rated variants in Luke cite $\mathfrak{P}^{75}$ as a witness; while 89 percent of *A* rated variants and 73 percent of *B* rated variants in Acts cite $\mathfrak{P}^{74}$ as a witness. This reveals, at least to some extent, the importance of these two papyri in calculating A and B rated variants in the books of Luke and Acts. The fact that $\mathfrak{P}^{75}$ is cited in only 36 percent of the C rated variants in Luke, while $\mathfrak{P}^{74}$ is cited in only 36 percent of the C rated variants in Acts, may provide further indirect support that these two papyri play a more significant role in determining those variants that are given an A and B rating, as opposed to those that are given a C rating. It is possible that many of those variants in Luke or Acts not having $\mathfrak{P}^{75}$ or $\mathfrak{P}^{74}$ cited as a witness are, therefore, given a C letter-rating, with the obvious result being that there are fewer C rated passages that cite one of these two papyri.

The second insight gained from Appendix VI is as follows. Of the 167 variants listed in the Gospel of Luke, 105 (63%) of these have papyri cited as a witness in the first variant option of a variant unit (i.e. the variant reading or option that appears in the *UBSGNT*[4] text). Of the 198 variants listed in the book of Acts, 147 (74%) of these have papyri cited as a witness in the first variant option of a variant unit. These two figures are significant because they reveal that very often that reading selected to represent the *UBSGNT*[4] text has papyri evidence cited as a witness. Although this does not specifically clarify the role that the papyri have in ascribing letter-ratings to variants, it does exhibit that those readings or options within an entire variant unit that have the support of a papyrus manuscript often hold the place of primacy in representing the *UBSGNT*[4] text.

A third insight is seen when one considers those variants within the *UBSGNT*[4] that experience a letter-rating upgrade. In the Gospel of Luke, there are 78 upgraded variants. This figure is calculated by simply adding together all variants improving one, two, and three steps in their letter-ratings. Of these 78 variants, 58 (74%) have papyri cited as witnesses. In the book of Acts, there are 92 variants that experience a letter-rating upgrade. Of these 92 variants, 61 (66%) have papyri cited as witnesses. These figures are significant because they show that a large number of variants that have papyri cited as witnesses experience letter-rating upgrades in the *UBSGNT*[4]. Therefore, once again, the citation of a papyrus manuscript in a variant seems to affect the letter-rating given to that variant. One could make this conclusion with even greater force if it were possible to examine the papyri evidence cited in variants that experienced decreasing letter-ratings. The problem here, however, is that there are no variants of this type in the books of Luke and Acts within the *UBSGNT*[4].

The final insight gained from Appendix VI pertains to the citation of papyri evidence within the exceptional variants. Once again, an exceptional variant is defined by the following parameters: (1) the variant contains a rating that increases or decreases by at least two letter grades, (2) the variant contains irregular fluctuating ratings involving at least three differing letters, or (3) the variant consists of fluctuating ratings that repeatedly contradict previous editorial decisions made in earlier editions. In the *UBSGNT*[4], there is a total of 98 exceptional variants. Of these 98 variants, 2 (2%) undergo *D-A* letter-rating improvements, 51 (52%) undergo *C-A* letter-rating improvements, 29 (30%) undergo *D-B* letter-rating improvements, and 16 (16%) are fluctuating variants. Of the 51 exceptional variants that are upgraded from a *C* to an *A* rating, 28 (55%) of these have papyri cited as witnesses in their first variant option of the variant unit. Of the 29 exceptional variants that are upgraded from a *D* to a *B* rating, 19 (66%) of these have papyri cited as witnesses in their first variant option of the variant unit. Of the two exceptional variants that are upgraded from a *D* to an *A* rating, only one (50%) has papyri cited as witnesses in its first variant option of the variant unit (again, these two variants are Lk. 19.25 and Acts 2.44, with the Acts variant containing $\mathfrak{P}^{74}$ as a witness). Lastly, of the 16 exceptional variants that have fluctuating letter-ratings, seven (44%) of these have papyri cited as witnesses in their first variant option of the variant unit. Of the 98 exceptional variants, 55 (56%) of these have papyri cited as witnesses in their first variant option, while 43 (44%) do not cite the papyri. These figures reveal that a significant number of exceptional variants contain papyri manuscripts as witness citations. However, for these figures to be of greater value in assessing the role the papyri might play in the ascribing of letter-ratings, one would need to see a higher number of exceptional variants containing papyri citations. Based upon this last set of figures, one can only speculate that the presence of papyri manuscripts in a variant affects the letter-rating given to that variant. However, despite the fragmentary nature of the papyri, when one considers the entire discussion concerning older manuscripts and this idea of a new consensus, there is convincing evidence supporting the conclusion that the papyri, like the high percentage manuscript groupings, play a role in and have some influence upon the ascribing of letter-ratings to specific *UBSGNT*[4] variants. In other words, those variants within the *UBSGNT*[4] that have papyri cited as a witness tend to receive ratings with higher degrees of certainty, that is, *A* and *B* letter-ratings.

There are, however, a number of problems in assuming that a new consensus concerning the papyri acts as the sole basis for the incredible *UBSGNT*[4] upgrades. This hypothesis needs to be tempered and contextualized. As seen in the *UBSGNT*[4] and other earlier *UBSGNT* editions, and as clearly presented in the previous discussion, a significant number of those variant passages that experience letter-rating upgrades have no papyri manuscripts cited as witnesses. As one examines the critical apparatus of the *UBSGNT*[4], it becomes apparent that many of the papyri, due to their fragmentary nature, are inconsistently cited and often do not represent enough of the *UBSGNT*[4] text to completely warrant the kind of upgrades that occur.

External evidence constitutes the second reason for a cautious assertion that a new consensus among scholars concerning the papyri forges the much higher textual quality present in the *UBSGNT*[4]. If the *UBSGNT*[4] alterations are, in fact, founded completely upon the presence of papyri in particular variants, then the *UBSGNT* editorial committee would be responsible for basing their revision upon external evidence alone. This would indeed be questionable. Even though the papyri provide, in some cases, persuasive evidence for variant readings, do they provide the kind of evidence that seems to cause the exceptional and conclusive *UBSGNT*[4] upgrades? Do they have enough influence to allow one to make textual decisions based exclusively upon external evidence? Do the papyri hold enough authority to cause modification to a large majority of the critical apparatus letter-ratings, regardless of the fact that a significant number of variants are without papyri citations? Although it seems that the papyri sway or influence, at least to some extent, variant letter-ratings, one should be cautious in claiming that they are the sole cause of this wholesale upgrade within the *UBSGNT*[4].

Furthermore, if a new consensus regarding the weight of the papyri has given rise to the *UBSGNT*[4] revisions, why were there not revisions of this nature made to the *UBSGNT*[3] and *UBSGNT*[3corr.]? One must question whether we have come so far since the publication of these two previous editions. Although a great deal of research has been poured into the study of biblical papyri, and although their importance has been continually reassessed and affirmed in the last decade, there have been no grand findings that would, once again, allow one to conclude that the papyri alone have induced the *UBSGNT*[4] upgrades. The weight of evidence, rather than falling entirely upon the biblical papyri, seems to lie in some type of corroboration between the papyri and the great uncials.

Indeed, since the publication of the earlier *UBSGNT* editions, there has, as of yet, been no decisive resolution among scholars that would place the papyri into the position of sole dominance and supremacy among biblical manuscripts. In spite of the fact that the papyri are of great importance to textual criticism, it seems unlikely that they alone can be held responsible for the extent of modification present in the *UBSGNT*[4]. Yet to claim they have played no part at all in the upgrades may be equally fallacious.

Again, one should not forget the earlier argument of omission. The *UBSGNT* editorial committee distinctively ascribes the *UBSGNT*[4] upgrades to a redefining of the letter-rating categories. If a new consensus concerning the papyri were the sole cause of the letter-rating upgrades in the *UBSGNT*[4], why would the editorial committee not explain this clearly to their readers, and thus provide a valid reason for the modifications? For the editorial committee to explain to their readership that the new upgrades are founded on one basis, and then to knowingly change that basis is questionable scholarship. Absent within the *UBSGNT*[4], however, is any explicit statement shedding light upon a new consensus concerning the papyri. Yet, implicitly, it seems that the papyri, along with the high percentage manuscript groupings, have played a significant role in determining the letter-ratings of many variants that cite such witnesses. In consideration of the above points, one must conclude that although the papyri might reflect the optimistic new ratings for a significant number of variant passages, they do not give sufficient justification on their own for the overall and extensive upgrades that occur in this latest *UBSGNT* edition.

An Emphasis upon the Older Manuscripts and a Marginalization of the Byzantine Text-Type

Rather than contend that the much more certain *UBSGNT*[4] text is the result of one primary determinant, perhaps the upgrades within this edition are the product of a combination of factors and considerations. The editorial committee makes it clear that the textual apparatus of the *UBSGNT*[4] is founded upon an entirely new collation of the Greek manuscript tradition undertaken by the Institute for New Testament Textual Research at Münster/Westfalen. The committee states on page 3* of the *UBSGNT*[4] Introduction:

> The purpose of selecting witnesses for the critical apparatus was generally to provide a broad number of witnesses that would be significant and representative of the whole tradition for the limited number of instances noted

in the apparatus in this edition. The emphasis is therefore naturally on Greek manuscripts of the New Testament. The result was a completely new selection, based on verifiable tests of the entire Greek manuscript tradition in the Institute for New Testament Textual Research at Münster.[74]

In questioning the criteria used by the *UBSGNT*[4] committee in omitting or including certain variants, and in the ascribing of letter-ratings, Silva makes an interesting point. He states:

> [O]ne is tempted to infer that the evidence of Codex D and its allies is now being treated with significantly less regard than it had been earlier. This inference would be in keeping with Kurt Aland's well-known criticisms of the so-called Western Text, but the introduction to the new edition says nothing that would help us confirm or set aside such an interpretation. And that is in fact the point of my comments: we are not given enough information to determine the criteria by which these decisions were made.[75]

Perhaps one further inference, not unlike Silva's, might be put forward. Could it be that Münster's new collation of the Greek manuscripts has brought about, among the *UBSGNT* committee members, some type of heightened collaboration between the great uncials and ancient papyri, and/or a newly expressed optimism and greater confidence in these older witnesses (as can be substantiated, one must grant at least to some degree, by the earlier discussions concerning the apparent importance of high percentage manuscript groupings and papyri citations)? Assuming this to be the case, perhaps this new optimism and confidence in the great uncials and ancient papyri have lowered the regard for not the Western text (or not *just* the Western text), but the already faltering and much later Byzantine text, with the overall result that the *UBSGNT*[4] letter-ratings see an enormous upgrading. This inference would be in even greater accord with not only Aland's well-known criticisms of the Byzantine text, but those criticisms of a large majority of textual scholars as well.[76] Indeed, textual critics have tended to marginalize the Byzantine

74. For further references to an entirely new collation of manuscripts, see the *UBSGNT*[4], pp. vi*, 2*, 19* regarding the lectionaries, 23* regarding the versions, and 29* regarding the Fathers. See also Elliott, 'The Fourth Edition', col. 13.

75. Silva, 'Symposium', p. 351.

76. Numerous scholars place the importance of the Byzantine text-type far below that of the older manuscripts, most notably the Alexandrian uncials and papyri. In addition to the examples about to follow, see K. and B. Aland, *The Text of the New Testament*, p. 318; Greenlee, *Textual Criticism*, p. 76; Metzger, *The Text of the New*

text-type, with the result being that it is firmly relegated to an increasingly low status while the older and more ancient manuscripts (particularly the uncials and papyri) are ascribed the greatest weight and place of authority in determining textual matters.[77] D.A. Carson states: 'But almost universally accepted today is the contention of Westcott and Hort that the Byzantine tradition does not antedate the middle of the fourth century and represents a relatively late conflation'.[78] Fee, in dealing with the Byzantine text-type, explains that:

> Most of the readings peculiar to this text are generally recognized to be of a secondary nature. A great number of them smooth out grammar; remove ambiguity in word order; add nouns, pronouns, and prepositional phrases; and harmonize one passage with another. Its many conflate readings...where the Byzantine text-type combines the alternative variants of the Egyptian and Western texts, also reflect this secondary process.[79]

One gains a clearer picture of the Byzantine text when reading two of the standard works on textual criticism, the Alands' *The Text of the New Testament* and Metzger's book of the same title. Opinions like the following are prominent in these publications:

> The most serious defect of the first edition of the Greek New Testament [i.e. Erasmus's edition] was not so much its innumerable errors as the type of text it represented. Erasmus relied on manuscripts of the twelfth/ thirteenth century which represented the Byzantine Imperial text, the Koine text, or the Majority text—however it may be known—the most recent and the poorest of the various New Testament text types...[80]

The Alands' Category Rating System (see n. 72 of this chapter) reveals this very same trend where the vast majority of purely Byzantine manuscripts are placed into category V, this being the least important

---

Testament, pp. 161, 238; *idem, A Textual Commentary*, 1994, pp. 7*-10*; and Vaganay and Amphoux, *An Introduction*, p. 109.

77. This strong emphasis upon the older manuscripts has often been referred to by scholars, particularly those discussing Westcott and Hort's reliance upon Codex Vaticanus, as 'the cult of the best manuscript'. However, the phrase has also been used specifically to criticize the *UBSGNT* committee's over-reliance upon the older manuscripts. For examples, see Black, 'A Reply', p. 120; Elliott, 'Recent Studies', p. 43; *idem*, 'An Evaluation', pp. 281, 290; *idem*, 'Textual Commentary', p. 132; and Epp, 'Reflections', p. 226, note 29.

78. Carson, *King James*, p. 41.

79. Fee, 'Textual Criticism', p. 8.

80. K. and B. Aland, *The Text of the New Testament*, p. 4.

textual category, while the older manuscripts are consistently placed in category I, this being the most important textual category. The relevance of the other three categories is determined, to a large degree, by the extent of Byzantine textual influences and readings within the manuscripts. Those manuscripts with little Byzantine influence are, on the basis of their textual 'purity', given greater weight concerning text-critical matters, while those manuscripts with more Byzantine influence are heeded as less important.[81] All these considerations indicate the low standing and secondary position accorded the Byzantine text by a majority of textual critics, especially when seen in the light of the older manuscripts. Despite several movements of resurgence in this secondary text-type, this remains the scholarly position and consensus.[82]

81. See Epp 'Reflections', pp. 225-26, where he assesses the Alands' rating system. The choosing of manuscripts for citation in the *UBSGNT*[4] is decided upon by using the Alands' category rating system. It is claimed that 'The Committee made use of these categories in selecting manuscripts because they provide the only tool presently available for classifying the whole manuscript tradition of the New Testament on an objective statistical basis'. See pp. 4*-5* in the *UBSGNT*[4]. In the Nestle-Aland[27] a similar method is used to select witnesses for the textual apparatus. Greek manuscripts are cited 'consistently, frequently, or only occasionally, depending on the significance of the individual manuscript for establishing the text'. *Consistently cited witnesses* include those Greek manuscripts which are of the greatest value and authority for establishing the text. *Frequently cited witnesses* include manuscripts that are of outstanding significance in establishing the history of the text, or readings of interest for their content. *Occasionally cited witnesses* include manuscripts that essentially represent the Koine (Byzantine) text-type. These are explicitly cited only when they diverge from the Koine text in passages of special interest for the history of the text or for exegesis. The editors of the Nestle-Aland[27] break down the consistently cited witnesses into two further categories, or orders, based upon their quality and the way they are cited. The *first order of consistently cited witnesses* includes the papyri and the uncials which are independent of the Byzantine Koine text-type, and a small number of minuscules which preserve an early form of the text. The *second order of consistently cited witnesses* includes the more important uncials of the Koine text-type, and a group of minuscules which are of special interest for the history of the text although they are related to the Byzantine Koine text-type. See Nestle-Aland[27], pp. 50*-51*. The methods used for selecting manuscripts in both the *UBSGNT*[4] and the Nestle-Aland[27] seem to reflect further some type of marginalization and the secondary nature accorded to the Byzantine text. Elliott also points out that the Nestle-Aland[27] manuscript classifications are 'based on the level of their difference from the Byzantine, majority (= M), text-type'. See Elliott, 'The Twentyseventh Edition', col. 21.

82. Again, this resurgence can be clearly seen in a number of works written

Is it possible that the *UBSGNT* editorial committee holds a newly expressed optimism for the great uncials and ancient papyri, while, at the same time, their view of the Byzantine text, spurred on by this new optimism and the views of the wider scholarly community, has been more pessimistic? That the presence of these older manuscript clusters within a variant often results in that variant receiving an *A* or *B* letter-rating, as seen in earlier discussions, tends to add support to the estimation that the older manuscripts are regarded as more important while the Byzantine manuscripts are marginalized. When the critical apparatus of the *UBSGNT* is closely examined, particularly the *UBSGNT*[4], one is able to detect the prominence and authority given to the more ancient manuscripts such as Codex Sinaiticus, Codex Vaticanus, and a number of the papyri. Aland himself has not been timid in making strong assertions regarding the importance of these older witnesses. He claims:

> The new 'standard text' [the text present in the *UBSGNT*[3] and Nestle-Aland[26]] has passed the test of the early papyri and uncials. It corresponds, in fact, to the text of the early time... At no place and at no time do we find readings here [i.e., in the earliest papyri and uncials] that require a change in the 'standard text'. If the investigation conducted here in all its brevity and compactness could be presented fully, the detailed apparatus accompanying each variant would convince the last doubter. A hundred years after Westcott-Hort, the goal of an edition of the New Testament 'in the original Greek' seems to have been reached... In the framework of the present possibilities, the desired goal appears now to have been attained, to offer the writings of the New Testament in the form of the text that comes nearest to that which, from the hand of their authors or redactors, they set out on their journey in the church of the 1st and 2d centuries.[83]

For Aland at least, the overwhelming importance of the older manuscripts, especially the great uncials and ancient papyri, cannot be

---

within the past few decades. See Hills, *The King James Defended!*; Fuller, *Which Bible?*; Sturz, *The Byzantine Text-Type*; Pickering, *Identity of the New Testament*; and Hodges and Farstad, *The Greek New Testament*.

83. This statement was first made by K. Aland, 'Der neue "Standard Text" in seinem Verhältnis zu den frühen Papyri und Majuskeln', in E.J. Epp and G.D. Fee, *New Testament Textual Criticism: Its Significance for Exegesis: Essays in Honour of Bruce M. Metzger* (Oxford: Clarendon Press, 1981), p. 275. This English translation appears in E.J. Epp, 'A Continuing Interlude in New Testament Textual Criticism', in Epp and Fee, *Studies in the Theory*, pp. 121-22, and n. 17. Compare this quotation with n. 73 above.

mistaken. The earlier words of Edwards, Hodges, and Moir concerning manuscript groupings seem to ring clear.[84] In fact, as was already mentioned, it is this external dependence upon the older manuscripts that has, in the past, been one of the criticisms leveled at the *UBSGNT* editions.[85] It seems obvious that external evidence (especially the date and character of the manuscripts) has been considered. But the opposite must be asked: To what degree has internal evidence been utilized in the attempt to ascribe variant letter-ratings? Similar to Silva's previous insight, the *UBSGNT*[4] introduction says very little that would help us confirm or set aside the hypothesis that a new collation of the Greek manuscripts has brought about some type of heightened concurrence between the uncials and papyri, and/or a new optimism and greater confidence in these older witnesses, while at the same time lowering regard for the Byzantine text. The overall result of this polarization of witnesses is that those textual variants in the *UBSGNT*[4] that cite the older manuscripts are given even higher letter-ratings than in previous *UBSGNT* editions in view of the new optimism and greater confidence in these more ancient witnesses. And again, like Silva, one should express disappointment that 'we are not given enough information to determine the criteria by which these decisions were made'. Although this argument is postulative, meaning that the *UBSGNT* editors have not specifically defended the *UBSGNT*[4] upgrades with this line of reasoning, could it, nonetheless, be viable?[86] Not only would it seem to support the

84. See the earlier references in nn. 68, 69, and 71.

85. Again, for this criticism, see especially Elliott, 'An Evaluation', pp. 292-300; *idem*, 'A Short Examination', p. 138; Ross, 'The United Bible', p. 121; and Omanson, 'A Perspective', p. 121.

86. It was greatly encouraging to discuss this entire theory with Dr Eugene A. Nida, who not only acted as the impetus for the formation of the United Bible Societies, but has also been intimately involved with the work on the *UBSGNT* editions. In conversation with Dr Nida (18 September, 1995), and in later correspondence (26 January, 1996), he affirmed the primary tenets in this hypothesis, concluding that 'There are many things that have occurred to justify this kind of re-evaluation. In the first place, the team in Münster has done a remarkable job in evaluating not just the evidence from critical texts but also from the manuscripts. They have computerized most of the relevant data and are in a position to judge both qualitatively and quantitatively. Furthermore, their study of the Byzantine tradition has shown that there are significant differences within the Byzantine tradition, and this leads therefore to greater confidence in the major early codices. There is probably negative evidence for this shift, because those who have been working with the material published by the UBS have on the whole been quite satisfied with the

immense shift displayed in the *A*, *B*, *C*, and *D* ratings present in this most recent *UBSGNT* edition, but it also answers a large number of questions that the *UBSGNT* committee remains silent upon.[87]

Concluding Summary

In this fourth and final section of Chapter 2, we have discussed various reasons for the letter-rating alterations present in the *UBSGNT*[4] and have sought to ascertain their validity. Five possible defenses for the rating upgrades have been advanced: (1) a redefining of the letter-rating levels, (2) the addition of new manuscripts adding further information, (3) manuscript groupings that affect the letter-ratings, (4) a new consensus concerning an old group of manuscripts, and lastly (5) an emphasis upon the older manuscripts and a marginalization of the Byzantine text-type. A number of these five justifications seem tenable. It must be emphasized that no explicit reasoning can be found in any of the *UBSGNT* editions, or for that matter in any handbook or article, that clearly elucidates why these letter-rating fluctuations have occurred. On the other hand, a number of criticisms have been pointed out pertaining

results. And the text prepared primarily for translators, as well as the so-called Nestle-Aland text (27th edition), have been generally accepted as the more satisfactory texts for textual scholarship of the New Testament.'

87. Perhaps a secondary note is that in the climate of textual criticism present in the earlier *UBSGNT* editions, the equality of the Byzantine text for determining textual matters (not necessarily its equality in textual 'weight', but more its equality for consideration) was still supported to some degree by scholars. Possibly the 'faith' that some academics and churchmen placed in the Majority text created moderate pressure that prevented (1) a complete marginalization of the Byzantine tradition, and (2) a fuller reliance upon the older manuscripts. However, in the climate of textual criticism present in the *UBSGNT*[4] (18 years removed from the *UBSGNT*[3], and ten years removed from the very similar *UBSGNT*[3corr.]) could it be that the field and discipline of New Testament textual criticism has changed? With the recent Münster manuscript collations, is it possible that a new optimism and confidence in the great uncials and the ancient papyri is being expressed, while the Byzantine tradition, seemingly losing its last foothold (again, as evident from much scholarly discussion and the present modern consensus), has left the field to these older manuscripts? Perhaps the eclectic tradition, with its supporting manuscripts, has risen to a more prominent and certain position, and with the marginalization of the Byzantine tradition, there is little opposition to a newly expressed degree of certainty in the great uncials and the ancient papyri. Is it conceivable that a progression of this nature has been revealed in the *UBSGNT*[4] by the dramatic improvement of letter-ratings and, therefore, a much more certain text?

to the weakness of letter-rating upgrades within the *UBSGNT* editions.[88] This general flaw of omission (i.e. the lack of explanation detailing adequate reasons for the rating fluctuations made between *UBSGNT* editions) is also to be noted regarding the shared Nestle-Aland and *UBSGNT* text. Epp comments:

> Something that is omitted in the Alands' volume [*The Text of the New Testament*]... is an adequate statement of the theoretical base for this so-called 'Standard text' [i.e. Nestle-Aland and *UBSGNT*]. In view of the many pages devoted to it in the volume, it is surprising to discover that the description of this text largely concerns procedural aspects of the committee's work, the story of how the text of the Nestle-Aland NT and the *UBSGNT* came together, and the differing formats of the two editions. There is little on the theory of the text itself...[89]

The fact that these rating changes have occurred in the *UBSGNT*[4] is problematic. However, the real crisis results when reasons adequately and precisely detailing the theory behind these changes are not clearly provided for users of the *UBSGNT*. Instead, brief allusion and insufficient defenses are given in their place. A detailed explanation as to why the letter-ratings in the *UBSGNT*[4] have been changed from past editions is clearly discarded.

---

88. Once again, see articles such as Elliott, 'The Third Edition', pp. 69-74; *idem*, 'The Fourth Edition', cols. 18-19; *idem*, 'Two New Editions', p. 95; Moir, 'Greek New Testament', pp. 141-42; and Ross, 'The United Bible', p. 118.

89. Epp, 'Reflections', p. 224.

Chapter 3

AN EVALUATION OF TWO SPECIFIC TEXT-CRITICAL PROBLEMS IN THE *UBSGNT*[4]

This final chapter will seek to apply the findings of the previous chapters to specific textual problems. Chapter 1 acts as the historical basis of this textual inquiry. Understanding the history and methodology of textual criticism from the time of Westcott and Hort until the present assists the reader in understanding the background of the discipline, seeing where text-critical methodology has shifted, and discerning areas in which advancement has occurred. As seen throughout this monograph, the methodology of Westcott and Hort has made an indelible imprint upon the approach and praxis of the *UBSGNT* editorial committee.[1] Although one will observe distinguishable differences between a modern approach to textual criticism and the classical approach as put forth by Westcott and Hort, the reader may be surprised by the obvious similarities and close relationship that forms between the two methods.

Chapter 2, which provides a statistical analysis of the *UBSGNT*[4], has revealed several of the more exceptional variants. In fact, two of them are analyzed in this chapter, Lk. 19.25 and Acts 2.44. Each variant undergoes a letter-rating increase of three grades, rising from an initial *D* rating to an *A* rating in the *UBSGNT*[4]. These two passages are considered exceptional because they are the only two variants within the entire *UBSGNT* tradition to experience a change of this extensive nature.[2] Several other aspects of the second chapter, such as the

---

1. See again Metzger, *A Textual Commentary*, 1994, p. 10*.

2. Since Lk. 19.25 and Acts 2.44 are the two variants that undergo the greatest level of upgrade in the *UBSGNT*[4], some may conclude that they are too extreme to act as representatives or examples of letter-rating changes in this latest edition. The complete opposite, however, is true. Luke 19.25 and Acts 2.44 are the most obvious examples of unwarranted letter-rating increase. If immoderate rating changes are allowed to occur in variants of this nature, where they obviously should not, what

discussion describing the high percentage manuscript groupings in the *UBSGNT*[4], will also be reconsidered.

An examination of these two variant units will fulfill several functions and goals: (1) the information and insight gained from an analysis of Lk. 19.25 and Acts 2.44 will serve as a paradigm for use with other exceptional and fluctuating *UBSGNT*[4] passages, (2) conclusions will be formed regarding the decision-making process of the *UBSGNT* editors as they sought to accord letter-ratings to each variant unit, and (3) the justifiability and integrity of the remarkable letter-rating changes present in the *UBSGNT*[4] will be evaluated.

1. A Textual Inquiry into the Exceptional Variant at Luke 19.25

Description of Each Variant in the Entire Variant Unit of Luke 19.25

Variant 1 includes v. 25 in the text: καὶ εἶπαν αὐτῷ, Κύριε, ἔχει δέκα μνᾶς (And they said to him, 'Lord, he has ten minas').
Variant 2 omits v. 25 from the text.

Letter-Ratings and Manuscript Changes to the Citations in the Apparatus at Luke 19.25 as Seen throughout Each UBSGNT *Edition*
Lk. 19.25 is given the following letter-ratings in each of the *UBSGNT* editions: *UBSGNT*[1]: *D* rating, *UBSGNT*[2]: *D* rating, *UBSGNT*[3]: *C* rating, *UBSGNT*[3corr.]: *C* rating, *UBSGNT*[4]: *A* rating. One can clearly observe the three-step increase from a *D* rating to an *A* rating.

The headings that follow simply list the changes to the critical apparatus as they occur in each subsequent edition. This section focuses predominantly upon matters of external evidence in order to reveal if there have been manuscript additions or perhaps deletions that warrant the increase in letter-ratings throughout each *UBSGNT* edition. Both added and deleted manuscripts for each edition are recorded. The changes to

then of variants that are upgraded by only one letter-rating? If the *UBSGNT*[4] editorial committee introduces unfounded upgrades of this excessive nature, how likely are they to modify variants with more moderate fluctuations? Are the new ratings of these more moderate variants equally unfounded? Again, because of the extent of letter-rating increases, Lk. 19.25 and Acts 2.44 are the two most obvious examples where this degree of upgrade should not have occurred. Can the *UBSGNT*[4] committee justify upgrades of this nature? If the editors of the fourth edition can take such liberties with these extreme variant fluctuations, what of variants with more modest fluctuations? Have these likewise been unjustifiably upgraded?

the apparatus of each edition are based upon the apparatus of each previous edition (i.e. the *UBSGNT*[1] is not used as the standard for each subsequent edition. Thus changes to the *UBSGNT*[3] are determined by the manuscripts cited in the *UBSGNT*[2], etc.)

UBSGNT[1] *and UBSGNT*[2] *Additions and Deletions*: In the *UBSGNT*[1] and the *UBSGNT*[2] the manuscript citation is identical. There are no additions or deletions.

UBSGNT[3] *Additions*: In the *UBSGNT*[3], the minuscule 565 (a category III manuscript from the ninth century representing the Caesarean text, with a *lower* importance in Luke) and the Byzantine lectionary *l*[1761] (fifteenth century) are added to the apparatus of the first variant.

UBSGNT[3] *Deletions from the First Variant*: The Byzantine lectionary *l*[883] (from the eleventh century) recorded in the *UBSGNT*[2] is removed from the *UBSGNT*[3] apparatus (according to the *UBSGNT* manuscript lists, this lectionary contains the text of Acts rather than Luke, which is the likely reason for its removal).

UBSGNT[3] *Deletions from the Second Variant*: Minuscule 565 is removed from the second variant of this unit in the *UBSGNT*[3], but as seen above, it is placed into the first variant option (apparently correcting a mis-categorization).

UBSGNT[3corr.] *Additions and Deletions:* The *UBSGNT*[3corr.] apparatus remains identical to the *UBSGNT*[3].

UBSGNT[4] *Additions:*[3] In the *UBSGNT*[4], the manuscript citation

---

3.   A number of these *UBSGNT*[4] additions to the first variant in Lk. 19.25 include newly recorded minuscules and uncials with Byzantine readings. Some may conclude that the addition of these manuscripts with a Byzantine influence invalidates that part of the earlier hypothesis presented in Chapter 2, Section 4, which tentatively asserted that this text-type had been to some degree marginalized. If new Byzantine witnesses are being added into the critical apparatus of the *UBSGNT*[4], one could claim that it is unlikely that this text-type is being marginalized. Although this may be true, the primary assertion of my hypothesis, that there seems to be some type of new consensus or greater confidence in the older witnesses, is not affected. The idea of a Byzantine marginalization is of secondary importance. Regardless, one should keep in mind that these manuscripts which have been newly added, although containing Byzantine readings, at the same time record a mixture of readings including representatives of the more ancient text and other peculiar variants. Given the nature of the *UBSGNT*[4] text with its prejudice for those readings attested by the more ancient manuscripts, it would be plausible to assume that these newly cited witnesses are added to the apparatus in order to provide support for those readings that represent an earlier or peculiar textual tradition rather than those readings that represent the much later Byzantine or Majority tradition. After all, this distinction between readings of

appears to change extensively. Additions to the *UBSGNT*[4] apparatus include:

Variant 1
* the uncial 0233 (eighth century, category III).

primary significance (i.e. those supported by the older witnesses such as the ancient papyri and great uncials) and readings of secondary significance (i.e. those supported by a majority of Byzantine witnesses) is clearly made by the editors of both the *UBSGNT*[4] and the Nestle-Aland[27]. Furthermore, the much later Byzantine readings, if used at all, generally serve the secondary purpose of rounding out the textual history of a variant rather than the primary purpose of establishing the reading of the original text. This place of prominence is reserved for those manuscripts that contain the more ancient readings or those readings of a more ancient origin. The variant here in Lk. 19.25 adds support to this idea. The majority of manuscripts that contain a high number of Byzantine readings and that are cited for this variant, and in fact most Byzantine manuscripts in general, are characterized as category III or category V witnesses. Again, these tend to be of more importance in rounding out the history of the textual tradition rather than confirming the correct reading of the original text. An evaluation of these newly added manuscripts on the basis of the categories presented in the Nestle-Aland[27] reveals further support. None are categorized as consistently cited witnesses of the first order (these being witnesses independent of the Byzantine Koine text-type, witnesses of the greatest value for establishing the text, and witnesses whose readings accordingly have the greatest authority). Only three (N022, 579, and 1424) are categorized as consistently cited witnesses of the second order (these being the more important uncials of the Byzantine Koine text-type, and a group of minuscules which are of special interest for the *history of the text*). The remainder of the manuscripts that are added to Lk. 19.25 in the *UBSGNT*[4] would appear to be either frequently cited witnesses (manuscripts of outstanding significance for the *history of the text*, or with readings of interest for their content), or occasionally cited witnesses (manuscripts representing the Byzantine Koine text-type). For these categories see Nestle-Aland[27], pp. 50*-51*, and 684-718. With Byzantine readings, and Byzantine manuscripts in general, being used for the secondary purpose of rounding out the text's history rather than the primary purpose of establishing the original text, one can still interpret this as some type of marginalization. This need not be viewed in a negative light. The fact is that the Byzantine text is a later, secondary text-type, as is seen from the *UBSGNT*[4], the Nestle-Aland[27], and the present scholarly consensus. Therefore, it serves a secondary role in New Testament textual criticism. Finally, regarding the Byzantine minuscules specifically, the Alands state that a large majority 'exhibit a purely or predominantly Byzantine text'. They add 'this is not a peculiarity of the minuscules, but a characteristic they share with a considerable number of uncials. They are all irrelevant for textual criticism, at least for establishing the original form of the text and its development in the early centuries'. See K. and B. Aland, *The Text of the New Testament*, p. 142.

- the minuscules 157 (twelfth century, category III), 180 (twelfth century, category III), 205 (fifteenth century, category III), 579 (thirteenth century, category II in Luke), 597 (thirteenth century, category V), 1006 (eleventh century, category V), 1243 (eleventh century, category III), 1292 (thirteenth century, category V), 1342 (thirteenth/fourteenth century, category II only in Mark), 1424 (ninth/tenth century, category III-V), 1505 (eleventh century, category V).
- the category V Byzantine uncials E07, F09, G011, H013, N022.
- the group symbol *Lect.* replacing various Byzantine lectionaries.
- the ancient versions of the Old Latin it^c, Ethiopic, and Slavonic translations.

Variant 2
- the lectionaries $l^{211, 384, 387, 770, 773, 1780}$ substituted for the group symbol *Lect.*

UBSGNT^4 Deletions: Deletions from the *UBSGNT*^{4} apparatus include:

Variant 1
- the category V Byzantine uncials K, Π, 063.
- the minuscules 1009, 1079, 1195, 1216, 1242, 1344, 1365, 1546, 1646, and 2148.
- the Byzantine lectionaries $l^{76, 150, 184, 185, 299, 950, 1761}$ are dropped and replaced by the group symbol *Lect.* as explained immediately above.
- the ancient versions of the Old Latin it^e and Gothic translations.

Variant 2
- minuscules 1230 and 1253, and the Greek Father Cyril.

Taking into account the previous data, it appears doubtful that these minor manuscript changes warrant an increase from a *D* rating in the *UBSGNT*^{1} and *UBSGNT*^{2} to a *C* rating in the *UBSGNT*^{3} and *UBSGNT*$^{3corr.}$. The addition of minuscule 565 (a category III manuscript from the ninth century with a *lower* importance in Luke) and the Byzantine lectionary l^{1761} into the apparatus of the *UBSGNT*^{3} and *UBSGNT*$^{3corr.}$ does not warrant this new *C* letter-rating. In what way does the addition of these two manuscripts change the *UBSGNT* committee's 'very high degree of doubt concerning the reading selected for the text' to 'considerable degree of doubt whether the text or the apparatus contains the superior reading'? One could argue that the additional textual information provided by the inclusion of minuscule 565 and l^{1761}, manuscripts that are more important for establishing textual history rather than the original text, provides little weight in ascribing a new *C* rating to this variant. However, this fluctuation is minor when compared to that present in the *UBSGNT*[4]. Although the changes to the *UBSGNT*[4] apparatus look extensive, in reality they are not. Manuscripts of approximately equal value seem to have been exchanged rather than added. Those removed are replaced by others of similar weight. Other than the addition of the uncials N022 (a category V Byzantine witness) and 0233 (eighth century, category III), the minuscules 579 (thirteenth century, category II in Luke) and 1424 (ninth/tenth century, category III), and several ancient versions, there are no significant manuscript additions to the *UBSGNT*[4] apparatus. The addition of these manuscripts into the apparatus of the *UBSGNT*[4]—even though minuscule 579 carries some weight and authority—seems very unlikely to give occasion to the letter-rating changing from a *C* in the *UBSGNT*[3] and *UBSGNT*[3corr.] to an *A* in this latest edition.[4]

4.   Once again, the most important manuscript additions to this variant are the category V Byzantine uncial N022, the category III uncial 0233, the category II minuscule 579, and the category III minuscule 1424. Based upon the category ratings used in the *UBSGNT*[4], only the category II minuscule 579 holds any type of authority or weight. When evaluated by the Nestle-Aland[27] categories, none of these manuscripts are considered to be consistently cited witnesses of the first order (which are important for establishing the reading of the original text). Three of these four manuscripts (N022, 579, and 1424) are regarded as consistently cited witnesses of the second order (which are of more importance for the history of the text although they are related to the Byzantine Koine text-type). Taking into account the categories that these manuscripts fall into, it seems unlikely that their addition should give rise to the letter-rating changing from a *C* in the *UBSGNT*[3] and *UBSGNT*[3corr.] to an *A* in the *UBSGNT*[4]. On the other hand, if the addition of these witnesses is responsible for the letter-rating modification here in Lk. 19.25, why are these manuscripts not all considered category I or consistently cited witnesses of the first order, especially if they are deemed so influential in ascribing letter-ratings? Perhaps there would be more justification for this rating upgrade if these manuscripts fell into category I or were regarded as consistently cited witnesses of the first order. An attempt was also made to compare the citation of manuscripts for Lk. 19.25 in both the *UBSGNT*[4] and the Nestle-Aland[27]. With the Nestle-Aland[27] citing only those witnesses of utmost importance in establishing the original text, it was hoped that a comparison of the two Greek editions would further delineate those manuscripts of greater weight cited within the *UBSGNT*[4]. Unfortunately, in Nestle-Aland[27], a

Evaluation of Variants Based upon Internal Evidence
Transcriptional probabilities. The more difficult reading would appear
to be the inclusion of v. 25 in the passage. The ambiguity of the subject
of εἶπαν supports this. Who said Κύριε, ἔχει δέκα μνᾶς? Was it the
bystanders in v. 24 or those listening to the parable? The addition of this
verse makes the transition to v. 26 more difficult as well. Verse 25 does
not seem to fit the context in which it is placed and its removal would
not adversely affect the passage, but would instead make the text
smoother and perhaps somewhat easier to understand contextually. The
shorter reading obviously omits the passage, therefore, one can see some
tension between the two maxims pertaining to *the more difficult reading*
and *the shorter reading*. Overall, the text-critical rule of the more
difficult variant probably prevails in this case and therefore may attest to
the verse's genuineness.

Unintentional alterations play almost no role in this variant. It seems
very unlikely that a scribe would accidentally include this verse in the
text. There may be some slight possibility that he unknowingly recorded
a marginal note from his exemplar, but this is extremely doubtful as one
would have a problem explaining the origin of the marginal note.
Instead, the length of v. 25 may indicate that it was purposely placed
into the text. Whether this was done by the original author or by a later
scribe is not certain. However, if this variant is not original, an intentional alteration by a scribe would make better sense than an unintentional alteration. On the other hand, the authenticity of this verse may go
back to the Lukan author, as the purposeful addition of this passage due
to scribal clarification or reinterpretation seems unlikely since the scribe
leaves the subject of εἶπαν ambiguous. There is no elimination of discrepancies and no harmonization involved as the parallel passage (some
scholars question if it is a parallel passage) is recorded without the verse
in Mt. 25.28-29. It may be possible that a scribe would include v. 25 out
of a desire to exclude nothing, or, through the process of conflation.
However, one must once again explain where this verse originated. One

'negative apparatus' is used for the variant in Lk. 19.25. This negative apparatus is
given for variants which are cited mainly for their relevance to the history of the text
or its interpretation. For these readings, only the evidence against the text is shown,
not the evidence representing the text. Therefore, it was not possible to compare the
manuscripts selected to support the reading in the text within both Greek editions.
See Nestle-Aland[27], p. 50* for an explanation of both the positive and negative
apparatus.

could more likely explain the assimilation and harmonization of several witnesses (such as D05, W032, 565, *l*[211, 384, 387, 770, 773, 1780], it[b, d, e, ff2], syr[c,s], and cop[bo]) with the Matthean parallel, where v. 25 is omitted. It could also be possible that a style-conscious scribe purposely removed the verse due to its lack of flow and congruency with its surrounding context and with v. 26. Therefore, the passage's more problematic presence here may well attest to its originality.

Intrinsic probabilities. Very little intrinsic probability figures into this passage. It is used in no other New Testament context.

Evaluation of Variants Based upon External Evidence

Relative date and character of manuscripts. Variant 1 holds the prominent position in view of the date and character of the manuscripts involved. The older manuscripts tend to align themselves with the inclusion of v. 25. The earliest and most important witnesses that attest to the inclusion of this verse, with their dates in brackets, are the uncials ℵ01 (4th cent.), A02 (5th cent.), and B03 (4th cent.). There is also support for this variant in a number of the earlier versions such as the Old Latin manuscript it[a] (4th cent.), the Vulgate (4th cent.), and the Coptic versions cop[sa] (4th cent.) and cop[bo] (9th cent.). On the other hand, the earliest support for variant 2 and the omission of this verse are the later fifth-century uncials D05 and W032. There is also support for the exclusion of this verse in a number of the earlier versions such as the Old Latin witnesses it[b] (5th cent.) and it[d] (5th cent.), and the Syriac versions syr[c] (4th cent.) and syr[s] (4th cent.). The omission of this verse is also attested by the Latin Father Lucifer of Calaris (4th cent.).

Geographical distribution. Variant 1 holds the greater geographical representation. Its witnesses spread from (1) Rome with a western influence (attested to by B03); (2) Asia Minor and Constantinople with an eastern influence (attested by many of the Byzantine manuscripts such as E07 and F09, a large number of the lectionaries and minuscules, and the Armenian and Georgian versions); (3) North Africa, Egypt, and Alexandria with a southern influence (attested to by A02, Δ037, many Old Latin manuscripts such as it[a] and it[i], the Syriac manuscripts syr[p] and syr[h], the Coptic manuscripts cop[sa] and cop[bo], and the Ethiopic version); and (4) Palestine with a central geographical influence (attested to by ℵ01 and θ038). Whereas the geographic spread of variant 1 is complete and thorough, variant 2 holds a more limited geographical representation. Its witnesses spread from (1) North Africa with the southern influence (attested by D05, W032, and Old Latin versions such as it^b and it^d); (2) Asia Minor with an eastern influence (attested by a number of the lectionaries); and, although limited (3) Palestine with a central influence (attested by the Syriac versions syr^c and syr^s).

Genealogical relationships and text-types. Variant 1 shows a broader genealogical and textual basis than variant 2. The inclusion of v. 25 is supported by witnesses such as ℵ01, B03, L019, 33, 579, 892, cop^{sa}, and cop^{bo} for the Alexandrian text. Manuscripts like Q038 (the chief witness), N022, f^1, f^{13}, 28, 565, 700, and the Armenian and Georgian versions represent the Caesarean text. Witnesses such as A02, Δ037, E07, F09, G011, H013, 597 and numerous other minuscules, and the lectionaries are representatives of the Byzantine text. And lastly, the Western text, the least represented text-type in this first variant, is supported by manuscripts like the Old Latin versions and the Syriac version syr^h. Variant 2 is strongly represented by the Western text manuscripts such as D05, a number of the Old Latin versions like syr^c and syr^s, and Lucifer of Calaris. This second variant is also represented, although to a limited degree, by the uncial W032 and a number of later Byzantine lectionaries; however, the Western text is the only strongly supported text-type that omits v. 25 from Luke 19. It may be that this second variant represents a peculiarity of the Western text-type.

Relative quality of witnesses. Variant 1, when the maxim that *manuscripts should be weighed and not counted* is applied, once again holds the position of prominence. A large number of uncials, minuscules, lectionaries, and ancient versions all support the presence of v. 25, while a considerably smaller number of uncials, lectionaries, ancient versions, and one Greek Father support the omission of the passage. But, again, one must weigh rather than count the manuscript evidence. Clearly, with the combined presence of ℵ01, A02, and B03, v. 25 is supported by the most important uncial representation and tradition possible for a textual variant. On the other hand, the omission of this verse is represented by the weaker Western tradition.

The question of which variant best accounts for the rise of the other variants is really not applicable to this situation. However, when one considers which variant makes the most sense in the context, in opposition to the previous external evidence, one should side with variant 2 and the exclusion of v. 25. Again, this verse does not seem to fit the context in which it is placed.

Summary of Textual Inquiry into Luke 19.25

Based upon the evaluation of both internal evidence (specifically pertaining to transcriptional probabilities) and external evidence, one should likely conclude that v. 25 (the first variant option of this unit) is original to the Gospel of Luke and not a later addition by scribes. However, in disagreement with the editors of the *UBSGNT*[4], this variant should not receive the assuredness of an *A* letter-rating. As one can see from the above discussion, the evidence is not conclusive. Considerations such as the preference of a shorter reading, the possibility of later additions to the text through the assimilation of a marginal note, and the omission of this variant making the most contextual sense, would leave the debate open, even if only slightly. At best, only a *B* rating would be justifiable.

Even Metzger reveals the apparent difficulty that the *UBSGNT* editors had in reaching a decision regarding this textual variant. His statements in the 1971 edition of the supplemental textual commentary (intended for use with the *UBSGNT*[3]), along with the ascription of a *C* letter-rating for this variant, indicates that a judgment was made, but with some difficulty, and not with conclusive support.[5] It must be kept in mind that the 1971 edition of this commentary was written based upon the more easily attainable definitions of the *A*, *B*, *C*, and *D* letter-rating categories used in the *UBSGNT*[3]. Again, in this edition Lk. 19.25 receives a *C* rating. Of even greater interest is Metzger's comment on this same variant in the 1994 edition of the supplemental textual commentary (intended for use with the new *UBSGNT*[4]).[6] Although in the *UBSGNT*[4] Lk. 19.25 is upgraded to an *A* letter-rating, supposedly attesting to its definite certainty, Metzger's explanation of this variant in the 1994 edition of the textual commentary remains essentially identical to his explanation in the 1971 edition of the commentary. It is dramatically clear that Metzger's explanation of Lk. 19.25 in the 1994 commentary is in direct contrast to the committee's ascription of an *A* letter-rating in the *UBSGNT*[4]. As in the 1971 edition of the textual commentary, Metzger states in the 1994 edition that

> a *majority* of the Committee considered it to be *more probable* that the words were omitted in several Western witnesses... A *majority* of the Committee considered that, *on balance*, both external attestation and

5.   See Metzger, *A Textual Commentary*, 1971, p. 169.
6.   See Metzger, *A Textual Commentary*, 1994, p. 144.

transcriptional probabilities *favor* the retention of the words in the text
[italics added].[7]

Even Metzger's use of the words 'majority', 'more probable', 'on balance', and 'favor' clearly do not correspond to the degree of certainty
necessary for a variant to receive an *A* letter-rating. Why is there a con-
tradiction here? According to Metzger's commentary, it would seem
more justifiable that this variant receive a *C* letter-rating. It appears that
the *UBSGNT* committee were not hesitant enough in making a decision
regarding this variant, even though the redefined *A*, *B*, *C*, and *D* letter-
rating categories as recorded in the *UBSGNT*[4] should be more difficult
to attain than in the previous *UBSGNT* editions. Why was Lk. 19.25 not
accorded an *A* rating in the *UBSGNT*[3], where it would fall under the
less rigorous definition of 'virtual/almost certainty' rather than the more
rigorous definition of 'complete certainty' which is required of *A* variants in the *UBSGNT*[4]? What caused this change in the minds of the
UBSGNT committee? It must be remembered that there is no new primary manuscript support added to the *UBSGNT*[4] apparatus at Lk. 19.25
thereby enabling and justifying the improved *A* rating. In consideration
of the external manuscript evidence, dealing strictly with manuscripts
alone, there is approximately the same weight of witnesses in the
UBSGNT[3] apparatus as in the *UBSGNT*[4] apparatus. Why the change in
letter-ratings at Lk. 19.25? Internal evidence is not absolutely certain
(as Metzger indicates in his textual commentary). It would seem that
Lk. 19.25 increased to an *A* rating for no apparent reason. Based upon
the discussion of internal and external evidence, as well as upon Metzger's
comments, there appears to be an illogical and fallacious increase in
letter-ratings, from *C* to *A*, at Lk. 19.25.

Bearing in mind the earlier discussion of Chapter 2, Section 4, regarding various possible reasons for the rating changes from previous
UBSGNT editions to the *UBSGNT*[4], it may be possible that the
UBSGNT committee re-evaluated Lk. 19.25 in the *UBSGNT*[4] on the
basis of (1) specific high percentage manuscript groupings present in
each variant (i.e. predominantly external evidence alone), and (2) on the
basis of a newly expressed optimism and greater respect for the older
witnesses. If we take into account this optimism for the earlier ancient
manuscripts, and then apply the results gained from the high percentage
manuscript groupings of Chapter 2 to the variant in Lk. 19.25, it can be

7.   See Metzger, *A Textual Commentary*, 1994, p. 144.

seen that Lk. 19.25 almost perfectly coincides with the high percentage manuscript cluster determined earlier for Luke 1–8. In Chapter 2 it was revealed that a large percentage of *A* rated variants in Luke 1–8 contained the following manuscripts in the apparatus:

A Rated Variants

Mss	Type/Category	Percent
B03	uncial (I)	100%
W032	uncial (III)	100%
ℵ01	uncial (I)	94%
L019	uncial (II)	89%
cop^{sa}	coptic	89%
579	minuscule (II)	78%
1241	minuscule (III)	72%
cop^{bo}	coptic	72%

In Lk. 19.25 the manuscripts recorded in the *UBSGNT*[4] critical apparatus are very similar to those found in the high percentage manuscript grouping above. The only manuscript present in the high percentage grouping that is not present in Lk. 19.25 is Codex Freerianus (W032); in fact, this witness is cited as a manuscript for the second variant of Lk. 19.25. There is, therefore, almost a perfect match. It would seem viable that these manuscript groups do indeed act as some type of model for ascribing letter-ratings.[8] Nevertheless, even if this provides only a

---

8.   A number of witnesses with Byzantine readings are cited not only in the *A* rated variant of Lk. 19.25 (as discussed in n. 3 above), but also in the high percentage manuscript grouping calculated for the first eight chapters of Luke. Again, some may decide that the inclusion of these witnesses with a Byzantine influence invalidates that part of the earlier hypothesis presented in Chapter 2, Section 4, which tentatively asserted that this text-type has been to some degree marginalized. If Byzantine witnesses are included in the high percentage manuscript grouping (therefore representing consistent use in the critical apparatus of the *UBSGNT*[4]), the claim could be made that this text-type has not been marginalized. However, even though this point may be true, the primary assertion of the hypothesis, that there seems to be some type of new consensus or greater confidence in the older witnesses, is not affected. The idea of a Byzantine marginalization is of secondary importance. Yet in following through with this thought, one might keep in mind that these manuscripts, although containing Byzantine readings, at the same time record a mixture of readings including representatives of the more ancient text and other peculiar variants. Considering again the nature of the *UBSGNT*[4] text with its prejudice for those readings attested by the more ancient manuscripts, it would be plausible to assume that these witnesses with a mixed text are included in the apparatus in order to provide support for those readings that represent an earlier or peculiar textual tradition rather than those readings that represent the much later Byzantine tradition or

partial explanation for the letter-rating increase in Lk. 19.25 (and it may, along with earlier considerations, have some merit), not once in the *UBSGNT*[4] is the reader presented with a logical and clear justification of why the letter-ratings have increased so dramatically; and this is certainly necessary. Unfortunately, this explanation is seemingly based upon external evidence alone, with little regard being given to internal evidence.

Majority text. As mentioned earlier, a distinction between readings of primary significance (i.e. those supported by the older witnesses such as the ancient papyri and great uncials) and readings of secondary significance (i.e. those supported by a majority of Byzantine witnesses) is clearly made by the editors of both the *UBSGNT*[4] and the Nestle-Aland[27]. Furthermore, the much later Byzantine readings, if used at all, generally serve the secondary purpose of rounding out the textual history of a variant rather than the primary purpose of establishing the reading of the original text. The place of prominence is reserved for those manuscripts that contain the more ancient readings or those readings of a more ancient origin. The variant here in Lk. 19.25 and the high percentage manuscript grouping for the first eight chapters of Luke add support to this idea, especially if the relative weight of each witness is considered. The majority of Byzantine manuscripts and manuscripts with a high proportion of Byzantine readings are characterized as category III or category V witnesses. Aside from the category II minuscule 579 (which records a predominantly Alexandrian text in Luke), the other manuscripts with a high proportion of Byzantine readings that are cited in the high percentage manuscript grouping for this book (minuscule 1241 which also contains Alexandrian readings in Luke, and the Western uncial W032 recording primarily Byzantine readings in Luke) are considered category III witnesses. Again, these tend to be of more importance in rounding out the history of the textual tradition rather than confirming the correct reading of the original text, particularly where the manuscript's Byzantine readings are concerned. The Nestle-Aland[27] categories shed further light on this issue. Of these three manuscripts with Byzantine readings, only one (W032) is a consistently cited witness of the first order and of greatest value for establishing the text (and this probably not due to its Byzantine readings in Matthew and Luke, but because of a number of its curious readings such as the Freer logion). The other two witnesses (minuscules 579 and 1241) are considered to be consistently cited witnesses of the second order and are of more importance for the history of the text. Therefore, the *A* letter-rating given to the variant here in Lk. 19.25 is probably ascribed on the basis of the superior category I and category II manuscripts that contain the more ancient readings or those readings of a more ancient origin, rather than those category III manuscripts or readings that represent the later Byzantine or Majority text. Taking into account these above considerations, it may still be possible to assert that the addition of these witnesses serves to broaden the textual history rather than to establish the original reading of the text, and therefore, it is equally possible to claim that the Byzantine text has been to some degree marginalized.

2. A Textual Inquiry into the Exceptional Variant at Acts 2.44

Description of Each Variant in the Entire Variant Unit of Acts 2.44

Variant 1 includes the full ἦσαν ἐπὶ τὸ αὐτὸ καί in v. 44:

> Πάντες δὲ οἱ πιστεύοντες *ἦσαν ἐπὶ τὸ αὐτὸ καὶ* εἶχον ἅπαντα κοινὰ
> And all the ones believing *were in the same place and* were having all
> things in common.

Variant 2 includes only ἐπὶ τὸ αὐτό:

> Πάντες δὲ οἱ πιστεύοντες *ἐπὶ τὸ αὐτό* εἶχον ἅπαντα κοινὰ
> And all the ones believing *in the same place* were having all things in
> common.

Variant 3 omits ἦσαν ἐπὶ τὸ αὐτὸ καί.

Letter-Ratings and Manuscript Changes to the Citations in the Apparatus at Acts 2.44 as Seen throughout Each UBSGNT Edition

Acts 2.44 is given the following letter-ratings in each of the *UBSGNT* editions: *UBSGNT*[1]: *D* rating, *UBSGNT*[2]: *D* rating, *UBSGNT*[3]: *D* rating, *UBSGNT*[3corr.]: *D* rating, *UBSGNT*[4]: *A* rating. As with Lk. 19.25, there is a three-step letter increase from a *D* rating to an *A* rating. However, here in Acts 2.44, this radical improvement occurs only in the *UBSGNT*[4], while all previous editions remain constant.

A list of the changes to the critical apparatus as they occur in each subsequent edition follows. These changes to the apparatus of each edition are based upon the apparatus of each previous edition (i.e. the *UBSGNT*[1] is not used as the standard for each subsequent edition. Thus changes to the *UBSGNT*[3] are determined by the manuscripts cited in the *UBSGNT*[2], etc.) It should also be noted that in each of the first four *UBSGNT* editions there are four variant options in the entire variant unit of Acts 2.44. However, the *UBSGNT*[4] omits the second option given in each of these earlier editions (ἐπὶ τὸ αὐτὸ καί) and, therefore, only lists three variant options.

UBSGNT[1] *and UBSGNT*[2] *Additions and Deletions*: In the *UBSGNT*[1] and the *UBSGNT*[2] the manuscript citation is identical in all four variant options. There are no additions or deletions.

UBSGNT[3] *Additions and Deletions*: In the *UBSGNT*[3], the minuscule 234 is added to the third variant option (ἐπὶ τὸ αὐτό) of the four variant unit.

UBSGNT[3corr.] *Additions and Deletions*: In the *UBSGNT*[3corr.], the Greek Church Father, Basil the Great, is added to the first variant option (ἦσαν ἐπὶ τὸ αὐτὸ καί) of the four variant unit.

UBSGNT[4] *Additions*:[9] Whereas in the first four *UBSGNT* editions there were four variant options listed in the entire variant unit, the *UBSGNT*[4] , by omitting the second option given in each of these earlier editions (ἐπὶ τὸ αὐτὸ καί), only lists three variant options. As in Lk. 19.25, the *UBSGNT*[4] manuscript citation appears to change extensively here in Acts 2.44. Additions to the *UBSGNT*[4] apparatus include:

Variant 1

- the minuscules 36 (twelfth century, category II), 307 (tenth century, category III), 453 (fourteenth century, category III), 610 (twelfth century, category III), 1175 (eleventh century, category I manuscript important for the history of the text), 1409 (fourteenth century, category II), 1678 (fourteenth century, category III?), 1891 (tenth century, category II), and 2344 (eleventh century, category III).
- the category V uncial P025 now follows the newly added *Byz*. symbol.

9.   Similar to Lk. 19.25, the variant here at Acts 2.44 also adds to the critical apparatus of the *UBSGNT*[4] a number of uncials and minuscules with Byzantine readings. Along with the initial considerations recorded in n. 3 above, the evaluation of this variant's witnesses in the light of the *UBSGNT*[4] and Nestle-Aland[27] manuscript categories is also of direct relevance. According to the *UBSGNT*[4] categories, the most important newly added witnesses with Byzantine readings would appear to be the category I minuscule 1175 (on p. 151 of *The Text of the New Testament*, the Alands claim it is significant for establishing the history of the text), and the category II minuscules 36, 1409, and 1891. On the basis of the Nestle-Aland[27] categories, there are no newly added *UBSGNT*[4] manuscripts in Acts 2.44 that are designated as consistently cited witnesses of the first order. Only two manuscripts are considered to be consistently cited witnesses of the second order (1175 and *l*[884]), while two others (36 and 453) are specifically designated as frequently cited witnesses. The remainder of these newly added manuscripts appear to be occasionally cited witnesses. In view of these considerations, one may justifiably conclude that the addition of these Byzantine manuscripts and Byzantine readings serves the secondary purpose of rounding out this variant's textual history while the primary purpose of establishing the reading of the original text is reserved for those manuscripts that contain the more ancient readings or those readings of a more ancient origin. If the Byzantine manuscripts and readings play this secondary role, the notion of a marginalization could still hold true.

- the lectionaries l^{884} and l^{1178}.
- the ancient versions of the Old Latin it[c, dem, ph, ro, t, w], and the Ethiopic and Slavonic translations.
- the Greek Church Father Chrysostom.

Variant 2 (variant 3 in each of the first four *UBSGNT* editions)
- the ancient version of the Old Latin it[r].
- the Latin Church Father Speculum.

Variant 3 (variant 4 in each of the first four *UBSGNT* editions)
- this third variant option remains unchanged in all of the *UBSGNT* editions.

UBSGNT[4] *Deletions*: Deletions from the *UBSGNT*[4] apparatus include:

Variant 1
- the category V uncial P025 now follows the newly added *Byz.* symbol.
- the category V Byzantine uncials 049, 056, 0142.
- the minuscules 88, 104, 326, 330, 436, 451, 614, 629, 630, 1241, 1505, 1877, 2127, 2412, and 2492.
- the ancient Syriac version syr[p], and the Coptic versions cop[sa, bo].

Variant 2 (variant 3 in each of the first four *UBSGNT* editions)
- the ancient version of the Old Latin it[m].

Variant 3 (variant 4 in each of the first four *UBSGNT* editions)
- this third variant option remains unchanged in all of the *UBSGNT* editions.

Upon observing the above data detailing the manuscript changes to the *UBSGNT* editions, particularly those of the *UBSGNT*[4], one must ask the following question: Is there a persuasive and influential addition or alteration in the critical apparatus of this fourth edition that would justify a consistent *D* rated variant leaping to an *A* rated variant? Although the changes to the *UBSGNT*[4] apparatus look extensive, the only appreciable modification lies in the addition of numerous important minuscules such as 36, 1175, 1409 and 1891, and a number of Old Latin manuscripts. There is no addition of new information in the form of a major papyrus or uncial witness. Therefore, as we consider this significant letter-rating change, the main focus must fall upon the four new minuscule additions. Does the inclusion of these minuscules warrant the upheaval of the consistent *D* letter-rating that is present in the *UBSGNT*[1] through to the *UBSGNT*[3corr.]? One should probably answer this question in the negative—it is not sufficient to base a rating change of such proportions upon the evidence of these four newly added witnesses. Although the importance of a select group of minuscules has been more recently reassessed, resulting in the elevation of these manuscripts, it is unlikely that the addition of these four witnesses is able to support such a high degree of letter-rating modification.[10] Regardless of the inclusion of these manuscripts, it seems a great leap for the *UBSGNT* committee to move from a 'very high degree of doubt concerning the reading selected for the text', as recorded in the *UBSGNT*[1] to the *UBSGNT*[3corr.], to 'the text is certain', as stated in the *UBSGNT*[4]. These manuscripts may add further weight to the inclusion of ἦσαν ἐπὶ τὸ αὐτὸ καί, along with $\mathfrak{P}$[74] and Codex Sinaiticus (א01), but they do not completely dispel the reading that is supported by Codex Vaticanus (B03) and hence provide undivided certainty regarding the correct reading of the text.[11]

10. See K. and B. Aland, *The Text of the New Testament*, pp. 128-29 regarding this reassessment of the minuscules.

11. As already discussed in n. 9 above, the category evidence would suggest that the addition of these four manuscripts (36, 1174, 1409, and 1891) serves to add to this variant's textual history instead of supporting the consistent *D* rating climbing to an *A* rating. There would be more justification for this letter-rating upgrade if these manuscripts fell into category I or were regarded as consistently cited witnesses of the first order. However, with the nature and extent of modification that occurs, even this is highly unlikely. As with Lk. 19.25, the variant at Acts 2.44 was compared in both the *UBSGNT*[4] and the Nestle-Aland[27]. The manuscript citations that both editions have in common are $\mathfrak{P}$[74], א, A, C, D, E, Ψ, 33, 1739, and syr[h]. Instead of listing the rest of the minuscules included in the *UBSGNT*[4], it may be that the Nestle-Aland[27] subsumes these under the group symbol 𝔐 representing the majority text, including the Byzantine Koine text. The Nestle-Aland[27] states that 𝔐 represents the witness of the Koine text-type, together with the witness of all consistently cited manuscripts of the second order which agree with it in a given reading. However, the symbol itself has the status of a consistently cited witness of the first order. See the Nestle-Aland[27], p. 55*. It is interesting to note that the Nestle-Aland[27] apparatus does not cite any of the newly added *UBSGNT*[4] manuscripts such as 36, 1175, 1409, and 1891. Does this reflect the idea that the Nestle-Aland[27], which cites, because of space limitations, only those manuscripts of greatest priority, regards these witnesses as less valuable in establishing the reading of the original text? If true, this provides one further piece of evidence that the addition of these manuscripts in the *UBSGNT*[4] does not warrant the *D–A* letter-rating upgrade present in Acts 2.44. Even if these witnesses are subsumed under the symbol 𝔐, they are still regarded as manuscripts of the Koine text-type and are consistently cited witnesses of

Evaluation of Variants Based upon Internal Evidence

Evaluation of this passage can begin by eliminating the possibility of variant 3. It seems unlikely that this phrase would be entirely omitted from the passage. This assumption is made on the following grounds. First, the phrase is common in classical Greek and in the Septuagint and even acquired a 'quasi-technical' meaning in the early church.[12] Therefore, its appearance here could very well be likely. Secondly, the manuscript evidence supporting the presence of this phrase, as it appears in variant 1 or variant 2, is extensive, while the evidence supporting its omission in variant 3 is extremely limited. Thirdly, the inclusion of this phrase, in one form or another, would be consistent with the earlier usage of ἦσαν in v. 42, and with the later usage of ἐπὶ τὸ αὐτό in v. 47, and would continue to emphasize and contribute to the theme of unity.[13] Taking into account the internal evidence, perhaps the scribe who copied the later Old Latin manuscript it[gig], in which this variant is omitted, purposely removed the phrase ἦσαν ἐπὶ τὸ αὐτὸ καί because he too was confused as to which form it should appear in. However, this is speculative. It is more likely that he intended to provide a smoother, more direct reading and, therefore, omitted the text.

Transcriptional probabilities. As in Lk. 19.25, consideration must be given to the shorter reading and the more difficult reading. The second variant is the shorter of the two more likely textual options in Acts 2.44. Variant 1 contains the longer reading, which provides further clarification by supplying the verb ἦσαν and the coordinating conjunction καί. With the inclusion of these two elements, a further clause and greater explanation of the statement is given. Instead of simply saying 'And all the believers together had everything in common', one gains a better understanding with the more complete text 'And all the believers were together and had everything in common'. Upon initial consideration one may conclude that variant 1, due to the addition of the verb

the second order. They are of more interest for the history of the text. Furthermore, if the addition of these manuscripts is a reason behind the incredible letter-rating upgrade in Acts 2.44, why were these apparently significant witnesses not likewise included in the apparatus of the Nestle-Aland[27]? Similarly, why are these manuscripts not all considered category I or consistently cited witnesses of the first order if they hold such a great degree of influence in ascribing letter-ratings?

12. Metzger, *A Textual Commentary*, 1994, p. 265.

13. Metzger notes that the phrase ἐπὶ τὸ αὐτό signifies the union of the Christian body, and could possibly be rendered 'in church fellowship'. See Metzger, *A Textual Commentary*, 1994, p. 265.

ἦσαν and the coordinating conjunction καί, is the more difficult of the two readings, while variant 2, which streamlines the phrase, uses fewer grammatical components. On the other hand, given the paratactic character of variant 2, that is, the clauses arranged without connectives, this second variant would likely assume the place of the more difficult reading while the first variant, which brings more clarity and information to the text by including additional grammatical components, would be seen as the least difficult of the two readings. Therefore, taking into account the text-critical axioms concerning the shorter and more difficult readings, the place of priority should most likely be given to variant 2 which includes the reading ἐπὶ τὸ αὐτό. This is in contrast to the decision made by the *UBSGNT* committee who chooses variant 1, ἦσαν ἐπὶ τὸ αὐτὸ καί, to represent the original text.

Again, as in Lk. 19.25, unintentional errors do not play a significant role in this variant unit. An error of judgment or memory may have occurred where the scribe forgot to add ἦσαν and καί, and therefore shortened the phrase as he wrote, but this is improbable and cannot be explained. The occurrence of an intentional alteration may be possible. Perhaps the scribe of variant 1 added the extra words for the sake of clarity or out of a desire to harmonize. It is feasible that the phrase ἐπὶ τὸ αὐτό is original and is again repeated in v. 47.[14] But this is only speculation. Nevertheless, it would seem that a correction of style is present here in Acts 2.44. However, it is difficult to conclude which variant received the stylistic change. Was it a scribe who sought to add more information and clarity by including the full phrase? Or was it a scribe who sought to make the reading more streamlined and concise? It may be the case that, as Metzger states in his textual commentary, the reading ἐπὶ τὸ αὐτό could be a later stylistic improvement where all superfluity of expression is pared away.[15] Regardless of how one decides, and there does appear to be a dilemma between the shorter and more difficult reading versus stylistic considerations, if variant 1 is original, then there is an error of omission in variant 2. But if variant 2 is original, then there is an error of addition to variant 1.

14. It may be of interest to note that in the variant located at Acts 2.47 the *UBSGNT* committee chooses as the original text the bare phrase ἐπὶ τὸ αὐτό without any other grammatical items. Yet, as we have seen in Acts 2.44, instead of choosing ἐπὶ τὸ αὐτό, the committee decided that the original text should be represented by the reading ἦσαν ἐπὶ τὸ αὐτὸ καί.

15. Metzger, *A Textual Commentary*, 1994, p. 263.

Intrinsic probabilities. It is very difficult to determine the intrinsic probabilities inherent to this passage. As stated earlier, the phrase ἐπὶ τὸ αὐτό is commonly used in both classical Greek and in the Septuagint, and in the New Testament has gained a semi-technical sense meaning 'in church fellowship'.[16] F.F. Bruce notes that these believers may have constituted a kind of synagogue within the wider Jewish community.[17] Other scholars have stated that the phrase is a mistranslation of a Judean Aramaic word meaning 'great'.[18] The author of Acts, on a number of occasions, clearly makes use of the phrase in describing the unity of believers (1.15; 2.1, 47). The term is also used in this way by Paul in 1 Cor. 11.20 and 14.23. But, on the basis of Lukan style, it becomes very difficult to determine if the additional words of variant 1 are original. This type of questioning becomes too intricate, and as one can see in this verse, the omission of one variant over another has little change on the meaning of the passage. The same theme of unity is still emphasized.

Evaluation of Variants Based upon External Evidence
Relative date and character of manuscripts. The evidence here is split between the first and second variant. Variant 1 is represented by numerous manuscripts, including the following selection with their dates in brackets: the Bodmer papyrus $\mathfrak{P}^{74}$ (7th cent.), the uncials ℵ01 (4th cent.), A02 (5th cent.), C04 (5th cent.), D05 (5th cent.), E^{a}08 (6th cent.), the minuscules 33 (9th cent.) and 1175 (11th cent.), and the Old Latin witnesses it^d (5th cent.), and it^e (6th cent.). On the other hand, variant 2 is attested by B03 (4th cent.), by far the most significant uncial, the Old Latin witnesses it^p (12th cent.), it^r (7th/8th cent.), and readings from Origen (253/254 CE). Variant 3 would follow far behind with its sole representative it^{gig} (13th cent.). If one strictly considers the number of manuscripts per variant, the verdict would unquestionably be to choose variant 1 as the original. The date of the manuscripts would also tend to support the first variant. However, this is based upon manuscript numbers and not weight.

Geographical distribution. Variant 1 is clearly to be preferred with regard to geographical distribution of manuscripts. This is based upon the number of manuscripts attesting to this option. There is strong

16. See again Metzger, *A Textual Commentary*, 1994, p. 265.
17. F.F. Bruce, *The Book of Acts* (Grand Rapids: Eerdmans, rev. edn, 1988), p. 72 n. 108.
18. See Metzger, *A Textual Commentary*, 1994, pp. 264-65.

manuscript evidence for this first variant from (1) Asia Minor and Constantinople with an eastern influence (attested by many of the Byzantine manuscripts with the symbol *Byz* and the manuscript [P], the lectionaries l^{884} and l^{1178}, the Armenian and Georgian versions, and a number of minuscules); (2) North Africa, Egypt, and Alexandria with a southern influence (seen in manuscripts such as A02, many Old Latin manuscripts such as it^a and it^d, the Syriac manuscript syr^h, the Vulgate, and the Ethiopic version); and (3) Palestine with a central geographical influence (represented primarily by the uncial ℵ01). Variant 2 is represented in the Roman or western regions (endorsed primarily by B03), and in North Africa with a southern influence (supported by several Old Latin manuscripts), while variant 3 is limited to one manuscript. The geographic range of variant 1 is more widespread than variant 2, and therefore, one should probably choose the first variant in matters concerning geographical distribution.

Genealogical relationships and text-types. Variant 1 holds the place of prominence over variant 2 and variant 3. The inclusion of ἦσαν ἐπὶ τὸ αὐτὸ καί is supported by witnesses such as $\mathfrak{P}^{74}$, ℵ01, A02, C04 although with a mixed text, Ψ044, 33, 81, and 1175 for the Alexandrian text. Manuscripts like [P], l^{884}, l^{1178}, the Armenian and Georgian versions, and a number of minuscules uphold the Byzantine text. The Western text is represented by witnesses such as D05, 614, 1739, and several of the Old Latin versions. Variant 2 is supported by both the Alexandrian text, with the citation of B03 and the Church Father Origen, and the Western text, with the citation of it^p and it^r.

Relative quality of witnesses. When one considers that *manuscripts should be weighed and not counted*, it is slightly more difficult to determine which variant holds the place of authority. One papyrus, a number of important uncials and minuscules, and numerous ancient versions all support variant 1. A considerably smaller number of witnesses support variant 2. However, this variant is attested to by B03, by far the most important uncial and the most valuable witness to the text of the New Testament we have to date. With the presence of $\mathfrak{P}^{74}$, the category I Bodmer papyrus, in variant 1, the weight may lean more towards this option. But there is clearly a dilemma with this variant unit. The most influential manuscript evidence is split between the two main variant readings. One might also consider variant 3 when the quality of witnesses is considered. As Metzger states, Codex Gigas, which represents variant 3, is considered valuable because in the book of Acts it preserves a form of the Old Latin text which agrees with scriptural quotations made by Lucifer of Cagliari dating back to the fourth century (yet, in consideration of the other forms of internal and external evidence, this third variant has little weight).[19]

The question of which variant best accounts for the rise of the other variants is difficult to answer. However, variant 3 with its omission of the text is eliminated. Again, one is forced to decide if variant 1 or variant 2 is the original reading. If the choice is given to the first variant, then an error of omission has resulted in variant 2. However, if the choice is made for the second variant, then there exists an error of addition in variant 1.

Summary of Textual Inquiry into Acts 2.44

Although one may conclude that the first variant, the inclusion of ἦσαν ἐπὶ τὸ αὐτὸ καί, is more likely to be the original reading due to the sheer amount of manuscript support, contrary to the decision made by the *UBSGNT*[4] committee, the matter seems to warrant more reflection and a good deal of caution. With Codex Vaticanus (B03) endorsing the reading of the second variant, ἐπὶ τὸ αὐτό, it seems obvious that the decision is, at best, somewhat clouded. A firm choice cannot be so confidently made, and Metzger points this out in the 1971 edition of his textual commentary. He cautiously asserts that 'The reading ἐπὶ τὸ αὐτό *gives the impression* of being a stylistic improvement...', while on the next page of the commentary he explains that a number of difficulties are inherent to a consideration of the phrase ἐπὶ τὸ αὐτό because of its obscurity.[20] Like Metzger's comments, the *UBSGNT* committee's decision to label this variant with a *D* letter-rating in all editions prior to the *UBSGNT*[4], thereby revealing among the committee 'a very high degree of doubt concerning the reading selected for the text', is reflective of a cautious consideration of this variant. In dramatic contrast to this is the *UBSGNT*[4] committee's decision to change this consistent *D* letter-rating to an *A* letter-rating. However, as in Lk. 19.25, the remarks for Acts 2.44 in the 1994 edition of Metzger's commentary remain essentially unchanged, despite the new *A* letter-rating.[21] There is

19. See Metzger, *The Text of the New Testament*, p. 75.

20. Metzger, *A Textual Commentary*, 1971, pp. 303-305. In this 1971 edition, the minuscule 254 is mistakenly recorded for what should be 234. This is corrected in the 1994 edition.

21. This appears to be a common occurrence throughout the new edition of

no mention of the addition of new manuscripts, such as the more significant minuscules 36, 1175, 1409 and 1891, which would perhaps allow for some type of letter-rating upgrade; however, it is unlikely that even this would justify the extent of change that occurs in the *UBSGNT*[4].

Even though this variant is not of great importance to the text of the New Testament, it is interesting to observe how the *UBSGNT* editorial committee has dealt with this minor variant. One must question if this is the manner in which other minor variants are dealt with in the *UBSGNT*[4]. As in Lk. 19.25, this variant seems unworthy of the assuredness of an *A* letter-rating. The above discussion reveals that the evidence is not entirely conclusive, and in fact may be less conclusive than that for Lk. 19.25. Both internal and external considerations are insufficient to justify the consistent *D* letter-rating in the first four editions leaping to an *A* rating in the *UBSGNT*[4]. Has this variant been promoted simply because it is of minor significance? If this is the case, regardless of how insignificant this variant is, problems of methodology and integrity emerge. Arguably, a *D* or *C* letter-rating, at best, should have been accorded to this passage, not an *A* rating, which designates complete certainty. Again, one must question the editors of the *UBSGNT*[4] as to their criteria for ascribing letter-ratings. It seems to be in opposition to the balanced criteria of both internal and external evidence employed within the rational eclectic method. It would appear that

---

Metzger's textual commentary. For the majority of variants that have been upgraded from previous *UBSGNT* editions, there is no explanation as to why these upgrades take place. In fact, for most variants, other than a change of sentence structure and the rearrangement of a small number of manuscripts, the textual notes remain almost identical between the 1971 and 1994 editions. There is for the most part silence concerning the new letter-rating upgrades. On numerous occasions within the 1994 edition, the new letter-rating is in almost direct contrast to the comments provided. One example is the variant located at Mk 1.41. The ascription of a *B* letter-rating in the commentary, signifying in the *UBSGNT*[4] that 'the text is almost certain', is in contrast to the comment 'It is difficult to come to a firm decision concerning the original text'. A second example is the first variant located at 2 Cor. 1.10. Although this variant receives a *B* letter-rating, the remarks in Metzger's textual commentary claim that 'The text is doubtful'. See Metzger, *A Textual Commentary*, 1994, pp. 65 and 506 respectively. A number of other examples where this type of discrepancy occurs include variants at Lk. 7.10; 24.47; Jn 8.16; 8.34; Acts 4.6; and 21.1. It is unfortunate that Metzger's new textual commentary has failed to provide vital explanatory information regarding the *UBSGNT* committee's decisions.

external evidence alone is given the position of prominence. Yet, even in the case of Acts 2.44, external evidence does not warrant an *A* letter-rating.

Once again, it should be remembered that this *A* rating was given to Acts 2.44 in conjunction with the more difficult to attain standards defining *A* letter-ratings newly delineated in the *UBSGNT*[4]. This variant went from a standard claiming a 'very high degree of doubt concerning the reading selected for the text' (the definition of a *D* rating in the *UBSGNT*[1]–*UBSGNT*[3corr.]), to 'the text is certain' (the definition of an *A* rating in the *UBSGNT*[4]). Bearing this in mind, one must ask of Acts 2.44, why was this passage not accorded an *A* rating in the *UBSGNT*[3corr.], where it would only have needed to be 'virtually (almost) certain', rather than completely certain as in the *UBSGNT*[4]? What evidence caused this change in the minds of the *UBSGNT* committee? The only notable evidence change that occurs is the addition of several important minuscules and various versional manuscripts. There is no addition of new primary manuscript evidence in the *UBSGNT*[4] apparatus that would sanction the extent of upgrade one sees in the variant at Acts 2.44. Why then the improved *A* rating? Again, based upon the discussion of internal and external evidence, it would seem that there is an illogical and fallacious increase in letter-ratings.

As was explained in the discussion of Lk. 19.25, it would appear to be possible and plausible that the *UBSGNT*[4] committee gave a good deal of weight to, or re-evaluated letter-ratings on the basis of specific high percentage manuscript groupings present in each variant (predominantly external evidence alone). This may, once more, ring true here in Acts 2.44. Taking into account the optimism for and confidence in the earlier ancient manuscripts, if one applies the results gained from the high percentage manuscript groupings of Chapter 2, Section 4 to the variant in Acts 2.44, we see once more the validity of our analysis. Acts 2.44 almost perfectly represents the higher percentage manuscript grouping calculated for the first eight chapters of Acts. In fact, because of the increased number of similarities despite the more numerous manuscripts representing this variant, Acts 2.44 may hold even greater credibility for our proposal than Lk. 19.25. In Chapter 2, it was revealed that a large percentage of *A* rated variants in Acts contained the following manuscripts in the apparatus:

A Rated Variants

Mss	Type/Category	Percent
ℵ01	uncial (I)	100%
A02	uncial (I)	100%
1175	minuscule (I)	100%
B03	uncial (I)	95%
$\mathfrak{P}^{74}$	papyrus (I)	90%
181	minuscule (III)	90%
it^{ph}	old latin	90%
it^{ro}	old latin	90%
Ψ044	uncial (III)	86%
1409	minuscule (II)	86%
2344	minuscule (III)	86%
it^{c}	old latin	86%
it^{dem}	old latin	86%
cop^{sa}	coptic	86%
arm	armenian	86%
geo	georgian	86%
33	minuscule (I)	81%
307	minuscule (III)	81%
453	minuscule (III)	81%
614	minuscule (III)	81%
945	minuscule (III)	81%
1678	minuscule (III)	81%
1739	minuscule (II)	81%
vg	vulgate	81%
cop^{bo}	coptic	81%
Chrys.	greek father	81%
36a	minuscule (II)	76%
610	minuscule (III)	76%
1891	minuscule (II)	76%
it^{w}(a)	old latin	76%
syr^{h}	syriac	76%
eth	ethiopic	76%
81	minuscule (II)	74%
C04	uncial (II)	71%
E08	uncial (II)	71%
it^{ar}	old latin	71%

In Acts 2.44 the manuscripts recorded in the *UBSGNT*[4] critical apparatus are just short of identical to those found in the above high percentage manuscript grouping. The only manuscripts present in the high percentage grouping that are not present in Acts 2.44 are Codex Vaticanus (B03), and the two Coptic versions, cop^{sa} and cop^{bo}. Codex Vaticanus is cited as a witness for the second variant option of Acts 2.44. Once more, there is almost a perfect match even though a greater number of manuscripts is cited in the grouping. This becomes more remarkable when we consider that there are only eight other manuscripts cited in the apparatus of Acts 2.44 that are not included in the manuscript cluster for this book. Almost all the citations in our passage are included in the high percentage manuscript group. As in Lk. 19.25, it would seem more than viable that these manuscript groups act as some type of standard of evaluation for ascribing letter-ratings to the *UBSGNT*[4] variant units and passages. The presence of high percentage manuscript groupings that dictate specific letter-ratings seems to be in operation, at least to some extent. If this justification is true, as it may well be, it is clear that it is founded upon external evidence alone, with little regard being given to internal evidence.[22]

22. As in Lk. 19.25 (see n. 8 above), a number of witnesses with Byzantine readings are cited not only here in the *A* rated variant of Acts 2.44, but also in the high percentage manuscript grouping calculated from the first eight chapters of Acts. In fact, the variant at Acts 2.44 reveals a greater Byzantine representation than what was previously seen in Lk. 19.25. As already stated, some may decide that the inclusion of these manuscripts with a Byzantine influence invalidates that part of the earlier hypothesis presented in Chapter 2, Section 4, which tentatively asserted as a secondary consideration that this text-type had been to some degree marginalized. If Byzantine witnesses are included in the high percentage manuscript grouping calculated for the first eight chapters of Acts, one could claim that it is unlikely that this text-type is being marginalized. However, along with the initial considerations included in n. 3 and especially n. 8 above, several further points should be kept in mind. First, although Acts 2.44 cites Byzantine manuscripts and manuscripts with Byzantine readings, the most strongly supported texts in this variant are Alexandrian and Western—these being the two distinct text-types that the book of Acts apparently circulated in within the early church. Secondly, when these witnesses containing Byzantine readings are examined in the light of the *UBSGNT*[4] and Nestle-Aland[27] manuscript categories, it is revealed that the majority are of a secondary nature. None of these manuscripts are placed into category I or are considered consistently cited witnesses of the first order. Only one manuscript, the category III minuscule 945, is recorded as a consistently cited witness of the second order. Three manuscripts fall into category II (36, 1409, and 1891); however, none of these are regarded to be more than frequently cited witnesses. The rest of those manuscripts containing a high proportion of Byzantine readings in Acts are placed within category III and would appear to be occasionally cited witnesses. These include the minuscules 181, 307, 453, 610, 1678, and 2344. The Ethiopic version, while containing Byzantine readings in Acts, is also mixed in textual character. The remaining uncials and minuscules that are cited in this *A* rated variant and also in the high percentage manuscript grouping, include, as mentioned, predominantly Alexandrian or Western readings in Acts. Taking into account these considerations, one may possibly conclude that the addition of these Byzantine manuscripts and Byzantine readings serves the secondary purpose of rounding out this variant's textual history while the primary purpose of establishing the reading of the original text is reserved for those manuscripts that

3. *Concluding Summary of the Textual Inquiry*
into the Exceptional Variants

In examining both Lk. 19.25 and Acts 2.44, a number of flaws and fallacies in both methodology and logic have been observed in the ascription of letter-ratings to variant units by the *UBSGNT*[4] editorial committee. In consideration of these methodological flaws and logical fallacies, one must ask for an explanation from this committee. What principles and techniques were foundational for the ascertainment of letter-ratings in the *UBSGNT*[4]? As discussed earlier in Chapter 2, Section 4, the following statement made by the committee in the preface to the fourth edition, page v of the *UBSGNT*[4], does not logically or adequately explain the letter-rating upgrades that represent this much more certain *UBSGNT* text:

> Further, the Committee also redefined the various levels in the evaluation
> of evidence on the basis of their relative degrees of certainty. Thus the
> evaluations of all the 1437 sets of variants cited in the apparatus have been
> completely reconsidered.

Therefore, it would appear evident that the *UBSGNT* committee based their fourth edition letter-ratings on some other unknown and unexplained methodology. Was this unknown methodology founded to some extent upon high percentage manuscript groupings? It must be emphasized once more that there is a definite exigency and obligation for the committee to provide their readers with (1) a more thorough reasoning for the employment and use of letter-ratings, and (2) a clearer and perhaps more honest explanation pertaining to the methodology used for the assigning of letter-ratings to variant units. In the light of this request, it is appropriate to apply the previously quoted words of E.J. Epp, concerning the Alands' book *The Text of the New Testament*, to the context of the *UBSGNT*[4] letter-ratings:

contain the more ancient readings or those readings of a more ancient origin. If the Byzantine manuscripts and Byzantine readings play this secondary role, the notion of a marginalization could still hold true. Therefore, if by a new collation of the Greek manuscripts in Münster a greater optimism in the older witnesses has resulted (and possibly the marginalization of the Byzantine tradition), perhaps this has been expressed in the *UBSGNT*[4] through the dramatic upgrading of variant letter-ratings resulting in a much more confident text.

Something that is omitted in the Alands' volume—in addition to what has been said earlier—is an adequate statement of the theoretical base for this so-called 'Standard text' [i.e. Nestle-Aland and *UBSGNT*]. In view of the many pages devoted to it in the volume, it is surprising to discover that the description of this text largely concerns procedural aspects of the committee's work, the story of how the text of the Nestle-Aland NT and the *UBSGNT* came together, and the differing formats of the two editions. There is little on the theory of the text itself...[23]

After assessing various editions of the *UBSGNT*, a number of individuals have pointed out the need for a reappraisal and restructuring of the evaluation of evidence letter-ratings. Omanson, commenting on the *UBSGNT*[3], states:

The UBS text is the only edition ever to rate the relative degree of certainty of the readings adopted in the text. Ranging from A-D, an A evaluation means that the text is virtually certain (for these editors) and a D means a very high degree of doubt exists. Judging by the ratings in the third edition, the editors have become less confident than they were in 1966. The purpose of this rating system is to help translators scattered around the world to have some idea of when they may more safely depart from the UBS text and when they should stay with it. It would be interesting and perhaps useful if, for the C and D ratings, the editors would indicate their second choice for the probable text.[24]

Ross points out some of the problems with the use of letter-ratings in the *UBSGNT* editions, and then provides several helpful options:

The attempt to indicate by the letters A B C and D the judgment of the editors as to the probability of the printed text represents an important advance on all previous editions, but these markings do not turn out in practice to be as useful as they promised to be at first sight. The scale of four grades from A to D is over-subtle... A further weakness of these markings is that in cases where there are several variants the user of the book who doubts the correctness of the reading in the text is given no guidance as to the probability of the various alternatives. These are evidently not always placed in the order of preference in the *apparatus criticus*... What is really wanted is not an estimate of the probability of the reading in the text, but an estimate of each rejected reading. It would be of great value to translators and other students if instead of the existing symbols there were a different set of symbols to be attached to each variant, along the following lines:

23. Epp, 'Reflections', p. 224.
24. Omanson, 'A Perspective', p. 122.

X, meaning, 'The reading in the text is, we think, the most probable, but the issue is very evenly balanced and many good scholars prefer this variant.'

Y, meaning, 'We think the reading in the text much more probable, but a case can be made out for this variant and anyone who prefers it to the reading in the text would not be without scholarly support.'

Z, meaning, 'We have mentioned this variant for the sake of interest or completeness, but no reputable scholar today thinks it original.'[25]

Perhaps the solution to letter-rating problems lies in the combining of the original *A*, *B*, *C*, and *D* guidelines and a method for evaluating each variant in the entire variant unit. A letter-rating could again be ascribed to the entire unit; however, by providing a numerical indicator revealing the order of preference for the other variants in the unit, one dilemma would thus be solved. Regardless, there remains a responsibility upon the *UBSGNT*[4] editorial committee to reconsider more logically the evaluation of evidence letter-ratings and to provide readers with a firmly founded explanation of their methodology and theoretical basis.

---

25. Ross, 'The United Bible', pp. 117-18.

CONCLUSION

A great deal of territory has been covered throughout these pages. However, the primary goal has remained unchanged. This analysis has sought to reveal, first, whether the $UBSGNT^4$ has introduced an extreme change to the critical apparatus letter-ratings for a large number of variants, especially as compared to its earlier editions. This has indeed been verified. There has been a considerable and substantial modification in the variant letter-ratings of the $UBSGNT^4$. As a result of these modifications, the text of the $UBSGNT^4$ is, by far, presented as a much more confident and much more certain text than any of the earlier *UBSGNT* editions.

Secondly, this analysis has explored various reasons why these remarkable changes have occurred, whether they are justifiable, or whether the editorial committee have been over-presumptuous in revising the ratings of many textual variants and/or inconsistent in their standards of variant ratings within the $UBSGNT^4$. Again, our research has indicated various possibilities that may have given rise to these large upgrades. However, for the most part, these letter-rating alterations are not logically or adequately justified. Therefore, one must conclude that the editorial committee have been too bold in revising the ratings of many textual variants, and, presupposing the trends of fluctuation present in the earlier *UBSGNT* editions, have also been inconsistent in the delineation of their standards of variant ratings within the $UBSGNT^4$.

Based upon these outcomes, it is necessary to request from the $UBSGNT^4$ editorial committee a much more detailed explanation of their methodology and the theoretical basis underlying these letter-rating enhancements. Although the United Bible Societies' *Greek New Testament* has been, throughout its entire history, one of the most up-to-date and valuable critical Greek editions offered to both student and scholar alike, there remains a need to sort out several of its methodological flaws. This is indeed obvious here in the $UBSGNT^4$. The problematic letter-ratings do not supply the Bible translator, the beginning student, or the working scholar with a reliable basis for assessing the certainty of the Greek text. In the light of this dilemma, perhaps a reconsideration of the evaluation of evidence letter-ratings, among a few other concerns, needs to take place for future *UBSGNT* editions. The development of a more effective and more sound means of evaluating the Greek text through the use of letter-ratings seems warranted. If the *UBSGNT* editorial committee desires to break away from the established norms of earlier editions, this is well and good. However, it is essential that their readers be clearly informed as to the basis of their methodology and praxis. To draw upon Elliott one last time, he comments on the *UBSGNT*[4] letter-ratings:

> To be told that the ratings result from a simple majority vote among members of the committee does not satisfy the requirements of a critical edition which, in the words of A.E. Housman, is an inappropriate name if an editor is not 'called to account and asked for his reasons'.[1]

Nor does the committee's explanation that the *UBSGNT*[4] letter-rating upgrades are founded upon a redefinition of the various levels in the evaluation of evidence criteria 'satisfy the requirements of a critical edition'. The fact that these rating changes have occurred in the *UBSGNT*[4] is somewhat problematic. However, of greater concern is the resulting lack of explanation that leaves users of the *UBSGNT* in the dark when it comes to matters concerning the details of the theory and methodology behind these changes. An adequate and more precise presentation of these facets should have been incorporated within the *UBSGNT*[4] Introduction. Instead, it would appear that brief allusion and insufficient defenses are given in their place. As it now stands, an unfounded letter-rating upgrade appears to have taken place and may instill in users of the *UBSGNT*[4] a false sense of textual optimism.

---

1. Elliott, 'The Fourth Edition', col. 18. See also A.E. Housman, *M. Manilius's Astronomicon* (5 vols.; London: Richards Press, 1930), V, p. xxxiii. Immediately following on pp. 18-19, Elliott goes on to say that 'Until Metzger's revised *Commentary* [the 1994 edition] is published to reveal the reasons for some of these changes in the voting for the rating of letters, we are left wondering what the new committee's motives were'. As explained in n. 21 of Chapter 3, it is unfortunate that for the most part Metzger's commentary does not address these issues.

Appendix I

Variants and Ratings Charts

Appendix I includes the data that are discussed in Chapter 2, Section 1. These charts are straightforward. Each biblical book is dealt with. All *UBSGNT* variant passages that have been assigned a letter-rating are situated under the heading '*VRNT*', meaning 'variant'. By simply locating a particular passage and moving horizontally from edition to edition, one can observe the exact changes made to the letter-rating in that variant. If a variant is absent from an edition, the backslash symbol (/) is used to signify this vacancy. The following examples demonstrate the usefulness of this appendix in aiding one to understand the rating changes that occur throughout the *UBSGNT* editions.

In the *UBSGNT*[1], Mt. 5.11 is represented by a *C* rating. In the *UBSGNT*[2] it is modified to a lower *D* rating. In the *UBSGNT*[3] and the *UBSGNT*[3corr.], the variant maintains its *D* rating. Yet, in the *UBSGNT*[4], Mt. 5.11 is once again altered to a *C* rating. Mt. 7.18 acts as a second illustration. From the *UBSGNT*[1] to the *UBSGNT*[3corr.], a constant *B* letter-rating occurs. However, in the *UBSGNT*[4] this variant has been removed from the edition. One final example is seen in the second variant of Mt. 11.2, where the backslash symbol (/) appears within each of the first four editions, revealing that this variant is not included in these earlier works. However, the *UBSGNT*[4] cites this verse as a *B* rated passage, confirming it as a new addition to the *UBSGNT* tradition.

The reader must keep in mind that this appendix records only the letter-ratings of the variant passage. Detailed explanations, manuscript citations, and specific reordering of variant options etc. are not represented in these charts. One should consult the relevant *UBSGNT* editions when working with individual passages or important textual issues. The reader may also wish to consult the few footnotes provided in this section in order to take advantage of additional information pertaining to the charts of Appendix I.

VARIANTS AND RATINGS CHART: MATTHEW						VARIANTS AND RATINGS CHART: MARK				
VRNT	UBS1	UBS2	UBS3	UBS3^C	UBS4	VRNT	UBS1	UBS2	UBS3	UBS3^C	UBS4
1.7-8	B	B	B	B	B	1.1	C	C	C	C	C
1.10	B	B	B	B	B	1.2	A	A	A	A	A
1.11	B	B	B	B	A	1.4	C	C	C	C	C
1.16	B	B	B	B	A	1.6	/	/	/	/	A
1.18	C	C	C	C	B	1.8	B	B	B	B	B
1.18	B	B	B	B	B	1.8	A	A	A	A	/
1.25	A	A	A	A	A	1.11	C	C	C	C	B
2.18	C	C	C	C	C	1.14	A	A	A	A	A
3.12	C	C	C	C	/	1.21	C	C	C	C	/
3.16	C	C	C	C	C	1.27	C	C	C	C	B
3.16	B	C	C	C	C	1.29	C	C	C	C	B
4.10	B	B	B	B	A	1.34	A	A	A	A	A
4.17	B	B	B	B	A	1.39	C	C	C	C	B
4.23	C	C	C	C	/	1.39	B	B	B	B	/
5.4-5	B	B	B	B	B	1.40	D	D	D	D	C
5.11	C	D	D	D	C	1.41	C	D	D	D	B
5.13	C	C	C	C	/	2.4	C	C	C	C	B
5.22	C	C	C	C	B	2.5	B	B	B	B	B
5.25	B	B	B	B	/	2.9	B	B	B	B	B
5.32	B	B	C	C	B	2.10	B	B	B	B	/
5.37	B	B	B	B	/	2.14	A	A	A	A	A
5.44	B	A	A	A	A	2.15-16	C	C	C	C	C
5.44	B	A	A	A	A	2.16	B	B	B	B	B
5.47	B	B	B	B	B	2.22	C	C	C	C	C
6.4	B	B	B	B	B	2.22	C	C	C	C	C
6.6	B	B	B	B	B	2.26	A	A	A	A	/
6.8	A	A	A	A	A	3.7-8	D	D	D	D	C
6.13	A	A	A	A	A	3.8	B	B	B	B	/
6.15	C	D	D	D	C	3.8	B	B	B	B	A
6.18	A	A	A	A	A	3.14	C	C	C	C	C
6.25	C	C	C	C	C	3.16	C	C	C	C	C
6.28	B	B	B	B	B	3.18	A	A	A	A	A
6.33	C	C	C	C	C	3.19	B	B	B	B	/
7.13	C	C	C	C	B	3.20	C	C	C	C	B
7.14	B	B	B	B	B	3.21	A	A	A	A	A
7.14	B	B	B	B	A	3.29	A	A	B	B	/
7.18	B	B	B	B	/	3.29	A	A	B	B	B
7.24	C	C	C	C	B	3.32	B	B	C	C	C
8.8	C	C	C	C	/	4.8	C	C	C	C	C
8.9	B	B	B	B	/	4.8	C	C	C	C	C
8.10	B	B	B	B	B	4.15	/	/	/	/	C
8.12	C	C	C	C	/	4.16	B	B	B	B	/
8.13	B	B	B	B	/	4.20	B	B	B	B	C
8.18	D	D	D	D	C	4.24	A	A	A	A	A
8.21	C	C	C	C	C	4.28	/	/	/	/	C
8.23	C	C	C	C	/	4.40	A	A	A	A	A
8.25	C	C	C	C	B	5.1	C	C	C	C	C
8.25	C	C	B	B	B	5.21	B	B	D	D	C
8.28	B	B	C	C	C	5.21	C	C	D	D	/
9.4	C	C	C	C	B	5.27	C	C	C	C	/
9.8	B	B	B	B	A	5.36	A	B	B	B	B
9.14	C	C	C	C	C	5.42	D	D	D	D	/
9.26	B	B	B	B	/	6.2	A	A	A	A	/
9.34	C	C	C	C	B	6.2	B	B	C	C	C
10.3	B	B	B	B	B	6.3	A	A	A	A	A
10.4	B	B	B	B	/	6.3	/	/	/	/	B
10.23	C	C	C	C	C	6.14	B	B	B	B	B

VARIANTS AND RATINGS CHART: MATTHEW

VRNT	UBS1	UBS2	UBS3	UBS3^C	UBS4
10.37	B	B	B	B	/
10.42	C	C	C	C	/
11.2	C	C	C	C	/
11.2	/	/	/	/	B
11.9	B	B	C	C	B
11.15	C	C	C	C	B
11.17	C	C	C	C	B
11.19	B	B	B	B	B
11.23	B	B	B	B	B
11.23	C	C	D	D	C
11.27	/	/	/	/	A
12.4	C	C	C	C	C
12.15	C	C	C	C	C
12.25	C	C	C	C	C
12.30	A	A	A	A	/
12.31	B	B	B	B	/
12.47	C	C	C	C	C
13.9	C	C	C	C	B
13.13	B	B	B	B	B
13.35	C	C	C	C	C
13.35	C	C	C	C	C
13.40	C	C	C	C	/
13.43	C	C	C	C	B
13.44	C	C	C	C	/
13.55	B	B	B	B	B
14.3	C	C	C	C	/
14.3	C	B	B	B	A
14.9	B	B	B	B	B
14.22	C	C	C	C	/
14.22	B	B	B	B	/
14.24	D	D	D	D	C
14.27	D	D	D	D	/
14.29	B	B	B	B	B
14.30	C	C	C	C	C
15.4	C	C	C	C	B
15.6	D	D	D	D	C
15.6	B	B	B	B	B
15.14	C	C	C	C	C
15.15	C	C	C	C	C
15.26	C	C	C	C	/
15.31	C	C	C	C	C
15.36	B	B	B	B	/
15.38	D	D	D	D	/
15.39	C	C	C	C	C
16.2-3	C	C	D	D	C
16.5	A	A	A	A	/
16.8	C	C	C	C	/
16.12	D	D	D	D	C
16.13	B	B	B	B	B
16.20	/	/	/	/	B
16.21	C	C	C	C	/
16.27	/	/	/	/	B
17.2	/	/	/	/	A
17.4	/	/	/	/	B
17.10	C	C	C	C	/
17.15	B	B	C	C	/
17.20	B	B	B	B	A
17.20	B	B	B	B	A

VARIANTS AND RATINGS CHART: MARK

VRNT	UBS1	UBS2	UBS3	UBS3^C	UBS4
6.20	C	C	D	D	C
6.22	D	D	D	D	C
6.23	C	C	C	C	C
6.23	C	C	D	D	C
6.33	B	B	B	B	B
6.39	B	B	B	B	/
6.41	C	C	C	C	C
6.44	C	C	C	C	C
6.45	/	/	/	/	A
6.47	C	C	C	C	B
6.50	B	B	B	B	/
6.51	/	/	/	/	C
6.51	C	C	C	C	B
7.3	A	A	A	A	A
7.4	A	A	A	A	A
7.4	A	A	B	B	B
7.4	C	C	C	C	C
7.6	B	B	B	B	/
7.7-8	A	A	A	A	A
7.9	C	C	D	D	D
7.15	B	B	B	B	A
7.19	A	A	A	A	A
7.24	A	A	A	A	B
7.28	B	B	B	B	B
7.31	A	A	A	A	A
7.35	C	C	C	C	C
7.35	B	B	B	B	/
7.37	C	C	C	C	/
8.7	B	B	B	B	B
8.10	B	B	B	B	B
8.13	C	C	C	C	/
8.15	C	C	C	C	/
8.15	A	A	A	A	A
8.16	C	C	C	C	/
8.16	C	C	C	C	/
8.17	B	B	B	B	/
8.26	B	B	B	B	B
8.35	C	C	C	C	/
8.38	A	B	B	B	B
8.38	B	B	B	B	A
9.14	/	/	/	/	B
9.23	B	B	B	B	B
9.24	A	A	A	A	A
9.29	A	A	A	A	A
9.34	B	B	B	B	/
9.38	C	C	C	C	B
9.41	A	A	A	A	A
9.42	C	C	C	C	C
9.43	A	B	B	B	/
9.43	A	A	A	A	A
9.45	A	A	A	A	A
9.45	A	A	A	A	A
9.49	B	B	B	B	B
10.1	C	C	C	C	C
10.2	C	C	C	C	B
10.6	B	B	B	B	B
10.7	C	C	D	D	C
10.13	/	/	/	/	A

VARIANTS AND RATINGS CHART: MATTHEW

VRNT	UBS1	UBS2	UBS3	UBS3^C	UBS4
17.22	C	C	C	C	B
17.26	C	C	C	C	B
18.7	C	C	C	C	/
18.10	B	B	B	B	B
18.14	C	C	C	C	C
18.15	C	C	C	C	C
18.19	/	/	/	/	C
18.21	C	C	C	C	/
18.26	B	B	B	B	A
18.34	C	C	C	C	/
19.3	C	C	C	C	/
19.3	C	C	C	C	/
19.4	B	B	B	B	B
19.7	C	C	C	C	C
19.9	B	B	C	C	B
19.9	B	B	C	C	B
19.10	C	C	C	C	C
19.11	C	C	C	C	C
19.16	B	B	B	B	A
19.17	B	B	B	B	A
19.20	/	/	/	/	A
19.22	C	C	C	C	/
19.24	/	/	/	/	A
19.25	B	B	B	B	/
19.29	C	C	C	C	C
19.29	B	B	B	B	B
20.10	/	/	/	/	C
20.15	C	C	C	C	C
20.16	/	/	/	/	A
20.17	C	C	C	C	/
20.17	C	C	C	C	C
20.17	B	B	B	B	/
20.22	/	/	/	/	A
20.23	/	/	/	/	C
20.26	C	C	C	C	B
20.30	C	C	D	D	C
20.31	/	/	/	/	C
21.12	B	B	B	B	B
21.29-31	C	C	C	C	C
21.39	B	B	B	B	A
21.44	C	C	C	C	C
22.10	B	B	B	B	B
22.23	A	B	B	B	B
22.30	C	C	C	C	B
22.32	C	C	C	C	C
22.35	C	C	C	C	C
23.4	C	C	C	C	C
23.9	/	/	/	/	B
23.13	B	B	B	B	A
23.19	C	C	C	C	B
23.23	/	/	/	/	C
23.25	/	/	/	/	A
23.26	D	D	D	D	D
23.38	B	B	C	C	B
24.6	B	B	B	B	B
24.7	/	/	/	/	B
24.31	B	B	B	B	B
24.36	C	C	C	C	B

VARIANTS AND RATINGS CHART: MARK

VRNT	UBS1	UBS2	UBS3	UBS3^C	UBS4
10.14	C	C	C	C	/
10.19	C	C	C	C	A
10.21	/	/	/	/	A
10.24	C	C	C	C	B
10.25	/	/	/	/	A
10.26	B	B	B	B	B
10.31	/	/	/	/	C
10.34	A	A	A	A	A
10.36	/	/	/	/	C
10.40	A	A	A	A	A
10.40	B	B	B	B	A
10.43	A	A	A	A	A
10.46	C	C	C	C	/
10.47	A	A	A	A	/
11.3	B	B	B	B	B
11.19	C	C	C	C	C
11.22	B	B	B	B	B
11.24	A	A	A	A	A
11.25	A	A	A	A	A
11.31	C	C	C	C	/
11.32	B	B	B	B	B
12.23	D	D	D	D	C
12.26	/	/	/	/	C
12.34	/	/	/	/	C
12.36	C	C	C	C	C
12.40	A	A	A	A	/
12.41	A	B	B	B	B
13.2	B	B	B	B	B
13.8	B	B	B	B	B
13.22	B	B	B	B	/
13.33	D	C	C	C	B
14.4	C	C	C	C	/
14.5	B	B	B	B	A
14.10	B	B	B	B	/
14.20	B	B	B	B	/
14.24	B	B	B	B	A
14.25	C	C	C	C	C
14.30	B	B	B	B	/
14.30	C	C	C	C	C
14.39	A	A	A	A	A
14.41	B	B	B	B	B
14.52	C	C	C	C	/
14.60	A	B	B	B	/
14.65	/	/	/	/	A
14.65	C	C	C	C	B
14.68	D	D	D	D	C
14.72	C	C	C	C	B
14.72	B	B	B	B	B
14.72	B	B	B	B	B
15.1	B	B	B	B	/
15.8	B	B	B	B	B
15.10	B	B	B	B	/
15.12	D	D	D	D	C
15.12	C	C	C	C	C
15.25	A	A	A	A	/
15.27	A	A	A	A	A
15.34	B	B	B	B	B
15.39	B	B	B	B	/

VARIANTS AND RATINGS CHART: MATTHEW

VRNT	UBS1	UBS2	UBS3	UBS3^C	UBS4
24.38	/	/	/	/	C
24.42	/	/	/	/	B
25.1	C	C	C	C	B
25.13	/	/	/	/	A
25.15-16	C	C	C	C	B
25.17	B	B	B	B	/
25.41	B	B	B	B	/
26.14	B	B	B	B	/
26.20	C	C	C	C	C
26.27	C	C	C	C	B
26.28	B	B	B	B	B
26.61	C	C	C	C	/
26.63	C	C	C	C	/
26.71	B	B	B	B	B
27.2	C	C	C	C	B
27.4	B	B	B	B	A
27.5	D	D	D	D	/
27.9	/	/	/	/	A
27.10	C	C	C	C	B
27.16	C	C	C	C	C
27.17	C	C	C	C	C
27.24	B	B	B	B	B
27.28	B	B	B	B	B
27.29	B	B	B	B	B
27.35	/	/	/	/	A
27.40	C	C	C	C	C
27.42	B	B	B	B	B
27.43	C	C	C	C	/
27.49	B	B	B	B	B
27.64	A	A	A	A	/
28.6	B	B	B	B	A
28.7	C	C	C	C	/
28.8	/	/	/	/	B
28.9	B	B	B	B	A
28.11	/	/	/	/	B
28.15	/	/	/	/	C
28.17	C	C	C	C	/
28.20	B	B	B	B	A

VARIANTS AND RATINGS CHART: LUKE

VRNT	UBS1	UBS2	UBS3	UBS3^C	UBS4
1.17	A	A	A	A	/
1.28	B	B	B	B	A
1.35	B	B	B	B	A
1.37	B	B	B	B	/
1.46	B	B	B	B	A
1.66	B	B	B	B	A

VARIANTS AND RATINGS CHART: MARK

VRNT	UBS1	UBS2	UBS3	UBS3^C	UBS4
15.39	B	C	C	C	C
15.44	C	C	C	C	B
16.1	A	A	A	A	A
16.2	/	/	/	/	A
16.8	/	/	/	/	A
16.9	A	A	A	A	/
16.14	A	A	A	A	/
16.14-15	A	A	A	A	A
16.17	B	B	B	B	B
16.18	C	C	C	C	C
16.19	C	C	C	C	C
16.20	B	B	B	B	B
Short End	A	A	A	A	A
Short End	C	C	C	C	B
Short End		see *UBS*, p. 198^i			/

VARIANTS AND RATINGS CHART: JOHN

VRNT	UBS1	UBS2	UBS3	UBS3^C	UBS4
1.3-4	C	C	C	C	B
1.4	A	A	A	A	A
1.13	A	A	A	A	A
1.13	/	/	/	/	A
1.15	A	A	A	A	/
1.18	B	B	B	B	B
1.19	/	/	/	/	C
1.21	D	D	D	D	C
1.26	B	B	B	B	B
1.28	C	C	C	C	C
1.34	B	B	B	B	B
1.41	B	B	B	B	B
1.42	B	B	B	B	B
2.12	/	/	/	/	C
2.12	B	B	B	B	/
2.15	A	B	B	B	B
2.24	/	/	/	/	C
3.5	A	A	A	A	/
3.13	A	C	C	C	B
3.15	B	B	B	B	B
3.20	C	C	C	C	/
3.25	C	C	C	C	B
3.28	C	C	C	C	/
3.31-32	C	C	C	C	C
3.34	/	/	/	/	B
4.1	B	B	C	C	C
4.3	/	/	/	/	A
4.5	/	/	/	/	A
4.9	C	C	C	C	A

i.   Occasionally in these charts the phrase 'see *UBS*, p. ....' occurs. The reasons for this phrase are: 1) the variant should be specifically examined to see how it has changed in each edition or to gain further information that the *UBSGNT* editors have provided (a good example is Jn 5.3-4); 2) the variant has not been given a letter-rating but again, further information is provided pertaining to the variant (a good example here is Jn 21.25 in the *UBSGNT*[3] and *UBSGNT*[3corr.]); and 3) there have been major changes to the ordering of the variant that require a specific examination. Compare Jn 21.25 in the *UBSGNT*[3] and *UBSGNT*[3corr.] with the *UBSGNT*[4] where the actual variant options are changed in their order.

VARIANTS AND RATINGS CHART: LUKE   *VARIANTS AND RATINGS CHART: JOHN*

VRNT	UBS1	UBS2	UBS3	UBS3^C	UBS4		UBS1	UBS2	UBS3	UBS3^C	UBS4
1.68	B	B	B	B	/	4.11	B	B	C	C	C
1.70	B	B	B	B	/	4.25	A	A	A	A	/
1.74	C	C	C	C	B	4.35-36	/	/	/	/	B
1.78	C	C	C	C	B	4.51	B	B	B	B	B
2.9	C	C	C	C	B	5.1	A	A	A	A	A
2.11	A	A	A	A	A	5.2	B	B	B	B	/
2.14	B	B	B	B	A	5.2	D	D	D	D	C
2.15	D	D	D	D	/	5.3	A	A	A	A	A
2.22	C	C	C	C	/	5.3	A	A	A	A	A
2.33	B	B	B	B	B	Vs. 4 added		see *UBS*, pp. 338, 330			
2.38	B	B	B	B	A	Vnt. 6; v. 4	B	B	B	B	/
3.9	C	C	C	C	/	Vnt. 7; v. 4	B	B	B	B	/
3.22	C	C	C	C	B	Vnt. 8; v. 4	B	B	B	B	/
3.32	B	B	B	B	B	Vnt. 9; v. 4	A	A	A	A	/
3.33	C	C	C	C	C	Vnt. 10; v. 4	C	C	C	C	/
4.4	B	B	B	B	B	5.9	B	B	B	B	/
4.17	C	C	C	C	B	5.17	C	C	C	C	C
4.18	/	/	/	/	A	5.32	B	B	B	B	A
4.44	B	B	B	B	B	5.44	B	B	B	B	B
5.17	C	C	C	C	B	6.1	B	B	B	B	A
5.17	B	B	B	B	A	6.14	B	B	B	B	B
5.33	C	C	C	C	B	6.15	B	B	B	B	A
5.38	B	B	B	B	B	6.22	A	A	A	A	A
5.39	/	/	/	/	C	6.23	B	C	C	C	C
5.39a^{ii}	B	B	B	B	5.39b A	6.23	C	C	C	C	B
5.39b	B	B	B	B	5.39a A	6.27	B	B	B	B	A
6.1	C	C	C	C	C	6.36	C	C	C	C	C
6.1	B	B	B	B	/	6.42	B	B	B	B	/
6.2	B	B	B	B	/	6.42	C	C	C	C	/
6.4	C	C	C	C	A	6.47	A	A	A	A	A
6.4	/	/	/	/	A	6.52	C	C	C	C	C
6.5	C	C	C	C	B	6.55	C	C	C	C	/
6.10	C	C	C	C	A	6.58	A	A	A	A	A
6.16	C	C	C	C	/	6.64	B	B	B	B	B
6.26	C	C	C	C	/	6.69	A	A	A	A	A
6.31	C	C	C	C	B	6.71	C	C	C	C	/
6.35	C	C	C	C	B	7.1	B	B	B	B	A
6.38	C	C	C	C	/	7.4	C	C	C	C	/
6.42	C	C	C	C	/	7.8	C	C	C	C	C
6.48	B	B	B	B	A	7.9	B	B	B	B	B
7.7	C	C	C	C	B	7.10	B	B	D	D	C
7.10	C	C	C	C	A	7.12	D	D	D	D	/
7.11	C	C	C	C	B	7.31	B	B	B	B	/
7.11	C	C	C	C	B	7.36		see *UBS*, pp. 353, 344			
7.19	C	C	C	C	C	7.37	B	B	B	B	B
7.28	C	C	C	C	/	7.39	C	C	C	C	B
7.28	C	C	C	C	B	7.39	A	A	A	A	A
7.32	/	/	/	/	B	7.46	B	B	B	B	B
7.35	/	/	/	/	B	7.52	/	/	/	/	B
7.39	C	C	C	C	A	7.53–8.11	A	A	A	A	A^{iii}
7.42	C	C	C	C	/	8.16	B	B	B	B	/

     ii.   5.39 is listed with an 'a' and 'b' suffix in the last two of its three references to show the change in order within the *UBSGNT*[4].

     iii.   Metzger notes that the citation of an *A* rating at Jn 7.53–8.11, the pericope concerning the adulterer, is incorrectly applied to the inclusion of this variant into the New Testament text instead of to its absence. See Metzger, *The Text of the New Testament*, p. 280.

VARIANTS AND RATINGS CHART: LUKE

VRNT	UBS1	UBS2	UBS3	UBS3^C	UBS4
7.45	/	/	/	/	A
8.3	B	B	B	B	B
8.5	B	B	B	B	/
8.26	D	D	D	D	C
8.27	C	C	C	C	/
8.37	D	D	D	D	C
8.43	D	D	D	D	C
8.44	C	C	C	C	B
8.45	B	B	B	B	B
8.45	C	C	C	C	B
8.49	C	C	C	C	B
9.1	C	C	C	C	B
9.2	C	C	C	C	C
9.3	C	C	C	C	C
9.10	/	/	/	/	B
9.26	B	B	B	B	A
9.35	B	B	B	B	B
9.47	C	C	C	C	C
9.49	/	/	/	/	B
9.54	C	C	C	C	B
9.55	C	/	/	/	/
9.55-56	/	C	C	C	A
9.59	C	C	C	C	C
9.62	/	/	/	/	C
9.62	C	C	C	C	C
9.62	C	C	C	C	/
10.1	C	C	C	C	/
10.1	C	C	C	C	C
10.15	D	D	D	D	C
10.17	C	C	C	C	C
10.21	C	C	C	C	C
10.22	B	B	B	B	A
10.38	C	C	C	C	B
10.41-42	C	C	C	C	C
11.2	A	A	A	A	A
11.2	B	B	B	B	A
11.2	A	A	A	A	A
11.4	A	A	A	A	A
11.10	C	C	C	C	C
11.11	B	B	B	C	B
11.11	C	C	C	C	C
11.12	C	C	C	C	C
11.13	D	D	D	D	C
11.13	B	B	B	B	B
11.14	D	D	D	D	C
11.23	A	A	A	A	A
11.24	C	C	C	C	C
11.25	B	B	B	B	B
11.33	D	D	D	D	C
11.42	B	B	B	B	B
11.48	C	C	C	C	B
12.1	C	C	C	C	/
12.11	C	C	C	C	/
12.14	B	B	B	B	B
12.20	D	D	D	D	/
12.21	B	B	B	B	A
12.22	C	C	C	C	C
12.27	D	D	D	D	B

VARIANTS AND RATINGS CHART: JOHN

VRNT	UBS1	UBS2	UBS3	UBS3^C	UBS4
8.16	C	C	C	C	A
8.25	B	B	B	B	B
8.34	C	C	C	C	A
8.38	B	B	B	B	B
8.38	C	C	C	C	B
8.38	C	C	C	C	/
8.39	C	C	C	C	B
8.44	D	D	D	D	C
8.53	C	C	C	C	/
8.54	C	C	C	C	B
8.57	B	B	B	B	B
8.59	A	A	A	A	A
9.4	C	C	D	D	C
9.4	C	C	D	D	/
9.6	B	B	B	B	/
9.11	C	C	C	C	/
9.28	C	C	C	C	/
9.35	A	A	A	A	A
9.36	C	C	C	C	/
9.38-39	/	/	/	/	B
10.8	C	C	C	C	C
10.11	B	B	B	B	B
10.15	C	C	C	C	B
10.16	C	C	C	C	C
10.18	C	C	C	C	B
10.19	/	/	/	/	B
10.22	C	C	C	C	B
10.26	A	B	B	B	B
10.29	D	D	D	D	D
10.29	C	C	C	C	/
10.32	C	C	C	C	/
10.34	B	B	B	B	/
10.38	C	C	C	C	B
10.39	/	/	/	/	C
11.19	B	B	B	B	/
11.21	/	/	/	/	A
11.25	B	B	B	B	A
11.31	B	B	B	B	B
11.45	B	B	B	B	/
11.50	B	B	B	B	B
12.1	B	B	B	B	A
12.4	C	C	C	C	/
12.8	C	C	C	C	A
12.9	C	C	C	C	C
12.12	C	C	C	C	/
12.17	C	C	C	C	B
12.28	B	B	B	B	A
12.32	D	D	D	D	B
12.40	C	C	C	C	C
12.41	B	B	B	B	B
13.2	C	C	C	C	B
13.2	C	C	C	C	C
13.10	B	B	B	B	B
13.18	D	D	D	D	C
13.24	B	B	B	B	/
13.26	C	C	C	C	C
13.26	C	C	C	C	C
13.26	C	C	C	C	/

VARIANTS AND RATINGS CHART: LUKE

VRNT	UBS1	UBS2	UBS3	UBS3^C	UBS4
12.31	C	C	C	C	B
12.39	B	B	B	B	B
12.56	C	C	C	C	B
13.7	C	C	C	C	C
13.9	C	C	C	C	B
13.19	C	C	C	C	B
13.27	C	C	C	C	C
13.27	C	C	C	C	C
13.35	/	/	/	/	B
13.35	D	D	D	D	C
14.5	B	B	B	B	B
14.17	C	C	C	C	C
15.1	/	/	/	/	A
15.16	C	C	C	C	B
15.21	B	B	B	B	A
16.12	B	B	B	B	A
16.14	C	C	C	C	/
16.21	B	B	B	B	B
16.21	/	/	/	/	A
16.22-23	/	/	/	/	A
17.3	/	/	/	/	A
17.9	C	C	C	C	B
17.23	D	D	D	D	C
17.23	C	C	C	C	/
17.24	C	C	C	C	C
17.33	C	C	C	C	B
17.35	B	B	B	B	A
18.11	D	D	D	D	C
18.24	D	D	D	D	C
18.25	/	/	/	/	A
19.15	C	C	C	C	B
19.25	D	D	C	C	A
19.38	C	C	C	C	C
19.42	C	C	C	C	B
19.42	C	C	C	C	B
20.9	C	C	C	C	C
20.20	C	C	C	C	/
20.26	C	C	C	C	/
20.27	C	C	C	C	C
20.34	/	/	/	/	A
20.36	/	/	/	/	B
20.45	C	C	C	C	C
21.4	B	B	B	B	B
21.6	C	C	C	C	/
21.11	D	D	D	D	C
21.19	D	D	D	D	C
21.35	C	C	C	C	B
21.38	A	A	A	A	A
22.16	C	C	C	C	B
22.17-20	B	B	C	C	B
22.31	/	/	/	/	B
22.42	C	C	/	/	/
22.43-44	/	/	C	C	A
22.52	C	C	C	C	/
22.62	C	C	C	C	A
22.68	C	C	C	C	B
23.11	C	C	C	C	C
23.15	C	C	C	C	A

VARIANTS AND RATINGS CHART: JOHN

VRNT	UBS1	UBS2	UBS3	UBS3^C	UBS4
13.32	C	C	C	C	C
13.32	B	B	B	B	B
13.37	C	C	C	C	A
14.2	C	C	C	C	B
14.4	C	C	C	C	B
14.7	C	C	C	C	C
14.7	C	C	C	C	C
14.11	B	B	B	B	B
14.14	B	B	B	B	A
14.14	B	B	B	B	B
14.15	C	C	C	C	C
14.17	D	D	D	D	C
14.22	A	A	A	A	A
15.8	D	D	D	D	C
16.3	C	C	C	C	/
16.4	C	C	C	C	B
16.13	B	B	B	B	B
16.16	/	/	/	/	A
16.18	/	/	/	/	C
16.22	C	C	C	C	B
16.22	C	C	C	C	B
16.23	/	/	/	/	B
16.23	C	C	C	C	C
16.27	C	C	C	C	C
16.28	C	C	C	C	C
17.1	C	C	C	C	B
17.11	C	C	C	C	B
17.12	C	C	C	C	B
17.14	/	/	/	/	A
17.21	C	C	C	C	B
17.23	/	/	/	/	A
17.24	B	B	B	B	B
18.5	C	C	C	C	C
18.13	see *UBS*, pp. 400, 402				/
18.16	C	C	C	C	/
18.13-27	A	A	A	A	A
18.30	B	B	B	B	B
19.16	/	/	/	/	B
19.24	/	/	/	/	C
19.29	A	A	A	A	A
19.39	C	C	C	C	B
20.11	C	C	C	C	/
20.16	B	B	B	B	/
20.17	C	C	C	C	/
20.19	/	/	/	/	A
20.21	/	/	/	/	C
20.23	B	B	B	B	B
20.30	C	C	C	C	C
20.31	C	C	C	C	C
21.15	/	/	/	/	B
21.16	/	/	/	/	B
21.17	/	/	/	/	B
21.18	C	C	C	C	/
21.23	/	/	/	/	C
21.24	see *UBS*, p. 413		/	/	/
21.25	/	/	see *UBS*, pp. 415, 406		
7.53–8.11	Insert end Jn.		Insert at 7.52		
7.53–8.11	A	A	A	A	A

VARIANTS AND RATINGS CHART: LUKE

VRNT	UBS1	UBS2	UBS3	UBS3^C	UBS4
23.16	B	B	B	B	A
23.23	C	C	C	C	B
23.34	C	C	C	C	A
23.38	B	B	B	B	A
23.42	C	C	C	C	B
23.45	B	B	B	B	B
24.3	D	D	D	D	B
24.6	D	D	D	D	B
24.9	D	D	D	D	/
24.10	C	C	C	C	B
24.12	D	D	D	D	B
24.13	B	B	B	B	B
24.17	/	/	/	/	B
24.19	C	C	C	C	B
24.32	C	C	C	C	C
24.36	D	D	D	D	B
24.40	D	D	D	D	B
24.42	B	B	B	B	B
24.47	D	D	D	D	B
24.47	C	C	C	C	B
24.49	C	C	C	C	C
24.51	D	D	D	D	B
24.52	D	D	D	D	B
24.53	C	C	C	C	B
24.53	B	B	B	B	A
24.53	/	/	see *UBS*, p. 319		/

VARIANTS AND RATINGS CHART: ACTS

VRNT	UBS1	UBS2	UBS3	UBS3^C	UBS4
1.2	/	/	/	/	A
1.9	B	B	B	B	/
1.11	C	C	C	C	A
1.18	A	A	A	A	/
1.23	/	/	/	/	A
1.25	B	B	B	B	B
1.26	B	B	B	B	B
1.26	A	A	A	A	/
2.5	B	B	B	B	B
2.7	B	B	B	B	/
2.16	C	D	D	D	B
2.18	C	C	C	C	A
2.18	B	B	B	B	A
2.19	B	B	B	B	A
2.24	B	B	B	B	A
2.30	B	B	B	B	B
2.37	B	B	B	B	A
2.43	C	C	C	C	C
2.44	D	D	D	D	A
2.47–3.1	B	B	B	B	B
3.6	B	B	D	D	C
3.13	C	C	C	C	/
3.14	/	/	/	/	A
3.21	C	C	C	C	B
3.22	B	B	B	B	B
3.22	C	C	C	C	C
3.25	C	C	C	C	C
4.1	C	C	C	C	B

VARIANTS AND RATINGS CHART: JOHN

VRNT	UBS1	UBS2	UBS3	UBS3^C	UBS4
8.2	B	B	B	B	/
8.3	C	C	C	C	/
8.4	A	A	A	A	/
8.6	/	/	/	/	A
8.7	/	/	/	/	A
8.7	/	/	/	/	A
8.8	A	A	A	A	/
8.9	A	A	A	A	A
8.9	A	A	A	A	A
8.10	A	A	A	A	A
8.10	A	A	A	A	A

VARIANTS AND RATINGS CHART: ROMANS

VRNT	UBS1	UBS2	UBS3	UBS3^C	UBS4
1.1	/	/	/	/	B
1.7	B	B	B	B	A
1.7	B	B	B	B	/
1.13	A	A	A	A	A
1.15	B	B	B	B	A
1.29	C	C	C	C	C
1.31	/	/	/	/	A
2.2	B	B	B	B	/
2.16	/	/	/	/	C
3.7	C	C	C	C	B
3.9	B	B	B	B	/
3.12	C	C	C	C	C
3.22	B	B	B	B	B
3.25	B	B	D	D	C
3.26	C	C	C	C	/
3.28	C	C	C	C	B
4.1	B	B	B	B	B
4.11	C	C	C	C	C
4.15	/	/	/	/	B
4.19	C	C	C	C	C
4.19	C	C	C	C	C
4.22	C	C	C	C	C
5.1	C	C	C	C	A
5.2	C	C	C	C	C
5.6	C	D	D	D	C
5.12	C	C	C	C	/
5.17	B	B	B	B	/
6.4	/	/	/	/	A
6.8	/	/	/	/	A
6.11	B	B	B	B	A
6.12	C	C	C	C	B
6.16	C	C	C	C	/
7.6	B	B	B	B	/
7.14	/	/	/	/	A
7.18	C	C	C	C	B
7.20	/	/	/	/	C
7.22	/	/	/	/	A
7.23	B	B	B	B	/
7.25	C	C	C	C	B
8.1	A	A	A	A	A
8.2	C	C	D	D	B
8.11	D	D	D	D	/
8.11	C	C	C	C	B

VARIANTS AND RATINGS CHART: ACTS						VARIANTS AND RATINGS CHART: ROMANS				
VRNT	UBS1	UBS2	UBS3	UBS3^C	UBS4	VRNT	UBS1	UBS2	UBS3	UBS3^C	UBS4
4.6	B	B	C	C	A	8.21	C	C	C	C	A
4.8	C	C	C	C	B	8.23	C	C	C	C	A
4.10	A	A	A	A	A	8.24	C	C	C	C	B
4.12	A	A	A	A	A	8.24	C	C	C	C	B
4.24	B	B	B	B	B	8.26	B	B	B	B	A
4.25	D	D	D	D	C	8.28	C	C	C	C	B
4.33	C	C	C	C	C	8.34	/	/	/	/	C
5.3	C	C	C	C	B	8.34	C	C	C	C	/
5.16	C	C	C	C	B	8.35	B	B	B	B	A
5.17	/	/	/	/	A	8.38	/	/	/	/	A
5.28	C	C	C	C	C	9.4	B	B	C	C	B
5.29	/	/	/	/	A	9.23	B	B	B	B	A
5.32	C	C	C	rtng^{iv}	B	9.28	A	A	A	A	A
5.32	B	B	B	B	/	9.32	B	B	B	B	B
5.33	C	C	C	C	B	9.33	B	B	B	B	A
5.37	B	B	B	B	A	10.1	A	A	A	A	A
5.37	C	C	C	C	/	10.5	C	C	C	C	/
5.39	/	/	/	/	A	10.5	C	C	C	C	/
6.3	C	C	C	C	C	10.9	B	B	B	B	/
6.7	B	B	B	B	B	10.15	A	A	A	A	A
6.9	B	B	B	B	/	10.17	B	B	B	B	A
7.16	D	D	D	D	C	11.1	B	B	B	B	A
7.17	C	C	C	C	B	11.6	A	A	A	A	A
7.18	C	C	C	C	C	11.16	B	B	B	B	/
7.19	C	C	C	C	C	11.17	C	C	C	C	B
7.32	C	C	C	C	/	11.21	C	C	C	C	C
7.38	B	B	B	B	B	11.25	/	/	/	/	C
7.46	C	C	C	C	B	11.31	B	B	D	D	C
8.5	/	/	/	/	C	11.32	B	B	B	B	A
8.10	B	B	B	B	A	12.11	A	A	A	A	A
8.18	C	C	C	C	B	12.14	C	C	C	C	C
8.24	/	/	/	/	A	13.1	C	C	C	C	A
8.36	A	A	A	A	A	13.5	B	B	B	B	/
8.39	/	/	/	/	A	13.9	B	B	B	B	B
9.4	A	A	A	A	/	13.11	C	C	C	C	B
9.5-6	A	A	A	A	/	13.12	/	/	/	/	A
9.12	C	C	C	C	C	14.4	A	A	A	A	A
9.29	/	/	/	/	A	14.5	C	C	C	C	C
9.31	B	B	B	B	A	14.9	B	B	B	B	A
10.5	B	B	B	B	B	14.10	B	B	B	B	B
10.11	C	C	C	C	C	14.12	B	C	C	C	C
10.12	B	B	B	B	B	14.16	C	C	C	C	/
10.16	C	C	C	C	B	14.19	D	D	D	D	D
10.17	C	C	C	C	/	14.21	C	C	C	C	B
10.19	C	C	C	C	B	14.22	C	C	C	C	C
10.24	C	C	C	C	C	14.23	A	A	A	A	A
10.30	D	D	D	D	B	15.7	B	B	B	B	A
10.32	C	C	C	C	B	15.19	C	C	C	C	C
10.33	C	C	C	C	/	15.23	B	B	B	B	/
10.33	C	C	C	C	C	15.24	/	/	/	/	A
10.36	C	C	C	C	C	15.29	B	B	B	B	A
10.37	/	/	/	/	B	15.31	B	B	B	B	A
10.40	C	C	C	C	C	15.32	C	C	C	C	C

iv.　Apparently the editors left the rating out of Acts 5.32 in the *UBSGNT*[3corr.] edition. It is most likely a *C* rating based upon the previous editions and in the light of the similarity of ratings from the *UBSGNT*[1] to the *UBSGNT*[3corr.].

VARIANTS AND RATINGS CHART: ACTS

VRNT	UBS1	UBS2	UBS3	UBS3^C	UBS4
10.48	C	C	C	C	B
11.2	/	/	/	/	A
11.9	C	C	C	C	/
11.11	C	C	C	C	C
11.12	C	C	C	C	C
11.17	/	/	/	/	A
11.17	/	/	/	/	A
11.20	C	C	C	C	C
11.22	/	/	/	/	C
11.23	B	B	B	B	B
11.28	/	/	/	/	A
12.10	/	/	/	/	A
12.18	C	C	C	C	/
12.23	/	/	/	/	A
12.25	D	D	D	D	C
13.14	B	B	B	B	/
13.18	D	D	D	D	C
13.19	C	C	C	C	B
13.20	D	D	D	D	C
13.23	B	B	B	B	B
13.25	/	/	/	/	B
13.26	B	B	B	B	B
13.27	/	/	/	/	A
13.33	D	D	D	D	C
13.33	D	D	D	D	B
13.40	C	C	C	C	B
13.42	A	A	A	A	A
13.42	C	C	C	C	B
13.43	/	/	/	/	A
13.43	/	/	/	/	A
13.44	C	C	C	C	C
13.45	B	B	B	B	B
13.48	C	C	C	C	C
14.18	C	C	B	B	/
14.19	C	C	C	C	/
14.19	C	C	C	C	/
14.25	/	/	/	/	B
15.2	/	/	/	/	A
15.6	/	/	/	/	A
15.7	/	/	/	/	A
15.7	B	B	B	B	/
15.12	/	/	/	/	A
15.17-18	/	/	/	/	B
15.18	C	C	C	C	/
15.20	B	B	B	B	A
15.20	C	C	C	C	C
15.20	A	A	A	A	A
15.23	B	B	B	B	/
15.23	B	B	B	B	B
15.24	C	C	C	C	C
15.24	B	B	B	B	A
15.25	C	C	C	C	C
15.29	B	B	B	B	B
15.29	B	B	B	B	A
15.29	B	B	B	B	A
15.33	B	B	B	B	A
15.40	/	/	/	/	B
15.41	/	/	/	/	A

VARIANTS AND RATINGS CHART: ROMANS

VRNT	UBS1	UBS2	UBS3	UBS3^C	UBS4
15.33	A	A	B	B	A
16.7	A	A	A	A	A
16.7	C	C	C	C	/
16.15	A	A	A	A	A
16.20	B	B	B	B	A
16.23	B	B	B	B	A
16.25-27	C	C	C	C	C
16.27	C	C	C	C	/
16.27	C	C	C	C	A

VARIANTS AND RATINGS CHART: 1 COR.

VRNT	UBS1	UBS2	UBS3	UBS3^C	UBS4
1.1	/	/	/	/	B
1.4	B	B	B	B	A
1.8	C	C	C	C	C
1.13	C	C	B	B	A
1.14	B	B	D	D	C
1.28	C	C	C	C	B
2.1	C	C	C	C	B
2.4	D	D	D	D	C
2.10	C	C	C	C	B
2.14	B	C	C	C	/
2.15	D	D	D	D	C
2.16	/	/	/	/	B
3.2	/	/	/	/	A
3.3	C	C	C	C	B
3.5	/	/	/	/	A
3.10	C	C	C	C	/
3.17	C	C	C	C	B
4.17	C	C	C	C	/
4.17	/	/	/	/	C
5.4	D	D	D	D	C
5.5	C	C	C	C	B
5.13	C	C	C	C	/
6.11	C	C	C	C	C
6.14	/	/	/	/	B
6.20	B	A	A	A	A
7.5	A	A	A	A	A
7.7	B	B	B	B	B
7.13	D	D	D	D	/
7.14	B	B	B	B	A
7.15	C	C	C	C	B
7.34	D	D	D	D	D
7.40	/	/	/	/	A
8.2	B	B	B	B	/
8.3	B	B	B	B	A
8.3	C	C	C	C	/
8.7	B	B	B	B	A
8.12	A	A	A	A	A
9.15	C	C	C	C	B
9.20	A	A	A	A	A
9.22	/	/	/	/	A
10.2	C	C	C	C	C
10.9	B	C	C	C	B
10.10	C	C	C	C	/
10.11	C	C	C	C	B
10.20	C	C	C	C	C

VARIANTS AND RATINGS CHART: ACTS

VRNT	UBS1	UBS2	UBS3	UBS3^C	UBS4
16.7	/	/	/	/	A
16.10	B	B	B	B	B
16.11	/	/	/	/	B
16.12	D	D	D	D	D
16.13	D	D	D	D	C
16.17	B	B	B	B	B
16.32	B	B	B	B	B
16.35	/	/	/	/	A
16.35	/	/	/	/	A
16.36	B	B	B	B	A
16.39	/	/	/	/	A
17.3	D	D	D	D	C
17.4	/	/	/	/	B
17.4	B	B	B	B	A
17.13	B	B	B	B	B
17.14	B	B	B	B	/
17.26	D	D	D	D	B
17.27	C	C	C	C	A
17.27	C	C	C	C	/
17.28	C	C	C	C	A
17.30	C	C	C	C	/
17.31	/	/	/	/	A
18.1	B	B	B	B	B
18.3	B	B	B	B	B
18.5	B	B	B	B	B
18.7	D	D	D	D	C
18.8	/	/	/	/	A
18.17	C	C	C	C	B
18.19	B	B	B	B	B
18.19	C	C	C	C	/
18.21	B	B	B	B	A
18.21-22	B	B	B	B	/
18.25	B	B	B	B	A
18.26	C	C	C	C	C
19.1	/	/	/	/	A
19.2	B	B	B	B	/
19.9	B	B	B	B	B
19.20	C	C	C	C	B
19.28	/	/	/	/	A
19.33	B	B	B	B	B
19.37	B	B	B	B	B
19.39	C	C	C	C	B
19.40	D	D	D	D	C
20.4	C	C	C	C	B
20.4	B	B	B	B	B
20.4	C	C	C	C	B
20.5	C	C	C	C	/
20.13	B	C	C	C	/
20.15	C	C	C	C	B
20.21	C	B	B	B	B
20.28	C	C	C	C	C
20.28	B	B	B	B	A
20.32	B	B	B	B	B
21.1	C	C	C	C	A
21.8	A	A	A	A	A
21.13	B	B	B	B	B

VARIANTS AND RATINGS CHART: 1 COR.

VRNT	UBS1	UBS2	UBS3	UBS3^C	UBS4
10.28	A	A	A	A	A
11.10	A	A	A	A	A
11.15	/	/	/	/	C
11.24	/	/	/	/	A
11.24	B	B	B	B	A
11.29	C	C	C	C	A
11.29	C	C	C	C	A
12.9	B	B	B	B	A
13.3	C	C	C	C	C
13.4	/	/	/	/	C
13.5	/	/	/	/	A
14.19	C	B	B	B	/
14.34-35	B	B	B	B	B
14.37	C	C	C	C	/
14.38	B	B	B	B	B
14.39	D	D	D	D	/
14.40	B	B	B	B	B
15.10	C	C	C	C	C
15.14	C	C	C	C	B
15.31	C	C	C	C	C
15.47	A	A	A	A	A
15.49	C	C	C	C	B
15.51	A	A	A	A	A
15.54	C	C	C	C	B
15.55	B	B	B	B	B
16.24	C	C	C	C	B

VARIANTS AND RATINGS CHART: 2 COR.

VRNT	UBS1	UBS2	UBS3	UBS3^C	UBS4
1.6-7	B	B	B	B	A
1.10	D	D	D	D	B
1.10	C	C	C	C	B
1.10	C	C	C	C	C
1.11	C	C	C	C	B
1.12	D	D	D	D	B
1.14	C	C	C	C	C
1.15	C	C	C	C	B
2.1	C	C	C	C	C
2.7	C	C	C	C	/
2.9	B	B	B	B	A
2.17	C	C	C	C	B
3.2	B	C	C	C	A
3.3	/	/	/	/	A
3.9	C	C	C	C	B
4.5	C	C	C	C	B
4.14	C	C	C	C	B
5.3	/	/	/	/	C
5.17	B	B	B	B	A
6.16	C	C	C	C	B
7.8	C	C	D	D	C
8.7	D	D	D	D	C
8.9	/	/	/	/	B
8.19	D	D	D	D	/
8.19	/	/	/	/	C
9.4	C	C	C	C	B

VARIANTS AND RATINGS CHART: ACTS

VRNT	UBS1	UBS2	UBS3	UBS3^C	UBS4
21.16-17	/	/	/	/	A
21.20	B	B	B	B	/
21.22	C	C	C	C	B
21.23	D	D	D	D	/
21.25	C	C	C	C	C
21.25	C	C	C	C	B
21.25	C	C	C	C	B
22.9	C	C	C	C	B
22.12	C	C	C	C	B
22.13	C	C	C	C	/
22.26	C	B	B	B	A
23.12	B	B	B	B	B
23.20	C	C	C	C	/
23.28	C	C	C	C	/
23.29	/	/	/	/	A
23.30	C	C	C	C	B
23.30	C	C	C	C	B
24.6-8	D	D	D	D	B
24.15	B	A	A	A	/
24.20	C	B	B	B	B
24.24	C	C	C	C	B
24.27	/	/	/	/	A
25.13	B	B	B	B	/
25.18	C	C	C	C	C
26.16	C	C	C	C	C
26.28	B	B	B	B	A
27.5	B	B	B	B	A
27.14	B	B	B	B	B
27.16	B	B	B	B	B
27.27	D	D	D	D	/
27.34	B	B	B	B	/
27.35	/	/	/	/	A
27.37	B	B	B	B	B
27.39	B	B	B	B	A
27.41	C	C	C	C	C
28.1	B	B	B	B	A
28.13	D	D	D	D	C
28.14	C	C	C	C	/
28.16	B	B	B	B	A
28.19	/	/	/	/	A
28.25	B	B	B	B	B
28.28	B	B	B	B	A
28.31	/	/	/	/	A

VARIANTS AND RATINGS CHART: EPHESIANS

VRNT	UBS1	UBS2	UBS3	UBS3^C	UBS4
1.1	C	C	C	C	C
1.6	/	/	/	/	A
1.14	C	C	C	C	B
1.15	B	B	B	B	B
1.18	/	/	/	/	C
2.5	C	C	C	C	B
2.5	/	/	/	/	A
2.21	B	B	B	B	B
3.1	/	/	/	/	C
3.9	D	D	D	D	C

VARIANTS AND RATINGS CHART: 2 COR.

VRNT	UBS1	UBS2	UBS3	UBS3^C	UBS4
9.4	/	/	/	/	B
9.12	B	B	B	B	/
10.12-13	C	C	C	C	B
11.3	C	C	C	C	C
11.17	/	/	/	/	A
11.21	/	/	/	/	B
11.32	C	C	C	C	B
12.1	B	C	C	C	A
12.1	B	C	C	C	A
12.7	D	D	D	D	C
12.7	D	C	C	C	B
12.9	/	/	/	/	A
12.10	C	C	C	C	/
12.15	B	B	B	B	B
12.15	C	C	C	C	C
12.19	/	/	/	/	A
13.4	B	B	B	B	A
13.4	/	/	/	/	A

VARIANTS AND RATINGS CHART: GALATIANS

VRNT	UBS1	UBS2	UBS3	UBS3^C	UBS4
1.3	C	C	C	C	B
1.6	D	D	D	D	C
1.8	D	D	D	D	C
1.11	/	/	/	/	C
1.15	B	B	D	D	C
2.1	B	B	B	B	A
2.5	B	B	B	B	A
2.12	A	A	A	A	A
2.12	B	B	B	B	A
2.20	B	B	B	B	A
3.14	B	B	B	B	A
3.17	B	B	B	B	A
3.19	/	/	/	/	A
3.21	C	C	C	C	C
3.28	/	/	/	/	A
4.6	B	B	B	B	A
4.7	B	B	B	B	A
4.14	B	B	B	B	A
4.25	D	D	D	D	C
4.26	B	B	B	B	A
4.28	B	B	B	B	B
5.1	C	C	C	C	B
5.21	D	D	D	D	C
5.23	/	/	/	/	A
5.24	/	/	/	/	C
6.2	C	C	C	C	C
6.10	/	/	/	/	A
6.13	C	C	C	C	/
6.15	/	/	/	/	A

VARIANTS AND RATINGS CHART: PHILIPPIANS

VRNT	UBS1	UBS2	UBS3	UBS3^C	UBS4
1.11	C	C	B	B	A
1.14	D	D	D	D	B

VARIANTS AND RATINGS CHART: EPHESIANS

VRNT	UBS1	UBS2	UBS3	UBS3C	UBS4
3.13	/	/	/	/	A
3.14	B	B	B	B	B
3.19	B	B	B	B	A
3.20	/	/	/	/	A
4.6	/	/	/	/	A
4.8	C	C	C	C	B
4.9	B	B	B	B	A
4.9	/	/	/	/	C
4.19	/	/	/	/	A
4.28	C	D	D	D	C
4.29	/	/	/	/	A
4.32	B	B	B	B	B
5.2	C	C	C	C	B
5.2	B	B	B	B	A
5.9	B	B	B	B	A
5.14	/	/	/	/	A
5.15	B	B	B	B	B
5.19	B	C	C	C	B
5.20	C	C	C	C	/
5.22	D	C	C	C	B
5.30	B	B	B	B	A
6.1	C	C	C	C	C
6.12	D	D	D	D	B
6.19	B	B	B	B	A
6.20	/	/	/	/	C
6.24	/	/	/	/	A

VARIANTS AND RATINGS CHART: 1 THESS.

VRNT	UBS1	UBS2	UBS3	UBS3C	UBS4
1.1	B	B	B	B	A
1.5	/	/	/	/	A
2.7	C	C	C	C	B
2.12	C	C	C	C	B
2.15	A	A	A	A	A
2.16	/	/	/	/	A
3.2	B	B	B	B	B
3.13	B	B	C	C	C
4.1	/	/	/	/	A
4.11	/	/	/	/	C
4.17	/	/	/	/	A
5.4	A	A	A	A	A
5.21	C	C	C	C	/
5.25	C	C	C	C	C
5.27	B	B	B	B	A
5.28	B	B	B	B	A

VARIANTS AND RATINGS CHART: 2 THESS.

VRNT	UBS1	UBS2	UBS3	UBS3C	UBS4
1.2	C	C	C	C	C
2.3	C	C	C	C	B
2.4	B	B	B	B	A
2.8	C	C	C	C	C

VARIANTS AND RATING CHARTS: PHILIPPIANS

VRNT	UBS1	UBS2	UBS3	UBS3C	UBS4
2.2	B	B	B	B	/
2.4	B	B	B	B	/
2.5	C	C	C	C	B
2.9	/	/	/	/	B
2.11	/	/	/	/	C
2.11	/	/	/	/	A
2.12	B	B	B	B	A
2.26	C	C	C	C	C
2.30	C	C	C	C	B
3.3	C	C	C	C	B
3.12	B	B	B	B	/
3.12	/	/	/	/	C
3.13	C	C	C	C	B
3.15	/	/	/	/	A
3.16	B	B	B	B	A
3.21	B	B	B	B	/
4.3	B	B	B	B	A
4.7	/	/	/	/	A
4.8	/	/	/	/	A
4.13	/	/	/	/	A
4.16	C	C	C	C	C
4.19	/	/	/	/	B
4.23	B	B	B	B	A

VARIANTS AND RATINGS CHART: COLOSSIANS

VRNT	UBS1	UBS2	UBS3	UBS3C	UBS4
1.2	B	B	B	B	A
1.3	D	D	D	D	C
1.7	C	C	C	C	B
1.12	C	C	C	C	B
1.12	/	/	/	/	B
1.12	C	C	C	C	B
1.14	/	/	/	/	A
1.20	D	D	D	D	C
1.22	D	D	D	D	C
2.2	B	B	B	B	B
2.7	/	/	/	/	A
2.7	C	C	C	C	B
2.12	C	C	C	C	/
2.13	C	C	C	C	B
2.13	/	/	/	/	A
2.18	B	B	B	B	B
2.23	D	D	D	D	C
3.4	C	C	C	C	B
3.6	D	D	D	D	C
3.13	C	C	C	C	C
3.16	B	B	B	B	A
3.16	B	B	B	B	A
3.17	C	C	C	C	B
3.21	/	/	/	/	B
4.3	/	/	/	/	A
4.8	C	C	C	C	B
4.12	/	/	/	/	C

VARIANTS AND RATINGS CHART: 2 THESS.

VRNT	UBS1	UBS2	UBS3	UBS3^C	UBS4
2.8	C	C	C	C	/
2.13	C	C	C	C	B
3.6	C	C	C	C	B
3.16	B	B	B	B	A
3.18	C	C	C	C	A

VARIANTS AND RATINGS CHART: 2 TIMOTHY

VRNT	UBS1	UBS2	UBS3	UBS3^C	UBS4
1.11	C	C	C	C	B
2.14	C	C	C	C	B
2.18	C	C	C	C	C
2.22	C	C	C	C	/
3.14	/	/	/	/	B
4.1	C	C	C	C	B
4.8	C	C	C	C	/
4.10	B	B	B	B	A
4.22	/	/	/	/	B
4.22	B	B	B	B	A

VARIANTS AND RATINGS CHART: TITUS

VRNT	UBS1	UBS2	UBS3	UBS3^C	UBS4
1.4	B	B	B	B	A
1.10	C	C	C	C	C
3.1	C	C	C	C	B
3.15	B	B	B	B	A

VARIANTS AND RATINGS CHART: HEBREWS

VRNT	UBS1	UBS2	UBS3	UBS3^C	UBS4
1.3	C	C	C	C	B
1.8	C	C	C	C	B
1.12	/	/	/	/	A
1.12	C	C	C	C	B
2.7	C	C	C	C	B
2.8	/	/	/	/	C
2.9	B	B	B	B	A
3.2	C	C	D	D	C
3.6	B	B	B	B	A
3.6	C	C	C	C	B
4.2	C	C	C	C	B
4.3	B	B	B	B	A
4.3	/	/	/	/	C
5.12	C	C	C	C	C
6.2	B	B	B	B	A
6.3	B	B	B	B	A
7.21	/	/	/	/	A
8.8	C	C	C	C	B
8.11	B	B	B	B	A
9.1	/	/	/	/	C
9.10	B	B	B	B	A
9.11	C	C	C	C	B
9.14	/	/	/	/	A
9.14	C	C	C	C	C
9.17	/	/	/	/	A
9.19	C	C	C	C	C

VARIANTS AND RATINGS CHART: COLOSSIANS

VRNT	UBS1	UBS2	UBS3	UBS3^C	UBS4
4.15	C	C	C	C	C
4.18	A	A	A	A	A

VARIANTS AND RATINGS CHART: 1 TIMOTHY

VRNT	UBS1	UBS2	UBS3	UBS3^C	UBS4
1.1	/	/	/	/	A
1.4	/	/	/	/	B
1.4	/	/	/	/	A
1.12	B	B	B	B	/
1.15	A	A	A	A	A
1.17	/	/	/	/	A
2.1	/	/	/	/	A
2.7	B	B	B	B	A
3.1	B	B	B	B	A
3.16	B	B	B	B	A
4.10	C	C	C	C	C
5.16	C	C	C	C	B
5.18	/	/	/	/	A
6.5	A	A	A	A	A
6.7	C	C	C	C	A
6.9	/	/	/	/	A
6.13	/	/	/	/	C
6.17	/	/	/	/	A
6.19	B	B	B	B	A
6.21	C	C	C	C	A

VARIANTS AND RATINGS CHART: PHILEMON

VRNT	UBS1	UBS2	UBS3	UBS3^C	UBS4
1.2	/	/	/	/	A
1.6	C	C	C	C	B
1.12	B	B	B	B	B
1.25	C	C	C	C	B
1.25	B	B	B	B	A

VARIANTS AND RATINGS CHART: JAMES

VRNT	UBS1	UBS2	UBS3	UBS3^C	UBS4
1.3	C	B	B	B	A
1.12	C	B	B	B	A
1.17	B	C	C	C	B
1.19	B	B	B	B	B
1.27	B	B	B	B	/
2.3	C	C	C	C	B
2.19	C	C	C	C	B
2.20	B	B	B	B	B
2.25	/	/	/	/	A
3.3	C	D	D	D	C
3.8	/	/	/	/	B
3.9	/	/	/	/	A
3.12	B	B	B	B	B
4.4	A	A	A	A	A
4.5	C	C	C	C	B
4.12	/	/	/	/	C
4.14	D	D	C	C	B
4.14	C	C	C	C	B

VARIANTS AND RATINGS CHART: HEBREWS

VRNT	UBS1	UBS2	UBS3	UBS3^C	UBS4
10.1	A	A	A	A	A
10.1	C	C	C	C	B
10.11	B	B	B	B	A
10.34	B	B	B	B	B
10.34	B	B	B	B	A
10.38	C	C	C	C	B
11.1	/	/	/	/	A
11.4	C	C	C	C	/
11.4	C	C	C	C	/
11.11	D	D	D	D	C
11.23	/	/	/	/	A
11.37	D	D	D	D	C
12.1	B	B	B	B	A
12.3	D	D	D	D	C
12.18	D	D	C	C	B
13.15	D	D	D	D	C
13.21	A	A	A	A	A
13.21	C	C	C	C	/
13.21	C	B	B	B	A
13.21	C	C	C	C	C
13.25	C	C	C	C	A

VARIANTS AND RATINGS CHART: 1 PETER

VRNT	UBS1	UBS2	UBS3	UBS3^C	UBS4
1.7	C	B	B	B	A
1.8	B	B	B	B	A
1.9	/	/	/	/	C
1.12	C	C	C	C	C
1.22	C	C	C	C	A
1.22	C	C	C	C	C
2.3	C	C	C	C	B
2.19	/	/	/	/	B
2.19	/	/	/	/	B
2.21	B	B	B	B	A
2.21	B	B	B	B	A
2.25	/	/	/	/	B
3.1	/	/	/	/	C
3.7	C	C	C	C	B
3.7	/	/	/	/	B
3.8	/	/	/	/	A
3.14	/	/	/	/	A
3.15	B	B	B	B	A
3.16	B	B	B	B	A
3.18	D	D	D	D	B
3.18	C	C	see *UBS*, pp. 798, 793		
3.18	C	C	C	C	C
3.21	C	C	C	C	A
4.1	B	B	B	B	A
4.1	B	B	B	B	/
4.3	B	B	B	B	/
4.14	B	B	B	B	A
4.14	A	A	A	A	A
5.2	C	C	C	C	C
5.3	/	/	/	/	A
5.6	/	/	/	/	A
5.8	D	D	D	D	C

VARIANTS AND RATINGS CHART: JAMES

VRNT	UBS1	UBS2	UBS3	UBS3^C	UBS4
4.14	D	C	D	D	C
5.4	/	/	/	/	A
5.7	B	B	B	B	B
5.14	/	/	/	/	A
5.20	D	D	C	C	B
5.20	D	D	D	D	C

VARIANTS AND RATINGS CHART: 2 PETER

VRNT	UBS1	UBS2	UBS3	UBS3^C	UBS4
1.1	C	C	C	C	B
1.2	/	/	/	/	A
1.3	D	D	D	D	B
1.4	/	/	/	/	B
1.5	/	/	/	/	B
1.10	B	B	B	B	A
1.17	C	C	C	C	B
1.21	B	B	B	B	A
2.4	D	D	D	D	C
2.6	D	D	D	D	C
2.6	C	C	C	C	C
2.11	C	C	D	D	C
2.13	C	C	C	C	B
2.13	/	/	/	/	A
2.13	D	D	C	C	B
2.14	/	/	/	/	A
2.15	B	B	B	B	A
2.18	C	C	C	C	A
2.20	C	C	C	C	C
2.21	C	C	C	C	/
3.9	B	B	B	B	A
3.10	D	D	D	D	D
3.11	C	C	C	C	B
3.11	C	C	C	C	C
3.18	D	D	D	D	C

VARIANTS AND RATINGS CHART: REVELATION

VRNT	UBS1	UBS2	UBS3	UBS3^C	UBS4
1.5	B	B	B	B	A
1.6	C	C	C	C	C
1.8	B	B	B	B	A
1.15	D	D	D	D	C
2.2	C	C	C	C	/
2.7	/	/	/	/	A
2.10	C	C	C	C	/
2.10	C	C	C	C	/
2.13	C	C	C	C	/
2.13	C	C	C	C	/
2.20	C	C	C	C	B
2.22	A	A	A	A	A
2.22	B	B	B	B	A
2.23	B	B	B	B	/
3.2	C	C	C	C	/
3.5	C	C	C	C	B
4.7	C	C	C	C	/
4.11	/	/	/	/	A

VARIANTS AND RATINGS CHART: 1 PETER

VRNT	UBS1	UBS2	UBS3	UBS3^C	UBS4
5.10	/	/	/	/	A
5.10	C	C	C	C	C
5.10	C	C	C	C	B
5.11	C	C	C	C	B
5.11	C	C	C	C	A
5.13	/	/	/	/	A
5.14	/	/	/	/	A
5.14	C	C	C	C	A
5.14	C	C	C	C	/

VARIANTS AND RATINGS CHART: 1 JOHN

VRNT	UBS1	UBS2	UBS3	UBS3^C	UBS4
1.4	C	C	C	C	B
1.4	B	B	B	B	A
2.4	/	/	/	/	A
2.6	/	/	/	/	C
2.14	/	/	/	/	A
2.17	C	B	B	B	/
2.18	/	/	/	/	B
2.20	D	D	D	D	B
2.25	B	B	B	B	A
3.1	B	B	B	B	A
3.5	C	C	C	C	A
3.13	D	D	D	D	C
3.14	C	C	C	C	A
3.19	C	C	D	D	C
3.19	/	/	/	/	A
3.21	C	C	C	C	C
3.21	C	C	C	C	B
4.3	B	B	B	B	A
4.3	B	B	B	B	A
4.10	/	/	/	/	B
4.19	B	B	B	B	A
4.20	B	B	B	B	A
5.1	C	C	C	C	C
5.2	C	C	C	C	B
5.6	B	B	B	B	A
5.7-8	A	A	A	A	A
5.10	B	B	B	B	B
5.10	B	B	B	B	A
5.17	/	/	/	/	A
5.18	/	/	/	/	A
5.18	C	C	C	C	B
5.20	B	B	B	B	A
5.21	A	A	A	A	A

VARIANTS AND RATINGS CHART: 2 JOHN

VRNT	UBS1	UBS2	UBS3	UBS3^C	UBS4
1.3	C	B	B	B	A
1.8	B	B	B	B	A
1.8	C	C	C	C	B
1.9	B	B	B	B	A

VARIANTS AND RATINGS CHART: REVELATION

VRNT	UBS1	UBS2	UBS3	UBS3^C	UBS4
5.1	B	B	B	B	/
5.4	C	C	C	C	/
5.6	C	C	C	C	C
5.9	C	C	C	C	A
5.10	/	/	/	/	A
5.10	C	C	C	C	A
5.13	C	C	C	C	B
6.1	C	C	C	C	B
6.2	C	C	C	C	B
6.3	C	C	C	C	/
6.3-4	/	/	/	/	B
6.4	C	C	C	C	/
6.5	C	C	C	C	B
6.5	C	C	C	C	B
6.7	C	C	C	C	B
6.8	C	C	C	C	B
6.8	C	C	C	C	/
6.11	C	C	C	C	/
6.12	B	B	B	B	/
6.17	C	C	C	C	A
7.12	C	C	C	C	/
8.8	C	C	C	C	/
9.7	C	C	C	C	/
9.13	C	C	C	C	C
9.20	C	C	C	C	/
9.21	C	C	C	C	/
10.4	C	C	C	C	B
10.6	B	B	B	B	A
10.7	C	C	C	C	/
11.1	/	/	/	/	A
11.2	B	B	B	B	A
11.12	/	/	/	/	B
11.17	C	C	C	C	B
11.19	C	C	C	C	/
12.18	C	C	C	C	B
13.1	C	C	C	C	C
13.6	C	C	C	C	B
13.7	B	B	B	B	A
13.8	C	C	C	C	/
13.10	C	C	C	C	B
13.10	C	C	C	C	B
13.15	C	C	D	D	C
13.17	C	C	C	C	A
13.18	B	B	B	B	A
14.1	/	/	/	/	A
14.3	C	C	C	C	C
14.5	C	C	C	C	/
14.6	C	C	C	C	B
14.8	C	C	C	C	B
14.13	B	B	B	B	A
14.18	C	C	C	C	C
14.19	C	C	C	C	/
15.3	C	C	C	C	B
15.4	C	C	C	C	/

VARIANTS AND RATINGS CHART: 2 JOHN				
VRNT	UBS1	UBS2	UBS3	UBS3^C	UBS4
1.12	C	C	C	C	B
1.13	B	B	B	B	A

VARIANTS AND RATINGS CHART: 3 JOHN				
VRNT	UBS1	UBS2	UBS3	UBS3^C	UBS4
1.3	C	C	C	C	/
1.4	B	B	B	B	A
1.9	C	C	C	C	B

VARIANTS AND RATINGS CHART: JUDE				
VRNT	UBS1	UBS2	UBS3	UBS3^C	UBS4
1.1	B	B	B	B	A
1.1	/	/	/	/	A
1.3	B	B	B	B	A
1.4	/	/	/	/	A
1.4	/	/	/	/	A
1.5	D	D	D	D	D
1.8	/	/	/	/	A
1.12	/	/	/	/	A
1.19	/	/	/	/	A
1.22	C	C	C	C	C
1.23	C	C	C	C	C
1.23	C	C	C	C	C
1.25	/	/	/	/	A

VARIANTS AND RATINGS CHART: REVELATION				
VRNT	UBS1	UBS2	UBS3	UBS3^C	UBS4
15.6	B	B	B	B	B
16.4	C	C	C	C	B
16.17	/	/	/	/	A
16.18	C	C	C	C	/
17.4	C	C	C	C	B
17.8	C	C	C	C	B
18.2	/	/	/	/	C
18.3	C	C	C	C	B
18.3	D	D	D	D	D
18.8	C	C	C	C	/
18.11	C	C	C	C	/
18.12	/	/	/	/	A
18.17	C	C	C	C	B
18.22	C	C	C	C	B
19.5	C	C	C	C	C
19.6	C	C	C	C	C
19.7	D	D	D	D	C
19.11	C	C	C	C	C
19.12	C	C	C	C	C
19.13	C	C	C	C	B
20.6	C	C	C	C	C
20.9	C	C	C	C	A
21.3	D	D	D	D	B
21.3	D	D	D	D	C
21.4	C	C	C	C	C
21.5	C	C	C	C	/
21.12	/	/	/	/	C
22.14	B	B	B	B	A
22.21	B	B	B	B	A
22.21	C	C	C	C	B
22.21	C	C	C	C	/

APPENDIX II

Analysis of Variants and Ratings (A, B, C, D) within Each UBSGNT Edition and within Each Biblical Book

Appendix II collates the charts of Appendix I. Both appendices represent the foundational data utilized in developing the arguments discussed in Chapter 2, Section 1. Once again, the statistics contained in this second appendix are relatively easy to understand. Each *UBSGNT* edition is listed. Under each edition the four possible variant ratings (*A, B, C,* and *D*) are supplied. The number appearing directly after each rating portrays the number of times the particular rating occurs in the given book and the given edition (Chart 1, in Chapter 2, Section 1, is based upon these figures). This is followed by a percentage statistic which is calculated by dividing the number of times the particular variant rating occurs by the number of total variants in that edition. This percentage figure displays the particular variant rating in relationship to the other three ratings (Chart 2, in Chapter 2, Section 1, is based upon these percentage figures).[i] Finally, the total number of variants in the edition are recorded. This is calculated by simply adding together all four variant ratings that appear in the given edition (these figures constitute the '*Tot.*' column in the charts of Chapter 2, Section 1).[ii]

The first book presented is Matthew. In the *UBSGNT*[1] (represented by the title '*FIRST EDITION VARIANTS and RATINGS*') the *A* letter-rating occurs eight times, four percent of the total number of variants ($8 \div 185 = 4.3\%$). *B* occurs 76 times in the first edition, 41 percent of the total number of variants ($76 \div 185 = 41\%$). *C* occurs 93 times, 50 percent of the total number of variants ($93 \div 185 = 50.2\%$). *D* occurs eight times, four percent of the total number of variants ($8 \div 185 = 4.3\%$). The total number of variants listed is 185 ($8 [A] + 76 [B] + 93 [C] + 8 [D] = 185$ total variants). The *UBSGNT*[1] is then followed by the other editions. By examining each *UBSGNT* edition in the light of the others, one is able to evaluate the changes that result in the Gospel of Matthew.

---

i.   The percentage calculations are rounded off to the nearest whole number based upon the first decimal figure.

ii.   The 'Total # Of Variants' figure is based upon variants that have a letter-rating. Variants without the *A, B, C,* or *D* letter-rating are not calculated.

MATTHEW:
FIRST EDITION VARIANTS AND RATINGS:

A	8	=	4%	
B	76	=	41%	TOTAL = 185
C	93	=	50%	
D	8	=	4%	

SECOND EDITION VARIANTS AND RATINGS:

A	9	=	5%	
B	75	=	41%	TOTAL = 185
C	91	=	49%	
D	10	=	5%	

THIRD EDITION VARIANTS AND RATINGS:

A	9	=	5%	
B	69	=	37%	TOTAL = 185
C	94	=	51%	
D	13	=	7%	

THIRD COR. EDITION VARIANTS AND RATINGS:

A	9	=	5%	
B	69	=	37%	TOTAL = 185
C	94	=	51%	
D	13	=	7%	

FOURTH EDITION VARIANTS AND RATINGS:

A	34	=	21%	
B	73	=	45%	TOTAL = 161
C	53	=	33%	
D	1	=	1%	

MARK:
FIRST EDITION VARIANTS AND RATINGS:

A	49	=	29%	
B	54	=	32%	TOTAL = 170
C	59	=	35%	
D	8	=	5%	

SECOND EDITION VARIANTS AND RATINGS:

A	43	=	25%	
B	59	=	35%	TOTAL = 170
C	60	=	35%	
D	8	=	5%	

THIRD EDITION VARIANTS AND RATINGS:

A	40	=	24%	
B	59	=	35%	TOTAL = 170
C	57	=	34%	
D	14	=	8%	

THIRD COR. EDITION VARIANTS AND RATINGS:

A	40	=	24%	
B	59	=	35%	TOTAL = 170
C	57	=	34%	
D	14	=	8%	

FOURTH EDITION VARIANTS AND RATINGS:

A	46	=	32%	
B	50	=	35%	TOTAL = 142
C	45	=	32%	
D	1	=	1%	

LUKE:
FIRST EDITION VARIANTS AND RATINGS:

A	7	=	4%	
B	47	=	27%	TOTAL = 177
C	97	=	55%	
D	26	=	15%	

SECOND EDITION VARIANTS AND RATINGS:

A	7	=	4%	
B	47	=	27%	TOTAL = 177
C	97	=	55%	
D	26	=	15%	

THIRD EDITION VARIANTS AND RATINGS:

A	7	=	4%	
B	45	=	25%	TOTAL = 177
C	100	=	56%	
D	25	=	14%	

THIRD COR. EDITION VARIANTS AND RATINGS:

A	7	=	4%	
B	45	=	25%	TOTAL = 177
C	100	=	56%	
D	25	=	14%	

FOURTH EDITION VARIANTS AND RATINGS:

A	45	=	27%	
B	78	=	47%	TOTAL = 167
C	44	=	26%	
D	0	=	0%	

JOHN:
FIRST EDITION VARIANTS AND RATINGS:

A	30	=	17%	
B	57	=	33%	TOTAL = 172
C	76	=	44%	
D	9	=	5%	

SECOND EDITION VARIANTS AND RATINGS:

A	27	=	16%	
B	58	=	34%	TOTAL = 172
C	78	=	45%	
D	9	=	5%	

THIRD EDITION VARIANTS AND RATINGS:

A	27	=	16%	
B	55	=	32%	TOTAL = 172
C	78	=	45%	
D	12	=	7%	

THIRD COR. EDITION VARIANTS AND RATINGS:

A	27	=	16%	
B	55	=	32%	TOTAL = 172
C	78	=	45%	
D	12	=	7%	

FOURTH EDITION VARIANTS AND RATINGS:

A	46	=	30%	
B	65	=	42%	TOTAL = 154
C	42	=	27%	
D	1	=	1%	

ACTS:
FIRST EDITION VARIANTS AND RATINGS:

A	10	=	5%
B	76	=	40% TOTAL = 192
C	87	=	45%
D	19	=	10%

SECOND EDITION VARIANTS AND RATINGS:

A	11	=	6%
B	77	=	40% TOTAL = 192
C	84	=	44%
D	20	=	10%

THIRD EDITION VARIANTS AND RATINGS:

A	11	=	6%
B	76	=	40% TOTAL = 192
C	84	=	43%
D	21	=	11%

THIRD COR. EDITION VARIANTS AND RATINGS:

A	11	=	6%
B	76	=	40% TOTAL = 191[iii]
C	83	=	43%
D	21	=	11%

FOURTH EDITION VARIANTS AND RATINGS:

A	74	=	37%
B	81	=	41% TOTAL = 198
C	42	=	21%
D	1	=	1%

ROMANS:
FIRST EDITION VARIANTS AND RATINGS:

A	12	=	13%
B	35	=	39% TOTAL = 91
C	42	=	46%
D	2	=	2%

SECOND EDITION VARIANTS AND RATINGS:

A	12	=	13%
B	34	=	37% TOTAL = 91
C	42	=	46%
D	3	=	3%

THIRD EDITION VARIANTS AND RATINGS:

A	11	=	12%
B	32	=	35% TOTAL = 91
C	42	=	46%
D	6	=	7%

THIRD COR. EDITION VARIANTS AND RATINGS:

A	11	=	12%
B	32	=	35% TOTAL = 91
C	42	=	46%
D	6	=	7%

FOURTH EDITION VARIANTS AND RATINGS:

A	41	=	48%
B	21	=	25% TOTAL = 85
C	22	=	26%
D	1	=	1%

1 CORINTHIANS:
FIRST EDITION VARIANTS AND RATINGS:

A	7	=	12%
B	16	=	27% TOTAL = 59
C	30	=	51%
D	6	=	10%

SECOND EDITION VARIANTS AND RATINGS:

A	8	=	14%
B	14	=	24% TOTAL = 59
C	31	=	53%
D	6	=	10%

THIRD EDITION VARIANTS AND RATINGS:

A	8	=	14%
B	14	=	24% TOTAL = 59
C	30	=	51%
D	7	=	12%

THIRD COR. EDITION VARIANTS AND RATINGS:

A	8	=	14%
B	14	=	24% TOTAL = 59
C	30	=	51%
D	7	=	12%

FOURTH EDITION VARIANTS AND RATINGS:

A	23	=	38%
B	22	=	37% TOTAL = 60
C	14	=	23%
D	1	=	2%

2 CORINTHIANS:
FIRST EDITION VARIANTS AND RATINGS:

A	0	=	0%
B	9	=	26% TOTAL = 34
C	19	=	56%
D	6	=	18%

SECOND EDITION VARIANTS AND RATINGS:

A	0	=	0%
B	6	=	18% TOTAL = 34
C	23	=	68%
D	5	=	15%

THIRD EDITION VARIANTS AND RATINGS:

A	0	=	0%
B	6	=	18% TOTAL = 34
C	22	=	65%
D	6	=	18%

THIRD COR. EDITION VARIANTS AND RATINGS:

A	0	=	0%
B	6	=	18% TOTAL = 34
C	22	=	65%
D	6	=	18%

FOURTH EDITION VARIANTS AND RATINGS:

A	12	=	30%
B	18	=	45% TOTAL = 40
C	10	=	25%
D	0	=	0%

---

iii   One variant rating is missing at Acts 5.32 in the *UBSGNT*[3corr.]. It should most probably be a *C* rated variant.

GALATIANS:
FIRST EDITION VARIANTS AND RATINGS:
A 1 = 5%
B 12 = 55%   TOTAL = 22
C 5 = 23%
D 4 = 18%
SECOND EDITION VARIANTS AND RATINGS:
A 1 = 5%
B 12 = 55%   TOTAL = 22
C 5 = 23%
D 4 = 18%
THIRD EDITION VARIANTS AND RATINGS:
A 1 = 5%
B 11 = 50%   TOTAL = 22
C 5 = 23%
D 5 = 23%
THIRD COR. EDITION VARIANTS AND RATINGS:
A 1 = 5%
B 11 = 50%   TOTAL = 22
C 5 = 23%
D 5 = 23%
FOURTH EDITION VARIANTS AND RATINGS:
A 16 = 57%
B 3 = 11%   TOTAL = 28
C 9 = 32%
D 0 = 0%

EPHESIANS:
FIRST EDITION VARIANTS AND RATINGS:
A 0 = 0%
B 12 = 52%   TOTAL = 23
C 8 = 35%
D 3 = 13%
SECOND EDITION VARIANTS AND RATINGS:
A 0 = 0%
B 11 = 48%   TOTAL = 23
C 9 = 39%
D 3 = 13%
THIRD EDITION VARIANTS AND RATINGS:
A 0 = 0%
B 11 = 48%   TOTAL = 23
C 9 = 39%
D 3 = 13%
THIRD COR. EDITION VARIANTS AND RATINGS:
A 0 = 0%
B 11 = 48%   TOTAL = 23
C 9 = 39%
D 3 = 13%
FOURTH EDITION VARIANTS AND RATINGS:
A 15 = 43%
B 12 = 34%   TOTAL = 35
C 8 = 23%
D 0 = 0%

PHILIPPIANS:
FIRST EDITION VARIANTS AND RATINGS:
A 0 = 0%
B 8 = 50%   TOTAL = 16
C 7 = 44%
D 1 = 6%
SECOND EDITION VARIANTS AND RATINGS:
A 0 = 0%
B 8 = 50%   TOTAL = 16
C 7 = 44%
D 1 = 6%
THIRD EDITION VARIANTS AND RATINGS:
A 0 = 0%
B 9 = 56%   TOTAL = 16
C 6 = 38%
D 1 = 6%
THIRD COR. EDITION VARIANTS AND RATINGS:
A 0 = 0%
B 9 = 56%   TOTAL = 16
C 6 = 38%
D 1 = 6%
FOURTH EDITION VARIANTS AND RATINGS:
A 10 = 48%
B 7 = 33%   TOTAL = 21
C 4 = 19%
D 0 = 0%

COLOSSIANS:
FIRST EDITION VARIANTS AND RATINGS:
A 1 = 5%
B 5 = 23%   TOTAL = 22
C 11 = 50%
D 5 = 23%
SECOND EDITION VARIANTS AND RATINGS:
A 1 = 5%
B 5 = 23%   TOTAL = 22
C 11 = 50%
D 5 = 23%
THIRD EDITION VARIANTS AND RATINGS:
A 1 = 5%
B 5 = 23%   TOTAL = 22
C 11 = 50%
D 5 = 23%
THIRD COR. EDITION VARIANTS AND RATINGS:
A 1 = 5%
B 5 = 23%   TOTAL = 22
C 11 = 50%
D 5 = 23%
FOURTH EDITION VARIANTS AND RATINGS:
A 8 = 29%
B 12 = 43%   TOTAL = 28
C 8 = 29%
D 0 = 0%

1 THESSALONIANS:
FIRST EDITION VARIANTS AND RATINGS:
A	2	=	18%	
B	5	=	45%	TOTAL = 11
C	4	=	36%	
D	0	=	0%	

SECOND EDITION VARIANTS AND RATINGS:
A	2	=	18%	
B	5	=	45%	TOTAL = 11
C	4	=	36%	
D	0	=	0%	

THIRD EDITION VARIANTS AND RATINGS:
A	2	=	18%	
B	4	=	36%	TOTAL = 11
C	5	=	45%	
D	0	=	0%	

THIRD COR. EDITION VARIANTS AND RATINGS:
A	2	=	18%	
B	4	=	36%	TOTAL = 11
C	5	=	45%	
D	0	=	0%	

FOURTH EDITION VARIANTS AND RATINGS:
A	9	=	60%	
B	3	=	20%	TOTAL = 15
C	3	=	20%	
D	0	=	0%	

2 THESSALONIANS:
FIRST EDITION VARIANTS AND RATINGS:
A	0	=	0%	
B	2	=	22%	TOTAL = 9
C	7	=	78%	
D	0	=	0%	

SECOND EDITION VARIANTS AND RATINGS:
A	0	=	0%	
B	2	=	22%	TOTAL = 9
C	7	=	78%	
D	0	=	0%	

THIRD EDITION VARIANTS AND RATINGS:
A	0	=	0%	
B	2	=	22%	TOTAL = 9
C	7	=	78%	
D	0	=	0%	

THIRD COR. EDITION VARIANTS AND RATINGS:
A	0	=	0%	
B	2	=	22%	TOTAL = 9
C	7	=	78%	
D	0	=	0%	

FOURTH EDITION VARIANTS AND RATINGS:
A	3	=	38%	
B	3	=	38%	TOTAL = 8
C	2	=	25%	
D	0	=	0%	

1 TIMOTHY:
FIRST EDITION VARIANTS AND RATINGS:
A	2	=	18%	
B	5	=	45%	TOTAL = 11
C	4	=	36%	
D	0	=	0%	

SECOND EDITION VARIANTS AND RATINGS:
A	2	=	18%	
B	5	=	45%	TOTAL = 11
C	4	=	36%	
D	0	=	0%	

THIRD EDITION VARIANTS AND RATINGS:
A	2	=	18%	
B	5	=	45%	TOTAL = 11
C	4	=	36%	
D	0	=	0%	

THIRD COR. EDITION VARIANTS AND RATINGS:
A	2	=	18%	
B	5	=	45%	TOTAL = 11
C	4	=	36%	
D	0	=	0%	

FOURTH EDITION VARIANTS AND RATINGS:
A	15	=	79%	
B	2	=	11%	TOTAL = 19
C	2	=	11%	
D	0	=	0%	

2 TIMOTHY:
FIRST EDITION VARIANTS AND RATINGS:
A	0	=	0%	
B	2	=	25%	TOTAL = 8
C	6	=	75%	
D	0	=	0%	

SECOND EDITION VARIANTS AND RATINGS:
A	0	=	0%	
B	2	=	25%	TOTAL = 8
C	6	=	75%	
D	0	=	0%	

THIRD EDITION VARIANTS AND RATINGS:
A	0	=	0%	
B	2	=	25%	TOTAL = 8
C	6	=	75%	
D	0	=	0%	

THIRD COR. EDITION VARIANTS AND RATINGS:
A	0	=	0%	
B	2	=	25%.	TOTAL = 8
C	6	=	75%	
D	0	=	0%	

FOURTH EDITION VARIANTS AND RATINGS:
A	2	=	25%	
B	5	=	63%	TOTAL = 8
C	1	=	13%	
D	0	=	0%	

TITUS:
FIRST EDITION VARIANTS AND RATINGS:

A	0	=	0%	
B	2	=	50%	TOTAL = 4
C	2	=	50%	
D	0	=	0%	

SECOND EDITION VARIANTS AND RATINGS:

A	0	=	0%	
B	2	=	50%	TOTAL = 4
C	2	=	50%	
D	0	=	0%	

THIRD EDITION VARIANTS AND RATINGS:

A	0	=	0%	
B	2	=	50%	TOTAL = 4
C	2	=	50%	
D	0	=	0%	

THIRD COR. EDITION VARIANTS AND RATINGS:

A	0	=	0%	
B	2	=	50%	TOTAL = 4
C	2	=	50%	
D	0	=	0%	

FOURTH EDITION VARIANTS AND RATINGS:

A	2	=	50%	
B	1	=	25%	TOTAL = 4
C	1	=	25%	
D	0	=	0%	

PHILEMON:
FIRST EDITION VARIANTS AND RATINGS:

A	0	=	0%	
B	2	=	50%	TOTAL = 4
C	2	=	50%	
D	0	=	0%	

SECOND EDITION VARIANTS AND RATINGS:

A	0	=	0%	
B	2	=	50%	TOTAL = 4
C	2	=	50%	
D	0	=	0%	

THIRD EDITION VARIANTS AND RATINGS:

A	0	=	0%	
B	2	=	50%	TOTAL = 4
C	2	=	50%	
D	0	=	0%	

THIRD COR. EDITION VARIANTS AND RATINGS:

A	0	=	0%	
B	2	=	50%	TOTAL = 4
C	2	=	50%	
D	0	=	0%	

FOURTH EDITION VARIANTS AND RATINGS:

A	2	=	40%	
B	3	=	60%	TOTAL = 5
C	0	=	0%	
D	0	=	0%	

HEBREWS:
FIRST EDITION VARIANTS AND RATINGS:

A	2	=	5%	
B	11	=	29%	TOTAL = 38
C	20	=	53%	
D	5	=	13%	

SECOND EDITION VARIANTS AND RATINGS:

A	2	=	5%	
B	12	=	32%	TOTAL = 38
C	19	=	50%	
D	5	=	13%	

THIRD EDITION VARIANTS AND RATINGS:

A	2	=	5%	
B	12	=	32%	TOTAL = 38
C	19	=	50%	
D	5	=	13%	

THIRD COR. EDITION VARIANTS AND RATINGS:

A	2	=	5%	
B	12	=	32%	TOTAL = 44
C	19	=	50%	
D	5	=	13%	

FOURTH EDITION VARIANTS AND RATINGS:

A	20	=	45%	
B	12	=	27%	TOTAL = 44
C	12	=	27%	
D	0	=	0%	

JAMES:
FIRST EDITION VARIANTS AND RATINGS:

A	1	=	6%	
B	6	=	33%	TOTAL = 18
C	7	=	39%	
D	4	=	22%	

SECOND EDITION VARIANTS AND RATINGS:

A	1	=	6%	
B	7	=	39%	TOTAL = 18
C	6	=	33%	
D	4	=	22%	

THIRD EDITION VARIANTS AND RATINGS:

A	1	=	6%	
B	7	=	39%	TOTAL = 18
C	7	=	39%	
D	3	=	17%	

THIRD COR. EDITION VARIANTS AND RATINGS:

A	1	=	6%	
B	7	=	39%	TOTAL = 18
C	7	=	39%	
D	3	=	17%	

FOURTH EDITION VARIANTS AND RATINGS:

A	7	=	30%	
B	12	=	52%	TOTAL = 23
C	4	=	17%	
D	0	=	0%	

1 PETER:
FIRST EDITION VARIANTS AND RATINGS:
A	1	=	4%	
B	9	=	32%	TOTAL = 28
C	16	=	57%	
D	2	=	7%	

SECOND EDITION VARIANTS AND RATINGS:
A	1	=	4%	
B	10	=	36%	TOTAL = 28
C	15	=	54%	
D	2	=	7%	

THIRD EDITION VARIANTS AND RATINGS:
A	1	=	4%	
B	10	=	37%	TOTAL = 27
C	14	=	52%	
D	2	=	7%	

THIRD COR. EDITION VARIANTS AND RATINGS:
A	1	=	4%	
B	10	=	37%	TOTAL = 27
C	14	=	52%	
D	2	=	7%	

FOURTH EDITION VARIANTS AND RATINGS:
A	20	=	54%	
B	9	=	24%	TOTAL = 37
C	8	=	22%	
D	0	=	0%	

2 PETER:
FIRST EDITION VARIANTS AND RATINGS:
A	0	=	0%	
B	4	=	20%	TOTAL = 20
C	10	=	50%	
D	6	=	30%	

SECOND EDITION VARIANTS AND RATINGS:
A	0	=	0%	
B	4	=	20%	TOTAL = 20
C	10	=	50%	
D	6	=	30%	

THIRD EDITION VARIANTS AND RATINGS:
A	0	=	0%	
B	4	=	20%	TOTAL = 20
C	10	=	50%	
D	6	=	30%	

THIRD COR. EDITION VARIANTS AND RATINGS:
A	0	=	0%	
B	4	=	20%	TOTAL = 20
C	10	=	50%	
D	6	=	30%	

FOURTH EDITION VARIANTS AND RATINGS:
A	8	=	33%	
B	8	=	33%	TOTAL = 24
C	7	=	29%	
D	1	=	4%	

1 JOHN:
FIRST EDITION VARIANTS AND RATINGS:
A	2	=	8%	
B	11	=	44%	TOTAL = 25
C	10	=	40%	
D	2	=	8%	

SECOND EDITION VARIANTS AND RATINGS:
A	2	=	8%	
B	12	=	48%	TOTAL = 25
C	9	=	36%	
D	2	=	8%	

THIRD EDITION VARIANTS AND RATINGS:
A	2	=	8%	
B	12	=	48%	TOTAL = 25
C	8	=	32%	
D	3	=	12%	

THIRD COR. EDITION VARIANTS AND RATINGS:
A	2	=	8%	
B	12	=	48%	TOTAL = 25
C	8	=	32%	
D	3	=	12%	

FOURTH EDITION VARIANTS AND RATINGS:
A	19	=	59%	
B	8	=	25%	TOTAL = 32
C	5	=	16%	
D	0	=	0%	

2 JOHN:
FIRST EDITION VARIANTS AND RATINGS:
A	0	=	0%	
B	3	=	50%	TOTAL = 6
C	3	=	50%	
D	0	=	0%	

SECOND EDITION VARIANTS AND RATINGS:
A	0	=	0%	
B	4	=	67%	TOTAL = 6
C	2	=	33%	
D	0	=	0%	

THIRD EDITION VARIANTS AND RATINGS:
A	0	=	0%	
B	4	=	67%	TOTAL = 6
C	2	=	33%	
D	0	=	0%	

THIRD COR. EDITION VARIANTS AND RATINGS:
A	0	=	0%	
B	4	=	67%	TOTAL = 6
C	2	=	33%	
D	0	=	0%	

FOURTH EDITION VARIANTS AND RATINGS:
A	4	=	67%	
B	2	=	33%	TOTAL = 6
C	0	=	0%	
D	0	=	0%	

3 JOHN:
FIRST EDITION VARIANTS AND RATINGS:
A   0   =   0%
B   1   =   33%   TOTAL = 3
C   2   =   67%
D   0   =   0%
SECOND EDITION VARIANTS AND RATINGS:
A   0   =   0%
B   1   =   33%   TOTAL = 3
C   2   =   67%
D   0   =   0%
THIRD EDITION VARIANTS AND RATINGS:
A   0   =   0%
B   1   =   33%   TOTAL = 3
C   2   =   67%
D   0   =   0%
THIRD COR. EDITION VARIANTS AND RATINGS:
A   0   =   0%
B   1   =   33%   TOTAL = 3
C   2   =   67%
D   0   =   0%
FOURTH EDITION VARIANTS AND RATINGS:
A   1   =   50%
B   1   =   50%   TOTAL = 2
C   0   =   0%
D   0   =   0%

JUDE:
FIRST EDITION VARIANTS AND RATINGS:
A   0   =   0%
B   2   =   33%   TOTAL = 6
C   3   =   50%
D   1   =   17%
SECOND EDITION VARIANTS AND RATINGS:
A   0   =   0%
B   2   =   33%   TOTAL = 6
C   3   =   50%
D   1   =   17%
THIRD EDITION VARIANTS AND RATINGS:
A   0   =   0%
B   2   =   33%   TOTAL = 6
C   3   =   50%
D   1   =   17%
THIRD COR. EDITION VARIANTS AND RATINGS:
A   0   =   0%
B   2   =   33%   TOTAL = 6
C   3   =   50%
D   1   =   17%
FOURTH EDITION VARIANTS AND RATINGS:
A   9   =   69%
B   0   =   0%   TOTAL = 13
C   3   =   23%
D   1   =   8%

REVELATION:
FIRST EDITION VARIANTS AND RATINGS:
A   1   =   1%
B   14   =   15%   TOTAL = 92
C   72   =   78%
D   5   =   5%
SECOND EDITION VARIANTS AND RATINGS:
A   1   =   1%
B   14   =   15%   TOTAL = 92
C   72   =   78%
D   5   =   5%
THIRD EDITION VARIANTS AND RATINGS:
A   1   =   1%
B   14   =   15%   TOTAL = 92
C   71   =   77%
D   6   =   7%
THIRD COR. EDITION VARIANTS AND RATINGS:
A   1   =   1%
B   14   =   15%   TOTAL = 92
C   71   =   77%
D   6   =   7%
FOURTH EDITION VARIANTS AND RATINGS:
A   23   =   32%
B   30   =   42%   TOTAL = 72
C   18   =   25%
D   1   =   1%

APPENDIX III

Analysis of Variants and Ratings (A, B, C, D) as Compared throughout All Editions and within Each Biblical Book

This third appendix contains the raw data used to build the argument of Chapter 2, Section 3. Chart 3 of this same chapter and section is based directly upon the figures presented here. The statistics compiled here are straightforward, given that one understands the classifications presented in the main body of this monograph. Each biblical book is represented. Following this, the grand total statistics are provided. This final group of data simply adds the figures of each biblical book together arriving at overall totals or, as mentioned, grand totals. A close observance of the footnotes in this section will provide additional information regarding several of the calculations. On numerous occasions specific passage references are recorded under certain categories. This is due to questions regarding where a particular variant should be placed. It could have perhaps been placed in several categories, or it did not perfectly characterize any one category. Therefore, to remedy this uncertainty, the variant has been specifically listed as to its location.

MARK:
NUMBER OF VARIANTS WITH RATINGS IMPROVING ONE STEP:
D–C = 6
C–B = 15
B–A = 6
NUMBER OF VARIANTS WITH RATINGS IMPROVING TWO STEPS:
D–B = 1
C–A = 1
NUMBER OF VARIANTS WITH RATINGS IMPROVING THREE STEPS:
D–A = 0
NUMBER OF VARIANTS WITH RATINGS DECREASING ONE STEP:
A–B = 10
B–C = 4
C–D = 2
NUMBER OF VARIANTS WITH RATINGS DECREASING TWO STEPS:
A–C = 0
B–D = 0
NUMBER OF VARIANTS WITH RATINGS DECREASING THREE STEPS:
A–D = 0
NUMBER OF VARIANTS WITH CONSISTENT RATINGS THROUGHOUT ALL OCCURRING EDITIONS:
A = 39
B = 44
C = 36
D = 1
NUMBER OF VARIANTS WITH FLUCTUATING RATINGS: 5
NUMBER OF NEW VARIANTS ADDED INTO THE UBSGNT[4]:
A = 8
B = 2
C = 7
D = 0
NUMBER OF OLD VARIANTS DROPPED OUT OF THE UBSGNT[4]: 45
TOTAL NUMBER OF VARIANTS REFERENCED: 187

MATTHEW:
NUMBER OF VARIANTS WITH RATINGS IMPROVING ONE STEP:
D–C = 4
C–B = 24
B–A = 19
NUMBER OF VARIANTS WITH RATINGS IMPROVING TWO STEPS:
D–B = 0
C–A = 1
NUMBER OF VARIANTS WITH RATINGS IMPROVING THREE STEPS:
D–A = 0
NUMBER OF VARIANTS WITH RATINGS DECREASING ONE STEP:
A–B = 1
B–C = 3
C–D = 0
NUMBER OF VARIANTS WITH RATINGS DECREASING TWO STEPS:
A–C = 0
B–D = 0
NUMBER OF VARIANTS WITH RATINGS DECREASING THREE STEPS:
A–D = 0
NUMBER OF VARIANTS WITH CONSISTENT RATINGS THROUGHOUT ALL OCCURRING EDITIONS:
A = 7
B = 49
C = 63
D = 4
NUMBER OF VARIANTS WITH FLUCTUATING RATINGS: 10
NUMBER OF NEW VARIANTS ADDED INTO THE UBSGNT[4]:
A = 10
B = 9
C = 7
D = 0
NUMBER OF OLD VARIANTS DROPPED OUT OF THE UBSGNT[4]: 51
TOTAL NUMBER OF VARIANTS REFERENCED: 211

LUKE:
NUMBER OF VARIANTS WITH RATINGS IMPROVING ONE STEP:
D–C = 13
C–B = 40
B–A = 20
NUMBER OF VARIANTS WITH RATINGS IMPROVING TWO STEPS:
D–B = 9
C–A = 9 (Lk. 9.55-56; 22.43-44)
NUMBER OF VARIANTS WITH RATINGS IMPROVING THREE STEPS:
D–A = 1
NUMBER OF VARIANTS WITH RATINGS DECREASING ONE STEP:
A–B = 0
B–C = 0
C–D = 0
NUMBER OF VARIANTS WITH RATINGS DECREASING TWO STEPS:
A–C = 0
B–D = 0
NUMBER OF VARIANTS WITH RATINGS DECREASING THREE STEPS:
A–D = 0
NUMBER OF VARIANTS WITH CONSISTENT RATINGS
THROUGHOUT ALL OCCURRING EDITIONS:
A = 7
B = 25
C = 50 (Lk. 9.55; 22.42)
D = 3
NUMBER OF VARIANTS WITH FLUCTUATING RATINGS: 2
NUMBER OF NEW VARIANTS ADDED INTO THE UBSGNT[4]:
A = 9
B = 8
C = 2
D = 0
NUMBER OF OLD VARIANTS DROPPED OUT OF THE UBSGNT[4]: 29
TOTAL NUMBER OF VARIANTS REFERENCED: 198

JOHN:
NUMBER OF VARIANTS WITH RATINGS IMPROVING ONE STEP:
D–C = 6
C–B = 23
B–A = 9
NUMBER OF VARIANTS WITH RATINGS IMPROVING TWO STEPS:
D–B = 1
C–A = 5
NUMBER OF VARIANTS WITH RATINGS IMPROVING THREE STEPS:
D–A = 0
NUMBER OF VARIANTS WITH RATINGS DECREASING ONE STEP:
A–B = 2
B–C = 3
C–D = 1
NUMBER OF VARIANTS WITH RATINGS DECREASING TWO STEPS:
A–C = 0
B–D = 0
NUMBER OF VARIANTS WITH RATINGS DECREASING THREE STEPS:
A–D = 0
NUMBER OF VARIANTS WITH CONSISTENT RATINGS
THROUGHOUT ALL OCCURRING EDITIONS:
A = 27
B = 44
C = 46
D = 2
NUMBER OF VARIANTS WITH FLUCTUATING RATINGS: 3
NUMBER OF NEW VARIANTS ADDED INTO THE UBSGNT[4]:
A = 11
B = 10
C = 8
D = 0
NUMBER OF OLD VARIANTS DROPPED OUT OF THE UBSGNT[4]: 47
TOTAL NUMBER OF VARIANTS REFERENCED: 201

ACTS:

NUMBER OF VARIANTS WITH RATINGS IMPROVING ONE STEP:
D–C = 11
C–B = 34
B–A = 24
NUMBER OF VARIANTS WITH RATINGS IMPROVING TWO STEPS:
D–B = 4
C–A = 6
NUMBER OF VARIANTS WITH RATINGS IMPROVING THREE STEPS:
D–A = 1
NUMBER OF VARIANTS WITH RATINGS DECREASING ONE STEP:
A–B = 0
B–C = 1
C–D = 0
NUMBER OF VARIANTS WITH RATINGS DECREASING TWO STEPS:
A–C = 0
B–D = 0
NUMBER OF VARIANTS WITH RATINGS DECREASING THREE STEPS:
A–D = 0
*NUMBER OF VARIANTS WITH CONSISTENT RATINGS
THROUGHOUT ALL OCCURRING EDITIONS:*
A = 10
B = 49
C = 46
D = 3
NUMBER OF VARIANTS WITH FLUCTUATING RATINGS: 3
NUMBER OF NEW VARIANTS ADDED INTO THE UBSGNT[4]:
A = 37
B = 7
C = 2
D = 0
NUMBER OF OLD VARIANTS DROPPED OUT OF THE UBSGNT[4]: 40
TOTAL NUMBER OF VARIANTS REFERENCED: 238

ROMANS:

NUMBER OF VARIANTS WITH RATINGS IMPROVING ONE STEP:
D–C = 0
C–B = 12
B–A = 16
NUMBER OF VARIANTS WITH RATINGS IMPROVING TWO STEPS:
D–B = 0
C–A = 5
NUMBER OF VARIANTS WITH RATINGS IMPROVING THREE STEPS:
D–A = 0
NUMBER OF VARIANTS WITH RATINGS DECREASING ONE STEP:
A–B = 0
B–C = 1
C–D = 0
NUMBER OF VARIANTS WITH RATINGS DECREASING TWO STEPS:
A–C = 0
B–D = 0
NUMBER OF VARIANTS WITH RATINGS DECREASING THREE STEPS:
A–D = 0
*NUMBER OF VARIANTS WITH CONSISTENT RATINGS
THROUGHOUT ALL OCCURRING EDITIONS:*
A = 11
B = 15
C = 23
D = 2
NUMBER OF VARIANTS WITH FLUCTUATING RATINGS: 6
NUMBER OF NEW VARIANTS ADDED INTO THE UBSGNT[4]:
A = 8
B = 2
C = 4
D = 0
NUMBER OF OLD VARIANTS DROPPED OUT OF THE UBSGNT[4]: 20
TOTAL NUMBER OF VARIANTS REFERENCED: 105

1 CORINTHIANS:

NUMBER OF VARIANTS WITH RATINGS IMPROVING ONE STEP:
D–C = 3
C–B = 13
B–A = 7

NUMBER OF VARIANTS WITH RATINGS IMPROVING TWO STEPS:
D–B = 0
C–A = 3

NUMBER OF VARIANTS WITH RATINGS IMPROVING THREE STEPS:
D–A = 0

NUMBER OF VARIANTS WITH RATINGS DECREASING ONE STEP:
A–B = 0
B–C = 1
C–D = 0

NUMBER OF VARIANTS WITH RATINGS DECREASING TWO STEPS:
A–C = 0
B–D = 0

NUMBER OF VARIANTS WITH RATINGS DECREASING THREE STEPS:
A–D = 0

NUMBER OF VARIANTS WITH CONSISTENT RATINGS
THROUGHOUT ALL OCCURRING EDITIONS:
A = 7
B = 6
C = 13
D = 3

NUMBER OF VARIANTS WITH FLUCTUATING RATINGS: 2
NUMBER OF NEW VARIANTS ADDED INTO THE UBSGNT[4].
A = 6
B = 3
C = 3
D = 0

NUMBER OF OLD VARIANTS DROPPED OUT OF THE UBSGNT[4]. 11
TOTAL NUMBER OF VARIANTS REFERENCED: 70

2 CORINTHIANS:

NUMBER OF VARIANTS WITH RATINGS IMPROVING ONE STEP:
D–C = 2
C–B = 11
B–A = 4

NUMBER OF VARIANTS WITH RATINGS IMPROVING TWO STEPS:
D–B = 3
C–A = 0

NUMBER OF VARIANTS WITH RATINGS IMPROVING THREE STEPS:
D–A = 0

NUMBER OF VARIANTS WITH RATINGS DECREASING ONE STEP:
A–B = 0
B–C = 0
C–D = 0

NUMBER OF VARIANTS WITH RATINGS DECREASING TWO STEPS:
A–C = 0
B–D = 0

NUMBER OF VARIANTS WITH RATINGS DECREASING THREE STEPS:
A–D = 0

NUMBER OF VARIANTS WITH CONSISTENT RATINGS
THROUGHOUT ALL OCCURRING EDITIONS:
A = 0
B = 2
C = 7
D = 1

NUMBER OF VARIANTS WITH FLUCTUATING RATINGS: 4
NUMBER OF NEW VARIANTS ADDED INTO THE UBSGNT[4].
A = 5
B = 3
C = 2
D = 0

NUMBER OF OLD VARIANTS DROPPED OUT OF THE UBSGNT[4]. 4
TOTAL NUMBER OF VARIANTS REFERENCED: 44

GALATIANS:
NUMBER OF VARIANTS WITH RATINGS IMPROVING ONE STEP:
D–C = 4
C–B = 2
B–A = 10
NUMBER OF VARIANTS WITH RATINGS IMPROVING TWO STEPS:
D–B = 0
C–A = 0
NUMBER OF VARIANTS WITH RATINGS IMPROVING THREE STEPS:
D–A = 0
NUMBER OF VARIANTS WITH RATINGS DECREASING ONE STEP:
A–B = 0
B–C = 0
C–D = 0
NUMBER OF VARIANTS WITH RATINGS DECREASING TWO STEPS:
A–C = 0
B–D = 0
NUMBER OF VARIANTS WITH RATINGS DECREASING THREE STEPS:
A–D = 0
NUMBER OF VARIANTS WITH CONSISTENT RATINGS
THROUGHOUT ALL OCCURRING EDITIONS:
A = 1
B = 1
C = 3
D = 0
NUMBER OF VARIANTS WITH FLUCTUATING RATINGS: 1
NUMBER OF NEW VARIANTS ADDED INTO THE UBSGNT[4]:
A = 5
B = 0
C = 2
D = 0
NUMBER OF OLD VARIANTS DROPPED OUT OF THE UBSGNT[4]. 1
TOTAL NUMBER OF VARIANTS REFERENCED: 29

EPHESIANS:
NUMBER OF VARIANTS WITH RATINGS IMPROVING ONE STEP:
D–C = 1
C–B = 4
B–A = 6
NUMBER OF VARIANTS WITH RATINGS IMPROVING TWO STEPS:
D–B = 2
C–A = 0
NUMBER OF VARIANTS WITH RATINGS IMPROVING THREE STEPS:
D–A = 0
NUMBER OF VARIANTS WITH RATINGS DECREASING ONE STEP:
A–B = 0
B–C = 0
C–D = 0
NUMBER OF VARIANTS WITH RATINGS DECREASING TWO STEPS:
A–C = 0
B–D = 0
NUMBER OF VARIANTS WITH RATINGS DECREASING THREE STEPS:
A–D = 0
NUMBER OF VARIANTS WITH CONSISTENT RATINGS
THROUGHOUT ALL OCCURRING EDITIONS:
A = 0
B = 5
C = 3
D = 0
NUMBER OF VARIANTS WITH FLUCTUATING RATINGS: 2
NUMBER OF NEW VARIANTS ADDED INTO THE UBSGNT[4]:
A = 9
B = 0
C = 4
D = 0
NUMBER OF OLD VARIANTS DROPPED OUT OF THE UBSGNT[4]. 1
TOTAL NUMBER OF VARIANTS REFERENCED: 36

PHILIPPIANS:
NUMBER OF VARIANTS WITH RATINGS IMPROVING ONE STEP:
D–C = 0
C–B = 4
B–A = 4
NUMBER OF VARIANTS WITH RATINGS IMPROVING TWO STEPS:
D–B = 1
C–A = 1
NUMBER OF VARIANTS WITH RATINGS IMPROVING THREE STEPS:
D–A = 0
NUMBER OF VARIANTS WITH RATINGS DECREASING ONE STEP:
A–B = 0
B–C = 0
C–D = 0
NUMBER OF VARIANTS WITH RATINGS DECREASING TWO STEPS:
A–C = 0
B–D = 0
NUMBER OF VARIANTS WITH RATINGS DECREASING THREE STEPS:
A–D = 0
NUMBER OF VARIANTS WITH CONSISTENT RATINGS
THROUGHOUT ALL OCCURRING EDITIONS:
A = 0
B = 4
C = 2
D = 0
NUMBER OF VARIANTS WITH FLUCTUATING RATINGS: 0
NUMBER OF NEW VARIANTS ADDED INTO THE UBSGNT[4]:
A = 5
B = 2
C = 2
D = 0
NUMBER OF OLD VARIANTS DROPPED OUT OF THE UBSGNT[4]. 4
TOTAL NUMBER OF VARIANTS REFERENCED: 25

COLOSSIANS:
NUMBER OF VARIANTS WITH RATINGS IMPROVING ONE STEP:
D–C = 5
C–B = 8
B–A = 3
NUMBER OF VARIANTS WITH RATINGS IMPROVING TWO STEPS:
D–B = 0
C–A = 0
NUMBER OF VARIANTS WITH RATINGS IMPROVING THREE STEPS:
D–A = 0
NUMBER OF VARIANTS WITH RATINGS DECREASING ONE STEP:
A–B = 0
B–C = 0
C–D = 0
NUMBER OF VARIANTS WITH RATINGS DECREASING TWO STEPS:
A–C = 0
B–D = 0
NUMBER OF VARIANTS WITH RATINGS DECREASING THREE STEPS:
A–D = 0
NUMBER OF VARIANTS WITH CONSISTENT RATINGS
THROUGHOUT ALL OCCURRING EDITIONS:
A = 1
B = 2
C = 3
D = 0
NUMBER OF VARIANTS WITH FLUCTUATING RATINGS: 0
NUMBER OF NEW VARIANTS ADDED INTO THE UBSGNT[4]:
A = 4
B = 2
C = 1
D = 0
NUMBER OF OLD VARIANTS DROPPED OUT OF THE UBSGNT[4]. 1
TOTAL NUMBER OF VARIANTS REFERENCED: 29

1 THESSALONIANS:
NUMBER OF VARIANTS WITH RATINGS IMPROVING ONE STEP:
D–C = 0
C–B = 2
B–A = 3
NUMBER OF VARIANTS WITH RATINGS IMPROVING TWO STEPS:
D–B = 0
C–A = 0
NUMBER OF VARIANTS WITH RATINGS IMPROVING THREE STEPS:
D–A = 0
NUMBER OF VARIANTS WITH RATINGS DECREASING ONE STEP:
A–B = 0
B–C = 1
C–D = 0
NUMBER OF VARIANTS WITH RATINGS DECREASING TWO STEPS:
A–C = 0
B–D = 0
NUMBER OF VARIANTS WITH RATINGS DECREASING THREE STEPS:
A–D = 0
NUMBER OF VARIANTS WITH CONSISTENT RATINGS
THROUGHOUT ALL OCCURRING EDITIONS:
A = 2
B = 1
C = 2
D = 0
NUMBER OF VARIANTS WITH FLUCTUATING RATINGS: 0
NUMBER OF NEW VARIANTS ADDED INTO THE UBSGNT[4].
A = 4
B = 0
C = 1
D = 0
NUMBER OF OLD VARIANTS DROPPED OUT OF THE UBSGNT[4]. 1
TOTAL NUMBER OF VARIANTS REFERENCED: 16

2 THESSALONIANS:
NUMBER OF VARIANTS WITH RATINGS IMPROVING ONE STEP:
D–C = 0
C–B = 3
B–A = 2
NUMBER OF VARIANTS WITH RATINGS IMPROVING TWO STEPS:
D–B = 0
C–A = 1
NUMBER OF VARIANTS WITH RATINGS IMPROVING THREE STEPS:
D–A = 0
NUMBER OF VARIANTS WITH RATINGS DECREASING ONE STEP:
A–B = 0
B–C = 0
C–D = 0
NUMBER OF VARIANTS WITH RATINGS DECREASING TWO STEPS:
A–C = 0
B–D = 0
NUMBER OF VARIANTS WITH RATINGS DECREASING THREE STEPS:
A–D = 0
NUMBER OF VARIANTS WITH CONSISTENT RATINGS
THROUGHOUT ALL OCCURRING EDITIONS:
A = 0
B = 0
C = 3
D = 0
NUMBER OF VARIANTS WITH FLUCTUATING RATINGS: 0
NUMBER OF NEW VARIANTS ADDED INTO THE UBSGNT[4].
A = 0
B = 0
C = 0
D = 0
NUMBER OF OLD VARIANTS DROPPED OUT OF THE UBSGNT[4]. 1
TOTAL NUMBER OF VARIANTS REFERENCED: 9

1 TIMOTHY:
NUMBER OF VARIANTS WITH RATINGS IMPROVING ONE STEP:
D–C = 0
C–B = 1
B–A = 4
NUMBER OF VARIANTS WITH RATINGS IMPROVING TWO STEPS:
D–B = 0
C–A = 2
NUMBER OF VARIANTS WITH RATINGS IMPROVING THREE STEPS:
D–A = 0
NUMBER OF VARIANTS WITH RATINGS DECREASING ONE STEP:
A–B = 0
B–C = 0
C–D = 0
NUMBER OF VARIANTS WITH RATINGS DECREASING TWO STEPS:
A–C = 0
B–D = 0
NUMBER OF VARIANTS WITH RATINGS DECREASING THREE STEPS:
A–D = 0
NUMBER OF VARIANTS WITH CONSISTENT RATINGS THROUGHOUT ALL OCCURRING EDITIONS:
A = 2
B = 1
C = 1
D = 0
NUMBER OF VARIANTS WITH FLUCTUATING RATINGS: 0
NUMBER OF NEW VARIANTS ADDED INTO THE UBSGNT[4]:
A = 7
B = 7
C = 1
D = 0
NUMBER OF OLD VARIANTS DROPPED OUT OF THE UBSGNT[4]: 1
TOTAL NUMBER OF VARIANTS REFERENCED: 20

2 TIMOTHY:
NUMBER OF VARIANTS WITH RATINGS IMPROVING ONE STEP:
D–C = 0
C–B = 3
B–A = 2
NUMBER OF VARIANTS WITH RATINGS IMPROVING TWO STEPS:
D–B = 0
C–A = 0
NUMBER OF VARIANTS WITH RATINGS IMPROVING THREE STEPS:
D–A = 0
NUMBER OF VARIANTS WITH RATINGS DECREASING ONE STEP:
A–B = 0
B–C = 0
C–D = 0
NUMBER OF VARIANTS WITH RATINGS DECREASING TWO STEPS:
A–C = 0
B–D = 0
NUMBER OF VARIANTS WITH RATINGS DECREASING THREE STEPS:
A–D = 0
NUMBER OF VARIANTS WITH CONSISTENT RATINGS THROUGHOUT ALL OCCURRING EDITIONS:
A = 0
B = 0
C = 3
D = 0
NUMBER OF VARIANTS WITH FLUCTUATING RATINGS: 0
NUMBER OF NEW VARIANTS ADDED INTO THE UBSGNT[4]:
A = 0
B = 2
C = 0
D = 0
NUMBER OF OLD VARIANTS DROPPED OUT OF THE UBSGNT[4]: 2
TOTAL NUMBER OF VARIANTS REFERENCED: 10

TITUS:
NUMBER OF VARIANTS WITH RATINGS IMPROVING ONE STEP:
D–C = 0
C–B = 1
B–A = 2
NUMBER OF VARIANTS WITH RATINGS IMPROVING TWO STEPS:
D–B = 0
C–A = 0
NUMBER OF VARIANTS WITH RATINGS IMPROVING THREE STEPS:
D–A = 0
NUMBER OF VARIANTS WITH RATINGS DECREASING ONE STEP:
A–B = 0
B–C = 0
C–D = 0
NUMBER OF VARIANTS WITH RATINGS DECREASING TWO STEPS:
A–C = 0
B–D = 0
NUMBER OF VARIANTS WITH RATINGS DECREASING THREE STEPS:
A–D = 0
NUMBER OF VARIANTS WITH CONSISTENT RATINGS
THROUGHOUT ALL OCCURRING EDITIONS:
A = 0
B = 0
C = 1
D = 0
NUMBER OF VARIANTS WITH FLUCTUATING RATINGS: 0
NUMBER OF NEW VARIANTS ADDED INTO THE UBSGNT[4]:
A = 0
B = 0
C = 0
D = 0
NUMBER OF OLD VARIANTS DROPPED OUT OF THE UBSGNT[4]: 0
TOTAL NUMBER OF VARIANTS REFERENCED: 4

PHILEMON:
NUMBER OF VARIANTS WITH RATINGS IMPROVING ONE STEP:
D–C = 0
C–B = 2
B–A = 1
NUMBER OF VARIANTS WITH RATINGS IMPROVING TWO STEPS:
D–B = 0
C–A = 0
NUMBER OF VARIANTS WITH RATINGS IMPROVING THREE STEPS:
D–A = 0
NUMBER OF VARIANTS WITH RATINGS DECREASING ONE STEP:
A–B = 0
B–C = 0
C–D = 0
NUMBER OF VARIANTS WITH RATINGS DECREASING TWO STEPS:
A–C = 0
B–D = 0
NUMBER OF VARIANTS WITH RATINGS DECREASING THREE STEPS:
A–D = 0
NUMBER OF VARIANTS WITH CONSISTENT RATINGS
THROUGHOUT ALL OCCURRING EDITIONS:
A = 0
B = 1
C = 0
D = 0
NUMBER OF VARIANTS WITH FLUCTUATING RATINGS: 0
NUMBER OF NEW VARIANTS ADDED INTO THE UBSGNT[4]:
A = 1
B = 0
C = 0
D = 0
NUMBER OF OLD VARIANTS DROPPED OUT OF THE UBSGNT[4]: 0
TOTAL NUMBER OF VARIANTS REFERENCED: 5

HEBREWS:

NUMBER OF VARIANTS WITH RATINGS IMPROVING ONE STEP:
D–C = 4
C–B = 10
B–A = 10

NUMBER OF VARIANTS WITH RATINGS IMPROVING TWO STEPS:
D–B = 1
C–A = 2

NUMBER OF VARIANTS WITH RATINGS IMPROVING THREE STEPS:
D–A = 0

NUMBER OF VARIANTS WITH RATINGS DECREASING ONE STEP:
A–B = 0
B–C = 0
C–D = 0

NUMBER OF VARIANTS WITH RATINGS DECREASING TWO STEPS:
A–C = 0
B–D = 0

NUMBER OF VARIANTS WITH RATINGS DECREASING THREE STEPS:
A–D = 0

NUMBER OF VARIANTS WITH CONSISTENT RATINGS THROUGHOUT ALL OCCURRING EDITIONS:
A = 2
B = 1
C = 7
D = 0

NUMBER OF VARIANTS WITH FLUCTUATING RATINGS: 1

NUMBER OF NEW VARIANTS ADDED INTO THE UBSGNT[4]:
A = 6
B = 0
C = 3
D = 0

NUMBER OF OLD VARIANTS DROPPED OUT OF THE UBSGNT[4]: 3
TOTAL NUMBER OF VARIANTS REFERENCED: 47

JAMES:

NUMBER OF VARIANTS WITH RATINGS IMPROVING ONE STEP:
D–C = 1
C–B = 4
B–A = 0

NUMBER OF VARIANTS WITH RATINGS IMPROVING TWO STEPS:
D–B = 2
C–A = 2

NUMBER OF VARIANTS WITH RATINGS IMPROVING THREE STEPS:
D–A = 0

NUMBER OF VARIANTS WITH RATINGS DECREASING ONE STEP:
A–B = 0
B–C = 0
C–D = 0

NUMBER OF VARIANTS WITH RATINGS DECREASING TWO STEPS:
A–C = 0
B–D = 0

NUMBER OF VARIANTS WITH RATINGS DECREASING THREE STEPS:
A–D = 0

NUMBER OF VARIANTS WITH CONSISTENT RATINGS THROUGHOUT ALL OCCURRING EDITIONS:
A = 1
B = 5
C = 0
D = 0

NUMBER OF VARIANTS WITH FLUCTUATING RATINGS: 3

NUMBER OF NEW VARIANTS ADDED INTO THE UBSGNT[4]:
A = 4
B = 1
C = 1
D = 0

NUMBER OF OLD VARIANTS DROPPED OUT OF THE UBSGNT[4]: 1
TOTAL NUMBER OF VARIANTS REFERENCED: 24

1 PETER:
NUMBER OF VARIANTS WITH RATINGS IMPROVING ONE STEP:
D–C = 1
C–B = 4
B–A = 7
NUMBER OF VARIANTS WITH RATINGS IMPROVING TWO STEPS:
D–B = 1
C–A = 5
NUMBER OF VARIANTS WITH RATINGS IMPROVING THREE STEPS:
D–A = 0
NUMBER OF VARIANTS WITH RATINGS DECREASING ONE STEP:
A–B = 0
B–C = 0
C–D = 0
NUMBER OF VARIANTS WITH RATINGS DECREASING TWO STEPS:
A–C = 0
B–D = 0
NUMBER OF VARIANTS WITH RATINGS DECREASING THREE STEPS:
A–D = 0
NUMBER OF VARIANTS WITH CONSISTENT RATINGS
THROUGHOUT ALL OCCURRING EDITIONS:
A = 1
B = 2
C = 6 (1 Peter 3.18[2] included here)
D = 0
NUMBER OF VARIANTS WITH FLUCTUATING RATINGS: 0
NUMBER OF NEW VARIANTS ADDED INTO THE UBSGNT[4]:
A = 7
B = 4
C = 2
D = 0
NUMBER OF OLD VARIANTS DROPPED OUT OF THE UBSGNT[4]: 3
TOTAL NUMBER OF VARIANTS REFERENCED: 40

2 PETER:
NUMBER OF VARIANTS WITH RATINGS IMPROVING ONE STEP:
D–C = 3
C–B = 4
B–A = 4
NUMBER OF VARIANTS WITH RATINGS IMPROVING TWO STEPS:
D–B = 2
C–A = 1
NUMBER OF VARIANTS WITH RATINGS IMPROVING THREE STEPS:
D–A = 0
NUMBER OF VARIANTS WITH RATINGS DECREASING ONE STEP:
A–B = 0
B–C = 0
C–D = 0
NUMBER OF VARIANTS WITH RATINGS DECREASING TWO STEPS:
A–C = 0
B–D = 0
NUMBER OF VARIANTS WITH RATINGS DECREASING THREE STEPS:
A–D = 0
NUMBER OF VARIANTS WITH CONSISTENT RATINGS
THROUGHOUT ALL OCCURRING EDITIONS:
A = 0
B = 0
C = 4
D = 1
NUMBER OF VARIANTS WITH FLUCTUATING RATINGS: 1
NUMBER OF NEW VARIANTS ADDED INTO THE UBSGNT[4]:
A = 3
B = 2
C = 0
D = 0
NUMBER OF OLD VARIANTS DROPPED OUT OF THE UBSGNT[4]: 1
TOTAL NUMBER OF VARIANTS REFERENCED: 25

1 JOHN:
NUMBER OF VARIANTS WITH RATINGS IMPROVING ONE STEP:
D–C = 1
C–B = 5
B–A = 10
NUMBER OF VARIANTS WITH RATINGS IMPROVING TWO STEPS:
D–B = 1
C–A = 2
NUMBER OF VARIANTS WITH RATINGS IMPROVING THREE STEPS:
D–A = 0
NUMBER OF VARIANTS WITH RATINGS DECREASING ONE STEP:
A–B = 0
B–C = 0
C–D = 0
NUMBER OF VARIANTS WITH RATINGS DECREASING TWO STEPS:
A–C = 0
B–D = 0
NUMBER OF VARIANTS WITH RATINGS DECREASING THREE STEPS:
A–D = 0
NUMBER OF VARIANTS WITH CONSISTENT RATINGS THROUGHOUT ALL OCCURRING EDITIONS:
A = 2
B = 1
C = 2
D = 0
NUMBER OF VARIANTS WITH FLUCTUATING RATINGS: 1
NUMBER OF NEW VARIANTS ADDED INTO THE UBSGNT[4]:
A = 5
B = 2
C = 1
D = 0
NUMBER OF OLD VARIANTS DROPPED OUT OF THE UBSGNT[4]: 1
TOTAL NUMBER OF VARIANTS REFERENCED: 33

2 JOHN:
NUMBER OF VARIANTS WITH RATINGS IMPROVING ONE STEP:
D–C = 0
C–B = 2
B–A = 3
NUMBER OF VARIANTS WITH RATINGS IMPROVING TWO STEPS:
D–B = 0
C–A = 1
NUMBER OF VARIANTS WITH RATINGS IMPROVING THREE STEPS:
D–A = 0
NUMBER OF VARIANTS WITH RATINGS DECREASING ONE STEP:
A–B = 0
B–C = 0
C–D = 0
NUMBER OF VARIANTS WITH RATINGS DECREASING TWO STEPS:
A–C = 0
B–D = 0
NUMBER OF VARIANTS WITH RATINGS DECREASING THREE STEPS:
A–D = 0
NUMBER OF VARIANTS WITH CONSISTENT RATINGS THROUGHOUT ALL OCCURRING EDITIONS:
A = 0
B = 0
C = 0
D = 0
NUMBER OF VARIANTS WITH FLUCTUATING RATINGS: 0
NUMBER OF NEW VARIANTS ADDED INTO THE UBSGNT[4]:
A = 0
B = 0
C = 0
D = 0
NUMBER OF OLD VARIANTS DROPPED OUT OF THE UBSGNT[4]: 0
TOTAL NUMBER OF VARIANTS REFERENCED: 6

3 JOHN:

NUMBER OF VARIANTS WITH RATINGS IMPROVING ONE STEP:
D–C   =   0
C–B   =   1
B–A   =   1
NUMBER OF VARIANTS WITH RATINGS IMPROVING TWO STEPS:
D–B   =   0
C–A   =   0
NUMBER OF VARIANTS WITH RATINGS IMPROVING THREE STEPS:
D–A   =   0
NUMBER OF VARIANTS WITH RATINGS DECREASING ONE STEP:
A–B   =   0
B–C   =   0
C–D   =   0
NUMBER OF VARIANTS WITH RATINGS DECREASING TWO STEPS:
A–C   =   0
B–D   =   0
NUMBER OF VARIANTS WITH RATINGS DECREASING THREE STEPS:
A–D   =   0
NUMBER OF VARIANTS WITH CONSISTENT RATINGS
THROUGHOUT ALL OCCURRING EDITIONS:
A   =   0
B   =   0
C   =   1
D   =   0
NUMBER OF VARIANTS WITH FLUCTUATING RATINGS: 0
NUMBER OF NEW VARIANTS ADDED INTO THE UBSGNT[4]:
A   =   0
B   =   0
C   =   0
D   =   0
NUMBER OF OLD VARIANTS DROPPED OUT OF THE UBSGNT[4]:   1
TOTAL NUMBER OF VARIANTS REFERENCED: 3

JUDE:

NUMBER OF VARIANTS WITH RATINGS IMPROVING ONE STEP:
D–C   =   0
C–B   =   0
B–A   =   2
NUMBER OF VARIANTS WITH RATINGS IMPROVING TWO STEPS:
D–B   =   0
C–A   =   0
NUMBER OF VARIANTS WITH RATINGS IMPROVING THREE STEPS:
D–A   =   0
NUMBER OF VARIANTS WITH RATINGS DECREASING ONE STEP:
A–B   =   0
B–C   =   0
C–D   =   0
NUMBER OF VARIANTS WITH RATINGS DECREASING TWO STEPS:
A–C   =   0
B–D   =   0
NUMBER OF VARIANTS WITH RATINGS DECREASING THREE STEPS:
A–D   =   0
NUMBER OF VARIANTS WITH CONSISTENT RATINGS
THROUGHOUT ALL OCCURRING EDITIONS:
A   =   0
B   =   0
C   =   3
D   =   1
NUMBER OF VARIANTS WITH FLUCTUATING RATINGS: 0
NUMBER OF NEW VARIANTS ADDED INTO THE UBSGNT[4]:
A   =   7
B   =   0
C   =   0
D   =   0
NUMBER OF OLD VARIANTS DROPPED OUT OF THE UBSGNT[4]:   0
TOTAL NUMBER OF VARIANTS REFERENCED: 13

REVELATION:

NUMBER OF VARIANTS WITH RATINGS IMPROVING ONE STEP:
D–C = 3
C–B = 26
B–A = 10

NUMBER OF VARIANTS WITH RATINGS IMPROVING TWO STEPS:
D–B = 1
C–A = 5

NUMBER OF VARIANTS WITH RATINGS IMPROVING THREE STEPS:
D–A = 0

NUMBER OF VARIANTS WITH RATINGS DECREASING ONE STEP:
A–B = 0
B–C = 0
C–D = 0

NUMBER OF VARIANTS WITH RATINGS DECREASING TWO STEPS:
A–C = 0
B–D = 0

NUMBER OF VARIANTS WITH RATINGS DECREASING THREE STEPS:
A–D = 0

NUMBER OF VARIANTS WITH CONSISTENT RATINGS THROUGHOUT ALL OCCURRING EDITIONS:
A = 1
B = 4
C = 40
D = 1

NUMBER OF VARIANTS WITH FLUCTUATING RATINGS: 1
NUMBER OF NEW VARIANTS ADDED INTO THE UBSGNT[4].
A = 7
B = 2
C = 2
D = 0

NUMBER OF OLD VARIANTS DROPPED OUT OF THE UBSGNT[4]. 31
TOTAL NUMBER OF VARIANTS REFERENCED: 103

GRAND TOTAL FIGURES[i]:

TOTAL NUMBER OF VARIANTS WITH RATINGS IMPROVING ONE STEP:
D–C = 68
C–B = 258
B–A = 189

TOTAL NUMBER OF VARIANTS WITH RATINGS IMPROVING TWO STEPS:
D–B = 29
C–A = 52

TOTAL NUMBER OF VARIANTS WITH RATINGS IMPROVING THREE STEPS:
D–A = 2

TOTAL NUMBER OF VARIANTS WITH RATINGS DECREASING ONE STEP:
A–B = 13
B–C = 14
C–D = 3

TOTAL NUMBER OF VARIANTS WITH RATINGS DECREASING TWO STEPS:
A–C = 0
B–D = 0

TOTAL NUMBER OF VARIANTS WITH RATINGS DECREASING THREE STEPS:
A–D = 0

TOTAL NUMBER OF VARIANTS WITH CONSISTENT RATINGS THROUGHOUT ALL OCCURRING EDITIONS:
A = 121
B = 262
C = 368
D = 22

TOTAL NUMBER OF VARIANTS WITH FLUCTUATING RATINGS: 45
TOTAL NUMBER OF NEW VARIANTS ADDED INTO THE UBSGNT[4].
A = 168
B = 62
C = 55   (285 Total Rated Passages)[ii]
D = 0

TOTAL NUMBER OF OLD VARIANTS DROPPED OUT OF THE UBSGNT[4].
A = 23
B = 99   300 Total Rated Passages
                (273 from *UBSGNT*[3] to the *UBSGNT*[4])[iii]
C = 162
D = 16

TOTAL NUMBER OF VARIANTS REFERENCED:
1731[iv] (1437-1438 in the *UBSGNT*[4])

Notes to Appendix III

i.   If any figure in this list shows a discrepancy with the *UBSGNT* committee's figures, it is footnoted and discussed. All figures were checked at least three times when a discrepancy was revealed. This often involved recalculating the statistics of an entire section. The following explanations also provide insight into the discrepancies existing in these figures: 1) in defining their numerical additions and deletions, the *UBSGNT* committee appendix has used the term 'passages' (see p. 2* of the *UBSGNT*⁴ Introduction). Discrepancies may result because this term denotes an actual biblical passage that may include more than one variant. 2) This chapter provides statistics only for variants that have been ascribed a letter-rating. If a variant has not been given this rating, it will not appear in these tables or statistics.

ii.   When the four totals recorded in this category (168, 62, 55, 0) are added together, the calculation comes to 285 new variants added to the *UBSGNT*⁴ (i.e. 168 [A] + 62 [B] + 55 [C] + 0 [D] = 285). On p. 2* of the *UBSGNT*⁴ Introduction, 284 new passages are said to be added. The statistical differences between this chart and the totals given in the *UBSGNT*⁴ are negligible. However, although the discrepancy here is minor, one can consult the list of 'New Variants Added to the *UBSGNT*⁴' in Chapter 2, Section 2, in order to examine the exact passages included in this tally.

iii.   On p. 2* of the *UBSGNT*⁴, we are told that 273 'passages' were removed. Again, the first point in note i above may account for some, if not all, of the discrepancy here. However, one may wish to consult the list entitled 'Variants Dropped Out of the *UBSGNT*⁴', in Chapter 2, Section 2, in order to examine the actual 300 omitted variants.

iv.   On p. v of the preface to the *UBSGNT*⁴ the total number of variants given is 1437. On p. 2* of the Introduction, 1438 passages are said to be the scope of the apparatus. It is uncertain whether the term 'passages' refers to individual variants or to actual biblical passages where variants occur. Yet the reason for this minor discrepancy within the *UBSGNT*⁴ is uncertain. Regardless, the figure given here is 1731 total variants referenced. It should be kept in mind that this number indicates all variants examined within all editions, not just the *UBSGNT*⁴. This includes variants that may have only occurred in one edition and were later removed. Therefore, in all the *UBSGNT* editions combined, a total of 1731 letter-rated passages have been dealt with (this figure does not include unrated variants which provided little information for this monograph). In Chapter 2, Section 1, the total number of variants recorded in the *UBSGNT*⁴ comes to 1431 (514 [A] + 541 [B] + 367 [C] + 9 [D] = 1431). As already stated immediately above, the *UBSGNT*⁴ committee claim there are either 1437 or 1438 variant passages. The discrepancy here (between 1431 or 1437-38 variant passages) may well be due to any number of the above explanations, yet it should be noted that this difference has no sizable effect whatsoever upon the conclusions of this monograph.

APPENDIX IV

Principal Manuscript Evidence in Selected Portions of the UBSGNT⁴

Appendix IV contains data that are one stage prior to the information presented in Appendix V. Appendix IV also contains the raw material used to develop the 'High Percentage Manuscript Groupings' charts of Chapter 2, Section 4. Like the charts in Section 4, this appendix records all *UBSGNT⁴* manuscript citations given in every variant that occurs within the first eight chapters of Luke, Acts, Romans, and Revelation, and the entire book of 1 Peter. The manuscript types that are represented in these charts follow in this order: papyri, uncials, minuscules, lectionaries, Old Latin versions, Vulgate versions, Syriac versions, Coptic versions, Armenian versions, Ethiopic versions, Georgian versions, Greek Father quotations, and Latin Father quotations.

Only the manuscripts cited within the first variant option of an entire variant unit (i.e. the variant reading that appears in the *UBSGNT⁴* text) are recorded in this appendix. Alternative variant options are not listed. These charts are fairly simple to understand. Every textual variant is listed with its reference (chapter and verse), and with its *UBSGNT⁴* letter-rating (*A*, *B*, *C*, and *D*). These appear at the top of each column. Every manuscript that is cited in the given chapters of a given book is listed along the far left column. If a particular manuscript is present within a variant passage, it is marked with an 'X'. If no 'X' is present, the manuscript is not cited for that variant. Often special abbreviations (such as brackets '( )', or superscript numerals like '1/2' etc.) are cited along with the particular manuscript (again, marked by the 'X'). For an explanation of these one should consult page 47* of the *UBSGNT⁴* which contains the 'Master List Of Symbols And Abbreviations'. If the symbols are too detailed to record within a chart, they are reproduced (in the same form as they appear in the *UBSGNT⁴*) in a list located at the end of this appendix. More information concerning these symbols and listings can be found there. What these charts are in essence producing is the *UBSGNT⁴* critical apparatus as it appears for the first variant option cited in each textual variant. By paying close attention to the footnotes, the reader will come across further details regarding these charts, the *UBSGNT⁴* apparatus, and particular points of interest pertaining to various manuscripts.

Textual Optimism

Principal Manuscript Evidence in the First Eight Chapters of Luke
Papyri Evidence (UBSGNT[4])

Variant	1.28	1.35	1.46	1.66	1.74	1.78	2.9	2.11	2.14	2.33	2.38
Rating	A	A	A	A	B	B	B	A	A	B	A
Papyri 𝔓4[i]				X[vid]							

Variant	3.22	3.32	3.33	4.4	4.17	4.18	4.44	5.17	5.17	5.33	5.38
Rating	B	B	C	B	B	A	B	B	A	B	B
Papyri 𝔓4	X	X								X	X
𝔓75							X				X[vid]

Variant	5.39	5.39a	5.39b	6.1	6.4	6.4	6.5	6.10	6.31	6.35	6.48
Rating	C	A	A	C	A	A	B	A	B	B	A
Papyri 𝔓4		X	X	X			X	X			
𝔓75			X						X[vid]		X[vid]

Variant	7.7	7.10	7.11	7.11	7.19	7.28	7.32	7.35	7.39	7.45	8.3
Rating	B	A	B	B	C	B	B	B	A	A	B
Papyri 𝔓75	X[vid]	X	X	X		X					

Variant	8.26	8.37	8.43	8.44	8.45	8.45	8.49
Rating	C	C	C	B	B	B	B
Papyri 𝔓75	X	X		X	X	X	X

i. Numerous papyri are footnoted throughout the papyri evidence charts because of their early age and importance to textual criticism. Both 𝔓4, containing various portions of the first six chapters in Luke, and 𝔓75, containing large sections of Luke and John, are significant (at least from the view of external evidence which is partially concerned with the age of manuscripts) in that they are dated from the third century with 𝔓75 given a very early third-century date. The Alands list both papyri as category I manuscripts in *The Text of the New Testament*, pp. 96-101.

Principal Manuscript Evidence in the First Eight Chapters of Luke
Uncial Evidence (UBSGNT^4)

Variant	1.28	1.35	1.46	1.66	1.74	1.78	2.9	2.11	2.14	2.33	2.38
Rating	A	A	A	A	B	B	B	A	A	B	A
Uncials											
ℵ01	X	X	X	X	X	X*	X	X	X*	X¹ (X*)	X
A02		X	X	X				X	X		
B03	X	X	X	X	X	X	X	X	X*	X	X
C04		X²	X² (X*)	X							
D05		X	(X)					X	X	X	
[E07]^{ii}		X	X	X				X			
[F09]			X	X				X			
[G011]		X	X	X				X			
[H013]		X	X	X				X			
L019	X	X	X	X	X	(X)	X	X		(X)	
[P024]								X			
W032	X	X	X	X	X	X	X	(X)	X	X	X
Δ037		X	X	X				X			
Θ038			X	X		X		X			
Ξ040			X				X	X			X
Ψ044	X	X	X	X				X			
0130				X	(X)						
0177						X					
0233											X

Variant	3.22	3.32	3.33	4.4	4.17	4.18	4.44	5.17	5.17	5.33	5.38
Rating	B	B	C	B	B	A	B	B	A	B	B
Uncials											
ℵ01	X	X*	X²	X	X	X	X	X¹	X	X¹	X¹ (X*)
A02	X							Xᶜ			
B03	X	X		X		X	X	X	X	X	X
C04							X	X			
D05					Xᶜ (X*)	X					
[E07]	X				X			X			
[F09]					X						
[G011]	X				X						
[H013]	X				X			X			
L019	X		X	X		X	X	X	X	X	X
[N022]	X		(X*)					X			
[Q026]							Xᵛⁱᵈ				
W032	X			X		X	(X)	X	X	X	(X)
Δ037					X			X			
Θ038	X				X			X			
Ξ040						X		X	X	X	
Ψ044	X			X				X			
070	X										
0233	Xᵛⁱᵈ				X						

ii. Manuscripts placed in brackets are uncials that have a Byzantine text. These manuscripts would be cited following the group symbol *Byz*, as indicated in the footnotes on p. 904 of the *UBSGNT^4*.

Variant Rating	5.39 C	5.39a A	5.39b A	6.1 C	6.4 A	6.4 A	6.5 B	6.10 A	6.31 B	6.35 B	6.48 A
Uncials											
ℵ01	X*	X	X	X		X	X	X			X
A02	X		X			X		X		X	
B03		X	X	X	X	X	X	X	X	X	X
C04	X		X								
D05										X	
[E07]	X		X			X		X		X	
[F09]	X		X								
[H013]	X		X			X				X	
L019	X	X	X	X	X	X		X		X	X
W032	X	X	X	X	X	X	X	X			X
Δ037	X		X			X		X		X	
Θ038	X		X			X				X	
Ξ040											X
Ψ044	X		X		X	X		X		X	
0233	X		X			X					

Variant Rating	7.7 B	7.10 A	7.11 B	7.11 B	7.19 C	7.28 B	7.32 B	7.35 B	7.39 A	7.45 A	8.3 B
Uncials											
ℵ01		X	X^2	X		X	X		X	X	
A02			X						X	X	
B03	X	X	X	X	X	X	X	X	X^2	X	X
D05				X			X		X	X	X
[E07]			X^{pt}						X	X	X^{pt}
[F09]			X^{pt}						X	X	X^{pt}
[G011]			X^{pt}						X	X	X^{pt}
[H013]			X^{pt}						X	X	X^{pt}
L019	X	X	X	X	X	X	X		X	X^c	
[P024]									X	X	
W032		X		X		X	X	X	X	X	X
Δ037			X						X	X	X
Θ038			X				X		X	X	X
Ξ040				X	X	X	X		X		
Ψ044			X						X	X	
079										X	

Variant Rating	8.26 C	8.37 C	8.43 C	8.44 B	8.45 B	8.45 B	8.49 B
Uncials							
ℵ01			X^2	X		X	X
A02		X		X			
B03	X	X		X	X	X	X
C04		X*		X			
D05	X	X					X
[E07]			X	X			
[G011]			X	X			
[H013]			X	X			
L019			X	X	X		
[P024]			X	X			
W032			X	X			
Δ037			X	X			
Θ038			X	X			
Ξ040			X	X			

Principal Manuscript Evidence in the First Eight Chapters of Luke
Minuscule Evidence (UBSGNT⁴)

Variant Rating	1.28 A	1.35 A	1.46 A	1.66 A	1.74 B	1.78 B	2.9 B	2.11 A	2.14 A	2.33 B	2.38 A
Minusc.											
f1	X		X	(X)				X		X	
f13		X	X	X	X			X			
1					X						X
28		X	X	X				X			
33			X	X				X^{vid}			
157		X	X	X				X			
180		X	X	X				X			
205		X	X	X				X			
565	X	X	X	X	X		X	X			X
579	X	X	X	X			X	X			
597		X	X	X				X			
700	X	X	X	X			X	X		X	
892		X	X	X	X			X			
1006		X	X	X				X			
1010		X	X	X				X			
1071		X	X	X				X			
1241	X	X	X	X			X	X		X	
1243		X	X	X				X			
1292		X	X	X				X			
1342		X	X	X				X			
1424		X	X	X				X			
1505		X	X	X				X			

Variant Rating	3.22 B	3.32 B	3.33 C	4.4 B	4.17 B	4.18 A	4.44 B	5.17 B	5.17 A	5.33 B	5.38 B
Minusc.											
f1	X				X		X				X
f13	X		(X)		X	X					
28	X				X			X			
33	X					X				X	X
157	X		X		X		X	X		X	X
180	X				X			X			
205	X				X		X				X
565	X				X			X			
579	X					X	X	X	X		X
597	X			X				X			
700	(X)				X	X		X			X
892	X					X*	X	X		X*	
1006	X			X				X			
1010	X			X				X			
1071	X			X				X			
1241	X			X			X	X		X	X
1243	X				X			X			
1292	X				X			X			
1342	X				X			X			
1424	X				X			X			
1505	X				X			X			

Variant Rating	5.39 C	5.39a A	5.39b A	6.1 C	6.4 A	6.4 A	6.5 B	6.10 A	6.31 B	6.35 B	6.48 A
Minusc.											
f1	X		X	X	X	X				X	
f13	X		X			X				X	
28	X		X			X		X		X	
33	X		X	X		X		X		X	
157	X	X	X	X						X	X
180	X		X			X		X		X	
205	X		X	X	X	X				X	
565	X		X			X		X		X	
579			X	X		X		X	X	X	X
597	X		X			X		X		X	
700			X			X		X	X	X	
892			X			X		X		X	X
1006	X		X			X		X		X	
1010	X		X			X		X		X	
1071	X		X			X					
1241		X	X	X		X	X	X	X	X	X
1243	X		X			X				X	
1292	X		X			X		X		X	
1342	X	X	X			X		X		X	X
1424	X		X			X		X		X	
1505	X		X					X		X	

Variant Rating	7.7 B	7.10 A	7.11 B	7.11 B	7.19 C	7.28 B	7.32 B	7.35 B	7.39 A	7.45 A	8.3 B
Minusc.											
f1		X	X			X			X	X	
f13			X		X		X	X	X		X
28									X	X	X
33			X		X				X	X	
157		X	X	X	X	X		X	X		X
180			X						X	X	X
205		X	X						X		
565									X	X	
579		X	X	X		X		X	X	X	
597			X						X	X	X
700		X	X						X	X	X
892		X*					X	X	X	X	X
1006			X						X	X	X
1010			X						X	X	
1071									X		X
1241	X	X	X	X			X		X	X	
1243			X						X		
1292			X						X	X	
1342		X	X	X	X		X		X	X	
1424									X	X	X
1505			X						X	X	X

Variant	8.26	8.37	8.43	8.44	8.45	8.45	8.49
Rating	C	C	C	B	B	B	B
Minusc.							
fl			X	X		X	
f13			X	X			
28			X	X			
33			X	X			
157				X		X	
180			X	X			
205			X	X		(X)	
565			X	X			
579		X	(X)	X			X
597			X	X			
700			(X)	X	X*		
892			X	X			
1006			X	X			
1010			(X)	X			
1241			X	X		X	
1243			X	X			
1292			X	X			
1342			X	X			
1424				X			
1505			X	X			

Principal Manuscript Evidence in the First Eight Chapters of Luke
Lectionary Evidence (UBSGNT⁴)

Variant	1.28	1.35	1.46	1.66	1.74	1.78	2.9	2.11	2.14	2.33	2.38
Rating	A	A	A	A	B	B	B	A	A	B	A
Lection.											
Lect.[iii]		X	X	X				X			
L253[iv]											X

Variant	3.22	3.32	3.33	4.4	4.17	4.18	4.44	5.17	5.17	5.33	5.38
Rating	B	B	C	B	B	A	B	B	A	B	B
Lection.											
Lect.	X				X		X	X			
L68							(X)				
L76							(X)				
L387							(X)				
L673							(X)				
L813							(X)				
L1223							(X)				

iii. The '*Lect*' symbol represents the reading of the majority of the lectionaries selected, together with the text of the edition published by Apostoliki Diakonia, Athens. This is explained on p. 50* of the *UBSGNT*⁴.

iv. Throughout these charts the regular small-cap letter '*l*', generally used as the lectionary symbol, is replaced with the capital letter '*L*'.

Variant	5.39	5.39a	5.39b	6.1	6.4	6.4	6.5	6.10	6.31	6.35	6.48
Rating	C	A	A	C	A	A	B	A	B	B	A
Lection.											
Lect.	X		X			X		X		X	
L524					X						

Variant	7.7	7.10	7.11	7.11	7.19	7.28	7.32	7.35	7.39	7.45	8.3
Rating	B	A	B	B	C	B	B	B	A	A	B
Lection.											
Lect.									X	$X^{pt,AD}$	X^{pt}

Variant	8.26	8.37	8.43	8.44	8.45	8.45	8.49
Rating	C	C	C	B	B	B	B
Lection.							
Lect.			X	X			

Principal Manuscript Evidence in the First Eight Chapters of Luke
Old Latin Evidence (UBSGNT⁴)

Variant	1.28	1.35	1.46	1.66	1.74	1.78	2.9	2.11	2.14	2.33	2.38
Rating	A	A	A	A	B	B	B	A	A	B	A
Old Latin											
it^{a}								X			
it^{aur}		X	(X)	X				X			X
$it^{b}\,(e)^{v}$		X		(X)				X			X
it^{β}					X						X
it^{c}			(X)	X				X			X
$it^{d}\,(ea)$		X	(X)						X	X	
$it^{e}\,(e)$			(X)	X	(X)						X
$it^{f}\,(e)$		X	(X)	X				X			X
it^{ff2}		X	(X)					X			X
$it^{l}\,(e)$		X						X			X
it^{n}											X
$it^{q}\,(e)$		X	(X)					X			
it^{rl}			(X)								

v.   When two manuscripts with identical lettering or numbering are listed in the Old Latin evidence chart, they are distinguished by placing the contents of each manuscript within brackets. The abbreviations are as given in the section entitled 'Principal Manuscripts And Versions Cited In The Textual Apparatus', beginning on p. 903 of the *UBSGNT⁴* (this information is also often included in a small pamphlet provided by the United Bible Society and placed inside their *UBSGNT*). The particular abbreviations are as follows: e-Gospels; a-Acts; p-Pauline Epistles; c-Catholic or General Epistles; and r-Revelation.

Variant	3.22	3.32	3.33	4.4	4.17	4.18	4.44	5.17	5.17	5.33	5.38
Rating	B	B	C	B	B	A	B	B	A	B	B
Old Latin											
it^a					X	X					
it^{aur}	X				X	X		X			
$it^b(e)$					X	X		X			
it^c					X	X		X			
$it^d(ea)$					X	X					
$it^e(e)$	X				X						
$it^f(e)$					X			X			
it^{ff2}					X	X		X			
$it^l(e)$					X	X		X			
$it^q(e)$	X				X	X		X			
it^{rl}					X	X		X			

Variant	5.39	5.39a	5.39b	6.1	6.4	6.4	6.5	6.10	6.31	6.35	6.48
Rating	C	A	A	C	A	A	B	A	B	B	A
Old Latin											
it^a					X	X			(X)	X	
it^{aur}	X		X		X	X			X	X	
$it^b(e)$			X	X	X	X				X	
it^c				X	(X)	X				X	
$it^d(ea)$										X	
$it^e(e)$					(X)	X				X	
$it^f(e)$	X		X		X	X		X		X	
it^{ff2}					X	X			X	X	
$it^l(e)$				X	X	X			X	X	
$it^q(e)$	X		X	X	X	X				X	
it^{rl}				X	X	X				X	

Variant	7.7	7.10	7.11	7.11	7.19	7.28	7.32	7.35	7.39	7.45	8.3
Rating	B	A	B	B	C	B	B	B	A	A	B
Old Latin											
it^a		X	X	X	X			X			
it^{aur}		X	X	X			(X)	X			
$it^b(e)$		X	X					X		X	
it^c		X					X	X		X	X
$it^d(ea)$			X				X			X	X
$it^e(e)$		X	X				X				X
$it^f(e)$			X					X		X	X
it^{ff2}	X	X	X		X			X			X
$it^l(e)$	X	X	X				X	(X)		X	
$it^q(e)$	X	X						X		X	
it^{rl}	X	X	X				X			X	X

| Variant | 8.26 | 8.37 | 8.43 | 8.44 | 8.45 | 8.45 | 8.49 |
Rating	C	C	C	B	B	B	B
Old Latin							
it^a	X	X	X				
it^{aur}	X	X		X			
$it^b(e)$	X	X		(X)			
it^c	X	X		X			
$it^d(ea)$	X	X					X
$it^e(e)$	X						
$it^f(e)$	X	X	X	X			
it^{ff2}	X	X					
$it^l(e)$	X	X					
$it^q(e)$	X	X		X			
it^{rl}	X	X	X				

Principal Manuscript Evidence in the First Eight Chapters of Luke
Vulgate Evidence (UBSGNT[4])

| Variant | 1.28 | 1.35 | 1.46 | 1.66 | 1.74 | 1.78 | 2.9 | 2.11 | 2.14 | 2.33 | 2.38 |
Rating	A	A	A	A	B	B	B	A	A	B	A
Vulgate											
vg			(X)	X	X^{mss}	X^{ms}	X			$X(X^{ms})$	
vg^{ww}		X							X		X
vg^{st}		X							X		X

| Variant | 3.22 | 3.32 | 3.33 | 4.4 | 4.17 | 4.18 | 4.44 | 5.17 | 5.17 | 5.33 | 5.38 |
Rating	B	B	C	B	B	A	B	B	A	B	B
Vulgate											
vg	X				X			X			
vg^{ww}						X					
vg^{st}						X					

| Variant | 5.39 | 5.39a | 5.39b | 6.1 | 6.4 | 6.4 | 6.5 | 6.10 | 6.31 | 6.35 | 6.48 |
Rating	C	A	A	C	A	A	B	A	B	B	A
Vulgate											
vg	X		X		X	X		X			
vg^{cl}										(X)	
vg^{ww}										(X)	
vg^{st}										X	

| Variant | 7.7 | 7.10 | 7.11 | 7.11 | 7.19 | 7.28 | 7.32 | 7.35 | 7.39 | 7.45 | 8.3 |
Rating	B	A	B	B	C	B	B	B	A	A	B
Vulgate											
vg		X^{ms}	X	X			X	X		X^{mss}	
vg^{ww}					X						X
vg^{st}					X						X

| Variant | 8.26 | 8.37 | 8.43 | 8.44 | 8.45 | 8.45 | 8.49 |
Rating	C	C	C	B	B	B	B
Vulgate							
vg	X	X	X^{mss}	X			

Principal Manuscript Evidence in the First Eight Chapters of Luke
Syriac Evidence (UBSGNT⁴)

Variant	1.28	1.35	1.46	1.66	1.74	1.78	2.9	2.11	2.14	2.33	2.38
Rating	A	A	A	A	B	B	B	A	A	B	A
Syriac											
syr^s			X			X		(X)		(X)	X
syr^p			X	X		X		(X)			X
syr^{pal}	X	X^{mss}	X	X			X^{ms}				
syr^h		X	X	X				X		(X^{mg})	

Variant	3.22	3.32	3.33	4.4	4.17	4.18	4.44	5.17	5.17	5.33	5.38
Rating	B	B	C	B	B	A	B	B	A	B	B
Syriac											
syr^s		X		X		X	X			X	
syr^p									X		
syr^{pal}		X							X		
syr^h	X						X		X		

Variant	5.39	5.39a	5.39b	6.1	6.4	6.4	6.5	6.10	6.31	6.35	6.48
Rating	C	A	A	C	A	A	B	A	B	B	A
Syriac											
syr^s									X		
syr^p	X	X	X	X	X	X	X	X			
syr^{pal}	X		X	X	X^{ms}	X	(X)				
syr^h	X		X	X^{mg}		X				X	X^{mg}

Variant	7.7	7.10	7.11	7.11	7.19	7.28	7.32	7.35	7.39	7.45	8.3
Rating	B	A	B	B	C	B	B	B	A	A	B
Syriac											
syr^s		X	X	X							X
syr^c											X
syr^p				X							X
syr^{pal}		X	X	X		X					X^{mss}
syr^h										X^{mg}	X^{mg}

Variant	8.26	8.37	8.43	8.44	8.45	8.45	8.49
Rating	C	C	C	B	B	B	B
Syriac							
syr^s				X	X		
syr^c				X	X		
syr^p				X			
syr^{pal}				X	X	X^{mss}	
syr^h	X^{mg}			X			X

Principal Manuscript Evidence in the First Eight Chapters of Luke
Coptic Evidence (UBSGNT⁴)

Variant	1.28	1.35	1.46	1.66	1.74	1.78	2.9	2.11	2.14	2.33	2.38
Rating	A	A	A	A	B	B	B	A	A	B	A
Coptic											
cop^{sa}	X	X	(X)	X		X		X	X	(X)	X
cop^{bo}	X	X	$X(X^{ms})$	X		X		$X(X^{ms})$		(X^{pt})	X

Variant	3.22	3.32	3.33	4.4	4.17	4.18	4.44	5.17	5.17	5.33	5.38
Rating	B	B	C	B	B	A	B	B	A	B	B
Coptic											
cop^{sa}	X	X		X		X	X	X	X	X	
cop^{bo}	X^{pt}	X^{mss}	X	X^{pt}		X	X^{pt}			X^{pt}	

Variant	5.39	5.39a	5.39b	6.1	6.4	6.4	6.5	6.10	6.31	6.35	6.48
Rating	C	A	A	C	A	A	B	A	B	B	A
Coptic											
cop^{sa}			X	X	X	X	(X)	X		X	X
cop^{bo}	X		X	X^{pt}		X	X $^{(pt)}$	X		X	X^{pt}

Variant	7.7	7.10	7.11	7.11	7.19	7.28	7.32	7.35	7.39	7.45	8.3
Rating	B	A	B	B	C	B	B	B	A	A	B
Coptic											
cop^{sa}	X	X	X	X	X	X^{mss}	X			X^{mss}	
cop^{bo}	X^{mss}	X		X	X^{mss}	X^{pt}	X			X^{pt}	

Variant	8.26	8.37	8.43	8.44	8.45	8.45	8.49
Rating	C	C	C	B	B	B	B
Coptic							
cop^{sa}	X	X			X	X	X
cop^{bo}	X^{ms}					X	

Principal Manuscript Evidence in the First Eight Chapters of Luke
Armenian Evidence (UBSGNT^4)

Variant	1.28	1.35	1.46	1.66	1.74	1.78	2.9	2.11	2.14	2.33	2.38
Rating	A	A	A	A	B	B	B	A	A	B	A
Armenian Kunz. Zohr.	X	X	X	X	X^{mss}		X			(X)	X

Variant	3.22	3.32	3.33	4.4	4.17	4.18	4.44	5.17	5.17	5.33	5.38
Rating	B	B	C	B	B	A	B	B	A	B	B
Armenian Kunz. Zohr.	X^{mss}					X					

Variant	5.39	5.39a	5.39b	6.1	6.4	6.4	6.5	6.10	6.31	6.35	6.48
Rating	C	A	A	C	A	A	B	A	B	B	A
Armenian Kunz. Zohr.	X		X		X	(X)					

Variant	7.7	7.10	7.11	7.11	7.19	7.28	7.32	7.35	7.39	7.45	8.3
Rating	B	A	B	B	C	B	B	B	A	A	B
Armenian Kunz. Zohr.				X	X		X		X	X	

Variant	8.26	8.37	8.43	8.44	8.45	8.45	8.49
Rating	C	C	C	B	B	B	B
Armenian Kunz. Zohr.				X		X	

Principal Manuscript Evidence in the First Eight Chapters of Luke
Ethiopic Evidence (UBSGNT[4])

Variant	1.28	1.35	1.46	1.66	1.74	1.78	2.9	2.11	2.14	2.33	2.38
Rating	A	A	A	A	B	B	B	A	A	B	A
Ethiopic eth			X					X			X

Variant	3.22	3.32	3.33	4.4	4.17	4.18	4.44	5.17	5.17	5.33	5.38
Rating	B	B	C	B	B	A	B	B	A	B	B
Ethiopic eth	X					X		X	X		

Variant	5.39	5.39a	5.39b	6.1	6.4	6.4	6.5	6.10	6.31	6.35	6.48
Rating	C	A	A	C	A	A	B	A	B	B	A
Ethiopic eth	X		X	X	X^{TH}	X	X	X^{TH}			

Variant	7.7	7.10	7.11	7.11	7.19	7.28	7.32	7.35	7.39	7.45	8.3
Rating	B	A	B	B	C	B	B	B	A	A	B
Ethiopic eth		X		X				X	X	X	

Variant	8.26	8.37	8.43	8.44	8.45	8.45	8.49
Rating	C	C	C	B	B	B	B
Ethiopic eth						X	

Principal Manuscript Evidence in the First Eight Chapters of Luke
Georgian Evidence (UBSGNT[4])

Variant	1.28	1.35	1.46	1.66	1.74	1.78	2.9	2.11	2.14	2.33	2.38
Rating	A	A	A	A	B	B	B	A	A	B	A
Georgian geo	X	X	X	X			X	X			
geo[1]					X					(X)	
geo[2]										X	X

Variant	3.22	3.32	3.33	4.4	4.17	4.18	4.44	5.17	5.17	5.33	5.38
Rating	B	B	C	B	B	A	B	B	A	B	B
Georgian geo	X							X			

Variant	5.39	5.39a	5.39b	6.1	6.4	6.4	6.5	6.10	6.31	6.35	6.48
Rating	C	A	A	C	A	A	B	A	B	B	A
Georgian geo	X		X		X	X		X			
geo[2]										X	

Variant	7.7	7.10	7.11	7.11	7.19	7.28	7.32	7.35	7.39	7.45	8.3
Rating	B	A	B	B	C	B	B	B	A	A	B
Georgian											
geo		(X)		X			X				
geo^2											X

Variant	8.26	8.37	8.43	8.44	8.45	8.45	8.49
Rating	C	C	C	B	B	B	B
Georgian							
geo				X	X		

Principal Manuscript Evidence in the First Eight Chapters of Luke
Greek Church Father Evidence (UBSGNT[4])[vi]

Variant	1.28	1.35	1.46	1.66	1.74	1.78	2.9	2.11
Rating	A	A	A	A	B	B	B	A
Greek Church Fathers								
Amphilochius								X
Apollinaris, of Laodicea		X						
Cyril, of Alexandria		X						X
Cyril-Jerusalem		X						X
Diatessaron, of Tatian			X					X^{syr}
Didymus		X^{dub}						X
Epiphanius	X	X$^{3/8}$						
Eusebius, of Caesarea		X					X	X
Gregory-Nyssa	X^{vid}	X				(X$^{1/2}$)		X
Hesychius, of Jerusalem	X	X						
Irenaeus			(X$^{lat1/2}$)		X^{lat}			X^{lat}
John-Damascus	X	X						
Marcus-Eremita		X$^{1/2}$						
Origen	X^{lem}	X^{lat}			X^{lat}		X^{lat}	X$^{gr?, lat}$
Orsiesius								X^{lat}
Peter-Alexandria	X^{Cyril}	X^{Cyril}						
Ps-Dionysius		X						X
Ps-Gregory-Thaumaturgus	X		X					
Ps-Hippolytus		X						
Serapion	X							
Severian								X
Theodoret, of Cyrrhus		X						X

Variant	2.14	2.33	2.38	3.22	3.32	3.33	4.4	4.17
Rating	A	B	A	B	B	C	B	B
Greek Church Fathers								
Cyril-Jerusalem	X	(X)						
Eusebius, of Caesarea								X$^{1/2}$
Irenaeus			X^{lat}					
Origen	X$^{gr, 2/5lat}$	X^{lat}	X^{lat}				X$^{gr,1/2lat}$	X^{lat}
Severian								X

vi.   Various other early authors or writings have not been included in this chart because they offer no witness of significance for the critical apparatus of the *UBSGNT*[4]. This is also stated on p. 34* of the *UBSGNT*[4].

Variant	4.18	4.44	5.17	5.17	5.33	5.38	5.39	5.39a
Rating	A	B	B	A	B	B	C	A
Greek Church Fathers								
Cyril, of Alexandria				$X^{1/2}$				
Didymus	X			X				
Eusebius, of Caesarea	X							
Nestorius	X							
Origen	$X^{gr,\,lat}$							
Peter-Alexandria	X							

Variant	5.39b	6.1	6.4	6.4	6.5	6.10	6.31	6.35
Rating	A	C	A	A	B	A	B	B
Greek Church Fathers								
Clement, of Alexandria							X	
Diatessaron, of Tatian					X			
Eusebian Canons	X				X			
Irenaeus			X^{lat}	X^{lat}			X^{lat}	

Variant	6.48	7.7	7.10	7.11	7.11	7.19	7.28	7.32
Rating	A	B	A	B	B	C	B	B
Greek Church Fathers								
Diatessaron, of Tatian		(X)					X	
Didymus							X	
Origen							$X^{1/3}$	

Variant	7.35	7.39	7.45	8.3	8.26	8.37	8.43	8.44
Rating	B	A	A	B	C	C	C	B
Greek Church Fathers								
Amphilochius		X						
(John) Chrysostom		X	X					
Cyril, of Alexandria								X
Diatessaron, of Tatian			$X^{arm,\,ms}$					(X^{arm})
Origen					(X)			
Titus-Bostra					X			X

Variant	8.45	8.45	8.49
Rating	B	B	B
Greek Church Fathers			
Cyril, of Alexandria		X	
Diatessaron, of Tatian	X		
Epiphanius			X
Gregory-Nyssa		X	
Origen	X^{vid}	X^{lat}	

Principal Manuscript Evidence in the First Eight Chapters of Luke
Latin Church Father Evidence (UBSGNT⁴)

Variant	1.28	1.35	1.46	1.66	1.74	1.78	2.9	2.11
Rating	A	A	A	A	B	B	B	A
Latin Church Fathers								
Ambrose		$X^{1/4}$	(X)					X
Ambrosiaster								X
Augustine		$X^{2/15}$	(X)	$X^{2/3}$				X
Chromatius								X
Cyprian		X						
Gaudentius								X
Jerome	X					X		X
Priscillian		X						
Quodvultdeus	X							

Variant	2.14	2.33	2.38	3.22	3.32	3.33	4.4	4.17
Rating	A	B	A	B	B	C	B	B
Latin Church Fathers								
Ambrose				(X)				
Augustine	$X^{2/41}$	X	X	X				X
Gaudentius	X							
Jerome	$X^{4/15}$	X	$X^{1/2}$					

Variant	4.18	4.44	5.17	5.17	5.33	5.38	5.39	5.39a
Rating	A	B	B	A	B	B	C	A
Latin Church Fathers								
Ambrose	X							
Augustine	X		X					
Jerome	X							

Variant	5.39b	6.1	6.4	6.4	6.5	6.10	6.31	6.35
Rating	A	C	A	A	B	A	B	B
Latin Church Fathers								
Ambrose			X	X			X	(X)

Variant	6.48	7.7	7.10	7.11	7.11	7.19	7.28	7.32
Rating	A	B	A	B	B	C	B	B
Latin Church Fathers								
Ambrose		X						X
Augustine								X

Variant	7.35	7.39	7.45	8.3	8.26	8.37	8.43	8.44
Rating	B	A	A	B	C	C	C	B
Latin Church Fathers								
Ambrose	X		X				X	
Ambrosiaster				X				
Augustine	X			X				
Chromatius							X	
Jerome							X	

Variant	8.45	8.45	8.49
Rating	B	B	B
Latin Church Fathers			
Augustine			X

Principal Manuscript Evidence in the First Eight Chapters of Acts
Papyri Evidence (UBSGNT[4])

Variant Rating	1.2 A	1.11 A	1.23 A	1.25 B	1.26 B	2.5 B	2.16 B	2.18 A	2.18 A	2.19 A	2.24 A
Papyri 𝔓74	X^{vid}			X				X	X	X^{vid}	X^{vid}

Variant Rating	2.30 B	2.37 A	2.43 C	2.44 A	2.47–3.1 B	3.6 C	3.14 A	3.21 B	3.22 B	3.22 C	3.25 C
Papyri 𝔓74		X^{vid}		X	X^{vid}		X	X	X^{vid}		X
𝔓91					X^{vid}						

Variant Rating	4.1 B	4.6 A	4.8 B	4.10 A	4.12 A	4.24 B	4.25 C	4.33 C	5.3 B	5.16 B	5.17 A
Papyri 𝔓8							X	X			
𝔓45vii											X
𝔓74		X	X	X	X^{vid}	X	X			X	X

Variants Rating	5.28 C	5.29 A	5.32 B	5.33 B	5.37 A	5.39 A	6.3 C	6.7 B	7.16 C	7.17 B	7.18 C
Papyri 𝔓33+58											X^{vid}
𝔓74		X	X^{vid}		X	X		X		X	X

Variants Rating	7.19 C	7.38 B	7.46 B	8.5 C	8.10 A	8.18 B	8.24 A	8.36 A	8.39 A
Papyri 𝔓45							X	X	X
𝔓74		X	X	X			X	X	X

Principal Manuscript Evidence in the First Eight Chapters of Acts
Uncial Evidence (UBSGNT[4])

Variant Rating	1.2 A	1.11 A	1.23 A	1.25 B	1.26 B	2.5 B	2.16 B	2.18 A	2.18 A	2.19 A	2.24 A
Uncials ℵ01	X	X	X		X		X	X	X	X	X
A02	X	X	X		X		X	X	X	X	X
B03	X	X	X	X	X	X	X	X	X	X	X
C04	X^{vid}	X	X	X*	X	(X)(X*)	X	X	X	X	X
D05			X^1	X	X^1	(X)					
E08	X	X	X			(X)					
[P024]							X	X	X	X	X
Ψ044	X	X	X	X		X	X	X	X	X	X
076							X^{vid}	X	X^{vid}	X	
095											X^{vid}
096						X					

vii. 𝔓^{45}, one of the most important papyri, and part of the Chester Beatty collection along with 𝔓^{46} and 𝔓^{47}, is dated in the third century. This papyrus contains sizable portions of the Gospels and Acts 4.27–17.7. The Alands classify it as a category I manuscript in *Text of the New Testament*, pp. 98-99.

Variant	2.30	2.37	2.43	2.44	2.47–3.1	3.6	3.14	3.21	3.22	3.22	3.25
Rating	B	A	C	A	B	C	A	B	B	C	C
Uncials											
ℵ01	X	X		X	X		X	X*	X	X²	X²
A02	X	X		X	X	X	X	X	X	X	X
B03	X	X	X		X		X	X*	X		X
C04	X	X		X	X	X	X	X	X		
D05	(X¹)		X	X						X	
E08		X		X		X	X				X
[P024]		X	X	X		X	X				
Ψ044		X		X		X	X				
095					X	X					

Variant	4.1	4.6	4.8	4.10	4.12	4.24	4.25	4.33	5.3	5.16	5.17
Rating	B	A	B	A	A	B	C	C	B	B	A
Uncials											
ℵ01	X	X	X	X	X	X	X		X²	X	X
A02	X	X	X	X	X	X	X		X	X	X
B03		X	X	X	X	X	X	(X)	X	X	X
D05	X			X					X		X
E08	X				X		X		X		
[P024]	X			X	X			X	X		X
Ψ044	X			X	X		X	X	X		X
0165	X	X	X	X	X						
0189									X	X	X

Variant	5.28	5.29	5.32	5.33	5.37	5.39	6.3	6.7	7.16	7.17	7.18
Rating	C	A	B	B	A	A	C	B	C	B	C
Uncials											
ℵ01	X²	X	X		X	X	X	X	X*	X	X
A02		X		X	X*	X		X		X	X
B03		X		X	X	X	X	X	X	X	X
C04						X²		X	X	X	X
D05	X		X*								
E08	X	X		X							
[P024]	X	X							X		
Ψ044	(X)	X		X		X					X

Variant	7.19	7.38	7.46	8.5	8.10	8.18	8.24	8.36	8.39
Rating	C	B	B	C	A	B	A	A	A
Uncials									
ℵ01			X*	X	X	X	X	X	X
A02	X	X		X	X		X	X	X*
B03			X	X	X	X	X	X	X
C04	X	X			X		(X)	X	X
D05		X	X		X				
E08	X	X			X		(X)		X
[L020]							(X)	X	X
[P024]	X	X					X	X	X
Ψ044	X	X					X	X	X

Principal Manuscript Evidence in the First Eight Chapters of Acts
Minuscule Evidence (UBSGNT⁴)

Variant Rating	1.2 A	1.11 A	1.23 A	1.25 B	1.26 B	2.5 B	2.16 B	2.18 A	2.18 A	2.19 A	2.24 A
Minusc.											
33	X		X		X	X	X	X	X	X	X
36a	X	X				X	X	X	X	X	X
81	X	X	X		X	X	X	X	X	X	X
181	X	X	X			X	X	X	X	X	X
307	X	X	X			X	X	X	X	X	X
453	X	X	X			X	X	X	X	X	X
610	X	X	X			X	X	X	X	X	X
614	X	X	X			X	X	X	X	X	X
945	X	X	X		X	X	X	(X)	X	X	X
1175	X	X	X		X	X	X	X	X	X	X
1409	X	X	X		X	X	X	X	X	X	X
1678	X	X	X			X	X	X	X	X	X
1739	X	X	X		X	X	X	X	X	X	X
1891	X	X						X	X	X	X
2344	X	X	X		X	X	X	X	X	X	X

Variant Rating	2.30 B	2.37 A	2.43 C	2.44 A	2.47–3.1 B	3.6 C	3.14 A	3.21 B	3.22 B	3.22 C	3.25 C
Minusc.											
33		X		X		X	X				
36a		X		X		X	X		X	X	
81	X	X	X	X	X	X	X	X	X	X	X
181		X		X		X	X			X	
307		X		X		X	X	X	X	X	
453		X		X		X	X	X	X	X	X
610		X		X		X	X		X	X	
614		X		X		X	X				
945		X	X	X		X	X			X	X
1175	X	X		X	X	X	X	X	X	X	X
1409		X		X		X	X				
1678		X		X		X	X		X	X	
1739		X	X	X		X	X	X		X	X
1891		X	X	X		X	X	(X*)		X	
2344		X		X		X	X				X

Variant Rating	4.1 B	4.6 A	4.8 B	4.10 A	4.12 A	4.24 B	4.25 C	4.33 C	5.3 B	5.16 B	5.17 A
Minusc.											
33	X			X	X		X		X^{vid}		X
36a	X	X		X	(X)		X		X		X
81	X	X									
181	X			X	X			X	X		X
307	X	X		X	(X)		X		X		X
453	X	X		X	(X)		X		X		X
610	X	X		X	(X)		X		X		X
614	X			X	X			X	X		X
945	X			X	X		(X)		X		X
1175	X	X	X	X	X		X		X		X
1409	X		X*	X	X		X^{vid}		X		X
1678	X	X		X	(X)		(X)		X		X
1739	X			X	X		X		X		X
1891	X			X	X		X		X		X
2344	X			X	X		X	X	X		X

Variant Rating	5.28 C	5.29 A	5.32 B	5.33 B	5.37 A	5.39 A	6.3 C	6.7 B	7.16 C	7.17 B	7.18 C
Minusc.											
33		X^{vid}						X			
36a	X	(X)		X		X		X	X	X*	X
181	X	X	X			X		X	X		X
307	X	(X)				X		X	X	X	X
453	X	(X)				X		X	X	X	X
610	X	X				X		X	X	X	X
614	X	X	X	X							
945	X	X				X		X	X		X
1175		X	X		X	X		X	X	X	X
1409	X	(X)						X			X
1678	X	(X)				X		X	X	X	X
1739	X	X				X*		X	X		X
1891	X	X				X		X	X		X
2344	X	X						X^{vid}	X		X

Variant Rating	7.19 C	7.38 B	7.46 B	8.5 C	8.10 A	8.18 B	8.24 A	8.36 A	8.39 A
Minusc.									
33		X			X		X	X^{vid}	X^{vid}
36a	X						X		
81	X	X			X		X	X	X
181	X	X		X	X		X	X	X
307	X						X		
453	X						X		
610	X						X		
614	X	X					X	X	X
945	X	X			X		X		
1175		X		X	X		X	X	X
1409					X		X	X	X
1678	X						X		
1739	X	X			X		X		
1891	X	X			X		X		
2344	X	X	X	X	X		X	X	X

Principal Manuscript Evidence in the First Eight Chapters of Acts
Lectionary Evidence (UBSGNT⁴)

Variant	1.2	1.11	1.23	1.25	1.26	2.5	2.16	2.18	2.18	2.19	2.24
Rating	A	A	A	B	B	B	B	A	A	A	A
Lection.											
Lect.	X	X	X			X	X	X	X	X	X
L165								(X)			
L680									(X)		
L1021								(X)			
L1178					X						
L1441											(X)

Variant	2.30	2.37	2.43	2.44	2.47–3.1	3.6	3.14	3.21	3.22	3.22	3.25
Rating	B	A	C	A	B	C	A	B	B	C	C
Lection.											
Lect.			X^{pt,AD}			X	X			X^{pt,AD}	
L60									X		
L884				X							
L1178		X		X							X

Variant	4.1	4.6	4.8	4.10	4.12	4.24	4.25	4.33	5.3	5.16	5.17
Rating	B	A	B	A	A	B	C	C	B	B	A
Lection.											
Lect.	X			X					X		X
L60							X				
L1178							X				

Variant	5.28	5.29	5.32	5.33	5.37	5.39	6.3	6.7	7.16	7.17	7.18
Rating	C	A	B	B	A	A	C	B	C	B	C
Lection.											
Lect.	X	X						X			
L60		(X)	X								
L422				X							
L591	(X)		X								
L597		(X)	(X)								
L680			X								
L883	(X)	(X)	X								
L921		(X)									
L1021		(X)									
L1154	(X)	(X)									
L1178						X			X		X
L1356	(X)										
L1441			X								
L1977	(X)										

Variant	7.19	7.38	7.46	8.5	8.10	8.18	8.24	8.36	8.39
Rating	C	B	B	C	A	B	A	A	A
Lection.									
Lect.						X	X	X	
L1178	X	X			X				

Principal Manuscript Evidence in the First Eight Chapters of Acts
Old Latin Evidence (UBSGNT⁴)

Variant Rating	1.2 A	1.11 A	1.23 A	1.25 B	1.26 B	2.5 B	2.16 B	2.18 A	2.18 A	2.19 A	2.24 A
Old Latin											
it^{ar}		X	X	X		X	X	X	X	X	
it^{c}	X	X	X	X	X	X	X	X	X	X	
it^{d} *(ea)*				X		(X)					
it^{dem}	X	X	X	X	X	X	X	X	X	X	
it^{e} *(a)*	X	X	X			(X)	X	X	X	X	
it^{gig}				X		X	(X)		X		
it^{p} *(a)*	X	X	X	X		X	X	X			
it^{ph}	X	X	X	X	X		X	X	X	X	
it^{r} *(a)*						X			X		
it^{ro}	X	X	X	X	X	X	X	X^2	X	X	
it^{sa}			X	X							
it^{t} *(acpr)*		X	X	X		X	X	X	X	X	
it^{w} *(a)*	X	X	X	X	X	X	X	X	X	X	

Variant Rating	2.30 B	2.37 A	2.43 C	2.44 A	2.47–3.1 B	3.6 C	3.14 A	3.21 B	3.22 B	3.22 C	3.25 C
Old Latin											
it^{ar}	X	X		X	X	X	X		X	X	
it^{c}	X	X		X	X	X	X		X	X	
it^{d} *(ea)*			X	X						X	
it^{dem}	X	X		X	X	X	X		X	X	
it^{e} *(a)*		X		X		X	X	X			X
it^{gig}	X		X			X	X			X	
it^{h} *(acr)*						X	X				
it^{p} *(a)*	X	X	X*			X(*)	X				
it^{ph}	X	X		X	X		X		X	X	
it^{r} *(a)*	X		X			X					
it^{ro}	X	X		X	X	X	X		X	X	
it^{t} *(acpr)*	X	X		X							
it^{w} *(a)*	X	X		X	X	X	X		X	X	

Variant Rating	4.1 B	4.6 A	4.8 B	4.10 A	4.12 A	4.24 B	4.25 C	4.33 C	5.3 B	5.16 B	5.17 A
Old Latin											
it^{ar}	X	X	X	X	X		(X)			X	
it^{c}	X	X	X	X	X	X	(X)				X
it^{d} *(ea)*	X			X					X		X
it^{dem}	X	X		X	X	X	(X)			X	X
it^{e} *(a)*	X				X		X		X		
it^{gig}				X	X		(X)	X	X	X	X
it^{h} *(acr)*	X	X								X	X
it^{p} *(a)*	X	X^{mg}		X	X^2		(X)	X	X*	X	
it^{ph}	X	X	X	X	X	X	(X)			X	X
it^{r} *(a)*									X		
it^{ro}	X	X		X	X	X	(X)			X	X
it^{t} *(acpr)*								X	X	X	X
it^{w} *(a)*	X	X		X	X	X	(X)			X	X

Variant	5.28	5.29	5.32	5.33	5.37	5.39	6.3	6.7	7.16	7.17	7.18
Rating	C	A	B	B	A	A	C	B	C	B	C
Old Latin											
it^{ar}		X	X		X			X		X	X
it^c		X	X		X					X	X
it^d (ea)					X						
it^{dem}		X	X		X			X		(X)	X
it^e (a)	X	X									
it^{gig}		X						X			
it^h (acr)	X										
it^p (a)	X	(X)				X					
it^{ph}		X	X		X	X				X	X
it^{ro}		X	X		X	X				X	X
it^w (a)	X	X	X				X			X	X

Variant	7.19	7.38	7.46	8.5	8.10	8.18	8.24	8.36	8.39
Rating	C	B	B	C	A	B	A	A	A
Old Latin									
it^{ar}		X			X		X^{txt}		
it^c	X	X			X		X	X	
it^d (ea)		X	X		X				
it^{dem}	X	X			X		X		X
it^e (a)	X	X			X				X
it^{gig}	X	X			X		X		X
it^p (a)	X				X		X		
it^{ph}	X	X			X		X		X
it^r (a)					X		X		X
it^{ro}	X	X			X		(X)		X
it^t (acpr)							X		X
it^w (a)	X	X			X		X		X

Principal Manuscript Evidence in the First Eight Chapters of Acts
Vulgate Evidence (UBSGNT^4)

Variant	1.2	1.11	1.23	1.25	1.26	2.5	2.16	2.18	2.18	2.19	2.24
Rating	A	A	A	B	B	B	B	A	A	A	A
Vulgate											
vg	X		X	X	X	X	X	X	X	X	

Variant	2.30	2.37	2.43	2.44	2.47–3.1	3.6	3.14	3.21	3.22	3.22	3.25
Rating	B	A	C	A	B	C	A	B	B	C	C
Vulgate											
vg	X	X		X	X	X	X		X	X	
vg^{ww}											X
vgst											X

Variant	4.1	4.6	4.8	4.10	4.12	4.24	4.25	4.33	5.3	5.16	5.17
Rating	B	A	B	A	A	B	C	C	B	B	A
Vulgate											
vg	X	X	X	X	X	X^{cl}	(X)			X	X

Variant	5.28	5.29	5.32	5.33	5.37	5.39	6.3	6.7	7.16	7.17	7.18
Rating	C	A	B	B	A	A	C	B	C	B	C
Vulgate											
vg		X	X		X					X	(X)X^{mss}
vg^{ww}						X		X			
vgst						X		X			

Variant	7.19	7.38	7.46	8.5	8.10	8.18	8.24	8.36	8.39
Rating	C	B	B	C	A	B	A	A	A
Vulgate									
vg		X			X		X	X	
vg^{cl}	X								
vg^{ww}							X		
vgst							X		

Principal Manuscript Evidence in the First Eight Chapters of Acts
Syriac Evidence (UBSGNT^4)

Variant	1.2	1.11	1.23	1.25	1.26	2.5	2.16	2.18	2.18	2.19	2.24
Rating	A	A	A	B	B	B	B	A	A	A	A
Syriac											
syr^p		X	X			X	X	X	X	X	
syr^{pal}		X				X	X	X	X	X	X
syr^h	X	X	X	X^{mg}		X	X	X	X	X	X

Variant	2.30	2.37	2.43	2.44	2.47–3.1	3.6	3.14	3.21	3.22	3.22	3.25
Rating	B	A	C	A	B	C	A	B	B	C	C
Syriac											
syr^p	X	X				X	X		X		
syr^{pal}	X										
syr^h		X	X	X		X	X				

Variant	4.1	4.6	4.8	4.10	4.12	4.24	4.25	4.33	5.3	5.16	5.17
Rating	B	A	B	A	A	B	C	C	B	B	A
Syriac											
syr^p	X	X		X	X				X	X	
syr^h	X	X		X	X			X	X	X	X

Variant	5.28	5.29	5.32	5.33	5.37	5.39	6.3	6.7	7.16	7.17	7.18
Rating	C	A	B	B	A	A	C	B	C	B	C
Syriac											
syr^p	X							X			X
syr^h	X	X								X^{mg}	X^{mg}

Variant	7.19	7.38	7.46	8.5	8.10	8.18	8.24	8.36	8.39
Rating	C	B	B	C	A	B	A	A	A
Syriac									
syr^p	X	X					X	X	X
syr^h	X	X					X		

Principal Manuscript Evidence in the First Eight Chapters of Acts
Coptic Evidence (UBSGNT⁴)

Variant	1.2	1.11	1.23	1.25	1.26	2.5	2.16	2.18	2.18	2.19	2.24
Rating	A	A	A	B	B	B	B	A	A	A	A
Coptic											
cop^{sa}		X	X	X	X	X	(X)	X	X	X	X
cop^{bo}		X	X	X	X	X	X	$X^{(mss)}$	X	X	
cop^{meg}		X	X	X	X	X	(X)	X	X	X	

Variant	2.30	2.37	2.43	2.44	2.47–3.1	3.6	3.14	3.21	3.22	3.22	3.25
Rating	B	A	C	A	B	C	A	B	B	C	C
Coptic											
cop^{sa}	X	X	X		X		X				X^{mss}
cop^{bo}	X	X			X	X	X		X		X^{mss}
cop^{meg}		X				X	X				

Variant	4.1	4.6	4.8	4.10	4.12	4.24	4.25	4.33	5.3	5.16	5.17
Rating	B	A	B	A	A	B	C	C	B	B	A
Coptic											
cop^{sa}	X	X	X	X	X			X	X		X
cop^{bo}	X	X	X	X	X	X			X		X
cop^{meg}	X	X			X				X		

Variant	5.28	5.29	5.32	5.33	5.37	5.39	6.3	6.7	7.16	7.17	7.18
Rating	C	A	B	B	A	A	C	B	C	B	C
Coptic											
cop^{sa}	X^{mss}	(X)	X	X	X^{mss}	X^{ms}	X^{mss}	X	X	X	X
cop^{bo}		(X)	X	X		X		X	X		X
cop^{meg}		(X)	X	X				X			X
cop^{fay}									X		X

Variant	7.19	7.38	7.46	8.5	8.10	8.18	8.24	8.36	8.39
Rating	C	B	B	C	A	B	A	A	A
Coptic									
cop^{sa}	X		X^{ms}			X	X	X	X
cop^{bo}	X				X		X	X	X
cop^{meg}	X					X			
cop^{fay}	X								

Principal Manuscript Evidence in the First Eight Chapters of Acts
Armenian Evidence (UBSGNT⁴)

Variant	1.2	1.11	1.23	1.25	1.26	2.5	2.16	2.18	2.18	2.19	2.24
Rating	A	A	A	B	B	B	B	A	A	A	A
Armenian Kunz. Zohr.	X	X^{mss}	X			X	X	X	X	X	X

Variant	2.30	2.37	2.43	2.44	2.47–3.1	3.6	3.14	3.21	3.22	3.22	3.25
Rating	B	A	C	A	B	C	A	B	B	C	C
Armenian Kunz. Zohr.	X	X	(X)	X	X	X	X		X^{mss}	X	X^{mss}

Variant	4.1	4.6	4.8	4.10	4.12	4.24	4.25	4.33	5.3	5.16	5.17
Rating	B	A	B	A	A	B	C	C	B	B	A
Armenian Kunz. Zohr.	X^{mss}	X		X	X			X^{mss}	X		X

Variant	5.28	5.29	5.32	5.33	5.37	5.39	6.3	6.7	7.16	7.17	7.18
Rating	C	A	B	B	A	A	C	B	C	B	C
Armenian Kunz. Zohr.	X	X	X^{mss}			X		X	X		X

Variant	7.19	7.38	7.46	8.5	8.10	8.18	8.24	8.36	8.39
Rating	C	B	B	C	A	B	A	A	A
Armenian Kunz. Zohr.	X^{mss}	X			X		X		

Principal Manuscript Evidence in the First Eight Chapters of Acts
Ethiopic Evidence (UBSGNT^4)

Variant	1.2	1.11	1.23	1.25	1.26	2.5	2.16	2.18	2.18	2.19	2.24
Rating	A	A	A	B	B	B	B	A	A	A	A
Ethiopic eth	X	X	X		X	(X)	(X)	(X)	X	X	X

Variant	2.30	2.37	2.43	2.44	2.47–3.1	3.6	3.14	3.21	3.22	3.22	3.25
Rating	B	A	C	A	B	C	A	B	B	C	C
Ethiopic eth	X		(X)	X	X	X	X				

Variant	4.1	4.6	4.8	4.10	4.12	4.24	4.25	4.33	5.3	5.16	5.17
Rating	B	A	B	A	A	B	C	C	B	B	A
Ethiopic eth		X	X	X	X		(X)	X	X	X	

Variant	5.28	5.29	5.32	5.33	5.37	5.39	6.3	6.7	7.16	7.17	7.18
Rating	C	A	B	B	A	A	C	B	C	B	C
Ethiopic eth	X	(X)	X	X		X				X	X

Variant	7.19	7.38	7.46	8.5	8.10	8.18	8.24	8.36	8.39
Rating	C	B	B	C	A	B	A	A	A
Ethiopic eth	X	X					X	X	
eth^{pp}							X		

Principal Manuscript Evidence in the First Eight Chapters of Acts
Georgian Evidence (UBSGNT^4)

Variant	1.2	1.11	1.23	1.25	1.26	2.5	2.16	2.18	2.18	2.19	2.24
Rating	A	A	A	B	B	B	B	A	A	A	A
Georgian geo	X	X	X		X	X	X	X	X	X	X

Variant	2.30	2.37	2.43	2.44	2.47–3.1	3.6	3.14	3.21	3.22	3.22	3.25
Rating	B	A	C	A	B	C	A	B	B	C	C
Georgian geo		X		X		X	X		X	X	X

Variant	4.1	4.6	4.8	4.10	4.12	4.24	4.25	4.33	5.3	5.16	5.17
Rating	B	A	B	A	A	B	C	C	B	B	A
Georgian geo	X	X		X	X		(X)		X		X

Variant	5.28	5.29	5.32	5.33	5.37	5.39	6.3	6.7	7.16	7.17	7.18
Rating	C	A	B	B	A	A	C	B	C	B	C
Georgian geo		X				X			X		X

Variant	7.19	7.38	7.46	8.5	8.10	8.18	8.24	8.36	8.39
Rating	C	B	B	C	A	B	A	A	A
Georgian geo	X				X		X		

Principal Manuscript Evidence in the First Eight Chapters of Acts
Greek Church Father Evidence (UBSGNT[4])

Variant	1.2	1.11	1.23	1.25	1.26	2.5	2.16	2.18
Rating	A	A	A	B	B	B	B	A
Greek Church Fathers								
Basil, the Great	X		X				X	
(John) Chrysostom	X	X	X			X	X	X
Cyril-Jerusalem							X	X
Didymus				X				
Epiphanius		X						
Eusebius, of Caesarea		X	X			(X)		
Nestorius	X							
Proclus		X						
Ps-Dionysius							X	
Ps-Ignatius		X						
Severian	X						X	
Theodoret, of Cyrrhus		X[3/4]						

Variant	2.18	2.19	2.24	2.30	2.37	2.43	2.44	2.47–3.1
Rating	A	A	A	B	A	C	A	B
Greek Church Fathers								
Asterius, Sophist	X							
Athanasius, of Alexandria			X					
Basil, the Great					X		X	
(John) Chrysostom	X	X	X		X[lem]	X	X	
Cyril, of Alexandria			X	X				
Cyril-Jerusalem	X							
Didymus	X	X						
Eusebius, of Caesarea			X	X				
Gregory-Nyssa			X					
Hippolytus						X		
Irenaeus				X[lat]				
Ps-Athanasius			X					
Severian		X						
Theodotus-Ancyra			X					

Variant	3.6	3.14	3.21	3.22	3.22	3.25	4.1	4.6
Rating	C	A	B	B	C	C	B	A
Greek Church Fathers								
Basil, the Great	X							
(John) Chrysostom	X	X			X	X	X	
Cyril, of Alexandria		X			X			
Didymus		X, X[dub]						
Eusebius, of Caesarea	X							
Irenaeus	X[lat]				X[lat]	X[lat]		
Origen	X				X[gr3/4,lat]			
Severian					X			
Theodoret, of Cyrrhus	X							
Theodotus-Ancyra		X						

Variant	4.8	4.10	4.12	4.24	4.25	4.33	5.3	5.16
Rating	B	A	A	B	C	C	B	B
Greek Church Fathers								
Athanasius, of Alexandria		X			X			
(John) Chrysostom		X	X				X	
Cyril, of Alexandria	X	X	X					
Cyril-Jerusalem							X	
Didymus				X[dub]			X[,dub1/2]	
Epiphanius							X[2/4]	
Gregory-Nyssa							X	
Hesychius, of Jerusalem					X			
Irenaeus		X[lat]			(X[lat])	X[lat]		
Marcellus, of Ancyra							X	
Origen							X[gk,lat]	
Orsiesius						X[lat]		

Variant	5.17	5.28	5.29	5.32	5.33	5.37	5.39	6.3
Rating	A	C	A	B	B	A	A	C
Greek Church Fathers								
Basil, the Great	X	X	X					
(John) Chrysostom	X	X	X		X			
Cyril, of Alexandria	X[1/3]							
Didymus				X[dub]				
Eusebius, of Caesarea						X		

Variant	6.7	7.16	7.17	7.18	7.19	7.38	7.46	8.5
Rating	B	C	B	C	C	B	B	C
Greek Church Fathers								
(John) Chrysostom					X	X		
Cyril, of Alexandria						X		

Variant	8.10	8.18	8.24	8.36	8.39
Rating	A	B	A	A	A
Greek Church Fathers					
Apostolic Constitutions		X	X		
(John) Chrysostom			X	X	X
Didymus					X^{lat}
Irenaeus	X^{lat}				
Origen	X				

Principal Manuscript Evidence in the First Eight Chapters of Acts
Latin Church Father Evidence (UBSGNT[4])

Variant	1.2	1.11	1.23	1.25	1.26	2.5	2.16	2.18
Rating	A	A	A	B	B	B	B	A
Latin Church Fathers								
Augustine		$X^{2/6}$		X		(X)		
Gaudentius							(X)	
Hilary						X		
Jerome		X				X	X	
Quodvultdeus		$X^{1/2}$						

Variant	2.18	2.19	2.24	2.30	2.37	2.43	2.44	2.47–3.1
Rating	A	A	A	B	A	C	A	B
Latin Church Fathers								
Bede			X					
Jerome				X				
Victorinus-Rome, Marius				X				

Variant	3.6	3.14	3.21	3.22	3.22	3.25	4.1	4.6
Rating	C	A	B	B	C	C	B	A
Latin Church Fathers								
Ambrose	X			X				
Chromatius	X			X	X			
Cyprian	X							
Hilary	X							
Jerome	X	X						
Lucifer, of Calaris	X							
Maximus, of Turin	X							
Priscillian	X							
Quodvultdeus		X						

Variant	4.8	4.10	4.12	4.24	4.25	4.33	5.3	5.16
Rating	B	A	A	B	C	C	B	B
Latin Church Fathers								
Ambrose		X					X	
Ambrosiaster							X	
Augustine				(X)	(X)	X		
Bede							X	
Cyprian							X	
Fulgentius							X	
Hilary				(X)	(X)			
Lucifer, of Calaris							X	X
Quodvultdeus							X	

Variant	5.17	5.28	5.29	5.32	5.33	5.37	5.39	6.3
Rating	A	C	A	B	B	A	A	C
Latin Church Fathers								
Ambrosiaster		X						
Bede		X						
Lucifer, of Calaris	X		X					

Variant	6.7	7.16	7.17	7.18	7.19	7.38	7.46	8.5
Rating	B	C	B	C	C	B	B	C
Latin Church Fathers								

Variant	8.10	8.18	8.24	8.36	8.39
Rating	A	B	A	A	A
Latin Church Fathers					
Ambrose				X	
Jerome					$X^{1/2}$
Rebaptism (De Rebaptismate)					X

Principal Manuscript Evidence in the First Eight Chapters of Romans
Papyri Evidence (UBSGNT⁴)

Variant Rating	1.1 B	1.7 A	1.13 A	1.15 A	1.29 C	1.31 A	2.16 C	3.7 B	3.12 C	3.22 B	3.25 C
Papyri											
𝔓10	X	X									
𝔓26		Xvid		Xvid							
𝔓40viii										X	Xvid

Variant Rating	3.28 B	4.1 B	4.11 C	4.15 B	4.19 C	4.19 C	4.22 C	5.1 A	5.2 C	5.6 C	6.4 A
Papyri											

Variant Rating	6.8 A	6.11 A	6.12 B	7.14 A	7.18 B	7.20 C	7.22 A	7.25 B	8.1 A	8.2 B	8.11 B
Papyri											
𝔓46		X									
𝔓94			X								

Variant Rating	8.21 A	8.23 A	8.24 B	8.24 B	8.26 A	8.28 B	8.34 C	8.35 A	8.38 A
Papyri									
𝔓27			Xvid					Xvid	
𝔓46	X		X	X				(X)	

Principal Manuscript Evidence in the First Eight Chapters of Romans
Uncial Evidence (UBSGNT⁴)

Variant Rating	1.1 B	1.7 A	1.13 A	1.15 A	1.29 C	1.31 A	2.16 C	3.7 B	3.12 C	3.22 B	3.25 C
Uncials											
ℵ01		X	X	X		X*	X*vid	X	X	X*	
A02		X	X	X		X		X	X	X	
B03	X	X	X	X	X	X	X			X	X
C04		X	X	X						X	X³
D06		Xabs1	Xc	X		X			X		X²
G012						X			X		
[K018]		X	X	X					X		
[L020]		X	X	X					X		X
[P024]		X	X	X					X		X
P025										X	
Ψ044		X		X					X	X	X
0172					Xvid						

viii. Once again, several papyri listed in this chart are important because of their early date. 𝔓40 contains portions of the first nine chapters of Romans and is given a third-century date. Although it is described by the Alands as 'carelessly written' it still maintains a category I rating in light of its age. 𝔓46 preserves portions of Romans, 1 and 2 Corinthians, Galatians, Ephesians, Philippians, Colossians, 1 Thessalonians, and Hebrews. It too is a category I manuscript, and like 𝔓45 and 𝔓47, one of the famous Chester Beatty papyri. 𝔓46 is one of the earliest manuscripts we have to date (around 200 CE). And finally 𝔓27 contains portions of chs. 8 and 9 in Romans. It is dated in the third century and like the other papyri listed here, is given a category I rating by the Alands in *The Text of the New Testament*, pp. 97-99.

| Variant | 3.28 | 4.1 | 4.11 | 4.15 | 4.19 | 4.19 | 4.22 | 5.1 | 5.2 | 5.6 | 6.4 |
Rating	B	B	C	B	C	C	C	A	C	C	A
Uncials											
ℵ01	X	$X^{*,2}$	X^2	X^*	X	X	X	X^1	$X^{*,2}$	X	X
A02	X	X		X	X	X	X			X	X
B03				X	X			X^2			X
C04		X^*	X	X	X	X	X		X	X^{vid}	X
D06	X^*		X			X	X^1			X^*	X
[F010]	X		X						X		X
G012	X		X						X		X
[K018]			X			X	X		X		X
[L020]			X			X	X		X		X
[P024]			X			X	X	X	X		X
Ψ044	X					X	X	X	X		X

| Variant | 6.8 | 6.11 | 6.12 | 7.14 | 7.18 | 7.20 | 7.22 | 7.25 | 8.1 | 8.2 | 8.11 |
Rating	A	A	B	A	B	C	A	B	A	B	B
Uncials											
ℵ01	X		X		X	X	X	X^1	X^*	X	X
A02	X	X	X		X	X	X			X	X
B03	X	X	X	X^2	X				X	X	
C04	X		X^*		X			X	$X^1(X^*)$	$X^2(X^*)$	X
D06	X	X		X^2			X		X^*		
[F010]		X					X		X	X	
G012		X					X		X	X	
[K018]	X			X		X	X				
[L020]	X			X		X	X				
[P024]	X						X				
P025											X^{c}
Ψ044	X	X				X	X	X			

| Variant | 8.21 | 8.23 | 8.24 | 8.24 | 8.26 | 8.28 | 8.34 | 8.35 | 8.38 |
Rating	A	A	B	B	A	B	C	A	A
Uncials									
ℵ01		X		X^2	X^*	X	X		X
A02	X	X			X		X		X
B03	X	X	X^*	X	X				X
C04	X	X		X		X	X	X	
D06	X^2			X	X	X		X	
[F010]				X	X	X	X	X	X
G012				X	X	X	X	X	X
[K018]	X	X		X		X		X	
[L020]	X	X		X		X	X		
[P024]	X	X		X		X			
Ψ044	X	X		X			X	X	

Principal Manuscript Evidence in the First Eight Chapters of Romans
Minuscule Evidence (UBSGNT[4])

| Variant | 1.1 | 1.7 | 1.13 | 1.15 | 1.29 | 1.31 | 2.16 | 3.7 | 3.12 | 3.22 | 3.25 |
Rating	B	A	A	A	C	A	C	B	C	B	C
Minusc.											
6		X	X	X	X	X				X	
33		X		X					X		X
81	X	X	(X)	X			X	X	X	X	X
104		X	X	X					X	X	
256		X	X	X				X	X		
263		X	X	X				X	X	X	X
365								X	X		
424c		X	X	X	X				X*	X	X*
436		X	X	X					X	X	
459		X	X	X					X	X	
1175		X	X	X					X		X
1241		X	X	X					X		X
1319		X	X	X				X*	X		
1506		X	X	X		X	X	X	X	X	
1573		X	X	X				X	X		
1739		X	X	X	X	X				X	
1852		X	X	X				X	X		
1881		X	X	X	X				X	X	
1912		Xvid	X	X					X		X
1962		X	X	X					X		
2127		X	X	X				X	X		
2200		X	X	X					X	X	X
2464		X	X	X					X		X

| Variant | 3.28 | 4.1 | 4.11 | 4.15 | 4.19 | 4.19 | 4.22 | 5.1 | 5.2 | 5.6 | 6.4 |
Rating	B	B	C	B	C	C	C	A	C	C	A
Minusc.											
6				X	X	X	X	X	X		X
33					X	X	X		X		X
81	X	X		X	X	X	X		X	X	X
104			X	X	X	X	X	X	X	X	X
256	X	X	X		X	X	X	X	X	X	X
263	X	X	X		X	X	X	X	X	X	X
365	X	(X)	X		X	X		X	X	(X)	X
424c			X*		Xc	X	X	X	X	X	X
436	X		X	X		X	X		X		X
459			X		X	X	X	X	X	X	X
1175			X		X	X			X		X
1241			X		X	X		X	X	X	X
1319	X	X*	X		X*	X	X	X	X	X	X
1506	X	X		X	X	X	X	X	X	X	
1573	X		X		X	X	X	X	X	X	X
1739	X				X		X	X	X		X
1852	X		X	X		X	X	X	X	(X)	X
1881	X						X	X	X		X
1912			X		X		X		X		X
1962	X		X		X		X				X
2127	X	X	X		X		X	X	X	X	X
2200	X						X	X	X		X
2464					X		X	X	X		X

Variant Rating	6.8 A	6.11 A	6.12 B	7.14 A	7.18 B	7.20 C	7.22 A	7.25 B	8.1 A	8.2 B	8.11 B
Minusc.											
6	X		X	X	X	X	X		X		
33						X	X	X			
81	X		X	X	X	X	X	X			X
104	X			X			X	X			X
256	X		X	X			X	X			X
263	X		X	X			X	(X)			X
365	X		X	X			X	X			
424[c]	X		X	X	X[c]	X	X		X[c]		
436	X		X	X	X		X	X	X		X
459	X			X		X	X	X			
1175	X			X		X	X				
1241	X			X			X				
1319	X		X	X			X	X			X
1506	X		X	X			X	X	X	X*	X
1573	X		X	X			X	X			X
1739	X	X*	X	X	X	X	X		X	X*	
1852	X	(X)	X	X	X		X	X			X
1881	X		X	X	X	X	X		X		
1912	X			X		X	X				
1962	X		X	X		X	X				X
2127	X		X	X			X	X			X
2200	X	X	X	X	X	X	X				
2464	X			X			X				

Variant Rating	8.21 A	8.23 A	8.24 B	8.24 B	8.26 A	8.28 B	8.34 C	8.35 A	8.38 A
Minusc.									
6	X	X		X	X	X	X	X	
33	X	X		X		X	X	X	
81	X	X		X	X		X	X	
104	X	X		X		X	X	X	
256	X	X		X	X	X	X	X	
263	X	X		X	X	X		X	
365							X		X
424[c]	X	X		X	X[c]	X	X[c]	X	
436	X	X		X		X	X	X	
459	X	X		X		X		X	
1175	X	X		X		X		X	
1241		X		X		X		X	
1319	X	X		X	X	X	X	X	X
1506	X	X		X	X	X			X
1573	X	X		X	X	X	X	X	X
1739	X	X	X[v.r.]	X*	X	X		X	X
1852	X	X		X		X	X	X	
1881	X	X		X	X	X		X	X
1912	X	X		X		X		X	
1962	X	X		X		X	X	X	X
2127		X		X	X	X	X	X	X
2200	X	X		X		X		X	
2464	X	X		X		X		X	

Principal Manuscript Evidence in the First Eight Chapters of Romans
Lectionary Evidence (UBSGNT⁴)

Variant	1.1	1.7	1.13	1.15	1.29	1.31	2.16	3.7	3.12	3.22	3.25
Rating	B	A	A	A	C	A	C	B	C	B	C
Lection.											
Lect.		X	X	X					X		X
L60										X	
L593										(X)	
L596					X						
L598										X	
L599										X	
L603			(X)								
L617										X	

Variant	3.28	4.1	4.11	4.15	4.19	4.19	4.22	5.1	5.2	5.6	6.4
Rating	B	B	C	B	C	C	C	A	C	C	A
Lection.											
Lect.			X			X	X	$X^{pt,AD}$	X		X
L598										X	
L599										X	

Variant	6.8	6.11	6.12	7.14	7.18	7.20	7.22	7.25	8.1	8.2	8.11
Rating	A	A	B	A	B	C	A	B	A	B	B
Lection.											
Lect.	X			X		X	X				
L59											$X^{1/2}$
L147											$X^{1/2}$
L596								X			X
L921											$X^{1/2}$
L1298											X
L1365											X
L1441											$X^{1/2}$
L1590											$X^{1/2}$

Variant	8.21	8.23	8.24	8.24	8.26	8.28	8.34	8.35	8.38
Rating	A	A	B	B	A	B	C	A	A
Lection.									
Lect.	X	X		X		X		X	

Principal Manuscript Evidence in the First Eight Chapters of Romans
Old Latin Evidence (UBSGNT⁴)

Variant	1.1	1.7	1.13	1.15	1.29	1.31	2.16	3.7	3.12	3.22	3.25
Rating	B	A	A	A	C	A	C	B	C	B	C
Old Latin											
it^ar	X	X	X	X			X		X		
it^b (p)		X		X			X		X		
it^d (p)		X		X			X		X		
it^g							X		X		
it^mon	X	(X)	X	X			X		X		
it^o (p)		X		X			X		X		

Variant	3.28	4.1	4.11	4.15	4.19	4.19	4.22	5.1	5.2	5.6	6.4
Rating	B	B	C	B	C	C	C	A	C	C	A
Old Latin											
it^{ar}	X						X	X	X		
it^{b} (p)	X								X		
it^{d} (p)	X		X						X²		X
it^{f} (p)	X		X								X
it^{g}	X		X								X
it^{mon}			X		X*	X			X		
it^{o} (p)	X					X			X		

Variant	6.8	6.11	6.12	7.14	7.18	7.20	7.22	7.25	8.1	8.2	8.11
Rating	A	A	B	A	B	C	A	B	A	B	B
Old Latin											
it^{ar}		X	X	X						X	
it^{b} (p)	X	X		X			X		X	X	
it^{d} (p)	X	X	X²	X			X		X*		
it^{f} (p)	X	X		X			X				X
it^{g}	X	X		X			X		X	X	
it^{mon}	X	X	X	X			X		X*		X
it^{o} (p)		X		X			X			X	
it^{r} (p)	X		X								

Variant	8.21	8.23	8.24	8.24	8.26	8.28	8.34	8.35	8.38
Rating	A	A	B	B	A	B	C	A	A
Old Latin									
it^{ar}		X		X		X		X	(X)
it^{b} (p)		X		X	X	X	X	X	
it^{d} (p)			X	X*		X	X	X	(X)
it^{f} (p)			X			X	X	X	(X)
it^{g}			X		X	X	X	X	(X)
it^{mon}		X	X*	X		X		X	
it^{o} (p)			X			X		X	(X)

Principal Manuscript Evidence in the First Eight Chapters of Romans
Vulgate Evidence (UBSGNT⁴)

Variant	1.1	1.7	1.13	1.15	1.29	1.31	2.16	3.7	3.12	3.22	3.25
Rating	B	A	A	A	C	A	C	B	C	B	C
Vulgate											
vg		X	X	X		X^mss		X^mss	X		
vg^ww	X										
vg^st	X										

Variant	3.28	4.1	4.11	4.15	4.19	4.19	4.22	5.1	5.2	5.6	6.4
Rating	B	B	C	B	C	C	C	A	C	C	A
Vulgate											
vg	X		X	X^mss		X^mss	X	X^mss	X		
vg^ww					X						
vg^st					X						

Variant	6.8	6.11	6.12	7.14	7.18	7.20	7.22	7.25	8.1	8.2	8.11
Rating	A	A	B	A	B	C	A	B	A	B	B
Vulgate											
vg	X		X	X			X				
vg^{ww}		X									
vgst		X									

Variant	8.21	8.23	8.24	8.24	8.26	8.28	8.34	8.35	8.38
Rating	A	A	B	B	A	B	C	A	A
Vulgate									
vg		X		X		X	X	X	
vg^{ww}									X
vgst									X

Principal Manuscript Evidence in the First Eight Chapters of Romans
Syriac Evidence (UBSGNT^4)

Variant	1.1	1.7	1.13	1.15	1.29	1.31	2.16	3.7	3.12	3.22	3.25
Rating	B	A	A	A	C	A	C	B	C	B	C
Syriac											
syr^{p}		X	(X)	X							
syr^{pal}		X		X						X	
syr^{h}		X	X	X					X		

Variant	3.28	4.1	4.11	4.15	4.19	4.19	4.22	5.1	5.2	5.6	6.4
Rating	B	B	C	B	C	C	C	A	C	C	A
Syriac											
syr^{p}		(X)	X		X				X		
syr^{pal}	X	X	X						X		X
syr^{h}			X	X^{mg}		X^{with*}	X		X	X	X

Variant	6.8	6.11	6.12	7.14	7.18	7.20	7.22	7.25	8.1	8.2	8.11
Rating	A	A	B	A	B	C	A	B	A	B	B
Syriac											
syr^{p}			X	X			X			X	
syr^{pal}	X										
syr^{h}	X	X		X		X	X				X

Variant	8.21	8.23	8.24	8.24	8.26	8.28	8.34	8.35	8.38
Rating	A	A	B	B	A	B	C	A	A
Syriac									
syr^{p}	X	X				X		X	
syr^{h}		X		X		X	X	X	

Principal Manuscript Evidence in the First Eight Chapters of Romans
Coptic Evidence (UBSGNT^4)

Variant	1.1	1.7	1.13	1.15	1.29	1.31	2.16	3.7	3.12	3.22	3.25
Rating	B	A	A	A	C	A	C	B	C	B	C
Coptic											
cop^{sa}		X	(X)	X		X^{ms}			X	X	
cop^{bo}		X	X	X		X		X	X	X	

Variant Rating	3.28 B	4.1 B	4.11 C	4.15 B	4.19 C	4.19 C	4.22 C	5.1 A	5.2 C	5.6 C	6.4 A
Coptic cop^{sa}	X	X	X	X	X			X			X^{mss}
cop^{bo}	X	(X)		X	X	X			X		X
cop^{fay}					X						

Variant Rating	6.8 A	6.11 A	6.12 B	7.14 A	7.18 B	7.20 C	7.22 A	7.25 B	8.1 A	8.2 B	8.11 B
Coptic cop^{sa}	X	X	X	X	X		X		X		X
cop^{bo}	X		X	X	X	X	X	X	X		X

Variant Rating	8.21 A	8.23 A	8.24 B	8.24 B	8.26 A	8.28 B	8.34 C	8.35 A	8.38 A
Coptic cop^{sa}		X						X	
cop^{bo}		X	X	X^{ms}		X	X	X	X

Principal Manuscript Evidence in the First Eight Chapters of Romans
Armenian Evidence (UBSGNT^4)

Variant Rating	1.1 B	1.7 A	1.13 A	1.15 A	1.29 C	1.31 A	2.16 C	3.7 B	3.12 C	3.22 B	3.25 C
Armenian Kunz. Zohr.	X^{ms}	X	X	X					X	X	

Variant Rating	3.28 B	4.1 B	4.11 C	4.15 B	4.19 C	4.19 C	4.22 C	5.1 A	5.2 C	5.6 C	6.4 A
Armenian Kunz. Zohr.		X	X	X	(X)	X			X		

Variant Rating	6.8 A	6.11 A	6.12 B	7.14 A	7.18 B	7.20 C	7.22 A	7.25 B	8.1 A	8.2 B	8.11 B
Armenian Kunz. Zohr.	X		X	X^{ms}	X			X	X^{ms}		X

Variant Rating	8.21 A	8.23 A	8.24 B	8.24 B	8.26 A	8.28 B	8.34 C	8.35 A	8.38 A
Armenian Kunz. Zohr.	X	X		X	X	X	X	X	X

Principal Manuscript Evidence in the First Eight Chapters of Romans
Ethiopic Evidence (UBSGNT^4)

Variant Rating	1.1 B	1.7 A	1.13 A	1.15 A	1.29 C	1.31 A	2.16 C	3.7 B	3.12 C	3.22 B	3.25 C
Ethiopic eth		X	(X)	(X)					X		

Variant	3.28	4.1	4.11	4.15	4.19	4.19	4.22	5.1	5.2	5.6	6.4
Rating	B	B	C	B	C	C	C	A	C	C	A
Ethiopic eth	X		(X)	X	X		X		X		X

Variant	6.8	6.11	6.12	7.14	7.18	7.20	7.22	7.25	8.1	8.2	8.11
Rating	A	A	B	A	B	C	A	B	A	B	B
Ethiopic eth	X		X	X			X		(X)		X

Variant	8.21	8.23	8.24	8.24	8.26	8.28	8.34	8.35	8.38
Rating	A	A	B	B	A	B	C	A	A
Ethiopic eth	X	X				X	X	X	X

Principal Manuscript Evidence in the First Eight Chapters of Romans
Georgian Evidence (UBSGNT⁴)

Variant	1.1	1.7	1.13	1.15	1.29	1.31	2.16	3.7	3.12	3.22	3.25
Rating	B	A	A	A	C	A	C	B	C	B	C
Georgian geo		X	X	X					X		
geo¹							X				

Variant	3.28	4.1	4.11	4.15	4.19	4.19	4.22	5.1	5.2	5.6	6.4
Rating	B	B	C	B	C	C	C	A	C	C	A
Georgian geo				X			X	X	X		
geo²						X					

Variant	6.8	6.11	6.12	7.14	7.18	7.20	7.22	7.25	8.1	8.2	8.11
Rating	A	A	B	A	B	C	A	B	A	B	B
Georgian geo	X			X							X
geo¹		X						X	X	X	

Variant	8.21	8.23	8.24	8.24	8.26	8.28	8.34	8.35	8.38
Rating	A	A	B	B	A	B	C	A	A
Georgian geo	X	X		X				X	
geo¹							(X)		
geo²							X		

Principal Manuscript Evidence in the First Eight Chapters of Romans
Greek Church Father Evidence (UBSGNT⁴)

Variant	1.1	1.7	1.13	1.15	1.29	1.31	2.16	3.7
Rating	B	A	A	A	C	A	C	B
Greek Church Fathers								
Basil, the Great						$X^{1/2}$		
(John) Chrysostom		X	X	X	X			
Irenaeus	X^{lat}							
Origen	$X^{2/3}$	$X^{gr,\,lat}$	X^{lat}	$X^{lat1/2}$		$X^{lat1/2}$	(X)	
Theodore, of Mopsuestia			X					
Theodoret, of Cyrrhus		X						

Variant	3.12	3.22	3.25	3.28	4.1	4.11	4.15	4.19
Rating	C	B	C	B	B	C	B	C
Greek Church Fathers								
Apollinaris, of Laodicea		X						
(John) Chrysostom	X^{lem}		X					$X^{1/4}$
Clement, of Alexandria		X						
Cyril, of Alexandria	(X)	X		X	X			
Cyril-Jerusalem								X
Didymus		X						
Hesychius, of Jerusalem			$X^{1/2}$					
Origen	X^{lat}	$X^{lat5/6}$		X^{lat}	$X^{gr\ lem}$	$X^{lat1/3}$	$X^{lat6/7}$	$X^{gr,lat1/3}$
Severian			X					
Theodoret, of Cyrrhus							X^{lem}	

Variant	4.19	4.22	5.1	5.2	5.6	6.4	6.8	6.11
Rating	C	C	A	C	C	A	A	A
Greek Church Fathers								
Basil, the Great	X	X	X			X		X
(John) Chrysostom				$X^{1/2}$		X	X	
Cyril, of Alexandria			$X^{4/5}$	X		$X^{4/6}$		X
Cyril-Jerusalem	X					X, X^{dub}		
Didymus			X^{dub}					
Epiphanius	X^{vid}		X					
Eusebius, of Caesarea							X	
Gregory-Nyssa			X^{mss}					
Marcion *according to* Tertullian/Origen/Adamantius/Epiphanius					X			
Origen	$X^{gr,\,lat3/4}$	X^{lat}	$X^{lat2/5}$				X^{lat}	$X^{gr,lat}$ 1/11(1/11)
Theodore, of Mopsuestia						X		
Theodoret, of Cyrrhus								X

Variant	6.12	7.14	7.18	7.20	7.22	7.25	8.1	8.2
Rating	B	A	B	C	A	B	A	B
Greek Church Fathers								
Athanasius, of Alexandria							X	
Basil, the Great		X		X				
(John) Chrysostom		X		X	X			
Clement, of Alexandria				X				
Cyril, of Alexandria	X	X^{lem}	X^{com}	X	X	X	X	
Didymus	X	X^{dub}	X		X	X$^{1/3}$	X	
Diodore							X	
Epiphanius					X			
Eusebius, of Caesarea					X			
Gregory-Nyssa		X						
Marcion *according to* Tertullian/Origen/Adamantius/Epiphanius							X	
Methodius	X	X	X		X	X^{ms}		
Nilus					X			
Origen	X$^{(gr)lat}$ 6/7	X$^{gr,\ lat}$		X^{lat}			X^{lat}	
Serapion		X						
Theodore, of Mopsuestia		X			X			
Theodoret, of Cyrrhus		X			X			

Variant	8.11	8.21	8.23	8.24	8.24	8.26	8.28	8.34
Rating	B	A	A	B	B	A	B	C
Greek Church Fathers								
Apollinaris, of Laodicea	X		X					
Athanasius, of Alexandria	X							
Basil, the Great	X							
(John) Chrysostom		X	X		X		X	
Clement, of Alexandria	X	X			X		X	
Cyril, of Alexandria	X		X				X	X
Cyril-Jerusalem	X						X	
Didymus	X$^{lat1/2}$ X^{dub}	X	X				X	
Epiphanius	X					X$^{1/4}$		
Eunomians								
Eusebius, of Caesarea	X						X	
Gregory-Nyssa					X		(X)	
Hesychius, of Jerusalem							X	
Hippolytus	X							
Macarius/Symeon	X						X	
Marcellus, of Ancyra	X							
Methodius	X$^{1/2}$	X	X					
Origen		X	X^{lat}	X$^{gr,\ lat}$		(X)	X$^{gr,\ lat}$	X^{lat}
Ps-Athanasius	X							
Severian		X						
Theodore, of Mopsuestia			X^{lat}					
Theodoret, of Cyrrhus		X			X		X	

Variant	8.35	8.38
Rating	A	A
Greek Church Fathers		
Amphilochius	X	
Athanasius, of Alexandria	X	
Basil, the Great	X	
(John) Chrysostom	X$^{2/3}$	
Cyril, of Alexandria	X	X
Cyril-Jerusalem	X	
Didymus	X$^{1/8}$	
Diodore	X	
Eusebius, of Caesarea	X$^{1/4}$	X
Hesychius, of Jerusalem	X	
Macarius/Symeon	X$^{2/3}$	
Marcus-Eremita	X	
Methodius	X	
Origen	X^{gr,lat} 3/11 X^{dub}	X^{gr,lat} 2(2)/19
Proclus	X	
Severian	X	
Theodoret, of Cyrrhus	X	

Principal Manuscript Evidence in the First Eight Chapters of Romans
Latin Church Father Evidence (UBSGNT^4)

Variant	1.1	1.7	1.13	1.15	1.29	1.31	2.16	3.7
Rating	B	A	A	A	C	A	C	B
Latin Church Fathers								
Ambrose	X$^{2/3}$			X				
Ambrosiaster		X				X		
Augustine	X$^{9/14}$	X		X		X		X
Gildas						X		
Lucifer, of Calaris						X		
Pelagius		X		X		X		
Rebaptism (De Rebaptismate)							X	
Victorinus-Rome, Marius	X							

Variant	3.12	3.22	3.25	3.28	4.1	4.11	4.15	4.19
Rating	C	B	C	B	B	C	B	C
Latin Church Fathers								
Ambrose				X			X	
Ambrosiaster	X			X		X		
Augustine		X		X$^{3/7}$		X	X$^{2/30}$	
Julian-Eclanum							X	X
Pelagius	X			X				
Primasius							X	

Variant	4.19	4.22	5.1	5.2	5.6	6.4	6.8	6.11
Rating	C	C	A	C	C	A	A	A
Latin Church Fathers								
Ambrose							X	
Ambrosiaster						X	X	
Augustine						$X^{8/15}$	X	$X^{8/14}$
Bede	X							
Chromatius						$X^{2/3}$		
Hilary								X
Julian-Eclanum	X	X				X		
Pacian						X		
Pelagius		X					X	X
Speculum						X	X	X
Tertullian						X	X	$X^{1/2,(1/2)}$

Variant	6.12	7.14	7.18	7.20	7.22	7.25	8.1	8.2
Rating	B	A	B	C	A	B	A	B
Latin Church Fathers								
Ambrose	X	X			X			
Ambrosiaster		X			X		X	X
Augustine	X	X	$X^{18/38}$	$X^{8/15}$	X		X	$X^{10/13}$
Gregory-Elvira					X			
Hilary		X						
Jerome	X	$X^{9/10}$	$X^{2/5}$	$X^{2/4}$	X			
Pelagius	X	X			X			X
Speculum								X
Tertullian								$X^{1/2}$
Varimadum								X
Victorinus-Rome, Marius								X

Variant	8.11	8.21	8.23	8.24	8.24	8.26	8.28	8.34
Rating	B	A	A	B	B	A	B	C
Latin Church Fathers								
Ambrose	$X^{2/3}$		X		X		X	
Ambrosiaster					X		X	
Augustine	$X^{28/43}$		X		X	$X^{14/17}$	X	$X^{3/4}$
Bede	X							
Cyprian					X			
Jerome	$X^{1/3}$						X	
Lucifer, of Calaris							X	
Pelagius			X		X		X	X
Priscillian	X							
Ps-Vigilius	X							
Varimadum	X							X
Victorinus-Rome, Marius	X							
Vigilius	X							

Variant	8.35	8.38
Rating	A	A
Latin Church Fathers		
Ambrose	$X^{7/9}$	
Ambrosiaster	X	
Augustine	$X^{24/25}$	$(X^{5/8})$
Cyprian	X	
Gaudentius	X	
Gregory-Elvira	X	
Hilary	$X^{1/3}$	
Jerome	$X^{6/7}$	$X^{1(6)/7}$
Lucifer, of Calaris	X	
Novatian	X	
Pelagius	X	X
Quodvultdeus	$X^{1/2}$	
Tertullian	X	

Principal Manuscript Evidence in the Five Chapters of 1 Peter
Papyri Evidence (UBSGNT[4])

Variant	1.7	1.8	1.9	1.12	1.22	1.22	2.3	2.19	2.19	2.21	2.21
Rating	A	A	C	C	A	C	B	B	B	A	A
Papyri											
$\mathfrak{P}72^{ix}$		X			X	X	X	X		X	X
$\mathfrak{P}74$	X										

Variant	2.25	3.1	3.7	3.7	3.8	3.14	3.15	3.16	3.18	3.18	3.21
Rating	B	C	B	B	A	A	A	A	B	C	A
Papyri											
$\mathfrak{P}72$		X	X		X		X	X		X	
$\mathfrak{P}81$			X	X^{vid}							

Variant	4.1	4.14	4.14	5.2	5.3	5.6	5.8	5.10	5.10	5.10	5.11
Rating	A	A	A	C	A	A	C	A	C	B	B
Papyri											
$\mathfrak{P}72$	X	X		X	X	X		X	X		(X)

Variant	5.11	5.13	5.14	5.14
Rating	A	A	A	A
Papyri				
$\mathfrak{P}72$	X	X	X	

ix. $\mathfrak{P}^{72}$ is another vital papyrus that makes up part of the Bodmer collection, along with $\mathfrak{P}^{66}$, $\mathfrak{P}^{72}$, and $\mathfrak{P}^{75}$. It contains the Epistles of Peter and Jude in their entirety. This papyrus is dated around the late third or early fourth century and although containing what the Alands call 'peculiarities', it is rated a category I manuscript. See K. and B. Aland, *The Text of the New Testament*, p. 100.

Principal Manuscript Evidence in the Five Chapters of 1 Peter
Uncial Evidence (UBSGNT^4)

Variant	1.7	1.8	1.9	1.12	1.22	1.22	2.3	2.19	2.19	2.21	2.21
Rating	A	A	C	C	A	C	B	B	B	A	A
Uncials											
ℵ01	X	X	X	X	X	X*	X*	X	X		X
A02	X		X		X		X	X	X^c	X	X
B03	X	X			X		X	X	X	X	X
C04	X	X	X	X	X	X				X	X
[K018]	X		X	X		X		X	X	X	
[L020]	X		X	X		X		X	X	X	
[P024]	X		X	X		X		X	X	X	
Ψ044	X		X		X	X					X
048	X		X								

Variant	2.25	3.1	3.7	3.7	3.8	3.14	3.15	3.16	3.18	3.18	3.21
Rating	B	C	B	B	A	A	A	A	B	C	A
Uncials											
ℵ01	X	X^2	X^2,(X*)		X	X	X				X^2
A02	X				X	X	X				X
B03	X		X	X	X		X	X	X	X	X
C04		X		X*	X	X	X				X
[K018]		X				X			X		X
[L020]		X		X							X
[P024]		X		X		X			X	X	X
Ψ044		X		X	X	X	X	X		X	X

Variant	4.1	4.14	4.14	5.2	5.3	5.6	5.8	5.10	5.10	5.10	5.11
Rating	A	A	A	C	A	A	C	A	C	B	B
Uncials											
ℵ01			X*	X^2	X	X	X	X		X	
A02				X	X			X	X		X
B03	X	X	X			X		X			X
C04	X										
[K018]		X			X	X	X	X	X		
[L020]		X			X	X	X	X	X		
[P024]					X			X	X		
P025				X			X				
Ψ044	X	X		X	X			X	X		X
0206						X					

Variant	5.11	5.13	5.14	5.14
Rating	A	A	A	A
Uncials				
ℵ01			X	
A02		X	X	X
B03	X	X	X	X
[K018]		X	X	
[L020]		X	X	
[P024]		X	X	
Ψ044		X	X	X

Principal Manuscript Evidence in the Five Chapters of 1 Peter
Minuscules Evidence (UBSGNT[4])

Variant Rating	1.7 A	1.8 A	1.9 C	1.12 C	1.22 A	1.22 C	2.3 B	2.19 B	2.19 B	2.21 A	2.21 A
Minusc.											
33	X		X		X	X				X	
81	X		X	X	X	X		X		X	X
322	X	X	X	X	X	X				X	
323	X	X	X	X	X	X				X	
436	X		X		X	X			X	X	
945	X	X	X	X	X	X				X	X
1067	X		X		X	X			X		
1175	X	X	X	X		X				X	X
1241	X		X	X	X	X				X	X
1243	X		X	X	X	X				X	
1292	X		X	X		X					Xvid
1409	X		X		X	X			X	X	
1505	X			X		X				X	
1611	X		X	X		X				X	X
1735	X		X			X	X	X	X	X	X
1739	X	X	X	X	X	X				X	X
1852		X	X			X				X	X
1881			X	X	X		X			X	
2138			X	X		X				X	X
2298		X	X	X		X				X	
2344	X		X		X	X				X	
2464	X		X		X	X			X		

Variant Rating	2.25 B	3.1 C	3.7 B	3.7 B	3.8 A	3.14 A	3.15 A	3.16 A	3.18 B	3.18 C	3.21 A
Minusc.											
33		X	X	X	X	X	X				X
81				X	X	X					X
322		X	X	X	X	X					X
323		X	X	X	X	X					X
436		X			X	X	X				
945		X		X	X	X	X				X
1067		X			X	X	X				
1175	X	X	X	X	X	X	X	X		X	
1241		X	X	X	X	X		X		X	X
1243		X	X	X	X	X	X			X	X
1292	X	X			X			X		X	X
1409		X			X	X					
1505	X				X			X		X	X
1611		X			X		X	X		X	X
1735	X	X		X	X	X				X	X
1739		X	X	X	X	X	X	X			X
1852		X	X	X	X		X	X		X	X
1881		X	X	X	X	X	X	X		X	X
2138		X			X		X	X		X	X
2298		X	X	X	X	X		X			X
2344		X	X	X	X	X					X
2464	X	X	X		X	X	X				X

Variant Rating	4.1 A	4.14 A	4.14 A	5.2 C	5.3 A	5.6 A	5.8 C	5.10 A	5.10 C	5.10 B	5.11 B
Minusc.											
33				(X)	(X)			X	X	X^{vid}	
81				X	X	X	X	X	X		
322	X		X		X	X	X	X	X		
323	X		X		X	X	X	X	X		
436			X	X	X			X	X	X	
945				X	(X)	X		X		X	
1067			X	X	X			X	X	X	
1175					X	X		X	X		
1241				X	(X)	X	(X*[sic]*)	X	X	X	
1243	X			X	(X)	X	X	X	X		(X)
1292					(X)	X	X	X	X		
1409			X	X	X			X	X	X	
1505					X	X	X	X			
1611					(X)	X	X	X			
1735				X	(X)			X	X		
1739	X		X$^{v.r.}$	X	X	X	X	X	X	X*	
1852				X	X	X	X	X	X	X	
1881	X			X	(X)	X	X		X	X	
2138					(X)		X	X			
2298				X	X	X		X	X		
2344			X^{vid}	X^{vid}	X^{vid}			X	X	X	
2464				X	X		X	X	X	X	

Variant Rating	5.11 A	5.13 A	5.14 A	5.14 A
Minusc.				
81		X	X	
322		X	X	
323		X	X	
436		X		
945		X	X	
1067		X		
1175		X	X	
1241		X	X	
1243		X	X	
1292		X	X	
1409		X		
1505		X	X	
1611		X	X	
1735		X		
1739		X	X	
1852		X	X	
1881		X	X	
2138			X	
2298		X	X	
2344		X	X	X
2464		X		

Principal Manuscript Evidence in the Five Chapters of 1 Peter
Lectionary Evidence (UBSGNT[4])

Variant Rating	1.7 A	1.8 A	1.9 C	1.12 C	1.22 A	1.22 C	2.3 B	2.19 B	2.19 B	2.21 A	2.21 A
Lection.											
Lect.	X		X	X	X					X	
L751									X	X	
L1159										X	

Variant Rating	2.25 B	3.1 C	3.7 B	3.7 B	3.8 A	3.14 A	3.15 A	3.16 A	3.18 B	3.18 C	3.21 A
Lection.											
Lect.		X				X			X		X
L590										X	
L591										X	
L592				X							
L593									(X)	X	
L596			X		X						
L883									(X)		
L884				X							
L921										X	
L1154				X						X	
L1159				X							
L1178										X	
L1364				X							
L1441				X							

Variant Rating	4.1 A	4.14 A	4.14 A	5.2 C	5.3 A	5.6 A	5.8 C	5.10 A	5.10 C	5.10 B	5.11 B
Lection.											
Lect.					Xpt,AD (Xpt)	X		X	X		
L147		X									
L422		X									
L590		X									
L592							X				
L596				X							
L895							X				
L1159		X					X				
L1298							X				
L1365							X				
L1441		X									

Variant Rating	5.11 A	5.13 A	5.14 A	5.14 A
Lection.				
Lect.		X	X	
L1298	X			
L1365	X			

Principal Manuscript Evidence in the Five Chapters of 1 Peter
Old Latin Evidence (UBSGNT⁴)

Variant	1.7	1.8	1.9	1.12	1.22	1.22	2.3	2.19	2.19	2.21	2.21
Rating	A	A	C	C	A	C	B	B	B	A	A
Old Latin											
it^{ar}		X	X						X	X	X
it^{q} (c)			X							X	
it^{s} (ac)		X	X	X							
it^{t} (acpr)							X			X	(X)
it^{v} (e)								X	X	X	X
it^{z}								X	X	X	X

Variant	2.25	3.1	3.7	3.7	3.8	3.14	3.15	3.16	3.18	3.18	3.21
Rating	B	C	B	B	A	A	A	A	B	C	A
Old Latin											
it^{ar}	X		X	X	X	X	X				X
it^{l} (ac)				(X)	X						
it^{t} (acpr)	X		X	X	X	X	X				
it^{w} (c)					X	X	X				
it^{z}	X		X	X	X	X	X			X	X

Variant	4.1	4.14	4.14	5.2	5.3	5.6	5.8	5.10	5.10	5.10	5.11
Rating	A	A	A	C	A	A	C	A	C	B	B
Old Latin											
it^{ar}	X			(X)	X			X			X
it^{h} (acr)				X	(X)		X	X			
it^{q} (c)				X			X	X			
it^{t} (acpr)				X	X			X			
it^{z}	X			X	X			X			

Variant	5.11	5.13	5.14	5.14
Rating	A	A	A	A
Old Latin				
it^{ar}			X	
it^{h} (acr)		X	X	
it^{q} (c)		X	X	
it^{z}				X

Principal Manuscript Evidence in the Five Chapters of 1 Peter
Vulgate Evidence (UBSGNT⁴)

Variant	1.7	1.8	1.9	1.12	1.22	1.22	2.3	2.19	2.19	2.21	2.21
Rating	A	A	C	C	A	C	B	B	B	A	A
Vulgate											
vg		X	X		X^{mss}	X^{mss}		X	X	X	
vg^{ww}											X
vg^{st}							X				X

Variant	2.25	3.1	3.7	3.7	3.8	3.14	3.15	3.16	3.18	3.18	3.21
Rating	B	C	B	B	A	A	A	A	B	C	A
Vulgate											
vg	X		X	X (X^{mss})	X	X	X			X^{mss}	X

Variant	4.1	4.14	4.14	5.2	5.3	5.6	5.8	5.10	5.10	5.10	5.11
Rating	A	A	A	C	A	A	C	A	C	B	B
Vulgate											
vg	X			X	X			X^mss	X		
vg^cl			X								
vg^ww											X
vg^st			X								X

Variant	5.11	5.13	5.14	5.14
Rating	A	A	A	A
Vulgate				
vg^st		X		X

Principal Manuscript Evidence in the Five Chapters of 1 Peter
Syriac Evidence (UBSGNT⁴)

Variant	1.7	1.8	1.9	1.12	1.22	1.22	2.3	2.19	2.19	2.21	2.21
Rating	A	A	C	C	A	C	B	B	B	A	A
Syriac											
syr^p	X	X	X		X	X					
syr^h	X	X	X		X	X				X	X

Variant	2.25	3.1	3.7	3.7	3.8	3.14	3.15	3.16	3.18	3.18	3.21
Rating	B	C	B	B	A	A	A	A	B	C	A
Syriac											
syr^p	X				X		X		X		
syr^h	X				X		X		X		

Variant	4.1	4.14	4.14	5.2	5.3	5.6	5.8	5.10	5.10	5.10	5.11
Rating	A	A	A	C	A	A	C	A	C	B	B
Syriac											
syr^p				(X)	(X)	X			(X)		
syr^h					(X)		X		X^with*		

Variant	5.11	5.13	5.14	5.14
Rating	A	A	A	A
Syriac				
syr^h		X	X	

Principal Manuscript Evidence in the Five Chapters of 1 Peter
Coptic Evidence (UBSGNT⁴)

Variant	1.7	1.8	1.9	1.12	1.22	1.22	2.3	2.19	2.19	2.21	2.21
Rating	A	A	C	C	A	C	B	B	B	A	A
Coptic											
cop^sa		X			X	X	X	X	X	X	X^mss
cop^bo			X		X	X	X	X	X	X	

Variant	2.25	3.1	3.7	3.7	3.8	3.14	3.15	3.16	3.18	3.18	3.21
Rating	B	C	B	B	A	A	A	A	B	C	A
Coptic											
cop^sa		X		X	X	X	X	X			
cop^bo		X^ms			X	X	X				

Variant	4.1	4.14	4.14	5.2	5.3	5.6	5.8	5.10	5.10	5.10	5.11
Rating	A	A	A	C	A	A	C	A	C	B	B
Coptic											
cop^sa	X				X	X		X	X^ms		
cop^bo				X	X		X	X	X		

Variant	5.11	5.13	5.14	5.14
Rating	A	A	A	A
Coptic				
cop^{sa}		X	X	X^{ms}
cop^{bo}	X	X	X	X^{mss}

Principal Manuscript Evidence in the Five Chapters of 1 Peter
Armenian Evidence (UBSGNT^4)

Variant	1.7	1.8	1.9	1.12	1.22	1.22	2.3	2.19	2.19	2.21	2.21
Rating	A	A	C	C	A	C	B	B	B	A	A
Armenian Kunz. Zohr.	X	X	X		X	(X)	X				X

Variant	2.25	3.1	3.7	3.7	3.8	3.14	3.15	3.16	3.18	3.18	3.21
Rating	B	C	B	B	A	A	A	A	B	C	A
Armenian Kunz. Zohr.			X	X	(X)	X	X			X	X

Variant	4.1	4.14	4.14	5.2	5.3	5.6	5.8	5.10	5.10	5.10	5.11
Rating	A	A	A	C	A	A	C	A	C	B	B
Armenian Kunz. Zohr.			X	X	X	X		X	X		

Variant	5.11	5.13	5.14	5.14
Rating	A	A	A	A
Armenian Kunz. Zohr.	X			

Principal Manuscript Evidence in the Five Chapters of 1 Peter
Ethiopic Evidence (UBSGNT^4)

Variant	1.7	1.8	1.9	1.12	1.22	1.22	2.3	2.19	2.19	2.21	2.21
Rating	A	A	C	C	A	C	B	B	B	A	A
Ethiopic eth	X	X	X	X	X					X	X

Variant	2.25	3.1	3.7	3.7	3.8	3.14	3.15	3.16	3.18	3.18	3.21
Rating	B	C	B	B	A	A	A	A	B	C	A
Ethiopic eth	X	X	X	(X)	(X)	X					

Variant	4.1	4.14	4.14	5.2	5.3	5.6	5.8	5.10	5.10	5.10	5.11
Rating	A	A	A	C	A	A	C	A	C	B	B
Ethiopic eth			X	X	(X)	(X)		X	(X)		

Variant	5.11	5.13	5.14	5.14
Rating	A	A	A	A
Ethiopic eth		X		

Principal Manuscript Evidence in the Five Chapters of 1 Peter
Georgian Evidence (UBSGNT[4])

Variant Rating	1.7 A	1.8 A	1.9 C	1.12 C	1.22 A	1.22 C	2.3 B	2.19 B	2.19 B	2.21 A	2.21 A
Georgian geo	X		X	X	X		X			X	X

Variant Rating	2.25 B	3.1 C	3.7 B	3.7 B	3.8 A	3.14 A	3.15 A	3.16 A	3.18 B	3.18 C	3.21 A
Georgian geo		X	X	X	X	X			(X)		X

Variant Rating	4.1 A	4.14 A	4.14 A	5.2 C	5.3 A	5.6 A	5.8 C	5.10 A	5.10 C	5.10 B	5.11 B
Georgian geo	X		X	X	X			X	X		X

Variant Rating	5.11 A	5.13 A	5.14 A	5.14 A
Georgian geo		X	X	

Principal Manuscript Evidence in the Five Chapters of 1 Peter
Greek Church Father Evidence (UBSGNT[4])

Variant Rating	1.7 A	1.8 A	1.9 C	1.12 C	1.22 A	1.22 C	2.3 B	2.19 B
Greek Church Fathers								
Ammonas	X							
Clement, of Alexandria	X		X[lat]				X	
Cyril, of Alexandria		X						
Didymus					X			
Irenaeus		X[lat]						
Origen	X							

Variant Rating	2.19 B	2.21 A	2.21 A	2.25 B	3.1 C	3.7 B	3.7 B	3.8 A
Greek Church Fathers								
(John) Chrysostom		X						
Clement, of Alexandria								X
Cyril, of Alexandria			X[1/3]					
Eusebius-Emesa		X						
Ps-Dionysius				X				

Variant Rating	3.14 A	3.15 A	3.16 A	3.18 B	3.18 C	3.21 A	4.1 A	4.14 A
Greek Church Fathers								
Clement, of Alexandria	X	X	X					X
Cyril, of Alexandria						X[1/2]		X[1/2]
Didymus						X[dub]		
Isidore, of Pelusium							X	
Nestorius							X[vid]	
Origen						X[lat1/2]		

Variant	4.14	5.2	5.3	5.6	5.8	5.10	5.10	5.10
Rating	A	C	A	A	C	A	C	B
Greek Church Fathers								
Clement, of Alexandria	X							
Cyril, of Alexandria			X					
Cyril-Jerusalem					X^{dub}			
Didymus			(X)	X			X^{dub}	
Eusebius, of Caesarea					X^{ms}			
Origen				X	$(X^{gr1/6})$			
Theodoret, of Cyrrhus	X							

Variant	5.11	5.11	5.13	5.14	5.14
Rating	B	A	A	A	A
Greek Church Fathers					
Cyril-Jerusalem				X^{dub}	
Eusebius, of Caesarea			X		
Origen			X		

Principal Manuscript Evidence in the Five Chapters of 1 Peter
Latin Church Father Evidence (UBSGNT^4)

Variant	1.7	1.8	1.9	1.12	1.22	1.22	2.3	2.19
Rating	A	A	C	C	A	C	B	B
Latin Church Fathers								
Augustine				X			$X^{1/2}$	
Jerome						X		
Varimadum			X					

Variant	2.19	2.21	2.21	2.25	3.1	3.7	3.7	3.8
Rating	B	A	A	B	C	B	B	A
Latin Church Fathers								
Ambrose			X				X	
Augustine		X	$X^{2/20}$			X		
Cyprian		X	X					
Jerome		X						
Pelagius								X
Quodvultdeus		X	$X^{3/4}$					
Speculum	X						(X)	X
Tertullian		X						
Varimadum		X						

Variant	3.14	3.15	3.16	3.18	3.18	3.21	4.1	4.14
Rating	A	A	A	B	C	A	A	A
Latin Church Fathers								
Ambrose							X	
Augustine				$X^{1/6}$	$X^{1/2}$	$X^{2/9}$	$X^{3/4}$	
Cyprian						X		
Jerome		(X)				X	$X^{2/3}$	
Niceta							X	
Tertullian								X
Varimadum						X		
Vigilius							X	

Variant	4.14	5.2	5.3	5.6	5.8	5.10	5.10	5.10
Rating	A	C	A	A	C	A	C	B
Latin Church Fathers								
Augustine			(X)					
Cyprian					X			
Hilary					(X)			
Jerome		$X^{2/3}$	X		$X^{1/9}$			
Speculum		(X)	(X)					
Tertullian	X							

Variant	5.11	5.11	5.13	5.14	5.14
Rating	B	A	A	A	A
Latin Church Fathers					
Cassiodorus				X	

Principal Manuscript Evidence in the First Eight Chapters of Revelation
Papyri Evidence (UBSGNT⁴)

Variant	1.5	1.6	1.8	1.15	2.7	2.20	2.22	2.22	3.5	4.11	5.6
Rating	A	C	A	C	A	B	A	A	B	A	C
Papyri											
$\mathfrak{P}18^{x}$	X										
$\mathfrak{P}24$											X

Variant	5.9	5.10	5.10	5.13	6.1	6.2	6.3-4	6.5	6.5	6.7	6.8
Rating	A	A	A	B	B	B	B	B	B	B	B
Papyri											

Variant	6.17
Rating	A
Papyri	

Principal Manuscript Evidence in the First Eight Chapters of Revelation
Uncial Evidence (UBSGNT⁴)

Variant	1.5	1.6	1.8	1.15	2.7	2.20	2.22	2.22	3.5	4.11	5.6
Rating	A	C	A	C	A	B	A	A	B	A	C
Uncials											
ℵ01	X²	X², (X*)	X¹		X	X	X	X	X*	X	X
A02	X		X	X	X				X	X	
C04	X	X	X	X	X	X	X	X	X		
[P024]			X				X	X			
P025					X	X					

Variant	5.9	5.10	5.10	5.13	6.1	6.2	6.3-4	6.5	6.5	6.7	6.8
Rating	A	A	A	B	B	B	B	B	B	B	B
Uncials											
ℵ01		X	X	X		X			X		X
A02	X	X			X	X	X	X	X	X^vid	X
C04					X	X	X	X	X	X	(X)
[P024]							X				
P025			X		X	X		X	X	X	X

Variant	6.17
Rating	A
Uncials	
ℵ01	X
C04	X

---

x. $\mathfrak{P}^{18}$, containing Rev. 1.4-7, is significant in that it is dated as early as the third or fourth century. The Alands list it as a category I manuscript in *The Text of the New Testament*, p. 97.

Principal Manuscript Evidence in the First Eight Chapters of Revelation
Minuscule Evidence (UBSGNT[4])

Variant Rating	1.5 A	1.6 C	1.8 A	1.15 C	2.7 A	2.20 B	2.22 A	2.22 A	3.5 B	4.11 A	5.6 C
Minusc.											
205		X			X	X	X			X	
209		X			X	X	X			X	
1006		X	X				X	X	X	X	
1611		X	X			X	X	X		X	
1841		X	X				X	X		X	
1854		X			X		X				X
2050	X					X	X	X			
2053		X	X			X	X	X		X	X
2062		X	X								
2329	X	X			X	X	X		X		X
2344						X	X		X		(X)
2351		X					X	X	X	X	X

Variant Rating	5.9 A	5.10 A	5.10 A	5.13 B	6.1 B	6.2 B	6.3-4 B	6.5 B	6.5 B	6.7 B	6.8 B
Minusc.											
205		X	X			X			X		X
209		X	X			X			X		X
1006		X			X	X	X	X	X	X	X
1611		X		X	X	X	X	X	X	X	X
1841		X			X	X	X	X	X	X	X
1854			X		X		X	(X)		X	
2050		X	X								
2053		X	X		X	X	X	X	X	X	(X)
2329							X			X	
2344		X	X			X					
2351		X	X		X		X	X		X	

Variant Rating	6.17 A
Minusc.	
1611	X
1854	X
2053	X
2329	X
2344	X

Principal Manuscript Evidence in the First Eight Chapters of Revelation
Lectionary Evidence (UBSGNT[4])

There are no Lectionary manuscripts cited in the first eight chapters of Revelation within the UBSGNT[4].

Principal Manuscript Evidence in the First Eight Chapters of Revelation
Old Latin Evidence (UBSGNT[4])

Variant Rating	1.5 A	1.6 C	1.8 A	1.15 C	2.7 A	2.20 B	2.22 A	2.22 A	3.5 B	4.11 A	5.6 C
Old Latin											
it^{ar}		X				X	X		X	X	
it^{gig}		X				X	X	X	X	X	X
it^{h} (acr)	X	X	X								
it^{l} (acpr)		X				X	X		X	X	

Variant Rating	5.9 A	5.10 A	5.10 A	5.13 B	6.1 B	6.2 B	6.3-4 B	6.5 B	6.5 B	6.7 B	6.8 B
Old Latin											
it^{ar}											X
it^{gig}			X	X		X		X			

Variant Rating	6.17 A
Old Latin	
it^{ar}	X
it^{gig}	X

Principal Manuscript Evidence in the First Eight Chapters of Revelation
Vulgate Evidence (UBSGNT[4])

Variant Rating	1.5 A	1.6 C	1.8 A	1.15 C	2.7 A	2.20 B	2.22 A	2.22 A	3.5 B	4.11 A	5.6 C
Vulgate											
vg		X				X	X		X	X	
vg^{cl}											X
vg^{ww}								X			
vg^{st}								X			

Variant Rating	5.9 A	5.10 A	5.10 A	5.13 B	6.1 B	6.2 B	6.3-4 B	6.5 B	6.5 B	6.7 B	6.8 B
Vulgate											
vg						X					
vg^{ww}			X	X			X	X	X	X	X
vg^{st}			X	X			X	X	X	X	X

Variant Rating	6.17 A
Vulgate	
vg	X

Principal Manuscript Evidence in the First Eight Chapters of Revelation
Syriac Evidence (UBSGNT[4])

Variant Rating	1.5 A	1.6 C	1.8 A	1.15 C	2.7 A	2.20 B	2.22 A	2.22 A	3.5 B	4.11 A	5.6 C
Syriac											
syr^{ph}		X	X		X		X		X		X
syr^{h}		X	X				X	X	X		X

Variant	5.9	5.10	5.10	5.13	6.1	6.2	6.3-4	6.5	6.5	6.7	6.8
Rating	A	A	A	B	B	B	B	B	B	B	B
Syriac											
syr^ph		X					X	X		X	X
syr^h		X		X	X	X			X		X

Variant	6.17
Rating	A
Syriac	
syr^ph	X
syr^h	X

Principal Manuscript Evidence in the First Eight Chapters of Revelation
Coptic Evidence (UBSGNT[4])

Variant	1.5	1.6	1.8	1.15	2.7	2.20	2.22	2.22	3.5	4.11	5.6
Rating	A	C	A	C	A	B	A	A	B	A	C
Coptic											
cop^sa						X			X		X
cop^bo						X	X		X		X

Variant	5.9	5.10	5.10	5.13	6.1	6.2	6.3-4	6.5	6.5	6.7	6.8
Rating	A	A	A	B	B	B	B	B	B	B	B
Coptic											
cop^sa			X	X	X	(X)	X	X		X	X^{ms} (X^{mss})
cop^bo		X	X	X^{pt}	X	X	X	X	X	X	X

Variant	6.17
Rating	A
Coptic	

Principal Manuscript Evidence in the First Eight Chapters of Revelation
Armenian Evidence (UBSGNT[4])

Variant	1.5	1.6	1.8	1.15	2.7	2.20	2.22	2.22	3.5	4.11	5.6
Rating	A	C	A	C	A	B	A	A	B	A	C
Armenian Kunz. Zohr.		(X)	X		X	X			X		X

Variant	5.9	5.10	5.10	5.13	6.1	6.2	6.3-4	6.5	6.5	6.7	6.8
Rating	A	A	A	B	B	B	B	B	B	B	B
Armenian Kunz. Zohr.		X		X	X	X	X	X	X	X	X

Variant	6.17
Rating	A
Armenian Kunz. Zohr.	

Principal Manuscript Evidence in the First Eight Chapters of Revelation
Ethiopic Evidence (UBSGNT[4])

Variant Rating	1.5 A	1.6 C	1.8 A	1.15 C	2.7 A	2.20 B	2.22 A	2.22 A	3.5 B	4.11 A	5.6 C
Ethiopic eth		X	X			X	(X)	X	X		

Variant Rating	5.9 A	5.10 A	5.10 A	5.13 B	6.1 B	6.2 B	6.3-4 B	6.5 B	6.5 B	6.7 B	6.8 B
Ethiopic eth	X	(X)		X		X					

Variant Rating	6.17 A
Ethiopic eth	

Principal Manuscript Evidence in the First Eight Chapters of Revelation
Georgian Evidence (UBSGNT[4])

There are no Georgian manuscripts cited in the first eight chapters of Revelation within the UBSGNT[4].

Principal Manuscript Evidence in the First Eight Chapters of Revelation
Greek Church Father Evidence (UBSGNT[4])

Variant Rating	1.5 A	1.6 C	1.8 A	1.15 C	2.7 A	2.20 B	2.22 A	2.22 A
Greek Church Fathers								
Andrew, of Caesarea	X	X			X	X	X	
Didymus		X						
Epiphanius			X			X		

Variant Rating	3.5 B	4.11 A	5.6 C	5.9 A	5.10 A	5.10 A	5.13 B	6.1 B
Greek Church Fathers								
Andrew, of Caesarea					X	X		X
Clement, of Alexandria			X[vid]					
Hippolytus			X			X		
Irenaeus			X[lat]					

Variant Rating	6.2 B	6.3-4 B	6.5 B	6.5 B	6.7 B	6.8 B	6.17 A
Greek Church Fathers							
Andrew, of Caesarea	X	X	X	X	X	X	

Principal Manuscript Evidence in the First Eight Chapters of Revelation
Latin Church Fathers Evidence (UBSGNT⁴)

Variant	1.5	1.6	1.8	1.15	2.7	2.20	2.22	2.22
Rating	A	C	A	C	A	B	A	A
Latin Church Fathers								
Ambrose			X					
Ambrosiaster						X	X	
Apringius		X						
Beatus		X				X		X
Cyprian							X	
Primasius	X		X				X	
Tertullian						X	X	X
Tyconius						X	X	X
Varimadum				X				
Victorinus-Pettau	X							

Variant	3.5	4.11	5.6	5.9	5.10	5.10	5.13	6.1
Rating	B	A	C	A	A	A	B	B
Latin Church Fathers								
Apringius		X						
Beatus		X	X				X	
Cassiodorus							X	
Cyprian			X	X	X			
Fulgentius			X		X			
Gregory-Elvira			X					
Primasius	X		X				X	
Tyconius			X					

Variant	6.2	6.3-4	6.5	6.5	6.7	6.8	6.17
Rating	B	B	B	B	B	B	A
Latin Church Fathers							
Fulgentius							X
Primasius				(X)			

Manuscripts Not Cited in the Principal Manuscript Evidence Charts

The following list contains manuscripts that have not been cited in the previous Principal Manuscript Evidence charts. They have not been included because 1) the citation is too detailed to record within a chart, and 2) the particular manuscript cited is not a principal witness.

Luke:
- 1.35 slav
- 1.46 (slav)
- 1.66 slav
- 2.11 slav
- 2.33 slav
- 3.22 slav
- 4.17 slav
- 5.17a (A* *illegible*)
- 5.17b slav
- 5.39 slav
- 5.39b slav

Acts:
- 1.2 slav
- 1.11 slav
- 1.23 slav
- 1.26 slav
- 2.5 slav
- 2.16 slav
- 2.18a slav
- 2.18b slav
- 2.19 slav
- 2.24 slav/Greek mss acc. to Bede
- 2.37 slav/l^{AD}

Romans:
- 1.7 slav
- 1.13 slav
- 1.15 slav
- 3.12 slav
- 4.11 slav
- 4.19 slav
- 4.22 slav
- 5.1 Byz^{pt}/slav
- 5.2 slav
- 6.4 slav
- 6.8 slav
- 6.12 slav

1 Peter:
- 1.7 slav
- 1.8 slav
- 1.9 slav
- 1.22 slav
- 2.19a slav
- 2.19b slav
- 3.7 l^{AD}
- 3.8 slav
- 3.14 slav
- 3.21 slav
- 4.1 slav^{ms}
- 4.14 Byz^{pt}

Revelation:
- 1.6 Byz [046]
- 1.8 Byz [P 046]
- 2.22a Byz [P 046]
- 2.22b Byz [P 046]
- 4.11 Byz/ Apringius mss acc.to Primasius
- 5.6 Byz [046]/ Maternus
- 5.10a Byz [046]/ Maternus
- 5.10b Maternus

Luke:
- 6.4a slav
- 6.4b slav
- 6.10 slav
- 6.35 slav
- 7.11 slav
- 7.35 slav[mss]
- 7.45 slav
- 8.26 mss acc. to Origen/Titus-Bostra
- 8.37 mss acc. to Origen/Titus-Bostra
- 8.43 slav[mss]
- 8.44 slav
- 8.49 syr[h with*, pal]

Acts:
- 2.43 (*Lect*[pt])
- 2.44 slav
- 3.6 slav
- 3.14 slav
- 3.22a *Byz*[pt]
- 3.22b slav[ms]
- 3.25 slav[ms]
- 4.1 slav
- 4.6 slav
- 4.10 slav
- 4.12 slav
- 4.24 2495
- 5.3 slav/Greek ms[acc. to Bede]
- 5.17 slav
- 5.28 slav/Greek ms[acc. to Bede]
- 5.29 (slav)/*l*[AD]
- 5.39 slav
- 6.7 slav[ms]
- 7.18 slav
- 7.19 slav
- 8.24 slav[(ms)]

Romans:
- 7.18 Greek mss acc. to Augustine
- 8.11 slav/Greek mss[acc. Ps-Athanasius]
- 8.21 slav[ms]/Clement[fm Theodotus]
- 8.23 slav
- 8.24 slav
- 8.28 slav
- 8.38 slav

1 Peter:
- 5.2 slav
- 5.3 slav
- 5.10a slav
- 5.10b slav
- 5.13 slav/Origen[acc. to Eusebius]
- 5.14 slav

Revelation:
- 6.3-4 *Byz*/[P 046]

APPENDIX V

Percentages Showing Important Manuscripts in Selected Portions of the UBSGNT[4]

Appendix V is based upon the collation of manuscripts in Appendix IV. This appendix also acts as the direct foundation of the 'High Percentage Manuscript Groupings' charts in Chapter 2, Section 4. However, these charts provide more information and greater detail. For example, the charts in Section 4 only list manuscripts that occur above 70 percent of the time in *A, B, C*, or *D* rated variants within a given book and given chapters. These charts list all manuscripts that are cited in a given book and given chapters. As in Appendix IV, the charts included here list manuscripts in the first eight chapters of Luke, Acts, Romans and Revelation, and the entirety of First Peter. Like Appendix IV, only manuscripts that are recorded in the first variant option (i.e. the variant reading that appears in the *UBSGNT*[4] text) are listed here. The manuscript types that are recorded follow the same progression as in the previous appendix: papyri, uncials, minuscules, lectionaries, Old Latin versions, Vulgate versions, Syriac versions, Coptic versions, Armenian versions, Ethiopic versions, Georgian versions, Greek Father quotations, and Latin Father quotations.

In contrast to the other charts presented here, this set is perhaps the most difficult to understand. By following the 'Rating' row (the 'Quality' row, located above the Rating row, simply reminds the reader that *A* and *B* rated variants have a higher degree of certainty, while *C* and *D* rated variants have a lower degree of certainty) horizontally across the page, from left to right, one can see that every letter-rating (*A, B, C*, and *D*) is recorded. Listed directly under each rating is the number of total particular letter-rated variants that occur in the given book and chapters. For example, in the first eight chapters of Luke, there are 18 total *A* rated variants, 26 total *B* rated variants, 7 total *C* rated variants, and no *D* rated variants. This accounts for 51 total variants in the first eight chapters of Luke (the 'Rating' row will function in a similar manner within each specific book that is presented, however, the figures will change from book to book).

Underneath the 'Rating' title the specific type of manuscript being dealt with is listed. Below the manuscript type a vertical list of all the witnesses that have been cited in the given book and chapters are recorded (this is the far left column). Each witness is represented by a horizontal column. Therefore, by following a straight line from left to right, information concerning any listed manuscript can be gained.

Underneath each of the *A*, *B*, *C*, and *D* rated variants headings, there are three vertical columns, '*COL 1*', '*COL 2*', and '*COL 3*'. Each column represents the identical type of statistic under each group of rated passages.

- *COL 1* indicates the number of times that a manuscript occurs in all the *A* rated variants, *B* rated variants, *C* rated variants, and *D* rated variants, respectively. One would explain this column in the following manner: *Manuscript X occurs in 17 out of a possible 18 A rated variants in the first eight chapters of Luke.*

- *COL 2* indicates the *percentage* that a given manuscript occurs in *A*, *B*, *C*, or *D* rated variants. This column simply takes the number recorded in *COL 1* and divides it by the total number of *A*, *B*, *C*, or *D* rated variants.[i] All percentage numbers listed as 70 percent and over appear in bold type. This is to help the reader distinguish between more and less frequently cited manuscripts. It is this column that provides the information given in the 'High Percentage Manuscript Groupings' charts in Chapter 2, Section 4. One would explain this column in the following manner: *Manuscript X occurs in 94 percent of all the A rated variants cited in the first eight chapters of Acts.*

- *COL 3* indicates the *percentage* that a given manuscript occurs in an *A*, *B*, *C*, or *D* rated variant, compared with its occurrence in the other three letter-rated variants. This column is calculated by dividing *COL 1* figures by *COL 4* figures. One would explain this column in the following manner: *Manuscript X occurs in 41 out of a total 51 rated variants in the first eight chapters of Luke. It occurs as an A rated variant 41 percent of the time, as a B rated variant 49 percent of the time, as a C rated variant 10 percent of the time, and as a D rated variant 0 percent of the time. Thus accounting for 100 percent of its occurrences.*

- *COL 4* (located at the far right margin) indicates the total number of variants that have the particular manuscript cited as a witness. Or, one could say it indicates the total number of times a given manuscript is cited in the given book and chapters. It is calculated by adding all four *A*, *B*, *C*, and *D COL 1* figures together (the box in the top right hand corner records the total number of variants in a particular book and chapters, calculated by adding all *A*, *B*, *C*, and *D* rated variants together). One would explain this column in the following manner: *Manuscript X is cited in 41 out of 51 variants in the first eight chapters of Luke.*

Examples

Codex Sinaiticus (ℵ*01*) will act as our example. It is listed as an uncial manuscript and is initially located in the first eight chapters of Luke (as seen in the chart entitled '*Percentages Showing Important Uncial Manuscripts in the First Eight Chapters of Luke [UBSGNT^4]*'). If one locates this manuscript in the extreme left hand column, and follows a horizontal line from left to right, the following data can be determined.

---

i.   As in previous percentage charts listed in this monograph, these figures have been either rounded up or rounded down based on the first decimal place.

COL 1 figures will be dealt with first. Under the '*A Rated Variants*' heading there are 18 total *A* rated variants in the first eight chapters of Luke. Under '*COL 1*', beneath the '*A Rated Variants*' heading, ℵ01 is cited in 17 of these 18 variants. Under the '*B Rated Variants*' heading there are 26 total *B* rated variants in the first eight chapters of Luke. Under '*COL 1*', beneath the '*B Rated Variants*' heading, ℵ01 is cited in 20 of these 26 variants. Under the '*C Rated Variants*' heading there are 7 total *C* rated variants in the first eight chapters of Luke. Under '*COL 1*', beneath the '*C Rated Variants*' heading, ℵ01 is cited in 4 of these 7 variants. And finally, under the '*D Rated Variants*' heading there are 0 total *D* rated variants in the first eight chapters of Luke. Under '*COL 1*', beneath the '*D Rated Variants*' heading, ℵ01 is cited, obviously, in no *D* rated variants. Adding together the number of all *A*, *B*, *C*, and *D* rated passages that are listed in the first eight chapters of Luke gives the total number of rated variants that occur as a whole (18 [*A*] + 26 [*B*] + 7 [*C*] + 0 [*D*] = 51 total variants in Luke 1–8). By adding all four *COL 1* figures together, we arrive at our *COL 4* figure. This records the total number of variants (out of 51 in Chapters 1–8 of this particular book) that have ℵ01 cited as a witness (17 [*A-COL1*] + 20 [*B-COL1*] + 4 [*C-COL1*] + 0 [*D-COL1*] = 41 out of 51 variants have ℵ01 cited.

Under '*COL 2*', beneath the '*A Rated Variants*' heading, ℵ01 occurs in 94 percent of all the *A* rated variants in the first eight chapters of Luke (17 [*COL1*] ÷ 18 total *A* rated variants = 0.944 or 94%). Therefore: 1) ℵ01 seems to be an important *A* rated witness, and 2) the *UBSGNT* editors likely have a high regard for ℵ01 in determining *A* rated variants. Under '*COL 2*', beneath the '*B Rated Variants*' heading, ℵ01 occurs in 77 percent of all the *B* rated variants in the first eight chapters of Luke (20 [*COL1*] ÷ 26 total *B* rated variants = 0.769 or 77%). Therefore: 1) ℵ01 seems to be an important *B* rated witness, and 2) the *UBSGNT* editors likely have a high regard for ℵ01 in determining *B* rated variants. Under '*COL 2*', beneath the '*C Rated Variants*' heading, ℵ01 occurs in 57 percent of all the *C* rated variants in the first eight chapters of Luke (4 [*COL1*] ÷ 7 total *C* rated variants = 0.571 or 57%). Because *C* ratings have a lower degree of certainty, and because *C* rated variants often do not include as many manuscripts, or as high a quality of manuscripts such as *A* and *B* rated variants, they tend to not be as useful in establishing conclusions. Under '*COL 2*', beneath the '*D Rated Variants*' heading, ℵ01 occurs in 0 percent, or no *D* rated variants.

Under *COL3*, beneath the '*A Rated Variants*' heading, the figure 41 percent is given (17 [*COL1*] ÷ 41 [*COL4*] = 0.414 or 41%). Under *COL3*, beneath the '*B Rated Variants*' heading, the figure 49 percent is given (20 [*COL1*] ÷ 41 [*COL4*] = 0.487 or 49%). Under *COL3*, beneath the '*C Rated Variants*' heading, the figure 10 percent is given (4 [*COL1*] ÷ 41 [*COL4*] = 0.097 or 10%). Under *COL3*, beneath the '*D Rated Variants*' heading, the figure 0 percent is given (0 [*COL1*] ÷ 41 [*COL4*] = 0.0 or 0%). Therefore, ℵ01 occurs in 41 out of a total 51 rated variants in the first eight chapters of Luke; ℵ01 occurs in *A* rated variants 41 percent of the time, *B* rated variants 49 percent of the time, *C* rated variants 10 percent of the time, and *D* rated variants 0 percent of the time, thus reaching 100 percent of its total occurrences.

Percentages Showing Important Papyri Manuscripts in the First Eight Chapters of Luke (UBSGNT[4])

Quality Rating	Above Average or Stronger Variants						Below Average or Weaker Variants						51 total variants in Lk. 1–8
	A Rated Variants (18 Possible Total)			B Rated Variants (26 Possible Total)			C Rated Variants (7 Possible Total)			D Rated Variants (0 Possible Total)			
Papyri	COL 1 # of times in A vrnts	COL 2 % in A vrnts	COL 3 % as A to B,C,D	COL 1 # of times in B vrnts	COL 2 % in B vrnts	COL 3 % as B to A,C,D 4	COL 1 # of times in C vrnts	COL 2 % in C vrnts	COL 3 % as C to A,B,D	COL 1 # of times in D vrnts	COL 2 % in D vrnts	COL 3 % as D to A,B,C	COL 4 # of variants with ms as a witness
𝔓[4ii]	5	28%	50%	4	15%	40%	1	14%	10%	0	0%	0%	10
𝔓[75]	3	17%	19%	11	42%	69%	2	29%	13%	0	0%	0%	16

ii.   Numerous papyri will be footnoted throughout the papyri evidence charts because of their early age and importance to textual criticism. Both 𝔓[4], containing various portions of the first six chapters in Luke, and 𝔓[75], containing large sections of Luke and John, are significant (at least from the view of external evidence which is partially concerned with the age of manuscripts) in that they are dated from the third century with 𝔓[75] given a very early third-century date. The Alands list both papyri as category I manuscripts in *The Text of the New Testament*, pp. 96-101.

*Percentages Showing Important Uncial Manuscripts in
the First Eight Chapters of Luke (UBSGNT⁴)*

Quality Rating	Above Average or Stronger Variants												51 total
	A Rated Variants (18 Possible Total)			B Rated Variants (26 Possible Total)			C Rated Variants (7 Possible Total)			D Rated Variants (0 Possible Total)			variants in Lk. 1–8
Uncials	COL 1 # of times in A vrnts	COL 2 % in A vrnts	COL 3 % as A to B,C,D	COL 1 # of times in B vrnts	COL 2 % in B vrnts	COL 3 % as B to A,C,D	COL 1 # of times in C vrnts	COL 2 % in C vrnts	COL 3 % as C to A,B,D	COL 1 # of times in D vrnts	COL 2 % in D vrnts	COL 3 % as D to A,B,C	COL 4 # of variants with ms as a witness
ℵ01	17	**94%**	41%	20	**77%**	49%	4	57%	10%	0	0%	0%	41
A02	10	56%	59%	5	19%	29%	2	29%	12%	0	0%	0%	17
B03	18	**100%**	38%	25	**96%**	53%	4	57%	9%	0	0%	0%	47
C04	4	22%	44%	3	12%	33%	2	29%	22%	0	0%	0%	9
D05	7	39%	44%	7	27%	44%	2	29%	13%	0	0%	0%	16
[E07]ⁱⁱⁱ	9	50%	50%	7	27%	39%	2	29%	11%	0	0%	0%	18
[F09]	6	33%	60%	3	12%	30%	1	14%	10%	0	0%	0%	10
[G011]	6	33%	50%	5	19%	42%	1	14%	8%	0	0%	0%	12
[H013]	8	44%	47%	7	27%	41%	2	29%	12%	0	0%	0%	17
L019	16	**89%**	41%	18	69%	46%	5	71%	13%	0	0%	0%	39
[N022]	0	0%	0%	2	8%	67%	1	14%	33%	0	0%	0%	3
[P024]	3	16%	60%	1	4%	20%	1	14%	20%	0	0%	0%	5
[Q026]	0	0%	0%	1	4%	100%	0	0%	0%	0	0%	0%	1
W032	18	**100%**	47%	17	65%	45%	3	43%	8%	0	0%	0%	38
Δ037	9	50%	53%	6	23%	35%	2	29%	12%	0	0%	0%	17
Θ038	7	39%	39%	9	35%	50%	2	29%	11%	0	0%	0%	18
Ξ040	7	39%	44%	7	27%	44%	2	29%	13%	0	0%	0%	16
Ψ044	11	61%	65%	5	19%	29%	1	14%	6%	0	0%	0%	17
070	0	0%	0%	1	4%	100%	0	0%	0%	0	0%	0%	1
079	1	6%	100%	0	0%	0%	0	0%	0%	0	0%	0%	1
0130	1	6%	50%	1	4%	50%	0	0%	0%	0	0%	0%	2
0177	0	0%	0%	1	4%	100%	0	0%	0%	0	0%	0%	1
0233	3	17%	50%	2	8%	33%	1	15%	17%	0	0%	0%	6

iii.   Manuscripts placed in brackets are uncials that have a Byzantine text. These manuscripts would be cited following the group symbol *Byz*, as indicated in the footnotes on p. 904 of the *UBSGNT*⁴.

*Percentages Showing Important Minuscule Manuscripts in
the First Eight Chapters of Luke (UBSGNT[4])*

| Quality Rating | Above Average or Stronger Variants | | | | | | | | | | | | 51 total variants in Lk. 1–8 |
| | A Rated Variants (18 Possible Total) | | | B Rated Variants (26 Possible Total) | | | C Rated Variants (7 Possible Total) | | | D Rated Variants (0 Possible Total) | | | |
Minusc.	COL 1 # of times in A vrnts	COL 2 % in A vrnts	COL 3 % as A to B,C,D	COL 1 # of times in B vrnts	COL 2 % in B vrnts	COL 3 % as B to A,C,D	COL 1 # of times in C vrnts	COL 2 % in C vrnts	COL 3 % as C to A,B,D	COL 1 # of times in D vrnts	COL 2 % in D vrnts	COL 3 % as D to A,B,C	COL 4 # of variants with ms as a witness
f1	10	56%	43%	10	38%	43%	3	43%	13%	0	0%	0%	23
f13	8	44%	38%	9	35%	43%	4	57%	19%	0	0%	0%	21
1	1	6%	50%	1	4%	50%	0	0%	0%	0	0%	0%	2
28	9	50%	53%	6	23%	35%	2	29%	12%	0	0%	0%	17
33	10	56%	50%	6	23%	30%	4	57%	20%	0	0%	0%	20
157	9	50%	33%	14	54%	52%	4	57%	15%	0	0%	0%	27
180	9	50%	50%	7	27%	39%	2	29%	11%	0	0%	0%	18
205	9	50%	45%	8	31%	40%	3	43%	15%	0	0%	0%	20
565	11	61%	55%	7	27%	35%	2	29%	10%	0	0%	0%	20
579	14	**78%**	47%	13	50%	43%	3	43%	10%	0	0%	0%	30
597	9	50%	50%	7	27%	39%	2	29%	11%	0	0%	0%	18
700	12	67%	48%	12	46%	48%	1	14%	4%	0	0%	0%	25
892	12	67%	52%	10	38%	43%	1	14%	4%	0	0%	0%	23
1006	9	50%	50%	7	27%	39%	2	29%	11%	0	0%	0%	18
1010	9	50%	53%	6	23%	35%	2	29%	12%	0	0%	0%	17
1071	7	39%	58%	4	15%	33%	1	14%	8%	0	0%	0%	12
1241	13	**72%**	41%	17	65%	53%	2	29%	6%	0	0%	0%	32
1243	7	39%	47%	6	23%	40%	2	29%	13%	0	0%	0%	15
1292	9	50%	53%	6	23%	35%	2	29%	12%	0	0%	0%	17
1342	12	67%	52%	8	31%	35%	3	43%	13%	0	0%	0%	23
1424	9	50%	56%	6	23%	38%	1	14%	6%	0	0%	0%	16
1505	8	44%	47%	7	27%	41%	2	29%	12%	0	0%	0%	17

Percentages Showing Important Lectionary Manuscripts in
the First Eight Chapters of Luke (UBSGNT[4])

Quality Rating	Above Average or Stronger Variants						Below Average or Weaker Variants						51 total variants in Lk. 1–8
	A Rated Variants (18 Possible Total)			B Rated Variants (26 Possible Total)			C Rated Variants (7 Possible Total)			D Rated Variants (0 Possible Total)			
Lection.	COL 1 # of times in A vrnts	COL 2 % in A vrnts	COL 3 % as A to B,C,D	COL 1 # of times in B vrnts	COL 2 % in B vrnts	COL 3 % as B to A,C,D	COL 1 # of times in C vrnts	COL 2 % in C vrnts	COL 3 % as C to A,B,D	COL 1 # of times in D vrnts	COL 2 % in D vrnts	COL 3 % as D to A,B,C	COL 4 # of variants with ms as a witness
Lect.[iv]	9	50%	50%	7	27%	39%	2	29%	11%	0	0%	0%	18
L68[v]	0	0%	0%	1	4%	100%	0	0%	0%	0	0%	0%	1
L76	0	0%	0%	1	4%	100%	0	0%	0%	0	0%	0%	1
L253	1	6%	100%	0	0%	0%	0	0%	0%	0	0%	0%	1
L387	0	0%	0%	1	4%	100%	0	0%	0%	0	0%	0%	1
L524	1	6%	100%	0	0%	0%	0	0%	0%	0	0%	0%	1
L673	0	0%	0%	1	4%	100%	0	0%	0%	0	0%	0%	1
L813	0	0%	0%	1	4%	100%	0	0%	0%	0	0%	0%	1
L1223	0	0%	0%	1	4%	100%	0	0%	0%	0	0%	0%	1

iv. The '*Lect*' symbol represents the reading of the majority of the lectionaries selected, together with the text of the edition published by Apostoliki Diakonia, Athens. This is explained on page 50* of the *UBSGNT[4]*.

v. Throughout these charts the regular small-cap letter '*l*', generally used as the lectionary symbol, is replaced with the capital letter '*L*'.

Percentages Showing Important Old Latin Manuscripts in the First Eight Chapters of Luke (UBSGNT[4])

| Quality Rating | Above Average or Stronger Variants | | | | | | Below Average or Weaker Variants | | | | | | 51 total variants in Lk. 1–8 |
| | A Rated Variants (18 Possible Total) | | | B Rated Variants (26 Possible Total) | | | C Rated Variants (7 Possible Total) | | | D Rated Variants (0 Possible Total) | | | |
Old Latin	COL 1 # of times in A vrnts	COL 2 % in A vrnts	COL 3 % as A to B,C,D	COL 1 # of times in B vrnts	COL 2 % in B vrnts	COL 3 % as B to A,C,D	COL 1 # of times in C vrnts	COL 2 % in C vrnts	COL 3 % as C to A,B,D	COL 1 # of times in D vrnts	COL 2 % in D vrnts	COL 3 % as D to A,B,C	COL 4 # of variants with ms as a witness
it[a]	5	28%	33%	6	23%	40%	4	57%	27%	0	0%	0%	15
it[aur]	10	56%	43%	10	38%	43%	3	43%	13%	0	0%	0%	23
it[b(e)vi]	9	50%	50%	6	23%	33%	3	43%	17%	0	0%	0%	18
it[b]	1	6%	50%	1	4%	50%	0	0%	0%	0	0%	0%	2
it[c]	9	50%	47%	7	27%	37%	3	43%	16%	0	0%	0%	19
it[d(ea)]	5	28%	36%	7	27%	50%	2	29%	14%	0	0%	0%	14
it[e(e)]	6	33%	40%	8	31%	53%	1	14%	7%	0	0%	0%	14
it[f(e)]	10	56%	48%	7	27%	33%	4	57%	19%	0	0%	0%	21
it[ff2]	8	44%	42%	8	31%	42%	3	43%	16%	0	0%	0%	19
it[l(e)]	8	44%	42%	8	31%	42%	3	43%	16%	0	0%	0%	19
it[n]	1	6%	100%	0	0%	0%	0	0%	0%	0	0%	0%	1
it[q(e)]	9	50%	45%	7	27%	35%	4	57%	20%	0	0%	0%	20
it[r1]	6	33%	35%	7	27%	41%	4	57%	24%	0	0%	0%	17

Percentages Showing Important Vulgate Manuscripts in the First Eight Chapters of Luke (UBSGNT[4])

| Quality Rating | Above Average or Stronger Variants | | | | | | Below Average or Weaker Variants | | | | | | 51 total variants in Lk. 1–8 |
| | A Rated Variants (18 Possible Total) | | | B Rated Variants (26 Possible Total) | | | C Rated Variants (7 Possible Total) | | | D Rated Variants (0 Possible Total) | | | |
Vulgate	COL 1 # of times in A vrnts	COL 2 % in A vrnts	COL 3 % as A to B,C,D	COL 1 # of times in B vrnts	COL 2 % in B vrnts	COL 3 % as B to A,C,D	COL 1 # of times in C vrnts	COL 2 % in C vrnts	COL 3 % as C to A,B,D	COL 1 # of times in D vrnts	COL 2 % in D vrnts	COL 3 % as D to A,B,C	COL 4 # of variants with ms as a witness
vg	9	50%	38%	11	42%	46%	4	57%	17%	0	0%	0%	24
vg[cl]	0	0%	0%	1	4%	100%	0	0%	0%	0	0%	0%	1
vg[ww]	4	22%	57%	2	8%	29%	1	14%	14%	0	0%	0%	7
vg[st]	4	22%	57%	2	8%	29%	1	14%	14%	0	0%	0%	7

vi.   When two manuscripts with identical lettering or numbering are listed in the Old Latin evidence chart, they are distinguished by placing the contents of each manuscript within brackets. The abbreviations are as given in the section entitled 'Principal Manuscripts And Versions Cited In The Textual Apparatus', beginning on p. 903 of the *UBSGNT[4]* (this information is also often included in a small pamphlet provided by the United Bible Society and placed inside their *UBSGNT*). The particular abbreviations are as follows: e-Gospels; a-Acts; p-Pauline Epistles; c-Catholic or General Epistles; and r-Revelation.

Percentages Showing Important Syriac Manuscripts in the First Eight Chapters of Luke (UBSGNT[4])

Quality Rating	Above Average or Stronger Variants						Below Average or Weaker Variants						51 total variants in Lk. 1–8
	A Rated Variants (18 Possible Total)			B Rated Variants (26 Possible Total)			C Rated Variants (7 Possible Total)			D Rated Variants (0 Possible Total)			
Syriac	COL 1	COL 2	COL 3	COL 1	COL 2	COL 3	COL 1	COL 2	COL 3	COL 1	COL 2	COL 3	COL 4
	# of times in A vrnts	% in A vrnts	% as A to B,C,D	# of times in B vrnts	% in B vrnts	% as B to A,C,D	# of times in C vrnts	% in C vrnts	% as C to A,B,D	# of times in D vrnts	% in D vrnts	% as D to A,B,C	# of variants with ms as a witness
syr[s]	6	33%	35%	11	42%	65%	0	0%	0%	0	0%	0%	17
syr[c]	0	0%	0%	3	12%	100%	0	0%	0%	0	0%	0%	3
syr[p]	9	50%	53%	6	23%	35%	2	29%	12%	0	0%	0%	17
syr[pal]	8	44%	38%	11	42%	52%	2	29%	10%	0	0%	0%	21
syr[h]	8	44%	42%	8	31%	42%	3	43%	16%	0	0%	0%	19

Percentages Showing Important Coptic Manuscripts in the First Eight Chapters of Luke (UBSGNT[4])

Quality Rating	Above Average or Stronger Variants						Below Average or Weaker Variants						51 total variants in Lk. 1–8
	A Rated Variants (18 Possible Total)			B Rated Variants (26 Possible Total)			C Rated Variants (7 Possible Total)			D Rated Variants (0 Possible Total)			
Coptic	COL 1	COL 2	COL 3	COL 1	COL 2	COL 3	COL 1	COL 2	COL 3	COL 1	COL 2	COL 3	COL 4
	# of times in A vrnts	% in A vrnts	% as A to B,C,D	# of times in B vrnts	% in B vrnts	% as B to A,C,D	# of times in C vrnts	% in C vrnts	% as C to A,B,D	# of times in D vrnts	% in D vrnts	% as D to A,B,C	# of variants with ms as a witness
cop[sa]	16	89%	42%	19	73%	50%	3	43%	8%	0	0%	0%	38
cop[bo]	13	72%	41%	14	54%	44%	5	71%	18%	0	0%	0%	32

Percentages Showing Important Armenian Manuscripts in the First Eight Chapters of Luke (UBSGNT[4])

Quality Rating	Above Average or Stronger Variants						Below Average or Weaker Variants						51 total variants in Lk. 1–8
	A Rated Variants (18 Possible Total)			B Rated Variants (26 Possible Total)			C Rated Variants (7 Possible Total)			D Rated Variants (0 Possible Total)			
Armen.	COL 1	COL 2	COL 3	COL 1	COL 2	COL 3	COL 1	COL 2	COL 3	COL 1	COL 2	COL 3	COL 4
	# of times in A vrnts	% in A vrnts	% as A to B,C,D	# of times in B vrnts	% in B vrnts	% as B to A,C,D	# of times in C vrnts	% in C vrnts	% as C to A,B,D	# of times in D vrnts	% in D vrnts	% as D to A,B,C	# of variants with ms as a witness
Armen.	11	61%	52%	9	35%	43%	1	14%	5%	0	0%	0%	21

Percentages Showing Important Ethiopic Manuscripts in the First Eight Chapters of Luke (UBSGNT[4])

Quality Rating	Above Average or Stronger Variants												51 total
	A Rated Variants (18 Possible Total)			B Rated Variants (26 Possible Total)			C Rated Variants (7 Possible Total)			D Rated Variants (0 Possible Total)			variants in Lk. 1–8
Ethiopic	COL 1	COL 2	COL 3	COL 1	COL 2	COL 3	COL 1	COL 2	COL 3	COL 1	COL 2	COL 3	COL 4
	# of times in A vrnts	% in A vrnts	% as A to B,C,D	# of times in B vrnts	% in B vrnts	% as B to A,C,D	# of times in C vrnts	% in C vrnts	% as C to A,B,D	# of times in D vrnts	% in D vrnts	% as D to A,B,C	# of variants with ms as a witness
eth	12	67%	60%	6	23%	30%	2	29%	10%	0	0%	0%	20

Percentages Showing Important Georgian Manuscripts in the First Eight Chapters of Luke (UBSGNT[4])

Quality Rating	Above Average or Stronger Variants						Below Average or Weaker Variants						51 total
	A Rated Variants (18 Possible Total)			B Rated Variants (26 Possible Total)			C Rated Variants (7 Possible Total)			D Rated Variants (0 Possible Total)			variants in Lk. 1–8
Georgn.	COL 1	COL 2	COL 3	COL 1	COL 2	COL 3	COL 1	COL 2	COL 3	COL 1	COL 2	COL 3	COL 4
	# of times in A vrnts	% in A vrnts	% as A to B,C,D	# of times in B vrnts	% in B vrnts	% as B to A,C,D	# of times in C vrnts	% in C vrnts	% as C to A,B,D	# of times in D vrnts	% in D vrnts	% as D to A,B,C	# of variants with ms as a witness
geo	10	56%	56%	7	27%	39%	1	14%	6%	0	0%	0%	18
geo[1]	0	0%	0%	2	8%	100%	0	0%	0%	0	0%	0%	2
geo[2]	1	6%	25%	3	12%	75%	0	0%	0%	0	0%	0%	4

Percentages Showing Important Greek Father Evidence in the First Eight Chapters of Luke (UBSGNT⁴)[vii]

Quality Rating	Above Average or Stronger Variants						Below Average or Weaker Variants						51 total variants in Lk. 1–8
	A Rated Variants (18 Possible Total)			B Rated Variants (26 Possible Total)			C Rated Variants (7 Possible Total)			D Rated Variants (0 Possible Total)			COL 4
Greek Church Fathers	COL 1 # of times in A vrnts	COL 2 % in A vrnts	COL 3 % as A to B,C,D	COL 1 # of times in B vrnts	COL 2 % in B vrnts	COL 3 % as B to A,C,D	COL 1 # of times in C vrnts	COL 2 % in C vrnts	COL 3 % as C to A,B,D	COL 1 # of times in D vrnts	COL 2 % in D vrnts	COL 3 % as D to A,B,C	# of variants with ms as a witness
Amphilochius	2	11%	100%	0	0%	0%	0	0%	0%	0	0%	0%	2
Apollinaris, of Laodicea	1	6%	100%	0	0%	0%	0	0%	0%	0	0%	0%	1
(John) Chrysostom	2	11%	100%	0	0%	0%	0	0%	0%	0	0%	0%	2
Clement, of Alexandria	2	11%	67%	1	4%	33%	0	0%	0%	0	0%	0%	3
Cyril, of Alexandria	2	11%	50%	2	8%	50%	0	0%	0%	0	0%	0%	4
Cyril-Jerusalem	3	17%	75%	1	4%	25%	0	0%	0%	0	0%	0%	4
Diatessaron, of Tatian	3	17%	38%	5	19%	63%	0	0%	0%	0	0%	0%	8
Didymus	4	22%	80%	1	4%	20%	0	0%	0%	0	0%	0%	5
Epiphanius	2	11%	67%	1	4%	33%	0	0%	0%	0	0%	0%	3
Eusebian Canons	2	11%	100%	0	0%	0%	0	0%	0%	0	0%	0%	2
Eusebius, of Caesarea	3	17%	60%	2	8%	40%	0	0%	0%	0	0%	0%	5
Gregory-Nyssa	3	17%	60%	2	8%	40%	0	0%	0%	0	0%	0%	5
Hesychius, of Jerusalem	2	11%	100%	0	0%	0%	0	0%	0%	0	0%	0%	2
Irenaeus	5	28%	83%	1	4%	17%	0	0%	0%	0	0%	0%	6
John-Damascus	2	11%	100%	0	0%	0%	0	0%	0%	0	0%	0%	2
Marcus-Eremita	1	6%	100%	0	0%	0%	0	0%	0%	0	0%	0%	1
Nestorius	1	6%	100%	0	0%	0%	0	0%	0%	0	0%	0%	1
Origen	6	33%	40%	9	35%	60%	0	0%	0%	0	0%	0%	15
Orsiesius	1	6%	100%	0	0%	0%	0	0%	0%	0	0%	0%	1
Peter-Alexandria	3	17%	100%	0	0%	0%	0	0%	0%	0	0%	0%	3

vii.   Various other early authors or writings have not been included in this chart because they offer no witness of significance for the critical apparatus of the *UBSGNT⁴*. This is also stated on page 34* of the *UBSGNT⁴*.

Important Greek Father Evidence (cont.)

	COL1	COL2	COL3	COL1	COL2	COL3	COL1	COL2	COL3	COL1	COL2	COL3	COL4
Ps-Dionysius	2	11%	100%	0	0%	0%	0	0%	0%	0	0%	0%	2
Ps-Gregory-Thaumaturgus	2	11%	100%	0	0%	0%	0	0%	0%	0	0%	0%	2
Ps-Hippolytus	1	6%	100%	0	0%	0%	0	0%	0%	0	0%	0%	1
Serapian	1	6%	100%	0	0%	0%	0	0%	0%	0	0%	0%	1
Severian	1	6%	50%	1	4%	50%	0	0%	0%	0	0%	0%	2
Theodoret, of Cyrrhus	2	11%	100%	0	0%	0%	0	0%	0%	0	0%	0%	2
Titus-Bostra	0	0%	0%	2	8%	100%	0	0%	0%	0	0%	0%	2

Percentages Showing Important Latin Father Evidence in the First Eight Chapters of Luke (UBSGNT4)

Quality	Above Average or Stronger Variants						Below Average or Weaker Variants						51 total variants in Lk. 1–8
Rating	A Rated Variants (18 Possible Total)			B Rated Variants (26 Possible Total)			C Rated Variants (7 Possible Total)			D Rated Variants (0 Possible Total)			
Latin Church Fathers	COL1 # of times in A vrnts	COL2 % in A vrnts	COL3 % as A to B,C,D	COL1 # of times in B vrnts	COL2 % in B vrnts	COL3 % as B to A,C,D	COL1 # times in C vrnts	COL2 % in C vrnts	COL3 % as C to A,B,D	COL1 # of times in D vrnts	COL2 % in D vrnts	COL3 % as D to A,B,C	COL4 # of variants with ms as a witness
Ambrose	7	39%	50%	6	23%	43%	1	14%	7%	0	0%	0%	14
Ambrosiaster	1	6%	50%	1	4%	50%	0	0%	0%	0	0%	0%	2
Augustine	7	39%	47%	8	31%	53%	0	0%	0%	0	0%	0%	15
Chromatius	1	6%	50%	0	0%	0%	1	14%	50%	0	0%	0%	2
Cyprian	1	6%	100%	0	0%	0%	0	0%	0%	0	0%	0%	1
Gaudentius	2	11%	100%	0	0%	0%	0	0%	0%	0	0%	0%	2
Jerome	5	28%	63%	2	8%	25%	1	14%	13%	0	0%	0%	8
Priscillian	1	6%	100%	0	0%	0%	0	0%	0%	0	0%	0%	1
Quodvultdeus	1	6%	100%	0	0%	0%	0	0%	0%	0	0%	0%	1

Percentages Showing Important Papyri Manuscripts in the First Eight Chapters of Acts (UBSGNT⁴)

| Quality | Above Average or Stronger Variants | | | | | | Below Average or Weaker Variants | | | | | | 53 total variants Acts1–8 |
| Rating | A Rated Variants (21 Possible Total) | | | B Rated Variants (20 Possible Total) | | | C Rated Variants (12 Possible Total) | | | D Rated Variants (0 Possible Total) | | | |
Papyri	COL 1 # of times in A vrnts	COL 2 % in A vrnts	COL 3 % as A to B,C,D	COL 1 # of times in B vrnts	COL 2 % in B vrnts	COL 3 % as B to A,C,D	COL 1 # of times in C vrnts	COL 2 % in C vrnts	COL 3 % as C to A,B,D	COL 1 # of times in D vrnts	COL 2 % in D vrnts	COL 3 % as D to A,B,C	COL 4 # of variants with ms as a witness
𝔓8	0	0%	0%	1	5%	50%	1	8%	50%	0	0%	0%	2
𝔓33+58	0	0%	0%	0	0%	0%	1	8%	100%	0	0%	0%	1
𝔓45viii	3	14%	100%	0	0%	0%	0	0%	0%	0	0%	0%	3
𝔓74	19	90%	56%	11	55%	32%	4	33%	12%	0	0%	0%	34
𝔓91	0	0%	0%	1	5%	100%	0	0%	0%	0	0%	0%	1

Percentages Showing Important Uncial Manuscripts in the First Eight Chapters of Acts (UBSGNT⁴)

| Quality | Above Average or Stronger Variants | | | | | | Below Average or Weaker Variants | | | | | | 53 total variants Acts1–8 |
| Rating | A Rated Variants (21 Possible Total) | | | B Rated Variants (20 Possible Total) | | | C Rated Variants (12 Possible Total) | | | D Rated Variants (0 Possible Total) | | | |
Uncials	COL 1 # of times in A vrnts	COL 2 % in A vrnts	COL 3 % as A to B,C,D	COL 1 # of times in B vrnts	COL 2 % in B vrnts	COL 3 % as B to A,C,D	COL 1 # of times in C vrnts	COL 2 % in C vrnts	COL 3 % as C to A,B,D	COL 1 # of times in D vrnts	COL 2 % in D vrnts	COL 3 % as D to A,B,C	COL 4 # of variants with ms as a witness
ℵ01	21	100%	47%	16	80%	36%	8	67%	18%	0	0%	0%	45
A02	21	100%	47%	17	85%	38%	7	58%	16%	0	0%	0%	45
B03	20	95%	44%	17	85%	38%	8	67%	18%	0	0%	0%	45
C04	15	71%	50%	11	55%	37%	4	33%	13%	0	0%	0%	30
D05	5	24%	29%	9	45%	53%	3	25%	18%	0	0%	0%	17
E08	15	71%	58%	6	30%	23%	5	42%	19%	0	0%	0%	26
[L020]	3	14%	100%	0	0%	0%	0	0%	0%	0	0%	0%	3
[P024]	14	67%	58%	5	25%	21%	5	42%	21%	0	0%	0%	24
Ψ044	18	86%	58%	7	35%	23%	6	50%	19%	0	0%	0%	31
076	3	14%	75%	1	5%	25%	0	0%	0%	0	0%	0%	4
095	1	5%	33%	1	5%	33%	1	8%	33%	0	0%	0%	3
096	0	0%	0%	1	5%	100%	0	0%	0%	0	0%	0%	1
0165	3	14%	60%	2	10%	40%	0	0%	0%	0	0%	0%	5
0189	1	5%	33%	2	10%	67%	0	0%	0%	0	0%	0%	3

viii. 𝔓⁴⁵, one of the most important papyri, and part of the Chester Beatty collection along with 𝔓⁴⁶ and 𝔓⁴⁷, is dated in the third century. This papyrus contains sizable portions of the Gospels and Acts 4.27–17.7. The Alands classify it as a category I manuscript in *The Text of the New Testament*, pp. 98-99.

*Percentages Showing Important Minuscule Manuscripts in
the First Eight Chapters of Acts (UBSGNT[4])*

| Quality Rating | Above Average or Stronger Variants | | | | | | Below Average or Weaker Variants | | | | | | 53 total variants Acts1–8 |
| | A Rated Variants (21 Possible Total) | | | B Rated Variants (20 Possible Total) | | | C Rated Variants (12 Possible Total) | | | D Rated Variants (0 Possible Total) | | | |
Minusc.	COL 1 # of times in A vrnts	COL 2 % in A vrnts	COL 3 % as A to B,C,D	COL 1 # of times in B vrnts	COL 2 % in B vrnts	COL 3 % as B to A,C,D	COL 1 # of times in C vrnts	COL 2 % in C vrnts	COL 3 % as C to A,B,D	COL 1 # of times in D vrnts	COL 2 % in D vrnts	COL 3 % as D to A,B,C	COL 4 # of variants with ms as a witness
33	17	81%	65%	7	35%	27%	2	17%	8%	0	0%	0%	26
36a	16	76%	52%	8	40%	26%	7	58%	23%	0	0%	0%	31
81	15	74%	52%	9	45%	31%	5	42%	17%	0	0%	0%	29
181	19	90%	56%	7	35%	21%	8	67%	24%	0	0%	0%	34
307	17	81%	53%	8	40%	25%	7	58%	22%	0	0%	0%	32
453	17	81%	52%	8	40%	24%	8	67%	24%	0	0%	0%	33
610	16	76%	52%	8	40%	26%	7	58%	23%	0	0%	0%	31
614	17	81%	61%	7	35%	25%	4	33%	14%	0	0%	0%	28
945	17	81%	52%	7	35%	21%	9	75%	27%	0	0%	0%	33
1175	21	100%	50%	14	70%	33%	7	58%	17%	0	0%	0%	42
1409	18	86%	62%	7	35%	24%	4	33%	14%	0	0%	0%	29
1678	17	81%	55%	7	35%	23%	7	58%	23%	0	0%	0%	31
1739	17	81%	50%	8	40%	24%	9	75%	26%	0	0%	0%	34
1891	16	76%	55%	5	25%	17%	8	67%	28%	0	0%	0%	29
2344	18	86%	55%	8	40%	24%	7	58%	21%	0	0%	0%	33

*Percentages Showing Important Lectionary Manuscripts in
the First Eight Chapters of Acts (UBSGNT[4])*

| Quality Rating | Above Average or Stronger Variants | | | | | | Below Average or Weaker Variants | | | | | | 53 total variants Acts1–8 |
| | A Rated Variants (21 Possible Total) | | | B Rated Variants (20 Possible Total) | | | C Rated Variants (12 Possible Total) | | | D Rated Variants (0 Possible Total) | | | |
Lection.	COL 1 # of times in A vrnts	COL 2 % in A vrnts	COL 3 % as A to B,C,D	COL 1 # of times in B vrnts	COL 2 % in B vrnts	COL 3 % as B to A,C,D	COL 1 # of times in C vrnts	COL 2 % in C vrnts	COL 3 % as C to A,B,D	COL 1 # of times in D vrnts	COL 2 % in D vrnts	COL 3 % as D to A,B,C	COL 4 # of variants with ms as a witness
Lect.	14	67%	61%	5	25%	22%	4	33%	17%	0	0%	0%	23
L60	1	5%	25%	2	10%	50%	1	8%	25%	0	0%	0%	4
L165	1	5%	100%	0	0%	0%	0	0%	0%	0	0%	0%	1
L422	0	0%	0%	1	5%	100%	0	0%	0%	0	0%	0%	1
L591	0	0%	0%	1	5%	50%	1	8%	50%	0	0%	0%	2
L597	1	5%	50%	1	5%	50%	0	0%	0%	0	0%	0%	2
L680	1	5%	50%	1	5%	50%	0	0%	0%	0	0%	0%	2
L883	1	5%	33%	1	5%	33%	1	8%	33%	0	0%	0%	3
L884	1	5%	100%	0	0%	0%	0	0%	0%	0	0%	0%	1
L921	1	5%	100%	0	0%	0%	0	0%	0%	0	0%	0%	1
L1021	2	10%	100%	0	0%	0%	0	0%	0%	0	0%	0%	2
L1154	1	5%	50%	0	0%	0%	1	8%	50%	0	0%	0%	2
L1178	4	19%	36%	2	10%	18%	5	42%	45%	0	0%	0%	11
L1356	0	0%	0%	0	0%	0%	1	8%	100%	0	0%	0%	1
L1441	1	5%	50%	1	5%	50%	0	0%	0%	0	0%	0%	2
L1977	0	0%	0%	0	0%	0%	1	8%	100%	0	0%	0%	1

Percentages Showing Important Old Latin Manuscripts in the First Eight Chapters of Acts (UBSGNT[4])

| Quality Rating | Above Average or Stronger Variants | | | | | | Below Average or Weaker Variants | | | | | | 53 total variants Acts1–8 |
| | A Rated Variants (21 Possible Total) | | | B Rated Variants (20 Possible Total) | | | C Rated Variants (12 Possible Total) | | | D Rated Variants (0 Possible Total) | | | |
Old Latin	COL 1 # of times in A vrnts	COL 2 % in A vrnts	COL 3 % as A to B,C,D	COL 1 # of times in B vrnts	COL 2 % in B vrnts	COL 3 % as B to A,C,D	COL 1 # of times in C vrnts	COL 2 % in C vrnts	COL 3 % as C to A,B,D	COL 1 # of times in D vrnts	COL 2 % in D vrnts	COL 3 % as D to A,B,C	COL 4 # of variants with ms as a witness
it^{ar}	15	71%	47%	13	65%	41%	4	33%	13%	0	0%	0%	32
it^{c}	18	86%	50%	13	65%	36%	5	42%	14%	0	0%	0%	36
$it^{d}(ea)$	5	24%	38%	6	30%	46%	2	17%	15%	0	0%	0%	13
it^{dem}	18	86%	49%	14	70%	38%	5	42%	14%	0	0%	0%	37
$it^{e}(a)$	13	62%	54%	6	30%	25%	5	42%	21%	0	0%	0%	24
it^{gig}	9	43%	38%	9	45%	38%	6	50%	25%	0	0%	0%	24
$it^{h}(acr)$	2	10%	40%	1	5%	20%	2	17%	40%	0	0%	0%	5
$it^{p}(a)$	13	62%	50%	7	35%	27%	6	50%	23%	0	0%	0%	26
it^{ph}	19	90%	53%	13	65%	36%	4	33%	11%	0	0%	0%	36
$it^{r}(a)$	4	19%	44%	3	15%	33%	2	17%	22%	0	0%	0%	9
it^{ro}	19	90%	51%	13	65%	35%	5	42%	14%	0	0%	0%	37
it^{sa}	1	5%	50%	1	5%	50%	0	0%	0%	0	0%	0%	2
$it^{t}(acpr)$	9	43%	56%	6	30%	38%	1	8%	6%	0	0%	0%	16
$it^{w}(a)$	16	76%	44%	13	65%	36%	7	58%	19%	0	0%	0%	36

Percentages Showing Important Vulgate Manuscripts in the First Eight Chapters of Acts (UBSGNT[4])

| Quality Rating | Above Average or Stronger Variants | | | | | | Below Average or Weaker Variants | | | | | | 53 total variants Acts1–8 |
| | A Rated Variants (21 Possible Total) | | | B Rated Variants (20 Possible Total) | | | C Rated Variants (12 Possible Total) | | | D Rated Variants (0 Possible Total) | | | |
Vulgate	COL 1 # of times in A vrnts	COL 2 % in A vrnts	COL 3 % as A to B,C,D	COL 1 # of times in B vrnts	COL 2 % in B vrnts	COL 3 % as B to A,C,D	COL 1 # of times in C vrnts	COL 2 % in C vrnts	COL 3 % as C to A,B,D	COL 1 # of times in D vrnts	COL 2 % in D vrnts	COL 3 % as D to A,B,C	COL 4 # of variants with ms as a witness
vg	17	81%	49%	14	70%	40%	4	33%	11%	0	0%	0%	35
vg^{cl}	0	0%	0%	0	0%	0%	1	8%	100%	0	0%	0%	1
vg^{ww}	2	10%	50%	1	5%	25%	1	8%	25%	0	0%	0%	4
vg^{st}	2	10%	50%	1	5%	25%	1	8%	25%	0	0%	0%	4

Percentages Showing Important Syriac Manuscripts in the First Eight Chapters of Acts (UBSGNT[4])

| Quality Rating | Above Average or Stronger Variants | | | | | | Below Average or Weaker Variants | | | | | | 53 total variants Acts1–8 |
| | A Rated Variants (21 Possible Total) | | | B Rated Variants (20 Possible Total) | | | C Rated Variants (12 Possible Total) | | | D Rated Variants (0 Possible Total) | | | |
Syriac	COL 1 # of times in A vrnts	COL 2 % in A vrnts	COL 3 % as A to B,C,D	COL 1 # of times in B vrnts	COL 2 % in B vrnts	COL 3 % as B to A,C,D	COL 1 # of times in C vrnts	COL 2 % in C vrnts	COL 3 % as C to A,B,D	COL 1 # of times in D vrnts	COL 2 % in D vrnts	COL 3 % as D to A,B,C	COL 4 # of variants with ms as a witness
syr^p	13	62%	50%	9	45%	35%	4	33%	15%	0	0%	0%	26
syr^pal	5	24%	63%	3	15%	38%	0	0%	0%	0	0%	0%	8
syr^h	16	76%	53%	8	40%	27%	6	50%	20%	0	0%	0%	30

Percentages Showing Important Coptic Manuscripts in the First Eight Chapters of Acts (UBSGNT[4])

| Quality Rating | Above Average or Stronger Variants | | | | | | Below Average or Weaker Variants | | | | | | 53 total variants Acts1–8 |
| | A Rated Variants (21 Possible Total) | | | B Rated Variants (20 Possible Total) | | | C Rated Variants (12 Possible Total) | | | D Rated Variants (0 Possible Total) | | | |
Coptic	COL 1 # of times in A vrnts	COL 2 % in A vrnts	COL 3 % as A to B,C,D	COL 1 # of times in B vrnts	COL 2 % in B vrnts	COL 3 % as B to A,C,D	COL 1 # of times in C vrnts	COL 2 % in C vrnts	COL 3 % as C to A,B,D	COL 1 # of times in D vrnts	COL 2 % in D vrnts	COL 3 % as D to A,B,C	COL 4 # of variants with ms as a witness
cop^sa	18	86%	44%	15	75%	37%	8	67%	20%	0	0%	0%	41
cop^bo	17	81%	47%	14	70%	39%	5	42%	14%	0	0%	0%	36
cop^meg	10	48%	43%	10	50%	43%	3	25%	13%	0	0%	0%	23
cop^fay	0	0%	0%	0	0%	0%	3	25%	100%	0	0%	0%	3

Percentages Showing Important Armenian Manuscripts in the First Eight Chapters of Acts (UBSGNT[4])

| Quality Rating | Above Average or Stronger Variants | | | | | | Below Average or Weaker Variants | | | | | | 53 total variants Acts1–8 |
| | A Rated Variants (21 Possible Total) | | | B Rated Variants (20 Possible Total) | | | C Rated Variants (12 Possible Total) | | | D Rated Variants (0 Possible Total) | | | |
Armen.	COL 1 # of times in A vrnts	COL 2 % in A vrnts	COL 3 % as A to B,C,D	COL 1 # of times in B vrnts	COL 2 % in B vrnts	COL 3 % as B to A,C,D	COL 1 # of times in C vrnts	COL 2 % in C vrnts	COL 3 % as C to A,B,D	COL 1 # of times in D vrnts	COL 2 % in D vrnts	COL 3 % as D to A,B,C	COL 4 # of variants with ms as a witness
Armen.	18	86%	49%	10	50%	27%	9	75%	24%	0	0%	0%	37

*Percentages Showing Important Ethiopic Manuscripts in
the First Eight Chapters of Acts (UBSGNT[4])*

Quality	Above Average or Stronger Variants						Below Average or Weaker Variants						53 total
Rating	A Rated Variants (21 Possible Total)			B Rated Variants (20 Possible Total)			C Rated Variants (12 Possible Total)			D Rated Variants (0 Possible Total)			variants Acts1–8
Ethiopic	COL 1 # of times in A vrnts	COL 2 % in A vrnts	COL 3 % as A to B,C,D	COL 1 # of times in B vrnts	COL 2 % in B vrnts	COL 3 % as B to A,C,D	COL 1 # of times in C vrnts	COL 2 % in C vrnts	COL 3 % as C to A,B,D	COL 1 # of times in D vrnts	COL 2 % in D vrnts	COL 3 % as D to A,B,C	COL 4 # of variants with ms as a witness
eth	16	76%	46%	12	60%	34%	7	58%	20%	0	0%	0%	35
eth[pp]	1	5%	100%	0	0%	0%	0	0%	0%	0	0%	0%	1

*Percentages Showing Important Georgian Manuscripts in
the First Eight Chapters of Acts (UBSGNT[4])*

Quality	Above Average or Stronger Variants						Below Average or Weaker Variants						53 total
Rating	A Rated Variants (21 Possible Total)			B Rated Variants (20 Possible Total)			C Rated Variants (12 Possible Total)			D Rated Variants (0 Possible Total)			variants Acts1–8
Georgn.	COL 1 # of times in A vrnts	COL 2 % in A vrnts	COL 3 % as A to B,C,D	COL 1 # of times in B vrnts	COL 2 % in B vrnts	COL 3 % as B to A,C,D	COL 1 # of times in C vrnts	COL 2 % in C vrnts	COL 3 % as C to A,B,D	COL 1 # of times in D vrnts	COL 2 % in D vrnts	COL 3 % as D to A,B,C	COL 4 # of variants with ms as a witness
geo	18	86%	58%	6	30%	19%	7	58%	23%	0	0%	0%	31

Percentages Showing Important Greek Father Evidence in the First Eight Chapters of Acts (UBSGNT⁴)

| Quality Rating / Greek Church Fathers | Above Average or Stronger Variants | | | | | | Below Average or Weaker Variants | | | | | | 53 total variants Acts 1–8 |
| | A Rated Variants (21 Possible Total) | | | B Rated Variants (20 Possible Total) | | | C Rated Variants (12 Possible Total) | | | D Rated Variants (0 Possible Total) | | | |
	COL1 A # of times in A vrnts	COL2 A % in A vrnts	COL3 A % as A to B,C,D	COL1 B # of times in B vrnts	COL2 B % in B vrnts	COL3 B % as B to A,C,D	COL1 C # of times in C vrnts	COL2 C % in C vrnts	COL3 C % as C to A,B,D	COL1 D # of times in D vrnts	COL2 D % in D vrnts	COL3 D % as D to A,B,C	COL4 # of variants with ms as a witness
Apostolic Constitutions	1	5%	50%	1	5%	50%	0	0%	0%	0	0%	0%	2
Asterius, Sophist	1	5%	100%	0	0%	0%	0	0%	0%	0	0%	0%	1
Athanasius, of Alexandria	2	10%	67%	0	0%	0%	1	8%	33%	0	0%	0%	3
Basil, the Great	6	29%	67%	1	5%	11%	2	17%	22%	0	0%	0%	9
(John) Chrysostom	17	**81%**	59%	6	30%	21%	6	50%	21%	0	0%	0%	29
Cyril, of Alexandria	5	24%	56%	3	15%	33%	1	8%	11%	0	0%	0%	9
Cyril-Jerusalem	2	10%	50%	2	10%	50%	0	0%	0%	0	0%	0%	4
Didymus	5	24%	63%	3	15%	38%	0	0%	0%	0	0%	0%	8
Epiphanius	1	5%	50%	1	5%	50%	0	0%	0%	0	0%	0%	2
Eusebius, of Caesarea	4	19%	57%	2	10%	29%	1	8%	14%	0	0%	0%	7
Gregory-Nyssa	1	5%	50%	1	5%	50%	0	0%	0%	0	0%	0%	2
Hesychius, of Jerusalem	0	0%	0%	0	0%	0%	1	8%	100%	0	0%	0%	1
Hippolytus	1	5%	100%	0	0%	0%	0	0%	0%	0	0%	0%	1
Irenaeus	2	10%	25%	1	5%	13%	5	42%	63%	0	0%	0%	8
Marcellus, of Ancyra	0	0%	0%	1	5%	100%	0	0%	0%	0	0%	0%	1
Nestorius	1	5%	100%	0	0%	0%	0	0%	0%	0	0%	0%	1
Origen	1	5%	25%	1	5%	25%	2	17%	50%	0	0%	0%	4
Orsiesius	0	0%	0%	0	0%	0%	1	8%	100%	0	0%	0%	1
Proclus	1	5%	100%	0	0%	0%	0	0%	0%	0	0%	0%	1
Ps-Athanasius	1	5%	100%	0	0%	0%	0	0%	0%	0	0%	0%	1
Ps-Dionysius	0	0%	0%	1	5%	100%	0	0%	0%	0	0%	0%	1
Ps-Ignatius	1	5%	100%	0	0%	0%	0	0%	0%	0	0%	0%	1

Important Greek Father Evidence (cont.)

	COL 1	COL 2	COL 3	COL 1	COL 2	COL 3	COL 1	COL 2	COL 3	COL 1	COL 2	COL 3	COL 4
Severian	2	10%	50%	1	5%	25%	1	8%	25%	0	0%	0%	4
Theodoret, of Cyrrhus	1	5%	50%	0	0%	0%	1	8%	50%	0	0%	0%	2
Theodotus-Ancyra	2	10%	100%	0	0%	0%	0	0%	0%	0	0%	0%	2

Percentages Showing Important Latin Father Evidence in the First Eight Chapters of Acts (UBSGNT[4])

Quality Rating / Latin Church Fathers	Above Average or Stronger Variants						Below Average or Weaker Variants						53 total variants Acts 1–8
	A Rated Variants (21 Possible Total)			B Rated Variants (20 Possible Total)			C Rated Variants (12 Possible Total)			D Rated Variants (0 Possible Total)			COL 4
	COL 1 # of times in A vrnts	COL 2 % in A vrnts	COL 3 % as A to B,C,D	COL 1 # of times in B vrnts	COL 2 % in B vrnts	COL 3 % as B to A,C,D	COL 1 # of times in C vrnts	COL 2 % in C vrnts	COL 3 % as C to A,B,D	COL 1 # of times in D vrnts	COL 2 % in D vrnts	COL 3 % as D to A,B,C	# of variants with ms as a witness
Ambrose	2	10%	40%	2	10%	40%	1	8%	20%	0	0%	0%	5
Ambrosiaster	0	0%	0%	1	5%	50%	1	8%	50%	0	0%	0%	2
Augustine	1	5%	17%	3	15%	50%	2	17%	33%	0	0%	0%	6
Bede	1	5%	33%	1	5%	33%	1	8%	33%	0	0%	0%	3
Chromatius	0	0%	0%	1	5%	33%	2	17%	67%	0	0%	0%	3
Cyprian	0	0%	0%	1	5%	50%	1	8%	50%	0	0%	0%	2
Fulgentius	0	0%	0%	1	5%	100%	0	0%	0%	0	0%	0%	1
Gaudentius	0	0%	0%	1	5%	100%	0	0%	0%	0	0%	0%	1
Hilary	0	0%	0%	2	10%	50%	2	17%	50%	0	0%	0%	4
Jerome	3	14%	43%	3	15%	43%	1	8%	14%	0	0%	0%	7
Lucifer, of Calaris	2	10%	40%	2	10%	40%	1	8%	20%	0	0%	0%	5
Maximus, of Turin	0	0%	0%	0	0%	0%	1	8%	100%	0	0%	0%	1
Priscillian	0	0%	0%	0	0%	0%	1	8%	100%	0	0%	0%	1
Quodvultdeus	2	10%	67%	1	5%	33%	0	0%	0%	0	0%	0%	3
Rebaptism (De Rebaptismate)	1	5%	100%	0	0%	0%	0	0%	0%	0	0%	0%	1
Victorinus-Rome, Marius	0	0%	0%	1	5%	100%	0	0%	0%	0	0%	0%	1

*Percentages Showing Important Papyri Manuscripts in
the First Eight Chapters of Romans (UBSGNT⁴)*

Quality	Above Average or Stronger Variants						Below Average or Weaker Variants						42 total
Rating	A Rated Variants (16 Possible Total)			B Rated Variants (14 Possible Total)			C Rated Variants (12 Possible Total)			D Rated Variants (0 Possible Total)			variants Rom. 1–8
Papyri	COL 1 # of times in A vrnts	COL 2 % in A vrnts	COL 3 % as A to B,C,D	COL 1 # of times in B vrnts	COL 2 % in B vrnts	COL 3 % as B to A,C,D	COL 1 # of times in C vrnts	COL 2 % in C vrnts	COL 3 % as C to A,B,D	COL 1 # of times in D vrnts	COL 2 % in D vrnts	COL 3 % as D to A,B,C	COL 4 # of variants with ms as a witness
𝔓10	1	6%	50%	1	7%	50%	0	0%	0%	0	0%	0%	2
𝔓26	2	13%	100%	0	0%	0%	0	0%	0%	0	0%	0%	2
𝔓27ⁱˣ	1	6%	50%	1	7%	50%	0	0%	0%	0	0%	0%	2
𝔓40	0	0%	0%	1	7%	50%	1	8%	50%	0	0%	0%	2
𝔓46	3	19%	60%	2	14%	40%	0	0%	0%	0	0%	0%	5
𝔓94	0	0%	0%	1	7%	100%	0	0%	0%	0	0%	0%	1

*Percentages Showing Important Uncial Manuscripts in
the First Eight Chapters of Romans (UBSGNT⁴)*

Quality	Above Average or Stronger Variants						Below Average or Weaker Variants						42 total
Rating	A Rated Variants (16 Possible Total)			B Rated Variants (14 Possible Total)			C Rated Variants (12 Possible Total)			D Rated Variants (0 Possible Total)			variants Rom. 1–8
Uncials	COL 1 # of times in A vrnts	COL 2 % in A vrnts	COL 3 % as A to B,C,D	COL 1 # of times in B vrnts	COL 2 % in B vrnts	COL 3 % as B to A,C,D	COL 1 # of times in C vrnts	COL 2 % in C vrnts	COL 3 % as C to A,B,D	COL 1 # of times in D vrnts	COL 2 % in D vrnts	COL 3 % as D to A,B,C	COL 4 # of variants with ms as a witness
ℵ01	12	**75%**	35%	12	**86%**	35%	10	**83%**	29%	0	0%	0%	34
A02	12	**75%**	44%	8	57%	30%	7	58%	26%	0	0%	0%	27
B03	14	**88%**	54%	8	57%	31%	4	33%	15%	0	0%	0%	26
C04	10	63%	37%	9	64%	33%	8	67%	30%	0	0%	0%	27
D06	13	**81%**	59%	3	21%	14%	6	50%	27%	0	0%	0%	22
[F010]	8	50%	57%	4	29%	29%	2	17%	14%	0	0%	0%	14
G012	9	56%	56%	4	29%	25%	3	25%	19%	0	0%	0%	16
[K018]	10	63%	53%	2	14%	11%	7	58%	37%	0	0%	0%	19
[L020]	10	63%	50%	2	14%	10%	8	67%	40%	0	0%	0%	20
[P024]	9	56%	50%	2	14%	11%	7	58%	39%	0	0%	0%	18
P025	0	0%	0%	2	14%	100%	0	0%	0%	0	0%	0%	2
Ψ044	10	63%	48%	4	29%	19%	7	58%	33%	0	0%	0%	21
0172	0	0%	0%	0	0%	0%	1	8%	100%	0	0%	0%	1

ix   Once again, several papyri listed in this chart are important because of their early date. 𝔓40 contains portions of the first nine chapters of Romans and is given a third-century date. Although it is described by the Alands as 'carelessly written' it still maintains a category I rating in the light of its age. 𝔓46 preserves portions of Romans, 1 and 2 Corinthians, Galatians, Ephesians, Philippians, Colossians, 1 Thessalonians, and Hebrews. It is again, like 𝔓45 and 𝔓47, one of the famous Chester Beatty papyri and is also one of the earliest manuscripts we have to date (around 200 CE). This important papyrus is a category I witness. And finally 𝔓27 contains portions of chs. 8 and 9 in Romans. It is dated in the third century and, like the other papyri listed here, is given a category I rating by the Alands in *The Text of the New Testament*, pp. 97-99.

Percentages Showing Important Minuscule Manuscripts in the First Eight Chapters of Romans (UBSGNT[4])

| Quality Rating | Above Average or Stronger Variants | | | | | | Below Average or Weaker Variants | | | | | | 42 total variants Rom. 1–8 |
| | A Rated Variants (16 Possible Total) | | | B Rated Variants (14 Possible Total) | | | C Rated Variants (12 Possible Total) | | | D Rated Variants (0 Possible Total) | | | |
Minusc.	COL 1 # of times in A vrnts	COL 2 % in A vrnts	COL 3 % as A to B,C,D	COL 1 # of times in B vrnts	COL 2 % in B vrnts	COL 3 % as B to A,C,D	COL 1 # of times in C vrnts	COL 2 % in C vrnts	COL 3 % as C to A,B,D	COL 1 # of times in D vrnts	COL 2 % in D vrnts	COL 3 % as D to A,B,C	COL 4 # of variants with ms as a witness
6	14	88%	54%	5	36%	19%	7	58%	27%	0	0%	0%	26
33	7	44%	41%	3	21%	18%	7	58%	41%	0	0%	0%	17
81	11	69%	34%	11	79%	34%	10	83%	31%	0	0%	0%	32
104	11	69%	46%	6	43%	25%	7	58%	29%	0	0%	0%	24
256	12	75%	43%	8	57%	29%	8	67%	29%	0	0%	0%	28
263	12	75%	41%	9	64%	31%	8	67%	28%	0	0%	0%	29
365	6	50%	33%	5	36%	28%	7	58%	39%	0	0%	0%	18
424c	13	81%	45%	5	36%	17%	11	92%	38%	0	0%	0%	29
436	10	63%	40%	9	64%	36%	6	50%	24%	0	0%	0%	25
459	11	69%	50%	4	29%	18%	7	58%	32%	0	0%	0%	22
1175	10	63%	53%	2	14%	11%	7	58%	37%	0	0%	0%	19
1241	10	63%	53%	2	14%	11%	7	58%	37%	0	0%	0%	19
1319	13	81%	45%	8	57%	28%	8	67%	28%	0	0%	0%	29
1506	13	81%	42%	11	79%	35%	7	58%	23%	0	0%	0%	31
1573	13	81%	46%	7	50%	25%	8	67%	29%	0	0%	0%	28
1739	16	100%	55%	8	57%	28%	5	42%	17%	0	0%	0%	29
1852	12	75%	43%	9	64%	32%	7	58%	25%	0	0%	0%	28
1881	14	88%	56%	6	43%	24%	5	42%	20%	0	0%	0%	25
1912	10	63%	53%	2	14%	11%	7	58%	37%	0	0%	0%	19
1962	11	69%	50%	5	36%	23%	6	50%	27%	0	0%	0%	22
2127	12	75%	43%	8	57%	29%	8	67%	29%	0	0%	0%	28
2200	12	75%	52%	6	43%	26%	5	42%	22%	0	0%	0%	23
2464	11	69%	61%	3	21%	17%	4	33%	22%	0	0%	0%	18

Percentages Showing Important Lectionary Manuscripts in the First Eight Chapters of Romans (UBSGNT[4])

| Quality Rating | Above Average or Stronger Variants | | | | | | Below Average or Weaker Variants | | | | | | 42 total variants Rom. 1–8 |
| | A Rated Variants (16 Possible Total) | | | B Rated Variants (14 Possible Total) | | | C Rated Variants (12 Possible Total) | | | D Rated Variants (0 Possible Total) | | | |
Lection.	COL 1 # of times in A vrnts	COL 2 % in A vrnts	COL 3 % as A to B,C,D	COL 1 # of times in B vrnts	COL 2 % in B vrnts	COL 3 % as B to A,C,D	COL 1 # of times in C vrnts	COL 2 % in C vrnts	COL 3 % as C to A,B,D	COL 1 # of times in D vrnts	COL 2 % in D vrnts	COL 3 % as D to A,B,C	COL 4 # of variants with ms as a witness
Lect.	10	63%	50%	2	14%	10%	8	67%	40%	0	0%	0%	20
L59	0	0%	0%	1	7%	100%	0	0%	0%	0	0%	0%	1
L60	0	0%	0%	1	7%	100%	0	0%	0%	0	0%	0%	1
L147	0	0%	0%	1	7%	100%	0	0%	0%	0	0%	0%	1
L593	0	0%	0%	1	7%	100%	0	0%	0%	0	0%	0%	1
L596	0	0%	0%	2	14%	67%	1	8%	33%	0	0%	0%	3
L598	0	0%	0%	1	7%	50%	1	8%	50%	0	0%	0%	2
L599	0	0%	0%	1	7%	50%	1	8%	50%	0	0%	0%	2
L603	1	6%	100%	0	0%	0%	0	0%	0%	0	0%	0%	1
L617	0	0%	0%	1	7%	100%	0	0%	0%	0	0%	0%	1
L921	0	0%	0%	1	7%	100%	0	0%	0%	0	0%	0%	1
L1298	0	0%	0%	1	7%	100%	0	0%	0%	0	0%	0%	1
L1365	0	0%	0%	1	7%	100%	0	0%	0%	0	0%	0%	1
L1441	0	0%	0%	1	7%	100%	0	0%	0%	0	0%	0%	1
L1590	0	0%	0%	1	7%	100%	0	0%	0%	0	0%	0%	1

Percentages Showing Important Old Latin Manuscripts in the First Eight Chapters of Romans (UBSGNT[4])

| Quality Rating | Above Average or Stronger Variants | | | | | | Below Average or Weaker Variants | | | | | | 42 total variants Rom. 1–8 |
| | A Rated Variants (16 Possible Total) | | | B Rated Variants (14 Possible Total) | | | C Rated Variants (12 Possible Total) | | | D Rated Variants (0 Possible Total) | | | |
Old Latin	COL 1 # of times in A vrnts	COL 2 % in A vrnts	COL 3 % as A to B,C,D	COL 1 # of times in B vrnts	COL 2 % in B vrnts	COL 3 % as B to A,C,D	COL 1 # of times in C vrnts	COL 2 % in C vrnts	COL 3 % as C to A,B,D	COL 1 # of times in D vrnts	COL 2 % in D vrnts	COL 3 % as D to A,B,C	COL 4 # of variants with ms as a witness
it^{ar}	10	63%	53%	6	43%	32%	3	25%	16%	0	0%	0%	19
it^{b}(p)	11	69%	61%	4	29%	22%	3	25%	17%	0	0%	0%	18
it^{d}(p)	12	75%	63%	4	29%	21%	3	25%	16%	0	0%	0%	19
it^{f}(p)	7	44%	50%	5	36%	36%	2	17%	14%	0	0%	0%	14
it^{g}	10	63%	59%	4	29%	24%	3	25%	18%	0	0%	0%	17
it^{mon}	11	69%	50%	6	43%	27%	5	42%	23%	0	0%	0%	22
it^{o}(p)	8	50%	53%	4	29%	27%	3	25%	20%	0	0%	0%	15
it^{r}(p)	1	6%	50%	1	7%	50%	0	0%	0%	0	0%	0%	2

Percentages Showing Important Vulgate Manuscripts in the First Eight Chapters of Romans (UBSGNT^4)

| Quality Rating | Above Average or Stronger Variants | | | | | | Below Average or Weaker Variants | | | | | | 42 total variants Rom. 1–8 |
| | A Rated Variants (16 Possible Total) | | | B Rated Variants (14 Possible Total) | | | C Rated Variants (12 Possible Total) | | | D Rated Variants (0 Possible Total) | | | |
Vulgate	COL 1 # of times in A vrnts	COL 2 % in A vrnts	COL 3 % as A to B,C,D	COL 1 # of times in B vrnts	COL 2 % in B vrnts	COL 3 % as B to A,C,D	COL 1 # of times in C vrnts	COL 2 % in C vrnts	COL 3 % as C to A,B,D	COL 1 # of times in D vrnts	COL 2 % in D vrnts	COL 3 % as D to A,B,C	COL 4 # of variants with ms as a witness
vg	10	63%	45%	6	43%	27%	6	50%	27%	0	0%	0%	22
vg^{ww}	2	13%	50%	1	7%	25%	1	8%	25%	0	0%	0%	4
vgst	2	13%	50%	1	7%	25%	1	8%	25%	0	0%	0%	4

Percentages Showing Important Syriac Manuscripts in the First Eight Chapters of Romans (UBSGNT^4)

| Quality Rating | Above Average or Stronger Variants | | | | | | Below Average or Weaker Variants | | | | | | 42 total variants Rom. 1–8 |
| | A Rated Variants (16 Possible Total) | | | B Rated Variants (14 Possible Total) | | | C Rated Variants (12 Possible Total) | | | D Rated Variants (0 Possible Total) | | | |
Syriac	COL 1 # of times in A vrnts	COL 2 % in A vrnts	COL 3 % as A to B,C,D	COL 1 # of times in B vrnts	COL 2 % in B vrnts	COL 3 % as B to A,C,D	COL 1 # of times in C vrnts	COL 2 % in C vrnts	COL 3 % as C to A,B,D	COL 1 # of times in D vrnts	COL 2 % in D vrnts	COL 3 % as D to A,B,C	COL 4 # of variants with ms as a witness
syr^p	8	50%	53%	4	29%	27%	3	25%	20%	0	0%	0%	15
syr^{pal}	4	25%	44%	3	21%	33%	2	17%	22%	0	0%	0%	9
syr^h	10	63%	45%	4	29%	18%	8	67%	36%	0	0%	0%	22

Percentages Showing Important Coptic Manuscripts in the First Eight Chapters of Romans (UBSGNT^4)

| Quality Rating | Above Average or Stronger Variants | | | | | | Below Average or Weaker Variants | | | | | | 42 total variants Rom. 1–8 |
| | A Rated Variants (16 Possible Total) | | | B Rated Variants (14 Possible Total) | | | C Rated Variants (12 Possible Total) | | | D Rated Variants (0 Possible Total) | | | |
Coptic	COL 1 # of times in A vrnts	COL 2 % in A vrnts	COL 3 % as A to B,C,D	COL 1 # of times in B vrnts	COL 2 % in B vrnts	COL 3 % as B to A,C,D	COL 1 # of times in C vrnts	COL 2 % in C vrnts	COL 3 % as C to A,B,D	COL 1 # of times in D vrnts	COL 2 % in D vrnts	COL 3 % as D to A,B,C	COL 4 # of variants with ms as a witness
cop^{sa}	13	**81%**	57%	7	50%	30%	3	25%	13%	0	0%	0%	23
cop^{bo}	12	**75%**	40%	12	**86%**	40%	6	50%	20%	0	0%	0%	30
cop^{fay}	0	0%	0%	0	0%	0%	1	8%	100%	0	0%	0%	1

Percentages Showing Important Armenian Manuscripts in the First Eight Chapters of Romans (UBSGNT[4])

Quality	Above Average or Stronger Variants						Below Average or Weaker Variants						42 total
Rating	A Rated Variants (16 Possible Total)			B Rated Variants (14 Possible Total)			C Rated Variants (12 Possible Total)			D Rated Variants (0 Possible Total)			variants Rom. 1–8
Armen.	COL 1 # of times in A vrnts	COL 2 % in A vrnts	COL 3 % as A to B,C,D	COL 1 # of times in B vrnts	COL 2 % in B vrnts	COL 3 % as B to A,C,D	COL 1 # of times in C vrnts	COL 2 % in C vrnts	COL 3 % as C to A,B,D	COL 1 # of times in D vrnts	COL 2 % in D vrnts	COL 3 % as D to A,B,C	COL 4 # of variants with ms as a witness
Armen.	11	69%	41%	10	71%	37%	6	50%	22%	0	0%	0%	27

Percentages Showing Important Ethiopic Manuscripts in the First Eight Chapters of Romans (UBSGNT[4])

Quality	Above Average or Stronger Variants						Below Average or Weaker Variants						42 total
Rating	A Rated Variants (16 Possible Total)			B Rated Variants (14 Possible Total)			C Rated Variants (12 Possible Total)			D Rated Variants (0 Possible Total)			variants Rom. 1–8
Ethiopic	COL 1 # of times in A vrnts	COL 2 % in A vrnts	COL 3 % as A to B,C,D	COL 1 # of times in B vrnts	COL 2 % in B vrnts	COL 3 % as B to A,C,D	COL 1 # of times in C vrnts	COL 2 % in C vrnts	COL 3 % as C to A,B,D	COL 1 # of times in D vrnts	COL 2 % in D vrnts	COL 3 % as D to A,B,C	COL 4 # of variants with ms as a witness
eth	12	75%	52%	5	36%	22%	6	50%	26%	0	0%	0%	23

Percentages Showing Important Georgian Manuscripts in the First Eight Chapters of Romans (UBSGNT[4])

Quality	Above Average or Stronger Variants						Below Average or Weaker Variants						42 total
Rating	A Rated Variants (16 Possible Total)			B Rated Variants (14 Possible Total)			C Rated Variants (12 Possible Total)			D Rated Variants (0 Possible Total)			variants Rom. 1–8
Georgn.	COL 1 # of times in A vrnts	COL 2 % in A vrnts	COL 3 % as A to B,C,D	COL 1 # of times in B vrnts	COL 2 % in B vrnts	COL 3 % as B to A,C,D	COL 1 # of times in C vrnts	COL 2 % in C vrnts	COL 3 % as C to A,B,D	COL 1 # of times in D vrnts	COL 2 % in D vrnts	COL 3 % as D to A,B,C	COL 4 # of variants with ms as a witness
geo	9	56%	60%	3	21%	20%	3	25%	20%	0	0%	0%	15
geo[1]	2	13%	33%	2	14%	33%	2	17%	33%	0	0%	0%	6
geo[2]	0	0%	0%	0	0%	0%	2	17%	100%	0	0%	0%	2

Percentages Showing Important Greek Father Evidence in the First Eight Chapters of Romans (UBSGNT⁴)

Quality	Above Average or Stronger Variants						Below Average or Weaker Variants						42 total variants Rom. 1–8
Rating	A Rated Variants (16 Possible Total)			B Rated Variants (14 Possible Total)			C Rated Variants (12 Possible Total)			D Rated Variants (0 Possible Total)			
Greek Church Fathers	COL 1 # of times in A vrnts	COL 2 % in A vrnts	COL 3 % as A to B,C,D	COL 1 # of times in B vrnts	COL 2 % in B vrnts	COL 3 % as B to A,C,D	COL 1 # of times in C vrnts	COL 2 % in C vrnts	COL 2 % as C to A,B,D	COL 1 # of times in D vrnts	COL 2 % in D vrnts	COL 3 % as D to A,B,C	COL 4 # of variants with ms as a witness
Amphilochius	1	6%	100%	0	0%	0%	0	0%	0%	0	0%	0%	1
Apollinaris, of Laodicea	1	6%	33%	2	14%	67%	0	0%	0%	0	0%	0%	3
Athanasius, of Alexandria	2	13%	67%	1	7%	33%	0	0%	0%	0	0%	0%	3
Basil, the Great	6	38%	60%	1	7%	10%	3	25%	30%	0	0%	0%	10
(John) Chrysostom	10	63%	56%	2	14%	11%	6	50%	33%	0	0%	0%	18
Clement, of Alexandria	1	6%	17%	4	29%	67%	1	8%	17%	0	0%	0%	6
Cyril, of Alexandria	9	56%	43%	8	57%	38%	4	33%	19%	0	0%	0%	21
Cyril-Jerusalem	2	13%	33%	2	14%	33%	2	17%	33%	0	0%	0%	6
Didymus	7	44%	54%	6	43%	46%	0	0%	0%	0	0%	0%	13
Diodore	2	13%	100%	0	0%	0%	0	0%	0%	0	0%	0%	2
Epiphanius	3	19%	60%	1	7%	20%	1	8%	20%	0	0%	0%	5
Eusebius, of Caesarea	4	25%	67%	2	14%	33%	0	0%	0%	0	0%	0%	6
Gregory-Nyssa	2	13%	50%	2	14%	50%	0	0%	0%	0	0%	0%	4
Hesychius, of Jerusalem	1	6%	33%	1	7%	33%	1	8%	33%	0	0%	0%	3
Hippolytus	0	0%	0%	1	7%	100%	0	0%	0%	0	0%	0%	1
Irenaeus	0	0%	0%	1	7%	100%	0	0%	0%	0	0%	0%	1
Macarius/Symeon	1	6%	33%	2	14%	67%	0	0%	0%	0	0%	0%	3
Marcellus, of Ancyra	0	0%	0%	1	7%	100%	0	0%	0%	0	0%	0%	1
Marcion according to Tertullian/Origen/Adamantius/Epiphanius	1	6%	50%	0	0%	0%	1	8%	50%	0	0%	0%	2
Marcus-Eremita	1	6%	100%	0	0%	0%	0	0%	0%	0	0%	0%	1
Methodius	5	31%	56%	4	29%	44%	0	0%	0%	0	0%	0%	9

Important Greek Father Evidence (cont.)

	COL 1	COL 2	COL 3	COL 1	COL 2	COL 3	COL 1	COL 2	COL 3	COL 1	COL 2	COL 3	COL 4
Origen	14	88%	47%	8	57%	27%	8	67%	27%	0	0%	0%	30
Proclus	1	6%	100%	0	0%	0%	0	0%	0%	0	0%	0%	1
Ps-Athanasius	0	0%	0%	1	7%	100%	0	0%	0%	0	0%	0%	1
Serapion	1	6%	100%	0	0%	0%	0	0%	0%	0	0%	0%	1
Severian	2	13%	67%	0	0%	0%	1	8%	33%	0	0%	0%	3
Theodore, of Mopsuestia	5	31%	100%	0	0%	0%	0	0%	0%	0	0%	0%	5
Theodoret, of Cyrrhus	6	38%	67%	3	21%	33%	0	0%	0%	0	0%	0%	9

Percentages Showing Important Latin Father Evidence in the First Eight Chapters of Romans (UBSGNT[4])

Quality Rating	Above Average or Stronger Variants						Below Average or Weaker Variants						42 total variants Rom. 1–8
	A Rated Variants (16 Possible Total)			B Rated Variants (14 Possible Total)			C Rated Variants (12 Possible Total)			D Rated Variants (0 Possible Total)			
Latin Church Fathers	COL 1 # of times in A vrnts	COL 2 % in A vrnts	COL 3 % as A to B,C,D	COL 1 # of times in B vrnts	COL 2 % in B vrnts	COL 3 % as B to A,C,D	COL 1 # of times in C vrnts	COL 2 % in C vrnts	COL 3 % as C to A,B,D	COL 1 # of times in D vrnts	COL 2 % in D vrnts	COL 3 % as D to A,B,C	COL 4 # of variants with ms as a witness
Ambrose	6	38%	46%	7	50%	54%	0	0%	0%	0	0%	0%	13
Ambrosiaster	8	50%	57%	4	29%	29%	2	17%	14%	0	0%	0%	14
Augustine	13	81%	48%	11	79%	41%	3	25%	11%	0	0%	0%	27
Bede	0	0%	0%	1	7%	50%	1	8%	50%	0	0%	0%	2
Chromatius	1	6%	100%	0	0%	0%	0	0%	0%	0	0%	0%	1
Cyprian	1	6%	50%	1	7%	50%	0	0%	0%	0	0%	0%	2
Gaudentius	1	6%	100%	0	0%	0%	0	0%	0%	0	0%	0%	1
Gildas	1	6%	100%	0	0%	0%	0	0%	0%	0	0%	0%	1
Gregory-Elvira	2	13%	100%	0	0%	0%	0	0%	0%	0	0%	0%	2
Hilary	3	19%	100%	0	0%	0%	0	0%	0%	0	0%	0%	3
Jerome	4	25%	44%	4	29%	44%	1	8%	11%	0	0%	0%	9
Julian-Eclanum	1	6%	20%	1	7%	20%	3	25%	60%	0	0%	0%	5

Important Latin Father Evidence (cont.)

Lucifer, of Calaris	2	13%	67%	1	7%	33%	0	0%	0%	0	0%	0%	3
Novation	1	6%	100%	0	0%	0%	0	0%	0%	0	0%	0%	1
Pacian	1	6%	100%	0	0%	0%	0	0%	0%	0	0%	0%	1
Pelagius	10	63%	56%	5	36%	28%	3	25%	17%	0	0%	0%	18
Primasius	0	0%	0%	1	7%	100%	0	0%	0%	0	0%	0%	1
Priscillian	0	0%	0%	1	7%	100%	0	0%	0%	0	0%	0%	1
Ps-Vigilius	0	0%	0%	1	7%	100%	0	0%	0%	0	0%	0%	1
Quodvultdeus	1	6%	100%	0	0%	0%	0	0%	0%	0	0%	0%	1
Rebaptism (De Rebaptismate)	0	0%	0%	0	0%	0%	1	8%	100%	0	0%	0%	1
Speculum	3	19%	75%	1	7%	25%	0	0%	0%	0	0%	0%	4
Tertullian	4	25%	80%	1	7%	20%	0	0%	0%	0	0%	0%	5
Varimadum	0	0%	0%	2	14%	67%	1	8%	33%	0	0%	0%	3
Victorinus-Rome, Marius	0	0%	0%	3	21%	100%	0	0%	0%	0	0%	0%	3
Vigilius	0	0%	0%	1	7%	100%	0	0%	0%	0	0%	0%	1

Textual Optimism

Percentages Showing Important Papyri Manuscripts in 1 Peter (UBSGNT^4)

| Quality Rating | Above Average or Stronger Variants | | | | | | Below Average or Weaker Variants | | | | | | 37 total variants 1 Peter |
| Papyri | A Rated Variants (20 Possible Total) | | | B Rated Variants (9 Possible Total) | | | C Rated Variants (8 Possible Total) | | | D Rated Variants (0 Possible Total) | | | |
	COL 1 # of times in A vrnts	COL 2 % in A vrnts	COL 3 % as A to B,C,D	COL 1 # of times in B vrnts	COL 2 % in B vrnts	COL 3 % as B to A,C,D	COL 1 # of times in C vrnts	COL 2 % in C vrnts	COL 3 % as C to A,B,D	COL 1 # of times in D vrnts	COL 2 % in D vrnts	COL 3 % as D to A,B,C	COL 4 # of variants with ms as a witness
𝔓72^x	15	75%	63%	4	44%	17%	5	63%	21%	0	0%	0%	24
𝔓74	1	5%	100%	0	0%	0%	0	0%	0%	0	0%	0%	1
𝔓81	0	0%	0%	2	22%	100%	0	0%	0%	0	0%	0%	2

Percentages Showing Important Uncial Manuscripts in 1 Peter (UBSGNT^4)

| Quality Rating | Above Average or Stronger Variants | | | | | | Below Average or Weaker Variants | | | | | | 37 total variants 1 Peter |
| Uncials | A Rated Variants (20 Possible Total) | | | B Rated Variants (9 Possible Total) | | | C Rated Variants (8 Possible Total) | | | D Rated Variants (0 Possible Total) | | | |
	COL 1 # of times in A vrnts	COL 2 % in A vrnts	COL 3 % as A to B,C,D	COL 1 # of times in B vrnts	COL 2 % in B vrnts	COL 3 % as B to A,C,D	COL 1 # of times in C vrnts	COL 2 % in C vrnts	COL 3 % as C to A,B,D	COL 1 # of times in D vrnts	COL 2 % in D vrnts	COL 3 % as D to A,B,C	COL 4 # of variants with ms as a witness
ℵ01	13	65%	52%	6	67%	24%	6	75%	24%	0	0%	0%	25
A02	13	65%	62%	5	56%	24%	3	38%	14%	0	0%	0%	21
B03	18	90%	67%	8	89%	30%	1	13%	4%	0	0%	0%	27
C04	10	50%	67%	1	11%	7%	4	50%	27%	0	0%	0%	15
[K018]	10	50%	53%	3	33%	16%	6	75%	32%	0	0%	0%	19
[L020]	9	45%	50%	3	33%	17%	6	75%	33%	0	0%	0%	18
[P024]	8	40%	44%	4	44%	22%	6	75%	33%	0	0%	0%	18
P025	0	0%	0%	0	0%	0%	2	25%	100%	0	0%	0%	2
Ψ044	15	75%	65%	2	22%	9%	6	75%	26%	0	0%	0%	23
048	1	5%	50%	0	0%	0%	1	13%	50%	0	0%	0%	2
0206	1	5%	100%	0	0%	0%	0	0%	0%	0	0%	0%	1

x.   𝔓^{72} is another vital papyrus that makes up part of the Bodmer collection, along with 𝔓^{66}, 𝔓^{72}, and 𝔓^{75}. It contains the Epistles of Peter and Jude in their entirety. This papyrus is dated around the late third or early fourth century and although containing what the Alands call 'peculiarities', it is rated by them as a category I manuscript in *The Text of the New Testament*, p. 100.

Percentages Showing Important Minuscule Manuscripts in
1 Peter (UBSGNT⁴)

| Quality Rating | Above Average or Stronger Variants | | | | | | Below Average or Weaker Variants | | | | | | 37 total variants 1 Peter |
| | A Rated Variants (20 Possible Total) | | | B Rated Variants (9 Possible Total) | | | C Rated Variants (8 Possible Total) | | | D Rated Variants (0 Possible Total) | | | |
Minusc.	COL 1 # of times in A vrnts	COL 2 % in A vrnts	COL 3 % as A to B,C,D	COL 1 # of times in B vrnts	COL 2 % in B vrnts	COL 3 % as B to A,C,D	COL 1 # of times in C vrnts	COL 2 % in C vrnts	COL 3 % as C to A,B,D	COL 1 # of times in D vrnts	COL 2 % in D vrnts	COL 3 % as D to A,B,C	COL 4 # of variants with ms as a witness
33	9	45%	53%	3	33%	18%	5	63%	29%	0	0%	0%	17
81	12	60%	60%	2	22%	10%	6	75%	30%	0	0%	0%	20
322	14	70%	64%	2	22%	9%	6	75%	27%	0	0%	0%	22
323	14	70%	64%	2	22%	9%	6	75%	27%	0	0%	0%	22
436	9	45%	53%	3	33%	18%	5	63%	29%	0	0%	0%	17
945	14	70%	67%	2	22%	10%	5	63%	24%	0	0%	0%	21
1067	8	40%	50%	3	33%	19%	5	63%	31%	0	0%	0%	16
1175	13	65%	59%	3	33%	14%	6	75%	27%	0	0%	0%	22
1241	13	65%	54%	3	33%	13%	8	100%	33%	0	0%	0%	24
1243	13	65%	54%	3	33%	13%	8	100%	33%	0	0%	0%	24
1292	9	45%	56%	1	11%	6%	6	75%	38%	0	0%	0%	16
1409	9	45%	53%	3	33%	18%	5	63%	29%	0	0%	0%	17
1505	10	50%	67%	1	11%	7%	4	50%	27%	0	0%	0%	15
1611	12	60%	67%	0	0%	0%	6	75%	33%	0	0%	0%	18
1735	9	45%	47%	5	56%	26%	5	63%	26%	0	0%	0%	19
1739	17	85%	63%	3	33%	11%	7	88%	26%	0	0%	0%	27
1852	13	65%	59%	3	33%	14%	6	75%	27%	0	0%	0%	22
1881	14	70%	64%	1	11%	5%	7	88%	32%	0	0%	0%	22
2138	9	45%	60%	0	0%	0%	6	75%	40%	0	0%	0%	15
2298	11	55%	58%	2	22%	11%	6	75%	32%	0	0%	0%	19
2344	11	55%	58%	3	33%	16%	5	63%	26%	0	0%	0%	19
2464	9	45%	47%	4	44%	21%	6	75%	32%	0	0%	0%	19

Percentages Showing Important Lectionary Manuscripts in 1 Peter (UBSGNT[4])

| Quality Rating Lection. | Above Average or Stronger Variants | | | | | | Below Average or Weaker Variants | | | | | | 37 total variants 1 Peter |
| | A Rated Variants (20 Possible Total) | | | B Rated Variants (9 Possible Total) | | | C Rated Variants (8 Possible Total) | | | D Rated Variants (0 Possible Total) | | | |
	COL 1 # of times in A vrnts	COL 2 % in A vrnts	COL 3 % as A to B,C,D	COL 1 # of times in B vrnts	COL 2 % in B vrnts	COL 3 % as B to A,C,D	COL 1 # of times in C vrnts	COL 2 % in C vrnts	COL 3 % as C to A,B,D	COL 1 # of times in D vrnts	COL 2 % in D vrnts	COL 3 % as D to A,B,C	COL 4 # of variants with ms as a witness
Lect.	9	45%	60%	1	11%	7%	5	42%	33%	0	0%	0%	15
L147	1	5%	100%	0	0%	0%	0	0%	0%	0	0%	0%	1
L422	1	5%	100%	0	0%	0%	0	0%	0%	0	0%	0%	1
L590	1	5%	33%	0	0%	0%	2	17%	67%	0	0%	0%	3
L591	0	0%	0%	0	0%	0%	1	8%	100%	0	0%	0%	1
L592	0	0%	0%	1	11%	50%	1	8%	50%	0	0%	0%	2
L593	0	0%	0%	1	11%	50%	1	8%	50%	0	0%	0%	2
L596	1	5%	33%	1	11%	33%	1	8%	33%	0	0%	0%	3
L751	1	5%	50%	1	11%	50%	0	0%	0%	0	0%	0%	2
L883	0	0%	0%	1	11%	100%	0	0%	0%	0	0%	0%	1
L884	0	0%	0%	1	11%	100%	0	0%	0%	0	0%	0%	1
L895	0	0%	0%	0	0%	0%	1	8%	100%	0	0%	0%	1
L921	0	0%	0%	0	0%	0%	1	8%	100%	0	0%	0%	1
L1154	0	0%	0%	1	11%	50%	1	8%	50%	0	0%	0%	2
L1159	2	10%	50%	1	11%	25%	1	8%	25%	0	0%	0%	4
L1178	0	0%	0%	0	0%	0%	1	8%	100%	0	0%	0%	1
L1298	1	5%	50%	0	0%	0%	1	8%	50%	0	0%	0%	2
L1364	0	0%	0%	1	11%	100%	0	0%	0%	0	0%	0%	1
L1365	1	5%	50%	0	0%	0%	1	8%	50%	0	0%	0%	2
L1441	1	5%	50%	1	11%	50%	0	0%	0%	0	0%	0%	2

Percentages Showing Important Old Latin Manuscripts in 1 Peter (UBSGNT[4])

| Quality Rating Old Latin | Above Average or Stronger Variants | | | | | | Below Average or Weaker Variants | | | | | | 37 total variants 1 Peter |
| | A Rated Variants (20 Possible Total) | | | B Rated Variants (9 Possible Total) | | | C Rated Variants (8 Possible Total) | | | D Rated Variants (0 Possible Total) | | | |
	COL 1 # of times in A vrnts	COL 2 % in A vrnts	COL 3 % as A to B,C,D	COL 1 # of times in B vrnts	COL 2 % in B vrnts	COL 3 % as B to A,C,D	COL 1 # of times in C vrnts	COL 2 % in C vrnts	COL 3 % as C to A,B,D	COL 1 # of times in D vrnts	COL 2 % in D vrnts	COL 3 % as D to A,B,C	COL 4 # of variants with ms as a witness
it^{ar}	10	50%	56%	5	56%	28%	3	38%	17%	0	0%	0%	18
$it^{h}(acr)$	4	20%	67%	0	0%	0%	2	25%	33%	0	0%	0%	6
$it^{l}(ac)$	1	5%	50%	1	11%	50%	0	0%	0%	0	0%	0%	2
$it^{q}(c)$	4	20%	57%	0	0%	0%	3	38%	43%	0	0%	0%	7
$it^{s}(ac)$	1	5%	33%	0	0%	0%	2	25%	67%	0	0%	0%	3
$it^{t}(acpr)$	6	30%	50%	4	44%	33%	2	25%	17%	0	0%	0%	12
$it^{w}(c)$	3	15%	100%	0	0%	0%	0	0%	0%	0	0%	0%	3
$it^{v}(e)$	2	10%	50%	2	22%	50%	0	0%	0%	0	0%	0%	4
it^{z}	9	45%	53%	5	56%	29%	3	38%	18%	0	0%	0%	17

Percentages Showing Important Vulgate Manuscripts in
1 Peter (UBSGNT⁴)

Quality	Above Average or Stronger Variants						Below Average or Weaker Variants						37 total
Rating	A Rated Variants (20 Possible Total)			B Rated Variants (9 Possible Total)			C Rated Variants (8 Possible Total)			D Rated Variants (0 Possible Total)			variants 1 Peter
Vulgate	COL 1	COL 2	COL 3	COL 1	COL 2	COL 3	COL 1	COL 2	COL 3	COL 1	COL 2	COL 3	COL 4
	# of times in A vrnts	% in A vrnts	% as A to B,C,D	# of times in B vrnts	% in B vrnts	% as B to A,C,D	# of times in C vrnts	% in C vrnts	% as C to A,B,D	# of times in D vrnts	% in D vrnts	% as D to A,B,C	# of variants with ms as a witness
vg	10	50%	50%	5	56%	25%	5	63%	25%	0	0%	0%	20
vg^{cl}	1	5%	100%	0	0%	0%	0	0%	0%	0	0%	0%	1
vg^{ww}	1	5%	100%	1	11%	100%	0	0%	0%	0	0%	0%	2
vgst	4	20%	67%	2	22%	33%	0	0%	0%	0	0%	0%	6

Percentages Showing Important Syriac Manuscripts in
1 Peter (UBSGNT⁴)

Quality	Above Average or Stronger Variants						Below Average or Weaker Variants						37 total
Rating	A Rated Variants (20 Possible Total)			B Rated Variants (9 Possible Total)			C Rated Variants (8 Possible Total)			D Rated Variants (0 Possible Total)			variants 1 Peter
Syriac	COL 1	COL 2	COL 3	COL 1	COL 2	COL 3	COL 1	COL 2	COL 3	COL 1	COL 2	COL 3	COL 4
	# of times in A vrnts	% in A vrnts	% as A to B,C,D	# of times in B vrnts	% in B vrnts	% as B to A,C,D	# of times in C vrnts	% in C vrnts	% as C to A,B,D	# of times in D vrnts	% in D vrnts	% as D to A,B,C	# of variants with ms as a witness
syr^p	7	35%	54%	1	11%	8%	5	63%	38%	0	0%	0%	13
syr^h	11	50%	69%	1	11%	6%	4	50%	25%	0	0%	0%	16

Percentages Showing Important Coptic Manuscripts in
1 Peter (UBSGNT⁴)

Quality	Above Average or Stronger Variants						Below Average or Weaker Variants						37 total
Rating	A Rated Variants (20 Possible Total)			B Rated Variants (9 Possible Total)			C Rated Variants (8 Possible Total)			D Rated Variants (0 Possible Total)			variants 1 Peter
Coptic	COL 1	COL 2	COL 3	COL 1	COL 2	COL 3	COL 1	COL 2	COL 3	COL 1	COL 2	COL 3	COL 4
	# of times in A vrnts	% in A vrnts	% as A to B,C,D	# of times in B vrnts	% in B vrnts	% as B to A,C,D	# of times in C vrnts	% in C vrnts	% as C to A,B,D	# of times in D vrnts	% in D vrnts	% as D to A,B,C	# of variants with ms as a witness
cop^{sa}	15	**75%**	68%	4	44%	18%	3	38%	14%	0	0%	0%	22
cop^{bo}	11	55%	55%	3	33%	15%	6	**75%**	30%	0	0%	0%	20

Percentages Showing Important Armenian Manuscripts in
1 Peter (UBSGNT[4])

Quality	Above Average or Stronger Variants						Below Average or Weaker Variants						37 total
Rating	A Rated Variants (20 Possible Total)			B Rated Variants (9 Possible Total)			C Rated Variants (8 Possible Total)			D Rated Variants (0 Possible Total)			variants 1 Peter
Armen.	COL 1	COL 2	COL 3	COL 1	COL 2	COL 3	COL 1	COL 2	COL 3	COL 1	COL 2	COL 3	COL 4
	# of times in A vrnts	% in A vrnts	% as A to B,C,D	# of times in B vrnts	% in B vrnts	% as B to A,C,D	# of times in C vrnts	% in C vrnts	% as C to A,B,D	# of times in D vrnts	% in D vrnts	% as D to A,B,C	# of variants with ms as a witness
Armen.	13	65%	62%	3	33%	14%	5	63%	24%	0	0%	0%	21

Percentages Showing Important Ethiopic Manuscripts in
1 Peter (UBSGNT[4])

Quality	Above Average or Stronger Variants						Below Average or Weaker Variants						37 total
Rating	A Rated Variants (20 Possible Total)			B Rated Variants (9 Possible Total)			C Rated Variants (8 Possible Total)			D Rated Variants (0 Possible Total)			variants 1 Peter
Ethiopic	COL 1	COL 2	COL 3	COL 1	COL 2	COL 3	COL 1	COL 2	COL 3	COL 1	COL 2	COL 3	COL 4
	# of times in A vrnts	% in A vrnts	% as A to B,C,D	# of times in B vrnts	% in B vrnts	% as B to A,C,D	# of times in C vrnts	% in C vrnts	% as C to A,B,D	# of times in D vrnts	% in D vrnts	% as D to A,B,C	# of variants with ms as a witness
eth	12	60%	60%	3	33%	15%	5	63%	25%	0	0%	0%	20

Percentages Showing Important Georgian Manuscripts in
1 Peter (UBSGNT[4])

Quality	Above Average or Stronger Variants						Below Average or Weaker Variants						37 total
Rating	A Rated Variants (20 Possible Total)			B Rated Variants (9 Possible Total)			C Rated Variants (8 Possible Total)			D Rated Variants (0 Possible Total)			variants 1 Peter
Georgn.	COL 1	COL 2	COL 3	COL 1	COL 2	COL 3	COL 1	COL 2	COL 3	COL 1	COL 2	COL 3	COL 4
	# of times in A vrnts	% in A vrnts	% as A to B,C,D	# of times in B vrnts	% in B vrnts	% as B to A,C,D	# of times in C vrnts	% in C vrnts	% as C to A,B,D	# of times in D vrnts	% in D vrnts	% as D to A,B,C	# of variants with ms as a witness
geo	14	**70%**	61%	5	56%	22%	4	50%	17%	0	0%	0%	23

Percentages Showing Important Greek Father Evidence in 1 Peter (UBSGNT[4])

Quality Rating / Greek Church Fathers	Above Average or Stronger Variants						Below Average or Weaker Variants						37 total variants 1 Peter
	A Rated Variants (20 Possible Total)			B Rated Variants (9 Possible Total)			C Rated Variants (8 Possible Total)			D Rated Variants (0 Possible Total)			
	COL 1 # of times in A vrnts	COL 2 % in A vrnts	COL 3 % as A to B,C,D	COL 1 # of times in B vrnts	COL 2 % in B vrnts	COL 3 % as B to A,C,D	COL 1 # of times in C vrnts	COL 2 % in C vrnts	COL 3 % as C to A,B,D	COL 1 # of times in D vrnts	COL 2 % in D vrnts	COL 3 % as D to A,B,C	COL 4 # of variants with ms as a witness
Ammonas	1	5%	100%	0	0%	0%	0	0%	0%	0	0%	0%	1
(John) Chrysostom	1	5%	100%	0	0%	0%	0	0%	0%	0	0%	0%	1
Clement, of Alexandria	7	35%	78%	1	11%	11%	1	13%	11%	0	0%	0%	9
Cyril, of Alexandria	5	25%	100%	0	0%	0%	0	0%	0%	0	0%	0%	5
Cyril-Jerusalem	1	5%	50%	0	0%	0%	1	13%	50%	0	0%	0%	2
Didymus	4	20%	80%	0	0%	0%	1	13%	20%	0	0%	0%	5
Eusebius, of Caesarea	1	5%	50%	0	0%	0%	1	13%	50%	0	0%	0%	2
Eusebius-Emesa	1	5%	100%	0	0%	0%	0	0%	0%	0	0%	0%	1
Irenaeus	1	5%	100%	0	0%	0%	0	0%	0%	0	0%	0%	1
Isidore, of Pelusium	1	5%	100%	0	0%	0%	0	0%	0%	0	0%	0%	1
Nestorius	1	5%	50%	0	0%	0%	1	13%	50%	0	0%	0%	2
Origen	4	20%	80%	0	0%	0%	1	13%	20%	0	0%	0%	5
Ps-Dionysius	0	0%	0%	1	11%	100%	0	0%	0%	0	0%	0%	1
Theodoret, of Cyrrhus	1	5%	100%	0	0%	0%	0	0%	0%	0	0%	0%	1

Percentages Showing Important Latin Father Evidence in 1 Peter (UBSGNT[4])

| Quality Rating / Latin Church Fathers | Above Average or Stronger Variants | | | | | | Below Average or Weaker Variants | | | | | | 37 total variants 1 Peter |
| | A Rated Variants (20 Possible Total) | | | B Rated Variants (9 Possible Total) | | | C Rated Variants (8 Possible Total) | | | D Rated Variants (0 Possible Total) | | | COL 4 |
	COL 1 # of times in A vrnts	COL 2 % in A vrnts	COL 3 % as A to B,C,D	COL 1 # of times in B vrnts	COL 2 % in B vrnts	COL 3 % as B to A,C,D	COL 1 # of times in C vrnts	COL 2 % in C vrnts	COL 3 % as C to A,B,D	COL 1 # of times in D vrnts	COL 2 % in D vrnts	COL 3 % as D to A,B,C	# of variants with ms as a witness
Ambrose	2	10%	67%	1	11%	33%	0	0%	0%	0	0%	0%	3
Augustine	5	25%	50%	3	33%	30%	2	25%	20%	0	0%	0%	10
Cassiodorus	1	5%	100%	0	0%	0%	0	0%	0%	0	0%	0%	1
Cyprian	3	15%	75%	0	0%	0%	1	13%	25%	0	0%	0%	4
Hilary	0	0%	0%	0	0%	0%	1	13%	100%	0	0%	0%	1
Jerome	6	30%	75%	0	0%	0%	2	25%	25%	0	0%	0%	8
Niceta	1	5%	100%	0	0%	0%	0	0%	0%	0	0%	0%	1
Pelagius	1	5%	100%	0	0%	0%	0	0%	0%	0	0%	0%	1
Quodvultdeus	2	10%	100%	0	0%	0%	0	0%	0%	0	0%	0%	2
Speculum	2	10%	40%	2	22%	40%	1	13%	20%	0	0%	0%	5
Tertullian	3	15%	100%	0	0%	0%	0	0%	0%	0	0%	0%	3
Varimadum	2	10%	67%	0	0%	0%	1	13%	33%	0	0%	0%	3
Vigilius	1	5%	100%	0	0%	0%	0	0%	0%	0	0%	0%	1

Percentages Showing Important Papyri Manuscripts in the First Eight Chapters of Revelation (UBSGNT⁴)

| Quality Rating | Above Average or Stronger Variants | | | | | | Below Average or Weaker Variants | | | | | | 23 total variants Rev. 1–8 |
| | A Rated Variants (10 Possible Total) | | | B Rated Variants (10 Possible Total) | | | C Rated Variants (3 Possible Total) | | | D Rated Variants (0 Possible Total) | | | |
Papyri	COL 1 # of times in A vrnts	COL 2 % in A vrnts	COL 3 % as A to B,C,D	COL 1 # of times in B vrnts	COL 2 % in B vrnts	COL 3 % as B to A,C,D	COL 1 # of times in C vrnts	COL 2 % in C vrnts	COL 3 % as C to A,B,D	COL 1 # of times in D vrnts	COL 2 % in D vrnts	COL 3 % as D to A,B,C	COL 4 # of variants with ms as a witness
𝔓18[xi]	1	10%	100%	0	0%	0%	0	0%	0%	0	0%	0%	1
𝔓24	0	0%	0%	0	0%	0%	1	33%	100%	0	0%	0%	1

Percentages Showing Important Uncial Manuscripts in the First Eight Chapters of Revelation (UBSGNT⁴)

| Quality Rating | Above Average or Stronger Variants | | | | | | Below Average or Weaker Variants | | | | | | 23 total variants Rev. 1–8 |
| | A Rated Variants (10 Possible Total) | | | B Rated Variants (10 Possible Total) | | | C Rated Variants (3 Possible Total) | | | D Rated Variants (0 Possible Total) | | | |
Uncials	COL 1 # of times in A vrnts	COL 2 % in A vrnts	COL 3 % as A to B,C,D	COL 1 # of times in B vrnts	COL 2 % in B vrnts	COL 3 % as B to A,C,D	COL 1 # of times in C vrnts	COL 2 % in C vrnts	COL 3 % as C to A,B,D	COL 1 # of times in D vrnts	COL 2 % in D vrnts	COL 3 % as D to A,B,C	COL 4 # of variants with ms as a witness
ℵ01	9	90%	53%	6	60%	35%	2	67%	12%	0	0%	0%	17
A02	6	60%	40%	8	80%	53%	1	33%	7%	0	0%	0%	15
C04	6	60%	35%	9	90%	53%	2	67%	12%	0	0%	0%	17
[P024]	3	30%	75%	1	10%	25%	0	0%	0%	0	0%	0%	4
P025	2	20%	22%	7	70%	78%	0	0%	0%	0	0%	0%	9

xi. 𝔓18, containing Rev. 1.4-7, is significant in that it is dated as early as the third or fourth century. The Alands list it as a category I manuscript in *The Text of the New Testament*, p. 97.

Percentages Showing Important Minuscule Manuscripts in the First Eight Chapters of Revelation (UBSGNT⁴)

Quality	Above Average or Stronger Variants						Below Average or Weaker Variants						23 total
Rating	A Rated Variants (10 Possible Total)			B Rated Variants (10 Possible Total)			C Rated Variants (3 Possible Total)			D Rated Variants (0 Possible Total)			variants Rev. 1–8
Minusc.	COL 1 # of times in A vrnts	COL 2 % in A vrnts	COL 3 % as A to B,C,D	COL 1 # of times in B vrnts	COL 2 % in B vrnts	COL 3 % as B to A,C,D	COL 1 # of times in C vrnts	COL 2 % in C vrnts	COL 3 % as C to A,B,D	COL 1 # of times in D vrnts	COL 2 % in D vrnts	COL 3 % as D to A,B,C	COL 4 # of variants with ms as a witness
205	5	50%	50%	4	40%	40%	1	33%	10%	0	0%	0%	10
209	5	50%	50%	4	40%	40%	1	33%	10%	0	0%	0%	10
1006	5	50%	36%	8	80%	57%	1	33%	7%	0	0%	0%	14
1611	6	60%	38%	9	90%	56%	1	33%	6%	0	0%	0%	16
1841	5	50%	38%	7	70%	54%	1	33%	8%	0	0%	0%	13
1854	4	40%	40%	4	40%	40%	2	67%	20%	0	0%	0%	10
2050	5	50%	83%	1	10%	17%	0	0%	0%	0	0%	0%	6
2053	7	70%	41%	8	80%	47%	2	67%	12%	0	0%	0%	17
2062	1	10%	50%	0	0%	0%	1	33%	50%	0	0%	0%	2
2329	4	40%	40%	4	40%	40%	2	67%	20%	0	0%	0%	10
2344	4	40%	50%	3	30%	38%	1	33%	13%	0	0%	0%	8
2351	5	50%	42%	5	50%	42%	2	67%	17%	0	0%	0%	12

Percentages Showing Important Lectionary Manuscripts in the First Eight Chapters of Revelation (UBSGNT⁴)

There are no Lectionary manuscripts cited in the first eight chapters of Revelation within the *UBSGNT⁴*.

Percentages Showing Important Old Latin Manuscripts in the First Eight Chapters of Revelation (UBSGNT⁴)

Quality	Above Average or Stronger Variants						Below Average or Weaker Variants						23 total
Rating	A Rated Variants (10 Possible Total)			B Rated Variants (10 Possible Total)			C Rated Variants (3 Possible Total)			D Rated Variants (0 Possible Total)			variants Rev. 1–8
Old Latin	COL 1 # of times in A vrnts	COL 2 % in A vrnts	COL 3 % as A to B,C,D	COL 1 # of times in B vrnts	COL 2 % in B vrnts	COL 3 % as B to A,C,D	COL 1 # of times in C vrnts	COL 2 % in C vrnts	COL 3 % as C to A,B,D	COL 1 # of times in D vrnts	COL 2 % in D vrnts	COL 3 % as D to A,B,C	COL 4 # of variants with ms as a witness
it*ar*	3	30%	43%	3	30%	43%	1	33%	14%	0	0%	0%	7
it*gig*	5	50%	42%	5	50%	42%	2	67%	17%	0	0%	0%	12
it*h(acr)*	2	20%	67%	0	0%	0%	1	33%	33%	0	0%	0%	3
it*t(acpr)*	2	20%	40%	2	20%	40%	1	33%	20%	0	0%	0%	5

Percentages Showing Important Vulgate Manuscripts in the First Eight Chapters of Revelation (UBSGNT[4])

Quality Rating	Above Average or Stronger Variants						Below Average or Weaker Variants						23 total variants Rev. 1–8
	A Rated Variants (10 Possible Total)			B Rated Variants (10 Possible Total)			C Rated Variants (3 Possible Total)			D Rated Variants (0 Possible Total)			
Vulgate	COL 1	COL 2	COL 3	COL 1	COL 2	COL 3	COL 1	COL 2	COL 3	COL 1	COL 2	COL 3	COL 4
	# of times in A vrnts	% in A vrnts	% as A to B,C,D	# of times in B vrnts	% in B vrnts	% as B to A,C,D	# of times in C vrnts	% in C vrnts	% as C to A,B,D	# of times in D vrnts	% in D vrnts	% as D to A,B,C	# of variants with ms as a witness
vg	3	30%	43%	3	30%	43%	1	33%	14%	0	0%	0%	7
vg^{cl}	0	0%	0%	0	0%	0%	1	33%	100%	0	0%	0%	1
vg^{ww}	3	30%	33%	6	60%	67%	0	0%	0%	0	0%	0%	9
vgst	3	30%	33%	6	60%	67%	0	0%	0%	0	0%	0%	9

Percentages Showing Important Syriac Manuscripts in the First Eight Chapters of Revelation (UBSGNT[4])

Quality Rating	Above Average or Stronger Variants						Below Average or Weaker Variants						23 total variants Rev. 1–8
	A Rated Variants (10 Possible Total)			B Rated Variants (10 Possible Total)			C Rated Variants (3 Possible Total)			D Rated Variants (0 Possible Total)			
Syriac	COL 1	COL 2	COL 3	COL 1	COL 2	COL 3	COL 1	COL 2	COL 3	COL 1	COL 2	COL 3	COL 4
	# of times in A vrnts	% in A vrnts	% as A to B,C,D	# of times in B vrnts	% in B vrnts	% as B to A,C,D	# of times in C vrnts	% in C vrnts	% as C to A,B,D	# of times in D vrnts	% in D vrnts	% as D to A,B,C	# of variants with ms as a witness
syr^{ph}	5	50%	42%	5	50%	42%	2	67%	17%	0	0%	0%	12
syr^{h}	5	50%	38%	6	60%	46%	2	67%	15%	0	0%	0%	13

Percentages Showing Important Coptic Manuscripts in the First Eight Chapters of Revelation (UBSGNT[4])

Quality Rating	Above Average or Stronger Variants						Below Average or Weaker Variants						23 total variants Rev. 1–8
	A Rated Variants (10 Possible Total)			B Rated Variants (10 Possible Total)			C Rated Variants (3 Possible Total)			D Rated Variants (0 Possible Total)			
Coptic	COL 1	COL 2	COL 3	COL 1	COL 2	COL 3	COL 1	COL 2	COL 3	COL 1	COL 2	COL 3	COL 4
	# of times in A vrnts	% in A vrnts	% as A to B,C,D	# of times in B vrnts	% in B vrnts	% as B to A,C,D	# of times in C vrnts	% in C vrnts	% as C to A,B,D	# of times in D vrnts	% in D vrnts	% as D to A,B,C	# of variants with ms as a witness
cop^{sa}	1	10%	9%	9	**90%**	82%	1	33%	9%	0	0%	0%	11
cop^{bo}	3	30%	21%	10	**100%**	71%	1	33%	7%	0	0%	0%	14

*Percentages Showing Important Armenian Manuscripts in
the First Eight Chapters of Revelation (UBSGNT⁴)*

Quality	Above Average or Stronger Variants						Below Average or Weaker Variants						23 total
Rating	A Rated Variants (10 Possible Total)			B Rated Variants (10 Possible Total)			C Rated Variants (3 Possible Total)			D Rated Variants (0 Possible Total)			variants Rev. 1–8
Armen.	COL 1 # of times in A vrnts	COL 2 % in A vrnts	COL 3 % as A to B,C,D	COL 1 # of times in B vrnts	COL 2 % in B vrnts	COL 3 % as B to A,C,D	COL 1 # of times in C vrnts	COL 2 % in C vrnts	COL 3 % as C to A,B,D	COL 1 # of times in D vrnts	COL 2 % in D vrnts	COL 3 % as D to A,B,C	COL 4 # of variants with ms as a witness
Armen.	3	30%	20%	10	100%	67%	2	20%	13%	0	0%	0%	15

*Percentages Showing Important Ethiopic Manuscripts in
the First Eight Chapters of Revelation (UBSGNT⁴)*

Quality	Above Average or Stronger Variants						Below Average or Weaker Variants						23 total
Rating	A Rated Variants (10 Possible Total)			B Rated Variants (10 Possible Total)			C Rated Variants (3 Possible Total)			D Rated Variants (0 Possible Total)			variants Rev. 1–8
Ethiopic	COL 1 # of times in A vrnts	COL 2 % in A vrnts	COL 3 % as A to B,C,D	COL 1 # of times in B vrnts	COL 2 % in B vrnts	COL 3 % as B to A,C,D	COL 1 # of times in C vrnts	COL 2 % in C vrnts	COL 3 % as C to A,B,D	COL 1 # of times in D vrnts	COL 2 % in D vrnts	COL 3 % as D to A,B,C	COL 4 # of variants with ms as a witness
eth	5	50%	50%	4	40%	40%	1	33%	10%	0	0%	0%	10%

*Percentages Showing Important Georgian Manuscripts in
the First Eight Chapters of Revelation (UBSGNT⁴)*

There are no Georgian manuscripts cited in the first eight chapters of Revelation within the *UBSGNT⁴*.

Percentages Showing Important Greek Father Evidence in the First Eight Chapters of Revelation (UBSGNT⁴)

| Quality Rating | Above Average or Stronger Variants | | | | | | Below Average or Weaker Variants | | | | | | 23 total variants Rev. 1–8 |
| | A Rated Variants (10 Possible Total) | | | B Rated Variants (10 Possible Total) | | | C Rated Variants (3 Possible Total) | | | D Rated Variants (0 Possible Total) | | | |
Greek Church Fathers	COL 1 # of times in A vrnts	COL 2 % in A vrnts	COL 3 % as A to B,C,D	COL 1 # of times in B vrnts	COL 2 % in B vrnts	COL 3 % as B to A,C,D	COL 1 # of times in C vrnts	COL 2 % in C vrnts	COL 3 % as C to A,B,D	COL 1 # of times in D vrnts	COL 2 % in D vrnts	COL 3 % as D to A,B,C	COL 4 # of variants with ms as a witness
Andrew, of Caesarea	5	50%	36%	8	**80%**	57%	1	33%	7%	0	0%	0%	14
Clement, of Alexandria	0	0%	0%	0	0%	0%	1	33%	100%	0	0%	0%	1
Didymus	0	0%	0%	0	0%	0%	1	33%	100%	0	0%	0%	1
Epiphanius	1	1%	50%	1	10%	50%	0	0%	0%	0	0%	0%	2
Hippolytus	1	1%	50%	0	0%	0%	1	33%	50%	0	0%	0%	2
Irenaeus	0	0%	0%	0	0%	0%	1	33%	100%	0	0%	0%	1

Percentages Showing Important Latin Father Evidence in the First Eight Chapters of Revelation (UBSGNT[4])

| Quality Rating | Above Average or Stronger Variants | | | | | | Below Average or Weaker Variants | | | | | | 23 total variants Rev. 1–8 |
| | A Rated Variants (10 Possible Total) | | | B Rated Variants (10 Possible Total) | | | C Rated Variants (3 Possible Total) | | | D Rated Variants (0 Possible Total) | | | |
Latin Church Fathers	COL1 # of times in A vrnts	COL2 % in A vrnts	COL3 % as A to B,C,D	COL1 # of times in B vrnts	COL2 % in B vrnts	COL3 % as B to A,C,D	COL1 # of times in C vrnts	COL2 % in C vrnts	COL3 % as C to A,B,D	COL1 # of times in D vrnts	COL2 % in D vrnts	COL3 % as D to A,B,C	COL4 # of variants with ms as a witness
Ambrose	1	10%	100%	0	0%	0%	0	0%	0%	0	0%	0%	1
Ambrosiaster	1	10%	50%	1	10%	50%	0	0%	0%	0	0%	0%	2
Apringius	1	10%	50%	0	0%	0%	1	33%	50%	0	0%	0%	2
Beatus	2	20%	33%	2	20%	33%	2	67%	33%	0	0%	0%	6
Cassiodorus	0	0%	0%	1	10%	100%	0	0%	0%	0	0%	0%	1
Cyprian	3	30%	75%	0	0%	0%	1	33%	25%	0	0%	0%	4
Fulgentius	2	20%	67%	0	0%	0%	1	33%	33%	0	0%	0%	3
Gregory-Elvira	0	0%	0%	0	0%	0%	1	33%	100%	0	0%	0%	1
Primasius	3	30%	43%	3	30%	43%	1	33%	14%	0	0%	0%	7
Tertullian	2	20%	67%	1	10%	33%	0	0%	0%	0	0%	0%	3
Tyconius	2	20%	50%	1	10%	25%	1	33%	25%	0	0%	0%	4
Varimadum	1	10%	100%	0	0%	0%	0	0%	0%	0	0%	0%	1
Victorinus-Pettau	1	10%	100%	0	0%	0%	0	0%	0%	0	0%	0%	1

APPENDIX VI

Principal Papyri Evidence in Luke, Acts, and the Exceptional Variants

This final appendix contains the data that corresponds to Chapter 2, Section 4, where the various possible reasons for the rating changes from previous *UBSGNT* editions to the *UBSGNT*⁴ are examined. More specifically, the tables and figures included here are necessary for investigating the role that the ancient papyri play in the ascribing of variant letter-ratings. Are the *UBSGNT*⁴ modifications founded upon a new consensus among scholars concerning the authority, importance, and merit of the ancient papyri? This appendix, using the Gospel of Luke, the book of Acts, and the exceptional variants (located in Chapter 2, Section 3) as a test case, presents the data that allow conclusions to be made regarding this question.

The first group of charts presented in this appendix closely resembles those found in Appendix IV. However, here, rather than recording the principal manuscript evidence (i.e. papyri, uncials, minuscules etc.) found in selected portions of the *UBSGNT*⁴, the entire papyri manuscript evidence for Luke, Acts, and the exceptional variants is recorded. This first set of charts also serve as the basis for the latter two sections of statistics recorded in this appendix.

Papyri manuscripts that are cited within the first variant option of an entire variant unit (i.e. the variant reading or option that appears in the *UBSGNT*⁴ text) as well as alternative variant options are listed. The first row of the charts, entitled '*Variant*', provides the reference (by chapter and verse) of every textual variant in the given book. If a particular passage records more than one variant a superscript numeral will be included in order to clarify which variant is being referred to. This number corresponds to the reference listings in the *UBSGNT*⁴ rather than in Appendix I. The second row, entitled '*Rating*', lists each variant's letter-rating trend, as seen throughout successive *UBSGNT* editions. The final *UBSGNT*⁴ letter-rating is always the last letter given (for example, if the rating trend '*C-A*' is given, the *UBSGNT*⁴ letter-rating for the particular variant is *A*). Some letter-ratings are preceded by the word '*new*', which signifies that it is a newly added variant within the *UBSGNT*⁴. Other letter-ratings are preceded by the abbreviation '*con.*', signifying a 'consistent' rating as defined in the categories delineated in Chapter 2, Section 3. Every papyri manuscript that is cited in the given book is listed along the far left column. If a particular papyri manuscript is cited in the first variant option of a variant unit or passage (i.e. the variant reading or option that appears in the *UBSGNT*⁴ text) it is marked by an 'X'. Often special abbreviations (such as [ ], or ᵛⁱᵈ) are cited along with the particular manuscript (again, marked by the 'X'). For an explanation of these abbreviations one should consult page 47* of the *UBSGNT*[4] which contains the 'Master List Of Symbols And Abbreviations'. Papyri manuscripts that are cited in alternative variant options (i.e. those variant options or readings that do not appear in the *UBSGNT*[4] text) are simply recorded by prefixing the letter 'v' to the number of the variant option where the papyri is cited within the complete variant unit. For example, 'v4' would indicate that a given papyri occurs as a witness in the fourth variant option of a complete variant unit. This first group of charts simply records every instance in Luke, Acts, and the exceptional variants where a papyrus manuscript is cited in the textual apparatus.

Papyri Evidence in the Gospel of Luke (UBSGNT[4])

Variant	1.28	1.35	1.46	1.66	1.74	1.78	2.9	2.11	2.14	2.33	2.38
Rating	B-A	B-A	B-A	B-A	C-B	C-B	C-B	con. A	B-A	con. B	B-A
Papyri											
𝔓4				X[vid]							

Variant	3.22	3.32	3.33	4.4	4.17	4.18	4.44	5.17[1]	5.17[2]	5.33	5.38
Rating	C-B	con. B	con. C	con. B	C-B	new A	con. B	C-B	B-A	C-B	con. B
Papyri											
𝔓4	X	X								X	X
𝔓75							X				X[vid]

Variant	5.39[1]	5.39a[2]	5.39b[3]	6.1[1]	6.4[1]	6.4[2]	6.5	6.10	6.31	6.35	6.48
Rating	new C	B-A	B-A	con. C	C-A	new A	C-B	C-A	C-B	C-B	B-A
Papyri											
𝔓4	v2	X	X	X		X		X			v3
𝔓75			X						X[vid]		X[vid]

Variant	7.7	7.10	7.11[1]	7.11[2]	7.19	7.28[2]	7.32	7.35	7.39	7.45	8.3
Rating	C-B	C-A	C-B	C-B	con. C	C-B	new B	new B	C-A	new A	con. B
Papyri											
𝔓75	X[vid]	X	X	X		X					

Variant	8.26	8.37	8.43	8.44	8.45[1]	8.45[2]	8.49	9.1	9.2	9.3	9.10
Rating	D-C	D-C	D-C	C-B	con. B	C-B	C-B	C-B	con. C	con. C	new B
Papyri											
𝔓75	X	X	v3	X	X	X	X	X			(X)

Variant	9.26	9.35	9.47	9.49	9.54	9.55-56	9.59	9.62[1]	9.62[2]	10.1[2]	10.15
Rating	B-A	con. B	con. C	new B	C-B	C-A	con. C	new C	con. C	con. C	D-C
Papyri											
𝔓45	X	X			X	X	X	v4	v3		v2
𝔓75	X[vid]	X		X[vid]	X	X	X	v4	(X)	X	X

Variant	10.17	10.21	10.22	10.38	vv.41-42	11.2[1]	11.2[2]	11.2[3]	11.4	11.10	11.11[1]
Rating	con. C	con. C	B-A	C-B	con. C	con. A	B-A	con. A	con. A	con. C	B-C-B
Papyri											
𝔓3				v2	v3						
𝔓45	X[vid]	v2	X[vid]	X	X					X	X
𝔓75	X	(X)	X	X	X	X	X	X	X	v3	(X)

Variant	11.11[2]	11.12	11.13[1]	11.13[2]	11.14	11.23	11.24	11.25	11.33	11.42	11.48
Rating	con. C	con. C	D-C	con. B	D-C	con. A	con. C	con. B	D-C	con. B	C-B
Papyri											
𝔓45	X	X	v5	v2	v2	X	v2		v2	v2	
𝔓75	X	X	v3	X	v2	(X)	X	X	v2	X	X

Variant	12.14	12.21	12.22	12.27	12.31	12.39	12.56	13.7	13.9	13.19	13.27¹
Rating	con. B	B-A	con. C	D-B	C-B	con. B	C-B	con. C	C-B	C-B	con. C
Papyri											
p45		X		X	v2		v2		v2	v4	
p75	X	X	v2	X	v4	X	X	X	X	X	Xc v2

Variant	13.27²	13.35¹	13.35²	14.5	14.17	15.1	15.16	15.21	16.12	16.21¹	16.21²
Rating	con. C	new B	D-C	con. B	con. C	new A	C-B	B-A	B-A	con. B	new A
Papyri											
p45		Xvid	v4	X							
p75	v3	X	v5	X	v2	X	X	X	X	X	X

Variant	vv.22-23	17.3	17.9	17.23¹	17.24	17.33	17.35	18.11	18.24	18.25	19.15
Rating	new A	new A	C-B	D-C	con. C	C-B	B-A	D-C	D-C	new A	C-B
Papyri											
p75	X		X	X	v3	X	X	v3			

Variant	19.25	19.38	19.42¹	19.42²	20.9	20.27	20.34	20.36	20.45	21.4	21.11
Rating	D-A	con. C	C-B	C-B	con. C	con. C	new A	new B	con. C	con. B	D-C
Papyri											

Variant	21.19	21.35	21.38	22.16	vv.17-20	22.31	vv.43-44	22.62	22.68	23.11	23.15
Rating	D-C	C-B	con. A	C-B	B-C-B	new B	C-A	C-A	C-B	con. C	C-A
Papyri											
p69							(Xvid)				
p75				Xvid	X	X	X	X	X	X	X

Variant	23.16	23.23	23.34	23.38	23.42	23.45	24.3	24.6	24.10	24.12	24.13
Rating	B-A	C-B	C-A	B-A	C-B	con. B	D-B	D-B	C-B	D-B	con. B
Papyri											
p75	X	X	X	X	X	X* v2	X	X	X	X	X

Variant	24.17	24.19	24.32	24.36	24.40	24.42	24.47¹	24.47²	24.49	24.51	24.52
Rating	new B	C-B	con. C	D-B	D-B	con. B	D-B	C-B	con. C	D-B	D-B
Papyri											
p75	X	X	v2	X	X	X	X	v3	v3	X	X

Variant	24.53¹	24.53²
Rating	C-B	B-A
Papyri		
p75	X	X

Variants Deleted from Luke in the UBSGNT⁴

Variant	1.17	1.37	1.68	1.70	2.15	2.22	3.9	6.1²	6.2	6.16	6.26
Rating	con. A	con. B	con. B	con. B	con. D	con. C	con. C	con. B	con. B	con. C	con. C
Papyri											
p4			v2	X			v3	X	X	X	
p75											X

Variant	6.38	6.42	7.28¹	7.42	8.5	8.27	9.62³	10.1¹	12.1	12.11	12.20
Rating	con. C	con. C	con. C	con. C	con. B	con. C	con. C	con. C	con. C	con. C	con. D
Papyri											
p3			Xvid								
p45	v6								v2	Xvid	
p75					X	Xvid	v2	X	X	X	v2

Variant	16.14	17.23²	20.20	20.26	21.6	22.52	24.9
Rating	con. C	con. C	con. C	con. C	con. C	con. C	con. D
Papyri							
p75	X	v4				X	X

Papyri Evidence in the Book of Acts (UBSGNT[4])

Variant	1.2	1.11	1.23	1.25	1.26[1]	2.5	2.16	2.18[1]	2.18[2]	2.19	2.24
Rating	new A	C-A	new A	con. B	con. B	con. B	C-D-B	C-A	B-A	B-A	B-A
Papyri											
𝔓74	X[vid]			X				X	X	X[vid]	X[vid]

Variant	2.30	2.37	2.43	2.44	2.47–3.1	3.6	3.14	3.21	3.22[1]	3.22[2]	3.25
Rating	con. B	B-A	con. C	D-A	con. B	B-D-C	new A	C-B	con. B	con. C	con. C
Papyri											
𝔓74		X[vid]	v3	X	X[vid]		X	X	X[vid]		X
𝔓91					X[vid]						

Variant	4.1	4.6	4.8	4.10	4.12	4.24	4.25	4.33	5.3	5.16	5.17
Rating	C-B	B-C-A	C-B	con. A	con. A	con. B	D-C	con. C	C-B	C-B	new A
Papyri											
𝔓8								X	X		
𝔓45											X
𝔓74		X	X	X	X[vid]	X	X		v2	X	X

Variant	5.28	5.29	5.32[1]	5.33	5.37[1]	5.39	6.3	6.7	7.16	7.17	7.18
Rating	con. C	new A	C-B	C-B	B-A	new A	con. C	con. B	D-C	C-B	con. C
Papyri											
𝔓33+58											X[vid]
𝔓45										v3	v2
𝔓74	v2	X	X[vid]		X	X	v5	X	v2	X	X

Variant	7.19	7.38	7.46	8.5	8.10	8.18	8.24	8.36	8.39	9.12	9.29
Rating	con. C	con. B	C-B	new C	B-A	C-B	new A	con. A	new A	con. C	new A
Papyri											
𝔓45						v2		X	X		
𝔓74	v2	v2	X	X	X	v2	X	X	X	v3	X

Variant	9.31	10.5	10.11	10.12	10.16	10.19	10.24	10.30	10.32	10.33[2]	10.36
Rating	B-A	con. B	con. C	con. B	C-B	C-B	con. C	D-B	C-B	con. C	con. C
Papyri											
𝔓45			v4		v2				X	X	
𝔓50								v2			
𝔓74	X		X	X	X	X	v2	X	X	v2	X

Variant	10.37	10.40	10.48	11.2	11.11	11.12	11.17[1]	11.17[2]	11.20	11.22	11.23
Rating	new B	con. C	C-B	new A	con. C	con. C	new A	new A	con. C	new C	con. B
Papyri											
𝔓45	v3			X	v2	v4					
𝔓74	v2	v2	X	X	X	(X)	X	X	v2	v2	X

Variant	11.28	12.10	12.23	12.25	13.18	13.19	13.20	13.23	13.25	13.26	13.27
Rating	new A	new A	new A	D-C	D-C	C-B	D-C	con. B	new B	con. B	new A
Papyri											
𝔓45									v2	v2	X
𝔓74	X	X	X	v3	v2	X	X	X	X	X	X

Variant	13.33[1]	13.33[2]	13.40	13.42[1]	13.42[2]	13.43[1]	13.43[2]	13.44	13.45	13.48	14.25
Rating	D-C	D-B	C-B	con. A	C-B	new A	new A	con. C	con. B	con. C	new B
Papyri											
𝔓45										X	
𝔓74	v2	X	X	X	X	X	X	X	X	X	v3

Variant	15.2	15.6	15.7¹	15.12	vv.17-18	15.20¹	15.20²	15.20³	15.23²	15.24¹	15.24²
Rating	new A	new A	new A	new A	new B	B-A	con. C	con. A	con. B	con. C	B-A
Papyri											
𝔓33									X	X	X
𝔓45		X^vid	v3			v3	X	X			X^vid
𝔓74	X	X	X	X	v4	X	v2	X	X	X	X

Variant	15.25	15.29¹	15.29²	15.29³	15.33	15.40	15.41	16.7	16.10	16.11	16.12
Rating	con. C	con. B	B-A	B-A	B-A	new B	new A	new A	con. B	new B	con. D
Papyri											
𝔓33			X	X							
𝔓45	X^vid					v2	X				
𝔓74		v2	X	v2	X	X	v2	X	X	X	v2

Variant	16.13	16.17	16.32	16.35¹	16.35²	16.36	16.39	17.3	17.4¹	17.4²	17.13
Rating	D-C	con. B	con. B	new A	new A	B-A	new A	D-C	new B	B-A	con. B
Papyri											
𝔓45			X	X	X	X^vid	X^vid				v3
𝔓74	v4	X	X	X	X	X	X	v3	v2	X	X

Variant	17.26	17.27¹	17.28	17.31	18.1	18.3	18.5	18.7	18.8	18.17	18.19¹
Rating	D-B	C-A	C-A	new A	con. B	con. B	con. B	D-C	new A	C-B	con. B
Papyri											
𝔓41				X	X						
𝔓74	X	X	v2	X	X	X	X		X	X	v2

Variant	18.21	18.25	18.26	19.1	19.9	19.20	19.28	19.33	19.37	19.39	19.40
Rating	B-A	B-A	con. C	new A	con. B	C-B	new A	con. B	con. B	C-B	D-C
Papyri											
𝔓38				v2							
𝔓41		v2									
𝔓74	X	X^vid	X	X	X	v2	X	X	X	X	v2

Variant	20.4¹	20.4²	20.4³	20.15	20.21	20.28¹	20.28²	20.32	21.1	21.8	21.13
Rating	C-B	con. B	C-B	C-B	C-B	con. C	B-A	con. B	C-A	con. A	con. B
Papyri											
𝔓41				X^vid					v2		
𝔓74	X	X	X	X	v2	v2	X	X	(X)	X	v2

Variant	vv.16-17	21.22	21.25¹	21.25²	21.25³	22.9	22.12	22.26	23.12	23.29	23.30¹
Rating	new A	C-B	con. C	C-B	C-B	C-B	C-B	C-A	con. B	new A	C-B
Papyri											
𝔓41							v3				
𝔓48									v3	v2	
𝔓74	X	v2	X	X	(X)	X	X	X	X	X	X

Variant	23.30²	24.6-8	24.20	24.24	24.27	25.18	26.16	26.28	27.5	27.14	27.16
Rating	C-B	D-B	C-B	C-B	new A	con. C	con. C	B-A	B-A	con. B	con. B
Papyri											
𝔓74		X	X	X	X	v2	v2	X	X	X	X

Variant	27.35	27.37	27.39	27.41	28.1	28.13	28.16	28.19	28.25	28.28	28.31
Rating	new A	con. B	B-A	con. C	B-A	D-C	B-A	new A	con. B	B-A	new A
Papyri											
𝔓74	X			X		v2	X^vid		X	X	X

Variants Deleted from Acts in the UBSGNT[4]

Variant	1.9	1.18	1.26[2]	2.7	3.13	5.32[2]	5.37[2]	6.9	7.32	9.4	9.5-6
Rating	con. B	con. A	con. A	con. B	con. C	con. B	con. C	con. B	con. C	con. A	con. A
Papyri											
𝔓8									X		
𝔓45						X	v2			X[vid]	
𝔓74				X	X		X	X	X	X[vid]	X

Variant	10.17	10.33[1]	11.9	12.18	13.14	14.18	14.19[1]	14.19[2]	15.7[2]	15.18	15.23[1]
Rating	con. C	con. C	con. C	con. C	con. B	C-B	con. C	con. C	con. B	con. C	con. B
Papyri											
𝔓45			X	X	X	X[vid]	(X)	X[vid]			X[vid]
𝔓74	X	X	X	X	X	X	X[vid]	X	X	v6	X

Variant	17.14	17.27[2]	17.30	18.19[2]	vv.21-22	19.2	20.5	20.13	21.20	21.23	22.13
Rating	con. B	con. C	con. C	con. C	con. B	con. B	con. C	B-C	con. B	con. D	con. C
Papyri											
𝔓38						v2					
𝔓41			X			v2		v5			v2
𝔓74	X	X	X	v5	X	X	X	X	(X)	X	X

Variant	23.20	23.28	24.15	25.13	27.27	27.34	28.14
Rating	con. C	con. C	B-A	con. B	con. D	con. B	con. C
Papyri							
𝔓8							
𝔓48		v2					
𝔓74	v2	X	X	X	X	X	X

Papyri Evidence in Exceptional Variants (UBSGNT[4])

Variant	Mt 14.3	Mk 1.41	Mk 5.21	Mk 10.19	Mk 13.33	Lk 6.4[1]	Lk 6.10	Lk 7.10	Lk 7.39	Lk 9.55-56	Lk 12.27
Rating	C-B-A	C-D-B	B-D-C	C-A	D-C-B	C-A	C-A	C-A	C-A	C-A	D-B
Papyri											
𝔓4							X				
𝔓45			v2							X	X
𝔓75									X	X	X

Variant	Lk 19.25	Lk 22.43-44	Lk 22.62	Lk 23.15	Lk 23.34	Lk 24.3	Lk 24.6	Lk 24.12	Lk 24.36	Lk 24.40	Lk 24.47[1]
Rating	D-C-A	C-A	C-A	C-A	C-A	D-B	D-B	D-B	D-B	D-B	D-B
Papyri											
𝔓69		(X[vid])									
𝔓75		X	X	X	X	X	X	X	X	X	X

Variant	Lk 24.51	Lk 24.52	Jn 3.13	Jn 4.9	Jn 7.10	Jn 8.16	Jn 8.34	Jn 12.8	Jn 12.32	Jn 13.37	Ac 1.11
Rating	D-B	D-B	A-C-B	C-A	B-D-C	C-A	C-A	C-A	D-B	C-A	C-A
Papyri											
𝔓39						X					
𝔓63				X							
𝔓66			X	X	X	X	X	X	v2	X	
𝔓75	X	X	X	X	X	X	X	v2	X[vid]		
𝔓76				X							

Variant	Ac 2.16	Ac 2.18[1]	Ac 2.44	Ac 3.6	Ac 4.6	Ac 10.30	Ac 13.33[2]	Ac 17.26	Ac 17.27	Ac 17.28	Ac 21.1
Rating	C-D-B	C-A	D-A	B-D-C	B-C-A	D-B	D-B	D-B	C-A	C-A	C-A
Papyri											
𝔓41											v2
𝔓50						v2					
𝔓45							v5				
𝔓74		X	X		X	X	X	X	X	v2	(X)

Variant	Ac 22.26	Ac 24.6-8	Rm 3.25	Rm 5.1	Rm 8.2	Rm 8.21	Rm 8.23	Rm 11.31	Rm 13.1	Rm 16.27	1 Cor 1.13
Rating	C-B-A	D-B	B-D-C	C-A	C-D-B	C-A	C-A	B-D-C	C-A	C-A	C-B-A
Papyri											
𝔓40			X[vid]								
𝔓46					X		v2	v2	v2	X	v2
𝔓61										v2	
𝔓74	X	X									

Variant	1 Cor 1.14	1 Cor 11.29[1]	1 Cor 11.29[2]	2 Cor 1.10[1]	2 Cor 1.12	2 Cor 3.2	2 Cor 12.1[1]	2 Cor 12.1[2]	2 Cor 12.7[2]	Gal 1.15	Eph 5.22
Rating	B-D-C	C-A	C-A	D-B	D-B	B-C-A	B-C-A	B-C-A	D-C-B	B-D-C	D-C-B
Papyri											
𝔓46		X	X	v2	v2	X	X	X	X	v2	X

Variant	Eph 6.12	Php 1.11	Php 1.14	2 Th 3.18	1 Tim 6.7	1 Tim 6.21	Hb 12.18	Hb 13.21[3]	Hb 13.25	Jm 1.3	Jm 1.12
Rating	D-B	C-B-A	D-B	C-A	C-A	C-A	D-C-B	C-B-A	C-A	C-B-A	C-B-A
Papyri											
𝔓23											X
𝔓46	v2	v4	X				X	X	X		
𝔓74										X[vid]	

Variant	Jm 4.14[1]	Jm 4.14[3]	Jm 5.20[1]	1 Pt 1.7	1 Pt 1.22[1]	1 Pt 3.18[1]	1 Pt 3.21	1 Pt 5.11[2]	1 Pt 5.14[2]	2 Pt 1.3	2 Pt 2.13[3]
Rating	D-C-B	D-C-D-C	D-C-B	C-B-A	C-A	D-B	C-A	C-A	C-A	D-B	D-C-B
Papyri											
𝔓72				v2	X	v2	v3	X		v2	X
𝔓74			v4	X							

Variant	1Jn 2.20	1Jn 3.5	1Jn 3.14	2Jn 1.3	Rv 5.9	Rv 5.10[2]	Rv 6.17	Rv 13.17	Rv 20.9	Rv 21.3[1]
Rating	D-B	C-A	C-A	C-B-A	C-A	C-A	C-A	C-A	C-A	D-B
Papyri										
𝔓47							X			

The second group of tables which follow are based upon the letter-rating categories developed in Chapter 2, Section 3, and are similar to those given in Appendix III. However, the tables in this appendix more specifically record the citation of papyri within each letter-rating category and, only those papyri within the first variant option of an entire variant unit (i.e. the variant reading or option that appears in the *UBSGNT*[4] text). The primary concern of these tables is to analyze whether the presence of papyri within a variant affects the type of upgrading, and therefore the type of classification that variant receives. The statistics compiled here are straight-forward, given that one understands the letter-rating classifications described in Chapter 2, Section 3. It should be noted that there are a number of small differences between the categories used in these tables and those used in Appendix III and

Chapter 2, Section 3. In order for a variant to be counted in the tables given in this appendix, it must be present in the *UBSGNT*[4]. In Appendix III, and in Chapter 2, Section 3, some variants that do not appear in the *UBSGNT*[4] are still recorded in categories such as 'Number of Variants with Consistent Ratings' and 'Total number of Variants Referenced'.

The Gospel of Luke and the book of Acts, in their entirety, are represented in the following tables. The number of variants that fall under each category and sub-category are broken down into those that have papyri cited as witnesses and those without papyri citations. For example, within the Gospel of Luke, and under the category 'Number of Variants with Ratings Improving One Step', one can observe that there are thirteen variants improving from a *D* letter-rating to a *C* letter-rating. Nine of these variants do not have papyri manuscripts cited as a witness (designated as '9w/o', which simply means nine are 'without' papyri citations) while four do have papyri manuscripts cited as a witness (designated as '4w', which simply means four 'with' papyri citations). After a similar consideration of the *C-B*, and *B-A* sub-categories, one can conclude that there are 73 variants that experience a one-step upgrade in the Gospel of Luke within the *UBSGNT*[4]. As the conclusion states, of these 73 variants, 45 (or 62%) have papyri cited as witnesses. Each category follows in a similar fashion allowing one to analyze which types of categories variants with papyri cited as witnesses fall into.

Papyri Presence in Specific Categories of Letter-Ratings
within the Gospel of Luke and in the UBSGNT[4]

NUMBER OF VARIANTS WITH RATINGS IMPROVING ONE STEP:
D - C   =   9w/o, 4w = 13
C - B   =   13w/o, 27w = 40
B - A   =   6w/o, 14w = 20
Conclusion: Out of 73 variants with one-step improvement, 45 (62%) have papyri cited as a witness.

NUMBER OF VARIANTS WITH RATINGS IMPROVING TWO STEPS:
D - B   =   0w/o, 9w = 9
C - A   =   2w/0, 9w = 9
Conclusion: Out of 18 variants with two-step improvement, 16 (89%) have papyri cited as a witness.

NUMBER OF VARIANTS WITH RATINGS IMPROVING THREE STEPS:
D - A   =   1w/o, 0w = 1
Conclusion: Out of 1 variant with three-step improvement, 0 (0%) have papyri cited as a witness.

NUMBER OF VARIANTS WITH RATINGS DECREASING ONE STEP:
A - B   =   0
B - C   =   0
C - D   =   0

NUMBER OF VARIANTS WITH RATINGS DECREASING TWO STEPS:
A - C   =   0
B - D   =   0

NUMBER OF VARIANTS WITH RATINGS DECREASING THREE STEPS:
A - D   =   0

NUMBER OF VARIANTS WITH CONSISTENT RATINGS IN UBSGNT^4:
A = 2w/o, 4w = 6
B = 5w/o, 14w = 19
C = 14w/o, 15w = 29
D = 0w/o, 0w = 0
Conclusion: Out of 54 consistent variants, 33 (61%) have papyri cited as a witness.

NUMBER OF VARIANTS WITH FLUCTUATING RATINGS IN UBSGNT^4: 0w/o, 2w = 2
Conclusion: Out of 2 fluctuating variants, 2 (100%) have papyri cited as a witness.

NUMBER OF NEW VARIANTS ADDED INTO THE UBSGNT^4:
A = 5w/o, 4w = 9
B = 3w/o, 5w = 8
C = 2w/o, 0w = 2
D = 0w/o, 0w = 0
Conclusion: Out of 19 new variants added, 9 (47%) have papyri cited as a witness.

NUMBER OF OLD VARIANTS DROPPED OUT OF UBSGNT^4: 15w/o, 14w = 29
Conclusion: Out of 29 variants dropped out, 14 (48%) have papyri cited as a witness.

TOTAL NUMBER OF VARIANTS REFERENCED IN UBSGNT^4: 62w/o, 105w = 167
Conclusion: Out of 167 variants displayed in the *UBSGNT^4* text of Luke, 105 (63%) have papyri cited as a witness in the first variant option of a variant unit (i.e. the variant reading or option that appears in the *UBSGNT^4* text).

Papyri Presence in Specific Categories of Letter-Ratings within the Book of Acts and in the UBSGNT^4

NUMBER OF VARIANTS WITH RATINGS IMPROVING ONE STEP:
D - C = 9w/o, 2w = 11
C - B = 7w/o, 26w = 33
B - A = 2w/o, 21w = 23
Conclusion: Out of 67 variants with one-step improvement, 49 (73%) have papyri cited as a witness.

NUMBER OF VARIANTS WITH RATINGS IMPROVING TWO STEPS:
D - B = 0w/o, 4w = 4
C - A = 2w/o, 4w = 6
Conclusion: Out of 10 variants with two-step improvement, 8 (80%) have papyri cited as a witness.

NUMBER OF VARIANTS WITH RATINGS IMPROVING THREE STEPS:
D - A = 0w/o, 1w = 1
Conclusion: Out of 1 variant with three-step improvement, 1 (100%) has papyri cited as a witness.

NUMBER OF VARIANTS WITH RATINGS DECREASING ONE STEP:
A - B = 0
B - C = 0
C - D = 0

NUMBER OF VARIANTS WITH RATINGS DECREASING TWO STEPS:
A - C = 0
B - D = 0

NUMBER OF VARIANTS WITH RATINGS DECREASING THREE STEPS:
A - D = 0

NUMBER OF VARIANTS WITH CONSISTENT RATINGS IN UBSGNT^4:
A = 0w/o, 6w = 6
B = 11w/o, 25w = 36
C = 12w/o, 16w = 28
D = 1w/o, 0w = 1
Conclusion: Out of 71 consistent variants, 47 (66%) have papyri cited as a witness.

NUMBER OF VARIANTS WITH FLUCTUATING RATINGS IN UBSGNT⁴: 2w/o, 1w = 3
Conclusion: Out of 3 fluctuating variants, 1 (33%) has papyri cited as a witness.

NUMBER OF NEW VARIANTS ADDED INTO THE UBSGNT⁴:
A = 2w/o, 35w = 37
B = 4w/o, 3w = 7
C = 1w/o, 1w = 2
D = 0w/o, 0w = 0
Conclusion: Out of 46 new variants added, 39 (85%) have papyri cited as a witness.

NUMBER OF OLD VARIANTS DROPPED OUT OF UBSGNT⁴: 6w/o, 34w = 40
Conclusion: Out of 40 variants dropped out, 34 (85%) have papyri cited as a witness.

TOTAL NUMBER OF VARIANTS REFERENCED IN UBSGNT⁴: 51w/o, 147w = 198
Conclusion: Out of 198 variants displayed in the *UBSGNT⁴* text of Acts, 147 (74%) have papyri cited as a witness in the first variant option of a variant unit (i.e. the variant reading or option that appears in the *UBSGNT⁴* text).

This final group of charts closely resembles those found in Appendix V. However, whereas Appendix V records the presence of all types of manuscripts (papyri, uncials, minuscules, etc.) within selected portions of a number of books (Luke, Acts, Romans, Revelation, and 1 Peter), this appendix records the presence of papyri manuscripts alone, within the entirety of Luke and Acts. Like Appendix V, only manuscripts that are recorded in the first variant option (i.e. the variant reading or option that appears in the *UBSGNT⁴* text) are of concern here. At the same time, papyri manuscripts that are cited in alternative variant options are likewise listed. This has been done in order that a complete picture of papyri dispersal might be gained (although these papyri are included in the following charts, no figures are able to be recorded for them as they do not represent the first variant reading or option that is chosen to represent the *UBSGNT⁴* text).

As with the charts in Appendix V, the charts provided in this appendix are perhaps more difficult to understand. Therefore, a thorough explanation, similar to that in Appendix V, follows. By following the *'Rating'* row horizontally across the page, from left to right, one can see that every letter-rating (*A, B, C,* and *D*) is recorded. Listed directly under each rating is the number of total particular letter-rated variants that occur in the given book and chapters. For example, in the entire Gospel of Luke, there are 45 total *A* rated variants, 78 total *B* rated variants, 44 total *C* rated variants, and no *D* rated variants. This accounts for 167 total variants within Luke.

Underneath the *'Rating'* title, the specific type of papyri manuscript being dealt with is listed. Here, a vertical list of all the papyri manuscripts that have been cited in the given book is recorded (this is the far left column). Each papyri witness is represented by a horizontal column. Therefore, by following a straight line from left to right, information concerning any of these listed papyri manuscripts can be gained.

Underneath each of the *A, B, C,* and *D* Rated Variants headings, there are three vertical columns, *'COL 1'*, *'COL 2'*, and *'COL 3'*. Each column represents the identical type of statistic under each group of rated variants.

- *COL 1* indicates the number of times that a papyri manuscript occurs in all the *A* rated variants, *B* rated variants, *C* rated variants, and *D* rated variants, respectively. One would explain this column in the following manner: *Papyri*

Manuscript X occurs in 25 out of a possible 45 A rated variants within the Book of Luke.

- *COL 2* indicates the percentage that a given manuscript occurs in *A, B, C,* or *D* rated variants. This column simply takes the number recorded in *COL 1* and divides it by the total number of *A, B, C,* or *D* rated variants.[1] All percentage numbers listed as 70 percent and over appear in bold type. This is to help the reader distinguish between more and less frequently cited manuscripts. One would explain this column in the following manner: *Papyri Manuscript X occurs in 89 percent of all the A rated variants cited within the book of Acts.*

- *COL 3* indicates the percentage that a given manuscript occurs in an *A, B, C,* or *D* rated variant, compared with its occurrence in the other three letter-rated variants. This column is calculated by dividing *COL 1* figures by *COL 4* figures. One would explain this column in the following manner: *Manuscript X occurs in 96 out of a total 167 rated variants in the Gospel of Luke. It occurs as an A rated variant 26 percent of the time, as a B rated variant 57 percent of the time, as a C rated variant 17 percent of the time, and as a D rated variant 0 percent of the time. Thus accounting for 100 percent of its occurrences.*

- *COL 4* (located at the far right margin) indicates the total number of variants that have the particular manuscript cited as a witness. Or, one could say it indicates the total number of times a given manuscript is cited in the given book. It is calculated by adding all four *A, B, C,* and *D COL 1* figures together (the box in the top right hand corner records the total number of variants in the particular book, calculated by adding all *A, B, C,* and *D* rated variants together). One would explain this column in the following manner: *Manuscript X is cited in 96 out of 167 variants in the Gospel of Luke.*

Examples

$\mathfrak{P}^{75}$ is listed as a papyri manuscript and is located within the Gospel of Luke (as seen in the chart entitled, '*Percentages Showing Important Papyri Manuscripts in the Gospel of Luke (UBSGNT⁴)*'). If one locates this manuscript in the extreme left hand column, and follows a horizontal line from left to right, the following data can be determined. *COL 1* figures will be dealt with first. Under the '*A Rated Variants*' heading, there are 45 total *A* rated variants in the Gospel of Luke. Under '*COL 1*', beneath the '*A Rated Variants*' heading, $\mathfrak{P}^{75}$ is cited in 25 of these 45 variants. Under the '*B Rated Variants*' heading, there are 78 total *B* rated variants in the Gospel of Luke. Under '*COL 1*', beneath the '*B Rated Variants*' heading, $\mathfrak{P}^{75}$ is cited in 55 of these 78 variants. Under the '*C Rated Variants*' heading, there are 44 total *C* rated variants in the Gospel of Luke. Under '*COL 1*', beneath the '*C Rated Variants*' heading, $\mathfrak{P}^{75}$ is cited in 16 of these 44 variants. And finally, under the

---

1. As in previous percentage charts listed in this monograph, these figures have been either rounded up or rounded down based on the first decimal place.

'*D Rated Variants*' heading, there are no *D* rated variants in the Gospel of Luke. Under '*COL 1*', beneath the '*D Rated Variants*' heading, $\mathfrak{P}^{75}$ is cited, obviously, in no *D* rated variants. Adding together the number of all *A*, *B*, *C*, and *D* rated variants that are listed in the Gospel of Luke gives the total number of rated variants that occur as a whole (45 [*A*] + 78 [*B*] + 44 [*C*] + 0 [*D*] = 167 total variants in Luke). By adding all four *COL 1* figures together, we arrive at our *COL 4* figure. This records the total number of variants (out of 167 in this particular book) that have $\mathfrak{P}^{75}$ cited as a witness (25 [*A-COL1*] + 55 [*B-COL1*] + 16 [*C-COL1*] + 0 [*D-COL1*] = 96 out of 167 variants have $\mathfrak{P}^{75}$ cited).

Under '*COL 2*', beneath the '*A Rated Variants*' heading, $\mathfrak{P}^{75}$ occurs in 56 percent of all the *A* rated variants in the Gospel of Luke (25 [*COL1*] ÷ 45 total *A* rated variants = 0.555 or 56%). Under '*COL 2*', beneath the '*B Rated Variants*' heading, $\mathfrak{P}^{75}$ occurs in 71 percent of all the *B* rated variants in the Gospel of Luke (55 [*COL1*] ÷ 78 total *B* rated variants = 0.705 or 75%). Under '*COL 2*', beneath the '*C Rated Variants*' heading, $\mathfrak{P}^{75}$ occurs in 36 percent of all the *C* rated variants in the Gospel of Luke (16 [*COL1*] ÷ 44 total *C* rated variants = 0.363 or 36%). Under '*COL 2*', beneath the '*D Rated Variants*' heading, $\mathfrak{P}^{75}$ occurs in 0 percent, or no *D* rated variants.

COL 3 calculations are the last to be described. Under *COL3*, beneath the '*A Rated Variants*' heading, the figure 26 percent is given (25 [*COL1*] ÷ 96 [*COL4*] = 0.260 or 26%). Under *COL3*, beneath the '*B Rated Variants*' heading, the figure 57 percent is given (55 [*COL1*] ÷ 96 [*COL4*] = 0.572 or 57%). Under *COL3*, beneath the '*C Rated Variants*' heading, the figure 17 percent is given (16 [*COL1*] ÷ 96 [*COL4*] = 0.166 or 17%). Under *COL3*, beneath the '*D Rated Variants*' heading, the figure 0 percent is given (0 [*COL1*] ÷ 96 [*COL4*] = 0.0 or 0%). Therefore, $\mathfrak{P}^{75}$ occurs in 96 out of a total 167 rated variants in the Gospel of Luke; $\mathfrak{P}^{75}$ occurs in *A* rated variants 26 percent of the time, *B* rated variants 57 percent of the time, *C* rated variants 17 percent of the time, and *D* rated variants 0 percent of the time, thus reaching 100 percent of its total occurrences.

Percentages Showing Important Papyri Manuscripts in
the Gospel of Luke (UBSGNT⁴)

Quality	Above Average or Stronger Variants												167 total
Rating	A Rated Variants (45 Possible Total)			B Rated Variants (78 Possible Total)			C Rated Variants (44 Possible Total)			D Rated Variants (0 Possible Total)			variants in Luke
Papyri	COL 1	COL 2	COL 3	COL 1	COL 2	COL 3	COL 1	COL 2	COL 3	COL 1	COL 2	COL 3	COL 4
	# of times in A vrnts	% in A vrnts	% as A to B,C,D	# of times in B vrnts	% in B vrnts	% as B to A,C,D	# of times in C vrnts	% in C vrnts	% as C to A,B,D	# of times in D vrnts	% in D vrnts	% as D to A,B,C	# of variants ms as a witness
$\mathfrak{P}$3	0	0%	0%	0	0%	0%	0	0%	0%	0	0%	0%	0
$\mathfrak{P}$4	5	11%	50%	4	5%	40%	1	2%	10%	0	0%	0%	10
$\mathfrak{P}$45	5	11%	28%	7	9%	39%	6	14%	33%	0	0%	0%	18
$\mathfrak{P}$69	1	2%	100%	0	0%	0%	0	0%	0%	0	0%	0%	1
$\mathfrak{P}$75	25	56%	26%	55	71%	57%	16	36%	17%	0	0%	0%	96

Percentages Showing Important Papyri Manuscripts in
the Book of Acts (UBSGNT⁴)

Quality	*Above Average or Stronger Variants*						*Below Average or Weaker Variants*						*198 total*
Rating	*A Rated Variants (74 Possible Total)*			*B Rated Variants (81 Possible Total)*			*C Rated Variants (42 Possible Total)*			*D Rated Variants (1 Possible Total)*			*variants in Acts*
Papyri	COL 1 # of times in A vrnts	COL 2 % in A vrnts	COL 3 % as A to B,C,D	COL 1 # of times in B vrnts	COL 2 % in B vrnts	COL 3 % as B to A,C,D	COL 1 # of times in C vrnts	COL 2 % in C vrnts	COL 3 % as C to A,B,D	COL 1 # of times in D vrnts	COL 2 % in D vrnts	COL 3 % as D to A,B,C	COL 4 # of variants with ms as a witness
𝔓8	0	0%	0%	1	1%	50%	1	2%	50%	0	0%	0%	2
𝔓33+ 58	3	4%	50%	1	1%	17%	2	5%	33%	0	0%	0%	6
𝔓38	0	0%	0%	0	0%	0%	0	0%	0%	0	0%	0%	0
𝔓41	1	1%	33%	2	2%	67%	0	0%	0%	0	0%	0%	3
𝔓45	13	18%	68%	2	2%	11%	4	10%	21%	0	0%	0%	19
𝔓48	0	0%	0%	0	0%	0%	0	0%	0%	0	0%	0%	0
𝔓50	0	0%	0%	0	0%	0%	0	0%	0%	0	0%	0%	0
𝔓74	66	**89%**	47%	59	**73%**	42%	15	36%	11%	0	0%	0%	140
𝔓91	0	0%	0%	1	1%	100%	0	0%	0%	0	0%	0%	1

BIBLIOGRAPHY

Aland, B., K. Aland, J. Karavidopoulos, C.M. Martini, and B.M. Metzger (eds.), *The Greek New Testament* (London: United Bible Societies, 4th edn, 1993).

Aland, K., 'The Significance of the Papyri for Progress in New Testament Research', in J.P. Hyatt (ed.), *The Bible in Modern Scholarship: Papers Read at the 100th Meeting of the Society for Biblical Literature, December 28-30, 1964* (Nashville/New York: Abingdon, 1965), pp. 325-46.

—'The Greek New Testament: Its Present and Future Editions', *JBL* 87 (1968), pp. 179-86.

—*Synopsis Quattuor Evangeliorum* (Stuttgart: Württembergische Bibelanstalt Stuttgart, 1976).

Aland, K., and B. Aland, *The Text of the New Testament* (Grand Rapids: Eerdmans; Leiden: Brill, 2nd edn, 1989).

Aland, K., M. Black, B.M. Metzger, and A. Wikgren (eds.), *The Greek New Testament* (London: United Bible Societies, 1st edn, 1966).

Aland, K., M. Black, C.M. Martini, B.M. Metzger, and A. Wikgren (eds.), *The Greek New Testament* (London: United Bible Societies, 2nd edn, 1968).

—*The Greek New Testament* (London: United Bible Societies, 3rd edn, 1975).

—*The Greek New Testament* (London: United Bible Societies, 3rd corr. edn, 1983).

American and British Committees of the International Greek New Testament Project (ed.), *The New Testament in Greek: The Gospel according to St Luke, Part One, Chapters 1–12* (Oxford: Oxford University Press, 1984).

Anonymous, 'Notes of Recent Exposition', *ExpTim* 77 (1966), pp. 353-54.

Bengel, J.A., *Novum Testamentum Graecum* (Tübingen: George Cottae, 1734).

Birdsall, J.N., 'The Text of the Fourth Gospel: Some Current Questions', *EvQ* (1957), p. 199.

—'The Recent History of New Testament Textual Criticism', *ANRW* II.26.1 (1992), pp. 99-197.

Black, D.A., and D.S. Dockery (eds.), *New Testament Criticism and Interpretation* (Grand Rapids: Zondervan, 1991).

Black, M., 'The Greek New Testament', *SJT* 19 (1966), pp. 486-88.

—'The United Bible Societies' Greek New Testament Evaluated—A Reply', *BT* 28 (1977), pp. 116-20.

Black, M., and W.A. Smalley (eds.), *On Language, Culture, and Religion: In Honor of Eugene A. Nida* (The Hague/Paris: Mouton, 1974).

Bruce, F.F., *The Book of Acts* (Grand Rapids: Eerdmans, rev. edn, 1988).

—*The Books and the Parchments* (London/Glasgow: Harper & Row, rev. edn, 1991).

Burkitt, F.C., 'Introduction', in P.M. Barnard, *The Biblical Text of Clement of Alexandria in the Four Gospels and the Acts of the Apostles* (Texts and Studies 5; Cambridge: Cambridge University Press, 1899), pp. vii-xix.

Carson, D.A., *The King James Version Debate: A Plea for Realism* (Grand Rapids: Baker, 1979).

Clark, A.C., *The Primitive Text of the Gospels and Acts* (Oxford: Oxford University Press, 1914).

Clark, K.W., 'The Effect of Recent Textual Criticism upon New Testament Studies', in W.D. Davies and D. Daube (eds.), *The Background of the New Testament and its Eschatology* (Cambridge: Cambridge University Press, 1954), pp. 27-50.

—'The Theological Relevance of Textual Variation in Current Criticism of the Greek New Testament', *JBL* 85 (1966), pp. 1-16.

—'Today's Problems with the Critical Text of the New Testament', in J.C. Rylaarsdam (ed.), *Transitions in Biblical Scholarship* (Essays in Divinity 6; Chicago/London: University of Chicago Press, 1968), pp. 157-69.

Clegg, F., *Simple Statistics* (Cambridge: Cambridge University Press, 1991).

Colwell, E.C., 'The Complex Character of the Later Byzantine Text of the Gospels', *JBL* 54 (1935), pp. 211-21.

—'Hort Redivivus: A Plea and a Program', in *Studies in Methodology in Textual Criticism of the New Testament* (NTTS 9; Leiden: Brill, 1969), pp. 148-71.

—*Studies in Methodology in Textual Criticism of the New Testament* (NTTS 9; Leiden: Brill, 1969).

Dahl, N.A., 'The Passion Narrative in Matthew', in *Jesus in the Memory of the Early Church* (Minneapolis, MN: Augsburg, 1976), pp. 37-51.

Drummond, J., *The Transmission of the Text of the New Testament* (London: The Sunday School Association, 1909).

Edwards, E.G., 'On Using the Textual Apparatus of the UBS Greek New Testament', *BT* 28 (1977), pp. 120-42.

Ellingworth, P., 'The UBS *Greek New Testament*, Fourth Revised Edition: A User's Response', *NTS* 42 (1996), pp. 282-87.

Elliott, J.K., 'The United Bible Societies' Greek New Testament: An Evaluation', *NovT* 15 (1973), pp. 278-300.

—'The United Bible Societies' Textual Commentary Evaluated', *NovT* 17 (1975), pp. 130-50.

—'The Third Edition of the Bible Societies' Greek New Testament', *NovT* 20 (1978), pp. 242-77.

—'The United Bible Societies' Greek New Testament: A Short Examination of the Third Edition', *BT* 30 (1979), pp. 135-38.

—'Textual Criticism, Assimilation and the Synoptic Gospels', *NTS* 26 (1980), pp. 231-42.

—'The Citation of Manuscripts in Recent Printed Editions of the Greek New Testament', *NovT* 25 (1983), pp. 97-132.

—'The Greek New Testament (Review of Third Corrected Edition)', *NovT* 26 (1984), pp. 377-79.

—'Keeping Up With Recent Studies XV: New Testament Textual Criticism', *ExpTim* 99 (1987), pp. 40-45.

—*A Survey of Manuscripts Used in Editions of the Greek New Testament* (Leiden: Brill, 1987).

—'Can We Recover the Original Text of the New Testament: An Examination of the Rôle of Thoroughgoing Eclecticism', in J.K. Elliott, *Essays and Studies in New Testament Textual Criticism* (FN 3; Cordoba: Ediciones El Almendro, 1992), pp. 17-43.

—*Essays and Studies in New Testament Textual Criticism* (FN 3; Cordoba: Ediciones El Almendro, 1992).

—'The New Testament in Greek: Two New Editions', *TLZ* 119 (1994), pp. 493-96.

—'The Fourth Edition of the United Bible Societies' Greek New Testament', *TRev* 90 (1994), cols. 9-20.

—'The Twentyseventh Edition of Nestle-Aland's Novum Testamentum Graece', *TRev* 90 (1994), cols. 19-24.

Elliott, J.K. (ed.), *The Principles and Practice of New Testament Textual Criticism: Collected Essays of G.D. Kilpatrick* (BETL 96; Leuven: Leuven University Press/Peeters, 1990).

Epp, E.J., 'New Testament Textual Criticism Past, Present, and Future: Reflections on the Alands' *Text of the New Testament*', *HTR* 82 (1989), pp. 213-29.

—'Decision Points in Past, Present, and Future New Testament Textual Criticism', in E.J. Epp and G.D. Fee, *Studies in the Theory and Method of New Testament Textual Criticism* (SD 45; Grand Rapids: Eerdmans, 1993), pp. 17-44.

—'Toward the Clarification of the Term "Textual Variant"', in E.J. Epp and G.D. Fee, *Studies in the Theory and Method of New Testament Textual Criticism* (SD 45; Grand Rapids: Eerdmans, 1993), pp. 47-61.

—'The Twentieth-Century Interlude in New Testament Textual Criticism', in E.J. Epp and G.D. Fee, *Studies in the Theory and Method of New Testament Textual Criticism* (SD 45; Grand Rapids: Eerdmans, 1993), pp. 83-108.

—'A Continuing Interlude in New Testament Textual Criticism', in E.J. Epp and G.D. Fee, *Studies in the Theory and Method of New Testament Textual Criticism* (SD 45; Grand Rapids: Eerdmans, 1993), pp. 109-23.

—'The Eclectic Method in New Testament Textual Criticism: Solution or Symptom?', in E.J. Epp and G.D. Fee, *Studies in the Theory and Method of New Testament Textual Criticism* (SD 45; Grand Rapids: Eerdmans, 1993), pp. 141-73.

—'The Significance of the Papyri for Determining the Nature of the New Testament Text in the Second Century: A Dynamic View of Textual Transmission', in E.J. Epp and G.D. Fee, *Studies in the Theory and Method of New Testament Textual Criticism* (SD 45; Grand Rapids: Eerdmans, 1993), pp. 274-97.

Epp, E.J., and G.D. Fee, *Studies in the Theory and Method of New Testament Textual Criticism* (SD 45; Grand Rapids: Eerdmans, 1993).

Epp, E.J., and G.D. Fee (eds.), *New Testament Textual Criticism: Its Significance for Exegesis: Essays in Honour of Bruce M. Metzger* (Oxford: Clarendon Press, 1981).

Erickson, B.H., and T.A. Nosanchuck, *Understanding Data* (Philadelphia: Open University Press, 1985).

Ewert, D., *From Ancient Tablets to Modern Translations* (Grand Rapids: Zondervan, 1983).

Fee, G.D., *Papyrus Bodmer II (P^{66}): Its Textual Relationships and Scribal Characteristics* (SD 34; Salt Lake City, UT: University of Utah Press, 1968).

—'Modern Textual Criticism and the Revival of the *Textus Receptus*', *JETS* 21 (1978), pp. 19-33.

—'Modern Textual Criticism and the Majority Text: A Rejoinder', *JETS* 21 (1978), pp. 157-60.

—'Textual Criticism of the New Testament', in E.J. Epp and G.D. Fee, *Studies in the Theory and Method of New Testament Textual Criticism* (SD 45; Grand Rapids: Eerdmans, 1993), pp. 3-16.

—'On the Types, Classification, and Presentation of Textual Variation', in E.J. Epp and G.D. Fee, *Studies in the Theory and Method of New Testament Textual Criticism* (SD 45; Grand Rapids: Eerdmans, 1993), pp. 62-79.

—'Rigorous or Reasoned Eclecticism—Which?', in E.J. Epp and G.D. Fee, *Studies in the Theory and Method of New Testament Textual Criticism* (SD 45; Grand Rapids: Eerdmans, 1993), pp. 124-40.

—'The Majority Text and the Original Text of the New Testament', in E.J. Epp and G.D. Fee, *Studies in the Theory and Method of New Testament Textual Criticism* (SD 45; Grand Rapids: Eerdmans, 1993), pp. 183-208.

—'Codex Sinaiticus in the Gospel of John: A Contribution to Methodology in Establishing Textual Relationships', in E.J. Epp and G.D. Fee, *Studies in the Theory and Method of New Testament Textual Criticism* (SD 45; Grand Rapids: Eerdmans, 1993), pp. 221-43.

—'P75, P66, and Origen: The Myth of Early Textual Recension in Alexandria', in E.J. Epp and G.D. Fee, *Studies in the Theory and Method of New Testament Textual Criticism* (SD 45; Grand Rapids: Eerdmans, 1993), pp. 247-73.

Finegan, J., *Encountering New Testament Manuscripts: A Working Introduction to Textual Criticism* (Grand Rapids: Eerdmans, 1974).

Fuller, D.O. (ed.), *Which Bible?* (Grand Rapids: Grand Rapids International Publications, 5th edn, 1975).

—*True or False? The Westcott-Hort Textual Theory Examined* (Grand Rapids: Grand Rapids International Publications, 1973).

Greenlee, J.H., *Introduction to New Testament Textual Criticism* (Peabody, MA: Hendrickson, rev. edn, 1995).

—*Scribes, Scrolls, and Scripture* (Grand Rapids: Eerdmans, 1985).

Gregory, C.R., *Prolegomena* [to Tischendorf, *Novum Testamentum Graece*] (Leipzig: Hinrichs, 1894).

Greisbach, J.J., *The Four Gospels in Greek* (London: John Taylor, 1832).

Hammond, C.E., *Outlines of Textual Criticism Applied to the New Testament* (Oxford: Clarendon Press, 3rd rev. edn, 1880).

Haufe, G., 'Neues Testament: The Greek New Testament', *TLZ* 92 (1967), col. 513.

Hills, E.F., *The King James Defended! A Space-Age Defense of the Historic Christian Faith* (Des Moines, IA: Christian Research Press, 3rd rev. edn, 1978).

Hodges, Z., 'The Greek Text of the King James Version', *BSac* 125 (1968), pp. 334-45.

—'Rationalism and Contemporary New Testament Textual Criticism', *BSac* 128 (1971), pp. 27-35.

—'Modern Textual Criticism and the Majority Text: A Response', *JETS* 21 (1978), pp. 143-55.

Hodges, Z.C., and A.L. Farstad (eds.), *The Greek New Testament according to the Majority Text* (Nashville: Thomas Nelson, 1982).

Holmes, M.W., 'Textual Criticism', in D.A. Black and D.S. Dockery (eds.), *New Testament Criticism and Interpretation* (Grand Rapids: Zondervan, 1991), pp. 101-34.

Hort, A.F., *Life and Letters of Fenton John Anthony Hort* (2 vols.; London: Macmillan, 1896).

Housman, A.E., *M. Manilius's Astronomicon* (5 vols.; London: Richards Press, 1930), V, p. xxxiii.

Hurtado, L.W., Review of Metzger's *Textual Commentary*, *JBL* 92 (1973), pp. 621-22.

Junack, K., 'The Reliability of the New Testament Text from the Perspective of Textual Criticism', *BT* 29 (1978), pp. 128-40.

Kenyon, F.G., *Handbook to the Textual Criticism of the New Testament* (London: Macmillan, 1912).

—*Recent Developments in the Textual Criticism of the Greek Bible* (Schweich Lectures; London: British Academy, 1933).

—*Our Bible and the Ancient Manuscripts* (London: Eyre & Spottiswoode, 4th rev. edn, 1941).

—*The Palaeography of Greek Papyri* (repr.; Chicago: Argonaut, Inc., 1970).

—*The Text of the Greek Bible* (rev. A.W. Adams; London: Duckworth, 3rd edn, 1975).

King, M.A., 'Should Conservatives Abandon Textual Criticism?', *BSac* 130 (1973), pp. 35-40.

Klijn, A.F.J., *A Survey of the Researches into the Western Text of the Gospels and Acts* (Utrecht: Kemink, 1949).

Krodel, G., 'New Manuscripts of the Greek New Testament', *JBL* 91 (1972), pp. 232-38.

Lachmann, K., and P. Buttmann, *Novum Testamentum: Graece et Latine* (2 vols.; Berlin: George Reimer, 1842–50).

Lake, K., *The Text of the New Testament* (Oxford Church Text Books; rev. Silva New; London: Rivingtons, 6th edn, 1928).

Lake, K., and R.P. Blake, 'The Text of the Gospels and the Koridethi Codex', *HTR* 16 (1923), pp. 267-86.

Lake, K., R.P. Blake, and S. New, 'The Caesarean Text of the Gospel of Mark', *HTR* 21 (1928), pp. 207-404.

Larson, S., 'The 26th Edition of the Nestle-Aland *Novum Testamentum Graece*: A Limited Examination of its Apparatus', *JSNT* 12 (1981), pp. 53-68.

Lewis, J.P., 'The Text of the New Testament', *ResQ* 27 (1984), pp. 65-74.

Markham, R.P., 'The Bible Societies' Greek Testament: The End of a Decade or Beginning of an Era', *BT* 17 (1966), pp. 106-13.

Markham, R.P., and E.A. Nida, *An Introduction to the Bible Societies' Greek New Testament* (New York: United Bible Societies, 1969).

Martini, C.M., 'Eclecticism and Atticism in the Textual Criticism of the Greek New Testament', in M. Black and W.A. Smalley (eds.), *On Language, Culture, and Religion: In Honor of Eugene A. Nida* (The Hague/Paris: Mouton, 1974), pp. 149-56.

—Review of D.E. Aune (ed.), *Studies in New Testament and Early Christian Literature: Essays in Honor of Allen P. Wikgren* (NovTSup 33; Leiden: Brill, 1972), *BT* 25 (1974), pp. 150-52.

Metzger, B.M., *Chapters in the History of New Testament Textual Criticism* (NTTS 4; Leiden: Brill, 1963).

—'Bibliographical Aids for the Study of the Manuscripts of the New Testament', *ATR* 48 (1966), pp. 339-55.

—'The Textual Criticism of the New Testament, Part 1', *ExpTim* (1967), pp. 324-27.

—'The Textual Criticism of the New Testament, Part 2', *ExpTim* (1967), pp. 372-75.

—*A Textual Commentary on the Greek New Testament* (London: United Bible Societies, 1971).

—'Patristic Evidence and the Textual Criticism of the New Testament', *NTS* 18 (1972), pp. 379-400.

—*Manuscripts of the Greek Bible: An Introduction to Greek Palaeography* (New York/Oxford: Oxford University Press, 1981).

—*The Text of the New Testament: Its Transmission, Corruption, and Restoration* (Oxford/New York: Oxford University Press, 3rd edn, 1992).

—*A Textual Commentary on the Greek New Testament* (London: United Bible Societies; Stuttgart: Deutsche Bibelgesellschaft, 2nd edn, 1994).

Moir, I.A., 'The Bible Societies' Greek New Testament', *NTS* 14 (1967), pp. 136-43.

—'Can We Risk Another "Textus Receptus"?', *JBL* 100 (1981), pp. 614-18.

Morris, C., *Quantitative Approaches in Business Studies* (London: Pitman Publishing, 3rd edn, 1993).

Neill, S., and T. Wright, *The Interpretation of the New Testament: 1861–1986* (Oxford/New York: Oxford University Press, 2nd edn, 1988).

Nestle, E., *Introduction to the Textual Criticism of the Greek New Testament* (New York: G.P. Putnam's Sons, 1901).

Nestle, E., and K. Aland, *Novum Testamentum Graece* (Stuttgart: Deutsche Bibelgesellschaft, 27th edn, 1993).

Nida, E.A., 'The "Harder Reading" in Textual Criticism: An Application of the Second Law of Thermodynamics', *BT* 32 (1981), pp. 101-107.

Omanson, R.L., 'A Perspective on the Study of the New Testament Text', *BT* 34 (1983), pp. 107-22.

Oudersluys, R.C., 'New New Testaments in Greek', *The Reformation Review* 20 (1966), pp. 41-44.

Pack, F., 'One Hundred Years since Westcott and Hort: 1881–1981', *ResQ* 26 (1983), pp. 65-79.

Parker, D., 'The Development of Textual Criticism since B.H. Streeter', *NTS* 24 (1977), pp. 149-62.

Parvis, M.M., and A.P. Wikgren, *New Testament Manuscript Studies: The Materials and the Making of a Critical Apparatus* (Chicago: University of Chicago Press, 1950).

Patrick, G.A., '1881–1981: The Centenary of the Westcott and Hort Text', *ExpTim* 92 (1981), pp. 359-64.

Pickering, W.N., *The Identity of the New Testament Text* (Nashville: Thomas Nelson, 1977).

Richards, W.L., 'An Examination of the Claremont Profile Method in the Gospel of Luke: A Study in Text-Critical Methodology', *NTS* 27 (1980), pp. 52-63.

Robertson, A.T., *An Introduction to the Textual Criticism of the New Testament* (Nashville: Broadman, 1925).

Ropes, J.H., 'The Text of Acts', in F.J. Foakes Jackson and K. Lake (eds.), *The Beginnings of Christianity: Part I, The Acts of the Apostles* (London: Macmillan, 1926), III.

Ross, J.M., 'The United Bible Societies' Greek New Testament', *JBL* 95 (1976), pp. 112-21.

—'Some Unnoticed Points in the Text of the New Testament', *NovT* 25 (1983), pp. 59-72.

Salmon, G., *Some Thoughts on the Textual Criticism of the New Testament* (London: John Murray, 1897).

Scanlin, H.P., 'Review Symposium of GNT[4]', *BT* 45 (1994), pp. 348-49.

Silva, M., 'Review Symposium of GNT[4]', *BT* 45 (1994), pp. 349-53.

Souter, A., *Text and Canon of the New Testament* (London: Duckworth, 1935).

—*Novum Testamentum Graece: Texti retractatoribus anglis adhibito brevem adnotationem criticam subiectit* (Oxford: Clarendon Press, 2nd edn, 1947).

Streeter, B.H., *The Four Gospels: A Study of Origins, Treating of the Manuscript Tradition, Sources, Authorship, and Dates* (London: Macmillan, 1924).

Sturz, H.A., *The Byzantine Text-Type and New Testament Textual Criticism* (Nashville: Thomas Nelson, 1984).

Tasker, R.V.G. (ed.), *The Greek New Testament, Being the Text Translated in the New English Bible* (Oxford: Oxford University Press; Cambridge: Cambridge University Press, 1964).

Taylor, V., *The Text of the New Testament: A Short Introduction* (London: Macmillan, 2nd edn, 1963).

Tischendorf, C., *Novum Testamentum Graece*. I–II. *Text* (3 vols.; Leipzig: Giesecke & Devrient, 8th edn, 1869–72).

Turner, E.G., *Greek Papyri: An Introduction* (Oxford: Clarendon Press, 1968).

Vaganay, L., and C. Amphoux, *An Introduction to New Testament Textual Criticism* (trans. J. Heimerdinger; Cambridge/New York: Cambridge University Press, 2nd edn, 1991 [1986]).

von Soden, H., *Die Schriften des Neuen Testaments in ihrer ältesten erreichbaren Textgestalt hergestellt auf Grund ihrer Textgeschichte* (2 vols.; Göttingen: Vandenhoeck & Ruprecht, 1902–10, 1913).

Wallace, D., 'Textual Criticism: Is it Relevant for the Bible Translator?', *Notes on Translation* 4 (1990), pp. 1-18.

Wallis, W.B., 'An Evaluation of the Bible Societies' Text of the Greek New Testament', *Bulletin of the Evangelical Theological Society* 10 (1967), pp. 111-13.

Westcott, A., *Life and Letters of Brooke Foss Westcott* (2 vols.; London: Macmillan, 1903).

Westcott, B.F., and F.J.A. Hort, *The New Testament in the Original Greek* (London: Macmillan, 1900).

—*Introduction to the New Testament in the Original Greek* (Peabody, MA: Hendrickson, repr. 1988 [1882]).

Wilson, J.M., *The Acts of the Apostles from Codex Bezae* (London: SPCK, 1923).

Wong, S., 'The United Bible Societies' Greek New Testament', [Chinese] *Jian Dao* 1 (1994), pp. 121-25.

Wright, R.L.D., *Understanding Statistics* (New York: Harcourt Brace Jovanovich, 1976).

Zuntz, G., *The Text of the Epistles: A Disquisition upon the Corpus Paulinum* (Schweich Lectures, 1946; London: British Academy, 1953).

INDEXES

INDEX OF REFERENCES

NEW TESTAMENT

INDEX OF AUTHORS

DATE DUE

			Printed in USA

Frommer's ®

9th
Edition

Philadelphia &
The Amish Country

by Jay Golan

Macmillan • USA

ABOUT THE AUTHOR

Jay Golan has been writing about travel in Europe, Asia, and the United States since college. Educated at Harvard, Oxford, and Columbia Universities, he has worked for major cultural institutions in Boston and New York for over a decade, most recently at Carnegie Hall. He and his young family live in New York City and frequently visit relatives and friends in Philadelphia.

MACMILLAN TRAVEL

A Simon & Schuster Macmillan Company
1633 Broadway
New York, NY 10019

Find us online at **http://www.mgr.com/travel**

ISBN 0-02-861168-3
ISSN 0899-3211

Editors: Robin Michaelson & Jim Moore
Production Editor: Phil Kitchel
Design by Michele Laseau
Digital Cartography by Jim Moore
Maps © copyright by Simon & Schuster, Inc.

Contents

List of Maps

AN INVITATION TO THE READER

In researching this book, I discovered many wonderful places. I'm sure you'll find others. Please tell me about them, so I can share the information with your fellow travelers in upcoming editions. If you were disappointed with a recommendation, I'd love to know that too. Please write to:

Jay Golan
Frommer's Philadelphia, 9th Edition
c/o Macmillan Travel
1633 Broadway
New York, NY 10019

AN ADDITIONAL NOTE

Please be advised that travel information is subject to change at any time—and this is especially true of prices. We therefore suggest that you write or call ahead for confirmation when making your travel plans. The author, editors, and publisher cannot be held responsible for the experiences of readers while traveling. Your safety is important to us, however, so we encourage you to stay alert and be aware of your surroundings. Keep a close eye on cameras, purses, and wallets, all favorite targets of thieves and pickpockets.

WHAT THE SYMBOLS MEAN

✪ Frommer's Favorites

Hotels, restaurants, attractions, and entertainment you should not miss.

⑤ Super-Special Values

Hotels and restaurants that offer great value for your money.

The following abbreviations are used for credit cards:

AE	American Express	EU	Eurocard
CB	Carte Blanche	JCB	Japan Credit Bank
DC	Diners Club	MC	MasterCard
DISC	Discover	V	Visa
ER	enRoute		

Introducing Philadelphia

Old history and new excitement—these are Philadelphia today. When you scratch the surface of William Penn's "Greene countrie town," you find a wealth of pleasures and pastimes.

Try these descriptions on for size: Philadelphia is the largest colonial district in the country, with dozens of treasures plus Independence National Historical Park. It boasts the most historic square mile in America, where the United States was conceived, declared, and ratified—and you can see the Liberty Bell to prove it. It offers some of the best dining values and several of the finest restaurants in America. It's a stroller's paradise of restored Georgian and Federal structures that are integrated with smart shops and contemporary row-house courts to create a working urban environment. Philadelphia is a center of professional and amateur sports, with over 7,800 acres of parkland within the city limits. It's a city filled with art, crafts, and music for every taste, with boulevards made for street fairs and parades all year long. From row-house boutiques to the Second Continental Congress's favorite tavern, from an Ivy League campus to street artists and musicians, from gleaming skyscrapers to Italian marketplaces, Philadelphia is a city of unexpected quality and pleasure.

The colonial view of Philadelphians as reflective, sophisticated, and tolerant has long been succeeded by the "Rocky" stereotype of brash, good-hearted ethnics. Of course, both characterizations have their points. There's a tremendous diversity of 1.6 million people over 129 square miles—there's a lot of distance between the boxes at the Academy of Music, the dining room of Zanzibar Blue, and the bleachers of Veterans Stadium.

Geographically, Philadelphia sits pretty. Some 60 miles inland, it's the country's busiest freshwater port, controlling the Delaware Valley. Philadelphia occupies a tongue of land at the confluence of the Delaware River—one of the largest U.S. rivers feeding into the Atlantic—and the Schuylkill River. The original settlement, and the heart of Center City today, is the band about 5 miles north that didn't dwindle into marshland in the 1600s. Since then, of course, the city has drained and used the entire tongue to the south and has exploded into the northeast and northwest. It's a natural stopping place between New York and Washington, D.C., with easy access by rail and road. And the casinos and beaches of Atlantic City, the revolutionary war sites of Valley Forge and Brandywine, the great Du Pont family mansions, and Pennsylvania Dutch country all lie within 90 minutes. In fact, 38% of the nation's population is within a $4^1/2$-hour drive from the city.

Economically, Philadelphia's a great deal too. A recent study of corporate travel showed that the city's average daily cost of lodging and meals—$132.50—was 51% of New York's, 68% of Washington's, and 78% of Boston's. Family-style travel is even more of a bargain.

1 Frommer's Favorite Philadelphia Experiences

- **Take Afternoon Tea at the Swann Lounge:** The quintessential luxury tea is held at the Four Seasons, overlooking one of the city's finest squares with its fountains on both sides.
- **Visit the Barnes Foundation:** The Barnes Foundation Gallery in Merion houses the world's most important private collection of Impressionist and early French modern paintings—for example, more Cézannes displayed than in all the museums in France put together. Try to schedule a visit around its open hours on Friday through Sunday.
- **Wander Through Fairmount Park:** Not even natives can cover this giant of urban parks, with 8,900 acres including 100 miles of trails, some virtually unchanged since Revolutionary times. We'll settle for the hundreds of flame azaleas in spring behind the Art Museum, and the dozen Georgian country mansions kept in immaculate condition.
- **Shop on First Friday:** On the first Friday of every month, the galleries, stores, and studios of Old City—just above Independence National Historical Park—remain open with refreshments until 9pm. Wander along the cobblestone streets, with stops in one of the many coffee bars and bistros.
- **Step Back in Time in Historic Philadelphia:** Everyone knows of the miraculous reclamation of this country's colonial capital, from the Liberty Bell to hundreds of row houses with their distinctive bricks and 18th-century formal gardens (and welcome benches). But the new tours, costumed town criers with free maps, and Revolutionary War–era street theater bring the experience even closer. Just wander; they'll find you.
- **Scarf Down Pretzels, Hoagies, and Philly's Famous Cheesesteaks:** Philadelphia has a rich tradition of cuisine from haute (as in the shad roe from fish caught in the Delaware River each April) to hot (the warm, soft, salty pretzels served slathered with mustard at stands all over town, or at the new Pretzel Museum on Market Street). The hoagie is something else—cold cuts, lettuce, and onions layered with oil and vinegar—along with its cousin the cheesesteak, also served in an enormous elongated bun.
- **Stroll Around Independence Square at Night:** The combination of history, elegance, and proportion among the three basic buildings that contained America's first government always induces a sense of wonder at this country's good fortune in its founding citizens. You might even feel the urge to jump aboard one of the horse-drawn carriages lined up in front of the square.
- **Listen to Hot Jazz and Blues:** There are at least half a dozen clubs with world-class, down-home, accessible, and affordable American music any night you're in town, very possibly with local sons like Grover Washington Jr. and Christian McBride.

Impressions

The question eagerly put to me by every one in Philadelphia is, "Don't you think the city greatly improved?" They seem to me to confound augmentation with improvement. It always was a fine city, since I first knew it; and it is very greatly augmented.
—William Cobbett, *A Year's Residence in the United States of America* (1817–19)

- **Tour an Open House:** If you're in the city at the right times, don't miss tours of restored mansions in Society Hill, Rittenhouse Square, or Fairmount Park for some true connoisseurship in interior design and Americana. I love the pre-Christmas season myself.
- **Check Out Penn's Landing and the Delaware Waterfront:** With the just-opened Independence Seaport Museum, historic ships, spanking-new sidewalks and streetlife, and throbbing pier lounges and discos, Philadelphia has definitively reclaimed its waterfront for tourism.
- **Breathe Deeply at the Philadelphia Flower Show:** In the last week of February, the scent-sational Flower Show—the largest and most prestigious indoor exhibition of its kind in the world—descends on the Pennsylvania Convention Center.
- **Rub Elbows at the Philadelphia Museum of Art:** It has a stupendous collection of masterpieces, period rooms, and crafts, and it's becoming one of the hottest museums in the country for special exhibitions. Look for more blockbusters like the recent Brancusi and Cézanne exhibitions. The late Wednesdays have become one of the city's hottest social scenes.
- **Cheer the Regattas Along the Schuylkill:** On all spring weekends, stand along Boathouse Row just north of the Philadelphia Museum of Art. Crews race each other every five minutes or so, with cheering friends along the riverbanks.
- **Stock Up at the Reading Terminal Market:** From Bassett's ice cream to Bain's turkey sandwiches and the food of the 12th Street Cantina, this is the century-old mother lode of unpackaged, fresh, honest-to-goodness provisions. The Amish farmers come in to sell their custards and scrapple on Wednesday through Saturday. And what could be more convenient than right underneath the Convention Center?
- **Explore South Philly:** Exuberant attitude punctuates every interchange you'll have, on a stroll with samples through the Italian Market or wandering further south, to seek out the area's great pizzas, cannoli, or famed cheesesteaks.
- **Dine on Walnut and Sydenham Streets:** Okay, it's provocative. But this particular corner near Rittenhouse Square has more world-class restaurants within mere feet—Le Bec Fin, Circa, Striped Bass, Susanna Foo, and Il Portico—than any other spot in the world. Whatever your taste or price range, you should try one of them.

2 The City Today

The 1990s have brought mixed fortunes to Philadelphia. Many of the problems that plague urban centers throughout America—homelessness, drugs, crime, and inadequate resources for public services—have hit large parts of the city and have crept into Center City. The city was technically bankrupt in 1990, and the 1995 closing of the Philadelphia Navy Yard also hit hard.

A Portrait of the Philadelphians

The waves of settlement and immigration witnessed by the area now known as Philadelphia are fascinating, starting with the Delaware or Lenape branch of the Algonquian Indians, who were found by the first European settlers from Sweden in the 1640s. Unusual tolerance, personified by Quakers, led to two separate strains of immigrants between this period and 1800. One was made up of entire European families of almost every sort—English, Scottish, Sephardic Jews, and German (*Deutsch* in German—whence the term Pennsylvania "Dutch")—who often made the decision to immigrate based on promises of cheap farmland. The other included thousands of London-based craftsmen, servants, and sailors who wanted to dwell in America's premier city.

After 1800, immigration was a push-pull thing; English commoners fled the industrialization of their countryside in the 1820s, Irish escaped from the 1840s potato famine, and waves of Germans and other central Europeans sought peace and stability throughout the 1870s. From the 1880s to the 1920s, Russians and Jews from eastern Europe, Italians, and free blacks from the American South all migrated in record numbers to the city. In recent years, Asian and Hispanic inflows have balanced the suburban outflow of descendants of earlier immigrants, creating a more multicultural Philadelphia than ever before. The classic pattern of these groups has been to stake out a section of the city as "home turf" in the first generation—South Philadelphia for Italians, South Street for Russian Jews, and North Philadelphia for blacks—and to move away from that section in later generations.

These various influences have shaped the modern city. To cite just one example, the Mummer's Parade mixes an English country-fair tradition with music of the black South of a century ago. The Philadelphia experience has not always been happy, however. The city has suffered from riots, protests, and bigotry along racial, religious, and economic lines. These have been most pronounced in times of economic distress.

The administration of Ed Rendell, first elected in 1991, has taken tremendous steps to reform waste in city government through selective privatization of services, more forceful collection of revenues (watch those parking violations!), and rooting out wasteful labor practices. Turning around the educational system under Superintendent David Hornbeck has become a major priority to retain the urban middle class. Rendell is also instilling a rejuvenated sense of community through tireless cheerleading, keeping business in town, and personal attention to major strategic areas like tourism and the arts. He won reelection in 1995 with 77% of the vote.

Unlike Portland, whose expanding economy creates new amenities for tourists and natives alike, or New York City, which is big enough to service both, Philadelphia's economy, particularly in recent years, has become more and more reliant on tourism. Recognition of this, and the resultant public and private investments based on visitors' needs, have not been easy for the city. If you go to the top of City Hall and look around, you'll see a panorama of factories, the old Navy Yard, warehouses, and docks—virtually all shuttered or turned to other uses. You'll also see block after block of row houses built by new immigrants a century ago, and whose more successful descendants have left for greener pastures. But there's also a gleaming inner Center

The Mid-Atlantic States

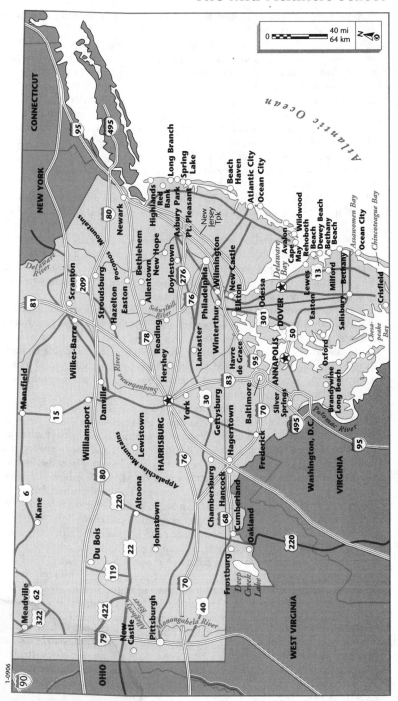

City core filled with new skyscrapers, the 1993 Pennsylvania Convention Center, and revitalized culture and streetlife.

The opening of the $522 million Pennsylvania Convention Center in June 1993, only minutes from both historic and business districts, has been tremendous for the city and its tourists. The Train Shed, Grand Hall, permanent art exhibition, and Ballroom are all breathtakingly beautiful, and it's a miracle that the historic Reading Terminal facade and its street-level Market have been preserved. The hundreds of conventions, millions of visitors, and billions of dollars projected in meeting revenues over the next decade are crucial to keeping afloat the restaurants, hotels, sights, and entertainments we recommend, after some lean years. There's appreciably more nightlife and sidewalk safety.

Pennsylvania Convention Center dollars also tie into great infrastructure improvements. By 1997, expect lots of repaving, new lighting, and curb cuts along lower Market Street, Columbus Boulevard and the waterfront, and the Italian Market. A dark blue "Direction Philadelphia" signage program that's clear and coherent can guide you on and off a reconstructed expressway system, now connecting I-95 and I-76 (along the two rivers), with plenty of easy entrances and exits. The airport is undergoing a $1 billion capital improvement, with new terminals, a new hotel connected to Terminal B, and new runways. The nation's second busiest Amtrak stop, 30th Street Station, has completed a $100 million restoration, with a new bakery, charcuterie, and rejuvenated services like bookstores.

Hot areas in town have radiated out from the city core. The northwest quadrant of Center City is indisputably the corporate center. The Delaware River waterfront's piers and warehouses have been transformed into frenetic pleasure domes: bars, clubs, sports palaces, and beach resorts, complete with a pleasant water taxi linking them every 20 minutes. On the other side, the once blue-collar terraced streets of Manayunk along the Schuylkill River host fashion from high to funky, cuisine, and shopping, along with a new farmer's market.

No one can ignore that Philadelphia has finally entered the age of the super-skyscraper with One Liberty Place, the energetic and gracious 945-foot spire. The 150,000-square-foot Shops at Liberty Place are the true flagships of city merchandising, with the demise of most downtown department stores and the rise of regional malls. Other megaliths completed are the 58-story Two Liberty Place; the 54-story One Mellon Center at 18th and Market Streets, 1919 Market St.; the Bell Atlantic Building; and a second tower at Commerce Square. These projects have left fabled Rittenhouse Square area, especially Chestnut Street, looking a bit seedy by comparison, and these locations are redeveloping to maintain their cachet.

The arts are finally attracting major projects and investment, particularly along South Broad Street, where the city is trying hard to establish a safe, convenient core zone of the performing arts. It's been called a strung-out Lincoln Center. The Philadelphia Orchestra is building a new home for itself along this $330 million "Avenue of the Arts" at Spruce Street, leaving the Academy of Music free to book traveling orchestras and the like. The Wilma Theater, the new Pennsylvania Ballet's home, and the new Arts Bank at South Street are also on the boards. In the historic district, Mayor Rendell is pushing for a $20 million National Constitution Center "theme park" adjacent to the Liberty Bell, and a $90 million dining and hotel complex on the Delaware River.

The sports complex of Veterans Stadium, the CoreStates Spectrum, and CoreStates Center combine all four professional teams—the Phillies in baseball, the Eagles in football, the Flyers in hockey, the 76ers in basketball—along with mass-market events, from rock shows to evangelical services and one-of-a-kind events.

3 The Philadelphia Story

Although Philadelphia may conjure up thoughts of William Penn and the revolutionary period in the minds of most Americans, it was in fact a tiny group of Swedish settlers who first established a foothold here in the 1640s. (You can see models of the two ships that brought them over in the Gloria Dei Church.) Where does William Penn fit in? Well, his father had been an admiral and a courtier under Charles II of England. The king was in debt to Admiral Penn, who died in 1670, and the younger Penn asked to collect the debt through a land grant on the west bank of the Delaware River, a grant that would eventually be named Pennsylvania, or "Penn's forest." At the time, Penn was in prison. His Quaker religion, anti-Anglican church attitudes, and contempt for authority had gotten him expelled from Oxford and arrested for conspiracy and "tumultuous assembling" numerous times. The chance for him to set up a utopia in the New World, based on Quaker principles, was too good to pass up. Since Swedish farmers owned most of the lower Delaware frontage, he decided to settle upriver, where the Schuylkill met the Delaware. The name he chose was Philadelphia—the City of Brotherly Love.

COLONIAL PHILADELPHIA In 1982 Philadelphia celebrated its 300th anniversary, and—incredibly—Penn's original city plan still adequately described the Center City, down to the public parks and the site for City Hall. Because of London's terrible 1666 fire, exacerbated by narrow streets and semidetached wooden buildings, the founder figured that broad avenues and city blocks arranged in a grid were the safest answer here. As he intended to treat Native Americans and fellow settlers equally, he planned no city walls or neighborhood borders. Front Street, naturally, faced the Delaware, as it still does, and parallel streets were numbered up to 24th Street and the Schuylkill. Streets running east to west were named after trees and plants (Sassafras became Race Street, for the horse-and-buggy contests run along it). To attract prospective investors, Penn promised bonus land grants in the "Liberties" (outlying countryside) to anyone who bought a city lot; he took one of the largest for himself, now Pennsbury Manor (26 miles north of town). Colonies were in the business of attracting settlers in those days, and Penn had to wear a variety of hats—those of financier, politician, religious leader, salesman, and manufacturer.

Dateline

- **1644** William Penn born.
- **1682** The 300-ton *Welcome,* with William Penn aboard, lands at New Castle (Delaware). Penn rows up to the tongue of land between the Delaware and Schuylkill Rivers and names the area Philadelphia.
- **1701** Penn leaves Philadelphia for the last time.
- **1718** William Penn dies in England.
- **1723** Sixteen-year-old Benjamin Franklin arrives by boat from Boston.
- **1745** Trim arcades of the Second Street Market, between Pine and Lombard Streets, built to house market stalls.
- **1748** First Philadelphia Assembly, an annual ball that in the 1990s still represents "making it" in social circles.
- **1749** First theater company in the colonies opens.
- **1752** Franklin performs his kite-flying experiment, proving that lightning is a form of electricity, in an open field that's now the location of St. Stephen's Episcopal Church at 10th and Ludlow Streets.
- **1755** Franklin and others open America's first hospital at 8th and Spruce Streets.
- **1765** Mass protests on news of English Parliament's passage of the Stamp Act, with boycotts of imports and office "strikes."
- **1774** First Continental Congress held in the State House (now Independence Hall).
- **1776** Declaration of Independence debated and adopted on July 2.

continues

- **1777** General Howe, moving up from Maryland, takes Germantown on October 4 and occupies Philadelphia soon after; members of the Continental Congress, with the Liberty Bell, flee to Lancaster.
- **1778** British troops abandon Philadelphia in June to advance on New York City.
- **1780** Pennsylvania becomes the first state to abolish slavery, calling for general emancipation by 1827.
- **1787** Constitutional Convention meets in the State House.
- **1790–1800** Philadelphia is the capital of the United States.
- **1805** First permanent bridge spans the Schuylkill, connecting the city to Pennsylvania's rich farmlands.
- **1812–15** English blockade of international trade shuts down Philadelphia shipping, though its Navy Yard outfits most of U.S. Navy.
- **1820s** Transformation of the seaport city into America's first major industrial city.
- **1832** Railroad to Germantown built.
- **1844** Riots over rail laying through Kensington for the Trenton route.
- **1840s** Anti-Catholic (Irish) riots; troops guard churches against "Know-Nothing" bigots.
- **1854** Consolidation Act expands Philadelphia tremendously, creating a city of 154 square miles.
- **1857–61** Bank panic, stagnation, and depression burden city until Civil War.
- **1860** First baseball game played in Philadelphia.
- **1861** Civil War begins. City elite, made wealthy through Southern trade, are against

continues

Homes and public buildings filled in the map, but slowly—that's why all the colonial row houses of Society Hill and Elfreth's Alley (continuously inhabited since the 1690s) are so near the Delaware docks. When he wrote the Declaration of Independence in 1776, almost a century later, Thomas Jefferson could still say of his boardinghouse on 7th and Market that it was away from the city noise and dirt! The city spread west to Broad Street even later, around 1800. Philadelphia grew along the river and not west as Penn had planned. Southwark, to the south, and the Northern Liberties, to the north, housed the less affluent, including most of the rougher sailors and their taverns set up in unofficial alleys. These were Philadelphia's first slums—unpaved, without public services, and populated by those without enough property or money to satisfy voting requirements.

Although Philadelphia had been founded after Boston and New York, manufacturing, financial services, excellent docking facilities, and fine Pennsylvania farm produce soon propelled it to the first city of the colonies—the largest English-speaking city in the British Empire except for London. Some 82 ships docked in 1682, in a cove that Dock Street has filled in and along docks at Front Street up to Vine. By 1770 the figure was 880 ships along 66 wharves.

Despite its urban problems, colonial Philadelphia was a thriving city in virtually every way, boasting public hospitals and streetlights, cultural institutions and newspapers, stately Georgian architecture and Chippendale furniture, imported tea and cloth, and, above all, commerce. William Penn put the stamp of his rough genius on the young city. However, the next generation turned away from his vision of brotherly love geographically, politically, and religiously, re-creating the institutions they had known in English towns. But in the third and fourth generations, men like James Logan, the first Biddles, and David Rittenhouse proved even more influential in determining a distinct Philadelphia style—genial, cooperative, and relaxed, though without the later Main Line inbred gentility. Alexander Graydon, a journalist, wrote in 1811, "of all the cities in the world, Philadelphia was for its size, perhaps, one of the most peaceable and unwarlike."

One man will always be linked with Philadelphia —multitalented, insatiably curious Benjamin Franklin. Franklin had an impulse to set things right, whether it be stoves, spectacles, or states. It sometimes seems that his hand appears in every aspect of the city worth exploring! The colonial

Impressions

Of all goodly villages, the very goodliest, probably, in the world; the very largest, and flattest, and smoothest. . . . The absence of the note of the perpetual perpendicular, the New York, the Chicago note, . . . seemed to symbolize exactly the principle of indefinite level extension and to offer, refreshingly, a challenge . . . to absolute centrifugal motion.

—Henry James, *The American Scene* (1905)

homes with the four-hand brass plaques were protected by his fire-insurance company; the post office at 3rd and Market Streets was his grandson's printing shop; the Free Library of Philadelphia, the University of Philadelphia, Pennsylvania Hospital at 8th and Spruce Streets, and the American Philosophical Society all were begun through Franklin's inspiration. He was an inventor, a printer, a statesman, a scientist, and a diplomat—an all-around genius.

FROM REVOLUTION TO CIVIL WAR Like most important Philadelphians, Franklin considered himself a loyal British subject until well into the 1770s, though he and the other colonists were increasingly subject to what they considered capricious English policy. Philadelphia lacked the radicalism of New England, but after Lexington and Concord and the meeting of the First and Second Continental Congresses, whose delegates were housed all over Philadelphia, tremendous political debate erupted. William Allen said, "We are to be England's Milch Cow, but if they are not prudent . . . we shall turn dry upon their hands." The moderates—wealthy citizens with friends and relatives in England—held out as long as they could. But with the April 1776 decision in Independence Hall to consider drafting a declaration of independence, revolutionary fervor became unstoppable.

"These are the times that try men's souls," wrote Thomas Paine in *The Crisis*—and they certainly were for Philadelphians, with so much to lose in a war with Britain. Thomas Jefferson and John Adams talked over the situation with George Washington, Robert Morris, and other delegates at City Tavern by night and at Carpenter's Hall and Independence Hall by day. On July 2, their declaration was passed by the general Congress; on July 6, it was read to a crowd of 8,000, who tumultuously approved.

Your visit to Independence National Historical Park will fill you in on the Revolution's effect on the City of Brotherly Love. Of the major colonial cities, Philadelphia had the fewest defenses. The war came

the war, despite strong popular antislavery sentiment.

- **1862** Philadelphia is an armed camp with tremendous demand for locomotives, uniforms, and supplies manufactured here.
- **1863** Battle of Gettysburg in July saves city from Confederate attack but brings loss of thousands of local troops.
- **1865** Antiblack riots culminate in an ordinance forbidding blacks to ride in the horsecars; Jim Crow laws persist until the 1870s. Lincoln's body lies in state in Independence Hall on its way to burial in Illinois.
- **1860–90** Rise of the saloon (6,000 by 1887) as a focus of German and Irish immigrant society.
- **1866–72** Chestnut Street bridge spurs the quick development of West Philadelphia; University of Pennsylvania moves there in 1872.
- **1874** Ground-breaking on July 4 for both City Hall and the Centennial Exhibition in Fairmount Park.
- **1876** President Grant and the emperor of Brazil open the Centennial Exhibition; 38 nations and 39 states and territories are represented. First public demonstration of the telephone and other wonders of the age.

continues

- **1878** First use of electric lighting for houses and offices; first Bell telephone exchange at 400 Chestnut St.
- **1884** Mayor King appoints the city's first African-American police officer.
- **1890** Drexel University founded at 32nd and Chestnut Streets.
- **1892** First trolley car, on Catharine and Bainbridge Streets.
- **1893** Reading Terminal built for Reading Railroad.
- **1899** First motor car arrives in Philadelphia, brought from France by a local merchant.
- **1900** More people own houses in Philadelphia than in any other city in the world; a middle-class house with seven rooms rents for $15 per month. City's population is over 1.25 million.
- **1901** First Mummer's Parade marches up Broad Street on New Year's Day. Wanamaker's department store and Bellevue Hotel open.
- **1908** Shibe Park, home of baseball's American League Athletics, opens.
- **1910** First airplane flight from New York City to Philadelphia.
- **1913** Women suffrage marches. President Wilson dedicates restored Congress Hall.
- **1917–18** Philadelphia is a beehive of activity in World War I, with the world's largest ship-construction plant.
- **1922–26** Delaware River Bridge connects Philadelphia and New Jersey; ferry trade persists until the 1950s.
- **1924** "The City Beautiful" movement, exemplified by Benjamin Franklin Parkway, designed along French lines.
- **1926** Sesquicentennial Exposition on site of present-day

continues

to the city itself because British troops occupied patriot homes during the harsh winter of 1777 to 1778. Woodford, a country mansion in what is now Fairmount Park, hosted many Tory balls, while Washington's troops drilled and shivered at Valley Forge. Washington's attempt to crack the British line at Germantown ended in a confused retreat. The city later greatly benefited from the British departure and the Peace of Paris (1783), which ended the war.

Problems with the new federal government brought a Constitutional Convention to Philadelphia in 1787. This body crafted the Constitution that the United States still follows. It's hard to say whether Philadelphia had an effect on the beautifully and strongly worded sessions that fostered both the Declaration of Independence and the Constitution, but its native tolerance and acuity must have stood the young country in good stead.

In the years between the ratification of the Constitution and the Civil War, Philadelphia prospered. For 10 of these years, 1790 to 1800, the U.S. government operated here, while the District of Columbia was still marshland. George Washington lived in an executive mansion where the Liberty Bell is now; the Supreme Court met in Old City Hall; Congress met in Congress Hall; and everybody met at City Tavern for balls and festivals.

In general the quality of life was high, despite a disastrous 1793 yellow fever epidemic. The legacies of Benjamin Franklin flourished, from printing and publishing to fire-insurance companies. The resources of the Library Company became available to the public, and both men and women received "modern" educations—that is, more emphasis on accounting and less on classics. The 1834 Free School Act established a democratic public school system, but such private academies as Germantown Friends School and Friends Select are still going strong today. The Walnut Street Theater, founded in 1809, is the oldest American theater still in constant use, and the Musical Fund Hall at 808 Locust St. (now apartments) hosted operas, symphony orchestras, and chamber ensembles. The 1805 Pennsylvania Academy of Fine Arts, now at Broad and Cherry Streets, taught such painters as Washington Allston and the younger Peales. Charles Willson Peale, the eccentric patriarch, set up the first American museum in the Long Hall of Independence Hall; its exhibits included a portrait gallery and the first lifelike arrangements of full-size stuffed animals.

It makes sense that Philadelphia retained the federal charter to mint money, build ships, and produce weapons even after the capital moved to Washington. The transportation revolution that made America's growth possible was fueled by the city's shipyards, ironworks, and locomotive works. Philadelphia vied with Baltimore and New York City for transport routes to agricultural production inland. New York eventually won out as a shipper, thanks to its natural harbor and the Erie Canal. Philadelphia, however, was the hands-down winner in becoming America's premier manufacturing city, and it ranked even with New York in finance. The need to harness Philadelphia's neighborhoods better for large-scale enterprises, in fact, led to the 1854 incorporation of outlying suburbs into one 154-square mile city.

During the Civil War, Philadelphia's manufacturers weren't above supplying both Yankees and Confederates with guns and rail equipment. Fortunately for the city, the Southern offensive met with bloody defeat at Gettysburg, not far away. With the end of the Civil War in 1865, port activity rebounded, as Southern cotton was spun and shipped from city textile looms. Philadelphia became the natural site for the first world's fair held on American soil: the Centennial Exposition. It's hard to imagine the excitement that filled Fairmount Park, with 200 pavilions and displays. There's a scale model in Memorial Hall, one of the few surviving structures in the park; it gives a good idea of how seriously the United States took this show of power and prestige. University City in West Philadelphia saw the establishment of campuses for Drexel University and the University of Pennsylvania, and public transport lines connected all the neighborhoods of the city.

20TH-CENTURY PHILADELPHIA   In the 20th century Philadelphia's fortunes have been checkered. Although port and petroleum-refining operations bolstered its position as an industrial center until the 1980s, manufacturing in general has moved out of the city and the region. Of the city's work force, 50% were employed in manufacturing; this figure has shrunk to 9% today. As industry has moved out, the city has tried to develop a tax base around service businesses. Tourism has become a major revenue source, and public and private efforts coordinate to create the relaxed but efficient attitude you'll find all over Center City. Major corporate headquarters in Philadelphia now include

Veterans Stadium; highlights are Jack Dempsey–Gene Tunney prizefight, movie "talkies," and electric refrigerator.

- **1928** Philadelphia Museum of Art opens.
- **1934** With repeal of Prohibition, establishment of state liquor stores (as opposed to those privately owned). Opening of 30th Street Station, the city's main railroad terminus.
- **1936** Special June Mummer's Parade entertains Democratic Party National Convention.
- **1944** Due to World War II labor shortages, black workers make substantial gains, despite union opposition.
- **1946** First computer, ENIAC, developed at University of Pennsylvania for the U.S. Army.
- **1950** Restoration and renovation of Society Hill begins.
- **1951** National Park Service establishes Independence National Historical Park.
- **1954** Philadelphia International Airport (domestic flights since 1940) dedicated.
- **1950s** Pop singing stars like Fabian, Frankie Avalon, and Chubby Checker emerge from Philadelphia neighborhoods.
- **1960** Dr. John Gibbons invents heart–lung machine at Jefferson Medical Center.
- **1964, 1967** Racial disturbances, said to have been aggravated by Police Commissioner Frank Rizzo, who would serve as mayor from 1972 to 1980.
- **1964** Society Hill Towers, symbolic of old and new in the neighborhood, constructed to design of I. M. Pei.

continues

- **1974** Chestnut Street urban mall project built; seen as a failure by 1980.
- **1976** Liberty Bell moved from Congress Hall to the new Independence Mall; America's bicentennial celebrated.
- **1982** Philadelphia's 300th anniversary celebration. Tall ships line Penn's Landing.
- **1984–92** Administration of Wilson Goode, Philadelphia's first black mayor, tainted by the 1985 MOVE bombing of a city block in West Philadelphia in the name of law and order.
- **1987** Bicentennial of U.S. Constitution celebrated at Independence Hall.
- **1993** Pennsylvania Convention Center opened with celebration and speech by Pres. Bill Clinton.
- **1994** Reading Terminal Train Shed at Convention Center reopens; City Hall reemerges from scaffolding.

SmithKline Beecham (pharmaceuticals); Aramark (food and hospitality); Core-States Bank; Advanta financial services; and CIGNA (insurance).

Politically, the city in 1900 was controlled by a small core of moderate Republican bosses, most with old-Philadelphia pedigrees. Immigrant populations united behind President Franklin D. Roosevelt to swing the city Democratic in the 1930s, and in the name of unions and the liberal state, they grew their own form of abuses of government. The period from 1949 to 1962, under mayors Joseph Clark (later a U.S. senator) and Richardson Dilworth, was the height of "good government" reform. It was succeeded in the 1970s by the controversial "law-and-order" administration of Frank Rizzo, who rose to fame as the police commissioner who tried to control the anti–Vietnam War and racial disturbances of the 1960s. Ironically, one of Rizzo's successors, Wilson Goode, is linked to the highly criticized leveling of a city block in West Philadelphia in order to protect public safety.

In terms of urban homeowners—an area in which Philadelphia led the world for decades—there have been good reasons for successful citizens to leave for more pleasant suburban areas. The urban-renewal projects at Society Hill, the boom period of expansion along the northeast and Parkway, and the establishment of Independence National Historical Park have combated the migration somewhat. The city boomed during a splendid bicentennial celebration of the 1787 drafting and signing of the U.S. Constitution.

Planning a Trip to Philadelphia

2

This chapter is devoted to the where, when, and how of your trip—the advance-planning issues required to get it together and take it on the road.

1 Visitor Information & Money

VISITOR INFORMATION

The **Philadelphia Visitors Center,** 16th Street and John F. Kennedy Boulevard, Philadelphia, PA 19102 (☎ **800/537-7676** or 215/636-1666), should be your first resource. They offer a wealth of publications, from seasonal calendars of events to maps; knowledgeable volunteers staff their phones. If you obtain nothing else, request the "Official Visitors Guide," an annual compendium. They also are the architects for an increasing number of package tours combining events like special museum exhibitions, concerts, or sporting events with discount hotel prices, free city transit passes, and Amtrak discounts. Once you're in town, note that many bus tours, historic trolley rides, and walking tours start from here, including tours of City Hall. The Visitors Center also maintains a helpful website (**http://www/libertynet.org/phila-visitor**).

Guest Informant and *Where* are two publications placed in most moderate to upscale hotel rooms.

MONEY

Except for truly deluxe experiences, you will find moderate prices in Philadelphia: less than those in New York and on par with or slightly above those in Washington, D.C. Expenses for a family of four staying in a hotel, with meals in restaurants and a healthy dose of sightseeing in Independence Park (all free) and museums, should run about $200 per day.

Minimal cash is required, since credit cards are accepted universally and automatic-teller machines linked to national networks are strewn around tourist destinations and increasingly within hotels. To get more specific information on the **Cirrus** network, call **800/424-7787**; for the **Plus** system, call **800/843-7587**. The three major traveler's check agencies are **American Express** (☎ **800/221-7282**); **BankAmerica** (☎ **800/227-3460**); and **VISA** (☎ **800/227-6811**).

What Things Cost in Philadelphia	U.S. $
Taxi from airport to Center City	27.00
Airport train to Center City (cash on board)	5.00
Local telephone call	.25
Double at Ritz-Carlton Philadelphia (deluxe)	225.00
Double at Doubletree Hotel Philadelphia (expensive)	199.00
Double at Holiday Inn—Independence Mall (moderate)	168.00
Double at Comfort Inn at Penn's Landing (budget)	119.00
Two-course lunch for one at The Garden (expensive)	21.00
Two-course lunch for one at the Food Court at Liberty Place (budget)	7.00
Three-course dinner for one at Dilullo Centro (expensive)	50.00
Three-course dinner at Circa (moderate)	36.00
Three-course dinner at Marabella's (inexpensive)	18.00
Bottle of beer	3.50
Coca-Cola	1.50
Cup of Coffee	1.50
Roll of ASA 100 color film, 36 exposures	6.00
Admission to Philadelphia Museum of Art	7.00
Movie ticket	7.50
Concert ticket at the Academy of Music	12.00–80.00

2 When to Go

Philadelphia has four distinct seasons with temperatures ranging from the 90s (°F) in summer to the 30s (°F) in winter, although below-zero (°F) temperatures normally hit only one out of every four winters. Summers tend to be humid. In the fall, the weather becomes drier. Spring temperatures are variable; count on comfortable breezes.

Average Temperatures and Precipitation in Philadelphia

	Jan	Feb	Mar	Apr	May	June	July	Aug	Sept	Oct	Nov	Dec
High °F	40	41	50	62	73	81	85	83	77	66	54	43
Low °F	26	26	33	43	53	63	68	66	60	49	39	29
Precip. in days	11	9	11	11	11	10	9	9	8	8	10	10

PHILADELPHIA CALENDAR OF EVENTS

For more details, contact the **Convention and Visitors Bureau**, 1515 John F. Kennedy Blvd., Philadelphia, PA 19102 (☎ **215/636-1666**).

January

✪ **Mummer's Parade.** On January 1 (or the following Saturday in case of bad weather), starting in late morning and lasting most of the day, 30,000 spangled strutters march with feathers and banjos in a celebration that must have been pagan in origin. The parade goes up Broad Street, from South Philadelphia up to City Hall. (There's talk of reversing the direction or winding up at the new Convention Center.) If you go to the Mummer's Museum, the gaudiness and elaborateness of the costumes won't amaze you quite so much. But the music (everyone ends up humming "Oh, Dem Golden Slippers" sooner or later) and gaiety will have you entranced. You can line up on Broad Street, or get reserved seats, available from early December at the Convention and Visitors Bureau for $2. Call **215/336-3050** for details.

- **Benjamin Franklin's Birthday.** On a Sunday in midmonth, the Franklin Institute celebrates its namesake's birthday. Call **215/448-1200** for details.

February

- **Chinese New Year.** You can enjoy dragons and fireworks at 11th and Arch Streets, traditional 10-course banquets, or a visit to the Chinese Cultural Center at 125 N. 10th Street. Call **215/923-6767** for details on the festivities, held between late January and midmonth.
- **Black History Month.** All month long, the Afro-American Museum, 7th and Arch Streets, offers a full complement of exhibitions, lectures, and music. Call **215/574-0380** for details.
- **George Washington's Birthday.** Valley Forge Historical Park holds a Cherries Jubilee weekend the third Sunday and Monday. Call **215/783-7700** for details.
- **Peco Energy Presidential Jazz Weekend.** On Presidents' Day weekend, more than 90 events are held around-the-clock, from concerts to screenings and meals. Call **215/636-1666** for information.
- **Comcast U.S. Indoor Tennis Championships.** This event, held the third weekend of February at the CoreStates Spectrum, features some of the world's best players. Call **215/947-2530** for particulars.

March

- **Philadelphia Flower Show.** It's the largest in the country, with acres of gardens and rustic settings. It runs from late February to early March, and is now held in the Convention Center. With the city-wide institution of Flower Show Week, it's even bigger and better than before. There are usually tickets at the door, but the Pennsylvania Horticultural Society at 325 Walnut St. sells them in advance. Call **215/625-8250** for information.
- ✪ **The Book and the Cook Festival.** For the past decade, Philadelphia has combined the love of reading and eating into this festival. For five days, eminent food critics, cookbook authors, and restaurateurs are invited to plan dream meals with participating city restaurants. If you're a "foodie," you know that the chance to stroll through Reading Terminal Market with Alice Waters, or to dine on what she turns up, is not to be declined. The festival has recently expanded into food samplings and wine and beer tastings all over town. It's usually held the third week in March. Call **215/686-3662** for a schedule and to make a reservation.
- **St. Patrick's Day Parade.** On March 17, the parade starts at noon on 20th Street and the Parkway. Call the Visitors Bureau for details. The Irish Pub at 2007 Walnut St. will be packed.

April

- **Philadelphia Antiques Show.** Started in 1961, this antiques show is probably the finest in the nation, with some 50-odd major English and American exhibitors. It's held the first weekend in April at the 103rd Engineers Armory, 33rd and Market Streets. Call **215/387-3500** for information.

- **American Music Theater Festival.** In its 12th year in 1995, this festival offers premieres of music-theater works by major American artists, ranging from traditional Broadway-bound musicals to avant-garde works. Call **215/893-1570** for information. The festival runs through June.
- **Easter Sunday.** This day brings fashion shows and music to Rittenhouse Square. The Easter Bunny usually makes an appearance at Wanamaker's and the Gallery. Call **215/686-2876** for details.
- **Spring Tour of Fairmount Park.** The dogwoods and cherry trees along both sides of the Schuylkill are in blossom. Trolleybuses make a special run along Wissahickon Creek, a lovely woodland minutes away from Center City. Call **215/636-1666** for details. The tour is held the last Sunday in April (or the first Sunday in May).

May

- **Philadelphia Open House.** These tours, held late April to early May, give you a rare chance to see Germantown, Society Hill, and University City mansions. Call **215/928-1188** for information.
- **Rittenhouse Square Flower Market.** This market, held the third Thursday, has been an annual event since 1914. Plants, flowers, baked goodies, and lemon sticks are some of the irresistibles for sale. Call **215/525-7182** for details.

   Also, the more than 2,000 azaleas and rhododendrons in bloom behind the Museum of Art literally stop traffic with their brilliance.
- **Mozart on the Square.** Also around Rittenhouse Square, this festival brings about 20 chamber performances of good younger talent to town all month. Performances cost $5 to $15; for information, contact P.O. Box 237, Merion Station, PA 19006 (☎ **215/668-1799**).
- **International Theater Festival for Children.** This festival runs the last week of the month, taking place on or near the University of Pennsylvania campus, based at 3680 Walnut St. Call **215/898-6791** for programs and prices.
- **Israel Independence Day.** This holiday, a Sunday in mid-May, brings a Center City parade and daylong Israeli bazaar to the Parkway. Call **215/922-7222** for details.
- **Jam on the River.** This was cooked up as a way for Philadelphia to pay homage to New Orleans, and has expanded to include blues as well as jazz. It's based at the Great Plaza at Penn's Landing. In recent years, Dr. John and the Preservation Hall Jazz Band have been in attendance. Call **215/636-1666** for particulars. It's held in late May.
- **Devon Horse Show,** Route 30, Devon. This event outside Philadelphia includes jumping competitions and carriage races and a great country fair, with plenty of food stalls—burgers as well as watercress sandwiches—under cheerful awnings. General admission is $6. Call **610/964-0550** for details on the end-of-the-month show.
- **Dad Vail Regatta.** This is one of the largest collegiate rowing events in the country, held the second week of May. You can picnic on East River Drive near Strawberry Mansion. Call **215/542-7844** for details.

June

- **Rittenhouse Square Fine Arts Annual.** Philadelphia moves outdoors with this event, in which hundreds of professional and student artworks go on sale the first two weeks of June. Call **215/634-5060** for details.
- **Head House Square.** Throughout the summer, local craftspeople, food vendors, and street artists set up shop on Saturday from noon to midnight and Sunday from noon to 6pm.

- **Elfreth's Alley Days.** The first weekend in June, the row-house dwellers, many in colonial costumes, open up their homes for inspection and admiration. There are reenactments of colonial crafts, as well as troops present. Call **215/574-0560** for details.
- **CoreStates Pro Cycling Championships.** The 156-mile-long course of this country's premier one-day cycling event starts and finishes on the Parkway. It's held the first weekend of June.
- **Betsy Ross House.** Flag Day festivities are held here on June 14.
- **Mellon Jazz Festival.** A top-drawer collection of artists are featured in the Mann Music Center and the Academy of Music, either the second or third week of the month.
- **Bloomsday.** On June 16, the Irish Pub at 2007 Walnut St. celebrates the 24-hour time span of James Joyce's novel, *Ulysses*.

July

☼ **Sunoco Welcome America!** The whole town turns out for this week-long festival to celebrate America's birthday with fountains, theater, free entertainment, and assorted pageantry. It's held the week before July 4, with fireworks on the Delaware River the night of the 3rd. The Fourth of July brings special ceremonies to Independence Square, including a reading of the Declaration of Independence, a presentation of the prestigious Freedom Medal, and an evening parade up the Parkway. There's also a Schuylkill regatta on the Fourth. Principal locations are the terrace by the Philadelphia Museum of Art, City Hall (to dive into the world's largest hoagie), and Independence Mall. Call **215/636-1666** for information.
- **Philadelphia Orchestra Summer Concerts,** Mann Music Center in Fairmount Park. The concerts are free on Monday, Wednesday, and Thursday through August. Also, there are pop concerts at low prices at Robin Hood Dell East and dance at Art Museum Terrace.

August

- **Philadelphia Folk Festival,** Suburban Poole Farm, Schwenksville. This festival, held late month, has a national reputation and brings major crowds. Call **215/242-0150** for details.
- **Pennsylvania Dutch Festival.** Every day the first week of August, Reading Terminal Market is the venue for quilts, music, food, crafts, and such.

September

- **Fairmount Park Festival.** This festival, which runs through November, includes the Harvest Show at Memorial Hall and parades of varying themes down the Parkway almost every weekend. Call **215/685-0052** for details.
- **Philadelphia Distance Run.** One of the nation's premier tests, it's a half marathon through Center City and Fairmount Park, usually held the third Sunday of September. In town, it's bigger than the November marathon and gets plenty of national running figures. Call **215/665-8500** if you wish to join the field of 7,500.

October

- **Columbus Day Parade.** There's a parade along the Parkway; also look for South Philadelphia fairs.
- ☼ **Super Sunday.** Think of a party for an entire city—that's Super Sunday, held on the Benjamin Franklin Parkway from Logan Circle to the Museum of Art. There are clowns, jugglers, mimes, rides, craft vendors, and a flea market. The museums and academies along the Parkway have sponsored this since 1970, rain or shine, and most have reduced admissions and special events. This is one day when

parking on the grass won't get you a ticket. It's the third Sunday in October. Call **215/665-1050** for information.

November
- **Philadelphia Marathon.** The finish line is at Independence Hall. The marathon is run on a Sunday at midmonth.
- **Virginia Slims Women's Tennis Championships.** The matches are played at the Spectrum during the second week of November. Call **215/568-4444** for details.
- **Thanksgiving Day Parade.** This parade features cartoon characters, bands, floats, and Santa Claus.

December
- **Holiday Activities Around Town.** It's not surprising that Christmas occasions many activities in Center City, beginning with the tree lighting in City Hall courtyard. The Gallery at Market East, "A Christmas Carol" at Strawbridge and Clothier, a Colonial Christmas Village at Market Place East, and Hecht's all host elaborate extravaganzas, with organs and choruses. The Society Hill and Germantown Christmas walking tours are lovely, with the same leafy decorations as Fairmount Park.
- **Christmas Tours of Fairmount Park and Germantown.** Colonial mansions sparkle with wreaths, holly, and fruit arrangements donated by local garden clubs. Call **215/787-5449** or 215/848-1777 for details. The tours begin midmonth.
- **Private Lights.** For an unusual Christmas experience, visit the 2700 block of South Colorado Street, south of Oregon Avenue, between 17th and 18th Streets. The sight of some 40 houses bathed in interconnected strands of holiday lights is not to be believed.
- **Lucia Fest,** Old Swedes' Church. It sounds Italian, but the Lucia Fest is a Swedish pageant held by candlelight. It's the first weekend of December.
- **Nutcracker Ballet.** Throughout the month, the Pennsylvania Ballet performs Tchaikovsky's classic at the Academy of Music. Call **215/551-7014** for details.
- **New Year's Eve.** Fireworks are held at the Great Plaza of Penn's Landing on December 31.

3 Tips for Travelers with Special Needs

FOR TRAVELERS WITH DISABILITIES   Travelers with disabilities will find the tourist areas of Philadelphia accessible. Even though some streets in Society Hill and bordering Independence National Historical Park have uneven brick sidewalks and Dock Street itself is paved with rough cobblestones, all curbs are well cut at intersections. The same is true for Chestnut Street, the Parkway, and the University of Pennsylvania campus. Virtually all theaters and stadiums accommodate wheelchairs. Call ahead to plan routes. To aid people with hearing impairments, the Academy of Music provides free infrared headsets for concerts; the Annenberg Center rents them for $2.

A national resource, the **Travel Information Service** at Moss Rehabilitation Hospital, will provide telephone information at **215/456-9603.**

For basic information, contact the **Mayor's Commission on People with Disabilities,** Room 143, City Hall, Philadelphia, PA 19107 (☎ **215/686-2798**). SEPTA publishes a special "Transit Guide for the Disabled"; you can request it from **SEPTA Special Services,** 130 S. 9th St., Philadelphia, PA 19107 (☎ **215/580-7365**). All SEPTA bus routes will be lift-equipped by 1998. Market East subway station is wheelchair accessible, but most other stops are not.

The Free Library of Philadelphia runs a **Library for the Blind and Physically Handicapped,** very conveniently located at 919 Walnut St. (☎ 215/925-3213); it's open Monday through Friday from 9am to 5pm. It adjoins the **Associated Services for the Blind,** which offers transcriptions into braille for a fee.

If you travel with Amtrak or Greyhound/Trailways, be aware that on the former you can receive a 25% discount and a special seat with advance notification (☎ 800/523-6590) and on the latter a free seat for a companion (☎ 800/345-3109). **Wheelers East, Inc.** (☎ 800/862-7475) will rent accessible vans and wheelchairs.

FOR GAY & LESBIAN TRAVELERS Center City is used to, and tolerant of, homosexual populations, and the rectangle bordered by 9th and 18th Streets and by Walnut and South Streets is filled with gay social services, restaurants, bookstores, and clubs. See Chapter 10 for specific clubs and bars. You might also check *Philadelphia Gay News,* which is widely available, and *Au Courant.* Both are weeklies. The lesbian-oriented *Labyrinth* is available free at Giovanni's Room and some newsstands.

With a diverse stock, **Giovanni's Room,** 345 S. 12th St., Philadelphia, PA 19107 (☎ 215/923-2960), is a national resource for publications produced by and for gays and lesbians, as well as for feminist and progressive literature.

A national **Gay/Lesbian Crisisline** (☎ 800/767-4297) can provide instant medical or legal counseling and local support listings as well. The **Gay Switchboard** (open daily from 7 to 10pm) is at **215/546-7100;** the **Lesbian Hotline** is at **215/222-5110.**

For meetings, classes, gallery exhibitions, and social events, consult **Penguin Place,** 201 S. Camac St. (☎ 215/723-2220). The **Blackwell Center for Women,** 1124 Walnut St. (☎ 215/923-7577), can direct you to health clinics. The **Women's Switchboard** is at **215/829-1976.**

To report antigay violence or discrimination, call the **Philadelphia Lesbian and Gay Task Force Hotline** at **215/563-4581. ACT UP/Philadelphia** meets on Monday; call **215/731-1844.**

FOR SENIORS Senior citizens should bring some form of photo ID because many city attractions grant special discounts, especially during weekdays. Some hotels, too, will shift their rates, particularly on weekends. The Convention and Visitors Bureau publishes "Seniors on the Go," which lists dozens of specific benefits around town—from flat taxi fares to museum admissions; write ahead or pick it up at the Visitors Center. They'll also give you a "Ben's Pass for Senior Citizens," good for a calendar year.

If you haven't already done so, think about joining the **American Association of Retired Persons (AARP),** 1909 K St. NW, Washington, DC 20049 (☎ 202/872-4700). Their Purchase Privilege Program unlocks an incredible chest of discounts.

Many seniors prefer places with convenient local transportation between sites, and Philadelphia is wonderful in this regard. Seniors might consider the SEPTA DayPass ($5), available at the Visitors Center at 16th Street and John F. Kennedy Boulevard, which offers unlimited on-off rides; the new purple PHLASH vans ($3), which loop around all day to Center City's most popular destinations; or the Ben Frankline, which goes from Society Hill up to the Art Museum and Zoo (50¢ per ride).

You can pick up a **Golden Age Passport** at Independence National Historical Park if you are 62 or over. Since this park is free, it won't matter there, but the passport provides free admission to all parks, monuments, and recreation areas operated by the National Park Service.

Some educational programs run by **Elderhostel** are in the Philadelphia area. You must be over 60 (and your spouse or companion over 50) to participate. For information, contact them at 75 Federal St., 3rd Floor, Boston, MA 02110 (☎ **617/ 426-7788**).

FOR FAMILIES   Planning is essential for success in Philadelphia—I know from personal experience! If your kids are old enough to appreciate the destination, let them read something about Philadelphia ahead of time.

Airlines and Amtrak both let children under 2 years old travel free and offer discounts for children and/or families. Once you arrive, children under 12 (in some cases 18) can stay free in the same room as their parents in virtually all Philadelphia hotels. Be sure to reserve cribs and playpens if needed in advance. Restaurants all over the country are increasingly aware of the need to provide the basics, and "Best Bets" in Chapter 6 will cover some favorites.

The best current resource for family travel in Philadelphia is *Metrokids*, a bimonthly newspaper available at the Visitors Center at 16th Street and John F. Kennedy Boulevard. It lists all special cultural attractions geared to families, along with theme issues on factory tours, the Camden aquarium, and the like. Call **215/ 735-7035** with specific questions.

FOR STUDENTS   It's not well known, but there probably are more colleges and universities in and around Philadelphia than any other city in the country. So accredited students will find a warm reception from area vendors and sites. With an **International Student Identity Card (ISIC),** available to any full-time high-school or university student, you are entitled to special discounts on cultural sites, accommodations, car rentals, and more. Contact your own campus or the **Council on International Educational Exchange (CIEE),** 205 East 42nd St., New York, NY 10017 (☎ **212/661-1414**). While in Philadelphia, students might head for the **University of Pennsylvania,** 34th and Walnut Streets (☎ **215/898-5000**); **Temple University,** Broad Street and Montgomery Avenue (☎ **215/787-8561**); or **International House,** 3701 Chestnut St. (☎ **215/387-5125**). All publish free papers listing lectures, performances, films, and social events.

4 Getting There

BY PLANE

THE MAJOR AIRLINES   You can check flight schedules and make reservations on the following domestic airlines:

American Airlines and American Eagle (☎ 800/433-7300 or 215/365-4000); **America West** (☎ 800/235-9292); **Continental** Airlines (☎ 800/525-0280); **Delta** Air Lines (☎ 800/221-1212 or 215/667-7720); **Midway** Airlines (☎ 800/ 446-4392); **Midwest Express** (☎ 800/452-2022); **Northwest** Airlines (☎ 800/ 225-2525 domestic, 800/447-4747 international); **TWA** (☎ 800/221-2000 or 215/923-2000 domestic, 800/892-4141 international); **United** Airlines (☎ 800/241-6522 or 215/568-2800); and **USAir** and USAir Express (☎ 800/428-4322). Midway Airlines and USAir use Philadelphia International Airport as a hub.

International carriers include Air Jamaica (☎ 800/523-5585); British Airways (☎ 800/247-9297); and Swissair (☎ 800/221-4750).

PHILADELPHIA'S AIRPORT   All flights into and from Philadelphia use **Philadelphia International Airport** (☎ **215/937-6800**), at the southwest corner of the city. For up-to-the-minute information on airline arrival and departure times and gate assignments, call **800/PHL-GATE.** There are flights to more than 100 cities in the United States and more than 1,000 arrivals and departures daily. By air, it's $2\frac{1}{2}$ hours to Miami or Chicago, 6 hours to the West Coast, and 10 hours to Zurich.

Under a $1 billion capital improvement plan, the new international Terminal A (Dilworth Terminal), additional garages, and the new 420-room Airport Marriott have been built; all other terminals have undergone cosmetic facelifts, with gourmet concessions to Parma for food and Jazz & Java for coffee. Future improvements call for consolidating Terminals B and C, resulting in a bigger ticket pavilion, moving sidewalks, a retail concession mall, and better baggage delivery.

The airport is laid out with a central corridor connecting the five basic depots. Terminal B is the place to catch taxis, buses, and hotel limousines. The areas with the most amenities are between Terminals B and C and between Terminals D and E.

If you're driving to the airport, long-term parking is available for $16 per day at the expanded indoor garages or in the more distant long-term parking lots. Short-term parking is $2.50 for the first 30 minutes, $12 for up to 3 hours, $16 for 3–4 hours, and $30 for 4–24 hours.

GETTING INTO TOWN   A taxi from the airport to Center City takes about 25 minutes and costs upward of $25 plus tip.

If you're interested in airport limousines or shuttles to garages, hotels, or area destinations, try **Airport-Limelight** (☎ 800/342-7121 or 215/342-5557), **BostonCoach** (☎ 800/672-7676), **Carey Limousine** (☎ 610/595-2800), or **A-1 Philadelphia Airport Shuttle** (☎ 215/969-1818). BostonCoach quotes sedan rates of $28 from the airport to a Center City address; $70 to Valley Forge; and $105 to Atlantic City; expect $50 more for a limo.

All major car-rental operations have desks at the airport. These include **Alamo** (☎ 215/492-3960); **Avis** (☎ 215/365-3600); **Budget** (☎ 800/824-7088); **Dollar** (☎ 800/800-4000); **Hertz** (☎ 215/492-7200); and **National** (☎ 800/283-7445).

A high-speed rail link with direct service between the airport and Center City was opened in 1985. The trains run daily every 30 minutes from 5:30am to 11:25pm. They leave the airport at 10 and 40 minutes past the hour. Trains to the airport depart from Market East (and a Convention Center connection), Suburban Station at 16th Street, and 30th Street Station. The 30-minute trip costs $5 for adults; children's fares are $1.50 weekdays and $1 weekends; and the family fare is $15.

BY CAR

Philadelphia is better served than ever before by a series of interstate highways that circle or pass through the city. Think of Center City as a rectangle. I-95 whizzes by its bottom and right sides. The Pennsylvania Turnpike (I-276) is the top edge, but I-76 splits off and snakes along the Schuylkill River along the left side into town. I-676 is a highway traversing Center City under Vine Street, connecting I-76 to adjacent Camden, New Jersey, via the Ben Franklin Bridge over the Delaware. The new "Blue Route" of I-476 is a suburban left edge about 15 miles west of town, connecting I-276 and I-76 at its northern end with I-95 to the south.

Philadelphia is some 300 miles (six or so hours) from Boston, 100 miles (two hours) from New York City, 135 miles (three hours) from Washington, D.C., and 450 miles (nine hours) from Montreal. Tolls between Philadelphia and either New York City or Washington come to about $12.

Here are directions to City Hall, in the very center of town, from various directions.

NEW JERSEY TURNPIKE SOUTHBOUND EXIT 6   Take the Pennsylvania Turnpike westbound to the first exit, Exit 29, and change to U.S. 13 southbound. Follow the signs a short distance to I-95 southbound and enter at Exit 22, heading south. Exit for Center City at I-676 (Vine Street Expressway) westbound to 15th Street, then turn left and travel southbound two blocks.

NEW JERSEY TURNPIKE EXIT 4   Take N.J. 73 northbound to N.J. 38 westbound, then change to U.S. 30 westbound (the signage is abominable) and follow it over the Ben Franklin Bridge ($2 this way, but free eastbound) to I-676. Go south on 6th Street to Walnut Street (historic district will be on the left), turn right, and travel westbound to 15th Street.

FROM I-95 NORTHBOUND   Just past Philadelphia International Airport, take Pa. 291 toward Center City, Philadelphia. Cross the George C. Platt Memorial Bridge and turn left onto 26th Street, then follow 26th Street directly onto I-76 (Schuylkill Expressway) westbound to Exit 39 (30th Street Station). Go one block to Market Street and turn right. Go east on Market Street to City Hall, which will be in front of you.

FROM THE PENNSYLVANIA TURNPIKE [I-76]   Take Exit 24 to I-76 (Schuylkill Expressway) eastbound to I-676 (Vine Street Expressway). Take I-676 eastbound to 15th Street, turn right, and proceed southbound two blocks.

BY TRAIN

Philadelphia is a major Amtrak stop. It's on the Boston–Washington, D.C., northeast corridor, which has extensions south, west to Pittsburgh and Chicago, and east to Atlantic City. The Amtrak terminal is Penn (30th Street) Station, about 15 blocks from City Hall. Regular service, called Northeast Direct, from New York City takes 85 minutes; Metroliner service is 15 minutes faster. Philadelphia is 5 hours from Boston and 100 minutes from Washington, D.C., by Metroliner (☎ **800/ USA-RAIL**).

SEPTA commuter trains also connect 30th Street Station and several Center City stations to Trenton, N.J., to the northeast, Harrisburg to the west, and directly to airport terminals to the south.

These are sample round-trip fares on Amtrak: New York City to Philadelphia, $90 peak, $72 excursion (not valid Friday or Sunday 11am to 11pm); Washington to Philadelphia, $96 peak, $74 excursion; and one train daily to or from Chicago, $148 to $262.

Keep in mind that Philadelphia trips can be much cheaper if you take **New Jersey Transit** (☎ **800/582-5946** or 215/569-3752) commuter trains out of Penn Station in New York City or Newark to Trenton, then switch across the platform to the R7 Philadelphia-bound SEPTA commuter train that makes several convenient Center City stops before heading out to Chestnut Hill. The off-peak round-trip costs $24.

BY BUS

Peter Pan/Trailways, the chief U.S. intercity operator, operates a great new office and terminal on 11th Street between Filbert and Arch Streets, right across from the Convention Center (☎ **800/343-9999** or 215/931-4000). **Greyhound Bus Lines** (☎ **800/231-2222**) stops here also. Depending on advance purchase and length of stay, a round-trip ticket to or from New York City is $26 for the 2-hour trip; one way is $14. The equivalent fare to or from Washington, D.C., is $28. New Jersey Transit (☎ **215/569-3752**) also operates buses out of Philadelphia, with terminals at Camden, Atlantic City, and other nearby destinations.

For Foreign Visitors 3

This chapter provides specific suggestions about getting to the United States as economically and effortlessly as possible, plus some helpful information about how things are done in Philadelphia—from receiving mail to making a local or long-distance telephone call.

1 Preparing for Your Trip

ENTRY REQUIREMENTS

DOCUMENT REGULATIONS   Canadian citizens may enter the United States without visas; they need only proof of residence.

British subjects and citizens of New Zealand, Japan, and most western European countries traveling on valid national (or EC) passports may not need visas for fewer than 90 days of holiday or business travel in the United States, providing that they hold round-trip or return tickets and they enter the United States on an airline or cruise line that participates in the visa waiver program. (Citizens of these visa-exempt countries who first enter the United States may then visit Mexico, Canada, Bermuda, and/or the Caribbean islands and then reenter the United States, by any mode of transportation, without needing a visa. Further information is available from any U.S. embassy or consulate.)

Citizens of countries other than those above, including citizens of Australia, must have two documents: (1) a valid passport, with an expiration date at least six months later than the scheduled end of the visit to the United States; and (2) a tourist visa, available without charge from the nearest U.S. consulate.

To obtain a visa, the traveler must submit a completed application form (either in person or by mail) with a 1 1/2-inch square photo and demonstrate binding ties to a residence abroad. Usually you can obtain a visa at once or within 24 hours, but it may take longer during the summer rush from June to August. If you cannot go in person, contact the nearest U.S. embassy or consulate for directions on applying by mail. Your travel agent or airline office may also be able to provide you with visa applications and instructions. The U.S. consulate that issues your visa will determine whether you will be issued a multiple- or single-entry visa and any restrictions regarding the length of your stay.

MEDICAL REQUIREMENTS   No inoculations are needed to enter the United States unless you are coming from, or have stopped over in, areas known to be suffering from epidemics, especially of cholera or yellow fever.

If you have a disease requiring treatment with medications containing narcotics or drugs requiring a syringe, carry a valid, signed prescription from your physician.

CUSTOM REQUIREMENTS   Every adult visitor may bring in free of duty: 1 liter of wine or hard liquor; 200 cigarettes or 100 cigars (but no cigars from Cuba) or 3 pounds of smoking tobacco; and $100 worth of gifts. These exemptions are offered to travelers who spend at least 72 hours in the United States and who have not claimed them within the preceding six months. It is altogether forbidden to bring into the country foodstuffs (particularly cheese, fruit, cooked meats, and canned goods) and plants (vegetables, seeds, tropical plants, and so on). Foreign tourists may bring in or take out up to $10,000 in U.S. or foreign currency with no formalities; larger sums must be declared to customs on entering or leaving.

INSURANCE

There is no national health-care system in the United States. Because the cost of medical care is extremely high, we strongly advise every traveler to secure health insurance coverage before setting out. You may want to take out a comprehensive travel policy that covers (for a relatively low premium) sickness or injury costs (medical, surgical, and hospital); loss or theft of your baggage; trip-cancellation costs; guarantee of bail in case of arrest; and costs associated with accident, repatriation, or death. Such packages (for example, "Europe Assistance" in Europe) are sold by automobile clubs at attractive rates, as well as by banks and travel agencies.

MONEY

CURRENCY & EXCHANGE   The U.S. monetary system has a decimal base: One American **dollar** ($1) = 100 **cents** (100¢). Dollar **bills** commonly come in $1 (a buck), $5, $10, $20, $50, and $100 denominations (the last two are not welcome when paying for small purchases, and are usually not accepted in taxis or at subway ticket booths). There are also $2 bills (seldom encountered).

There are six coin denominations: 1¢, (one cent, or "penny"); 5¢ (five cents or "nickel"); 10¢ (ten cents or "dime"); 25¢ (twenty-five cents or "quarter"); 50¢ (fifty cents or "half dollar"); and the $1 pieces (both the older, large silver dollar and the newer, small Susan B. Anthony coin).

TRAVELER'S CHECKS   Traveler's checks denominated in U.S. dollars are accepted at most hotels, motels, restaurants, and large stores. Sometimes picture identification is required. The best place to change traveler's checks is at a bank. Do not bring traveler's checks denominated in other currencies.

CREDIT CARDS   The method of payment most widely used is credit and charge cards: Visa (BarclayCard in Britain), MasterCard (EuroCard in Europe, Access in Britain, Diamond in Japan), American Express, Discover, Diners Club, enRoute, JCB, and Carte Blanche. You can save yourself trouble by using "plastic" rather than cash or traveler's checks in most hotels, motels, restaurants, and retail stores (a growing number of food and liquor stores now accept credit cards). You must have a credit card to rent a car. It can also be used as proof of identity, or as a "cash card," enabling you to draw money from automated teller machines (ATMs) that accept it.

You can telegraph (wire) money, or have it telegraphed to you very quickly using the **Westen Union** system (☎ 800/325-6000).

SAFETY

While tourist areas are generally safe, crime is on the increase everywhere, and U.S. urban areas tend to be less safe than those in Europe or Japan. Visitors should always stay alert. This is particularly true of large U.S. cities. It is wise to ask the city's or area's tourist office if you're in doubt about which neighborhoods are safe.

Remember also that hotels are open to the public, and in a large hotel, security may not be able to screen everyone entering. Always lock your door—don't assume that once inside your hotel you are automatically safe and no longer need to be aware of your surroundings.

DRIVING   Safety while driving is particularly important. Question your rental agency about personal safety, or ask for a brochure of traveler safety tips when you pick up your car. Obtain from the agency written directions, or a map with the route marked in red, to show you how to get to your destination. If possible, arrive and depart during daylight hours.

Recently more and more crime has involved cars and drivers. If you drive off a highway into a doubtful neighborhood, leave the area as quickly as possible. If you have an accident, even on the highway, stay in your car with the doors locked until you assess the situation or until the police arrive. If you are bumped from behind on the street or are involved in a minor accident with no injuries and the situation appears to be suspicious, motion for the other driver to follow you. *Never* get out of your car in such situations.

If you see someone on the road who indicates a need for help, do not stop. Take note of the location, drive on to a well-lighted area, and telephone the police by dialing 911. Park in a well-lighted, well-traveled area if possible.

Always keep your car doors locked, whether attended or unattended. Never leave any packages or valuables in sight. If someone attempts to rob you or steal your car, do not try to resist the thief/carjacker—report the incident to the police department immediately.

2   Getting to & Around the United States

GETTING TO THE U.S.

Overseas travelers can take advantage of the **APEX (Advance Purchase Excursion) fares** offered by major U.S. and European carriers. International carriers that fly into Philadelphia International Airport (☎ 215/937-6800) include **Air Canada** (☎ 800/268-7240 in Canada), **Air Jamaica** (☎ 800/523-5585); **British Airways** (☎ 0345/222-111 in London); and **Swissair** (☎ 01/258-3434 in Zurich or 022/799-5999 in Geneva). From Ireland, **Aer Lingus** (☎ 01/844-4747 in Dublin or 061/415-556 in Shannon) can fly you into New York and arrange an add-on flight to Philadelphia. From New Zealand and Australia, there are flights to Los Angeles on **Quantas** (☎ 008/177-767 in Australia) and on **Air New Zealand** (☎ 0800/737-000 in Auckland or 3/379-5200 in Christchurch); both airlines can book you through to Philadelphia.

The visitor arriving by air, no matter what port of entry, should cultivate patience and resignation before setting foot on U.S. soil. Getting through Immigration Control may take as long as two hours on some days, especially summer weekends. Add the time it takes to clear Customs and you should make a very generous allowance for delay in planning connections between international and domestic flights—figure on two or three hours at least.

In contrast, travelers arriving by car or by rail from Canada will find border-crossing formalities streamlined to the vanishing point. And air travelers from Canada, Bermuda, and some places in the Caribbean can sometimes go through Customs and Immigration at the point of departure, which is much quicker and less painful.

GETTING AROUND THE U.S.

BY PLANE   Some large airlines (for example, TWA, American Airlines, Northwest, United, and Delta) offer transatlantic and transpacific travelers special discount tickets under the name **Visit USA,** allowing travel between U.S. destinations at minimum rates. They are not on sale in the United States—they must be purchased before you leave your foreign point of departure. This system is the best, easiest, and fastest way to see the United States at low cost. You should obtain information well in advance from your travel agent or the office of the relevant airline, since the conditions attached to these discount tickets can change at any time.

BY TRAIN   Long-distance trains in the United States are operated by **Amtrak** (☎ **800/872-7245**). International visitors can also buy a **USA Railpass,** good for 15 or 30 days of unlimited travel on Amtrak. The pass is available through many foreign-travel agents. Prices in 1996 for a 15-day pass are $355 for nationwide travel, $175 if you stay in the Northeast; a 30-day pass costs $440 for nationwide travel, $205 for the Northeast only. (With a foreign passport, you can also buy passes at some Amtrak offices in the United States, including locations in San Francisco, Los Angeles, Chicago, New York, Miami, Boston, and Washington, D.C.). Reservations are generally required and should be made for each part of your trip as early as possible.

Visitors should also be aware of the limitations of long-distance rail travel in the United States. With a few notable exceptions (for instance, the Northeast Corridor line between Boston and Washington, D.C.), service and convenience are rarely up to European standards.

BY BUS   The cheapest way to travel the United States is by bus. Greyhound (☎ **800/231-2222**), the sole nationwide bus line, offers an **Ameripass** for unlimited travel. At press time, a 7-day pass was $179, a 15-day pass was $289, and a 30-day pass was $399. Bus travel in the United States can be both slow and uncomfortable, so this option is not for everyone.

BY CAR   To rent a car, you will need a major credit card. The minimum driver age is usually 21, and you'll need a valid driver's license.

The major car-rental agencies are **Hertz** (☎ 800/654-3131), **Avis** (☎ 800/831-2847), **National** (☎ 800/227-7368), **Budget** (☎ 800/824-7088), and **Alamo** (☎ 800/327-9633). Also check smaller local companies and car dealers like **Sheehy Ford** (☎ 215/698-7000).

For information on transportation to Philadelphia from elsewhere in the United States, see "Getting There" in Chapter 2.

FAST FACTS: For the Foreign Traveler

Automobile Organizations   Auto clubs can supply maps; recommended routes; guidebooks; accident and bail-bond insurance; and, most important, emergency road service. The major auto club in the United States, with 955 offices nationwide, is the **American Automobile Association (AAA),** with national headquarters at 1000 AAA Dr., Heathrow, FL 32745 (☎ **800/336-4357**). AAA can provide you with an international driving permit validating your foreign license. The local office is Keystone AAA, 2040 Market St., Philadelphia, PA 19103 (☎ 215/864-5000). For local emergency road service, call **569-4411.**

Business Hours   Public and private offices are usually open Monday through Friday from 9am to 5pm. Banks are generally open Monday through Friday from 9am to 3pm, in some cases Friday until 6pm and Saturday morning. Post offices are open Monday through Friday from 8am to 5:30 or 6pm, Saturday from 8am to noon. Store hours are Monday through Saturday from 9 or 10am to 5:30 or 6pm, though often on Wednesday until 9pm in Philadelphia. Most shopping centers, drugstores, and supermarkets are open Monday through Saturday from 9am to 9pm, with some open 24 hours a day.

Climate   See "When to Go" in Chapter 2.

Currency   See "Preparing for Your Trip" earlier in this chapter.

Currency Exchange   You can exchange money at the following places in Center City: American Express Travel Service, 2 Penn Center Plaza (☎ 215/587-2342 or 215/587-2343); Thomas Cook Currency Services, Inc., 1800 John F. Kennedy Blvd. (☎ 215/563-5544); CoreStates First Pennsylvania Bank, 16th and Market Streets (☎ 215/786-8880); Dickins Inn, Head House Square at 2nd Street (☎ 215/928-9307); First Fidelity Bank, Broad and Walnut Streets (☎ 215/985-7068); Mellon PSFS Bank, Broad and Chestnut Streets (☎ 215/553-2145); Meridian Bank, 1700 Arch St. (☎ 215/854-3549); MidAtlantic Bank, 1201 Chestnut St. (☎ 215/225-2424); and PNC Bank, Broad and Chestnut Streets (☎ 215/585-5000).

Drinking Laws   You must be 21 or older to consume alcohol in public. In Philadelphia, establishments may serve alcoholic beverages from 9am to 2am (private clubs may serve until 4am). Liquor purchasing in Pennsylvania is quite restricted (see Chapter 9).

Electricity   U.S. wall outlets give power at 110 to 120 volts, 60 cycles, compared to 220 to 240 volts, 50 cycles, in most of Europe. In addition to a 110-volt converter, small appliances of non-American manufacture, such as hair dryers and shavers, will require a plug adapter with two flat, parallel pins.

Embassies and Consulates   All embassies are located in Washington, D.C.; some consulates are located in major cities, and most nations have a mission to the United Nations in New York City. You can get the telephone number of your embassy by calling information in Washington, D.C. (☎ 202/555-1212).

   Most European countries have Philadelphia consulates; call information at 215/555-1212 for the telephone number. The British Consulate is at 226 Walnut St. (☎ 215/925-0118).

Emergencies   Call **911** to report a fire, call the police, or get an ambulance. This is a toll-free call (no coins are required at a public telephone). You can also report an emergency by dialing **0** (zero, *not* the letter "O") and contacting the telephone-company operator.

   If you encounter such travelers' problems as sickness, accident, or lost or stolen baggage, call the local chapter of the **Travelers Aid Society** at 215/546-0571. This organization specializes in helping distressed travelers, whether American or foreign.

   For medical emergencies at Philadelphia International Airport, call **215/937-3111.**

Gasoline (Petrol)   One U.S. gallon equals 3.75 liters, while 1.2 U.S. gallons equals 1 imperial gallon. You'll notice there are several grades (and price levels) of gasoline at most gas stations. And you'll also notice that their names change from company to company. The unleaded grades with the highest octane are the most expensive, but most rental cars take the least expensive "regular" unleaded. Leaded gasoline is rarely used anymore. Gas stations are both self-serve and full-service.

Holidays   On the following national legal holidays, banks, government offices, post offices, and many stores, restaurants, and museums are closed: January 1 (New Year's Day); third Monday in January (Martin Luther King Jr. Day); third Monday in February (Presidents' Day, marking Washington's and Lincoln's birthdays); last Monday in May (Memorial Day); July 4 (Independence Day); first Monday in September (Labor Day); second Monday in October (Columbus Day); November 11 (Veterans Day/Armistice Day); fourth Thursday in November (Thanksgiving Day); and December 25 (Christmas). The Tuesday following the first Monday in November is Election Day, and is a legal holiday in presidential election years (2000 is an election year).

Legal Aid   If you are stopped for a minor infraction (say, speeding on the highway), never attempt to pay the fine directly to a police officer; you may wind up arrested on the much more serious charge of attempted bribery. Pay fines by mail or directly to the clerk of a court. If you're accused of a more serious offense, say and do nothing before consulting a lawyer. Under U.S. law, an arrested person is allowed one telephone call to a party of his or her choice. Call your embassy or consulate.

Mail   If your mail is addressed to a U.S. destination, don't forget to add the five-figure postal code or ZIP code after the two-letter abbreviation of the state to which the mail is addressed (CA for California, MA for Massachusetts, NY for New York, PA for Pennsylvania, and so on).

Rates in 1996 for international mail are: post cards, 50¢ to everywhere except Mexico (35¢) and Canada (40¢); basic letters cost 60¢ to everywhere except Mexico (40¢) and Canada (46¢). Aerogrammes are 50¢. U.S. postage is 23¢ for postcards, 32¢ for letters.

Philadelphia's main post offices are located at 9th and Market Streets and across from Penn Station at 30th Street.

Safety   Whenever you're traveling in an unfamiliar city, stay alert. Be aware of your immediate surroundings. Wear a money belt—or, better yet, check valuables in a safety-deposit box at your hotel. Keep a close eye on your possessions and be sure to keep them in sight when you're seated in a restaurant, theater, or other public place. Don't leave valuables in your car—even in the trunk. While driving a car, be extremely cautious when unlocking doors or leaving your car for any reason.

Taxes   In the United States there is no VAT (value-added tax) at the national level. Every state, and each city in it, can levy its own local tax on purchases, including hotel and restaurant checks, airline tickets, and the like. It is automatically added to the price of certain services, such as public transportation, cab fares, phone calls, and gasoline. Philadelphia's sales tax is 7%, except for clothing, which makes visits to outlet malls such as Franklin Mills so popular with international tourists.

In addition, each locality can levy its own separate tax on hotel occupancy. In Philadelphia, in addition to your hotel rate, you pay 7% sales tax plus a 5% surcharge.

Telephone and Fax The telephone system in the United States is run by private corporations, so rates, especially for long-distance service and operator-assisted calls, can vary widely—even on calls made from public telephones. Local calls usally cost 25¢.

Generally, hotel surcharges on long-distance and local calls are astronomical. These are best avoided by using a public phone, calling collect, or using a telephone charge card.

Most long-distance or international calls can be dialed directly from any phone. For international calls, dial 011, followed by the country code and then by the city code and the number of the person you wish to call. For calls to Canada and other parts of the United States, dial 1 followed by the area code and seven-digit number.

For reversed-charge or collect calls, and for person-to-person calls, dial 0 (zero, *not* the letter "O") followed by the area code and number you want; an operator will then come on the line, and you should specify what you want. If your operator-assisted call is international, ask for the overseas operator.

For local directory assistance ("information"), dial 411; for long-distance information, dial 1, then the appropriate area code and **555-1212**.

Most hotels have fax machines available for their customers, and there is usually a charge to send or receive a facsimile. You will also see signs for public faxes in the windows of small shops.

Time The United States is divided into six time zones. From east to west, these are eastern standard time (EST), central standard time (CST), mountain standard time (MST), Pacific standard time (PST), Alaska standard time (AST), and Hawaii standard time (HST). Always keep changing time zones in your mind if you are traveling (or even telephoning) long distances in the United States. For example, noon in Philadelphia (EST) is 11am in Chicago (CST), 10am in Denver (MST), 9am in Los Angeles (PST), 8am in Anchorage (AST), and 7am in Honolulu (HST). Daylight saving time (DST) is in effect from the first Sunday in April through the last Saturday in October, except in Arizona, Hawaii, part of Indiana, and Puerto Rico. Daylight saving time moves the clock one hour ahead of standard time.

Tipping This is part of the American way of life, on the principle that you must pay for any service received. Bartenders should receive 10% to 15%; bellhops, 50¢ per bag; cab drivers, 15% of the fare; chambermaids, $1 a day; waiters, 15% to 20% of the check.

Toilets As elsewhere in the United States, there are no public kiosks; you must use restrooms within buildings. Most of the Independence National Historical Park sites have very clean, free restrooms. Within Center City, most hotel lobbies have public restrooms, and many restaurants will allow you to use theirs during off-peak hours.

4 Getting to Know Philadelphia

This chapter sets out to answer all your travel questions, furnishing you with all the practical information that you'll need during your stay in Philadelphia to handle any and every experience—from the city layout and transportation to emergencies and business hours.

1 Orientation

VISITOR INFORMATION

The **Philadelphia Convention and Visitors Bureau,** 1515 John F. Kennedy Blvd., Philadelphia, PA 19102 (☎ **800/537-7676** or 215/636-1666), is one of the very best in America. It looks like a shiny layer cake between Suburban Station and City Hall, and its reception desk is staffed by enthusiastic and knowledgeable volunteers. You can pick up coupons for reduced admissions to many museums and attractions, too, as well as free aids for persons who are blind or have disabilities.

The visitors bureau parcels out free tickets to the New Year's Day Mummer's Parade and to the Mann Music Center for summer concerts in the park. They also sell such tickets as the SEPTA DayPass ($5) and "A Gift of Gardens" for 14 regional sites. Many bus tours, trolley rides, and walking tours begin here for convenience. Some floor space has been devoted to a city gift shop.

The bureau is open daily from 9am to 5pm (except Christmas Day) and until 6pm on summer weekdays. If you think ahead, call **800/537-7676** to get material on all the special seasonal promotions. In summer, if you show up at noon, there's usually outdoor entertainment on the adjoining plaza, which anchors one end of the Benjamin Franklin Parkway (known simply as "the Parkway").

There's also an **International Visitors Center** at 1600 Arch St., Philadelphia, PA 19103 (☎ **215/686-4471**), to make foreign visitors feel at home. This center offers special services to visitors from overseas.

CITY LAYOUT

MAIN ARTERIES & STREETS Unlike Boston, Philadelphia has no colonial cowpaths that were turned into streets. If you can count and remember the names of trees, you'll know exactly where you are in the Center City grid. For the overview, go to (or pretend you're at) the top of **City Hall,** that overiced wedding cake in the very center of things, at the intersection of Broad and Market Streets.

Broad Street runs 4 miles south, where the Delaware and Schuylkill flow together, and 8 miles north—all perfectly straight. The other major north–south streets are numbered. Except for a few two-way exceptions, traffic on even-numbered streets heads south and on odd-numbered streets, north. **Front Street** (should be 1st Street), once at the Delaware's edge off to the right, and neighboring **2nd Street** were the major thoroughfares in colonial times. In-between streets are named. The major east–west streets in Philadelphia's Center City run from Spring Garden Street to the north to South Street. You'll spend much of your time between Arch and Pine Streets, especially south of Chestnut Street.

The colonial city, now **Independence National Historical Park** and reconstructed row houses, grew up along the Delaware north and south of **Market Street,** extending west to 6th Street by 1776. The 19th century saw the development of the western quadrants (including most museums and cultural centers) and suburbs in every direction. The city blocks planned by William Penn included five parks spaced between the two rivers. Four parks have been named for local notables (including George Washington, who headed the federal government here in the 1790s), and the fifth supports City Hall. A broad northwest boulevard, dividing the grid like a slice of Paris, ends in the majestic arms of the Philadelphia Museum of Art. The entire quadrant west and north of City Hall has been the site of intensive development of hotels, office buildings, and apartment houses.

Just beyond, the Schuylkill separates Philadelphia from West Philadelphia from 24th Street to about 30th Street—if you're looking for an address in this area, ask which side it's on. **Fairmount Park** lines both sides of the Schuylkill for miles above the museum.

FINDING AN ADDRESS   Addresses on these streets add 100 for every block away from the axis of Market Street (north–south) or Front Street (east–west); 1534 Chestnut St. is between 15th and 16th Streets, and 610 S. 5th St. is between six and seven blocks south of Market.

STREET MAPS   The **Philadelphia Convention and Visitors Bureau,** 1515 John F. Kennedy Blvd. (☎ **800/537-7676** or 215/636-1666), has a very good street map within its "Official Visitors Guide." You can pick it up at the Visitors Bureau and at all hotels.

NEIGHBORHOODS IN BRIEF

Philadelphia is more of a collection of neighborhoods than a unified metropolis. Here are ultra-short descriptions of those likely to come your way.

Chestnut Hill   This enclave of suburban gentility, with a "Main Street" flavor centered around upper Germantown Avenue, is the highest point within city limits. It's filled with galleries and boutiques, tearooms, and comfortable restaurants.

Chinatown   Nowadays it's largely commercial rather than residential, but there are lots of good restaurants and cheaper parking only 5 minutes from the Convention Center. And it stays up forever.

Germantown   One of Philadelphia's most ancient settlements, this area was founded by German émigrés attracted by Penn's religious tolerance. Outside of its wonderful historic mansions, however, it is not especially attractive now.

Manayunk   This neighborhood, 4 miles up the Schuylkill River from Center City, has rocketed to gentility in the last decade, with many of the city's hottest boutiques, galleries, and café/restaurants on Main Street, overlooking a 19th-century canal adjoining the river. It's a picturesque and vital place for an afternoon stroll, and there's a great farmer's market.

Philadelphia at a Glance

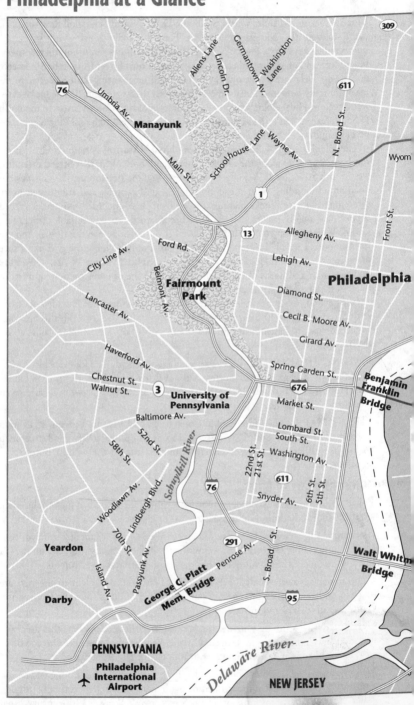

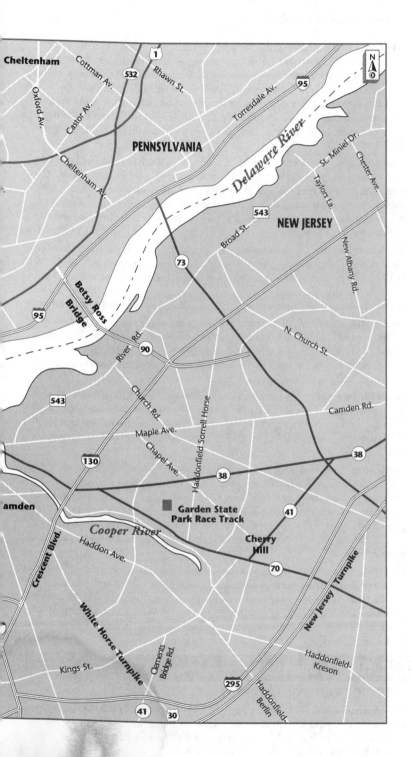

Old City   In the shadow of the Benjamin Franklin Bridge just north of Independence National Historical Park lies an eclectic blend of row houses dating from William Penn's time, 19th-century commercial warehouses, and 20th-century rehabs à la SoHo in New York City. If you're interested in either the very old or the very new, this is the place to spend a few hours, and the odd alleyways between the city grid streets provide nooks for quaint and quiet cafés and shops. The first Friday night of every month is like a giant block party, with all the galleries and stores open until 8pm.

Queen Village   On a pleasant day you'll want to walk south from Society Hill along the Delaware or 2nd Street (known as "Two Street" among old Philadelphians). The Swedish originally settled this area, along with river islands below the confluence with the Schuylkill, and some of their buildings remain. There are lots of small, reasonable cafés and bistros here, and pedestrian bridges constructed over I-95 have recently reconnected it to the waterfront.

Rittenhouse Square   This is not just an urban park, but a specific cultural connotation of elite Philadelphians' community for offices, shops, and mansions from 1950 to 1970. The world is much bigger and more diverse, but more than traces linger on. From the Rittenhouse Hotel on a sunny day, walk through the square to Walnut Street, which can rival any district in Paris or London for charm and sophistication.

Society Hill   This heart of reclaimed 18th-century Philadelphia is loosely bounded by Walnut and Lombard Streets and Front and 7th Streets. Today it's a fashionable section of the old city, just south of Independence National Historical Park, where you can stroll among restored Federal, colonial, and Georgian homes; even the contemporary "infill" is interesting and immaculately kept up.

South Philadelphia   It's Rocky Balboa and more. From 300 years of waves of immigration, this is Philadelphia's most colorful and ethnically diverse neighborhood, although the stereotypes and most of the restaurants and bars are Italian circa 1910s Calabria. I love strolling the Italian Market at 9th and Christian and heading south, snacking all along the way until dinner.

South Street   Located below Society Hill and above Queen Village, South Street was the city limit in William Penn's plan. The 1960s saw bohemian artists reclaim this street in the name of peace and love; newer spirits, just as young and somewhat more filled with attitude, have replaced the previous hipsters, but it's undeniably hopping day or night. Look for good retaurants and bars, bookstores, hoagie shops, handcrafted contemporary furniture stores, natural-food stores, European cafés, and art galleries.

University City   West Philadelphia was farmland until the University of Pennsylvania moved here from 9th and Chestnut Streets in the 1870s, and you ought to wander through the main campus, both for the architecture and for the cultural amenities. The original college quadrangle built in 1895 was based on Oxford and Cambridge models, with just a touch of Dutch gables. Even though it's mere blocks away from Center City, it has a slightly stranded feeling.

2 Getting Around

BY PUBLIC TRANSPORTATION

SEPTA (Southeastern Pennsylvania Transportation Authority) operates a complicated and extensive network of trolleys, buses, commuter trains, and subways. In the past 10 years the capital budget for new equipment has increased from $20 million to $120 million; new cars gleam on the Broad Street line.

Fares for any SEPTA route are $1.60, with 40¢ more for a transfer, and *exact change or tokens are required.* Anyone can purchase a 5-pack for $5.75 or a 10-pack for $11.50. Seniors pay nothing and the passengers with disabilities pay half-fare during off-peak hours. Certain buses and trolleys run 24 hours a day. The $5 DayPass is good for all buses, subways, and one ride on the Airport loop; a weekly TransPass, good from Monday to the next Sunday, is $16.

An **Information Center** (open Monday through Friday from 7am to 6pm, also on Saturday in summer) in the underground arcade at 15th and Market Streets will give you free timetables and routes for individual lines (take the down escalator across the street from City Hall and turn right). The official street and transit map, which puts the entire picture together, costs $1.50 and is available here or at newsstands. If you have questions about how to reach a specific destination, call SEPTA headquarters at **215/580-7800** between 6am and midnight—but expect to wait.

BY SUBWAY-SURFACE LINE This "local" connects City Hall and 30th Street Station, stopping at 19th and 22nd Streets along the way. West of the Amtrak station, it branches out, moving aboveground to the north and south.

BY RAPID TRANSIT In Center City, these fast cars speed under Broad Street and Market Street, intersecting under City Hall. The Broad Street line now connects directly to Pattison Avenue and Philadelphia sporting events to the south. The Market Street line stops at 2nd, 5th, 8th, 11th, 13th (Convention Center), 15th, and 30th Street stations and stretches to the west and northeast. Both run all night, but residents suggest caution during late-hour use.

BY PATCO This commuter rail line (☎ 215/922-4600) begins at Walnut and Locust Streets around Broad Street, connects with rapid transit at 8th and Market, and crosses the Ben Franklin Bridge to Camden. To get to the aquarium, get off at Broadway in Camden to transfer to the New Jersey Transit's Aqualink Shuttle. Transfers connect to the Jersey shore from Lindenwold.

BY BUS Since November 1995, those purple vans with the turquoise wings have been everywhere tourists want to go. Every 10 minutes between 10am and 12:30am in summer (until 6:30pm from mid-September to mid-May) the **PHLASH Bus** service (☎ 474-5274) links Independence Park sites, the Delaware waterfront, the Convention Center, Rittenhouse Square shopping, and the cultural institution at Logan Circle. The total loop takes 50 minutes and makes 30 stops. A one-time pass is $1.50, but take the all-day unlimited ride pass for $3. Passes are not transferable to SEPTA. Children under 6 ride free.

Route 76, the **Ben FrankLine,** is also a subsidized tourism deal at 50¢; it connects Society Hill at 3rd and Chestnut Streets to the Parkway all the way to the Museum of Art and the Zoo; it operates every 10 minutes weekdays, every 20 minutes weekends. The first trip from 3rd Street is at 9am, and the last pickup at the Museum of Art is at 6:11pm.

For a straight crosstown route, you'll often find yourself on the **Chestnut Street Transitway,** a stretch of Chestnut between 6th and 17th Streets open only to buses and taxis. Bus no. 42 swoops along Chestnut from West Philadelphia to 2nd at all hours. Several bus routes serve Market Street; the **Mid-City loop** ($1.50, with a 40¢ transfer to another bus) goes up Market and down Chestnut between 5th and 17th Streets. Route 32 goes up Broad Street and the Parkway and through Fairmount Park to Andorra; the full trip is 15 miles. New double buses now swivel through many major routes.

BY TROLLEY There are no more "true" city trolleys like in Boston or San Francisco. A privately operated **Penn's Landing Trolley** chugs along Christopher

Columbus Boulevard (formerly Delaware Avenue) between the Benjamin Franklin Bridge and Fitzwater Street; you can board at Dock Street or Spruce Street. The fare is $1.50 for adults, 75¢ for children, and the trolley runs Thursday through Sunday from 11am to dusk in the summer.

Replicas of 1930s open-air trolleys operate as 39-seat buses run by **American Trolley Bus** (☎ 215/333-0320) and **Old Town Trolley** (☎ 215/928-8687), with guides who point out all the high spots. Admission ranges from $6 to $14, depending on tour length and family size. Pickup spots include Liberty Bell Pavilion, Independence Park Visitors Center, and the Franklin Institute.

BY TRAIN   The Philadelphia area is served by one of the great commuter-rail networks in America. Chestnut Hill, a wealthy enclave of fine shops and restaurants, can be reached from both Suburban Station at 16th Street and John F. Kennedy Boulevard and Reading Terminal at 12th and Market Streets, now connected themselves by the new rail link. The famous term "Main Line" refers, in fact, to the old Pennsylvania Railroad line from Suburban (now Penn Center) Station to Harrisburg. What in the suburbs would interest you? Merion is home to the great Barnes Foundation art collection and the Buten Museum of Wedgwood. Bryn Mawr, Haverford, Swarthmore, and Villanova are sites of noted colleges. Devon hosts a great horse and country fair. One-way fares for all destinations are under $6, and you can buy tickets at station counters or vending machines.

BY CAR

Philadelphia's streets were once considered so wide that there was room for market stalls in the divides. Unfortunately, that was 200 years ago. So on Center City streets there's little room for parked or moving cars. You might try the streets below Chestnut. Locust, Spruce, and Pine are often the best. Be forewarned that *all streets are one-way*—except for lower Market Street, the Parkway, Vine Street, and Broad Street. The Convention and Visitors Bureau at the foot of the Parkway offers a Center City traffic map. Traffic around City Hall follows a counterclockwise pattern, but traffic lights seem to follow none.

Since Philadelphia is so walkable, it is easier to leave your car while you explore. Many hotels offer free or reduced-rate parking to registered guests.

If you need emergency car repair, try **Center City Auto Care,** 901 N. Broad St. (☎ 215/763-8328), or **Mina Motors,** Broad and Fitzwater Streets (☎ 215/735-2749), for same-day service. **Keystone AAA** is at 2040 Market St., Philadelphia, PA 19103 (☎ 215/864-5000).

RENTALS   Philadelphia has no shortage of cars and very good rental rates as a consequence. For example, you can pick up a weekend sedan from **Avis** (☎ 800/331-1212) for $42 per day, with unlimited mileage, at one of their lots: 2000 Arch St. (☎ 215/563-8976), 30th Street Station (☎ 215/386-6426), or under Independence Place at 6th and Locust Streets (☎ 215/928-1082). Avis and all other major renters maintain offices at the airport. These include **Budget** (☎ 800/824-7088, or 215/492-9400 at the airport, 215/557-0808 at 21st and Market); **Dollar** (☎ 800/800-4000, or 215/365-2700 at the airport); and **Hertz** (☎ 800/654-3131 for all locations).

PARKING   Call the Philadelphia Parking Authority (☎ 215/563-7670 or 215/977-7275) for current information.

Garage rates are fairly similar: Outside of hotels, no place exceeds $22 per day, with typical charges of $3.50 per hour and $10 for an evening out.

Parking can be found for **Independence Park** at 125 S. 2nd St. (Sansom Street is the cross street); Independence Mall Garage, 41 N. 6th St.; Spruce Street between 5th and 6th Streets (private lot); and Head House Square, 2nd and Lombard Streets (city meters). **Convention Center Area** parking includes Kinney Chinatown at 11th and Race Streets (private garage); Kinney underneath the Gallery II mall at 11th and Arch Streets; the Autopark beside the Gallery mall at 10th and Filbert Streets; or the garage underneath the adjoining Marriott at Arch and 13th Streets. **City Hall Area** parking is underneath Hecht's (formerly Wanamaker's), between Market and Chestnut Streets at 13th Street; a private garage adjoining the Doubletree Hotel at Broad and Spruce Streets; and Kennedy Plaza, 15th Street and John F. Kennedy Boulevard (underground city garage; enter on Arch, one block north of the plaza).

BY TAXI

Philadelphia's notorious shortage of taxis is improving, with about 1,400 currently licensed. Under 1991 legislation, gypsy cabs have been outlawed in return for increasing taxi medallions. Cabbies must pass stringent tests for city knowledge and maintain clean vehicles. Fares are currently $1.80 for the first one-seventh mile and 30¢ for each additional one-seventh mile or minute of stasis. Tips are expected, usually 15% of the fare.

If you need to call for a cab while in the city, the three largest outfits are **Olde City Taxi** (☎ 215/247-7678), **United Cab** (☎ 215/238-9500), and **Quaker City** (☎ 215/728-8000).

FAST FACTS: Philadelphia

American Express   There are AmEx offices at 16th Street and John F. Kennedy Boulevard (☎ 215/587/2342) and at the airport (☎ 215/492-4200).

Area Code   Philadelphia's telephone area code is **215.** Bucks County and half of Montgomery County use **215** also, but the Brandywine Valley area of Delaware, Chester, and half of Montgomery have switched to **610.** Lancaster County and the Pennsylvania Dutch region use area code **717.**

Babysitters   Check with your hotel, or contact Rocking Horse Child Care Center at the Curtis Center, Walnut and 6th Streets (☎ 215/592-8257); rates are $7 per hour for those under 2, $6 per hour for ages 3 to 6. Comparable is Call-A-Granni, Inc., 1133 E. Barringer St. (☎ 215/924-8723).

Business Hours   Banks are generally open Monday through Thursday from 10am to 3pm, Friday until 6pm, with some also open on Saturday from 9am to noon. Most bars and restaurants serve food until 10 or 10:30pm (some Chinatown places stay open until 3am), and social bars are open Friday and Saturday until 1 or 2am. Offices are open Monday through Friday from 9am to 5pm. Stores are open daily from 9am to 5pm, and most Center City locations keep the doors ajar later on Wednesday evening. Old City, South Street, the Delaware waterfront, and Head House Square are the most active late-night districts. Some SEPTA routes run all night, but the frequency of buses and trolleys drops dramatically after 6pm.

Car Rentals   See "Getting Around," earlier in this chapter.

Dentist   Call 215/925-6050 in a dental emergency.

Doctor   Call the Philadelphia County Medical Society at **215/563-5343.** You can always dial **911** in an emergency. Every hospital in town has an emergency room.

Drugstores   See "Pharmacies" below.

Embassies and Consulates   See Chapter 3.

Emergencies   In an extreme emergency, telephone **911.** In case of accidental poisoning, call **215/386-2100.** For police, call **215/231-3131;** for fire and rescue, call **215/922-6000.** Ambulance and emergency transportation can be summoned through Care & Emergency, Inc. (☎ **215/877-5900**), or SEPTA Paratransit (☎ **215/574-2780**).

Eyeglass Repair   Snyder Opticians at 251 S. 17th St. (☎ **215/735-5656**) does on-site repairs. Contact Lens Neun at 255 S. 17th St., sixth floor (☎ **215/545-7355**), promises same-day replacement.

Hospitals   Medical care in Philadelphia is excellent. Major hospitals include Children's Hospital, 34th Street and Civic Center Boulevard (☎ **215/590-1000**); Graduate Hospital, 1800 Lombard St. (☎ **215/893-2000**); Hahnemann, Broad and Vine Streets (☎ **215/762-7000**); University of Pennsylvania Hospital, 3400 Spruce St. (☎ **215/662-4000**); Pennsylvania Hospital, 8th and Spruce Streets (☎ **215/829-3000**); and Thomas Jefferson, 11th and Walnut Streets (☎ **215/955-6000**).

Information   See "Visitor Information," earlier in this chapter.

Liquor Laws   The legal drinking age is 21. You can only buy liquor in state stores, which are usually open Monday through Wednesday from 9am to 5pm and Thursday through Saturday from 9am to 9pm. See Chapter 9 for the best state store locations.

Lost Property   If you lose something on a SEPTA train or subway, try the stationmaster's office in Suburban Station.

Newspapers/Magazines   Philadelphia has two main print journals, both now owned by the same firm. You'll want to check out the Friday "Weekend" supplement of the *Inquirer* for listings and prices of entertainment as well as special events and tours. The *Daily News* is more close-to-home Philadelphia material. Free tabloid weeklies with surprisingly good articles and listings include *City Paper* and *Philadelphia Weekly;* you'll find them at record and bookstores and on street-corner boxes. For the most complete selection of journals and newspapers, try Avril 50, 3406 Sansom St. (☎ **215/222-6108**), in University City. The Society Hill equivalent is Popi, 526 S. 4th St. (☎ **215/922-4119**), and 116 S. 20th St. (☎ **215/557-8282**), near Rittenhouse Square.

Pharmacies   There's a 24-hour CVS at 6501 Harbison Ave. (☎ **215/333-4300**), but this is miles from Center City. The Medical Tower Pharmacy, 255 S. 17th St. (☎ **215/545-3525**), is open until 9pm on Monday through Friday and until 6pm on Saturday. During regular hours, try Barclay Pharmacy, 18th and Spruce Streets (☎ **215/735-1410**), and Green Drugs, 5th and South Streets (☎ **215/922-7440**).

Police   The emergency telephone number is **911.**

Post Office   The main post office at 2970 Market St. (☎ **215/596-5577**), just across the Schuylkill and next to 30th Street station, is always open; the number of its 24-hour window is **215/895-8989.** The post office on the subway concourse at 2 Penn Center, 15th Street and John F. Kennedy Boulevard, is open Monday through Friday from 7am to 6pm, Saturday from 9am to noon. You can also go to the post office that Ben Franklin used at 316 Market St.

Radio   There's intense competition among more than 60 stations, so the following programming emphasis is subject to change: all news, KYW (1060 AM);

album-oriented rock, WMMR (93.3 FM); classic rock, WYSP (94.1 FM); oldies, WOGL (98.1 FM); soft rock, WIOQ (102.1 FM); country, WCZN (1590 AM) and WXTU (92.5 FM); ethnic urban orientation, WUSL (98.9 FM), WDAS (1480 AM), and WHAT (1340 AM); classical music, WFLN (95.7 FM); and National Public Radio, WHYY (91.0 FM) and WXPN (88.5 FM).

Restrooms   Public restrooms can be found at 30th Street Station; the Independence National Historical Park Visitors Center; and at major shopping complexes like Liberty Place, the Bourse, the Gallery, and Downstairs at the Bellevue. You can usually use hotel lobby and restaurant facilities.

Safety   Philadelphia exhibits many preconditions of crime: It's large and populous, suffering from overall job losses in the last decade and a widening gap between haves and have-nots. You won't see too much of this underside if you concentrate on major tourist destinations, but stay alert and be aware of your immediate surroundings. Keep a close eye on your possessions. If you are planning to explore Philadelphia in unusual neighborhoods, around college campuses in West Philadelphia, at unusual hours, or in a style that makes you conspicuous, be especially careful. Center City has recently responded to visible signs of urban distress, including tourist crime, with a combination of police staffing and specially identified "Community Ambassadors," so incidents are rare under normal circumstances.

Taxes   Hotel-room charges incur a 7% state tax and a 5% city surcharge. There is a 7% tax on restaurant meals and on general sales. Clothing is tax-free.

Taxis   See "Getting Around," earlier in this chapter.

Television   Network affiliates include Channel 3 (CBS), KYW; Channel 6 (ABC), WPVI; Channel 10 (NBC), WCAU; Channel 12 (PBS), WHYY; and Channel 29 (FOX), WTXF. Most hotels have cable with offerings like Home Box Office, CNN, ESPN, and Disney.

Time Zone   Philadelphia is in the eastern time zone—eastern standard time (EST) or eastern daylight time, depending on the time of year, making it the same as New York and three hours ahead of the West Coast.

Transit Information   To find out how to reach a specific destination, call SEPTA headquarters at **215/574-7800**—but expect to wait.

Weather   Call **215/936-1212.**

5 Accommodations

A century ago, Philadelphia was full of inns, hostelries, and European-style hotels for all pocketbooks and tastes. The names and faces are different today, but the situation is again the same, after decades of frankly disappointing choices. Philadelphia, as part of its new reliance on tourism, has begun paying serious attention to the comfort of guests, and it shows.

Thanks to the dozens of conventions being booked by the new Pennsylvania Convention Center, Philadelphia hotels are currently booming. The adjoining Philadelphia Convention Center Marriott, even with 1,200 rooms (the largest in the state), can't soak up all this demand, so look for increased occupancy in Center City's other 5,600 hotel rooms. And consistent with the law of supply and demand, the increased demand for Philadelphia accommodations has caused prices to take a substantial jump in 1996. There's no indication that prices won't continue to rise, so you'll have to look a little harder for discounts and promotions by hotels—especially luxury and near luxury. Concentrate on those great weekend packages around town, and check out the increased bed-and-breakfast and smaller inn listings below for a cheaper, fresh alternative.

Geographically, look to hotels in the Rittenhouse Square area for larger, more individualized prewar spaces. Corporate activity in the northeast quadrant between City Hall and the Philadelphia Museum of Art has produced sleek 1980s hotels, with a lesser surge of smaller hotels in or near historic Society Hill. Outside Center City, West Philadelphia is only a bus ride away and rates are a bit cheaper.

Philadelphia has an additional 8,000 hotel beds within a 20-mile circumference out of town. This includes a full complement of airport hotels 20 minutes away, many of them recently opened in response to the growth of the airport itself. Two fine hotels sit atop a bluff near I-76 that overlooks the downtown skyline. Roosevelt Boulevard hides some smaller properties, about 20 minutes out of town.

Outlying countries are full of lovely old inns like the 1740 House in Bucks County; see Chapter 11 for listings as you go. The **Visitors Center,** 16th Street and John F. Kennedy Boulevard, Philadelphia, PA 19102 (☎ 215/636-1666), can help with any questions.

RATES Recommendations are divided here into four categories based on double occupancy rates per night: **very expensive** (more than $190), **expensive** ($140 to $190), **moderate** ($80 to $140), and **inexpensive** (less than $80). All rooms have private baths unless otherwise indicated, and you can count on a state tax of 7% plus a city surcharge of 5%. You can always try to bargain for lower rates, because there is keen competition to boost occupancy rates. Also, be sure to ask about parking and/or arrangements for children.

BED & BREAKFAST AGENCIES   One good agency to contact is **A Bed & Breakfast Connection/Bed & Breakfast of Philadelphia,** Box 21, Devon, PA 19333 (☎ 800/448-3169 or 610/687-3565; fax 610/995-9524). This reservation service represents more than 100 personally inspected accommodations in Philadelphia, Valley Forge, the Brandywine Valley, and Lancaster, Montgomery, and Bucks counties. The agency has assembled a group of interesting, warm hosts, including linguists, gourmet cooks, and therapists. Philadelphia accommodations include a contemporary loft with a spectacular view of the Delaware River, a mid-18th-century inn, a Victorian home with a magnificent three-story open staircase, and a town house tucked in an alley seconds from Rittenhouse Square. In greener pastures, you could pick from the second oldest house in Pennsylvania, a former stage-coach stop, or a converted carriage house complete with swimming pool.

Their prices range from $40 to $100 per night for a single person, $45 to $225 for a couple. Many at lower prices have shared baths, and children are a point to discuss. The agency will select a compatible lodging for you or send you their free brochure. American Express, VISA, and MasterCard are accepted; phone reservations can be made Monday through Friday from 9am to 7pm and on Saturday from 9am to 5pm.

Janice Archbold at **Guesthouses,** Box 2137, West Chester, PA 19380 (☎ 610/692-4575), has more than 200 host situations lined up, not only in Philadelphia but also throughout the Mid-Atlantic region. Most buildings are architecturally or historically significant, and rates average $100 and up. Monthly rentals are also available.

The **Association of Bed and Breakfasts in Philadelphia, Valley Forge, and Brandywine,** P.O. Box 562, Valley Forge, PA 19481 (☎ 800/344-0123 or 215/783-7838 for reservations from 9am to 9pm daily; fax 610/783-7783), is a no-fee reservation service with 600 rooms in more than 130 town-and-country choices from Main Line, Bucks County, Lancaster County, and West Chester. Singles start at $35 per night, and doubles at $45.

1 Best Bets

- **Best Historic Hotel:** Well, it's only the "lite" version of what it used to be, when Thomas Edison designed the fixtures and a top-floor ballroom cornered the market for swank. But the **Bellevue Hotel's** (☎ 215/893-1776) top-floor, occasionally oddly proportioned rooms carry traces of a century of history on South Broad Street.
- **Best for Business Travelers:** Even though it's the largest hotel in the state, you can still figure out the layout and amenities of the new **Philadelphia Marriott** (☎ 215/625-2900) pretty easily. The rooms have great workspaces with a second modem jack instead of a breakfast table, and the business center on the fifth floor is quite efficient. The service staff is truly excellent.
- **Best for a Romantic Getaway:** Some people like a slick, cosmopolitan suite in the clouds for romance. Give me the **Penn's View Inn** (☎ 215/922-7600) any day. Even at the noisy corner of Front and Market Streets, the upper floors feel like an

exquisite club with views over the Delaware River. And how could you vote against the largest wine bar in the world downstairs?

- **Best Hotel Lobby for Pretending That You're Rich:** There's no place like the cool, plush **Four Seasons Hotel** (☎ 215/963-1500) for rubbing elbows with the monied elite. The Swann Lounge overlooking Logan Circle is a constant stream of chic outfits, special occasions, custom suits, and the frequent black tie.
- **Best for Families:** It looks like a 1960s condo version of the Leaning Tower of Pisa—but the **Embassy Suites Center City** (☎ 215/561-1776) is actually a family's treasure house, with a stimulating play area with PC programs designed by the impeccable Please Touch Museum people, cute little open-air balconies (yes, the railings are good), and an opulent buffet breakfast at the TGI Friday's at street level. It's five minutes to the premier children's museums and Logan Circle. And, of course, all the rooms are suites, so parents can still have their privacy.
- **Best Moderately Priced Hotel:** Prices have jumped substantially since the opening of the Convention Center, so I would judge the **Penn Tower Hotel** (☎ 215/387-8333) in West Philadelphia as the best choice in its price range, with a "retail" double for $144 and packages from $99. It has excellent views and is located only minutes from Center City and the University of Pennsylvania by taxi or by walking from 30th Street Station. U. Penn., which in fact owns the building, keeps it first-rate.
- **Best B&B:** Many, many more B&Bs are listed through A Bed & Breakfast Connection/Bed & Breakfast of Philadelphia (see "Bed and Breakfast Agencies" above) than allow themselves to be listed independently. My favorite among the latter is **Shippen Way Inn** (☎ 215/627-7266), a tiny row house in Queen Village built around 1750 and lovingly maintained. During summer, you can wake up in a four-poster bed and have breakfast in the back herb garden for $70 to $105 per night.
- **Best Service:** The training process set up by COO Horst Schulze for every employee of every **Ritz-Carlton** (☎ 215/563-1600) hotel is legendary, and the hotel atop Liberty Place is no exception. Guests pay top prices (actually, quite affordable on weekend packages) to be pampered in preparation for a tough world outside. It's a fantasy land of amenities; service attendants earn points for thinking of extras like foam and down pillows in the same closet and bookmarks in the TV Guides. Think about this: "May I pour your first cup of coffee?"
- **Best Location:** Assuming we're tourists who have come to see Independence Park, why not wake up looking at it from the floral chintz curtains at the **Omni Hotel at Independence Park** (☎ 215/925-0000). All 155 guest rooms do—specifically, at the Greek Revival Second Bank of the U.S. and a half-dozen of America's Georgian jewels. The clip-clopping of horses and carriages below doesn't harm that sense of history.
- **Best Health Club: The Wyndham** (☎ 215/448-2000)—with 758 rooms, second only to the Convention Center Marriott—has the best facilities free to hotel guests, including a 45-foot indoor pool, track, three racquetball courts, three squash courts, outdoor handball, and two tennis courts—all on the third-floor lobby roof. Weights and Nautilus round out the picture inside.
- **Best Hotel Pool:** I'm actually cheating a tiny bit here, but part of the garage complex of the **Bellevue Hotel** (☎ 215/893-1776) is the Sporting Club, with its four-lane, junior Olympic pool. Only hotel guests and local members can use the pool.
- **Best Views:** Many of the hotel listings below specify one side or another as preferable. In Center City, rooms at **The Rittenhouse** (☎ 215/546-9000) are on

floors 5 through 9, and all have wonderful views, from the wonderfully colorful park below on the east, to the western view of the Schuylkill and the Parkway.

•**Best Hotel Restaurant:** The Zagat 1996 guide to local restaurants is only the latest ranking of **Fountain Restaurant** in the **Four Seasons** (☎ **215/963-1500**) as one of the country's top 50 dining spots. Natural light streams over fresh flowers, tapestries, and wide armchairs. It's virtually flawless, with prices to match.

2 Historic Area

VERY EXPENSIVE

Omni Hotel at Independence Park. 4th and Chestnut sts., Philadelphia, PA 19106. ☎ **800/843-6664** or 215/925-0000. Fax 215/925-1263. 141 rms, 9 suites. A/C MINIBAR TV TEL. $179–$229 double; $375–$750 suite. Weekend rates from $119 double per night. Children stay free in parents' room. AE, CB, DC, DISC, MC, V. Self-parking $13.50; valet parking $19.50.

This small, polished hotel opened in 1990 and has a terrific location in the middle of Independence National Historical Park, three blocks south of Ben Franklin Bridge (Chestnut Street runs one-way east, so approach from 6th Street). All rooms have Independence Park views, and horse-drawn carriages clip-clop past the valet parking dropoff and an elegant glass-and-steel canopy. The lobby is classic, with current newspapers, huge vases of flowers, and a bar featuring a piano or a jazz trio nightly.

Each room is cheery, with plants and original pastels of city views. State-of-the-art conveniences include plastic coded room keys, voice mail, VCR, two telephones, and fax- and computer-compatible jacks. All rooms have individual temperature controls, windows that open, and closets with three different kinds of hangers. Rooms for nonsmokers are available. The staff here is noteworthy for its quality and park knowledge.

Dining/Entertainment: The second-floor Azalea is one of Philadelphia's top restaurants; chef Aliza Green has created imaginative treatments of American regional dishes. The restaurant is open for breakfast, lunch, brunch, and dinner. Hearty (not English) afternoon tea is served in the lobby lounge, which also features a piano trio most nights.

Services: 24-hour room service, concierge, valet parking. Complimentary van to Center City stops, weekdays 7am to 7pm.

Facilities: Indoor lap pool (no lifeguard) available daily from 7am to 11pm; whirlpool and sauna adjoining, with Stairmaster and exercise area; Ritz 5 movie theater tucked into the back corner.

Sheraton Society Hill. 1 Dock St., Philadelphia, PA 19106. ☎ **800/325-3535** or 215/238-6000. Fax 215/922-2709. 365 rms, 17 suites. A/C MINIBAR TV TEL. $210–$220 double, depending on view; $450–$650 suite. Weekend rates $159–$179 double per night. Children under 17 stay free in parents' room. AE, DC, MC, V. Parking $12.50 per day.

Located three blocks from Head House Square and four blocks from Independence Hall, the 1986 Sheraton Society Hill sits nestled among the tree-lined cobblestone streets of this historic district. Set on a triangular 2¹/₂-acre site between Dock and South Front Streets, the building was designed in keeping with the area's Flemish Bond architecture. Its skylit, four-story atrium is entered via a circular courtyard with a splashing fountain.

The guest rooms—on the long, low second, third, and fourth floors (the only Delaware River views are from the latter)—are a bit smaller than you'd expect; half have one king-size bed, and the others have two double beds. The furnishings of each are top-quality Drexel Heritage mahogany, with four lamps, two-post headboards,

Philadelphia Accommodations

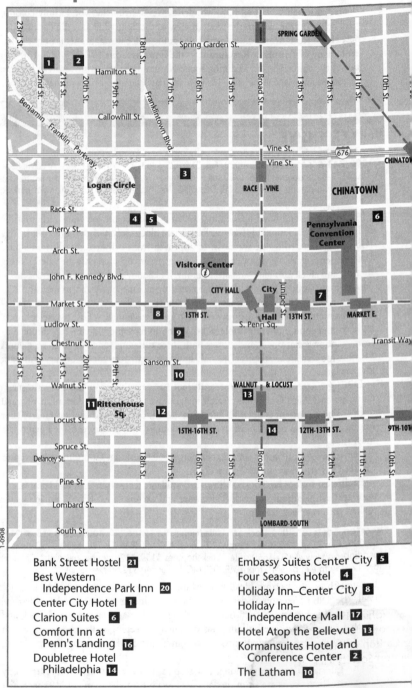

Bank Street Hostel **21**

Best Western
Independence Park Inn **20**

Center City Hotel **1**

Clarion Suites **6**

Comfort Inn at
Penn's Landing **16**

Doubletree Hotel
Philadelphia **14**

Embassy Suites Center City **5**

Four Seasons Hotel **4**

Holiday Inn–Center City **8**

Holiday Inn–
Independence Mall **17**

Hotel Atop the Bellevue **13**

Kormansuites Hotel and
Conference Center **2**

The Latham **10**

44

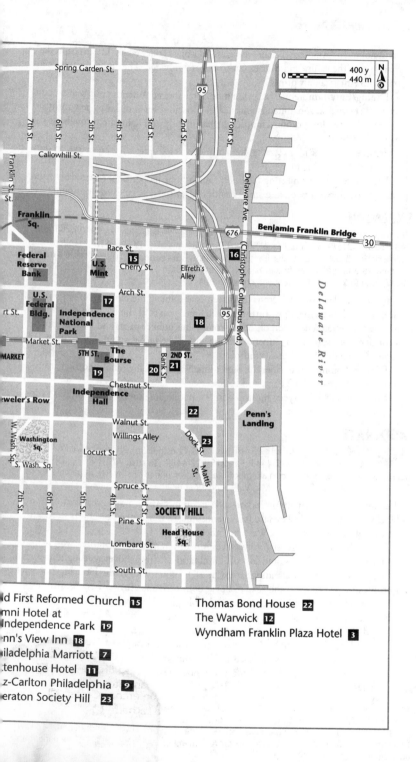

an upholstered loveseat and chair, and glass-and-brass coffee tables. In each bath, dark marble tops the vanity and Martex bathrobes are provided. The decor is gender neutral, with American art prints.

Dining/Entertainment: Hadleys, a moderately priced American bistro restaurant, features creative seasonal menus and health-conscious main dishes. The Courtyard has piano music for a cappuccino/dessert bar nightly and light fare throughout the day and evening.

Services: 24-hour room service, free shuttle van to Center City, concierge on duty daily from 6am to 11pm.

Facilities: Superior meeting facilities; fourth-floor indoor pool (open daily from 6am to 10pm), whirlpool, and small health club with trainers; third-floor sauna.

EXPENSIVE

Holiday Inn–Independence Mall. 4th and Arch sts., Philadelphia, PA 19106. ☎ **800/843-2355** or 215/923-8660. Fax 215/829-1796. 364 rms. A/C TV TEL. $168 standard with double or king bed. Weekend rates from $98 per night. Extra person $10 (up to four in a room). Children 18 and under stay free in parents' room; children 12 and under eat free. AE, DC, MC, V. Parking $10 per day; frequent airport shuttles.

This Holiday Inn, set back from the street, is absolutely the closest you're going to sleep to the Liberty Bell; just turn the corner and you're at the pavilion that houses it. The continued renovation of the bedrooms and public spaces and the addition of a concierge have given it a "superior" rating within the Holiday Inn organization. All rooms have individual climate control.

Dining: You might consider the buffet lunch served in the renovated Benjamin's, or the less expensive Café Plain and Fancy.

Facilities: Washer/dryers; rooftop outdoor pool; game room; and children's programs in the summer.

MODERATE

⑤ Best Western Independence Park Inn. 235 Chestnut St., Philadelphia, PA 19106. ☎ **800/528-1234** or 215/922-4443. Fax 215/922-4487. 36 rms. A/C TV TEL. $99–$135 double. Rates include breakfast and afternoon tea. Children under 12 stay free in parents' room. 15% AAA discount. AE, DC, DISC, MC, V. Parking $9 at nearby enclosed garage.

This top choice for bed-and-breakfast–style accommodations has a great location, two blocks from Independence Hall. It's a handsome 1856 former dry-goods store with renovated rooms, now a Best Western franchise.

The eight floors of guest rooms have four different color schemes; you'll find armoires, lathed bedposts, and lots of illumination, with an overhead light at each entrance foyer and four standing lamps in each room. The baths have big beveled mirrors, dropped ceilings, and soap dishes at both bath and shower heights. Although all the windows are triple casement and double glazed, specify an interior room if you're sensitive to noise from the traffic on Chestnut Street. A third bed can be wheeled into your room for a child, at no additional charge.

The Independence Park has no restaurant. However, it serves a very passable continental breakfast in a glass-enclosed garden courtyard, with the Dickens Inn (see Chapter 6) supplying a complimentary afternoon tea. Special discount coupons to nearby restaurants are available at the desk.

⑤ Comfort Inn at Penn's Landing. 100 N. Columbus Blvd. (formerly Delaware Avenue), Philadelphia, PA 19106. ☎ **800/228-5150** or 215/627-7900. Fax 215/238-0809. 185 rms. A/C MINIBAR TV TEL. $119 double. Rates include continental breakfast. Children under 18 stay free in parents' room. Ask about discounts for AAA members. AE, DC, MC, V. Free parking in adjacent lot.

Comfort Inn at Penn's Landing is the area's only waterfront hotel, nestled into a corner of Old City between I-95 and the Delaware River, three blocks from the northbound ramp off the expressway. A shuttle van to Center City stops here, and the crosstown subway line is two blocks away.

A basic steel skeleton hung with blue-and-white concrete panels, Comfort Inn has been built to airport-area noise specifications, with insulated windows and other features to lessen the din of traffic. The eastern views of the river on upper floors are stupendous. Comfort Inn has no restaurant, but a complimentary continental breakfast is served in the cocktail lounge. There's a coin laundry on the second floor, and half the rooms are designated for nonsmokers. Its fitness room stocks weights and cardio machines.

Penn's View Inn. Front and Market Strs., Philadelphia, PA 19106. ☎ **800/331-7634** or 215/922-7600. Fax 215/922-7642. 28 rms. A/C TV TEL. $132 double. Weekend rate is $99 per room; a package at $229 includes two nights, champagne upon arrival, and Panorama restaurant voucher for $50. Rates include continental breakfast. Guarantee requested on reservation. AE, DC, MC, V. Parking $7 at adjacent lot.

Tucked behind the Market Street ramp to I-95 in a renovated 1856 hardware store, this small, exquisite inn exudes a European flair—when you enter you'll feel like you're in a private club. It was developed by the Sena family, who started La Famiglia 150 yards south (see Chapter 6 for details) and have grown a small neighborhood empire.

The decor is floral and rich; the main concern is traffic noise, but the rooms are well insulated, with large framed mirrors, armoires, and efficient bath fixtures. The ceilings have been dropped for modern vents. A third bed can be wheeled into your room for $15. Ristorante Panorama offers excellent contemporary Italian cuisine at moderate prices. Next to the restaurant is a world-class wine bar, il Bar, that offers 120 different wines by the glass.

Thomas Bond House. 129 S. 2nd St., Philadelphia, PA 19106. ☎ **800/845-2663** or 215/923-8523. Fax 215/923-8504. 12 rms, 2 suites. A/C TV TEL. $90–$160 double, $160 suite. Rates include breakfast and afternoon wine and cheese. MC, V. Parking $9 at adjacent lot.

This 1769 Georgian row house sitting almost directly across from the back of Independence Park is owned by the federal government, which kept the shell and gutted the interior. The proprietors have turned the guest rooms into cheerful, comfortable colonial-style accommodations. Guests now enter through the former side entrance, encountering a basic cream-and-blue color scheme, with map illustrations and secretary desks. The charming parlor has pink sofas and a replica Chippendale double chair, while the breakfast room has four tables for four. All rooms are individually decorated and feature private baths and period furnishings. Fresh-baked cookies are put out each evening for bedtime snacking. The hotel is named for its first occupant, the doctor who cofounded Pennsylvania Hospital with Benjamin Franklin.

3 Center City

VERY EXPENSIVE

Bellevue Hotel. Broad and Walnut sts., or 1415 Chancellor Court (between Walnut and Locust Streets), Philadelphia, PA 19102. ☎ **800/221-0833** or 215/893-1776. Fax 215/893-9868. 170 rms. A/C MINIBAR TV TEL. $230 standard room; $260 deluxe room; $290 executive room. Weekend package (which includes free parking and a credit of $30 toward breakfast) at $185 often available. AE, DC, MC, V. Parking $14 per day at connected garage; valet parking $21.

The "grande dame of Broad Street" was the most opulent hotel in the country when it first opened in 1904, and it was fully renovated in 1989. A notch below the Four Seasons, Rittenhouse, or Ritz-Carlton, it's still a grand experience in a great location, and the value is substantial.

The luxury hotel is now managed by former officers of Cunard, Inc., which ran the Bellevue Hotel from 1989 to 1993. The ground floor houses internationally renowned retailers like Tiffany & Co. and Polo/Ralph Lauren, while the belowground level features quick and easy gourmet fare and take-out from a food court. A separate elevator lifts you to the 19th-floor registration area and foyer for the hotel restaurants.

The rooms, occupying floors 12 through 17, are as large as ever, and all slightly different, with a green-and-white decor and wall moldings reproduced from the 1904 designs. The makeover has added to each room extra-large goose-down pillows, three two-line phones with data ports, a VCR, a large bed, a writing desk, a round table, and four upholstered chairs. Closets have built-in tie racks and automatic lighting. The baths are dated but have amenities like hair dryers, TVs, and illuminated close-up mirrors.

Dining/Entertainment: Founders Dining Room (see Chapter 6), voted one of the top 50 restaurants in the nation by *Conde Nast Traveler,* has two spectacular semicircular windows draped with dramatic swags of brown and cream.

The Library Lounge is quiet and a bit precious. With a copy of a Gilbert Stuart full-length portrait and a collection of books by and about Philadelphians, the lounge is open all day but serves from 11am to 1am. The Ethel Barrymore Room serves afternoon tea with a view of the Philadelphia skyline Wednesday through Friday from 2 to 4:30pm, and Saturday from 2 to 5pm. At night, the Ethel Barrymore Room features live music, such as caberet performances, a musical theater festival, or the hotel's house swing band.

On the 12th floor is the equally impressive Conservatory, at the base of a dramatic 80-foot atrium carved out of the original hotel. It has a wonderful, whimsical cafe ambience, with trellises, oval cloud mural, porch swings, and two-story palms. It serves a generous breakfast buffet and lunch buffet on weekdays.

Services: 24-hour room service, concierge, complimentary glass of champagne or hot drink upon arrival, full-day child-care facility at the Sporting Club.

Facilities: A fourth-floor skywalk from the hotel at the ballroom level leads directly to the garage on the other side of Chancellor Court. It also goes to the Sporting Club, a Michael Graves–designed facility that boggles the eye with 93,000 square feet of health space, including a half-mile jogging track; a four-lane, 25-meter junior Olympic pool; and corridors of squash and racquetball courts. The club is open daily from 6:30am to 10pm and is available only to members and hotel guests.

✪ **Four Seasons Hotel.** One Logan Square, Philadelphia, PA 19103. ☎ **800/332-3442** or 215/963-1500. Fax 215/963-9506. 371 rms, 9 suites. A/C MINIBAR TV TEL. Doubles from $285; suites from $345. Weekend rates from $180 double per night. AE, DC, MC, V. Valet parking $24 weekdays, $18 weekends.

The Four Seasons, one of the two best hotels in Philadelphia, is a member of a distinguished luxury chain that includes New York's Pierre, the Four Seasons in Dallas and Washington, and London's Inn on the Park. Its luxury is spare, refined, and understated.

Built in 1983, the Four Seasons is an eight-story curlicue on Logan Square. It's separated from the "partner" CIGNA headquarters by a fountain and landscaped courtyard that opens as a café in summer. The hotel has landscaped the Logan Circle gardens as well.

As you're waved into the porte cochere on 18th Street, your first view is of enormous masses of flowers, with stepped-stone levels, water, and honeyed woods stretching far into the distance. The lounge and promenade serve as foyers to the dining and meeting facilities and are paneled in a rare white mahogany.

The guest rooms mix Federal-period furniture with richer, more Victorian color schemes. There is a very direct American elegance in each room: the desk, settee, armoire, and wing chair/ottoman combinations are top-quality Henredon. All the rooms have large windows or private verandas boasting marvelous views of Logan Circle or the interior courtyard.

Dining/Entertainment: The Four Seasons restaurants regularly collect raves from local reviewers. The Fountain Restaurant, serving all three meals, continues the low-key elegance of the hotel by combining luxury (150 seats in wide, comfortable armchairs) with intimacy. Natural light streams over tapestries, fresh flowers, and walnut paneling.

The Swann Lounge, closer to the lobby corridor, has marble-top tables and a colorful, civilized look out of a Maurice Prendergast sketch. It's open for an extensive lunch, afternoon tea, early evening cocktails, and dessert and drinks until midnight. As summer visitors can't help noticing, the Courtyard Café bubbles with light refreshments.

Services: Concierge, 24-hour room service, complimentary overnight shoe shine, terry-cloth robes, and town-car service within Center City.

Facilities: Besides European spa weekends, the basement health center includes a heated pool (large enough for laps), a superheated whirlpool, Universal machines, exercycles, and exercise mats—all spotlessly maintained. The hotel also has a full-service hair salon and a small sundries shop.

✪ **Rittenhouse Hotel.** 210 W. Rittenhouse Square, Philadelphia, PA 19103. ☎ **800/ 635-1042** or 215/546-9000. Fax 215/732-3364. 98 rms. A/C MINIBAR TV TEL. Doubles from $285. Weekend rates from $160 double per night. Packages including health club, dinners, and other amenities are usually available. AE, DC, MC, V. Parking $21.

Among Philadelphia's luxury hotels, the Rittenhouse has the fewest and largest rooms, the most satisfying views, and the more homegrown Philadelphia feel. Built in 1989, it's a jagged concrete-and-glass high-rise off the western edge of Philadelphia's most distinguished public square. The lobby is truly magnificent, with inlaid marble floors and a series of frosted-glass chandeliers and sconces. This and the Four Seasons (see above) are AAA's only 5 Diamond Award winners in the state.

The Rittenhouse Hotel has 98 guest rooms on floors 5 through 9; the other floors contain condominium residences. The rooms have bay windows, reinforced walls between rooms, and solid-wood doors. All have great views: The park is wonderfully green 9 months of the year, but the western view of the Schuylkill and the Parkway is even more dramatic. Spirited renderings of city scenes by local artists decorate the walls; amenities include VCRs and in-room fax machines.

Dining/Entertainment: Radio personality and executive chef James Coleman oversees the cuisine in the hotel's restaurant and two lounges. Tree Tops, which occupies the second floor and overlooks the park, is a sun-filled café offering regional American cuisine. It is open for breakfast, lunch, and dinner. The Boathouse Row Bar is a Ralph Lauren–style re-creation of an authentic boathouse, with an entire rowing scull mounted overhead and a lighted mural of boathouse row. The bar serves lunch, dinner, and late-night snacks.

Completing the picture is the ground-floor Cassatt Tea Room and Lounge serving traditional afternoon tea and cocktails daily. The site was the original town house of the painter Mary Cassatt's brother, and the Rittenhouse has adorned an ingenious trellised private garden triangle with three drypoints by this American master.

Services: 24-hour room service, one Clef d'Or concierge, turndown service with written weather report for the morrow and radio tuned to soft classical music, twice-daily room cleaning. Many cooking classes and/or lunch events are held for children.

Facilities: The third floor is split between Adolf Biecker hair salon and Toppers Spa, a fitness club with a five-lane indoor pool, a sundeck, and Cybex weight machines and aerobic equipment. Sauna, steam room, and spa-like amenities such as massages, facials, and body wraps are also offered. The floor above is devoted to an executive business center. There's an ATM in the building.

✪ **Ritz-Carlton Philadelphia.** 17th and Chestnut sts. at Liberty Place, Philadelphia, PA 19103. ☎ **800/241-3333** or 215/563-1600. Fax 215/564-9559. 290 rms, 17 suites. A/C MINIBAR TV TEL. $205–$245 double; $265 Ritz-Carlton Club; $325–$425 suite. Weekend rates from $169 double per night. Packages include valet parking and fitness center. AE, DC, MC, V. Self-parking $17.50; valet parking $22.

If the Four Seasons is luxury with a 20th-century slant and the Rittenhouse captures the 19th century, then the Ritz-Carlton claims the 18th century. Opened in 1990 as part of Liberty Place, the hotel is a superb blend of luxury amenities and service, steps away from the best in urban life.

A small porte cochere and a ground-floor lobby on 17th Street lead to a series of smaller, almost residential rooms that contain the front and concierge desks, the dining areas, and the elevators on the second floor.

The guest rooms feature bedside walnut tables, desks, beds with spindle-top headboards (with four pillows!), and Wedgwood or Sandwich glass lamps. Large walnut armoires house the TVs, clothing drawers, and minibars. The color schemes are muted, and all rooms are provided with two phone lines and data ports. The modern baths are outfitted with black-and-white marble, silverplate fixtures, magnifying mirrors, and lots of toiletries. The service is simply impeccable, as a result of fanatical training.

Dining/Entertainment: Three distinctive locations combine uncompromising cuisine with gracious service and ambience. (See also Chapter 6.) The Dining Room is decorated in American Federal and concentrates on contemporary American cuisine under the hand of chef Keith Mitchell. On the other side of the lounge fireplace, the mahogany-paneled and period-furnished Grill and Grill Bar have quickly become "Best of Philly" winners, with daily lunches and dinners of steaks, chops, and fish specialties. The Lobby Lounge has expanded its offerings to a continental breakfast, a formal tea, and hors d'oeuvres and desserts, with a constantly crackling fireplace. Classical and jazz music accompany afternoon and evening service.

Services: 24-hour room service, 24-hour concierge, nightly turndown, complimentary morning newspapers, transport to and from airport, car-rental arrangements, very frequent weekend or month-long festivals in connection with museum exhibitions or city theme events. These include a January through April Wine Festival, a February film weekend, a cigar smoker, children's events, and Philadelphia's "The Book and the Cook" culinary event.

Facilities: There are a small exercise and sauna facility, superb business meeting rooms, a fully equipped business center, and the like, but the most impressive extra is the internal connection to the 70 Shops at Liberty Place (see Chapter 9).

EXPENSIVE

Doubletree Hotel Philadelphia. Broad St. at Locust St., Philadelphia, PA 19107. ☎ **800/222-8733** or 215/893-1600. Fax 215/893-1663. 427 rms. A/C TV TEL. $199 double.

Weekday special rates $99–$119. Weekend package $99+ per night. "Dream Deal" weekend packages including full cooked-to-order breakfast at $114 per night. AE, DC, MC, V. Self-parking $13 in adjoining garage, valet parking $17.

In 1993, Sprint Hospitality Group took this property over and switched its management to Doubletree Hotels. Although the location is no longer ideal for business travelers, it is prime for tourists, and the weekend packages are quite affordable.

You'll probably enter through the corridor connecting the lobby to the garage on the block's southern side. The motor entrances ingeniously keep traffic flows separate for three floors of meeting facilities. During registration, take a good look at the four-story atrium: A web of steel struts finished in black enamel supports a diagonal sheet of glass panes, sloping down to a glass wall at street level. Decor features classic browns and whites, sky-blue tapestries, and Degas-style murals alluding to the orchestral and ballet life at the Academy of Music across the street.

The guest rooms, all completely renovated in the last three years, each have two views of town because of the sawtooth design. Obviously, the higher floors afford the better views; the views of the Delaware River (eastern corner) or City Hall (northeastern corner) are the most popular. Ten rooms, next to the elevators on certain floors, are designed for travelers with disabilities.

Dining: The Café Académie, an informal 220-seat restaurant and lounge, continues the glossy atrium connection. If you dine here (breakfast, lunch, and dinner served), ask for one of the tables overlooking the action outside. The decor is colonial-meets-California. The Lobby Bar, also being renovated, serves until midnight.

Services: Green boxes of great chocolate-chip cookies are delivered to your room upon arrival. Quick breakfasts are guaranteed. A guest services desk is staffed 16 hours daily. Budget will deliver rental cars to the hotel door.

Facilities: The fifth-floor Racquet and Health Club is free to all guests. You can tan, steam, swim in an indoor pool, whirlpool, or work out on CAM II exercise machines, Lifesteps, or Schwinn Airdynes. Two racquetball courts can be reserved for $10 per hour, with no equipment charge. A small jogging track circles a huge oak-planked deck, and summer brings many hotel parties and parade views.

Embassy Suites Center City. 1776 Benjamin Franklin Pkwy. at Logan Square, Philadelphia, PA 19103. ☎ **800/362-2779** or 215/561-1776. Fax 215/963-0122. 288 suites. A/C TV TEL. $184 suite. Weekend packages from $116 suite per night. Rates include full breakfast. AE, DC, MC, V. Parking $15.50 weekdays, $10 weekends in underground garage.

The big cylinder of marble and glass on the Parkway at 18th Street looks dated, but Bell Atlantic Properties (corporate headquarters are next door) and Embassy Suites have put $10 million into a 1993 refurbishment and it works quite well within their all-suite format.

The hotel has an interesting set of strengths and weaknesses. It was designed in the 1960s as luxury apartments radiating out from a central core—the Kelly family had the last penthouse here—but the quality of views varies widely, and the basic shape is weirdly disorienting. It's evident that the elevators and lobby weren't equipped to handle this volume. On the other hand, amenities such as the full breakfast at TGI Friday's (the connected restaurant), fitness room, nightly managers' reception, and Please Touch Too room for the kids all exceed expectations.

The suites themselves have a sleek severity, with black matte and putty surfaces for TV stands and a spare walnut inset bedroom armoire. The kitchenette eschews oven and dishwasher, but includes microwave, under-the-counter refrigerator, and coffeemaker; dishes and silverware are provided upon request. An especially nice 48-inch round table with four chairs overlooks the small balcony terraces with sliding doors. Baths have large Italian marble tiles, plush white towels, and hair dryers. With two double beds, the bedrooms don't have a lot of extra room. HVAC is customized to the room.

Dining/Entertainment: TGI Friday's is open until 1am daily, connected on two levels, and used for hotel breakfasts. The lobby lounge hosts happy hour.

Services: Valet parking; toiletries available at front desk upon request.

Facilities: The second-floor fitness center has Nordic Track, Stairmasters, rowing machine, and unisex sauna. The adjoining Please Touch Too room for children aged 2 to 9 is great, with a "store," interlocking foam tiles, hand puppets, and programmed "edugames" on PCs.

✪ **KormanSuites Hotel and Conference Center.** 2001 Hamilton St. (just off the Parkway), Philadelphia, PA 19130. ☎ **215/569-7300.** Fax 215/569-0584. 170 rms, 12 Grand Club suites. A/C TV TEL. $169 efficiency; $189 two-bedroom plus kitchen; $229 one-bedroom suite with connecting den. Other options available for stays of two weeks or more. Children stay free in parents' room. Rates include continental breakfast. AE, DC, MC, V. Free parking.

The amenities and the location of this hotel make it an excellent value at rack rates; the weekend packages make it outstanding. You'll recognize it by the bright neon scribble near its roof north of Logan Circle, visible from anywhere south.

KormanSuites is really a grand hotel, but it's in separate pieces. A 28-story tower is connected by a marble-and-mahogany lobby and a glass-enclosed corridor to the restaurant and lush Japanese sculpture garden and pool.

The standard rooms are unbelievably spacious, and a corridor contains a microwave, minibar, and coffeemaker. The suites add full kitchens with dishwashers, stoves, coffeemakers, and telephones. Each living area has a full dining table for four, TV, full couch, and three double closets. Each bedroom features a queen-size bed and another TV (in suites, with built-in VCR), and the adjoining bath has a stacked washer/dryer. The views are great: to the north, highlights of 19th-century manufacturing and churches; to the south, 20th-century Center City.

Dining: Catalina, the hotel restaurant, succeeds as a neighborhood favorite for moderate California-style mixtures of East Coast and West Coast. Hotel guests are offered complimentary continental breakfasts from 6 to 10am.

Services: Complimentary shuttle van running hourly through Center City to Independence Park, concierge, 24-hour message center, and garage attendants.

Facilities: Outdoor pool, Jacuzzi, two tennis and platform tennis courts, high-tech spa and fitness center, full-service hair salon, ATM on-site.

The Latham. 135 S. 17th St. at Walnut Street, Philadelphia, PA 19103. ☎ **800/528-4261** or 215/563-7474. Fax 215/563-4034. 140 rms, 3 suites. A/C MINIBAR TV TEL. $185 standard double; $195–$215 superior with king-size bed. Basic weekend package $99–$109 double per night. One or two children stay free in parents' room. Rates include breakfast and parking. AE, DC, MC, V. Valet parking $14.

An apartment house until 25 years ago, the Latham now brings to mind a small, superbly run Swiss hostelry, with its charm, congeniality, and small attentions. And the weekend packages are great bargains. However, some readers have recently complained about dropped standards and rude service.

On weekday mornings the lobby, a high-ceilinged salon with terrazzo highlights, is filled with refreshed executives who look as though the Latham truly is their home away from home. Dealings with the reception area are quick and professional, and newsstand and lobby phones are discreetly nestled in one corner. The Latham does no convention business. The guest rooms, renovated from 1988 to 1990, are not huge or lavish but perfectly proportioned and done in burgundy or light green. Each minibar combines a digital drink dispenser (with totals registered automatically) with space for storing your own supplies. Louis XIV–style writing tables, modern upholstered armchairs, and contemporary prints harmoniously mix the taste of different eras. The bathrooms feature Princess phones, embossed soaps, and Bic disposable razors. Full-wall mirrors, large marblelike basins, and oversize towels accentuate the white-toned interiors.

Dining: Michel's has gotten raves since its 1993 opening for its highly stylized variations of continental dishes.

Services: Concierge, turndown service with Godiva chocolate mints, valet parking.

Facilities: Free access to nearby fitness club with indoor pool.

Philadelphia Marriott. 12th and Market sts., Philadelphia, PA 19107. ☎ **800/228-9290** or 215/972-6700. Fax 215/972-6704. 1,200 rms. A/C TV TEL. $190 double; $169–$210 concierge-level rooms. Weekend rates from $138 double per night. AE, DC, MC, V. Parking $20, valet service only.

After more than a decade of planning and construction, the Marriott chain opened the biggest hotel in Pennsylvania in January 1995, linked by an elevated covered walkway to the Reading Terminal Shed of the Convention Center. The hotel's major auto entrance is on Filbert Street (two ways between Market and Arch Streets), with an equally grand pedestrian entrance adjoining Champions Sports Bar and retail on Market Street. The lobby is sliced up into a five-story atrium, enlivened by a 10,000-square-foot water sculpture, a lobby bar, and a Starbucks coffeeshop. Setbacks and terraces provide plenty of natural light and views from the hotel rooms in floors 6 through 23. Although tastefully outfitted with dark woods, maroon and green drapes and bedspreads, a TV armoire, club chair and ottoman, and round table plus a separate desk, the rooms are slightly less elegant than the top hotels. Comfortably sized baths have heavy chrome fixtures and tuck sinks and counters in the corners for more dressing room–type space. Closets are spacious. Concierge-level rooms feature private key access and use of a special lounge. Service is impeccable, thanks to the well-trained, knowledgeable staff.

Dining/Entertainment: J. W. Steakhouse overlooks the lobby atrium and Market Street; Champions, a sports bar with a lot of TVs, is on the east side along Market Street; Allie's serves casual meals all day, and a continental sidewalk café fronts 12th Street. There are also three lounges.

Services: The hotel offers all possible corporate and some luxury services. Concierge-floor rooms have special amenities.

Facilities: Complimentary seventh-floor health club with indoor lap pool, whirlpool, aerobics/fitness room, locker rooms, and wet and dry saunas. Direct internal connection to SEPTA subways and airport train.

The Warwick. 17th and Locust sts., Philadelphia, PA 19103. ☎ **800/523-4210** or 215/735-6000. Fax 215/790-7766. 180 rms, 20 suites. A/C MINIBAR TV TEL. $175 double; suites from $275. AE, DC, MC, V. Self-parking $14.75 in adjacent garage; valet parking $17.75.

If you wanted to live in a luxurious older apartment building, you'd head for The Warwick. Most recently renovated from 1991 to 1994, 200 rooms are rented or belong to condo owners, while 200 rooms and suites are the hotel's.

The Warwick's lobby mixes the old and the new: Many of the 1926 friezes and mantels have been reworked and repainted, while gleaming contemporary ensembles stretch themselves on Persian carpets. The mirrored pilasters may edge toward garishness, but the wall braziers and broad-leafed plants ensure a warm, splendid atmosphere. The guest rooms are basically done in English country; they're used by many meeting groups. Special touches include hand-milled sandalwood soap.

Dining: Mia's, with white tablecloths and dark-wood paneling, offers cuisine at moderate prices. It's open for mostly Italian breakfasts, lunches, and dinners. Capriccio's is a wonderful Italian-style espresso bar and sweetshop.

Services: Concierge (Betty George is one of the best in town), room service, overnight complimentary shoe shine.

Wyndham Franklin Plaza Hotel. 17th and Race sts., Philadelphia, PA 19103. ☎ **800/ 996-3426** or 215/448-2000. Fax 215/448-2864. 758 rms, 36 suites. A/C MINIBAR TV TEL. $175 double; $195–$215 deluxe; $300 and up suite. Weekend rate $99 double per night; a $149 package includes parking and next-day brunch. Children 18 and under stay free in parents' room. AE, DC, MC, V. Self-parking $13; valet parking $17.

The convention center four blocks away is finally filling this convention hotel. Nevertheless, the Wyndham has been functioning as a convenient meeting center and urban resort since 1980. The complex uses a full city block. The lobby, lounge, and two restaurants are beautifully integrated under a dramatic 70-foot glass roof. In terms of service and maintenance, the Wyndham has been showing signs of fatigue; look either for major renovations or for lots of discount deals to rebuild traffic, now that the Marriott is taking major convention business. Request a west view above the 19th floor to get an unobstructed peek at the Parkway, although be forewarned that the cathedral bells below ring hourly from 7am.

Dining/Entertainment: The Terrace is a coffee shop that serves excellent fare daily from 7am to 11pm. Between Friends, the flagship, features French tableside service for lunch and dinner in opulent surroundings of oil portraits, banks of flowers, and mirrored angle piers. A small atrium connects to the SmithKline building; the cafe is open daily from 7am to 3pm.

Services: Room service, travel service.

Facilities: The third-floor Clark's Uptown offers an indoor swimming pool (21 by 45 feet), a sauna, and a track—all free to hotel guests. An all-day fee of $10 gets you racquetball (three courts), squash (three courts), outdoor handball (three courts), and tennis (two courts). Around the latter is a one-eighth-mile jogging track. A sundeck, whirlpool, Nautilus machine, snack bar, and superb locker and exercise facilities round out the picture.

MODERATE

Abigail Adams Bed & Breakfast. 1208 Walnut St., Philadelphia, PA 19107. ☎ **800/ 887-1776** or 215/546-7336. Fax 215/546-7573. 20 rms, 6 suites. A/C TV TEL. $90 double; $120 suites. Rates include continental breakfast. AE, DC, MC, V.

Robert and Thomas Manning bought this late 1800s shell in 1992, in the expectation that the Convention Center and nearby hospitals would spin off at least 30 people per night who would want to save at least $50 from the Marriott's prices. They've constructed seven floors of comfortable, bigger-than-average rooms with solid-core doors and private baths. The front desk is attended 24 hours a day, and they are in the process of installing a 2,000-square-foot restaurant on the rear of the ground floor. All suites have gas fireplaces; the lobby has a pretty glass bow front.

Clarion Suites Convention Center. 1010 Race St., Philadelphia, PA 19107. ☎ **800/ 272-6232** or 215/922-1730. Fax 215/922-6258. 92 suites. A/C MINIBAR TV TEL. $130 double. Each additional person $10. Rates include continental breakfast. AE, DC, MC, V. Parking $8 validated (overnight) in garage next door.

You'll find spacious and reasonable accommodations at the Clarion Suites Convention Center in the heart of Philadelphia's Chinatown. The property was purchased at a low price and then properly renovated for high hotel occupancy. The building

👪 Family-Friendly Hotels

As mentioned above, a division of the Visitors Bureau, "Family Friendly Philadelphia," offers special packages at a number of hotels that include two nights, free parking and breakfast, and free admissions to attractions such as Sesame Place, the Franklin Institute, the Zoo, the Academy of Natural Sciences, the Please Touch Museum, and "The Liberty Tale Tour" run by the Historic Philadelphia people near Independence Hall. Call **800/770-5889** for details.

Embassy Suites Center City *(see page 51)*   There's an innovative play area designed by the Please Touch Museum, with hand puppets, CD-ROM interactive "edugames," and more—perfect for kids aged 2 to 9.

Four Seasons Hotel *(see page 48)*   The Saturday Lunch Club is a three-course meal for $21.50 designed for and presented to kids; it's featured on the first Saturday of the month.

Penn Tower Hotel *(see page 56)*   This West Philadelphia hotel has a courtesy shuttle to the historic district, free Disney and HBO on television, and a Children's Survival Kit and city tour packet for kids. It's also the closest hotel to the Zoo.

Rittenhouse Hotel *(see page 49)*   It intermittently offers children's cooking classes taught by Rena Coyle and also features some Saturday theme lunches for kids and their parents.

Sheraton Society Hill *(see page 43)*   There's a special children's check-in to the right of the lobby as well as concierge treatment with free snacks, the use of the game room, and so on.

---

itself, dating from the 1880s, is constructed of handsome dark-red brick with lots of terra-cotta tiling and wide arches. For many years a bentwood furniture factory, it retains 13-foot ceilings, solid floors, and wood cross beams. You'll enter the inn through large double Chinese doors flanked by Ming lions. The lobby is sea-green with wood touches; to the right is the breakfast room/bar, with the reception desk behind it. One-half flight up is a small new fitness center.

Clarion Suites Convention Center offers a couple special advantages for families. There's a very clean and well-stocked Chinese market directly across the street, and Reading Terminal Market is within two blocks. There is no hotel restaurant.

Holiday Inn–Center City. 18th and Market Streets, Philadelphia, PA 19103. ☎ **800/ 465-4329** or 215/561-7500. Fax 215/561-4484. 445 rms, 72 suites. A/C TV TEL. $190 double; B&B packages (including $6 per person toward breakfast), $134 Sunday through Thursday, $124 Friday and Saturday. Children under 19 stay free in parents' room; children 12 and under eat free with parents. AE, DC, MC, V. Parking $17.

The Holiday Inn was the only hotel to open in Philadelphia in the 1970s, and it underwent a $9.5 million refurbishment after Holiday Inn Worldwide bought it back from the local franchiser in 1993. It's very popular with conventioneers and relocating executives, but hotel policy is to leave at least 40% of the 445 rooms free for tourists. It offers solid accommodations with no real surprises.

The lobby, which dispenses coffee all day and looks like a club library in the evening, combines bowls of apples, plush armchairs, and entrances from both 18th Street and the garage. The glass marquee canopy on Market Street was added in 1994. Above lobby level, a parking garage and meeting halls occupy the next 6 floors, and rooms and several suites fill the next 17 floors.

By Philadelphia standards, the inn's guest rooms are large, each holding a Formica desk or table alongside the beds. Furnishings include deep carpeting and 1876 *Harper's* magazine prints of the city's Centennial Exposition. Baths are slightly shabby. Two floors are devoted to Executive Level suites, offering upgraded decor and complimentary breakfast.

Dining: The hotel restaurant, an English pub called Elephant & Castle, serves largely continental fare from 6:30am to 11pm.

Facilities: The outdoor pool perched atop the garage extension's roof (open daily from 10am to 9pm in summer) is free to guests, who can also use a weight room with rowing and Nautilus machines.

4 University City

EXPENSIVE

Penn Tower Hotel. Civic Center Boulevard at 34th St., Philadelphia, PA 19104. ☎ **800/ 356-7366** or 215/387-8333. Fax 215/386-8306. 175 rms, 7 suites. A/C TV TEL. $144 double; suites from $375. A 25% discount is offered to relatives of patients in University and Children's Hospitals. Packages available both weekdays and weekends starting at $99 per night. AE, DC, MC, V. Parking $9.

Penn Tower is a greatly improved version of a former Hilton, built with a direct sky-walk to University Hospital and within steps of the University of Pennsylvania, 30th Street Station, the Civic Center, and Drexel University. The University of Pennsylvania bought it in 1986 and uses the lower floors as medical offices; the hotel part of the tower comprises floors 11 through 20, as well as an enclosed garage and ground-floor restaurants and shops.

You'll have to get used to spirited displays of red and blue, the Penn colors, and a long lobby corridor of rough-textured concrete that leads to the reception desk. Those handsome chairs and rugs were picked up for a song from the Bellevue Hotel in 1986.

Dining/Entertainment: I.D.E.A.S. is the lobby cocktail lounge. P. T.'s, a casual restaurant-coffee shop, serves breakfast, lunch, and dinner.

Services: Complimentary van service to Independence Park/historic district; limo service to and from the airport.

Facilities: Penn Tower is fully accessible to travelers with disabilities. It offers complimentary guest passes to Penn's nearby Hutchinson Health Complex for its track and rowing machines and makes tennis reservations at courts one block away. There are also sundries shops and a florist on the ground floor.

Sheraton University City. 36th and Chestnut Streets, Philadelphia, PA 19104. ☎ **800/ 325-3535** or 215/387-8000. Fax 215/387-7920. 377 rms, 7 suites. A/C TV TEL. $145 double; suites from $195. Children 17 and under stay free in parents' room. Weekend and package rates from $104 per night. AE, DC, MC, V. Parking $10.

A favorite with business and academic visitors, located west of the Schuylkill River, this cheerful, moderately priced hotel is close to Center City via public transport or car. There's a fine view of the university and the Philadelphia skyline.

You'll enter the inn through a spacious Spanish-tiled lobby with access to the parking garage, located on the first 5 floors. The remaining 15 floors hold guest rooms with the same basic decor of floral-print bedspreads and curtains, dark-blue or gold carpeting, and beige wallpaper.

Dining/Entertainment: In the hotel are Smart Alex restaurant, a deli, and a cocktail lounge.

Facilities: Small outdoor pool open in summer, ice and soft drinks available on every other floor.

INEXPENSIVE

ⓢ Gables. 4520 Chester Ave. (at South 46th St.), Philadelphia, PA 19104.☎ **215/662-1921.** 9 rms, 5 with private bath. A/C TV. $60–$80 double. Rates include full breakfast. AE, MC, V. Free parking.

This 1889 Victorian mansion was one of West Philadelphia's first and finest, and it has been reclaimed from boardinghouse status in the last six years. The location is about eight blocks west of the University of Pennsylvania's main campus. It's right at the SEPTA trolley line stop into Center City and five minutes from 30th Street Station or 15 minutes from the airport. For visiting academics, parents of University of Pennsylvania students, prospective applicants, and relaxed tourists, it's an excellent value choice.

Donald Caskey and Warren Cederholm have outfitted the eight formal areas with antiques, including sitting rooms, breakfast room, and wraparound porch, as well as five private-bath and four shared-bath bedrooms on the top two floors. All rooms have gorgeous inlaid wood floors, and three have charming corner turrets; closets, armoires, lamps, and desks also fit the period. Home-baked muffins, breads, fresh fruit, and casseroles fill out breakfasts.

International House. 3701 Chestnut St., Philadelphia, PA 19104. ☎ **215/387-5125.** Fax 215/895-6535. 379 rms (most with shared bath). A/C. Students with I.D. only. $54 single; $65 double (private bath). Refundable deposit fee equal to one night's stay required on registration. No children allowed. MC, V. No parking arrangements; garages nearby.

This is a tremendous value, but it depends on who you are, since International House is not a formal hotel but a residence during the academic year for U.S. and foreign students and academics. Some (under 100) rooms for academically affiliated transients are generally available year-round, more in summer. Related facilities and programs include a low-cost International Bazaar shop; many coffee hours, concerts, and films at the student center, all at nominal costs; a full-service restaurant and bar; and a travel agent. To get here, you can take bus 21 on Walnut Street from Center City.

Most guest rooms will resemble your college dorm; doubles, when available, must be reserved 10 days in advance. Tough blue carpeting covers all floors, and the lighting is adequate, with two lamps and a vanity lamp above the mirror. The walls are solid and acoustically dead. Linen and towels are in the rooms, but soap and cups are your own responsibility. There are plenty of sparkling-clean showers, sinks, and bathrooms on each floor and a 24-hour security staff; there is also a coin-operated laundry.

University City Guest Houses. P.O. Box 28612, 2933 Morris Rd., Philadelphia, PA 19151. ☎ **215/387-3731.** A/C TEL. $60–$65 double. Children allowed in some situations. No credit cards; traveler's checks accepted.

This is basically a neighborhood collection of bed-and-breakfasts, most within walking distance of the University of Pennsylvania and University Hospital. Most hosts are academically affiliated. Parking is provided at most places.

5 Near the Airport

Hotel chain options are very well represented at the moderate to inexpensive level, including: **Holiday Inn Philadelphia Stadium,** 10th Street and Packer Avenue, Philadelphia, PA 19148 (☎ 800/424-0291 or 215/755-9500), which charges $120 double; **Airport Ramada Inn,** 76 Industrial Hwy., Essington, PA 19029 (☎ 800/228-2828 or 610/521-9600), with rates of $89 double, $69 weekends; **Days Inn,** 4101 Island Ave. (between I-95 and Pa. 291), Philadelphia, PA

19153 (☎ **800/325-2525** or 215/492-0400), charging $118 double, with specials from $69 to $79; **Comfort Inn Airport,** 53 Industrial Hwy., Essington, PA 19029 (☎ **800/228-5150** or 610/521-9800), with rates of $78 double, $62 weekends; and **Red Roof Inn,** 49 Industrial Hwy., Essington, PA 19029 (☎ **800/843-7663** or 610/521-5090), with rates of $55 double, $54 to $59 weekends.

EXPENSIVE

Doubletree Guest Suites. 4101 Island Ave., Philadelphia, PA 19153. ☎ **800/424-2900** or 215/365-6600. Fax 215/492-9858. 251 rms. A/C MINIBAR TV TEL. $165 double. Seasonal specials from $110; various other packages $116–$149. Children under 12 stay free in parents' room. Rates include full buffet breakfast. AE, DC, MC, V. Free parking.

For first-class prices you get deluxe suites of beautifully furnished bedrooms and living rooms that encircle dramatic multistory atriums containing restaurant and lounge seating. The occupancy rates are among the highest in town. The standard rooms have been recently redecorated in deep green and mauve, with a king-size bed, round dining room table for four, armoire concealing a TV, convertible sofa bed, and speaker-phone. HVAC controls are located near the wet bar, small refrigerator, and marble-topped vanity and bath. There is minimal airport noise.

Dining/Entertainment: The Terrace Lounge offers fairly lavish complimentary hors d'oeuvres and low drink prices on Friday to Sunday from 5 to 7pm; the Atrium Lounge and Café serves contemporary cuisine.

Services: *USA Today* delivered to door; complimentary coffee machines; Ambassador car rental in lobby; complimentary shuttle to and from airport.

Facilities: Complimentary indoor pool, whirlpool, sauna, and steam bath.

Philadelphia Airport Marriott Hotel. Arrivals Rd., Philadelphia, PA 19153. ☎ **800/228-9290** or 215/492-9000. Fax 215/3492-6799. 419 rms, 5 suites. A/C MINIBAR TV TEL. $139 double; $149 concierge-level room for up to five people; $200–$300 suite. Weekend rate $109 double per night. AE, DC, MC, V. Parking $8 in Level 2 of the airport garage at Terminal B.

Opened in 1995, this is the newest major hotel in the city—it's also the only one linked by skywalk to Philadelphia International Airport. The $55 million facility obviously specializes in business travelers, with voice mail, speakerphone, free incoming faxes, two data port jacks, and outlets set alongside oversized counter space for your laptop available in 70% of the rooms. However, it's not an unreasonable choice for families, since the soundproofed rooms are mostly angled away from the runways, and it's very convenient to I-95. When you throw in the full recreational activities, a reasonable restaurant, easy train or bus shuttle into Center City, and frequent weekend packages, it's worth considering.

Dining/Entertainment: Riverbend Bar & Grille, with a rowing motif, is open 24-hours.

Facilities: Indoor lap pool, whirlpool, exercise room (open daily 5:30am to 11pm).

MODERATE

Philadelphia Airport Hilton. 4509 Island Ave., Philadelphia, PA 19153. ☎ **800/HILTONS** or 215/365-4150. Fax 215/937-6382. 331 rms. A/C MINIBAR TV TEL. $88 double; weekend packages available. Free parking, with courtesy transport to and from the airport.

The Philadelphia Airport Hilton is removed from flight patterns, features a lobby and cocktail lounge built around a lushly planted indoor pool, and offers serious dining possibilities in two restaurants, plus a lounge. Like all airport hotels, business travelers predominate during the week, and reservations are desirable. The guest rooms, all renovated in 1993, are classically American—spacious, comfortable, and anonymously elegant. The barrel chairs and sofa bed, in tan and deep brown, show unusual understanding of human contours. Facilities include an indoor pool, whirlpool, health club (open daily 6:00am to 11pm), and sauna.

Radisson Hotel Philadelphia Airport. 500 Stevens Dr., Philadelphia, PA 19113. ☎ **800/ 333-3333** or 215/521-5900. Fax 215/521-4362. 350 rms, 52 suites. A/C TV TEL. $119–$129 double. Super-saver packages at $115 double. Weekend rate from $95 double per night. AE, DC, MC, V. Free parking.

Opened in March 1991, the Radisson is trading on its spanking new looks, sleek 12-story glass atrium, and corporate clout even while rates have declined to match the competition. The design is ingenious, with northward balcony views of Center City expanded by a second enclosed atrium, overlooking a pool and health club. The guest rooms have two phones (one a speakerphone), and the materials are mostly veneers and hollow core. To get here, drivers should take Route 291, one mile west of the airport, and follow the signs over a winding road. There are two lounges; a restaurant, Hampton Grille; and a coffee shop. Courtesy vans are provided to and from the airport and room service is available. Facilities include an indoor pool and health club.

6 City Line & Northeast

City Line Avenue (U.S. 1) just off the Schuylkill Expressway is a good jumping-off point for West Philadelphia, Bucks County, or Lancaster County. Its retail outlets are struggling with the emergence of the huge mall in King of Prussia, so sales at the nearby Saks Fifth Avenue and Lord & Taylor are frequent.

Thoroughly comfortable lodgings at representatives of national chains dot this area, including: **Holiday Inn City Line,** 4100 Presidential Blvd. (City Line Avenue at I-76), Philadelphia, PA 19131 (☎ **800/465-4329** or 215/477-0200), charging $109 double on weekdays and $129 double on weekends; and the **Best Western Philadelphia Northeast,** 11580 Roosevelt Blvd., Philadelphia, PA 19116 (☎ **800/ 528-1234** or 215/464-9500), charging $90–$100 double.

MODERATE

Adam's Mark Philadelphia. City Ave. and Monument Rd., Philadelphia, PA 19131. ☎ **800/444-2326** or 215/581-5000. Fax 215/581-5069. 515 rms, 9 suites. A/C TV TEL. $134 double; executive rooms $170 double; $425–$800 suite. Getaway weekend packages from $89 per night. AE, DC, MC, V. Free parking in front lots or rear-connected garage; valet parking $12.

The Adam's Mark looks like an airport control tower, but there's also an extensive brick complex of connected restaurants and function rooms. Eighty percent of the hotel's business is convention, since the lower levels contain 50,000 square feet of meeting space, making the hotel a bit ungainly in size—but the friendly service, good value, and individual touches make up for this. From customized plastic Safe-keys and clear elevator signage, to the 6 nonsmoking floors (out of 23) and recently replaced individual HVAC units, constant attention is at work. The 1992 renovation brought dark-green checks, beige carpets, and firm new beds. Each room maintains solid-core doors, two armchairs, a round wood table, and wall-length drapes. Baths, done the year before, have new counters and resurfaced tubs.

Dining/Entertainment: The Adam's Mark's food and beverage operation really shines. The gardenlike Appleby's is several notches above your average coffee shop, with all-you-can-eat meals, 30-foot ziggurat skylights, and local antiques. Lines start forming early at the Marker, an improbable re-creation of French château orangerie, paneled English library, and western ranch that's somehow relaxing. It seats 150 on three levels, and evenings bring French tableside service. Quincy's, with some of the city's best hors d'oeuvres complimentary to 7pm, offers backgammon, dancing to

1940s-style bands, or jazz nightly, and so forth in a decor of old copper and wood. There's no cover Monday through Thursday, $10 on Friday and Saturday (open from 8pm to 2am). Players, a sports bar, serves until 2am.

Services: Budget car rental in lobby; Barclay unisex hair salon; Squires travel service; extensive sundries shop.

Facilities: The excellent health-club operation, open 7am to 10pm, includes indoor and outdoor pools with sunken whirlpool in a comfortable, high-ceilinged room. Two racquetball courts rent for $10 for a 45-minute session. Stairmasters, treadmills, Lifecycles, a rowing machine, and eight-station Nautilus and sauna round out the area.

7 Hostels

Students or travelers on tight budgets might consider staying at one of the area's hostels. It might be worth joining **American Youth Hostels,** 733 15th St. NW, No. 840, Washington, DC 20005 (☎ **202/783-6161**). Membership costs $25 annually, and you'll get discounts on hostel rates.

Bank Street Hostel. 32 S. Bank St. (between 2nd and 3rd sts. and Market and Chestnut sts.), Philadelphia, PA 19106. ☎ **800/392-4678** or 215/922-0222. 70 beds (shared bath). $15 for AYH members; $18 for nonmembers; $2 sheet charge. No credit cards. Check in before 10am or after 4:30pm. SEPTA station three blocks east from 5th and Market. Parking $8–$10 per day at nearby garages.

David Herskowitz opened up this 140-year-old former factory and its two neighbors in 1992 to those who want Spartan accommodations on a budget, without wanting a flophouse. Managed by Scott and Betty Milling, it works quite well year-round in a very convenient part of town. The dormitory-style rooms are spread over four floors of the complex. Extras include free coffee and tea, use of kitchen facilities, a pool table, and lounge with large-screen TV. Baths are shared in clean dorm-style areas. Also, Scott has arranged many discounts for food and other items with area merchants.

Chamounix Hostel Mansion. West Fairmount Park, Philadelphia, PA 19131. ☎ **800/379-0017** or 215/878-3676. Fax 215/871-4313. $11 AYH members; $14 nonmembers; $2 sheet charge. Maximum three-day stay. MC, V. Closed Dec 15–Jan 15. By car: Take I-76 (Schuylkill Expressway) to Exit 33, City Line Avenue, turn right (south) on City Avenue to Belmont Avenue, left on Belmont to first traffic light at Ford Road, left on Ford, through stone tunnel to stop sign, then a left onto Chamounix Drive and follow to the end. By bus: Take SEPTA route 38 from John F. Kennedy Boulevard near City Hall to Ford and Cranston Streets (a 30-minute ride), then walk under the overpass and left onto Chamounix Drive to the end.

The oldest building offering accommodations in town, this renovated 1802 Quaker farmhouse is also the cheapest. Chamounix Mansion is a Federal-style edifice constructed as a country retreat at what is now the upper end of Fairmount Park. About 33 years ago the only thing about to cross the threshold was the wrecker's ball, but in 1964, it was converted into a youth hostel. It has 6 dormitory rooms for 44 people, with limited family arrangements, and another 37 spots in a fully renovated adjoining carriage house. Guests have use of the newly renovated self-serve kitchen. Write or call ahead for reservations, since the hostel is often 90% booked in summer by groups of boat crews or foreign students.

You can check in daily between 4:30 and midnight and show an American Youth Hostel card or IYHF card for member rates. Check out is from 8 to 11am. Call AYH directly at 215/925-6004 for information on hostel trips in the area.

Old First Reformed Church. 4th and Race sts., Philadelphia, PA 19106. ☎ **215/ 922-4566**. 20 beds (shared baths). Open July–Aug only. $11 singles ages 18–26 only. Rates include continental breakfast. Check-in 5–10pm. Maximum three-day stay. Parking $8 per day at garage on 5th Street between Market and Chestnut.

This church, built in 1837, has responded to the major lack of Center City student accommodations by making its basement social hall available. Showers and security for valuables are available. There's a midnight curfew, after which the church doors are locked. The church is situated one block east and two blocks north of the 5th and Market SEPTA station.

6 Dining

Philadelphia's restaurants reflect 300 years of influences. Some of the early Colonial favorites have been recaptured, and South Philadelphia has plenty of places that have Italian immigrant cuisine from the 1910s frozen in time. In the 1970s and 1980s a restaurant renaissance captured Philadelphia's imagination—new spots opened constantly, with distinctive menus, superb service, and cozy surroundings. The 1990s legacy? In a recent *Condé Nast Traveler*'s readers poll, the city had seven restaurants placed among America's top 50, including Le Bec-Fin, and The Fountain at the Four Seasons Hotel. Below them are literally dozens of young entrepreneurs turned on to excellent gourmet fare, combining tastes from around the world. The line between special-occasion restaurants and more casual, moderately priced, everyday bistros has blurred to the advantage of both.

Unfortunately, this chapter cannot include many of the more renowned Main Line and other suburban restaurants. If you're heading out that way, many volunteers staffing the desk at the **Convention and Visitors Bureau,** 16th Street and Kennedy Boulevard (☎ 215/568-1666), hail from those parts and have crackerjack knowledge.

Compared to places in New York, the average quality and attention in Philadelphia restaurants set a higher standard, and the prices fall between one-third and one-half less, particularly in the upper reaches. This chapter will categorize **very expensive** restaurants as those charging $45 or more per person for dinner without wine; **expensive** as $30 to $45 per person; **moderate** as $20 to $30; and **inexpensive** as under $20.

Meal tax is 7%, and standard tipping is 15% (the latter is occasionally included on the tab). For most restaurants I have given only summer hours; you can expect plenty of 9pm (as opposed to 10pm) closings in other seasons.

1 Best Bets

- **Best Spot for a Romantic Dinner:** Between its antique tables and the flowery back garden with its bright yellow umbrellas, **The Garden's** (☎ 215/546-4455) setting is perfect for lingering over a long meal. The predominance of chocolate, exemplified in the sampler plate dessert, is guaranteed to leave you on a high.

- **Best Spot for a Business Lunch: The Grill Room** of the Ritz-Carlton Hotel (☎ 215/563-1600) fulfills every requirement: It's quiet, the tables are well spaced, the decor and service are impressive, and the cuisine is top-of-the-line steak, chops, and fish, elegantly presented. You have to like Georgian and mahogany paneling, though.

- **Best Spot for a Celebration:** If you have a truly special occasion—even if it's just to celebrate being in Philadelphia—**Le Bec-Fin** (☎ 215/567-1000) is the only choice. The cuisine under Georges Perrier has an international reputation, and the opulence of the prix-fixe meal will stagger you. And those dessert carts—unforgettable! Advance reservations are a must.

- **Best Decor:** This is necessarily a personal evaluation, but I figure if you're in Philadelphia, you're interested in a sense of history and pre-20th-century elegance. With these criteria, I head for **Founders** (☎ 215/893-1776), the flagship restaurant on the 19th floor of the Bellevue Hotel in the center of town. With its arched windows, flourishes and swags of draperies, and statues of Philadelphia's historical greats surrounding you, you'll find yourself in for the whole evening.

- **Best View: The Chart House** (☎ 215/625-8383) is the Convention Center of Philadelphia restaurant, but the food is amazingly good considering this volume, and the views of the Delaware River from its own pier are spectacular. All this—plus reasonable prices for steak and lobster.

- **Best Wine List:** I can't resist mentioning two, because they're only a block apart and meant as a pair by the owners. **La Famiglia** (☎ 215/922-2803) offers one of the finest wine cellars in the world, according to *Wine Spectator* magazine. Bar manager William Eccleston says that **Panorama Restaurant** (☎ 215/922-7800), the charming Italian trattoria one block north in the Penn's View Inn, has the largest single wine-dispensing machine in the world, with 120 different bottles available by the glass ($2.75 to $30 per 5-ounce glass). What's really fun, though, is to order a "flight," or five glasses grouped around a theme, in the $12 to $16 range.

- **Best Value:** For an absolutely central location and elegant surroundings in this retrofitted bank, I'd be glad to dine in **Circa** (☎ 215/545-6800) anytime. The fact that all dinner entrees are below $20 makes it an outstanding choice; lunch is even more reasonable. And why not stick around for the great dance club action on weekends after 10pm?

- **Best for Kids:** If your kids are like mine, they are capable of working up to a seated meal with table service—but, especially on vacation, they like the broad selection and energy that a mall-type food court gives them. The **Food Court at Liberty Place** has branches of old city stalwarts like Bain's Deli and Bassett's Original Turkey, along with out-of-towners like Sbarro and Mentesini Pizza. It's spotless, large, and steps away from the city's best urban mall.

- **Best American Cuisine:** Jack McDavid is the *enfant terrible* of Philadelphia chefs, but his **Jack's Firehouse** (☎ 215/232-9000) features the most dramatic juxtapositions of American ingredients and flavors in town, with special emphasis on those that are rare and the inheritances of immigrant cultures. You won't be offered bear or beaver tail too often, or have such a selection of organic ingredients. Don't expect a temple of ascetic fanatics—it's warm and homey.

- **Best Chinese Cuisine:** A reserved former librarian, born in inner Mongolia and raised in northern China and Taiwan, has quietly built up a national reputation with **Susanna Foo** (☎ 215/545-2666). Her innovative style relies on reductions rather than dashes of soy sauce and ginger, and skillets and saucepans rather than a wok—many people think she's found a definitive answer to taking the best of the West to augment the strength of Chinese cuisine. The dim sum, or noshes served in appetizer-sized portions, are a city favorite.

- **Best Continental Cuisine: The Fountain** at the Four Seasons Hotel (☎ 215/ 963-1500) is consistently rated best in town for understated, complex extensions of classic continental dishes. Since dishes are so uniformly excellent, my advice is to go with the chef's choice on the prix-fixe menu rather than à la carte.
- **Best French Cuisine:** Most French have never tasted a meal remotely as good as what Georges Perrier prepares at **Le Bec-Fin** (☎ 215/567-1000)—a meal here can be the food event of one's life.
- **Best Italian Cuisine:** Philadelphia must have a thousand Italian restaurants, be- tween South Philly, the Northeast, and the normal complement in any northeast- ern urban center. Given that, I head for **The Saloon** (☎ 215/627-1811), the type of dignified, elegant surroundings that draw everyone in town sooner or later. For up-to-date style and modern interpretations of classic dishes, try **Aglio** (☎ 215/ 336-8008), also in South Philly. The best bargain Italian spot? I'd vote for **Ristorante Primavera** (☎ 215/925-7832), the poor-cousin version of the Monte Carlo Living Room, with absolutely fresh ingredients and family recipes; the tiramisù for dessert is outstanding.
- **Best Seafood:** You would expect Philadelphia to have a superb reputation for fish houses, but the best in town is only two years old—**Striped Bass** (☎ 215/ 732-4444), in the most chic dining block in the city. New chef Will Ternay has continued to create a menu breathtaking in its unusual treatment of fish and seafood.
- **Best Steakhouse:** Throughout its history, Philadelphia has always been more of a seafood and pasta town than a steak town. The top choices are either **Ruth's Chris Steak House** (☎ 215/790-1515), a butter-laden sizzling chain from New Orleans located in the heart of the Avenue of the Arts, or **Morton's of Chicago** (☎ 215/557-0724), a quiet refuge with a 24-ounce porterhouse (specify a booth when you reserve, though).
- **Best Burgers & Beer:** It's a bit upscale, but with Philadelphia's newfound love of microbrewery products, the choice is **Dock Street Brewing Company,** right off Logan Square (☎ 215/496-0413). It's got an onsite brewery that produces six different ales, porters, and lagers fresh each day. The burgers are constructed to match, and there's even a darts and game room.
- **Best Pizza: Marra's** (☎ 215/463-9249) in South Philadelphia has thin crusts and delicious, spicy traditional toppings, baked in decades-old brick ovens; enjoy them in those old wooden booths. In Center City, aficionados swear by **Savas** (☎ 215/ 564-1920), which combines similar crusts with more avant-garde variations, along with hoagies, cheesesteaks, and vegetarian fare.
- **Best Bakery:** It's "only" bread—but bakers Wendy Born and James Barrett do make it better at **Metropolitan Bakery,** 262 S. 19th St. (☎ 215/545-6655), and 1114 Pine St. (☎ 215/627-3433), than anyone else in Philadelphia. They use organic fruit starters rather than commercial yeast and they use French willow baskets for the final rise and bake in a steam-process brick oven. The results—try San Francisco Sourdough, Chocolate Cherry, and Olive Thyme—have wonder- ful crusts and texture.
- **Best Desserts:** Apart from the dessert cart at **Le Bec-Fin** (☎ 215/567-1000), the best sweet show in town is to be found at **Painted Parrot Cafe** (☎ 215/ 922-5971), near Independence National Historical Park; choices range from brownies and other chocolate delights to fruit tarts. Special mention goes to **Isgro Pastries** (☎ 215/923-3092), the city's oldest family-owned pasticceria at

1009 Christian St. in South Philadelphia, for their cannoli, tubes of baked dough filled with a sweet-flavored ricotta cheese.

- **Best Breakfast:** The **Down Home Diner** at Reading Terminal (☎ **215/627-1955**), open from 7am on, has wonderful blueberry pancakes, fresh eggs with garlic grits, and a breakfast "pizza" with sausage biscuits, smoked cheddar, and tomato. All ingredients are fanatically organic, from small-scale producers wherever possible. Lunch has its charms also, with meat loaf, black-eyed pea and ham-hock soup, and pecan pie. The vintage jukebox plays great old American tunes.

- **Best Brunch:** Nearly every restaurant offers Sunday brunch, ranging from standard bagels with spreads to full English breakfasts. The **White Dog Café** (☎ **215/386-9224**) in West Philadelphia can swing either way, in a completely comfortable, unpretentious environment.

- **Best People Watching:** No place is hotter than the district of Manayunk, halfway between Center City and Bryn Mawr. The window seats at **Sonoma** (☎ **215/483-9400**) on Main Street are great for seeing thousands of people stroll by, hour after hour, between noon and midnight. The vodka bar is legendary.

- **Best Afternoon Tea:** The advent of true luxury hotels in Philadelphia has brought exquisite afternoon teas all over town. I love the **Cassatt Lounge** (☎ **215/546-9000**) at the Rittenhouse Hotel because of its cheery decor, tucked-in garden, and the Mary Cassatt drawings, commemorating her brother's house that once stood on the site. For a more solid, English burgher version, try the **Dickens Inn** (☎ **215/928-9307**) in Head House Square.

- **Best for Pretheater Dinner:** It's had some ups and downs over the past decade, but I am partial to **DiLullo Centro** (☎ **215/546-2000**), steps from the Academy of Music and the Merriam. It's always looked spectacular, and now serves a simpler, less over-the-top Italian menu.

- **Best Outdoor Dining:** The back garden of **City Tavern** (☎ **215/413-1443**) belongs to Independence National Historical Park, and you're literally surrounded by century-old trees and Federal landmarks while imbibing strong ale or punch, or dining on a historically faithful 18th-century chop or pot pie. Weekend reservations are mandatory.

- **Best Late-Night Dining:** When it's after midnight, I head for Chinatown; restaurants have always stayed open late here, and the nearby Convention Center has only encouraged this. It's not much to look at, but **Shiao Lan Kung** (☎ **215/928-0282**) has wonderful hot pot dishes, and you can order fresh sea bass from the tank.

- **Best Fast Food:** I always enjoy a quick stop in **Marabella's,** either the 1420 Locust St. (☎ **215/545-1845**) or Benjamin Franklin Parkway at 17th Street (☎ **215/981-5555**) location. Both are reasonable, open until 11pm weeknights and midnight on the weekends, and offer colorful and upbeat settings for pizzas, simple Italian grazing breads and salads, and mesquite-grilled fish. It's great for families.

- **Best Ice Cream: Bassett's Ice Cream** (☎ **215/925-4315**), an original 1892 tenant of Reading Terminal Market, has long claimed supremacy for its rich and smooth flavors, and it makes a terrific milkshake. The second location at the Food Court at Liberty Place carries the quality but lacks that turn-of-the-century soda fountain ambience.

- **Best Picnic Fare:** A picnic in Philadelphia means either a trip to the Delaware waterfront on the east side of town or Fairmount Park to the west. For the former, **Famous Deli** (☎ **215/922-3274**) is the place. Before South Street turned funky, it was mostly Jewish, and under three generations of Auspitzes the 74-year-old

Famous has weathered the demographics. The deli roasts its own turkey and does a lot of carry-out of lox, whitefish, pastrami, and corned beef, with a more recent "best" in chocolate chip cookies. On the other side of town, **Charcuterie Francaise** (☎ 215/222-3299) at 30th Street Station has six different chicken salads and unusual pasta salads.

2 Restaurants by Cuisine

AMERICAN
Azalea (Historic Area, *M*)
Bookbinder's Seafood House
  (Center City, *E*)
Circa (Center City, *M*)
City Tavern (Historic Area, *M*)
Cutter's Grand Cafe and Bar
  (Center City, *M*)
Diner on the Square
  (Center City, *I*)
Grill Room (Center City, *VE*)
Jack's Firehouse (Center City, *E*)
Jake & Oliver's House of Brews
  (Historic Area, *M*)
Jim's Steaks (Local Favorites, *I*)
Judy's Cafe (Historic Area, *M*)
Le Bus Main Street (Manayunk, *M*)
Lee's Hoagies (Local Favorites, *I*)
Michel's (Center City, *E*)
New Deck Tavern (University
  City, *I*)
Old Original Bookbinder's
  (Historic Area, *VE*)
Pat's King of the Steaks (Local
  Favorites, *I*)
Philadelphia Fish & Company
  (Historic Area, *M*)
Rib It (Center City, *I*)
Samuel Adams Brew House
  (Center City, *I*)
Society Hill Hotel
  (Historic Area, *I*)
Sonoma (Manayunk, *M*)
White Dog Café
  (University City, *M*)

BRAZILIAN
Brasil's (Historic Area, *I*)

BRITISH
Dickens Inn (Historic Area, *M*)

CHINESE
Golden Pond (Chinatown, *M*)
Harmony Vegetarian Restaurant
  (Chinatown, *I*)
Imperial Inn (Chinatown, *I*)
Joe's Peking Duck House
  (Chinatown, *I*)
Ray's Coffee Shop (Chinatown, *I*)
Shiao Lan Kung (Chinatown, *I*)
Susanna Foo (Center City, *M*)

COFFEE
Ray's Coffee Shop (Chinatown, *I*)

CONTEMPORARY
The Dining Room (Center City, *VE*)
Jack's Firehouse (Center City, *E*)

CONTINENTAL
Dickens Inn (Historic Area, *M*)
Founder's (Center City, *I*)
Friday Saturday Sunday (Center
  City, *E*)
The Garden (Center City, *E*)
Jake & Oliver's House of Brews
  (Historic Area, *M*)
Palladium (University City, *M*)
The Saloon (South Philadelphia, *E*)
Zanzibar Blue (Center City, *I*)

DINER
Melrose Diner (South Philadelphia, *I*)

ECLECTIC
Le Bus (University City, *I*)
The Restaurant (University City, *I*)

ENGLISH
Grill Room (Center City, *VE*)
Samuel Adams Brew House
  (Center City, *I*)

Key to abbreviations: *E* = Expensive; *I* = Inexpensive; *M* = Moderate; *VE* = VeryExpensive

FRENCH

Ciboulette (Center City, *E*)
Le Bec-Fin (Center City, *VE*)
Jeannine's Bistro (Historic Area, *M*)
Michel's (Center City, *E*)

GREEK

Cafe Zesty (Manayunk, *M*)
Chef Theodore (Historic Area, *M*)

INDIAN

New Delhi (University City, *I*)

INTERNATIONAL

The Dining Room (Center City, *VE*)
Dock Street Brewing Company
(Center City, *I*)
The Fountain (Center City, *VE*)
Marabella's (Center City, *I*)

IRISH

Downey's Pub (Historic Area, *M*)
New Deck Tavern (University City, *I*)

ITALIAN

Aglio (South Philadelphia, *E*)
Cafe Zesty (Manayunk, *M*)
DiLullo Centro (Center City, *E*)
La Famiglia (Historic Area, *E*)
Marra's (South Philadelphia, *I*)
Pizzeria Uno (Local Favorites, *I*)
Ralph's (South Philadelphia, *I*)
Rex Pizza (Center City, *I*)
Ristorante Panorama (Historic
Area, *M*)
The Saloon (South Philadelphia, *E*)
Sfuzzi (Center City, *I*)
Sonoma (Manayunk, *M*)
Strolli's (South Philadelphia, *I*)
Tacconelli's (Local Favorites, *I*)
Triangle Tavern (South Phila-
delphia, *I*)
Victor's Cafe (South Philadelphia, *M*)

JAPANESE

Hikaru (Manayunk, *M*)
Meiji-en (Historic Area, *M*)

MEDITERRANEAN

Circa (Center City, *M*)
Tutto Misto (Historic Area, *M*)

MEXICAN

Zocalo (University City, *I*)

MIDDLE EASTERN

Sawan's Mediterranean Bistro
(Center City, *I*)

SEAFOOD

BLT Cobblefish
(Manayunk, *M*)
Bookbinder's Seafood House
(Center City, *E*)
Chart House (Historic Area, *E*)
DiNardo's Famous Crabs
(Historic Area, *M*)
Old Original Bookbinder's
(Historic Area, *VE*)
Philadelphia Fish & Company
(Historic Area, *M*)
Sansom Street Oyster House
(Center City, *M*)
Striped Bass (Center City, *E*)
Walt's King of the Crabs
(Historic Area, *I*)

SOUTHWESTERN

New Mexico Grille (Historic
Area, *I*)

STEAK

Chart House (Historic
Area, *E*)
Kansas City Prime
(Manayunk, *E*)
Morton's of Chicago (Center
City, *E*)
Ruth's Chris Steak House
(Center City, *M*)

THAI

Thai Palace (Historic Area, *I*)

VEGETARIAN

Harmony Vegetarian Restaurant (Chinatown, *I*)

VIETNAMESE

Capital (Chinatown, *I*)

3 Historic Area

VERY EXPENSIVE

Old Original Bookbinder's. 125 Walnut St. ☎ **215/925-7027.** Reservations recommended. Main courses $18–$42; lunch $6–$25. AE, DC, MC, V. Lunch Mon–Fri noon–2:45pm; dinner Mon–Fri 2:45–10pm; Sat noon–10pm; Sept–June, Sun 3–9pm; July–Aug Sun 3–10pm. SEAFOOD/AMERICAN.

If dining at an institution is your predilection, head for this place. Sam Bookbinder opened this seafood restaurant in 1865; his wife announced lunch by ringing a bell. The restaurant acquired status as the *only* place to dine in town for decades. The family sold to the Taxins, now operating it for the third generation, in the 1930s and moved to 15th Street (see Bookbinder's Seafood House under "Center City," below). Over the years this Bookbinder's has expanded to encompass almost the entire block across from the Sheraton Society Hill. The complex includes cigar-store Indian sentries, a ship's wheel, and a gift shop that sells pies and cans of the most popular soups—snapper with sherry, New England clam chowder, and Manhattan clam chowder. To the right the rooms stretch on and on—three bars and seven dining rooms, served by 185 staff members.

Bookbinder's is most renowned for lobsters, which it transports live from Maine in tanks. The less-expensive baked imperial crabmeat with pimientos, a touch of Worcestershire, and green peppers is beyond reproach. The dinner menu is huge: all sizes and kinds of shellfish and fish, steaks, and veal. Their shortcake, strawberry cheesecake, and apple-walnut pie have all won gastronomic awards. The wine list, fairly standard, offers plenty of domestic vintages for under $15.

EXPENSIVE

Chart House. 555 S. Columbus Blvd. (formerly Delaware Avenue) at Penn's Landing. ☎ **215/625-8383.** Reservations recommended. Main courses $16–$36. Sun prix-fixe brunch $20. Children's menu available. AE, DC, MC, V. Mon–Thurs 4–11pm; Fri 5pm–midnight, Sat 4pm–midnight, Sun 4–10pm; brunch Sun 10:30am–2pm. STEAKHOUSE/SEAFOOD.

The busiest restaurant in all Philadelphia has to be the Chart House, a convention center right on the Delaware River. You may not love everything about it—expect a spirited crowd and frequent birthday celebrations—but the Chart House chain has a track record for reasonably priced dinners, with soup, fresh molasses or sourdough bread, and an unlimited salad bar included. All seats have spectacular views, and the service will make you wish you had had camp counselors that enthusiastic.

Start with New England clam chowder, of course, or raw oysters. The unlimited salad bar is $12.95 by itself, with over 50 components including beets, cherry tomatoes, fresh fruit, and hearts of palm, or free with main courses such as prime rib or a steak of halibut, tuna, or other fish. The desserts are very sweet: mud pie, Key lime pie, cheesecakes, and ice creams.

✪ La Famiglia. 8 S. Front St. ☎ **215/922-2803.** Reservations required. Main courses $21–$35. AE, CB, DC, MC, V. Tues–Fri noon–2pm and 5:30–9:30pm, Sat 5:30–10pm, Sun 5–9pm. ITALIAN.

The name La Famiglia should tip you off that this place is a refined Italian restaurant—and in this case it refers to both the proprietors and the clientele. In the 1980s La Famiglia was chosen one of the 25 best Italian restaurants in the country by *Bon Appetit* magazine, and the wine cellar is legendary. The Neapolitan Sena family (parents and three children) aim for elegant dining, service, and presentation; their success here has spawned Penn's View Inn and its Ristorante Panorama (see below).

This restaurant seats 60 in a private, warm setting of hand-hammered Venetian chandeliers and majolica tiles. Recordings of arias give some of the best aural accompaniment in the city. Downstairs by the restrooms, you can see the privy excavations and 1680s foundations.

The chefs at La Famiglia make most of their own pasta, so you might concentrate on such dishes as gnocchi al pesto, which adds walnuts and pecorino cheese to the noodles. There's a choice of five or six vegetables with meals, and the marinated string beans and zucchini with pepper have never failed to please. For dessert, try a *mille foglie,* the Italian version of the napoleon, or the profiteroles in chocolate sauce. People often remain here well after the closing hour, lingering over Sambuca.

MODERATE

✪ **Azalea.** Omni Hotel, 4th and Chestnut sts. ☎ **215/931-4260.** Reservations recommended. Main courses $14–$27; breakfast $7–$14; lunch $8.50–$14. AE, CB, DC, MC, V. Mon–Fri 6:30–10:30am, Sat–Sun 7am–1pm; daily 11am–2pm; Sun–Thurs 5:30–10pm, Fri–Sat 5:30–11pm. AMERICAN.

For imaginative interpretations of American produce, including local dishes, this is one of the two best spots in town, with a treetop view of Independence National Historical Park. Azalea features arched windows, chandeliers, and comfortable armchairs.

The menu selections include such traditional Pennsylvania Dutch specialties as chicken-corn soup with saffron and apple fritters, shad in sorrel sauce (what saved the troops at Valley Forge), and pheasant pot pie. The menus change seasonally, and Kennett Square mushrooms, Lancaster County persimmons and quince, and elderberry preserve make an appearance. The local brook trout is sealed in cornmeal, then topped with smoky bacon. The desserts offer a choice of five freshly made sorbets or an old-fashioned apple-and-sour-cherry pie.

✪ **Chef Theodore.** 1100 S. Columbus Blvd. (formerly Delaware Avenue) at Washington Avenue ☎ **215/271-6800.** Reservations recommended. Main courses $11–$17. AE, CB, DC, MC, V. Tues–Sat 4–11pm, Sun 1–10pm. GREEK.

The best Greek restaurant along South Street migrated to the waterfront in 1989, to a Delaware Avenue shopping center near the multiplex Riverfront Plaza Theater. It's not practical to get there except by car, but an evening at Chef Theodore's, the movies, and perhaps the adjoining Cafe Casa Nova for dessert is a local favorite. While the decor is unassumingly white and the ambience is casual, the quality of the food is unusually good. Start with the enormous *mezze* (a combination platter of standards like baba, tarama, and octopus) or with the sausage or dry goat's milk cheese; both are flamed at your table. You can sample from more combination platters for a main course or stick with the salmon with roasted potatoes or the shrimp casserole. The service is unobtrusive and wine prices are reasonable.

✪ **City Tavern.** 138 S. 2nd St., near Walnut St. ☎ **215/413-1443.** Reservations recommended. Main courses $16–$26; lunch $8–$15. AE, CB, DC, MC, V. Mon–Fri 11:30am–10pm, Fri–Sat 11:30am–11pm, Sun 11:30am–9pm. AMERICAN.

If the hunger to relive those good old 1780s overcomes you in Independence Park, there's at least one authentic restaurant that will let you use that newfangled credit card to pay for colonial fare: City Tavern—the same tavern that members of the Constitutional Convention used as coffee shop, ballroom, and club some 200 years ago. The U.S. government now owns the building, which is operated by a concessionaire, Walter Staib. He's pumped in $500,000 to completely renovate and open up 10 dining areas plus garden and veranda, all serviced by a discreet state-of-the-art

Philadelphia Dining

Azalea **38**
Le Bec-Fin **17**
Ben's Restaurant **1**
Bookbinder's Seafood House **41**
Brasil's **46**
Capital **29**
The Chart House **57**
Ciboulette **22**
Circa **18**
City Tavern **47**
Cutter's Grand Cafe and Bar **6**

Dickins Inn **53**
DiLullo Centro **24**
DiNardo's Famous Crabs **56**
Diner on the Square **11**
The Dining Room **7**
Dock Street Brewing Company **3**
Downey's Pub **56**
Downstairs at the Bellevue **22**
Famous Deli **50**
Food Court at the Bourse **57**
Food Court at the Gallery **27**

Food Court at Liberty Place **8**
Founder's **22**
The Fountain, Four Seasons Hotel
Friday Saturday Sunday **10**
The Garden **14**
Golden Pond **29**
Grill Room, Ritz-Carlton **7**
Harmony Vegetarian Restaurant **4**
Imperial Inn **30**
Jake & Oliver's House of Brews **59**
Jeannine's Bistro **45**

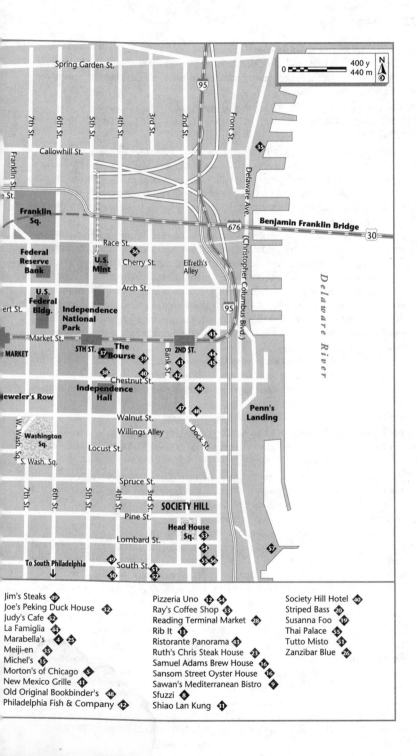

(well, almost—true to its roots, the only freezer space is for the ice cream!) kitchen. Chef Peter Chan rolls out hearty local brook trout, stews over noodles, and meat pies. The taproom features microbrewery and custom beers and ales, and the "shrubs" or punches also pack a wallop.

⑤ Dickens Inn. 421 S. 2nd St. ☎ **215/928-9307.** Reservations recommended. Main courses $12–$20; lunch $5–$8.50. AE, CD, DC, MC, V. Daily 11:30am–3pm; Mon–Sat 5:30–10pm; Sun 3–9pm; brunch Sun 11:30am–3pm. BRITISH/CONTINENTAL.

This three-story Federal town house on Head House Square has proved to have real staying power since it has survived with crumbling New Market behind it. The key elements here are atmosphere and friendly service. Opened in 1980 by the owners of the famous Dickens Inn by the Tower of London, the American version re-creates an English pub and restaurant (19th-century London is all over the walls and tables) that serves fine country-house cuisine.

Paneling lines the walls, and wooden tables, exposed beams, and frosted-glass lamps mix at every turn with lithographs of scenes from Dickens novels and framed Dickensiana. Main courses are extremely generous, tasty, and attractive, served on large speckled crockery. Traditional beef Wellington and prime rib with Yorkshire pudding are offered along with lighter dishes. The seafood choices displayed on a cart raw for your choice include bay scallops poached with basil, tomatoes, and muscadet. All main courses are served with a platter of steamed fresh vegetables. To finish, select a dessert from their own bakery or sample the English Stilton cheese with fresh fruit.

Lunch is a less ambitious affair, with Cornish pasty (traditional pastry filled with lamb, carrots, and potatoes and flavored with fresh herbs), shepherd's pie, trout filet, and a wild-mushroom-and-vegetable crêpe. A traditional homemade soup is offered daily.

There are four bars, with 14 English imported beers.

✪ DiNardo's Famous Crabs. 312 Race St. ☎ **215/925-5115.** Reservations required for six or more. Crabs $2.50 each; other main courses $12–$22; lunch $5–$9. AE, CB, DC, MC, V. Mon–Thurs 11am–11pm, Fri–Sat 11am–midnight, Sun 4–9pm. SEAFOOD.

DiNardo's Famous Crabs, a branch of the original Wilmington location, springs to mind as the best moderately priced spot in the area around the Betsy Ross House and Elfreth's Alley. The door nearest 3rd Street is the real entrance. Only William DiNardo and his son mix the secret crab seasonings.

DiNardo's has two unique factors—the site and the prices. The building at 312 Race St. was an inn for Tory soldiers in 1776, in the oldest part of town, and later served as an Underground Railroad stop and Prohibition-era brothel. Three ground-floor dining rooms were recently updated with eight murals depicting the history of the building from 1776 to the present, with 30 illuminated cases of local Mummers' headdresses and nautical equipment.

Prime live catches from the Gulf of Mexico are flown up north daily. Experienced hands dredge the crabs with the house seasoning of 24 spices and pack heavy-gauge steel hampers with them. Then the crabs are steamed, not boiled (this keeps the seasoning on), for 25 minutes. All crabs are served on plastic platters, with nutcrackers and red sauce. If you're not in a crabby mood, there are at least 30 other succulent items, from raw-bar oysters to seafood platters.

Downey's Pub. Northwest corner of Front and South sts. ☎ **215/629-9500.** Reservations recommended. Main courses $7–$20; lunch $8–$13. AE, DC, MC, V. Mon–Fri 11:30am–3pm and 4:30–10:45pm, Sat 11:30am–3pm and 4:30pm–12:30am, Sun 11:30am–3pm and 4:30–9:45pm. IRISH.

Two hundred fifty years ago Front Street from Race to Fitzwater Streets was a jumble of docks, shops, and public houses that reminded English and Irish seamen of home. Downey's Pub has succumbed to such modern blandishments as electricity and daily quiche, but it's still a place any Irish person would be proud to frequent. Much of the ground floor was lifted from a Dublin bank built in 1903; the upstairs is from a pub in Cork City.

Downey's obviously started off less "lace curtain" than it is now, since the downstairs walls are covered by yellowing shellacked newspapers, with brass rails, coat stands, and framed Victorian prints added since. In summer, café tables grace both the South Street and the river patios. Upstairs, which has a wraparound deck added in 1993, is tonier still, with Beerbohm caricatures, skylights, and beveled mirrors on beautiful wood paneling. The staff, in white shirts and Limerick-green bow ties, is gracious and lively.

Lunch and dinner retain some Irish dishes with American fillips, but are balanced by Italian and lighter fare. The soups are strong here—the potato soup and the lobster bisque use thick milk and have plenty of body. Crab cakes are Downey's most popular item, and roast beef and turkey are carved on your order. The fish of the day, done any way you like, is served with a fresh vegetable.

Live music is a staple of Downey's, both at the weekend brunches and in the upstairs Piano Bar on Friday and Saturday from 8pm to 1am.

Jake & Oliver's House of Brews. 22 S. 3rd St. ☎ **215/627-4825.** Reservations recommended for dinner. Main courses $10–$16; pizzas $8–$9. AE, DC, MC, V. Mon–Fri 11:30am–11:30pm, Sat–Sun 11:30am–12:30am. Bar and dancing daily until 2am. AMERICAN/CONTINENTAL.

David Cohen has transformed this 1837 Greek Revival church into a relaxed and improbably good combination of restaurant, bar, and nightclub, steps from Franklin Court. The first-floor restaurant, named for his two young sons, has a new oak floor and a back bar like a Georgian altar, featuring the products of 40 microbreweries from throughout the country. I love the murals of amber waves of grain (get it?) under clear blue skies. Chef Rowland Butler produces gourmet pizzas in a brick oven, along with simple, quickly braised or baked fish and poultry. If you come for dinner, you can stay for the dancing until 2am on Thursday through Saturday upstairs ($5 to $10 cover charge; see Chapter 10).

✪ Jeannine's Bistro. 10 S. Front St. ☎ **215/925-2928.** Reservations recommended. Main courses $10–$20. AE, MC, V. Tues–Fri noon–2pm, Tues–Sat 6–10pm. FRENCH BISTRO.

In 1991, the popular classic French restaurant downstairs decided to open a bistro, with cut-down dishes. Lunch is served downstairs, with dinner and entertainment upstairs. Owner Jeanne Mermet herself makes a vocal appearance on Friday to augment the guitar-and-violin duo that plays most nights. The chef, Todd Davies, has credentials from Aureole and the River Café in Manhattan.

The dining room is charming, with floral-print wallpaper and tablecloths, burgundy pillows, and candlelight. Watch the climb, though. The menu selections include braised pork, grilled fish, and poultry. The desserts are mostly like what restaurant diners get downstairs, with white-chocolate mousse and the like.

Judy's Cafe. 3rd and Bainbridge sts. ☎ **215/928-1968.** Reservations recommended for parties of four or more. Main courses $13–$22. AE, DC, MC, V. Mon–Thurs 6–10pm, Fri–Sat 6–11pm, Sun 5–9:30pm. AMERICAN.

An agreeable bistro that's long outgrown its countercultural beginnings, Judy's is one of the finest examples of the South Street renaissance. The place opened in 1976;

Judy left soon after, but the locale retains a neighborhood feeling, though it's not really a family place. The regulars banter with the waiters, who dine here on their nights off, and the service at the well-stocked bar may depend on how you strike the person behind it. Jonathan Demme, director of the film *Philadelphia*, ate here throughout film production.

Judy's two rooms are simply furnished: Photo-realist canvases coexist with a quizzical neon strip embracing the wall behind the bar. The main courses are eclectic. A Monday through Thursday special includes your choice of stir-fried duck, lamb stew, or the catch of the day with soup and coffee. Whatever seafood is on the menu will undoubtedly be fresh. The very, very chocolate cake could deserve a third *very;* for those not hooked on fudge, the carrot cake is moist and scrumptious. *Note:* Local papers often advertise two-for-one weeknight specials.

Meiji-en. Upstairs at Pier 19, on the Delaware River at Callowhill St. ☎ **215/592-7100.** Reservations recommended. Main courses $14–$28. AE, CB, DC, MC, V. Mon–Thurs 5–9:30pm, Fri–Sat 5–11pm, Sun 5–9pm; brunch Sun 10:30am–2:30pm. JAPANESE.

Meiji-en opened in 1988 as a huge harbinger of the waterfront development needed to support a 600-seat restaurant. The restaurant now enjoys high volume and offers consistent quality. Meiji-en falls somewhere between an indoor tennis court and a Japanese theme park; everyone from a romantic couple to a huge family can take pleasure in a visit. There are separate areas for sushi, tempura, teppanyaki (or stovetop at table), and regular table seating (the latter two feature river views to the east), as well as a bar with live jazz on Friday and Saturday. Everything is scrupulously clean, and the service is impeccable. The decor features lots of hanging rice-paper globes, blond-wood screens and seats, and comfortable black-and-red cushions.

Many of Meiji-en's dishes have the same basic ingredients—filets of fish and chicken—prepared in different ways, from boiled to quick grilled to diced in gyoza dumplings. Many dishes are marked as especially health conscious. The teppanyaki dishes are cheapest and most fun; your group will sit around horseshoe-shaped tables of granite-and-steel stovetops while you're served seared meat and greens. If you're ordering regular service, expect fish steaks or marbled beef that are beautifully presented.

Be sure to call ahead to request a water view and don't be deterred by the slightly forbidding Delaware Avenue approach, four blocks north of the Benjamin Franklin Bridge. Valet parking nearby is $6.

Philadelphia Fish & Company. 207 Chestnut St. ☎ **215/625-8605**. Reservations recommended. Main courses $11–$21. AE, MC, V. Mon–Fri 11:30am–4pm, Sat noon–3pm; Mon–Thurs 4–10pm, Fri–Sat 4pm–midnight, Sun 3–10pm. SEAFOOD/AMERICAN.

It's inevitable that you'll pass Philadelphia Fish & Company, given its location next to Independence National Historical Park sites and outdoor patio dining, weather permitting. I can confirm that the restaurant offers an *au courant* selection of fish and preparations, with premium freshness. You'll encounter lots of grilling over mesquite: yellowfin tuna, salmon, and rock cod, with increasing use of Asian spices, soys, and sesame oil. The $7.95 executive lunch is a great deal: a cup of soup, the fish special, green salad, and beverage. The wine list, skewed toward whites, is very reasonable for Philadelphia, with good quality. Late night here can get noisy amid the Windsor chairs and soft lighting.

Ⓢ Ristorante Panorama. Front and Market sts. ☎ **215/922-7800.** Reservations recommended. Main courses $9–$20. AE, CB, DC, MC, V. Daily noon–midnight, with dinner service Sun–Thurs 5:30–10pm and Fri–Sat 5:30–11pm. ITALIAN.

Although the Ristorante Panorama is on the waterfront, its view is a colorful mural of the Italian countryside. The cuisine is a wonderful, choice list of lighter Italian dishes. Pasta, salads, and fish predominate, with a few veal and beef favorites. The bread is served without butter but with a tiny bowl of pesto. Favorite appetizers are the fantasy platter of grilled vegetables, beautifully arranged, and the croquettes of shrimp and lamb served on a bed of arugula. The fish are usually grilled and lightly seasoned with garlic and tomatoes. The tiramisù, with its triple-creme mascarpone cheese drizzled with chocolate, needs either an espresso or a dessert wine as an accompaniment.

Panorama is also the city's best wine bar, with 120 (not all Italian) wines served in 3- or 5-ounce glasses from a Cruvinet system to a sophisticated, lively crowd. In fact, diners can take a "map" of their selections, with space for notes and ratings.

Tutto Misto. 603 S. 3rd St. ☎ **215/923-7220.** Reservations recommended. Main courses $6.50–$17. AE, DC, MC, V. Daily 4pm–midnight. MEDITERRANEAN.

There's always a need for a solid, interesting, and affordable restaurant on South Street with hours to match its late-night shopping. Tutto Misto brings together the owners of Cafe Nola and Copacabana with chef Louis Qualtieri; "tutto misto" means a lot of little dishes, and that's what they are best at delivering. Among entrees, try the four-cheese lasagna and the paella; fried olives, polenta, and marinated seafood punctuate the starters. The salads are particularly unusual; try endive, roquefort, and walnuts. The decor is basic with large mirrors and French commercial posters.

INEXPENSIVE

Brasil's. 112 Chestnut St. ☎ **215/413-1700.** Reservations recommended. Main courses $7–$13. AE, DC, MC, V. Sun–Fri 5–11pm, Sat 5pm–midnight. BRAZILIAN.

This warm new bistro in the heart of the historic district has gotten positive press for all-you-can-eat feijoada Sundays and churrasco Tuesdays. The former is the Brazilian national stew of black beans, sausage, seafood, and orange garnish; the latter a spicy grilled beef. There are plenty of more standard meat and poultry offerings, along with live entertainment on weekends.

New Mexico Grille. 50 S. 2nd St. ☎ **215/922-7061.** Reservations not accepted. Main courses $9–$20; combination Tex-Mex plates $9–$11. AE, DC, MC, V. Mon–Thurs 11:30am–10pm, Fri–Sat 11:30am–1am, Sun 11:30am–10pm. Bar open Mon–Sat until 2am. SOUTHWESTERN.

Unassuming, piquant touches encourage your eye to wander around New Mexico Grille's arcade of brick and pink stucco and a mural valance above the bar. Mike Shemeley recently decided to switch from Mexican to north of the border, with a new look and chef.

The appetizers are good examples of standard cuisine—nachos, guacamole, chili, a fondue of Mexican cheese. Entrees swing a bit more with pulled duck in blue corn tortillas and coriander-crusted chicken. A combination plate makes a satisfying light meal. Items with hot peppers are indicated. Exotic beers are available, as is a limited selection of wines and an annual tequila-based festival.

Society Hill Hotel. 301 Chestnut St. ☎ **215/925-1919.** Reservations not required. Main courses $6–$14. AE, CB, DC, MC, V. Daily 11am–1am; Sun brunch 11am–1:30pm. AMERICAN.

This is a very pleasant, lively spot opposite Independence National Historical Park, with outdoor bar service during the summer. The light menu includes burgers and club sandwiches, along with omelets and salads. Ted Gerike makes this one of the city's top piano bars.

Thai Palace. 117 South St. ☎ **215/925-2764.** Reservations recommended. Main courses $7–$13. AE, DC, MC, V. Dinner daily 5:30–10pm. THAI.

This longstanding Thai location has a new lease on life as Thai Palace, boasting all the sweet and hot pastes and spices you'd expect. It isn't much to look at—white, clean, and spare—so start right in on the satay, a highly spiced and marinated meat kebab. For something hot that doesn't sear the taste buds, try the chicken *ka prow* (chicken with fried hot pepper) done in an unusual basil-and-lemongrass sauce. The desserts here are not their strong points; perhaps dessert doesn't flourish in cultures accustomed to single-pot communal meals. BYOB.

Walt's King of the Crabs. 804–806 S. 2nd St. ☎ **215/339-9124.** Reservations not accepted. Main courses $8–$14. No credit cards. Mon–Sat 11am–12:30am; Sun 2–10pm. SEAFOOD.

Walt's makes no bones (or shells?) about the house specialty, and this little, unpretentious storefront hangout has acquired a fanatical following. Owner Ted Zalewski is an extremely nice, beefy Queen Villager who cares about serving lots of people well. Unless your taste includes both bizarre ocean-scene murals and Patti Page records, ignore the decor and dig in.

The platters include truly tasty coleslaw and french-fried potatoes. The deviled crab comes in a great minced patty, fried but never greasy. At last hearing, chicken lobsters were offered for $10 each. The house specialty features two jumbo shrimp stuffed with crabmeat. Draft beer costs $1 a glass or $6 a pitcher. Take-out costs 25¢ extra. You'd be advised to call ahead to find out about waiting time, because the lines in summer and on weekends are fierce.

4 Center City

VERY EXPENSIVE

The Dining Room. The Ritz-Carlton Philadelphia, Liberty Place (between Chestnut and Market sts. at 17th St.). ☎ **215/563-1600.** Reservations required. Dinner $32 (two courses), $38 (three courses), or $44 (four courses); lunch $35. Mon–Sat 6:30–11am and 11:30am–2:30pm; Tues–Sat 6–10pm. CONTEMPORARY/INTERNATIONAL.

Chef Troy Thompson and sommelier David Fischer preside over an operation that is elegant in every way. The room itself is stunning, with large crystal chandeliers, royal carpets, dark cabinets, and hand-blown cobalt-blue goblets. If you have reason to leave your seat, you'll find that your napkin is refolded when you return.

The menu has been lightened and reduced to six or seven choices per course. It's too dependent on seasonal market choices to quote from, so look for garnishes or reductions of fruit and root vegetables from Amish country or New Zealand.

✪ **The Fountain.** The Four Seasons Hotel, One Logan Square (between 18th St. and the Franklin Pkwy.). ☎ **215/963-1500.** Reservations required. Main courses $18–$30; lunch $8–$19; prix-fixe four-course menu $48. AE, CB, DC, MC, V. Mon–Fri 6:30–11:30am, Sat–Sun 7–11am; daily 11:30am–2:30pm and 6–11pm; brunch Sun 10am–2:30pm. Fri and Sat dessert and dancing in Swann Lounge. INTERNATIONAL.

The Zagat Restaurant Survey's 1996 edition ranked this Philadelphia's second most popular restaurant (right behind Le Bec-Fin) and *Food & Wine* magazine chose it as one of America's top 25. The views partially explain why: unparalleled plumes from the Swann Fountain in Logan Circle on one side, and the hotel's own courtyard cascade on the other. The chief reason is the wonderful cuisine, expertly prepared and quietly served in expansive surroundings.

The menu is complicated and understated, and my recommendation is to accept the $48 prix-fixe menu rather than go à la carte for 35% more. After a complimentary canape or two, you might have filet of skate with capers, a mesclun salad with pear and purple potato, sautéed lamb tenderloin and veal kidneys with mustard-seed sauce, a cheese tray, and fresh fruit pastry. A favorite à la carte starter is the pierogi of foie gras in Savoy cabbage with truffles. The main courses include salmon filet and pheasant with bacon and more Savoy cabbage.

Grill Room. The Ritz-Carlton Philadelphia, Liberty Place (between Market and Chestnut sts. at 17th St.). ☎ **215/563-1600.** Reservations required. $41 average for dinner; $30 for lunch. Daily 6:30–11am and 5:30–10pm; Mon–Sat 11:30am–2:30pm. AMERICAN/ENGLISH.

The Ritz-Carlton's Grill Room has become one of the city's chief spots for business lunches, and is easily equal to its formal Dining Room. The entrance bar features a marble bar and an antique wood-burning fireplace and opens into a clublike atmosphere with mahogany paneling and period furnishings and paintings. Under executive chef Thomas von Muenster (a veteran of the Ritz-Carlton in Boston), the Grill serves steaks, chops, and fish for lunch and dinner. A special Cuisine Vitale selection identifies the calories and nutritional values of six dishes.

✪ **Le Bec-Fin.** 1523 Walnut St. ☎ **215/567-1000.** Reservations required a week ahead for weeknights, months ahead for Fri–Sat. Prix-fixe lunch $32; prix-fixe dinner $94. AE, DC, MC, V. Lunch seatings Mon–Fri at 11:30am and 1:30pm; dinner seatings Mon–Thurs at 6 and 9pm, Fri–Sat at 6 and 9:30pm. Bar Lyonnais downstairs serves food and drink until midnight. FRENCH.

There's no doubt that Le Bec-Fin is the best in Philadelphia and certainly one of the top 10 in the country. Patron Georges Perrier hails from Lyon, France's gastronomic capital, and commands the respect of restaurateurs on two continents for his culinary accomplishments.

Le Bec-Fin looks exactly as it should—elegant and comfortable, with deep red silk covering acoustic panels. A portrait of one of Perrier's ancestors, a Russian émigré, peers benignly from the 18th century. Mirrors in back of wall brackets and candlelight add to the warm lighting—seeing your food can only enhance your meal. The table settings include bountiful bouquets; Christofle silver; and the same 18th-century Limoges pattern Paul Bocuse uses in his Lyon restaurant. In addition to the main dining room, the Blue Room (seating 25) may be reserved for private parties. As review after review has noted, it is virtually impossible not to enjoy yourself here, even before your meal begins.

With leisurely timing, an evening at Le Bec-Fin waltzes through hors d'oeuvres, a fish course, a main course, a salad, cheese, a dessert, and coffee with petits fours. Since most of the menu changes seasonally—and your special orders are welcome as well—dishes listed are illustrative. A roast lobster in a butter sauce infused with black truffles is unbelievably flavorful. The terrine of three fish contains a layer of turbot mousse, then a layer of salmon mousse, then one of sole mousse, each with its own dressing; the total effect, with shallots, couldn't be more subtle. The escargots au champagne are renowned as a first course, as the garlic butter also includes a touch of chartreuse and hazelnuts.

The main dishes give you the opportunity to try some rarities—pheasant, venison, and pigeon. The last (stuffed with goose liver, leeks, and mushrooms) comes in a truffle sauce. So does the mouth-watering dish of four filets of venison, covered by a thick milk-mustard sauce. The desserts become grand opera, with trays, tables, and ice cream and sherbets (in the little aluminum canisters they were churned in) zooming from guest to guest. With the addition of pastry chef Bobby Bennett—who just placed fifth in a worldwide World Cup of Pastry—the dessert tray looks and tastes like Dante's Paradiso, especially the 18-inch-high Mont Blanc with sides of sheet chocolate. The finest coffee in the city, served in Villeroy & Boch flowered china, makes those petits fours you really don't need easier to take. Cigars, cordials, liqueurs, and marcs and other fortified spirits gild the lily.

In 1991 M. Perrier opened the basement **Le Bar Lyonnais** for more affordable snacking and champagne toasts. Open until midnight, it has only four tables and bar stools, but trompe l'oeil pilasters and paisley wallpaper expand its effect. Expect to spend about $10 a nibble and $7 for a glass of house wine. The later it gets, the more likely dishes from upstairs are to arrive—and M. Perrier himself, for that matter. A larger, cheaper bistro is supposed to be signed and sealed by 1997—let's hope!

EXPENSIVE

Bookbinder's Seafood House. 215 S. 15th St. ☎ **215/545-1137.** Reservations recommended for Fri lunch and for dinner. Main courses $16–$30; lunch $5–$14. Occasional prix-fixe dinners from $27. AE, CB, DC, MC, V. Mon–Fri 11:30am–10pm, Sat 4–11pm, Sun 3–10pm. Dinner served from 3pm. AMERICAN/SEAFOOD.

A trip to Philadelphia once automatically meant a seafood meal at Old Original Bookbinder's (see "Historic Area," above). But even before the 1970s restaurant renaissance, the third generation of Bookbinders moved downtown and set up 400 seats on two floors.

The 15th Street Booky's is less self-congratulatory and has its own solid clientele. The high ceilings give plenty of room for the mounted fish, nautical chandeliers, oak paneling, and captain's chairs. The heavy wood tables hold goblets of croutons for chowder.

You might start with the famous snapper soup laced with sherry. All the seafood but the smoked fish comes from Chesapeake Bay trawling—the smelts get especially high marks for freshness. You can get that basket of clams you've been pining for, a large box of Chincoteague oysters, or lobsters from $21. The mussels in red sauce are probably the best known among Philadelphians. To adapt to modern tastes, more sauces are being served on the side and new imports, such as mako shark, have been added.

✪ **Ciboulette.** 200 S. Broad St. ☎ **215/790-1244.** Reservations strongly recommended. All items portioned as appetizers, $6–$14. Degustation five-course menu $60. AE, DC, MC, V. Mon–Thurs 5:30–9pm, Fri–Sat 5:30–10:30pm. FRENCH.

Ciboulette, French for "chives," is upward mobility in action. Bruce Lim was born in Singapore, raised in the south of France, and trained in France and across town at the Four Seasons, with a stint as George Harrison's private chef along the way. In 1993 he moved his inventive application of southern French cooking principles to the Bellevue's palatial digs vacated by Pierre Deux, turning out meals applauded by *Esquire* and *Travel/Holiday* for their elegance and service.

You'll enter a suite of French Renaissance rooms with an ornate fireplace, marble columns, and gilt-framed ormolu mirrors. In an effort to keep quality high and prices affordable, in 1996 Ciboulette offers all à la carte items *as appetizers,* so you'll have a choice of about 30 different dishes, in as many combinations as you wish. If you dislike decision making on this scale, the kitchen offers their own 5 items, usually off the regular menu, as a preplanned menu for $60. Lim uses virtually no butter or cream, relying on fresh reductions and virtually all organic meat and poultry, vegetables, and herbs. Look for tender, seared slices of squab or duck, or sea bass steamed in olive oil with organic artichokes and fennel. Desserts like lemon galette and crème brûlée are flawless.

DiLullo-Centro. 1407 Locust St. ☎ **215/546-2000.** Reservations recommended. Main courses $16–$25; lunch $5–$13. AE, CB, DC, MC, V. Mon–Fri 11:45am–2pm; Mon–Sat 5:30–10pm. ITALIAN.

This wonderful Italian restaurant, now a decade old, is undergoing a change of life, with proprietor Joe dying in 1995 and his widow handing the restaurant over to manager Toto Schiavone, who's changed the original Fox Chase base into Moonstruck. It's still close to the Academy of Music and theaters with such opulent and slightly decadent items as a huge copper antipasto cart, enlarged copies of impressionist and expressionist works, and a series of booths separated by etched glass, ebonied wood, and wrought-metal armchairs.

Begin a meal with an antipasto—sautéed buffalo-milk mozzarella slices, marinated pepperoni, sun-dried tomatoes, and the like on a single plate or a single seafood terrine or mousse. Italian meals of this quality demand a small first course of pasta; followed by a second of fish, meat, or poultry with vegetables; and finally optional fruit, sweets, and coffee. For a real splurge, the tagliatelle with black mushrooms is smoky and wild yet smooth. Main courses include thin-sliced fresh monkfish in lemon sauce and three slices of veal loin sautéed, then baked after a slow marinade in rosemary and garlic. If you order a grilled dish, be aware that many Americans perceive the Italian style as underdone. You'll want to finish with an espresso, which comes in a silver pot, and some dessert. DiLullo produces its own gelato, with ground fruits or beans and a splash of spirits.

Friday Saturday Sunday. 261 S. 21st St. (between Locust and Spruce sts.) ☎ **215/546-4232.** Reservations accepted. Main courses $13.50–$20. AE, CB, DC, MC, V. Mon–Fri 11:30am–2:30pm; Mon–Sat 5:30–10:30pm, Sun 5–10pm. CONTINENTAL.

There's a lot to be said for a restaurant that installed a window on Rittenhouse Street for the kitchen staff. Friday Saturday Sunday is a romantic survivor of the early restaurant renaissance that has adapted to the times, offering informality, abundant personal attention, and a relaxed confidence in cuisine. Chef Aliza Green of Azalea recently upgraded ingredients and found better suppliers for the 1990s.

Friday Saturday Sunday is classy but unostentatious: The cutlery and china don't match, flowers are rare, and the menu is a wall-mounted slate board with inscriptions in several Day-Glo colors. Pin lights frame a row of rectangular mirrors set in wood paneling, and fabric flecked with gold swathes the upstairs ceiling (downstairs, it's striped). An aquarium bubbles behind a cosmopolitan holding bar. Dress is anywhere from jeans to suits, and the service is vigilant but hands-off.

Try the fairly spicy Thai green salad with chicken breast, served over a marinade of soy, honey, and sesame. Or sample the colorful Szechuan salad with sweet red peppers and wok-fried beef slivers. The portions (both first and second courses) are well laden, so you're advised to split an appetizer and even a dessert between two. If you have any taste at all for duck, the double-baked and mildly curried half duck is excellent. The wine card lists about 30 vintages. The desserts change often.

✪ **The Garden.** 1617 Spruce St., near Rittenhouse Square. ☎ **215/546-4455.** Reservations recommended. Main courses $15–$25; lunch $10–$22. AE, CB, DC, MC, V. Mon–Fri 11:30am–1:45pm and 2:30–5:30pm; Mon–Sat 5:30–10pm. Closed Sat–Sun in July–Aug. CONTINENTAL.

Although it's 22 years old, Kathleen Mulhern's place captures the city's sense of style—taste without ornateness—better than any other spot I know. In this former music academy, the tables and bar are antiques, set off by the many 19th-century prints of fruit and animals. The three softly lit dining areas—Swan Room, with wooden decoys; Print Room, a floral back parlor; and the Main Room, a former concert hall with practice rooms—can become noisy when crowded. Thanks to 5 tons of soil and gravel brought in each spring, the gaily bedecked back garden is a fragrant and spectacularly quiet enclave, weather permitting; it's the preferable dining locale, either for candlelit evenings or for sun-shaded luncheons. Potted flowers vie with the yellow umbrellas for brightness. *Note:* The Garden now offers valet parking and reduced rates in a nearby garage.

The house's cuisine specializes in high-quality, comfortable dishes like breaded Dover sole, calves' liver with fried potato and shallots, and chateaubriand with roquefort sauce. Spinach gnocchi made by "Aunt Diddy" is feather light with a sweet Gorgonzola sauce. All main courses include vegetables. The French chocolate cake has been called the best dessert in Philadelphia by *Food & Wine* magazine, and the chocolate sampler plate is frighteningly good.

✪ **Jack's Firehouse.** 2130 Fairmount Ave. ☎ **215/232-9000.** Reservations recommended. Main courses $17–$23; prix-fixe menus $45 and $52. Bar service available; sandwiches from $7. AE, DC, MC, V. Mon–Sat 11:30am–10:30pm; Sun brunch 11am–3pm. Bar open nightly until 2am. CONTEMPORARY AMERICAN.

In many ways this is one of the most imaginative, and one of the most hotly debated, restaurants now operating in Philadelphia. Chef Jack McDavid, after raves for Reading Terminal's Down Home Diner and Reading Terminal Restaurant at 12th and Filbert Streets, has taken a turn-of-the-century firehouse and incorporated contemporary (and rotating) art by Philadelphia artists, a beautiful rowing shell, and a glass-and-walnut island bar. It's warm and homey, but the cuisine features dramatic juxtapositions of American ingredients and flavors, with special emphasis on the rare, the nearly lost varietal, and the inheritances of immigrant cultures. The game is outstanding, and McDavid's dressing and preparation of gopher, bear, bison, and beaver tail (to name a few) make this a national pilgrimage of sorts. The historical steeping in many dishes, such as Pennsylvania shad and bacon, is impeccable, and McDavid is fanatical on organic ingredients.

A typical menu starts with a basket of buttermilk muffins. It then presents main courses like suckling pig with a thin and slightly sweet sauce, garnished with lettuce and Granny Smith tempura; shrimp with fennel in a lime-pepper sauce; or three thick medallions of venison in a succulent berry-and-meat stock, served with haricots and baby carrots and a red-bean-and-wild-rice mélange. The desserts could be a smooth peanut-butter-and-chocolate cake or sweet pecan pie.

The same stretching of boundaries goes for the extensive all-American wine list, ranging from $16 to $90 per bottle. Several microbreweries, such as Stoudt's of Pennsylvania, are represented with quality beer, on tap and in bottles.

To save a bundle, try a simple meal of the black-eyed pea soup, the cornmeal crêpe, or a hearty sandwich for under $20 with your drink.

Michel's. Latham Hotel, 17th and Walnut sts. ☎ **215/563-9444.** Reservations recommended. Main courses $13–$19; breakfast $2–$9; lunch $7–$13. Mon–Fri 6:30–10:30am, Sat–Sun 7:30–11:30am; daily 12:30–2:30pm and 5:30–10:30pm. FRENCH/AMERICAN.

Michel Richard, a flamboyant French chef who found his true home in California, has been opening up a set of Eastern outposts, following his book *Home Cooking with a French Accent.* Michel's has a whimsical art-gallery feel. The cuisine aims to amuse and amaze you: Who else would stack a smoked salmon terrine with salmon mousse so it resembles a pastry? If you *do* want puff pastry, you can have it around almost anything, including crab cakes. Desserts are magnificent, and a dozen wines are available by the glass.

Morton's of Chicago. One Logan Square (19th and Cherry sts). ☎ **215/557-0724.** Reservations accepted for 5:30–7pm only. Jacket and tie required. Main courses $18–$32. AE, CB, DC, MC, V. Mon–Sat 11:30am–2:30pm; Mon–Thurs 5:30–11pm, Fri–Sat 5:30–11:30pm, Sun 5–10pm. STEAKHOUSE.

Looking for sirloin? Morton's of Chicago has become a staple both for business lunches near Logan Square and for celebratory evenings. Don't kid yourself about the specialty—the double-cut filets, sirloins, and T-bones come in aged, well-marbled tender masses. The house porterhouse weighs in at 24 ounces ($30); if you wish, the waiter will bring your cut of meat or fish raw to your table for precooking inspection. The cauliflower soup also is touted, and the Sicilian veal chop with garlic bread crumbs is a "hometown" hit. If you must branch out farther, sample the crab cocktail or the smoked salmon served on dark bread with horseradish cream, capers, and onions.

Morton's looks as sedate as you'd expect, with glass panels between the tables and booths and dim lighting that makes the brass glow. The art-deco bar has a wall lined with wine bottles, and the wine-by-the-glass list has a good selection of California cabernets.

✪ Striped Bass. 1500 Walnut St. ☎ **215/732-4444.** Reservations almost essential. Main courses $15–28; lunch $13.50–$20. AE, DC, MC, V. Mon–Fri 11:30am–2:30pm; Mon–Sun 5–11pm. Brunch Sat–Sun 11am–2:30pm. SEAFOOD.

This long-awaited 1994 creation of Neil Stein, formerly of The Fish Market, has an absolutely spectacular setting for what's called the hottest seafood restaurant in the country. In terms of ambience and setting, the 16-foot steel sculpture of a leaping bass poised over the exhibition kitchen sets the tone. With rows of plateaued banquettes, warm lighting, and carpeted floors to soak up all the din bouncing off marble walls, you'll experience a rare and exotic sense of theater.

The kitchen, under Will Ternay since June 1996, delivers creative, simple preparations of seafood, with the emphasis on fresh herbs and clean flavors. Appetizers include a potato mousseline caske with sevruga caviar and dill egg salad; Barshak calls it a "grown-up egg salad sandwich." The signature entree is the wild striped bass with garlic mash, spring onions, and vegetables; it's firm and flavorful. But take chances; this is the type of restaurant where you can feel comfortable asking the wait staff for advice—or the owners, who are religious about stopping by tables. An extensive raw bar features oysters from the East and West coasts, clams, shrimp, and caviars. Desserts and ice creams are extravagant. A mostly domestic wine list starts at $22.

MODERATE

Ⓢ Circa. 1518 Walnut St. ☎ **215/545-6800.** Reservations recommended. Main courses $9–$18; lunch $6–$13. AE, MC, V. Tues–Fri 11:30am–2:30pm; Mon–Thurs 4:30–10pm, Fri–Sat 4:30–11pm, Sun 4:30–9:30pm. Dancing Fri–Sat 10:30pm–2:20am, Labor Day to Memorial Day. AMERICAN/MEDITERRANEAN.

This 1994 labor of love is one of Philadelphia's hottest spots: It's got great food on a great restaurant block, it combines dinner with a sophisticated dance club, it's magnificent and yet engaging and comfortable, and it's cheaper than you think it's going to be. Owners Philippe Daouphars and David Mantelmacher took their club success at Xero on South Street into Center City, where they teamed up with thoughtful chef Albert Paris for Mediterranean cuisine with a twist up and westward.

The former bank building provides Circa with great beaux arts columns and windows along the east wall's long bar, opening up to a square, pleasant room upstairs—and also original steel-and-brass vault fittings downstairs. Chef Paris likes strong, congenial, flavorful food—you'll find choices like duck ravioli, goat cheese, and sun-dried cherries or roast salmon osso buco with scallop marron, cleverly chosen dishes that won't suffer from a complicated trip upstairs. Sauces, vegetables, and starches are expected to complement main meals, and every dish is a "signature": its ingredients are unique on the menu. Wines, from $18, are well chosen.

Circa is not a club, but at 11pm on Friday and Saturday (except in summer) the ground floor and mezzanine become a club with a jammed dance floor. The sound is excellent, and the lines go around the block.

Cutter's Grand Cafe and Bar. Commerce Square building, Market St. at 20th St. ☎ **215/851-6262.** Reservations recommended. Main courses $10–$24. AE, DC, DISC, MC, V. Mon–Fri 11:30am–4pm; Mon–Thurs 5–10pm, Fri–Sat 5–11pm, Sun 5–9pm. AMERICAN.

This place has all the things you'd expect of a restaurant in a big, impressive skyscraper: modern, cool lighting, and a huge bar (120 seats) for singles. But it's also an impeccable, convenient, 180-seat restaurant that's surprisingly warm for a romantic dinner, given that you're in white-collar clothes and paying white-collar prices.

The 20-foot bar is noted for its huge selection, with the bottles stacked vertically so that bartenders scamper up and down like gymnasts. Look for highly polished surfaces in wood and stone, handblown glass chandeliers, and oversized Rousseau mural reproductions in leafy hues. Fortunately the high ceilings soak up much of the din.

Cutter's showcases American edibles from Nebraska beef to pastas of all ethnicities, but their Seattle roots show most in the biggest single item, the filet of salmon (flown in fresh daily) grilled over mesquite wood. Pizza, lamb chops, steaks, herb-crusted beef, and chicken fill out the extensive menu, with delicious flat bread to nibble while you wait. The desserts are as good as you'd expect: lots of chocolate and a wonderful crème brûlée and pear bread pudding. The validated garage parking is complimentary after 5pm.

Founders. Broad and Walnut sts. ☎ **215/893-1776.** Reservations recommended. Main courses $26–$34. AE, CB, DC, MC, V. Mon–Sat 7–10am and 11:30am–2:30pm; Mon–Fri 5:30–10pm, Sat 5:30–10:30pm, Sun 5:30–9pm. CONTINENTAL.

Founders is actually the keystone of the Bellevue Hotel's restaurants, and its 19th-floor location makes it attractive for fans of views. The elegant dining room features arched windows, flourishes and swags of draperies, and plush armchairs. It's another winner in the 1994 *Conde Nast Traveler's* readers poll for America's top 50 restaurants. The "founders" are the statues of Philadelphia luminaries that surround you. At these prices, you will get fine preparations and large portions of dishes such as goat cheese and leek cakes, and baked chicken breast with berries. There's also live entertainment.

Ruth's Chris Steak House. 260 S. Broad St. ☎ **215/790-1515.** Reservations recommended. Main courses $15–$28; lunch $10–$16. AE, MC, V. Fri noon–5pm; Mon–Sat 5–11:30pm; Sun 5–10:30pm. STEAKHOUSE.

Ruth's Chris Steak House, just south of the Academy of Music, has gotten rave reviews since 1989. Ruth's Chris serves only U.S. prime beef that's custom aged, never frozen, and rushed to Philadelphia by the New Orleans distributor for the chain. The rib-eye steak in particular is presented lovingly, almost ritually, in a quiet and respectful setting, and garnishes are almost nonexistent. The portions are so large that you might want to skip the side dishes, although Ruth's Chris touts potatoes done nine ways. Several fish and chicken choices also are available. The desserts, mostly southern recipes with lots of sugar and nuts, average $6.

Ⓢ **Sansom Street Oyster House.** 1516 Sansom St. ☎ **215/567-7683.** Reservations not accepted. Main courses $11–$20; lunch $5–$11. Four-course prix-fixe dinner $18. AE, DC, MC, V. Mon–Sat 11am–10pm. SEAFOOD.

Chef David Mink knows oysters from every angle—where they come from, how their flavors differ, and how to prepare them. The Sansom Street Oyster House, located on one of Philadelphia's most colorful shopping blocks, is where David puts his acumen into action. In 1989, he added the Samuel Adams Brew House upstairs, the first brew pub in town, with two ales and porter on tap.

The ambience is that of a traditional seafood parlor, with such 20th-century concessions as a tiled floor (instead of sawdust) and plywood paneling. The blackboards listing the daily specials perch beside an endless collection of antique oyster plates and nautical lithographs.

You'll probably want an appetizer of several different types of oysters: metallic belons; cooler, meatier Long Island half-shells; the new, fruity Westcott hybrids from Washington State; and larger, fishier box oysters. All are opened right at the raw bar. For dinner, most people choose one of the specials—local shad or tilefish, for instance. The homemade bread pudding is the most reliable dessert. The liquor prices are moderate and draft Samuel Adams beer is $2.25. Free parking after 5pm at 15th and Sansom with $20 minimum.

✪ **Susanna Foo.** 1512 Walnut St. ☎ **215/545-2666.** Reservations recommended for dinner. Main courses $15–$24; lunch $9–$16. AE, MC, V. Mon–Fri 11:30am–2:30pm; Mon–Thurs 5–10pm, Fri–Sat 5–11pm. CHINESE.

Susanna Foo has been touted in *Gourmet* and *Esquire* magazines and just about everywhere else as one of the best blends of Asian and Western cuisines in this country. A fall 1993 redecoration incorporated her collection of Chinese art and textiles, a new kitchen, and a second-floor café.

The cuisine is the main thing, so expect to pay first-class prices. Appetizers feature such delicacies as curried chicken ravioli with grilled eggplant, slightly crispy but not oily. Noodle dishes, salads, and main courses similarly combine East and West: water chestnuts and radicchio, smoked duck and endive, grilled chicken with Thai lemongrass sauce, and spicy shrimp and pear curry. Ms. Foo does include French caramelizing of certain dishes but not any butter-based sauces or roux; the Asian technique is to sear small amounts of ingredients, combining them just before service. The wine list, designed to complement these dishes, specializes in French and Californian white wines. Desserts such as the ginger creme with strawberries and the hazelnut meringue are light and delicate.

A long-awaited dim-sum café and bar was opened upstairs at Susanna Foo's in 1993—diners graze from up to 30 choices of tidbit platters. These are exquisite, from pork-stuffed jalapeños and lamb wantons to tiny spring rolls.

INEXPENSIVE

Diner on the Square. 19th and Spruce sts. ☎ **215/735-5787.** Reservations not necessary. Sandwiches $4–$7; main courses $7–$9. Blue-plate dinner special $6.45 served 4–10pm. Always open. AMERICAN.

Say that you're strolling around Rittenhouse Square and have an urge for the type of square meal you'd associate with a roadside restaurant. A dressed-up place like that is waiting for you at Peter Bruhn's Diner on the Square. Don't let its pink neon fool you; it has booths at which homemade soups, burgers, hash browns, and the best milkshakes in Philadelphia make their cheerful appearances—for about $5 per person. The Diner also branches out as a deli, with a whitefish platter and delicious omelets, and offers some fancier cuisine, such as a chicken-breast sandwich. The lunch and Sunday brunch crowds can be fierce, so try to beat the rush.

Dock Street Brewing Company. Two Logan Square (corner of 18th and Cherry Streets). ☎ **215/496-0413.** Reservations required for six or more. Main courses $7–$15; lunch $5–$11.

Fresh-brewed tap beer $2.50–$3.50 per glass. AE, CB, DC, DISC, MC, V. Mon–Thurs 11am–midnight, Fri–Sat 11am–2am, Sun noon–11pm. INTERNATIONAL.

This brew pub is just right for the 1990s: relaxed, with a definite hook in the spotless on-premises microbrewery. Jeffrey Ware saw a market niche for a brewery that could operate in combination with a popular restaurant. You can take a tour, but at any time six or more fresh beers, ales, stouts, and porters will be on tap (Dock Street products only); sample the subtle distinctions in hops, yeast, temperature, length of fermentation, and filtration. The 200-seat restaurant features a 40-foot bar, a paneled billiard room to the rear, spacious banquettes, and high ceilings (it's ironic that this place is located in a brand-new corporate granite skyscraper!).

The lunch menu offers soups, several fresh salads, and pub-style sandwiches, including a grilled vegetable pita with black-bean hummus. Dinner main courses include maple-chipotle barbecued salmon, hand-carved roast beef, traditional English fish-and-chips with malt vinegar and house-made tartar, and a Stilton blue cheese tart in whole-wheat crust with apples and leeks.

Marabella's. 1420 Locust St. ☎ **215/545-1845.** Also at Benjamin Franklin Parkway at 17th Street. ☎ **215/981-5555.** Reservations not accepted for dinner. Main courses $9–$16; lunch $4–$7. AE, DC, MC, V. Mon–Thurs 11:30am–11pm, Fri–Sat 11:30am–midnight, Sun 3–11pm. INTERNATIONAL.

Are you looking for a trendy trattoria that offers pastas, pizza, sandwiches, and grilled seafood, all with contemporary flair? That's Marabella's, a restaurant that is not only fun and chic but also reasonably priced. Marabella's offers the same menu at lunch and dinner, with almost every item under $14. Both locations are convenient for families and posttheater dining. Before you order, your waiter will bring you bread and roasted peppers—hard to resist. The appetizers range from such old favorites as mussels in red or white sauce, fried mozzarella, and antipasto to a more unusual platter of fish and shellfish in sauce, something like a seafood stew. The roasted garlic cloves to be spread on the delicious bread are another pleasure. The wine list boasts a good selection of inexpensive California and Italian wines.

For a main course, try a contemporary dish such as tortellini with goat cheese, sun-dried tomatoes, and olives. The old standards, spaghetti and meatballs and lasagne with meat sauce, are very well done here; the pasta is homemade, and the sauces are carefully seasoned. If you want to go with pizza instead, the version with goat cheese, sun-dried tomatoes, and black olives is very popular. The desserts are gelati, ricotta cheesecake, burned-sugar custard, and a chocolate concoction called "original sin."

Rex Pizza. 20 S. 18th St. ☎ **215/564-2374.** Reservations not accepted. Pizza $4.50–$8.50; hoagies from $3.95. No credit cards. Mon–Sat 11am–1am. ITALIAN.

For those self-indulgent moments when you need a large pepperoni pizza or a tuna hero, one of the most convenient—and surprisingly good—spots is Rex Pizza. They do a fine, nongreasy, thick-crust pizza for about $6.95 and a full-scale submarine sandwich for $4.50. Even when they're busy, your wait will rarely exceed 10 minutes.

Rib-It. 1709 Walnut St. ☎ **215/568-1555.** Reservations not necessary. Main courses $7–$14. AE, DC, MC, V. Mon–Sat 11:30am–midnight; Sun noon–11pm. AMERICAN.

Rib-It does a lot of casual, off-the-street trade and gives wonderful value for ribs, an onion loaf, or a quick drink. Rib-It has a relaxed sense of comfort, featuring an old tin ceiling with cone moldings and soft lighting that sets a subdued tone. Swirling stained glass, much from the old Waldorf-Astoria in New York, decorates the bar and all the windows.

🎡 Family-Friendly Restaurants

Ben's Restaurant   In the Franklin Institute at Logan Circle, Ben's is well set up for kids with cafeteria food, hamburgers, and hot dogs. You can enter with or without museum admission.

Chinatown *(see page 90)*   Between 9th and 11th Streets and Race and Vine Streets are lots of family-oriented places.

Cutter's Grand Café and Bar *(see page 82)*   Lunch and dinner menus for children feature a $3.25 peanut butter and jelly sandwich, $5 fettuccine Alfredo, grilled cheese sandwiches, and fish-and-chips. Try for a window banquette.

Dave and Buster's   A playgound on the Delaware waterfront for kids of all ages, Dave and Buster's is a destination rather than a stop, since it's so far north of Independence National Historical Park and Penn's Landing. Arcade and carnival games are played in the Fun Factory from 11:30am daily.

Food Court at Liberty Place *(see page 96)*   Kids have their choice of cuisines from among 25 stalls, and they can wander without going out of sight.

Marabella's *(see page 84)*   You'll have plenty of family company at this natural in Center City. Its pizzas, burgers, and grilled chicken come quickly after you order them, and the noise and the colors are cheerful.

Vernon Hill dishes up a lean, smoky version of western barbecued baby-back ribs. The portions are quite large, to say the least. An appetizer called Wonder Wings dishes up over a pound of sauced chicken wings, and can easily make a meal for two. Whatever you order, don't leave without trying the onion-ring loaf, which consists of true onion rings pressed into a bread mold.

Samuel Adams Brew House. 1516 Sansom St., 2nd floor. ☎ **215/563-2326.** Reservations not required. Main courses $6–$17. AE, DC, MC, V. Mon–Fri 11am–11pm, Sat 11am–midnight. Bar Mon–Sat until 2am. ENGLISH/AMERICAN.

The 1989 Samuel Adams is a traditional, English-style pub with an American twist—a microbrewery. While you sit at the handsome hand-carved English bar, you can watch as up to five varieties of beer are made. In addition to best bitter, amber ale, and porter, they offer seasonal specials like Spring Bock. The menu features such English favorites as fish-and-chips and grilled sausage, plus such Americanisms as a 20-ounce Delmonico steak, burgers, crab cakes, and ribs. Cigar smoking is welcome in the bar, and local musicians play live Thursday through Saturday at 9:30pm.

Sawan's Mediterranean Bistro. 114–116 S. 18th St. ☎ **215/568-3050.** Reservations recommended. Main courses $7–$15. AE, DC, MC, V. Mon–Thurs 11am–11pm, Fri 11am–11:30pm, Sat noon–11:30pm, Sun noon–11pm. MIDDLE EASTERN.

The Sawan clan began in the South Street area with Cedars, and has continued with this agreeable 1996 effort near Sansom Street. I like to sit closer to the front of this narrow room and plunge into a selection of dips such as baba ghanouj and tzidziki, a yogurt laced with dill and a bit of garlic; three or four of these with pita bread makes a great light meal in itself. Stick to the ethnic entrees such as kabobs, though they do have some American choices on the menu. Service is wonderful.

Sfuzzi. 1650 Market St. (One Liberty Place). ☎ **215/851-8888.** Reservations recommended. Main courses $9–$15. AE, CB, DC, MC, V. Mon–Sat 11:30am–3pm; Mon–Wed 5:30–10pm, Fri–Sat 5:30–11pm, Sun 5–9pm; Sun brunch 10:30am–2:30pm. ITALIAN.

Clean, bright, and modern, Sfuzzi has a silent *S*. The service at the bar or at the tables concentrates on pastas, pizzas, desserts, and such Italian specialties as crispy pizza, fried calamari with aioli, and crispy chicken breast with romano cheese dustings. Kids under 12 eat free on Sunday.

Zanzibar Blue. 305 S. 11th St. ☎ **215/829-0300.** Reservations not required. Main courses $16–$22; Sunday brunch $15. Sun–Thurs 5:30–10pm, Fri–Sat 5:30–11pm; late supper, daily until 1am; Sun jazz brunch 11am–2pm. CONTINENTAL.

This café and restaurant between Pine and Spruce Streets is in a renovated building, with nightly jazz and roomy, sophisticated seating. The menu changes quarterly, but you can expect some Creole and latin spices and seafood, along with basic steaks and fish. Many people make a meal of the appetizers around a jazz set.

5 South Philadelphia

South Philly—literally square miles of basic row houses in straight lines between Bainbridge Street and the sports stadiums—is the best place on earth for one particular cuisine: adaptations of the dishes of south and central Italy to American ingredients and meal sizes. What makes South Philly interesting is that this "American cousin" is frozen sometime between 1920 and 1990, and you can always tell unmistakably by the decor, menu, and music what decade a particular restaurant is frozen in. So I've selected the best on their own terms.

EXPENSIVE

Aglio. 937 E. Passyunk Ave. ☎ **215/336-8008.** Reservations recommended. Main courses $13–$24. AE, DC, MC, V. Daily 5:30–11pm. Closed Sun–Mon in summer. ITALIAN.

Aglio, Italian for garlic, denotes the use of roasted garlic as a spread on the wheat bread distributed at this 1993 new-style Italian bistro. It also says something about owner Frank Audino's desire to get close to natural and unusual ingredients like sorrel, barley, brown rice, and risotto. Neighborhood regulars are applauding its elegance (in admittedly tight quarters), the flavored gnocchi made on the premises, and the freshness of the sauces.

The Saloon. 750 S. 7th St. ☎ **215/627-1811.** Reservations required. Main courses $14–$34. AE. Tues–Fri 11:30am–2pm; Mon–Thurs 5–10:30pm, Fri–Sat 5–11:30am. ITALIAN/CONTINENTAL.

The Santore family has tended here since the late 1960s, and the tastes of the time have again rolled around to the freshness and quality of their cuisine. The decor is solid wood paneling, soft, uplit sconces, and antiques and Tiffany lamps amid a second floor that is above one excellent bar and is surrounded by a second with an old National cash register.

The Saloon has a long menu and daily specials to consider over the pesto tapenade, parmesan, and olive oil delivered automatically with your bread. The Santores like standards like clams casino and crabmeat salads, but also serve sautéed radicchio with shiitake mushrooms and superb salads. The heavy artillery is the 12-ounce prime sirloin or the 26-ounce porterhouse with greens and roasted potatoes, and the lightly breaded veal slices with sweet and hot peppers. The wines are expensive, and the desserts high cholesterol and exquisite, thanks to the pastry chef on board.

MODERATE

✪ **Victor's Cafe.** 1303 Dickinson St. (follow Broad Street south to Dickinson, then two blocks east). ☎ **215/468-3040.** Reservations recommended. Main courses $13–$20. AE, CB, DC. Tues–Thurs 5–11pm, Fri–Sat 4:30pm–12:30am, Sun 4–9:30pm. ITALIAN.

Victor's is a South Philly shrine to opera, with waiters who deliver arias along with hearty Italian classics. Started in the 1930s by John Di Stefano, who covered the walls with photos of Toscanini, local Mario Lanza, and the like, the family still plays over 70,000 seventy-eights and hires the best voices they can find. The food has come in for some quizzical comments recently, though; best to stick to basics like the cannelloni Don Carlos, with its two enormous shells filled with beef and veal and covered in marinara.

INEXPENSIVE

Ⓢ Marra's. 1734 E. Passyunk Ave. (between Morris and Moore sts.). ☎ **215/463-9249.** Reservations not necessary. Main courses $5–$12. Basic pizza $5.75 small, $7 large. No credit cards. Tues–Thurs 11:30am–11pm, Fri–Sat 11:30am–midnight, Sun 2–11pm. ITALIAN.

No list of eateries would be complete without a pizzeria, and Marra's wins the "Best Pizza" award hands down. It's in the heart of South Philadelphia, and the brick ovens give these thin-crust versions a real Italian smokiness. Marra's has a large Italian menu in addition, and is noted for its homemade lasagne, its tomato sauce, and its squid on Friday.

Melrose Diner. 1501 Snyder St. (intersection of 15th St., Passyunk Avenue, and Snyder St., one block west of South Broad Street). ☎ **215/467-6644.** Reservations not accepted. Breakfast $2–$5; lunch and dinner $4–$10. No credit cards. Always open. DINER.

Somewhere between kitsch and postmodern, the Melrose's logo of a coffee cup with a clockface and knife-and-fork hands is eternal. Scrapple and eggs, creamed chipped beef, and the like are dished out 10 blocks north of the sporting stadiums in South Philly. If you hanker for the type of place where you'll be called "hon," the Melrose is paradise. They bake pies three times a day to ensure freshness, and turn out wonderful butter cookies and a great buttercream layer cake.

✪ Ralph's. 760 S. 9th St. ☎ **215/627-6011.** Reservations recommended. Main courses $9–$16; pasta $8. No credit cards. Sun–Thurs noon–9:45pm, Fri–Sat noon–10:45pm. ITALIAN.

This two-story restaurant a few blocks above the Italian Market is the epitome of the "red gravy" style: unpretentious, comfortable, reasonable, and owned by the same family for decades. The baked lasagne and spaghetti with sausage have fans all over the city, and the extensive menu features veal and chicken in particular. The service is friendly and attentive.

Ⓢ Strolli's. 1528 Dickinson St. (Follow Broad St. south to Dickinson, then walk two blocks west.) ☎ **215/336-3390.** Reservations essential. Main courses $6–$9; pasta $4. No credit cards. Mon–Sat 11:30am–1:30pm and 5–10pm, Sun 4–9pm. ITALIAN.

With all those Italians in South Philly, you'd figure on an extremely inexpensive, wholesome, family restaurant in the middle of a neighborhood, right? Right—and the place is Strolli's. It used to look like a burned-out storefront at the corner of Mole Street—now there's a sign and an identifiable side door. Implacable, pipe-puffing John Strolli presides over two plain rooms, with plywood paneling and bare plaster enlivened by an ancient cigarette machine and a life preserver dedicated to Strolli's wife, Carmela. Music emanates from a corner radio. You'll make your own atmosphere, and any description of the size, taste, or pricing of the dishes won't be believed.

You'll want to start with an antipasto; a medium-size one is fully 10 inches long and 4 inches high, so the large would suit three fine. All seafood platters come with tomato, lettuce, and coleslaw—would you believe a scallop-crammed plate for $6? The veal-cutlet platter is an extraordinary piece of sautéed red veal. While you're making reservations, you might ask for the special stuffed shells—they're legendary.

⭐ **Triangle Tavern.** 10th and Reed sts. (intersection with East Passyunk Avenue). ☎ **215/467-8683.** Reservations not encouraged. Main courses $6–$10. No credit cards. Mon–Sat 11am–2pm and 4pm–midnight, Sun 3pm–midnight. ITALIAN.

Inexpensive, heaping dishes of homemade pasta and bowls of mussels are served here amid the Fraiettas' 60-year-old steamy atmosphere of good humor. You'll enter through the neighborhood bar, complete with large-screen TV; keep pushing toward the back. Nothing costs more than $10, and most items are closer to $6: chicken cacciatore, gnocchi, and spaghetti in white clam sauce. The mussels in red sauce are famous. On Friday and Saturday nights, look for plenty of audience participation in helping the steady guitar trio along with old favorites. Be prepared to wait for a table.

6 University City (West Philadelphia)

MODERATE

Palladium. 3601 Locust Walk. ☎ **215/387-3463.** Reservations recommended. Main courses $10–$20; lunch $6.50–$11.50. AE, DC, MC, V. Mon–Fri 11:30am–2:30pm; Mon–Tues 5–9pm, Wed–Sat 5–10pm; late suppers daily. Closed Sun Jun–Aug. CONTINENTAL.

In the heart of the University of Pennsylvania campus (Wharton specifically) is Palladium, an elegantly appointed full-service restaurant and bar. It's reminiscent of an old-time faculty club—chesterfields and wing chairs with footstools face an old stone fireplace, while leaded-glass windows, oak wainscoting, and an ornate ceiling add the final touches. In the spacious dining room the atmosphere is similar, if slightly less cozy. The prices here are a little high to make the Palladium a student hangout, but they're quite reasonable given this restaurant's quality. You can choose à la carte dishes, a fixed-price menu, or a pretheater special.

Menus change completely four times a year, from Tunisian grilled shrimp to French classic lamb chops. Most main dishes are accompanied by potatoes au gratin (good enough to be a meal in themselves) and a mélange of fresh vegetables. Desserts do not quite live up to the standard set by the main courses, although the cold lime mousse is quite pleasantly tart. Pastries, homemade ice cream, and ices also are offered. Watch the (largely student) service, which is at best uneven, and sometimes downright slow.

Downstairs is The Gold Standard, a cafeteria that heats up with comedy, dinner theater, and the like.

⭐ **White Dog Café.** 3420 Sansom St. ☎ **215/386-9224.** Reservations recommended. Main courses $14–$19; lunch $8–$16. AE, DC, MC, V. Mon–Fri 11:30am–2:30pm; Mon–Thurs 5:30–10pm, Fri–Sat 5:30–11pm, Sun 5–10pm; brunch Sat–Sun 11am–2:30pm. Frequent theme dinners and parties. AMERICAN.

Judy Wicks is one of Philadelphia's great citizens: She led the fight against the University of Pennsylvania to save this block of Sansom Street and has evolved into a smart, tough, and fun-loving entrepreneur. All this comes through in the White Dog Café. The name is indebted to the mystic and theosophist Madame Blavatsky, who resided here a century ago. Blavatsky was about to have an infected leg amputated, when a white dog in the house slept across the leg and cured all. It has still got cure-all food under chef/partner Kevin von Klause.

You'll enter two row houses with the dividing wall knocked out and with the most sophisticated kitchen equipment and electronics concealed behind an eclectic mélange of checkered tablecloths, antique furniture and lights, and white dogs, dogs, and dogs. The friendly pups are everywhere—on the menu, holding matchbooks, pouring milk, and in family photographs.

From Sansom Street, the three-counter bar specializes in such all-American beers as McSorley's Ale, New Amsterdam, and Anchor Steam, as well as inexpensive American wines by the glass or bottle. Dining areas lie to the rear and right—there are several, and the White Dog has completed an ambitious glassed-in porch across the rear.

The staff offers frequently changing menus as well as "theme" dinners based on the season or a particular American region. They buy produce locally, which eliminates the middleman and results in dishes that underprice the market by $3–$5. Current starters include a lemon pepper grilled calamari salad and black olive crostini or fresh-made ravioli with European mushrooms, braised with white truffle oil and herbs. The grilled yellowtail filet with sweet-and-sour eggplant relish is delicious, and pastry chef Heather Carb turns out signature rolls and cakes.

The White Dog attracts everyone, from Penn students to the mayor. Just next door at 3424 Sansom St., **The Black Cat** (☎ **215/386-6664**) offers more of Judy's antiques and crafts; living-room articles are sold in the living room and so on. It's open Tuesday through Thursday from 11am to 11pm, Friday and Saturday from 11am to midnight, and Sunday and Monday from 11am to 9pm.

INEXPENSIVE

Le Bus. 3402 Sansom St. ☎ **215/387-3800.** No reservations accepted. Main courses $5–$11. No credit cards. Mon–Fri 7:30am–10pm, Sat 7:30am–11pm, Sun 10am–9pm. ECLECTIC.

Le Bus actually used to be a bus; stationary, it dispensed simple fare from four wheels in the funkier days of Sansom Street. It has since moved indoors to a simple row house, with the expected contemporary art on the walls, an uncluttered decor, and even a neon sign. You'll still learn about the homemade breads, baked goods, vegetarian lasagne, chili, soups, and salads from a blackboard over the counter, though, and you must bus them yourself to your table. Expect the main courses to be under $9, with unusual spices. The apple pie with sour cream is a wonderful dessert. A second, more substantial Le Bus has opened at 4266 Main St. in Manayunk (see below).

New Deck Tavern. 3408 Sansom St. ☎ **215/386-4600.** Reservations recommended. Main courses $6–$12. Daily 11am–2am. IRISH/AMERICAN.

Virtually next door to the White Dog (see above), the New Deck Tavern is less of a restaurant than a relaxed watering hole, with truly Irish beers and barmaids and a 37-foot solid cherrywood bar. The Tavern specializes in crab cakes, homemade soups, and Irish fare such as shepherd's pie. Specials abound at the 5 to 7pm happy hour. Try to catch Dottie Ford, a secretary to Penn's physics department, on the piano nightly between 7 and 9pm; she has an amazing range of thousands of show and other tunes, built up over the past 50 years.

New Delhi. 4004 Chestnut St. ☎ **215/386-1941.** Reservations not required. Main courses $4.50–$9; all-you-can-eat lunch buffet $5.95 daily; dinner buffet $8.95 Mon–Thurs only. AE, MC, V. Mon–Thurs noon–10pm, Fri–Sat noon–11pm. INDIAN.

New Delhi is a fairly good Indian restaurant near the University of Pennsylvania campus with an all-you-can-eat, 26-item buffet. It boasts quality ingredients, a tandoor clay oven, and friendly service. Look for discount coupons in student tabloids.

The Restaurant. 4207 Walnut St. ☎ **215/222-4200.** Reservations required on weekends, accepted after 3pm. $15 prix fixe for appetizer and main course; extra $3 for desserts. AE, CB, DC, MC, V. Tues–Sat 5:30–10pm. ECLECTIC.

The Restaurant is simply the final project for students at the Restaurant School, a cooking school central to Philadelphia dining and restaurateurs that emphasizes business and management. After eight months of instruction, teams plan a menu and kitchen protocol, then take over the ground floor for eight weeks at a time.

So why eat in this restored Victorian? There are several reasons, so Philadelphians say. The food is never downright bad and is often quite good. A month of Texan turkey recipes once left most people cold, but the following month a New Orleans menu was worth three times the price. In fact, it's popular to check out the month's crop, and it's not unusual for a good team to attract sufficient financial backing to set up elsewhere in town. Since the students are paying for the right to cook your meal, the prices are extremely low. The restaurant has acquired a liquor license and offers a fine selection of apéritifs, wines, and cocktails. You can count on at least one soup, one salad, and five main courses.

✪ **Zocalo.** 36th Street and Lancaster Avenue (one block north of Market St.). ☎ **215/895-0139.** Reservations recommended. Main courses $10–$16; three-course prix-fixe dinner $13.95 Mon–Thurs. AE, DC, MC, V. Mon–Fri noon–2:30pm; Mon–Thurs 5:30–10pm, Fri–Sat 5:30–11pm, Sun 5–9:30pm. MEXICAN.

This sparely decorated restaurant presents contemporary Mexican cuisine, from all the provinces, using fresh ingredients. It's undoubtedly the best Mexican place around, and its food is priced accordingly—from such traditional dishes as carne asada to such modern classics as fresh shrimp in adobo. There's lively Latin music on most nights, with a pleasant deck in back for use in summer.

7 Chinatown

MODERATE

Golden Pond. 1006 Race St. ☎ **215/923-0303.** Reservations recommended. Main courses $8–$16; lunch special $6. MC, V. Mon–Fri 11:30am–10pm, Sat–Sun noon–11pm. CHINESE.

This very stylish Hong Kong–style place costs a bit more than others in the neighborhood, but the impeccable service and the obviously fresh preparation are worth it. Wing Ming Tang, the chef, is a survivor of the Tiananmen Square riot in 1989 and has years of Hong Kong training. This Chinese cuisine features some potato dishes, chicken, duck, and seafood, but no pork or beef. It's one of the few places that serves brown rice.

INEXPENSIVE

✪ **Capital.** 1008 Race St. ☎ **215/925-2477.** Reservations recommended. Main courses $2.75–$6.75. MC, V. Daily 11am–10pm. VIETNAMESE.

The positive restaurant reviews placed at every table are not merely a major part of the decor, which was upgraded in 1993—Capital is one of the best spots in town for Vietnamese cuisine, which needs some explanation. Look for ground pork, sweet or pungent herbs and greens, and slight French touches. *Bun thit nuong* is a small, savory serving of pork with garlic flavor over rice noodles. You must bring your own bottle of liquor or wine.

Ⓢ **Harmony Vegetarian Restaurant.** 135 N. 9th St. ☎ **215/627-4520.** Reservations recommended. Main courses $7–$13. AE, MC, V. Sun–Thurs 11:30am–10:30pm, Fri–Sat 11:30am–midnight. VEGETARIAN/CHINESE.

This winner of the 1992 *Travel/Holiday* Good Value dining award is intimate and candlelit and prohibits smoking. Despite the menu listings for meat and fish, absolutely everything is made with vegetables (that also means no eggs or dairy). George Tang makes his own gluten by washing the starch out of flour; this miracle fiber is then deep-fried and marinated as appropriate to simulate "beef" or "chicken" or even "fish." Raves go to the hot-and-sour soup and the various mushroom dishes. BYOB.

Imperial Inn. 142–6 N. 10th St. ☎ **215/627-5588.** Reservations recommended. Main courses $8–$13. AE, CB, DC, MC, V. Mon–Thurs and Sun 11:30am–midnight, Fri–Sat 11:30am–2am. CHINESE.

The Imperial Inn has shown its true staying power in Chinatown under proprietor Luis Sust. The North 10th Street location, opened in 1973 and renovated in 1994, serves an enormous variety of Szechuan, Mandarin, and Cantonese dishes.

Lunch here features dim sum, appetizer-size dishes that are trundled around on carts for diners to take as the fancy strikes them, with $2 the average cost per dish. It's a great form of instant gratification for samples. For dinner, the lemon chicken features a sautéed boneless breast in egg batter, laced with a mild lemon sauce. You can order a full-course dinner, which includes a choice of soup, rice, a main course, and a dessert for about $3 more than the main course itself.

Joe's Peking Duck House. 925 Race St. ☎ **215/922-3277.** Reservations recommended. Main courses $6–$13. No credit cards. Daily 10:30am–11:30pm. CHINESE.

Chef Joe Poon, a graduate of the Culinary Institute of America, churns out Chinatown's best Peking duck, Szechuan duck, and barbecued pork with consistent quality. More recent menus have grown in low-fat items like steamed sea bass with light black-bean sauce. The decor is unassuming.

Ray's Coffee Shop. 141 N. 9th St. ☎ **215/922-5122.** Reservations not required. Main courses $6–$13; coffee $2.80–$5. AE, DC, MC, V. Mon–Thurs 9am–10pm, Fri 9am–midnight, Sat 9:30am–midnight, Sun 11am–9pm. CHINESE/COFFEE BAR.

This odd precursor of the city's penchant for coffee bars, located near the Convention Center, features an unusual combination of subtle Taiwanese cuisine (dumplings are especially touted) and a selection of dozens of exotic coffees, each brewed to order in little glass siphons and priced smartly. The iced coffee here is great.

Shiao Lan Kung. 930 Race St. ☎ **215/928-0282.** Reservations not necessary. Main courses $6–$11. AE, CB, DC, MC, V. Sun–Thurs 4pm–3am, Fri–Sat 4pm–4am. CHINESE.

This modest place is very close to the Convention Center, and the Lee family unassumingly turns out fresh and adventuresome dishes like jellyfish as well as most standards. It won the "Best of Philly" award for Chinese cuisine in 1992. The Pachen tofu in hot pot has ham, barbecued pork, fish balls, and several vegetables thrown together with unusual subtlety.

8 Manayunk

This neighborhood, 8 miles up the Schuylkill from the Art Museum and Center City, has rocketed to popularity in the last decade, with some of Philadelphia's hippest restaurants and shops (see Chapter 9 for the latter). Manayunk is particularly strong in long, thin bistros with urban vitality and in off-the-street temptations for snacks with appetizer-sized dishes. It helps that the geography is so simple; from the Belmont Avenue exit (north, crossing the Schuylkill River and its adjoining canal) off I-76 or one block south of the Green Lane SEPTA stop, just follow Main Street east alongside the river from the 4400 to 3900 addresses. Also, a cohesive local development group runs a continual series of attractive weekend festivals and events to attract business. Parking is plentiful, and store hours tend to run late to match dinner reservations.

EXPENSIVE

Kansas City Prime. 4417 Main St. ☎ **215/482-3700).** Reservations recommended. Main courses $16–$28; $56 porterhouse for two. AE, CB, DC, MC, V. Daily 6–11pm, late supper. STEAKHOUSE.

Derek Davis is the entrepreneur most associated with Manayunk as a restaurant destination, and this (along with Sonoma and Arroyo Grille, which is slated to open on the banks of the canal in 1996) was a real surprise—I mean, a 140-person steakhouse for yuppies? Well, it's a steakhouse with a difference. It's creamy, curving, and unclubby, deliberately attractive to couples. The cuisine has all the classics like rib-eye steak, at least five fish choices, and lobsters, but the side dishes throw in unusual combinations like spinach with raisins and pine nuts. Sauces like a reduced-cream béarnaise and condiments like sweet onion marmalade are superb. And if you're in for a splurge, try the Kobe beef from Japan—at $100 per order.

MODERATE

BLT Cobblefish. 443 Shurs Lane ☎ **215/483-5478.** Reservations recommended. Main courses $11–$22. AE, MC, V. Tues–Thurs 5:30–10pm, Fri–Sat 5:30pm–11pm. SEAFOOD.

Why the name? Bill and Lisa T. Shapiro started off with a catering kitchen here and expanded into a bistro; the address is in a cobblestoned former stable; and they serve fish, fish, fish. What it also explains is the determinedly incremental, nondesigned nature of the place; you will not find the expected salmon, swordfish, or tuna here. What you *do* get is sophisticated combinations, like Barbados flying fish with a Jamaican pepper hash, and shiitake-topped tilapia with mashed sweet potatoes. If you like Jack's Firehouse in town, the kitchen staff are alumni. Try to make reservations in advance, since waiting areas are not comfortable.

Hikaru. 4348 Main St. ☎ **215/487-3500.** Reservations recommended. Main courses $7–$15. AE, DC, MC, V. Mon–Fri noon–2:15pm; Sun–Thurs 5–10:30pm, Fri–Sat 5pm–midnight. JAPANESE.

This restaurant has added a top-notch Japanese element to Manayunk, with its elegant, height-accented greenhouse or more traditional tatami room. Hikaru, following up on branches in Queen Village and Rittenhouse Square, is known for its sushi selection, but the teppan grill is great fun in terms of tabletop drama, with a server searing meat, fish, or vegetables before your eyes.

Le Bus Main Street. 4266 Main St. ☎ **215/487-2663.** Reservations recommended. Main courses $9–$14. MC, V. Mon–Fri 11am–5pm; Sun–Tues 5–10pm, Wed–Thurs 5–11pm, Fri–Sat 5–11:30pm; Sun 10am–3pm. AMERICAN.

Le Bus graduated from the University of Pennsylvania neighborhood to Manayunk, but it also dishes out home-style, fresh, affordable cuisine featuring American classics, in a more substantial restaurant with new outdoor seating as well. The stone walls feature enormous paintings of farm landscapes. Homemade breads and pastries are baked fresh daily, and the weekend brunch features omelets, frittatas, and pancakes. The menu—from meat loaf to great pasta—and wholesomeness make it especially attractive to families. There are lines at peak hours.

Sonoma. 4411 Main St. ☎ **215/483-9400.** Reservations recommended. Main courses $13–$19. AE, DC, MC, V. Sun–Thurs 11am–11pm, Fri–Sat 11am–midnight, late bar. AMERICAN/ITALIAN.

In 1992, Sonoma was the original hot Manayunk restaurant, and its Italifornian cuisine and service have only gotten stronger. Set in a double storefront with 35-foot windows, three levels of seating, and a decor of black and brushed steel as a backdrop, this restaurant is crowded all the time between a hectic exposed kitchen, thin wait staff, and second-floor bar with 87 varieties of vodka. The food is wonderful—always Italian specialties like risotto, with American standards like roasted chicken. With this noise level, kids won't be noticed.

INEXPENSIVE

Cafe Zesty. 4382 Main St. ☎ **215/483-6226.** Reservations not necessary. Main courses and pizzas $5–12. AE, MC, V. Tues–Sat 11am–11pm, Sun 3pm–11pm. GREEK/ITALIAN.

This spot is an agreeable upgraded café featuring gourmet pizzas from a wood-burning brick oven, along with Italian and Greek dishes like pastas and moussaka. The enormous espresso and cappuccino machine in the center of the room highlights sweet desserts as well.

9 Local Favorites: Cheesesteaks, Hoagies & More

CHEESESTEAKS & HOAGIES

Philadelphia cheesesteak is nationally known. Preparing a cheesesteak is an art here—ribbons of thinly sliced steak are cooked quickly (with onions if you'd like) and then slapped onto a roll on top of overlapping slices of provolone or a thick smear of Cheez Wiz. Hoagies are the local name for the sandwiches known variously throughout the Northeast as submarines, grinders, or torpedoes.

✪ **Jim's Steaks.** 400 South St. ☎ **215/928-1911.** Reservations not accepted. Lunch and main courses $3.50–$4.75. No credit cards. Mon–Thurs 10am–1am, Fri–Sat 10am–2am, Sun noon–10pm. AMERICAN.

The best practitioner of the fine art of hoagiedom in this area is Jim's Steaks in Queen Village; they also do the mightiest steak sandwiches in town. Jim's has a certain art-deco charm, with a black-and-white enamel exterior and tile interior, plus omnipresent chrome. But most of the ground floor is taken up by the counters, containers, and ovens, although there is a counter with bar stools along the opposite wall. Take-out is highly recommended in pleasant weather.

Proper hoagie construction can be debated endlessly, but Jim's treatment of the Italian hoagie with prosciutto is a benchmark. A fresh Italian roll is slit before your eyes and layers of sliced salami, provolone, and prosciutto are laid over the open faces. You choose your condiment: mayonnaise or oil and vinegar. Salad fixings—lettuce, tomatoes, and green peppers, with options on onion and hot peppers—come next, with more seasoning at the end. The result is not subtle but pungent, filling, and delicious. The steak sandwiches are less succulent than in the past but also cheaper at $3.75; melted cheese (or Cheez Wiz) additional. Beer and soft drinks are sold in cans and bottles.

Lee's Hoagies. 44 S. 17th St. ☎ **215/564-1264.** Sandwiches $4–$10. No credit cards. Mon–Fri 10:30am–8pm, Sat 10:30am–6pm. AMERICAN.

For more than 30 years Lee's hoagies have captured the hearts and mouths of many native Philadelphians, at a low-slung complex between Market and Chestnut Streets and also on Chestnut itself between 13th and 14th Streets. The regular hoagie (basically an elongated spicy cold-cuts sandwich) measures about 8 inches long, the giant about twice as long. They will create various combinations, such as the Italian (four meats and provolone) and the turkey (with provolone and mayonnaise). Lee's minors in steak sandwiches, served with fried onions and sauce.

✪ **Pat's King of the Steaks.** 1237 E. Passyunk Ave. (between 9th and Wharton sts.). ☎ **215/468-1546.** $3.95–$10. No credit cards. Always open. AMERICAN.

Pat's, so its adherents claim, serves the best steak sandwiches this side of the equator. The location and hours make for an interesting mix at the take-out counter. The 24-hour competition with Geno's just across the street creates one of Philadelphia's liveliest late-night scenes.

PRETZELS

Soft, salted pretzels served warm with a dollop of mustard are an authentic local tradition, dating from the German settlers of the early 1700s. The best in town continue to be made by the Amish farmers who bring them to Reading Terminal Market. But you can make your own at the new **Pretzel Museum** at 312 Market St., open 10am to 3pm, Monday through Saturday. If you're outdoors, the vendor stand in front of the Franklin Institute has always caught my fancy.

PIZZA

I think **Marra's** (see "South Philadelphia" above) is the best of—literally—hundreds of pizza parlors and restaurants.

Pizzeria Uno. 509 S. 2nd St. ☎ **215/592-0400.** 18th and Locust sts. ☎ **215/ 790-9669.** Pizzas $8.45 and up. AE, CB, DC, MC, V. Sun–Thurs 11:30am–midnight, Fri–Sat 11:30am–1:30am. ITALIAN.

This national string of dark-green bar/cafés, festooned with signs and serves a reliable deep-dish Chicago pizza that's more like a meal-on-bread than a traditional pizza. The 1721 Locust Street location, just off Rittenhouse Square, is very convenient.

✪ **Tacconelli's.** Somerset St. at Aramingo Ave. ☎ **215/425-4983.** Reservations required; place pizza orders in advance. Pizzas $5.50–$12. MC, V. Wed–Sun 4–9pm. ITALIAN.

A real insider recommendation for pizza is Tacconelli's—not, as you'd think, in South Philly, but north of the new discos along Christopher Columbus Boulevard (formerly Delaware Avenue). The greatly expanded Tacconelli's is open until whenever the crusts run out (about 9pm). It's imperative to call ahead to reserve the type of pizza you want, which is prepared in a brick oven. The white pizza with garlic oil and the spinach and tomato pies are particularly recommended. To get here, take the Frankfort subway line from Market Street to Somerset Street, then walk eight blocks east. If you drive from Society Hill, take Front Street north, make a right onto Kensington Avenue, then make another right onto Somerset.

COFFEE BARS

In the last three years, Center City has been transformed with the addition of dozens of coffee bars serving versions of the arabica coffee bean, ranging from inky espresso to mocha caffe (chocolate milk for grown-ups). Depending on where you are, you can blow in for a two-minute respite at a stand-up counter, or linger for an hour at a window seat.

The best in Philadelphia? My wife, who is a true addict (and to whom this section is dedicated), adores **Torreo Coffee & Tea Company,** 130 S. 17th St. (near Liberty Place), open daily which roasts all their own coffees from light to full-bodied, and has a selection of premium loose teas. It also has a full espresso bar and excellent muffins, scones ($1.50), and biscotti. **Old City Coffee,** at 221 Church St. (behind Christ Church) and at Reading Terminal Market (they also set up at the Convention Center at larger events), is relaxed to the point of somnolence, but the coffee selection is rich, varied, and strong. The Church Street location has eclectic acoustic acts during Old City's "First Friday" festivals. **Melitta's Coffee World,** an outside import of the coffee accessory firm, has recently taken over the absolutely stunning corner space at 1601 Market St., with baked goods, sandwiches, and salads as well as take-out desserts. Everyone has heard of Seattle-based **Starbucks,** which has set up outposts at 1528 Walnut St. and in the Convention Center Marriott at Market and 11th Streets. In Manayunk, try **Péché** at 4436 Main St., with sinful selections of desserts along with the standard blends.

A Taste of Ethnic Philly: Reading Terminal Market

The ⑤ **Reading Terminal Market,** at 12th and Arch Streets (☎ **215/922-2317**), has been a greengrocer, snack shop, butcher, fish market, and sundries store for smart Philadelphians since the turn of the century. The idea was to use the space beneath the terminal's tracks for the food business so that commuters and businesses could stock up easily and cheaply. The basic format is rows of dozens of stalls, now half English covered market with cool brick floors and smells of fresh provender and baked bread and half gourmet grocer/charcuterie.

What's at Reading Terminal exactly? Scrapple, mangoes, clam chowder, pretzels—you name it, if it's fresh and unpackaged. The northwest corner (12th and Arch Streets) is where most of the "retail," as opposed to restaurant or institutional, Amish farm products come to market. You can still see the Amish in the big city on their market days of Wednesday and Saturday, and you can buy sticky buns at **Beiler's Pies,** soft pretzels made before your eyes at **Fisher's,** and individual egg custards (75¢) and chicken pot pies at **The Dutch Eating Place.** If you're in the market for meat, **Harry Ochs** and **Halteman Family** have the most extensive selections, with great country hams and local honey as well. **Reading Terminal Cheese Shop and Salumeria** offers gourmet cheeses and tinned goods, while **Margerum's,** now in its fourth generation, sells flours, spices, and coffee beans from barrels and kegs. The best coffee sold is **Old City Coffee's.**

If your stomach rumbles uncontrollably by now, **Termini Brothers Bakery** will still it with terrific bagels (40¢) or **Braverman's** will fill it with egg challah ($3.50), as well as danish and other pastry. For more protein, **Pearl's Oyster Bar** practically gives away six cherrystone clams for $4, and a shrimp platter with french fries, bread, and coleslaw goes for $6.95. Or try **Coastal Cave Trading Co.,** which has great clam chowder ($2.95), oyster crackers, and smoked fish. Just inside 12th Street, **Bassett's** purveys Philadelphia's entry in the best American ice-cream contest at $1.50 a cone. The shakes ($3.15) are no less enticing, and the turkey sandwiches ($4.95) are simply the best anywhere. And a new contender, **Old Post Road Farm,** has a cherry pie that tastes just like cherry.

The 1993 renovation of the market has left it with many more stools and counters. **Jill's Vorspeise** has a great selection of hearty soups, for starters. A lunch like linguine with clam sauce will cost $3 at **By George Pasta & Pizza; Spataro's,** an old-time favorite, vends fresh buttermilk, cottage cheese, and huge slabs of fresh pies. The **12th Street Cantina** sells not only tasty enchiladas and burritos but authentic ingredients, like blue cornmeal. Some consider **Rick's Philly Steaks**—a third generation of Pat's down in South Philly—the best in town. And the **Beer Garden** can draw pints of Yuengling Porter and Dock Street Beer, among other more mass-market brews.

The market is open Monday through Saturday from 9am to 6pm, but many vendors close at 5pm. Prices vary by vendor, and about half accept cash only. There are public rest rooms here.

FOOD COURTS & MARKETS

✪ **The Food Court at Liberty Place.** Second level (accessible by escalator or elevator) of Liberty Place between Chestnut and Market Streets and 16th and 17th Streets. Mon–Sat 9:30am–7pm, Sun noon–6pm. INTERNATIONAL/AMERICAN.

This court, in the heart of a gleaming urban mall in the heart of Center City, has Reading Terminal alumni like Bain's Deli, Bassett's Original Turkey, and Original Philly Steaks joined by Mandarin Express, Montesini Pizza and Pasta Gourmet, Sbarro, and Chick-fil-A. The prepared sandwiches at New World Coffee are outstanding. It's spotless, large, and reasonable, with full lunches from $3.50. You'll find it easy to keep your eyes on the kids as they wander.

Downstairs at the Bellevue. The Bellevue Hotel, S. Broad and Walnut sts.

This is a sparkling 1993 effort to attract a clientele willing to pay less than upscale prices while using this address. It's very appealing with bright tiles, great lighting, and public restrooms, and quiet center tables surrounding food-court vendors such as **Montesini Pizza,** the **Cajun Gourmet Grill, Rocco's Italian Hoagies** ($4.85 and up), **Bookbinder's Seafood Bar** (the crab-cake sandwiches are great, though the relationship is souring with the landlord here), and wonderful chocolate-chip cookies and coffee at **Café Monet.**

The Food Court. The Gallery, Market Street at 9th St.

The Gallery parades ropes of people up and down four floors of shops under a massive glass roof, and the lowest level near Gimbels houses an enclave of oyster bars; ice-cream stands; and stalls with baked potatoes, Greek snacks, and egg rolls.

The Food Court at The Bourse. 21 N. 5th St. (just east of the Liberty Bell).

This location has 10 snack/restaurant operations, all moderately priced and designed for take-out to be eaten at the tables that fill this cool and stunning restoration of the 1895 merchant exchange. Names of representative stalls include **Sbarro's** for pizza and pasta, **Bain's Delicatessen** for turkey sandwiches, and for sandwiches **Grande Olde Cheesesteak.**

Italian Market. 9th St. between Christian and Federal sts. Daily, dawn to dusk. Bus: 47 or 64.

While touring South Street or South Philadelphia, be sure to visit the Italian Market for the freshest produce, pasta, seafood, and other culinary delights. This is what shopping used to be like before supermarkets and malls. In cold weather, vendors light fires in the trash cans for warmth—but it's vibrant. It's increasingly safe, and 1997–98 will see a $2.5 million project to repave the streets and add new building facades, new awnings, and night lighting. It's most interesting to head for the market from South Street, which has been gentrified from Front to Ninth Streets. Only a couple of blocks filled with notable Italian restaurants—Ralph's, Felicia's, and Palumbo's—separate South Street from the market proper. Fast-talking vendors, opera-singing butchers, and try-it-before-you-buy-it cheese merchants hawk their wares here. The Market is also a great place to pick up ultra-cheap clothing, if you want to wade through racks of items. Fante's Cookware is famous nationally.

What to See & Do

Consider the sightseeing possibilities—the most historic square mile in America; more than 90 museums; innumerable colonial churches, row houses, and mansions; an Ivy League campus; more Impressionist art than you'd find in any place outside of Paris; and leafy, distinguished parks, including the largest one within city limits in the United States. Philadelphia has come a long way from what it was in 1876, when a guidebook recommended seeing the new Public Buildings at Broad and Market Streets, the Naval Yards, the old YMCA, and the fortresslike prison.

Most of what you'll want to see within the city falls inside the original grid plan, between the Delaware and Schuylkill Rivers and South and Spring Garden Streets. In fact, it's possible to organize your days into walking tours relatively easily—see Chapter 8 for suggestions. Even if you ramble on your own, nothing is that far away. A stroll from City Hall to the Philadelphia Museum of Art takes about 25 minutes, although you'll undoubtedly be sidetracked by the flags and flowers along the Parkway. A walk down Market or one of the "tree" streets (Chestnut, Spruce, Pine, Locust) to Independence National Historical Park and Society Hill should take a little less time—but it probably won't, since there's so much to entice you on the way. If you'd rather ride, the new PHLASH buses loop about every 10 minutes past most major attractions, and the all-day fare is $3. SEPTA also has an all-day fare for city buses, which is $5, but the two systems do *not* accept each other's passes.

Suggested Itineraries

If You Have 1 Day

Start at the Liberty Bell in Independence National Historical Park, then move south through Independence Hall and on to residential Society Hill, which is interwoven with U.S. history. In the evening, see what's on at the Academy of Music, the Annenberg Center at the University of Pennsylvania, or the CoreStates Spectrum for sports.

If You Have 2 Days

Day 1   Follow the itinerary given above.
Day 2   Starting at City Hall, walk up the Benjamin Franklin Parkway to Logan Circle and spend the afternoon at Franklin Institute

or the Philadelphia Museum of Art. Try to circle back to Rittenhouse Square and the Liberty Place complex before closing.

If You Have 3 Days

Days 1–2　Follow the itinerary given above.

Day 3　Spend the morning in Old City viewing its Christ Church and Elfreth's Alley, then explore the Delaware River waterfront and the new Independence Seaport Museum at Penn's Landing. Finally, either visit the New Jersey State Aquarium by ferry to Camden or continue shoreward to eclectic South Street. At night, hop by water taxi among the riverfront clubs and restaurants.

If You Have 5 Days or More

Days 1–3　Follow the itinerary given above.

Day 4　Explore the Rittenhouse Square/South Broad Street area, with a visit to the Academy of Fine Arts, winding up with a stroll through Reading Terminal Market (it closes at 5pm) and Chinatown.

Day 5　Fairmount Park's Zoo and many restored colonial mansions beckon. Further out, Franklin Mills or King of Prussia Court and Plaza have become magnets for literally millions of tourists who want to save on clothing from America's finest stores—retail and discounted—with no state tax.

1 Independence National Historical Park: America's Most Historic Square Mile

Is there anyone who doesn't know about the Liberty Bell in Independence Hall? It may not be there anymore, but you get the point: The United States was conceived on this ground in 1776, and the future of the young nation was assured by the Constitutional Convention held here in 1787. The choice of Philadelphia as a site was natural because of its centrality, wealth, and gentility. The delegates argued at Independence Hall (then known as the State House) and boarded and dined at City Tavern. Philadelphia was the nation's capital during Washington's second term, so the U.S. Congress and Supreme Court met here for 10 years while awaiting the construction of the new capital at Washington, D.C. From the first penny to the First Amendment, Philadelphia led the nation.

The ✪ **Independence National Historical Park** comprises 40 buildings on 45 acres of Center City real estate (see Walking Tour 1 in Chapter 8 for more information). Independence Hall and the Liberty Bell in its glass pavilion lie between 6th and 5th Streets. The Visitors Center, at the corner of 3rd and Chestnut Streets, is well equipped to illustrate the early history of this country.

This neighborhood ranks as a superb example of successful revitalization. Fifty years ago, this area had become overgrown with warehouses, office buildings, and rooming houses. The National Park Service stepped in, soon followed by the Washington Square East urban-renewal project now known as Society Hill. Buildings were bought and then torn down to create Independence Mall, a wide swath of greenery opposite Independence Hall. To the east, gardens replaced edifices as far as the Dock Street food market, which was replaced by Society Hill Towers in 1959. Graff House, City Tavern, Pemberton House, and Library Hall all were reconstructed on the original sites; Liberty Bell Pavilion, Franklin Court, and the Visitors Center are contemporary structures that were erected for the Bicentennial of the Declaration of Independence celebrations.

A park ranger must lead you through Independence Hall, and you must reserve a place for the free and frequent guided tours of the Bishop White House and the Todd House. This can be done in person at the **Visitors Center,** 3rd and Chestnut Streets (☎ **215/597-8974** voice, or **215/597-1785** TDD), which should be your first encounter with the park. Here you can pick up a map of the area and information in any of 13 languages. The modern bell tower houses a 6-ton bell given by Queen Elizabeth II of England to this country in 1976, and it rings at 11am and 3pm. The gift shop sells mementos and park publications, and every 30 minutes the center shows a John Huston feature, *Independence,* without charge.

It's open daily from 9am to 5pm, often later in the summer. Some of the park's building interiors require reservations, and other adjacent historic buildings have separate admissions.

To get here, you can take the SEPTA Market–Frankford Line to 5th and Market Streets or 2nd and Market Streets. By bus, take the PHLASH, 76, or any Chestnut Street Transitway bus from Center City.

If you're driving, from I-76, take I-676 east to 6th Street (last exit before the Ben Franklin Bridge), then turn south (right) along Independence Mall. From the Ben Franklin Bridge, make a left onto 6th Street and follow the same directions as above. From I-95 southbound, take the Center City exit to 2nd Street. From I-95 northbound, use the exit marked "Historic Area." Turn left on Columbus Boulevard (formerly Delaware Avenue) and follow it to the exit for Market Street (on right). There's metered parking along most streets, as well as parking facilities (all $10 per day) at 2nd and Sansom Streets, at Independence Mall between Arch and Market Streets, and at the corner of Dock and 2nd Streets.

✪ INDEPENDENCE HALL

Even if you knew nothing about Independence Hall, on Chestnut Street between 5th and 6th Streets, flanked by Old City Hall to the left and Congress Hall to the right, you could tell that noble and important works took place here. From an architectural standpoint, the ensemble is graceful and functional; from the standpoint of history and American myth, it's unforgettable. Independence Square sets you thinking about the boldness of forming an entirely sovereign state from a set of disparate colonies and about the strength and intelligence of the representatives who gathered here to do it.

Independence Hall is open daily from 9am to 5pm. Free tours are led by park rangers every 15 minutes; you can't walk around by yourself. You'll avoid waits by arriving early. You can get here by PHLASH or bus 76.

Although these buildings are best known for their national role, remember that city, county, and state governments used them at various times too. The French and Indian War (1754–63) required troops who, in turn, required money, and King George III believed the colonists should pay for their own defense through taxes. The colonists disagreed, and the idea that the king harbored tyrannical thoughts swept through the colonies but was felt most strongly in Virginia and Massachusetts. Philadelphia, as the wealthiest and most culturally anglophile of the seacoast cities, was leery of radical proposals of independence, as Franklin was in his role as American agent in London. But the news that British troops had fired on citizens defending their own property in Concord pushed most moderates to reconsider what they owed to England and what they deserved as free people endowed with natural rights.

The Second Continental Congress convened in May 1775 in the Pennsylvania Assembly Room, to the left of the Independence Hall entrance. Each colony had its

Philadelphia Attractions

Academy of Music ⑨
Academy of Natural Sciences ⑤
Afro-American Museum ⑪
Army-Navy Museum ㉖
Betsy Ross House ⑭
Chinatown ⑥
City Hall ⑦
Edgar Allen Poe National
   Historic Site ⑩

Elfreth's Alley ⑬
Franklin Court ⑲
Franklin Institute Science Museum
   & Science Park ③
Free Quaker Meeting House ⑮
The Graff House ⑰
Independence Hall ㉑
Independence National Historical Park ⑯
Kosciuszko National Memorial ㉙

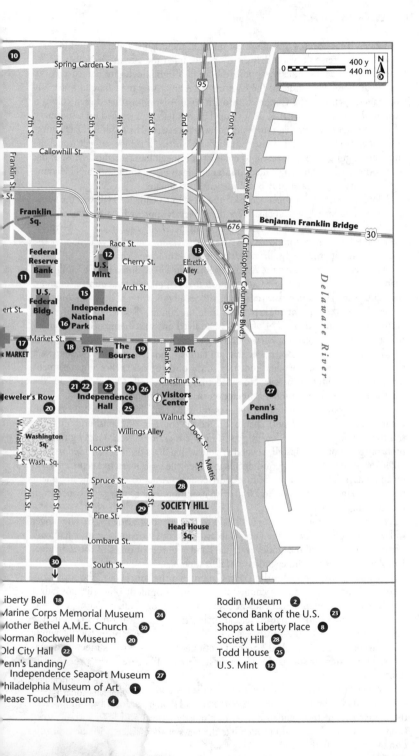

own green baize-covered table, but not much of the original room's furnishings escaped use as firewood when British troops occupied the city in December 1777. The Congress acted quickly, appointing a tall Virginia delegate named George Washington as commander of the Continental Army. After the failure of a last "olive branch" petition, the Congress, through John Adams, instructed each colony's government to reorganize itself as a state. Thomas Jefferson worked on a summary of why the colonists felt that independence was necessary. The resulting Declaration of Independence, wrote noted historian Richard Morris, "lifted the struggle from self-interested arguments over taxation to the exalted plane of human rights." Most of the signatories used Philip Syng's silver inkstand, which is still in the room. The country first heard the news on July 8 in Independence Square.

Before and after the British occupied the city, Independence Hall was the scene of the U.S. national government. Here the Congress approved ambassadors, pored over budgets, and adopted the Articles of Confederation, a loose and problematic structure for a country composed of states. Congress moved to New York after the war's end, and it grudgingly allowed delegates to recommend changes.

The delegates who met in the Assembly Room in Philadelphia in 1787 did more than that—they created a new Constitution that has guided the country for more than 200 years. Jefferson's cane rests here, as does a book of Franklin's. Washington, as president of the convention, kept order from the famous "Rising Sun Chair." Delegates were mature, urbane (24 of the 42 had lived or worked abroad), and trained to reason, and many had experience drafting state constitutions and laws. They decided on approaches to governance that are familiar today: a bicameral Congress, a single executive, an independent judiciary, and a philosophical belief in government by the people and for the people. No wonder John Adams called the convention "the greatest single effort of national deliberation that the world has ever seen."

Across the entrance hall from the Assembly Room, the courtroom served as Pennsylvania's Supreme Court chamber. Like the court at Williamsburg, Virginia, this room exemplifies pre–Bill of Rights justice—for example, your ranger guide will probably point out the tipstaff, a wooden pole with a brass tip that was used to keep onlookers subdued. Other period details include little coal boxes to keep feet warm on chilly days. This is one of the first courtrooms in America to hear the argument that disagreement with a political leader isn't sedition, one of the great concepts in modern Anglo-American law.

The stairwell of Independence Hall held the Liberty Bell until 1976. The ranger will conduct you upstairs to the Long Gallery. Now it's set up as a banquet hall with a harpsichord (some of the guides even play) and a rare set of maps of the individual 13 colonies. Its view of Independence Mall is superb.

Two smaller rooms adjoin the Long Gallery. To the southwest, the royal governors of Pennsylvania met in council in a setting of opulent blue curtains, silver candlesticks, and a grandfather clock. Beneath a portrait of William Penn, governors met with foreign and Native American delegations, in addition to conducting normal business. On the southeast side, the Committee Room fit the whole Pennsylvania Assembly while the Second Continental Congress was meeting downstairs. More often, it stored the assembly's reference library or arms for the city militia.

As you descend the stairs, look at leafy, calm **Independence Square,** with its statue of Commodore John Barry. The clerk of the Second Congress, John Nixon, first read the Declaration of Independence here, to a mostly radical and lower-strata crowd (Philadelphia merchants didn't much like the news at first, since it meant a disruption of trade, to say the least).

LIBERTY BELL

You can't leave Philadelphia without seeing the Liberty Bell at Chestnut Street between 5th and 6th Streets. During the first minute of 1976 it was taken out of Independence Hall and put by the park in its own glass Liberty Bell Pavilion across the street, once the site of the Executive Mansion. Admission is free; you can see the bell in summer daily from 9am to 8pm, and the rest of the year, daily from 9am to 5pm.

The Liberty Bell, America's symbol of independence, was commissioned in 1751 to mark the 50th anniversary of another noble event: William Penn, who governed Pennsylvania by himself under Crown charter terms, agreed that free colonials had a right to govern themselves, so he established the Philadelphia Assembly under a new Charter of Privileges. The bell, cast in England, cracked as it was tested, and the Philadelphia firm of Pass and Stow recast it by 1753. It hung in Independence Hall to "proclaim liberty throughout the land" as the Declaration of Independence was announced and survived a trip to an Allentown church in 1777 so the British wouldn't melt it down for ammunition. The last time it tolled was in 1846 to celebrate Washington's birthday. The term *Liberty Bell* was coined by the abolitionist movement, which recognized the potency of its inscription in the fight against slavery.

You can no longer touch the bell, but you can photograph it. You can even see it through the glass walls at night.

The brick arcades with terrazzo floors and marble benches one block north of the bell were built for the 1976 bicentennial, but they have been considered white elephants outside of special festivals and concerts. Some public hearings have taken place on one of Mayor Ed Rendell's pet projects, a proposed $170 million National Constitution Center, to replace this whole area. Don't look for quick visible progress.

✪ FRANKLIN COURT

Franklin Court, on Chestnut Street between 3rd and 4th Streets, with another entrance at 316–318 Market St., may just be the most imaginative, informative, and downright fun (and free) museum run in America by the National Park Service. Designed by noted architect Robert Venturi, it was very much a sleeper when it opened in April 1976, because the Market and Chestnut Streets' arched passages give little hint of the court within and the exhibit below.

Franklin Court once held the home of Benjamin Franklin, who'd resided with his family in smaller row houses in the neighborhood. Like Jefferson at Monticello, he planned many of the time-savers and interior decorations of the house; but unlike Jefferson, Franklin spent the building period as colonial emissary first to England, then to France. His wife, Deborah, oversaw the construction, as the engraved flagstones show, while Ben sent back continental goods and a constant stream of advice. Unfortunately, they were reunited only in the family plot at Christ Church Burial Ground, since Deborah died weeks before the end of Ben's 10-year absence. Under the stewardship of his daughter Sarah and her husband, Richard Bache, Franklin Court provided a gentle home for Ben until his 1790 death.

Since archeologists have no exact plans of the house, a simple frame in girders indicates the dimensions of the house and the smaller print shop. Excavations have uncovered wall foundations, bits of walls, and outdoor privy wells, and these have been left as protected cutaway pits. This is all very interesting—but enter the exhibition for the fun. After a portrait and furniture gallery, a mirrored room reflects Franklin's almost limitless interests as a scientist, an inventor, a statesman, a printer, and so on. At the Franklin Exchange, dial various American and European luminaries to hear what they thought of Franklin.

The middle part of the same hall has a 15-minute series of three climactic scenes in Franklin's career as a diplomat. On a sunken stage, costumed doll figures brief you, and each other, on the English Parliament in 1765 and its Stamp Act; the Court at Versailles when its members were wondering whether to aid America in its bid for independence; and the debates of the Constitution's framers in 1787, right around the corner at Independence Hall. Needless to say, Ben's pithy sagacity wins every time.

On your way in or out on the Market Street side, break for a snack at the pretzel factory next door, then stop in the 1786 houses that Ben rented out. One is the Printing Office and Bindery, where you can see colonial methods of printing and bookmaking in action. Next door, get a letter postmarked at the Benjamin Franklin Post Office (remember that Ben was postmaster general too!). Employees still hand stamp the marks. Upstairs, a postal museum is open in summer.

It's open daily from 9am to 5pm, including the post office and postal museum.

2 The Top Museums

✪ **Philadelphia Museum of Art.** 26th St. and Ben Franklin Pkwy. ☎ **215/763-8100** or 215/684-7500 for 24-hour information. Admission $7 adults, $4 students, seniors, and children 5–18; free for children under 5. Free Sun 10am–1pm. Tues–Sun 10am–5pm; Wed evening hours to 8:45pm with music, talks, movies, and socializing. Bus: 7, 32, 38, 43, or 76; this last is door-to-door, but runs only until 6pm. Car: From the Parkway headed west (away from City Hall), follow signs to Kelly Dr., and turn left at the first light at 25th St. to the lots at the rear entrance. Plentiful free parking.

Even on a hazy day you can see America's third-largest art museum from City Hall— resplendent, huge, a beautifully proportioned Greco-Roman temple on a hill. Because the museum, established in the 1870s, has relied on donors of great wealth and idiosyncratic taste, the collection does not aim to present a comprehensive picture of Western or Eastern art. But its strengths are dazzling; it's undoubtedly one of the finest groupings of art objects in America, and no visit to Philadelphia would be complete without at least a walk-through. Late hours on Wednesday have quickly become a city favorite.

The museum is designed simply, with L-shaped wings off the central court on two stories. A major rearrangement of the collections has just been completed, and they now mix paintings, sculptures, and decorative arts within set periods. The front entrance (facing City Hall) admits you to the first floor. Special exhibition galleries and American art are to the left; the collection emphasizes that Americans came from diverse cultures, which combined to create a new, distinctly national esthetic. French- and English-inspired domestic objects, like silver, predominate in the Colonial and Federal galleries, but don't neglect the fine rooms of Amish and sturdy Shaker crafts, more German in origin. The 19th-century gallery has many works of Philadelphia's Thomas Eakins, which evoke the spirit of the city in watercolors and oil portraits.

Controversial 19th- and 20th-century European art galleries highlight Cézanne's monumental *Bathers* and Marcel Duchamp's *Nude Descending a Staircase,* which doesn't seem nearly as revolutionary as it did in 1913. The recent gift of the McIlhenny $300 million collection of paintings is one of the last great donations of this type possible and adds French impressionist strength.

Upstairs is a chronological sweep in 83 galleries of European arts from medieval times through about 1850. The John G. Johnson Collection, a Renaissance treasure trove, has been integrated with the museum's other holdings. Roger van der Weyden's diptych *Virgin and Saint John* and *Christ on the Cross* is renowned for its exquisite sorrow and beauty. Van Eyck's *Saint Francis Receiving the Stigmata* is unbelievably precise (borrow the guard's magnifying glass). Other masterpieces include Poussin's frothy *Birth of Venus* (the USSR sold this and numerous other canvases in the early 1930s, and many were snapped up by American collectors) and Rubens's sprawling *Prometheus Bound.* The remainder of the floor takes you far abroad—to medieval Europe, 17th-century battlefields, Enlightenment salons, and Eastern temples.

The museum has excellent dining facilities as well. A cafeteria, open from 10am to 2:30pm on Tuesday through Friday and 10am to 3pm on Saturday and Sunday, dispenses simple hot lunches and salad plates for about $4. The museum restaurant down the hall is open from 11:45am to 2:15pm on Tuesday through Saturday, Sunday 11am to 2pm, and Wednesday 5 to 7pm.

The PMA has moved into the 20th century with recent shows of Jonathan Borofsky and Anselm Kiefer and a blockbuster on Picasso's still lifes. A massive exhibit on Cézanne's paintings, watercolors, and drawings in 1996 brought some 500,000 visitors—and $40 million to the local economy.

Museum of American Art of the Pennsylvania Academy of Fine Arts. 118 N. Broad St. at Cherry St. ☎ **215/972-7600.** Admission $5.95 adults, $4.95 seniors and students with ID, $3.95 children 5–12. Mon–Sat 10am–5pm; Sun 11am–5pm. Tours are free with admission. Leave from the Grand Stairhall Sat–Sun at 12:30 and 2pm. Bus: C or 48.

Located two blocks north of City Hall, the Museum of American Art of PAFA, the first art school in the country (1805) and at one time the unquestioned leader of American beaux arts, in 1976 got a healthy dose of Cinderella treatment as its headquarters celebrated its centennial at the same time as the U.S. bicentennial. At the end of all the scrubbing, repainting, and stuccoing, Philadelphians were amazed again at the imagination of the Frank Furness masterpiece built in 1876. Following six months of further renovation in late 1994, the academy unveiled a major reinstallation of 300 works done over 200 years.

The ground floor houses an excellent bookstore, a café, and the academy's classrooms. A splendid staircase, designed from archways to light fixtures by Furness, shines with red, gold, and blue walls. Each May the museum is devoted to the annual academy school exhibition. The school itself has moved to sparkling new quarters at 1301 Cherry St.

As is evident from the PAFA galleries, such early American painters as Gilbert Stuart, the Peale family, and Washington Allston congregated in Philadelphia, because it was America's capital and wealthiest city. The main galleries feature works from the museum's collection of over 6,000 canvases. The rotunda has been the scene of occasional events ever since Walt Whitman listened spellbound to concerts. The adjoining rooms display works from the illustrious years of the mid-19th century, when PAFA probably enjoyed its most innovative period.

Franklin Institute Science Museum. Logan Circle, 20th St. and Benjamin Franklin Pkwy. ☎ **215/448-1200** or 215/564-3375 for a taped message. Admission charges are confusing and depend on what you want. Basic admission to exhibitions and Futures Center $8.50 adults, $7.50 children; to Planetarium, Omniverse, and laser shows $6 adults, $5 children; combinations of the two $13.50 adults, $11.50 children. Science Center, daily 9:30am–5pm; Futures Center, Mon–Wed 9:30am–5pm, Thurs–Sat 9:30am–9pm, Sun 9:30am–6pm; CoreStates Science Park, May–Oct, daily 10am–4pm. Bus: 33, 76, or PHLASH.

The Franklin Institute Science Museum isn't just kid stuff. Everyone loves it because it's a thoroughly imaginative trip through the worlds of science showing us their influence on our lives. The complex actually has four parts. The first is the home of the Franklin National Memorial, with a 30-ton statue of its namesake and a collection of authentic Franklin artifacts and possessions.

The second part is a collection of 1940s through 1970s science- and technology-oriented exhibition areas that were pioneers in hands-on displays, from a gigantic walk-through heart with heartbeat recordings and explanations, to ship models and the Hall of Aviation, with its small planes and a chance to sit in a cockpit of a Wright brothers' biplane. For a hair-raising experience, plug into a Van de Graaff generator at the lightning gallery. On the third floor, an energy hall bursts with Rube Goldberg contraptions, noisemakers, and light shows. The nearby Discovery Theater gives afternoon shows featuring liquid air and other oddities. The fourth floor specializes in astronomy and mathematical puzzles. The basement Fels Planetarium (☎ 215/563-1363) rounds out the picture.

The third part of the Franklin Institute is the result of an ambitious 1991 campaign to construct a Futures Center addition funded by $22 million from the city and state and $36 million from private sources. Just past the Franklin National Memorial on the second floor, you'll enter an energy-charged atrium with cafés, ticket counters, and ramps and stairs leading to the new exhibits. Just beyond is a separate-admission Omnimax arena, showing films ranging from undersea explorations to the Rolling Stones in spectacular 70mm format. Besides the two-level atrium are eight permanent, interactive exhibits taking you into the 21st century with Disney World–style pizzazz, including ones on space, earth, computers, chemistry, and health. My personal favorites are the video driving exercise in "Future Vision," "The Jamming Room" of musical synthesizers, and the "See Yourself Age" computer program in "Future and You." The texts throughout are witty and disarming.

The fourth part is the 1995 CoreStates Science Park, a collaboration with the Please Touch Museum to use the 38,000-square-foot lawn between the two museums—it's free with admission to either one. The imaginative urban garden is filled with high-tech and play structures, including a high-wire tandem bicycle, 12-foot tire, step-on organ, maze, and optical illusions.

Of course, you'll eventually get hungry—with a family, the institute is a full afternoon. Your choices are excellent: a vending-machine space in the **Wawa Lunchroom** on the first floor, open only to museum goers; the new all-American with a nutritional twist **Ben's Restaurant** on the second floor, accessible without museum admission and open Monday through Friday from 8:30am to 2:30pm, Saturday and Sunday from 9am to 3:30pm; and the **Omni Café** in the Futures Center lobby, open daily from 11am to shortly before museum closing and serving beer and wine. Vendors outside sell Philadelphia soft pretzels with plenty of mustard.

3 More Attractions

Reading Terminal Market is an attraction in itself, as is the Italian Market if you're exploring South Philadelphia. Both are described in detail in the "Local Favorites" section of Chapter 6, "Dining."

ARCHITECTURAL HIGHLIGHTS

Benjamin Franklin Bridge. Entrance to free bicycle/pedestrian walkway at 5th and Vine sts. 6am–dusk. Bus 50.

An old fixture on the Old City landscape has jumped into the 21st century—the Benjamin Franklin Bridge, designed by Paul Cret, one of the architects of the Parkway across town. The largest single-span suspension bridge in the world (1.8 miles) when it was finished in 1926, it carries cars and commuter trains and also has a foot/bicycle path along its south side. For the bicentennial of the U.S. Constitution, a Philadelphia team, including Steven Izenour (of Venturi, Rauch, and Scott Brown), a leading American architect and planner, created a computer-driven system for illuminating each and every cable. At night Philadelphians are treated to the largest lighting effects short of Ben Franklin's lightning itself.

City Hall. Broad and Market sts. ☎ **215/569-3187.** Free admission. Daily 10am–3pm. During school year, Mon–Fri 10am–noon reserved for school groups. Last tour at 2:45pm. Interior tours daily at 12:30pm. Bus/Subway: Most lines converge beside or underneath the building.

When construction of City Hall began in 1871, it was planned to be the tallest structure in the world. But that elaborate 1901 wedding cake by John McArthur, Jr., with an inner courtyard straight out of a French château, was dated in more ways than one, and it still arouses wildly differing reactions, although there's general love for the crowning 37-foot statue of William Penn by A. M. Calder.

You may wish to wander inside its vast floors, which range from breathtaking to bureaucratically forlorn; both inside and out, City Hall boasts the richest sculptural decoration of any American building. The Mayor's Reception Room (Room 202) and the City Council Chamber (Room 400) are especially rich.

The highlight of City Hall is the **tower view.** The Juniper Street entrance is most convenient, but you can take any corner elevator to the seventh floor and follow the red tape (always indicative of city government). In this case, it leads to two escalators and a waiting area for the tower elevator. The elevator up to the Penn statue's recently renovated shoestrings, at 480 feet, can hold only eight people, and the outdoor cupola cannot hold many more. On the way, notice how thick the walls are—City Hall is the tallest building ever constructed without a skeleton of steel girders, so that recently cleaned white stone stretches 6 feet thick at the top and 22 feet at ground level. The simply stupefying view from the top encompasses not only the city but also the upper and lower Delaware Valley and port, western New Jersey, and suburban Philadelphia. It's windy up there, though. If you look straight down, you can see more of the hundreds of sculptures designed by Calder, the works of whose descendants—Alexander Sterling Calder (1870–1945) and Alexander Calder (1898–1976)—beautify Logan Circle and the Philadelphia Museum of Art.

Fisher Fine Arts (Furness) Library. 220 S. 34th St. at Locust Walk on the University of Pennsylvania campus. ☎ **215/898-8325.** Free admission. During academic year only, Mon–Fri 9am–10pm; summer hours, Mon–Fri 9am–5pm. Bus: 44.

Like the Pennsylvania Academy of Fine Arts building (see above), this citadel of learning has the characteristic chiseled thistle of Frank Furness, although it was built a decade later from 1888 to 1890. The use of 1890s leaded glass here is even richer. The library now houses, appropriately, the fine arts library of the University of Pennsylvania.

Pennsylvania Convention Center. Between 11th and 13th sts. and Market and Race sts. ☎ **215/418-4728.** Public tours are free; most shows charge admission. Public tours Tues and Thurs at 11:30am, 12:30pm, 1:30pm, and 2:15pm. Enter at the northwest corner of 12th and Arch sts. Subway: Rail lines (including Airport Express) stop at Market East Station; SEPTA at 11th and Market and 13th and Market; Bus 12, 17, 33, 44, or PHLASH. Car: separate exit from I-676, between I-95 and I-76.

A $522 million investment! With the July 1993 opening of the Convention Center, Philadelphia made clear that the future of the area depends on its ability to welcome tens of thousands of visitors weekly. The statistics are staggering: With 440,000 square feet of exhibit space, it's larger than 30th Street Station. But what's really great about the Convention Center is how solid, elegant, and in keeping with its surroundings it is. Architects Thompson, Ventulett, Stainback & Associates shoehorned blocks of brick and limestone between I-76 in the back and just five blocks from Independence National Historic Park in the front.

Unless you're one of the millions the PCC hopes to lure in for a meeting, you'll need to take the public tour for a peek inside. The highlight is a stupendous Grand Hall on the second level, evoking the Train Shed and Headhouse of the Reading Terminal it once was; gray and black Mexican marble alternates with waterfalls, steel, and terrazzo, with huge granite pylons for heating and cooling the mammoth space. Judy Pfaff's vast, kaleidoscopic *Cirque* extends airy steel and aluminum tubes over 70,000 square feet of space. Esplanades and corridors contain a veritable museum of 52 living artists (35 from Philadelphia) in one of the most successful public art projects of our time. In 1995, the Market Street entrance, the original Reading Railroad facade, was restored, with an escalator up to the Train Shed, and the Marriott next door has a skywalk into the Great Hall. And don't forget that the incomparable Reading Terminal Market is downstairs.

Philadelphia Merchants Exchange. Walnut and 3rd sts. ☎ **215/597-8974.** Not open to the public. Bus: 21, 42, or PHLASH.

This sloped site, alongside one of the city's original creeks emptying into a Delaware cove, was used by hometown architect William Strickland from 1832 to 1834 as a forerunner of a stock-and-trading market. It's a pity that this building, once obviously central to city life, isn't open to the public, because the exterior is fascinating—a Greek semicircular front end on the river side and a strong coffer of a building with a portico facing the city. The tower was built to provide instant information on arriving ships.

CEMETERIES

Christ Church Burial Ground. 5th and Arch sts. (enter on 5th Street). Open by appointment only. Bus: 48, 50, or PHLASH.

This 1719 expansion of the original graveyard of Christ Church (see below) contains the graves of Benjamin Franklin and his wife, Deborah, along with those of four other signers of the Declaration of Independence and many Revolutionary War heroes. It's a remarkably simple and peaceful place. There are always pennies on Ben's grave; tossing them there is a local tradition of wishing for good luck.

Laurel Hill Cemetery. 3822 Ridge Ave., East Fairmount Park. ☎ **215/228-8200.** Entrance may be restricted, since it's still in use as a private institution. The Friends of Laurel Hill arrange tours (☎ 215/228-8817). Tues–Sat 9:30am–1:30pm. Bus: 61. Car: Go north on East River Dr.; make a right on Ferry Rd., go one block to Ridge Ave., and turn right. The entrance is a half mile along on the right.

How come you find Benjamin Franklin buried in a small, flat plot next to a church (see above) while Civil War General George Meade is buried in a bucolic meadow? Basically, the views of death and the contemplation of nature got more romantic in the 19th century, and Laurel Hill was a result of that romanticism. Laurel Hill (1836), the first American cemetery designed by an architect, was the second (after Mount Auburn in Cambridge) to develop funerary monuments—even small Victorian palaces. Set amid the rolling, landscaped hills overlooking the Schuylkill, its 100 acres also house plenty of tomb sculpture, pre-Raphaelite stained glass, and art-nouveau sarcophagi. People picnicked here a century ago, but there's nothing but walking allowed now.

Mikveh Israel Cemetery. Spruce St. between 8th and 9th sts. ☎ **215/922-5446** (synagogue number). Summer Mon–Fri 10am–4pm; off-season, contact synagogue or park service. Bus: 47 or 90.

Philadelphia was an early center of American Jewish life, with the second-oldest synagogue (1740) organized by English and Sephardic Jews. While this congregation shifted location and is now adjacent to the Liberty Bell, the original cemetery—well outside the city at the time—was bought from the Penn family by Nathan Levy and later filled with the likes of Haym Solomon, a Polish immigrant who helped finance the revolutionary government, and Rebecca Gratz, the daughter of a fine local family who provided the model for Sir Walter Scott's Rebecca in his *Ivanhoe*.

CHURCHES

Arch Street Meeting House. 4th and Arch sts. ☎ **215/627-2667.** Guided tours year-round. Mon–Sat 10am–4pm. Services Thurs 10am and Sun 10:30am. Bus: 17, 33, 48, 50, or PHLASH.

This plain brick building dates from 1804, but William Penn gave the land to his Religious Society of Friends in 1693. In this capital city of Quakers, each year during the last week in March, the Meeting House opens its doors to the 12,000 local Quakers for worship and "threshing sessions." They use a Spartan chamber with no pulpit, with hand-hewn benches facing one another. Other areas of the meetinghouse display Bibles, clothing, and implements of Quaker life past and present, along with a simple history of the growth of the religion and the life of William Penn.

Christ Church. 2nd St. one-half block north of Market St. ☎ **215/922-1695.** Donations welcome. Mon–Sat 9am–5pm, Sun 1–5pm. Sun services at 9 and 11am. Closed Jan–Feb Mon–Tues and major holidays. Bus: 5, 17, 33, 48, or PHLASH.

The most beautiful colonial building north of Market Street has to be Christ Church (1727–54). Its spire gleams white from anywhere in the neighborhood, now that the buildings to the south have been replaced by a grassy park and a subway stop. The churchyard also has benches, tucked under trees or beside brick walls.

Christ Church, dating from the apex of English Palladianism, follows the proud and graceful tradition of Christopher Wren's churches in London. As in many of them, the interior spans one large arch, with galleries above the sides as demanded by the Anglican church. Behind the altar, the massive Palladian window—a central columned arch flanked by proportional rectangles of pane—was the wonder of worshipers and probably the model for the one in Independence Hall. The main chandelier was brought over from England in 1744. As in King's Chapel in Boston, seating is by pew—Washington's is marked with a plaque.

With all the stones, memorials, and plaques, it's impossible to avoid history. William Penn was baptized at the font, which All Hallows' Church in London sent over. Penn left the Anglican church at age 23 (he spent most of his 20s in English jails because of it), but his charter included a clause that an Anglican church could be founded if 20 residents requested it, which they did. The socially conscious Philadelphians of the next generations chose Anglicanism as the "proper" religion, switching to Episcopalianism after the Revolution.

There's also a small gift shop.

Gloria Dei (Old Swedes' Church). 916 Swanson St., near Christian and Delaware aves. ☎ **215/389-1513.** Apr–Oct, daily 9am–5pm. By appointment in the off-season. Bus: 5, 64, or 79. By foot or car: Take Swanson St. under I-95 at Christian St. in Queen Village, opposite Pier 34 and the Moshulu docked there, and then a turn onto Water St.

The National Park Service administers this oldest church in Pennsylvania (1700). At its dedication, the self-styled "Hermits of the Wissahickon" performed a public concert on viola, trumpets, and kettledrums. Inside the enclosing walls, you'll think you're in the 1700s, with a miniature parish hall, a rectory, and a graveyard amid the greenery. The one-room museum directly across from the church has a map of the good old days.

The thin, simple church interior has plenty of wonderful details. Everybody loves the ship models suspended from the ceiling: The *Key of Kalmar* and *Flying Griffin* carried the first Swedish settlers to these shores in 1638. And catch the silver crown in the vestry; any woman married here wears it during the ceremony.

Mother Bethel African Methodist Episcopal Church. 419 S. 6th St. ☎ **215/925-0616.** Donations welcome. Tues–Wed, Fri–Sat, 10am–3pm; Sun 2–4pm. Sun service, 10:45am.

This National Historic Landmark site is the oldest piece of land continuously owned by blacks in the United States. Richard Allen, born in 1760, was a slave in Germantown and bought his freedom in 1782, eventually walking out of St. George's down the street to found the African Methodist Episcopal order, today numbering some 5 million. His tomb and a small museum are below the church floor. This handsome, varnished-wood-and-stained-glass 1890 building is their mother church.

Old St. Joseph's Church. Willings Alley near 4th and Walnut sts. ☎ **215/923-1733.** Mon–Fri 10:30am–2pm, Sat 10:30am–6:30pm, Sun 7am–4pm. One daily mass Mon–Sat, four on Sun. Bus: 21, 42, or 50.

At its 1733 founding, St. Joseph's was the only place in the English-speaking world where Roman Catholics could celebrate mass publicly. The story goes that Benjamin Franklin advised Father Greaton to protect the church physically, since religious bigotry wasn't unknown even in the Quaker city. That's why the building is so unassuming from the street, a fact that didn't save it from damage during the anti-Catholic riots of the 1830s. Such French allies as Lafayette worshiped here. The present building (1838) is Greek Revival merging into Victorian, with wooden pews and such unusual colors as mustard and pale yellow, but the interior has preserved a colonial style unusual in a Catholic church.

St. Peter's Episcopal. 3rd and Pine sts. ☎ **215/925-5968.** Tues–Sat 9am–4pm, Sun 1–4pm. Guided tours Sat 10am–noon and 1–3pm, Sun 1–3pm. Bus: 50, 90, or PHLASH.

St. Peter's (1761) was originally established through the bishop of London and has remained continuously open since. So like all pre-Revolutionary Episcopal churches, St. Peter's started out as an Anglican shrine. But why was this so, with Christ Church at 2nd and Market? In one word—mud. In the words of a local historian, "the long tramp from Society Hill was more and more distasteful to fine gentlemen and beautiful belles."

Robert Smith, the builder of Carpenters' Hall, continued his penchant for red brick, pediments on the ends, and keystoned arches for gallery windows. The white box pews are evidence that not much has changed. Unlike in most churches, the wine-glass pulpit is set into the west end, but the chancel is at the east, so the minister had to do some walking during the service. George Washington and Mayor Samuel Powel sat in pew 41. The 1764 organ case blocks the east Palladian window. The steeple outside, constructed in 1842, was designed by William Strickland to house a chime of bells, which are still played.

The graveyard contains seven Native American chiefs, victims of the 1793 smallpox epidemic. Painter C. W. Peale, Stephen Decatur of naval fame, Nicholas Biddle of the Second Bank of the United States, and other notables also are interred here.

HISTORIC BUILDINGS & MONUMENTS

Betsy Ross House. 239 Arch St. ☎ **215/627-5343.** Suggested contribution $1 adults, 25¢ children. Tues–Sun 10am–5pm. Bus: 5, 17, 33, 48, or PHLASH.

One colonial home everybody knows about is this one near Christ Church, restored in 1937 and distinguished by the Stars and Stripes outside. Elizabeth (Betsy) Ross was a Quaker needlewoman, married in Gloria Dei Church and newly widowed in 1776. So she worked as a seamstress and upholsterer out of her home on Arch Street (nobody is quite sure if No. 239 was hers, though). Nobody knows if she did the original American flag of 13 stars set in a field of 13 red-and-white stripes, but she was commissioned to sew for the American fleet ship's flags that replaced the earlier Continental banners.

The house takes only a minute or two to walk through, and the wooden stairwell was designed for shorter colonial frames—certainly not Washington's! Since the house is set back from the street, the city maintains the Atwater Kent Park in front, where Ross and her last husband are buried. The upholstery shop, now a gift shop, opens into the period parlor. Other rooms include the cellar kitchen (standard placement for this room), tiny bedrooms, and model working areas for upholstering, making musket balls, and the like. Note such little touches as reusable note tablets made of ivory; pine cones, used to help start hearth fires; and the prominent kitchen hourglass.

Carpenters' Hall. 320 Chestnut St. ☎ **215/925-0167.** Free admission. Tues–Sun 10am–4pm (hours are curtailed because the Carpenters' Company still maintains it); Wed–Sun in Jan–Feb. Bus: 21, 42, 76, or PHLASH.

Carpenters' Hall (1773) was the guildhall for—guess who?—carpenters; at the time the city could use plenty, for 18th-century Philadelphia was the fastest-growing urban area in all the colonies and perhaps in the British Empire outside of London. Robert Smith, a Scottish member of the Carpenters' Company, designed the building (like most carpenters, he did architecture and contracting as well). He also designed the steeple of Christ Church, with the same calm Georgian lines. It's made of Flemish Bond brick in a checkerboard pattern, with stone window sills, superb woodwork, and a cupola that resembles a salt shaker.

You'll be surprised at how small Carpenters' Hall is because such great events transpired here. In 1774 the normal governmental channels to convey colonial complaints to the Crown were felt inadequate, and a popular Committee of Correspondence debated in Carpenters' Hall. The more radical delegates, led by Patrick Henry, had already expressed treasonous wishes for independence, but most wanted to exhaust possibilities of bettering their relationship with the Crown.

What's in there now isn't much—an exhibit of colonial building methods; some portraits; and Windsor chairs that seated the First Continental Congress. If some details look as if they're from a later period, you're right: The fan lights above the north and south doors date from the 1790s, and the gilding dates from 1857.

Declaration House (Graff House). 7th and Market sts. ☎ **215/597-2505.** Free admission (part of Independence National Historical Park). Daily 9am–5pm. Bus: 17, 33, 48, 76, or PHLASH.

Bricklayer Jacob Graff constructed a modest three-story home in the 1770s, figuring on renting out the second floor for added income. The Second Continental Congress soon brought to the house a thin, red-haired tenant—Thomas Jefferson—in search of a quiet room away from city noise. If the Declaration of Independence is any indication, he found it, because he drafted it here between June 10 and June 18, 1776.

The reconstruction uses the same Flemish Bond checkerboard pattern (only on visible walls; it was too expensive for party walls) for brick, windows with paneled shutters, and implements that the house exhibited in 1775. If you compare it with Society Hill homes, it's tiny and asymmetrical, with an off-center front door. You'll enter through a small garden and see a short film about Jefferson and a copy of

Jefferson's draft (which would have forbidden slavery in the United States, had the clause survived debate). The upstairs rooms are furnished as Jefferson would have seen them.

✪ **Elfreth's Alley.** 2nd St. between Arch and Race sts. ☎ **215/574-0560.** Admission Street is public; Mantua Maker's House $1 adults, 50¢ children, $2.50 families. Tues–Sat 10am–4pm, Sun noon–4pm. Bus: 5, 48, 76, or PHLASH.

The modern Benjamin Franklin Bridge shadows Elfreth's Alley, the oldest continuously inhabited street in America. Most of colonial Philadelphia looked much like this: cobblestone lanes between the major thoroughfares; small two-story homes; and pent eaves over doors and windows, a local trademark. Note the busybody mirrors that let residents see who is at their door (or someone else's) from the second-story bedroom. In 1700 the resident artisans and tradesmen worked with shipping, but 50 years later haberdashers, bakers, printers, and house carpenters set up shop. Families moved in and out rapidly, for noisy, dusty 2nd Street was the major north–south route in Philadelphia. Jews, blacks, Welsh, and Germans made it a miniature melting pot. Because of luck and the vigilant Elfreth's Alley Association, the destruction of the street was averted in 1937. The minuscule, sober facades hide some ultramodern interiors, and there are some restful shady benches under a Kentucky Coffee Bean tree on Bladen Court, off the north side of the street.

Number 126, the 1755 **Mantua Maker's House** (cape maker), built by blacksmith Jeremiah Elfreth, now serves as a museum and is the only house open to the public. An 18th-century garden in back has been restored, and the interiors include a dressmaker's shop and upstairs bedroom. You can also buy colonial candy and gifts and peek in some of the open windows on the street. On the first weekend in June all the houses are thrown open for inspection—don't miss this.

Masonic Temple. 1 N. Broad St. ☎ **215/988-1917.** Free admission. Tours Mon–Fri at 10 and 11am and 1, 2, and 3pm, Sat at 10 and 11am. Bus: 17, 33, 44, 48, or 76.

Quite apart from its Masonic lore, the temple—among the world's largest—is one of America's best on-site illustrations of the use of post-Civil War architecture and design, because the halls are more or less frozen in time and because no expense was spared. There are seven lodge halls, designed to capture the seven "ideal" architectures: Renaissance, Ionic, Oriental, Corinthian, Gothic, Egyptian, and Norman (notice that Renaissance was the most contemporary style that architect James Windrim could come up with!). This is actually the preeminent Masonic Temple of American Freemasonry; many of the Founding Fathers including Washington were Masons, and the museum has preserved their letters and emblems. Lafayette and Andrew Jackson also were Masons.

Pennsylvania Hospital. 8th and Spruce sts. ☎ **215/829-3971.** Free admission. Mon–Fri 9am–5pm. Guided tours are no longer obligatory; copies of a walking tour itinerary available from the Marketing Department on the 2nd floor of the Pine St. building. Bus: 47 or 90.

Pennsylvania Hospital, like so much in civic Philadelphia, owes its presence to Benjamin Franklin, who devised a rudimentary matching-grant scheme so that the Assembly wouldn't feel it was subsidizing something that private citizens didn't want. This was the first hospital in the colonies, and it seemed like a strange venture into social welfare at the time. Samuel Rhoads, a fine architect in the Carpenters' Company, designed the Georgian headquarters; the east wing, nearest 8th Street, was completed in 1755, and a west wing matched it in 1797. The grand Center Building by David Evans completed the ensemble in 1804. The marble pilasters and arched doorway of the middle structure add curving grace to the anchorlike wings. Instead of a dome, the hospital decided on a surgical amphitheater's skylight. In spring, the garden's azaleas brighten the neighborhood, and the beautifully designed herb garden is equally popular.

The hospital was the workplace of Philadelphia's many brilliant doctors, among them Philip Syng Physick, Benjamin Rush, and Caspar Wistar. The entrance on 8th Street, between Spruce and Pine, highlights the Benjamin West painting, *Christ Healing the Sick in the Temple.*

✪ **Powel House.** 244 S. 3rd St. ☎ **215/627-0364** or 215/925-2251. Admission $3 adults, $2 students; free for children under 6. Guided tours only. Call for current hours. Be sure to arrive at least 30 minutes before closing. Bus: 50, 76, or 90.

If Elfreth's Alley (see above) leaves you wondering about how someone really well-to-do lived in colonial Philadelphia, head for the Powel House. Samuel Powel was mayor, and he and his wife, Elizabeth, hosted every Founding Father and foreign dignitary around. (John Adams called these feasts "sinful dinners," which shows how far Samuel had come from a Quaker background.) He spent most of his 20s gallivanting in Europe, thanks to the family's wealth, collecting wares for this 1765 mansion.

Unbelievably, this most Georgian house was slated for demolition in 1930 because it had become a decrepit slum dwelling. Period rooms were removed to the Philadelphia Museum of Art and the Metropolitan Museum of Art in New York. But the Philadelphia Society for the Preservation of Landmarks saved it and has gradually refurnished the entire mansion as it was. The yellow satin Reception Room, off the entrance hall, has some gorgeous details, such as a wide-grain mahogany secretary. Upstairs, the magnificent ballroom features red damask drapes whose design is copied from a bolt of cloth found untouched in a colonial attic. There is also a 1790 Irish crystal chandelier and a letter from Benjamin Franklin's daughter referring to the lively dances held here. An 18th-century garden lies below.

LIBRARIES & LITERARY SITES

Athenaeum of Philadelphia. 219 S. 6th St. (Washington Square East). ☎ **215/925-2688.** Free admission. Mon–Fri 9am–5pm. Permission to enter and guided tours given on request. Bus: 21, 42, or 90.

The age when a group of private subscribers could fund the dissemination of useful knowledge—or even keep tabs on it in diverse fields—has long since passed, but a 15-minute peek into the Athenaeum will show you one of America's finest collections of Victorian-period architectural design and also give you the flavor of private 19th-century life for the proper Philadelphian. The building, beautifully restored in 1975, houses almost one million library items for the serious researcher in American architecture. Changing exhibitions of rare books, drawings, and photographs fill a recently constructed first-floor gallery.

Free Library of Philadelphia. Central Library, Logan Circle at 19th and Vine sts. ☎ **215/686-5322.** Mon–Wed 9am–9pm, Thurs–Fri 9am–6pm, Sat 9am–5pm, Sun 1–5pm. Bus: 33, 76, or PHLASH.

Splendidly sited on the north side of Logan Circle, the Free Library of Philadelphia rivals the public libraries of Boston and New York for magnificence and diversity. The library and its twin, the Municipal Court, are plagiarisms of buildings in the Place de la Concorde in Paris (the library's the one on the left). If you're hungry, the Library's Marietta's Skyline Cafe (open Monday through Friday from 9am to 4pm) is one of the nicest locations for a snack and one of the only Parkway dining areas.

The main lobby and the gallery always have some of the institution's riches on display, from medieval manuscripts to modern bookbinding. Greeting cards and stationery are sold for reasonable prices too. The second floor houses the best local history, travel, and resource collection in the city. The local map collection of 130,000 catalog items is fascinating. The third-floor rare-book room hosts visitors on Monday through Friday from 9am to 5pm, with tours at 11am or by appointment. If you're interested in manuscripts, children's literature, incunabula, and early American hornbooks, or just want to see a stuffed raven, this is the place.

There's also an active concert and film series.

Edgar Allan Poe National Historical Site. 532 N. 7th St. (near Spring Garden St.). ☎ **215/597-8780.** Free admission. Tues–Sat 9am–5pm. Bus: 47.

The acclaimed American author lived here from 1843 to 1844. "The Black Cat," "The Gold Bug," and "The Tell-Tale Heart" were published while he was a resident. It's a simple place—after all, Poe was badly off most of his life—and the National Park Service keeps it unfurnished. An adjoining building contains basic information on Poe's life and work, along with a reading room and slide presentation. The Park Service also runs intermittent discussions and candlelight tours on Saturday afternoon.

Rosenbach Museum and Library. 2010 Delancey Place (between Spruce and Pine sts). ☎ **215/732-1600.** Admission $3.50 adults, $2.50 children under 18 and seniors. Tues–Sun 11am–4pm; last tour at 2:45pm. Closed Aug. Bus: 17 or 90.

The Rosenbach specializes in books: illuminated manuscripts, parchment, rough drafts, and first editions. If you love the variations and beauty of the printed word, they'll love your presence.

You're not allowed absolute freedom in the opulent town-house galleries, or free rein among the 30,000 rare books and 270,000 documents. But the admission fee allows you a 75-minute tour with one of the trained volunteer guides. Some rooms preserve the Rosenbachs' elegant living quarters, with antique furniture and Sully paintings. Others are devoted to authors and illustrators: Marianne Moore's Greenwich Village study is reproduced in its entirety, and the Maurice Sendak drawings represent only the tip of the iceberg (or the forest). Holdings include the original manuscript of Joyce's *Ulysses* and first editions of Melville, in Melville's own bookcase. Small special exhibitions are tucked in throughout the house, and don't miss the shop behind the entrance, for bargains in greeting cards and a superb collection of Sendak.

MORE MUSEUMS & EXHIBITIONS

Academy of Natural Sciences. 19th St. and Benjamin Franklin Pkwy. ☎ **215/299-1000.** Admission $6.75 adults, $6 seniors, $5.75 children 3–12, free for children under 3. Mon–Fri 10am–4:30pm, Sat–Sun and holidays 10am–5pm. Bus: 32, 33, 76, or PHLASH.

If you're looking for dinosaurs, the Academy is the best place to find them. Kids love the big diorama halls, with cases of several species mounted and posed in authentic settings. A $2.5 million permanent display, "Discovering Dinosaurs," features more than a dozen specimens, including a huge *Tyrannosaurus rex* with jaws agape. The Dig (weekends only) gives you an opportunity to dig for fossils in a re-created field station. The North American Hall, on the first floor, has enormous moose, buffalo, and bears. A small marine exhibit shows how some fish look different in ultraviolet light and how the bed of the Delaware has changed since Penn landed in 1682.

The second floor features groupings of Asian and African flora and fauna. Many of the cases have nearby headphones that tell you more about what you're seeing. Five or six live demonstrations are given here every day; the handlers are expert in conducting these sessions with rocks, birds, plants, and animals. Several daily Eco Shows are given in the auditorium downstairs too. The Egyptian mummy, a priest of a late dynasty, seems a bit out of place.

Upstairs, "Outside In" is a touchable museum designed for children under 12, with a model campsite, fossils, minerals, shells, and other unbreakables. It stimulates almost every sense: Children can see, feel, hear, and smell live turtles, mice, bees in a beehive, and snakes (all caged) and wander around mock forests and deserts. A large bird hall and a hall of endangered species round out the picture, along with frequent films. There's a brown-bag lunchroom and vending area with drinks and snacks.

Afro-American Historical and Cultural Museum. 7th and Arch sts. ☎ 215/574-0380. Admission $4 adults, $2 children and seniors. Tues–Sat 10am–5pm, Sun noon–6pm. Bus: 47, 48, or PHLASH.

Three blocks northwest of the Liberty Bell is the only building in America in 20 years specifically constructed to display the history of African Americans. It's built in five split levels of ridged concrete, meant to evoke African mud housing, off a central atrium and ramp. As you ascend, you follow the path from African roots through to the role blacks have played in U.S. development. The specific exhibitions do change.

The ground floor contains the admissions office, the gift shop, and the African Heritage Gallery (here's your chance to see photographs of original cornrow hairstyles and customs). The second level, concentrating on slavery and captivity, is undoubtedly the most dramatic and informed section. It emphasizes that the slave trade was hardly exclusive to, or even predominant in, North America, and that it persisted in South America until 1870.

The upper three levels, dealing with black history and culture after emancipation, lose some focus since blacks slowly gained acceptance and/or visibility in so many areas of American life. Black cowboys, inventors, athletes, spokespeople, businesspeople—all are presented, along with such organizations as the NAACP and CORE and the civil rights movements of the 1960s.

American-Swedish Historical Museum. 1900 Pattison Ave. ☎ 215/389-1776. Admission $5 adults, $4 students and seniors, free for children under 12. Tues–Fri 10am–4pm, Sat noon–4pm. Bus: 17. Near the Naval Hospital and Veterans Stadium, at the southern edge of the city.

Modeled after a 17th-century Swedish manor house, this small museum chronicles in 14 galleries 350 years of the life and accomplishments of Swedish Americans. Specific rooms highlight John Ericsson, inventor of the Civil War ironclads, and 19th-century opera singer Jenny Lind. Traditional Swedish holidays are celebrated-year round, including *Valborgsmässoafton* (Spring Festival) in April, *Midsommarfest* in June, and the procession of St. Lucia and her attendants in December.

Atwater Kent Museum. 15 S. 7th St. ☎ 215/922-3031. Admission $2 adults, $1 children. Tues–Sat 10am–4pm. Bus: 17, 33, 42, 76, or PHLASH.

Across the street from the Balch Institute (see below), the small Atwater Kent Museum occupies an 1824 John Haviland building. Using more artifacts than the Visitors Center, the Atwater Kent shows you what Philadelphia was like from 1680 to 1880. The founder, you may remember, built most of America's early radios, and much of this fortune benefited Philadelphia gardens and societies. Nothing was too trivial to include—the collection jumps from dolls to dioramas, from cigar-store Indians to period toy shops. Sunbonnets, train tickets, rocking horses, ship models, and military uniforms are all part of the display.

Balch Institute for Ethnic Studies. 18 S. 7th St. ☎ 215/925-8090. Admission $2 adults, $1 students and seniors. Mon–Sat 10am–4pm. Bus: 17, 33, 42, 76, or PHLASH.

Philadelphia's Oddball Museums

Maybe it's something in the water—but Philadelphia has an amazing assortment of small single-interest museums, built out of the passions of, or inspired by, a single individual. Maybe you and your family are ready for these!

- The **Historical Dental Museum** at Temple University, Broad and Alleghany Streets (☎ 215/707-2816), houses a 1790 dentist's chair, early X-ray machines, and a battery-operated electrical device used in 1890s root-canal operations. It's open by appointment only.

- On the other end is the Pennsylvania College of Podiatric Medicine's **Shoe Museum,** 8th and Race Streets (☎ 215/625-5243, ext. 185). Even to contemplate some of those 3-inch shoes made for the bound feet of Chinese oligarchy is excruciating. The collection also includes Lucille Ball's hot-pink sandals, Sandy Duncan's Peter Pan boots, and other historical and celebrity footwear. It's open by appointment only.

- The Mummer's Parade on New Year's Day is uniquely Philadelphian; dozens of crews spend months practicing their musical and strutting skills with spectacular costumes. Talk about multicultural—mumming comes out of pagan celebrations picked up by Anglo-Saxon immigrants, and equally from African dancing and celebrations. The **Mummers Museum,** 2nd St. and Washington Ave. (☎ 215/336-3050), is devoted to the history and display of this phenomenon. It's open Tuesday through Saturday from 9:30am to 5pm and Sunday from noon to 5pm.

- It's a trip into the Northeast district of the city, but Steve Kanya's **Insectarium,** 8046 Frankford Ave. (☎ 215/338-3000), has taken off as a school-class destination, not to mention a *Wall Street Journal* write-up. Can you believe an admission of only $3 to watch more than 40,000 cockroaches, other bugs, and

---

Everyone comes from someplace—and the United States is virtually the only country where everyone (except the Native Americans) comes from someplace else and knows it and is proud of it. The institute has a terrific library that covers everything you've always wanted to know about your roots, if you're one of more than 100 ethnicities. The exhibition "Freedom's Doors" makes the point that one-third of all immigrants disembarked not at New York but at Boston, Miami, New Orleans, Los Angeles, and so forth. To the left, the exhibits change every couple of months; they range from ethnic images in World War I posters to African crafts.

Barnes Foundation. 300 N. Latches Lane, Merion Station, PA 19066. ☎ 610/667-0290. Admission $5 per person. Thurs 12:30–3pm, Fri–Sun 9:30am–5pm. Hours may expand in the future. SEPTA: Take Paoli local train to Merion; walk up Merion Ave. and turn left onto Latches Lane Bus: 44 to Old Lancaster Rd. and Latches Lane Car: I-76 (Schuylkill Expressway) north to City Line Ave., then south on City Line 1 1/2 miles to Old Lancaster Rd. Turn right onto Old Lancaster, continue four blocks, and turn left onto Latches Lane.

If you're interested in art, the Barnes Foundation will stun you with its magnificence. Albert Barnes crammed his French provincial mansion with over 1,000 masterpieces—180 Renoirs, 69 Cézannes, innumerable impressionists and postimpressionists, and a generous sampling of European art from the Italian primitives onward. Following a tour of more than 80 masterworks from the restored collection and renovation of the galleries, the Barnes reopened in November 1995.

their predators like scorpions and tarantulas? It's open Monday through Saturday from 10am to 4pm.

- Also not for the squeamish is the **Mutter Museum,** 19 S. 22nd St. (☎ **215/ 587-9919**), a collection of preserved human oddities assembled in the 1850s by a Philadelphia physician. Skeletons of giants and dwarves and row on row of plaster casts of abnormalities inhabit this varnished, musty place—it's so out, it's in. It's open Tuesday through Friday from 10am to 4pm.
- The massive **Eastern State Penitentiary,** 22nd St. and Fairmount Ave. (☎ **215/236-7236**), built in the 1820s by John Haviland to maximize solitary confinement and penitential hard work, revolutionized the way prisons were constructed all over the world, and was later the home of Willie Sutton and Al Capone. It finally closed in 1971, and is now open for guided tours, art installations, and performing arts. Sean Kelley, the program director, persuaded the National Park Service to adopt this flaking, evocative hulk. It's only minutes from great restaurants like Jack's Firehouse. It's open in May on Saturday and Sunday from 10am to 6pm, and from June to October, Thursday through Sunday from 10am to 6pm.
- Also from this era is the **Civil War Library and Museum,** 1805 Pine St. (☎ **215/735-8196**). Everyone loves the stuffed and mounted head of Old Baldy, the horse that carried General George Meade through Gettysburg. It's open Monday through Saturday from 10am to 4pm and Sunday from 11am to 4pm.
- What could belong more in South Philly than the **Mario Lanza Museum,** 416 Queen St. (☎ **215/468-3623**)? This tribute to actor/tenor Lanza is the scene of his first music lessons, with a life-size bust, clippings, and telegrams. It's open from September to June, Monday through Saturday from 10am to 3:30pm.

Barnes believed that art has a quality that can be studied scientifically—for example, one curve will be beautiful and hence art, and another that's slightly different will not be art. That's why the galleries display antique door latches, keyholes, keys, and household tools with strong geometric lines right next to the paintings. And the connections beg to be drawn between neighboring objects—an unusual van Gogh nude, an Amish chest, and New Mexico rural icons. Virtually every first-rank European artist is included: Degas, Seurat, Bosch, Tintoretto, Lorrain, Chardin, Daumier, Delacroix, Corot, and so forth. This is not a bad use of a fortune derived from selling patent medicine!

The bad news is that the foundation still suffers from the archaic rigidity that Mr. Barnes set up regarding its user-friendliness and open hours to those not attending classes. The current board is petitioning in state court to open six days a week, but this is pending.

Hill-Physick-Keith House. 321 S. 4th St. ☎ **215/925-7866** or 215/925-2251. Admission $4 adults, $2 students and seniors, free for children under 6. Guided tours only; call for current hours. Bus: 50, 90, or PHLASH.

As with the Powel and Bishop White homes (discussed earlier in the chapter), the Hill-Physick-Keith House combines attractiveness through design with interest of history on Society Hill. This home is, if anything, the area's most impressive—it's freestanding but not boxy, gracious but solid. Built during the 1780s boom, it soon wound up housing the father of American surgery, Philip Syng Physick, a very professional name for a physician. The usual pattern of descendants, neglect, and renovation has applied here, on an even grander scale.

All the cloths and wallpapers were fashioned expressly for use here, and the mansion as restored is a landmark of the Federal style from about 1815. The drawing room opens onto a lovely 19th-century walled garden and shows the excitement caused by the discovery of the buried city of Pompeii, including a Roman stool and 18th-century Italian art. Look for an inkstand tarnished by Ben Franklin's fingerprints. Dr. Physick treated Chief Justice Marshall, and Marshall's portrait and gift of a wine stand testify to the doctor's powers.

Independence Seaport Museum. Penn's Landing at 211 South Columbus Blvd. ☎ 215/925-5439. Admission $5 adults, $4 seniors, 2.50 children. Combined admission to the museum and Historic Ship Zone (USS *Olympia* and USS *Becuna*; see below) $7.50 adults, $6 seniors, $3.50 children. Daily 10am–5pm except for major holidays. RiverPass tickets, including admission to the museum, the Riverbus Ferry, and the New Jersey State Aquarium at Camden, $15 adults, $12 seniors, $10 children; this will take 5 hours at least.

Opposite Walnut Street, between the two dock areas, is this great new facility in the contemporary poured-concrete structure north of the Olympia jetty. The match between the 1981 state-owned building and the 1961 museum took several years to achieve, but was consummated in July 1995. Now the user-friendly maritime museum is the jewel in the crown of the city's waterfront.

The museum is beautifully laid out, blending a first-class maritime collection with interactive exhibits for a trip through time that engages all ages. Its 11,000-square-foot main gallery is the centerpiece for exhibits, educational outreach, and activities that are jazzy and eye-catching without being noisy or obtrusive. Twelve sections mix the professional, with call-up interviews with river pilots, Navy personnel, and shipbuilders, with the personal. My family loves the stories of immigrants who flooded Philadelphia between 1920 and 1970 and the rich reminiscences and memorabilia that make their lives real. And I defy anyone to ace the computer-screen quiz on how and why the river made Philadelphia's rich history possible.

One of the museum's most attractive features is the **Workshop on the Water,** where you can watch classes and amateurs undertake traditional wooden boat building and restoration throughout the year. Classmates bid on the chance to keep the boat they build.

National Museum of American Jewish History. 55 N. 5th St. ☎ 215/923-8811. Admission $2.50 adults; $1.75 students, seniors, and children; free for children under 5. Mon–Thurs 10am–5pm, Fri 10am–3pm, Sun noon–5pm. Bus: 17, 33, 48, 50, or PHLASH.

This is the only museum that's specifically dedicated to preserving and presenting Jewish participation in the development of the United States. Don't expect to walk into another colonial structure. The complex was built in the aftermath of the 1950s clearance that allowed for Independence Mall, although the congregation connected to it, Mikveh Israel, was established in Philadelphia in 1740 (see the "Cemeteries" section, above). The walkway between 4th and 3rd Streets displays an 1876 statue by Sir Moses Ezekiel, an English lord born in America, symbolizing religious freedom. It was fittingly given by the Jewish congregation in Philadelphia, and you can see how much lower the street level was a century ago. You'll enter close to 4th Street (passing Christ Church Cemetery, with Ben Franklin's grave the major attraction here) into a dark-brick lobby that serves both the museum and the adjoining Mikveh Israel Synagogue. The museum starts with a permanent exhibition, "The American Jewish Experience: From 1654 to the Present," combining dry-mounted reproductions of portraits and documents, actual books and letters, and utensils and religious articles to attest to the diversity and vitality of American Jews. It's a fascinating show, and the museum should be proud of sponsoring its recent tour. Smaller rotating exhibitions supplement this presentation. Official annual attendance clocks in at more than 40,000, but it's usually cool and restful and makes a good break from a hot Independence Park tour. A small gift shop is attached.

Curtis Center Museum of Norman Rockwell Art. 601 Walnut St. (lower level). ☎ **215/ 922-4345.** Admission $2 adults, $1.50 seniors, free for children under 12. Mon–Sat 10am–4pm, Sun 11am–4pm. Bus: 21, 42, or 90.

In the corner of the old headquarters of the Curtis Publishing Company on Washington Square, this attraction and souvenir shop—it's not really a museum—exhibits about 320 of Rockwell's famous covers for the *Saturday Evening Post.* None are originals. You can see the classic Four Freedoms posters, which stimulated war-bond sales in World War II.

Please Touch Museum. 210 N. 21st St. ☎ **215/963-0667.** Admission $6.95 adults and children; maximum of three children per adult. Voluntary donation Sun 9–10am. No strollers inside, but Snuglis available. Daily 9am–6pm. Bus: 7, 48, or 76.

The museum is the first in the country designed specifically for children 7 years and younger. Dedicated to a unique fun-filled educational, cultural, hands-on experience, the converted factories provide a window to the creative, exuberant, and receptive in us all. The location is great—just off the Parkway, two blocks south of Franklin Institute—and it's one of the best indoor activities in town for a younger family.

The museum shows its thoughtful design at the lobby: A separate gift shop, with plenty of cute and challenging items, can be entered without paying admission. Once you're in, you can park strollers, check coats, and buy tickets at counters that cater to kids. Exciting hands-on exhibits like "Growing Up" encourage parent/child participation and focus on specific social, cognitive, and emotional areas of child development. "Studio PTM," installed in 1993, allows children to experience being behind the camera and on stage in a television studio, including sound effects and camera angles. New in 1995 was an exhibit of oversized settings and creatures from celebrated author/illustrator Maurice Sendak. My own kids love "Nature's Nursery," with toy animals revealed through various pushes and pulls; "Play in Motion," which mixes gymnastics and science; and "Foodtastic Journey," with an extensive play farm to supermarket to kitchen route.

The museum collaborates with the Franklin Institute on operating the 38,000-square-foot CoreStates Science Park between May and October, on that green lawn between the two institutions. It's a great playground for the mind and body.

The Please Touch Museum is not a day-care center; you cannot simply drop the kids off, and you won't want to. Educational activities like storytelling and crafts are available daily from 11am to 3:30pm. It's also a great place to celebrate a child's birthday, if you care to plan ahead.

Rodin Museum. Benjamin Franklin Pkwy. between 21st and 22nd sts. ☎ **215/ 763-8100.** Donation requested. Free with same-day admission ticket from the Philadelphia Museum of Art (see above). Tues–Sun 10am–5pm. Bus: 32, 38, or 76.

The Rodin Museum exhibits the largest collection of the master's work—129 sculptures—outside the Musée Rodin in Paris. It has inherited a little of its sibling museum's romantic mystery, making a very French use of space within and boasting much greenery without. Entering from the Parkway, virtually across the street from the Franklin Institute (see above), you'll contemplate *The Thinker* contemplating other things, then pass through an imposing arch to a front garden of hardy shrubs and trees surrounding a fish pond. Before going into the museum, study the *Gates of Hell*. These gigantic doors reveal an awesome power to mold metal by the force of passionate imagination.

The galleries were restored to their original sparkle in 1989. The main hall holds authorized casts of *John the Baptist, The Cathedral,* and *The Burghers of Calais*. Several of the side chambers and the library hold powerful erotic plaster models. Drawings, sketchbooks, and Steichen photographic portraits of Rodin are exhibited periodically.

U.S. Mint. 5th and Arch sts. ☎ **215/597-7350.** Free admission. Sept–April, Mon–Fri 9am–4:30pm; May–June, Mon–Sat 9am–4:30pm; July–Aug, daily 9am–4:30pm. Closed New Year's Day, Christmas. Bus: 5, 48, or 76.

The U.S. Mint building was the first authorized by the government during Washington's first term. Fortunately for us, the present edifice, diagonally across from Liberty Bell Pavilion (see above), turns out enough cash to keep us all solvent, about 1.5 million coins every hour. This is one factory tour that's quite stingy with free samples, but a self-guided walk through the process has its own rewards.

The coinage process involves melting raw metal, rolling it to coin thinness, punching out blanks from these sheets, and pressing designs on them. The metal slabs and coils look cherry red from the heating they undergo, and after the coins are done a counting machine automatically sews lots of 5,000 into bags, headed for Federal Reserve Banks. Points along the route have prerecorded explanations, if you wish to listen (ever wonder how the layers in composite coins stick together?).

University of Pennsylvania Museum of Archaeology and Anthropology. 33rd and Spruce sts. ☎ **215/898-4000.** Admission $5 adults, $2.50 students and seniors, free for children under 6. Tues–Sat 10am–4:30pm, Sun 1–5pm. Closed Mon, holidays, and summer Sun Memorial Day–Labor Day. Bus: 21, 30 (from 30th Street Station), 40, 42, or 90.

Higher buildings may have left their Romanesque brickwork more secluded, but considering its contents, this museum has still seen quite a bit of the world. The University of Pennsylvania Museum, which celebrated its centennial in 1986–87, got into archeology and anthropology on the ground floor, and hundreds of excavations have endowed it with Benin bronzes, ancient cuneiform texts, Mesopotamian masterpieces, pre-Columbian gold, and artifacts of every continent.

The museum is intelligently explained. The basement Egyptian galleries, including colossal architectural remains from Memphis and "The Egyptian Mummy: Secrets and Science," are family favorites. Probably the most famous excavation display, located on the third floor, is a spectacular Sumerian trove of jewelry and household objects from the royal tombs of the ancient city of Ur. Adjoining this, huge cloisonné lions from Peking's (now Beijing's) Imperial Palace guard Chinese court treasures and tomb figures. The Ancient Greek Gallery in the classical-world collection, renovated in 1994, has 400 superb objects such as red-figure pottery—a flower of Greek civilization—and an unusual lead sarcophagus from Tyre that looks like a miniature house. Other galleries display Native American and Polynesian culture and a small but excellent African collection of bronze plaques and statues.

The glass-enclosed Museum Cafe, overlooking the museum's inner gardens, serves cafeteria-style snacks and light meals from 8:30am to 3:30pm on weekdays, from 10am to 4pm on Saturday, and from 1 to 5pm on Sunday. The Museum Shop has cards and jewelry and crafts from around the world, and the Pyramid Shop has children's items. There's also a very active range of events throughout the year.

OUTDOOR ART & PLAZAS

Since the late 1950s, Philadelphia has required that all new developments dedicate 1% of the total cost of the project toward public art. As a result, a burst of modern art has joined the inevitable war memorials, Alexander M. Calder's massive program for City Hall, and the early sculpture placed in Fairmount Park. Of the dozens of pieces, the most notable seem to be Claes Oldenburg's 1976 *Clothespin,* an enigmatic symbol of union opposite City Hall at 15th and Market Streets; Robert Indiana's 1978 *LOVE,* a slickly ironic statement opposite the Visitors Center at 16th Street and John F. Kennedy Boulevard; Isamu Noguchi's 1984 *Bolt of Lightning—Franklin Memorial,* at the entrance to the Franklin Bridge at 5th and Vine Streets; and, of course, the replica of Rocky Balboa in victory, at the entrance to the sports complex in South Philadelphia.

It's not exacly outdoors, but Judy Pfaff's *Cirque* in the Grand Hall of the Pennsylvania Convention Center is a spectacular double helix of metal and glass.

A UNIVERSITY

University of Pennsylvania. 34th and Walnut sts. and surrounding neighborhood. ☎ **215/898-5000.** Bus: 21, 30, 40, 42, or 90. Car: Market/Chestnut exit from I-76 (Schuylkill Expressway), six blocks west toward West Philadelphia.

This private, now coeducational Ivy League institution was founded by Benjamin Franklin and others in 1740. It boasts America's first medical (1765), law (1790), and business (1881) schools. Penn's liberal arts curriculum, dating to 1756, was the first to combine classical and practical subjects. Its progress and excellence have been revitalized in the last 25 years, thanks to extremely successful leadership, alumni, and fund-raising drives.

The campus core, moved to West Philadelphia in the 1870s, features dozens of serene Gothic-style buildings and specimen trees in a spacious quadrangle. More modern buildings punctuate the 20th-century expansion of the university to accommodate 22,000 students enrolled in 4 undergraduate and 12 graduate schools, spanning over 100 academic departments. Sites of most interest to visitors include the University Museum of Archaeology and Anthropology, the Annenberg Center for the Performing Arts, and the Institute for Contemporary Art.

A ZOO & AN AQUARIUM

✪ **Philadelphia Zoological Gardens.** 34th St. and Girard Ave. ☎ **215/243-1100.** Admission $8.50 adults, $6 seniors and children 2–11, free for children under 2. A family membership for $40 might be worth it. Parking spaces for 1,800 cars; $4 per vehicle. Fidelity Bank MAC ATM machine near North Gate. Mon–Fri 9:30am–5:45pm, Sat–Sun 9:30am–6pm. Closed Thanksgiving, Christmas, and New Year's Day. Bus: 76. Car: Separate exit off I-76 north of Center City.

The Philadelphia Zoo was the nation's first, opened in 1874, but by the late 1970s the 42 acres tucked into West Fairmount Park were run-down and had few financial resources. It has since become a national leader with more than 1,500 animals, although it has had a crisis of confidence and a run of bad luck, most recently with a December 1995 fire that destroyed the Primate House and dozens of animals.

The biggest attractions are the white lions: Two females arrived in June 1993, and one had a cub in April 1994, among a pride of six cats. The 1992 1½-acre, $6-million Carnivore Kingdom houses snow leopards and jaguars; feeding time is around 11am for smaller carnivores, 3pm for tigers and lions. The monkeys have a new home on four naturally planted islands, where a variety of primate species live together naturally.

The old Bird House has been changed to the new Jungle Bird Walk, where you can walk among free flying birds. Glass enclosures have been replaced with wire mesh so that the birds' songs can now be heard from both sides.

> ## ❓ Did You Know?
>
> - The "hex" signs that adorn barns and houses in Pennsylvania Dutch Country were a sign to travelers that German was spoken within.
> - It is still against the law in Philadelphia to sleep in a barber shop and to take a cow to Logan Circle.
> - The first public protest in America against slavery was held at the Germantown Friends (Quaker) Meeting House in 1688.
> - The Benjamin Franklin Parkway is one of the widest streets (250 feet) in the world.
> - Early fire-insurance companies offered rewards for stopping fires. This led to street battles between rival volunteer brigades racing to arrive at a blaze first, often while buildings burned down!
> - It was in Philadelphia that Charles Goodyear superheated sulfur to harden India rubber, at the same time preserving its pliancy.
> - Ben Franklin's kite-flying experiment in 1752 took place at what is now the corner of 10th and Ludlow Streets.
> - Thirty-two bridges span the Schuylkill River within the city limits.
> - George Washington lived in a mansion at the corner of 5th and Chestnut Streets for his entire two terms as president.
> - Philadelphian Robert Green's chance decision to combine ice cream and soda water has refreshed millions since 1861.
> - W. C. Fields's epitaph does *not* read, "On the whole, I'd rather be in Philadelphia."
> - The U.S. Congress held a rare session outside the capital for the special July 16, 1987, bicentennial celebration of the U.S. Constitution at Independence Mall.
> - The first law school (1790) and medical school (1765) in the United States were established at the University of Pennsylvania.

As part of the zoo's concern to educate zoo visitors about animal life, a spectacular children's exhibit, the Treehouse ($1), was opened in 1985. It contains six larger-than-life habitats for kids of all ages to explore—oversize eggs to hatch from, an oversize honeycomb to crawl through, and a four-story ficus tree to climb through and see life from a bird's-eye view. The very popular Camel Rides ($1.50) start next to the Treehouse. A Children's Zoo (50¢) portion of the gardens lets your kids pet and feed some baby zoo and farm animals; this closes 30 minutes before the zoo proper. Pony rides ($1) are also given here.

Other exhibits cover polar bears, the Reptile House, which bathes its snakes and tortoises with simulated tropical thunderstorms, and cavorting antelopes, zebras, and giraffes that coexist on the "African Plains" exhibit. For a quick survey, consider the Monorail Safari ($2 for adults, $1.50 for children, 50¢ more on weekends; operated April to November). It circumnavigates the zoo in 20 minutes and has a pre-recorded narrative.

The zoo has a McDonald's concession, across from the lion house.

New Jersey State Aquarium. 1 Riverside Dr., Camden, NJ 08103. ☎ **609/365-3300.** Admission $9.95 adults, $8.45 students and seniors, $6.95 children 2–11, free for children under 2. Reserved admission through TicketMaster (800/616-JAWS) is recommended (handling charge). Daily 9:30am–5:30pm. Closed Thanksgiving, Christmas, and New Year's Day. Ferry: The *Riverbus* ferry from Port of History Museum at Penn's Landing is $5 adults, $3 children, each way; hourly arrivals/departures. Car: From I-676 eastbound (Vine St. Expressway/Ben Franklin Bridge) or westbound from I-295/New Jersey Turnpike, take Mickle Blvd. exit and follow signs.

The aquarium opened in 1992 as a first step in reclaiming the once-vital (and now denuded) Camden waterfront with a hotel and marina, trade center, and office and commercial development. As an aquarium, it fills a true niche in the Delaware Valley.

Up to 3,000 fish live here. The main attraction is a 760,000-gallon tank, the second largest (next to Epcot Center's) in the country, with stepped seat/benches arranged in a Greek amphitheater on the first floor. Three times a day, a diver answers questions through a "scuba phone." This window wall is by far the best; parents of younger children will find few other flat edges for them to stand on for views. This "Ocean Base Atlantic" tank also contains sharks, rockfish, a shipwreck, and a mockup of the underwater Hudson canyon off the Jersey coast. Also on the first floor is a Caribbean outpost with 1,000 new tropical fish. The second floor has the 1996 "W.O.W.! Weird? or Wonderful?" featuring interactive exhibits and strange ocean dwellers. Touch tanks are on both floors.

The Riverview Café serves basic fast food; outdoor seating is frequently windy.

4 Parks & Penns Landing

BENJAMIN FRANKLIN PARKWAY

The Parkway, a broad diagonal swath linking City Hall to Fairmount Park, wasn't included in Penn's original plan. In the 1920s, however, Philadelphians thought that a grand boulevard in the style of the Champs Elysées was appropriate. In summer, a walk from the Visitors Center to the "Museum on the Hill" becomes a flower-bedecked and leafy stroll; but all year-round, institutions, public art, and museums enrich the avenue with their handsome facades. Most of the city's parades and festivals pass this way too.

Logan Circle, outside the Academy of Natural Sciences, Free Library of Philadelphia, and Franklin Institute (see above), used to be Logan Square before the Parkway was built, and it was a burying ground before becoming a park. The designers of the avenue cleverly made it into a low-landscaped fountain, with graceful figures cast by Alexander Sterling Calder. From this point, you can see how the rows of trees make sense of the diagonal thoroughfare, although all the buildings along the Parkway are aligned with the grid plan. Under the terms of the city permit, the Four Seasons Hotel now landscapes and tends Logan Circle, to magnificent effect.

Bus route 76 goes both ways every 20 minutes, and the PHLASH bus goes up as far as Logan Circle every 10 minutes.

FAIRMOUNT PARK

The northern end of the Benjamin Franklin Parkway leads into Fairmount Park, the world's largest landscaped city park, with 8,700 acres of winding creeks, rustic trails, and green meadows, plus 100 miles of jogging, bike, and bridle paths. In addition, this park (☎ 215/685-0000) features more than a dozen historical and cultural attractions, including 29 of America's finest colonial mansions (most are open year-round, including weekends, and standard admission is $2.50), as well as gardens, boathouses, America's first zoo, a youth hostel, and a Japanese teahouse. Visitors can rent sailboats and canoes, play tennis and golf, swim, or see free symphony concerts in the summer. See the Fairmount Park map as a reference.

You can get here by taking bus 76 to the Museum of Art entrance or 38 or 76 to the upper end. If you're driving, there are several entrances and exits off I-76; East and West River Drives are local roads flanking the Schuylkill River.

The park is generally divided by the Schuylkill River into East and West Fairmount Park. Before beginning a tour of the mansions, stop by the **Waterworks** (☎ **215/ 581-5111**). With the establishment of the 1812 Waterworks, land and machinery were combined in a 5-acre municipal park by 1822. You can still see the Greek Revival mill housings in back of the Art Museum and an ornamental pavilion connecting them that was added after the Civil War. Also on the east bank, don't miss **Boat House Row,** home of the "Schuylkill Navy" and its member rowing clubs. Now you know where Thomas Eakins got the models for all those sculling scenes in the Art Museum. These gingerbread Tudors along the riverbank appear magical at night, with hundreds of pinlights along their eaves.

The four most spectacular Colonial houses are all on the lower east quadrant of the park. **Lemon Hill** (☎ **215/232-4337**), just up the hill from Boat House Row, shows the influence of Robert Adam's architecture, with its generous windows, curved archways and doors, and beautiful oval parlors. John Adams described **Mount Pleasant** (☎ **215/763-8100**), built for a privateer in 1763 and once owned by Benedict Arnold, as "the most elegant seat in Pensylvania" for its carved designs and inlays. **Woodford** (☎ **215/229-6115**), the Tory center during their occupation of the city in 1779, is not to be missed, both for its architecture and for the Naomi Wood Collection of Colonial houseware. Only at Winterthur (see Chapter 11) is there another place where you can step into the full atmosphere of 18th-century home life, with all its ingenious gadgets and elegant objects. The next lawn over from Woodford is the park's largest mansion, **Strawberry Mansion** (☎ **215/228-8364**), with a Federal-style center section and Greek Revival wings.

Just north of this mansion is bucolic **Laurel Hill Cemetary** (see "Cemeteries," above, for a fuller description), but if you cross Strawberry Mansion Bridge, West Fairmount Park has many charms also. **Belmont Mansion** (☎ **215/878-8844**) hosted all the leaders of the Revolutionary cause, and is being restored now. South of this area, you'll enter the site occupied by the stupendous 1876 Centennial Exposition. Approximately 100 buildings were designed and constructed in under two years; only two remain today: Ohio House, built of that state's stone, and **Memorial Hall** (☎ **215/685-0000**), now the park's headquarters and a recreation site. The **Japanese House and Gardens** (☎ **215/878-5097**), on the grounds of the nearby Horticultural Center, is a typical 17th-century scholar's house, with its sliding screens and paper doors in place of walls and glass. It was originally presented to the Museum of Modern Art in New York. Since the Centennial Exposition had featured a similar house, it wound up here. The waterfall, grounds, and house are serene and simple, and were extensively refurbished in 1976 by a Japanese team as a bicentennial gift to the city. It's open during the summer only, Tuesday through Sunday from 11am to 4pm.

Two more major homes lie south of the Exposition's original concourses: **Cedar Grove** (☎ **215/763-8100**), a Quaker farmhouse built as a country retreat in 1748 and moved here in 1928, and **Sweetbriar** (☎ **215/222-1333**), a mixture of French Empire and English neoclassicism with wonderful river views. Continuing south past the Girard Avenue Bridge will bring you to the **Philadelphia Zoo** (see below), or a five-minute drive on I-76 to Center City.

If you have some time and really want to get away from it all, Wissahickon and Pennsylvania Creeks lie north of the park and don't allow access by automobiles— only trampers and horses. The trees and slopes of Valley Green block out city noise

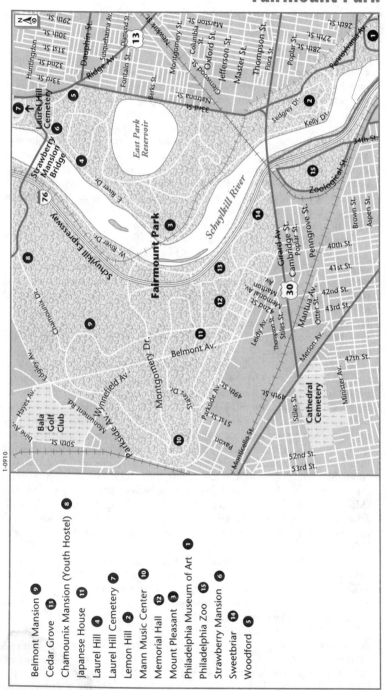

Belmont Mansion **9**
Cedar Grove **13**
Chamounix Mansion (Youth Hostel) **8**
Japanese House **11**
Laurel Hill **4**
Laurel Hill Cemetery **7**
Lemon Hill **2**
Mann Music Center **10**
Memorial Hall **12**
Mount Pleasant **3**
Philadelphia Museum of Art **1**
Philadelphia Zoo **15**
Strawberry Mansion **6**
Sweetbriar **14**
Woodford **5**

completely. Search out attractions like the 340-year-old Valley Green Inn and the only covered bridge left in an American city.

PENN'S LANDING

Philadelphia started out as a major freshwater port, and its tourism and services are increasingly nudging it back to the water after 50 years of neglect, typified by the placement of the I-95 superhighway between the city and its port. In 1945, 155 "finger" piers jutted out into the river; today, only 14 remain. Since 1976 the city has added on parts of a complete waterfront park at Penn's Landing (☎ 215/629-3200) on Columbus Boulevard (formerly Delaware Avenue) between Market and Lombard Streets, with a wonderful new museum and an assembly of historic ships, performance and park areas, cruise facilities, and a marina. This trend is accelerating with more pedestrian bridges over I-95; a 1996 project to install wider sidewalks, lighting, and kiosks along Columbus Boulevard; and more sites and transport connecting them all. So Penn's Landing has a pleasantly spacious feeling, and is getting more unified and coherent as an equivalent to Baltimore's Inner Harbor.

You can access the Penn's Landing waterfront by parking along the piers or by walking across several bridges spanning I-95 between Market Street, at the northern edge, and South Street to the south. There are pedestrian walkways across Front Street on Market, Chestnut, Walnut, Spruce, or South Streets; Front Street connects directly at Spruce Street. By bus, PHLASH, and nos. 17, 21, 33, and 76 go directly to Penn's Landing; 42 is an easy walk from 2nd Street. If you're driving, from I-95 use the Columbus Boulevard/Washington Street exit and turn left on to Columbus Boulevard. From I-76, take I-676 across Center City to I-95 south. There's ample parking available onsite.

Walking south from Market Street is an esplanade with pretty new blue guardrails and charts to help you identify the Camden shoreline opposite and the funnels of passing freighters. The hill that connects the shoreline with the current Front Street level has been enhanced with the festive **Great Plaza,** a multitiered, tree-lined amphitheater that hosts many Visitors and Convention Bureau festivals, such as Jam on the River. The terrace itself is a wonderfully landscaped and informative view of quirky facts about the site and city, with plenty of benches. Just north of the Great Plaza is the **Blue Cross RiverRink,** Philadelphia's only outdoor ice skating rink, open November through March night and day. In the other direction is a jetty/marina complex, anchored by the new **Independence Seaport Museum** (listed above in "More Attractions"), that's perfect for strolling and noshing. The sober 1987 **Philadelphia Vietnam Veteran Memorial** lists 641 local casualties, and nearby is the **International Sculpture Garden** with its new obelisk monument to Christopher Columbus.

There's also plenty to do in and near the water. The Penn's Landing Corporation coordinates more than 100 events annually, all designed to attract crowds with high-quality entertainment like the Jam on the River during Memorial Day weekend, the Sunoco Welcome America! festival punctuating July 4, and many others. So an aimless visit is likely to be greeted with sounds and performances.

Several ships and museums are berthed around a long jetty at Spruce Street, and the Independence Seaport Museum is slowly consolidating management of these as a **Historic Ship Zone.** From the north down, these attractions are the brig **Niagara,** built in 1813 for the War of 1812, and rededicated as the official flagship of Pennsylvania in 1990; the USS *Becuna,* a guppy-class submarine, commissioned in 1944 to serve in Admiral Halsey's South Pacific fleet; and the USS *Olympia,* Admiral Dewey's own flagship in the Spanish-American War, with a self-guided three-deck tour. (Separate admission to both the *Olympia* and the *Becuna* is $3.50 for adults, $1.75 for children under 12; both are open daily from 10am to 5pm.) Harbor cruise boats the ***Liberty Belle II*** (☎ 215/629-1131), ***Spirit of Philadelphia*** (☎ 215/923-1419), and a stop for the paddlewheeler ***Riverboat Queen*** (☎ 215/ 923-BOAT) are augmented by private yachts; Queen Elizabeth docked her yacht *Britannia* here in 1976. Anchoring the southern end is the **Chart House** restaurant, open for lunch and dinner, and the restored **Moshulu** four-masted floating restaurant at Pier 34 (see Chapter 6 for details).

Another group of boats occupies the landfill directly on the Delaware between Market and Walnut Streets. The ***Gazela Primiero,*** a working three-masted, square-rigged wooden ship launched from Portugal in 1883, has visiting hours on Saturday and Sunday from 12:30 to 5:30pm when it's in port. Adjoining are the ***Barnegat Lightship*** and the tugboat ***Jupiter;*** all the above are operated by the Philadelphia Ship Preservation Guild (☎ 215/923-9030); admission $3 adults, $2 students.

If you want to get onto the water, at the river's edge in front of the Independence Seaport Museum at Walnut Street, the ***Riverbus*** (☎ 609/364-1400) plies a round-trip route to the New Jersey State Aquarium in Camden every hour on the hour between 9am and 5pm. The trip takes 10 minutes, and the fare without museum admission on either end is $5 adults, $3 children each way. Penn's Landing also runs a free **Waterfront Shuttle** on Friday, Saturday, and Sunday evenings between 9pm and 2am in the summer. This is meant to reduce drunk driving between the many Columbus Boulevard clubs to the north of Penn's Landing, but it does stop here as well as at Pier 34 and the Moshulu. Call **215/629-3200** for more information.

5 Especially for Kids

Philadelphia is one of the country's great family destinations. It has a great many attractions for different types of kids, and because it's so walkable and neighborhood-like, a respite or an amenity is never far away. Since so many of the family attractions are explained in more detail elsewhere in this or other chapters, I'll restrict myself to a list of the basics. See "Fast Facts: Philadelphia" in Chapter 4 for babysitting options.

A monthly publication on what to do with kids in Philadelphia, *Metrokids,* is available at the Visitors Center, 16th Street and John F. Kennedy Boulevard. The center also coordinates and sells several packages that combine free admissions to much of what follows with accommodations at hotels such as the Penn Tower, Sheraton Society Hill, and Embassy Suites Center City; call the Family Friendly Funline at **800/770-5889**.

MUSEUMS & SIGHTS

In Center City, there are the **Please Touch Museum,** 210 N. 21st St.; **Franklin Institute,** Benjamin Franklin Parkway and 20th Street; **CoreStates Science Park** between these two on 21st Street; and the **Academy of Natural Sciences,** the Parkway and 19th Street. The **Free Library of Philadelphia Children's Department** across Logan Circle at Vine and 19th Streets is a joy, with a separate entrance, 100,000 books and microcomputers in a playground-like space, and weekend hours. Around Independence Hall are the **Liberty Bell** at Market and 5th Streets; **Franklin Court,** between Market and Chestnut Streets at 4th Street; the waterfront at **Penn's Landing,** off Front Street; and, of course, the guided tour of **Independence Hall.** You can also take the ferry from Penn's Landing and the great new **Independence Seaport Museum** to the **aquarium** in Camden. In Fairmount Park you'll find the **zoo** in West Fairmount Park.

PLAYGROUNDS

Rittenhouse Square at 18th and Walnut Streets has a small playground and space to eat and relax. Other imaginative urban playgrounds on this side of Center City are **Schuylkill River Park** at Pine and 26th Streets and at 26th Street and the Benjamin Franklin Parkway, opposite the art museum. Nearest Independence Hall, try **Delancey Park** at Delancey between 3rd and 4th Streets (with lots of fountains and animal sculptures to climb on) or **Starr Garden** at 6th and Lombard Streets. The best in Fairmount Park is the **Smith Memorial** (head north on 33rd Street, then take a left into the park at Oxford Avenue, near Woodford).

ENTERTAINMENT

The **Great Plaza** at Penn's Landing has free children's theater performances by American Family Theater on Friday at 7pm in July and August; call **215/629-3237** for details. **Philadelphia Marionette Theater** has heavily reserved programs in Belmont Mansion in West Fairmount Park on Monday through Friday at 10:30am; call **215/879-1213** for details.

The **Philadelphia Museum of Art** has dedicated itself to producing Sunday-morning and early-afternoon programs for children, without fail and at minimal or no charge. Your kids could wind up drawing pictures of armor or watching a puppet theater about dragons, visiting a Chinese court, or playing with Picasso-style cubism. Call **215/763-8100** or **215/684-7500** for 24-hour information.

ATTRACTIONS OUTSIDE PHILADELPHIA

In Bucks County, there are **Sesame Place,** based on public TV's *Sesame Street,* in Langhorne, and the restored antique carousel at **Peddler's Village** in Lahaska. To the northwest, try the 20th-century entertainment areas connected with **Franklin Mills,** and **Ridley Creek State Park** and its 17th-century working farm in Montgomery County. For Revolutionary War history in action, try Valley Forge or Washington Crossing National Historical Parks. And for fascinating real life, try a couple of days in Lancaster County—you can even stay on a working "Plain People" farm. See chapters 11 and 12 for directions and information.

6 Organized Tours

BUS TOURS   Those double-decker buses decked out like trolleys, clanging along the city streets, are from **American Trolley Tours** (☎ **215/333-2119**). Tours of historic areas, conducted by guides in the climate-controlled vehicles, leave mornings and afternoons from the Visitors Center at 16th Street and John F. Kennedy Boulevard and from the Independence National Park Visitors Center at 3rd and Walnut Streets. The tours cost $10 for adults, $5 for children.

Gray Line (☎ **800/577-7745**) has introduced year-round, three-hour excursions of historic Philadelphia, Philadelphia at night, and Valley Forge for $16 adults and $10 children ages 3 to 11. All tours leave from 30th Street Station but shuttles from hotels are available.

WALKING TOURS   Of course, the next chapter will give you some guided walking tours to follow. To explore the four-block historic district at your own pace with the benefit of a prerecorded commentary, you can rent an Audio Walk and Tour cassette player and tape. The narration describes each attraction as you walk from site to site. An illustrated souvenir map comes with the tape. Players and cassettes are available daily from **AudioWalk and Tour** at the Curtis Center Museum of Norman Rockwell Art, 601 Walnut St. (☎ **215/925-1234**), on Washington Square. It's open from 10am to 5pm daily; return equipment by 4pm. The charge is $8 for one person, $16 for two to six people. You can also purchase the cassette for $10.95 and use your own recorder.

There are many specific-interest tours such as African-American Philadelphia, architectural walks, Jewish sites in Society Hill, and the Italian Market. Check the Visitors Center (☎ **215/636-3300**) for information.

CANDLELIGHT STROLLS   From May through October, evening tours of the historic area, led by costumed guides, leave from Welcome Park at 2nd and Walnut Streets at 6:30pm. Tours of Old City (Friday) and Society Hill (Saturday) take 90 minutes; they cost $5 for adults, $4 for seniors and children. Call **215/735-3123** for reservations with **Centipede Tours, Inc.,** 1315 Walnut St.

HORSE & CARRIAGE TOURS   To get the feel of Philadelphia as it was (well, almost—asphalt is a lot smoother than cobblestones!), try a narrated horse-drawn carriage ride. Operated daily by the **76 Carriage Co.** (☎ **215/923-8516**), tours begin at 5th and Chestnut Streets in front of Independence Hall from 10am to 5pm, with later hours in summer. Fares range from $10 for 15 minutes to $20 for 30 minutes, with a maximum of four per carriage. Reservations are not necessary.

BOATING TOURS   Two choices are available at Penn's Landing. The *Spirit of Philadelphia* (☎ **215/923-1419**) at the Great Plaza combines lunch, brunch, or dinner with a cruise on a 600-person passenger ship, fully climate controlled, with two enclosed decks and two open-air decks. Trips, which require reservations, are $20 and up for two or three hours.

The newly redecorated *Liberty Belle II* (☎ **215/629-1131**) boards from Lombard Street Circle, near the Chart House restaurant at the southern end of Penn's Landing, and can accommodate up to 475 passengers on three decks. Meals and prices are comparable.

The *Riverbus* (☎ **609/365-1400**) provides a 10-minute crossing from a landing just outside the Independence Seaport Museum and the New Jersey State Aquarium. There's a large interior to the ferry, and the views of the Philadelphia skyline are great, although the aquarium is the only possible destination in New Jersey. Departures from Penn's Landing are on the hour, from Camden on the half hour, from 9am to 5pm daily. One-way fares are $5 for adults, $3 for children and seniors; the package admissions with the attractions are advantageous.

7 Outdoor Activities

I can't begin to make a complete list of all that you can do outdoors while in Philadelphia, so contact the Department of Recreation (☎ **215/686-3600**). The following is merely a sample.

BIKING   Plaisted Hall, the Fairmount Park rental spot for bikes and boats, burned in 1993; there are plans to reconstruct it, but no public rentals at press time. That's a shame, because the lower half of West River Drive along the Schuylkill is closed to vehicular traffic most weekend hours in summer. If you do get or have a bicycle—try **Via Bicycle** at 1134 Pine St. (☎ **215/627-3370**), or **Bike Line** at 13th and Locust Streets (☎ **215/735-1503**), which rents mountain bikes for $15 per day—the biking is flat near the Schuylkill on either side but loops up sharply near Laurel Hill Cemetery or Manayunk. Since anyone who enjoys cycling would love the outlying countryside, note that you can also rent bicycles in Lumberville, 8 miles north of New Hope on the Delaware (☎ **215/297-5388**), and in Lancaster, the heart of

Amish farmland (☎ 717/684-7226). And bicycles may be taken free on all SEPTA and PATCO trains, so you're well within some nice country rides.

Call the **Bicycle Club of Philadelphia** at **215/440-9483** for specific neighborhood recommendations.

BOATING   City rowers and sailors must also await Plaisted Hall's reconstruction. Outside of the city, try **Northbrook Canoe Co.,** north of Route 842 in Northbrook on Brandywine Creek (☎ 610/793-2279), or **Point Pleasant,** on Route 32, 7 miles north of the New Hope exit on I-95, with canoeing, inner tubing, and rafting on the Delaware River (☎ 215/297-8823).

FISHING   It's true that **Pennypack Creek** and **Wissahickon Creek** are stocked from mid-April through December with trout and muskie and provide good, even rustic, conditions. A required license of $12.25 for Pennsylvania residents or $20.25 for out-of-staters is available at such sporting-goods stores as I. Goldberg or at the Municipal Services Building near the Visitors Center. Out of the city, **Ridley Creek** and its **state park** (☎ 610/566-4800) and **Brandywine Creek** at Hibernia Park (☎ 610/384-0290) are stocked with several kinds of trout.

GOLF   The city of Philadelphia operates five municipal courses out of the more than 100 in the region. All have 18 holes, and the current fees range from $14 to $22 on Monday through Friday and $16 to $26 on Saturday and Sunday. Call **215/877-8813** or the numbers below for more information on **Cobbs Creek** and **Karakung** (two adjacent courses in West Philadelphia, which are considered among the best public courses in the area; Cobbs Creek is especially pretty and challenging), 7800 Lansdowne Ave. at 72nd Street (☎ 215/877-8707); **Franklin D. Roosevelt,** 20th Street and Pattison Avenue (☎ 215/462-8997); **J. F. Byrne,** Frankford Avenue and Eden Street (☎ 215/632-8666); **Juniata,** M and Cayuga Streets (☎ 215/743-4060); and **Walnut Lane,** Walnut Lane and Henry Avenue (☎ 215/482-3370).

Among the better public courses outside the city are **Montgomeryville Golf Club,** Route 202 (☎ 215/855-6112); **Paxon Hollow Golf Club,** Paxon Hollow Road in Marple Township (☎ 215/353-0220); and **Valley Forge Golf Club,** 401 N. Gulph Rd., King of Prussia (☎ 215/337-1776). Expect fees of $65 and up.

HEALTH CLUBS   The Philadelphia Marriott, Wyndham Franklin Plaza, Four Seasons, the Rittenhouse, and Sheraton Society Hill have in-house facilities free to guests but open to nonguests at an additional charge. The spectacular **Sporting Club** at the Bellevue Hotel charges everyone. Most other moderately priced hotels have at least a few exercycles and an aerobics space; the KormanSuites, four blocks from Logan Circle, has a full gym room, pool, and tennis court. Near Society Hill, the top health club that admits per-day guests is **Gold's Gym** with Ron Jaworski, 834 Chestnut St. (☎ 215/592-9644). It provides an understanding staff, large Universal weight machines, free weights, and several aerobics classes daily. The cost is $10 per guest, and it's open Monday through Friday from 6am to 10pm, Saturday and Sunday from 8am to 5pm. Another alternative closer to midtown is the **12th Street Gym,** 204 S. 12th St. (☎ 215/985-4092), a revamped version of a 1930s men's club with a pool, courts for squash and racquetball, and weights and aerobics rooms. It's open Monday through Friday from 5:30am to 11pm, Saturday from 7am to 7pm, and Sunday from 9am to 7pm. The basic rate is $10 per guest.

HIKING   Fairmount Park (☎ 215/686-3616) has dozens of miles of paths, and the extensions into Wissahickon Creek are quite unspoiled, with dirt roads and no auto traffic. Farther afield, **Horseshoe Trail** (☎ 215/664-0719) starts at Routes 23 and 252 in Valley Forge State Park and winds 120 miles west marked by yellow horseshoes until it meets the Appalachian Trail.

HORSEBACK RIDING   There are many riding trails in Fairmount Park, the Wissahickon, and Pennypack Park within city limits, and Chester and Brandywine counties are famous for horsemanship, from fox hunting to the Winterthur Point-to-Point races. Unfortunately, insurance costs have made it unprofitable for most riding stables to allow visitors to rent horses. The only riding stable within city limits that does is **Harry's Riding Stables** (☎ 215/335-9975), 2240 Holmesburg Ave., near Pennypack Park. It's open seven days a week from 9am to 8pm, and seven or eight horses are always available, with rates of $20 per hour for guided trail rides with western saddles. The easiest directions from Center City are via I-95 north. Take the Academy Road exit, following the exit ramp to the left onto Academy until the first light; then turn left onto Frankford Avenue and continue for 2 miles. After a hill, there's an intersection with a railroad trestle that passes above Frankford. Before going under it, take the dirt road on the left and follow 300 yards to the white barn building on the right.

ICE SKATING   One great improvement to the city has been the **Blue Cross RiverRink at Penn's Landing,** open for public skating near the intersection of Chestnut Street and Columbus Boulevard daily from late November to early March. Admission for one 2-hour session is $4 to 6, with skate rentals only $2. Call **215/925-RINK** for details; there's a nice food court, also.

RUNNING & JOGGING   Once again, **Fairmount Park** has more trails than you could cover in a week. An 8.2-mile loop starts at the front of the Museum of Art, up the east bank of the Schuylkill, across the river at Falls Bridge, and back down to the museum. At the north end, Forbidden Drive along the Wissahickon has loops of dirt/gravel of 5 miles and more, with no traffic. The Benjamin Franklin Bridge path from 5th and Vine Streets is 1.8 miles each way.

SWIMMING   Philadelphia has 86 municipal swimming pools, and many hotels have small lap versions. Municipal pools are open daily from 11am to 7pm and are free. Two of the best are **Cobbs Creek,** 63rd and Spruce Streets, and **FDR Pool,** Broad and Pattison in South Philadelphia. Call **215/686-1776** for details.

TENNIS   Some 115 courts are scattered throughout **Fairmount Park,** and you can get a tourist permit for their use by calling **215/686-0152.** You might also try the University of Pennsylvania's indoor courts at the **Robert P. Levy Tennis Pavilion,** 3130 Walnut St. (☎ 215/898-4741). Rates are $30 for two visitors until 4pm, $35 for two after 4pm.

8 Spectator Sports

Even in these days of frequently relocating professional teams, Philadelphia fields teams in every major sport and boasts a newly enhanced complex at the end of South Broad Street to house them all. **Veterans Stadium** (☎ 215/686-1776) is a graceful bowl with undulating ramps that can seat 58,000 for the Phillies in baseball and 68,000 for the Eagles in football. The new $230-million, 21,000-seat **CoreStates Center** houses the Philadelphia Flyers pro hockey and Philadelphia 76ers basketball teams. It couples with the 17,000 **CoreStates Spectrum,** which functions as one of the best rock-concert forums around and hosts the U.S. Pro Indoor Tennis Championships and other one-of-a-kind events.

All these are next to each other and can be reached via a 10-minute subway ride straight down South Broad Street to Pattison Avenue ($1.60). The same fare will put you on the SEPTA bus C, which goes down Broad Street slower but with a bit more safety late at night.

Professional sports aren't the only game in town, though. Philadelphia has a lot of colleges, and **Franklin Field** and the **Palestra** dominate West Philadelphia on 33rd below Walnut Street. The Penn Relays, the first intercollegiate and amateur track event in the nation, books Franklin Field on the last weekend in April. Regattas pull along the Schuylkill all spring, summer, and fall, within sight of Fairmount Park's mansions.

A call to Teletron (☎ **800/233-4050**) or TicketMaster (☎ **212/507-7171** in New York, **215/336-2000** in Philadelphia) can get you tickets in many cases before you hit town.

BASEBALL The **Philadelphia Phillies,** Box 7575, Philadelphia, PA 19101 (☎ **215/463-1000** for ticket information, **215/463-5300** for daily game information), won the National League pennant in 1993 and made playoffs in 1995. They play at Veterans Stadium, Broad Street and Pattison Avenue. Day games usually begin at 1:35pm, regular night games at 8:05pm on Friday, at 7:35pm on other days. When there's a twilight doubleheader, it begins at 5:35pm. The huge computerized scoreboard and the antics that follow a Phillies home run will leave you laughing and amazed.

Tickets for the Phillies have been increasing rapidly in cost; box seats overlooking the field are around $20, and the cheapest bleacher seats are $7.50 if you're over 14.

BASKETBALL The **Philadelphia 76ers,** Box 25050, Philadelphia, PA 19147, play about 40 games at the CoreStates Center between early November and late April. Call **215/339-7676** for ticket information; tickets range from $12 to $54. There's always a good halftime show, and the promotion department works overtime with special nights, especially involving 76ers T-shirts.

There are five major college basketball teams in the Philadelphia area, and the newspapers print schedules of their games. Most games are at the Palestra, with tickets going for $5 to $8. Call **215/898-4747** to find out about ticket availability.

BIKING The CoreStates Pro Cycling Championship, held each June, is actually a top event in the cycling world. The 156-mile race starts and finishes along the Benjamin Franklin Parkway, and watching the cyclists climb "The Wall" in Manayunk is terrifying.

BOATING From April to September, you can watch regattas on the Schuylkill River, which have been held since the earliest days of the "Schuylkill Navy" a century ago. The **National Association of Amateur Oarsmen** (☎ **215/769-2068**) and the **Boathouse Association** (☎ **215/686-0052**) have a complete schedule of races. The Dad Vail Regatta is one of the best known.

FOOTBALL Football, without a doubt, is Philadelphia's favorite sport. It will take all your ingenuity to come up with tickets for a game, since all **Philadelphia Eagles** games (at Veterans Stadium, Philadelphia, PA 19148) are popular, and 85% of all tickets are sold to season ticketholders. Call **215/463-5500** for ticket advice. The games start at 1 or 4pm, and tickets cost up to $75.

HORSE RACING **Philadelphia Park** (the old Keystone Track) has races every day except Monday from January 1 to February 13 (post time is 12:30pm) and from June 15 to December 31 (post time is 1pm). The $3 admission includes parking and a program; the park is on Street Road in Bensalem, half a mile from Exit 28 on the Pennsylvania Turnpike. Call **215/639-9000** for information.

For more thoroughbred horse racing, try **Garden State Park,** N.J. 70 and Haddonfield Road in Cherry Hill, New Jersey (☎ **609/488-8400**), which runs thoroughbred races in the spring and harness (standard bred) races in the fall. Call for exact schedules, but the first post time is usually 7:30pm Wednesday through Saturday.

Off-Track Wagering Parlor and Dining, 7 Penn Center, 1635 Market St., on the concourse and lower mezzanine levels (☎ **215/245-1556**), features 270 color video monitors and an ersatz art-deco design; it brings the wagering to you in the comfort of Center City.

ICE HOCKEY   The CoreStates Center rocks to the **Philadelphia Flyers,** led by star Eric Lindros, from fall to spring, and their tickets are even harder to get than the Eagles'—80% of tickets to the much smaller arena are sold by the season. Call **215/465-5500** for ticket information; if you can find some, they'll cost between $15 and $35.

TENNIS   Philadelphia has several world-class tournaments annually. February brings the **Comcast U.S. Professional Indoor Championships** at the Spectrum, with $600,000 in prize money; call **215/947-2530** for information. The women's invitational held at Haverford College (☎ **610/896-1000**) in late September has attracted top players, and Advanta sometimes brings the **Virginia Slims tour** to the Civic Center in November. The late-summer **USTA Senior Men's Grass Court Championships** at Germantown Cricket Club (☎ **215/438-9900**) can bring you face-to-face with former greats.

TRACK & FIELD   The city hosts the **Penn Relays,** the oldest and still the largest amateur track meet in the country, in late April at Franklin Field. There's a November annual **Marathon** and a September **Philadelphia Distance Run,** a half-marathon; the latter is becoming a world-class event. Call **215/686-0053** for more details.

8 City Strolls

Philadelphia is probably the most compact, walkable major city in the United States, just as it was in 1776. It's fascinating to see the progress of the centuries and unexpected juxtapositions on a random walk, always noting that the nearer you are to the Delaware, the older (and smaller) the buildings are likely to be. The walking tours mapped out below are specifically designed to enhance your ability to cover the most worthwhile attractions and to recoup your strength along the way.

1 Historic Highlights & Society Hill

Start: Visitors Center, 3rd and Walnut Streets.
Finish: City Tavern, 2nd and Walnut Streets; optional extension to Penn's Landing.
Time: 6–7 hours.
Best Time: Start between 9 and 11am to avoid hour-long waits for Independence Hall tours.

Start your tour at the:

1. **Visitors Center** in Independence National Historical Park, 3rd and Walnut Streets. This handsome brick building was built for the 1976 bicentennial celebration and maintains spotless restrooms and cool benches as well as providing pamphlets and maps of the park, free tickets (limited in number) for the Bishop White and Todd Houses (see below), and information about special tours or special daily events. The John Huston–directed film *Independence* is shown without charge every half hour. There is a small exhibition area and a substantial quality gift shop and bookstore.

   Just opposite the Visitor Centers is the:

2. **First Bank of the United States** (1795), not open to the public but a superb example of Federal architecture. It is as old and as graceful as a Roman rotunda. The idea for this building derived from Alexander Hamilton. The reliance on the currencies of the 13 new states hampered commerce and travel, and he proposed a single bank for loans and deposits. The bank started in Carpenters' Hall. The mahogany American eagle on the pediment over the Corinthian entrance columns is a famous—and rare—example of 18th-century sculpture.

Walking Tour—Historic Highlights & Society Hill

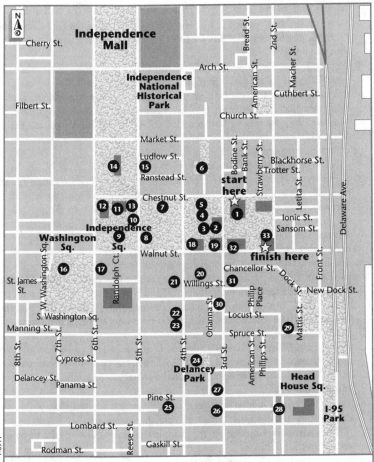

1. Visitor Center
2. First Bank of the United States
3. Carpenters' Hall
4. New Hall
5. Pemberton House
6. Franklin Court
7. Second Bank of the United States
8. Library Hall
9. Independence Square
10. Philosophical Hall
11. Independence Hall
12. Congress Hall
13. Old City Hall
14. The Liberty Bell
15. The Bourse
16. Washington Square
17. Athenaeum
18. Todd House
19. Bishop White House
20. St. Joseph's Church
21. Philadelphia Contributionship
22. Episcopal Diocese
23. Old St. Mary's Church
24. Hill-Physick-Keith House
25. Old Pine Presbyterian
26. St. Peter's Episcopal Church
27. Kosciuszko National Memorial
28. Head House Square
29. Man Full of Trouble Tavern
30. Powel House
31. St. Paul's Episcopal Church
32. Philadelphia Merchants' Exchange
33. City Tavern

Behind the First Bank, the Park Service cleared much of the block (as throughout the Historic Park area), leaving historic structures and establishing 18th-century gardens and lawns. To the right, a walkway leads to the midblock:

3. **Carpenters' Hall,** which was a newly built guildhall when the First Continental Congress met here in 1774 (see Chapter 7 for a fuller description). Just north of this, you'll find:

4. **New Hall,** a modern copy of a hall built in 1791 for rent by the Carpenters' Company. With the federal government based in Philadelphia until Washington, D.C., was habitable, the U.S. government took the space as the first headquarters of the War (now Defense) Department. This building now houses the Marine Corps Museum, since the marines were founded at Tun Tavern nearby; you can see uniforms and swords that fought on "the shores of Tripoli" as well as the medals that decorated those uniforms.

A few steps north on Chestnut Street proper is:

5. **Pemberton House,** another reconstruction. Joseph Pemberton, a Quaker merchant of sugar and Madeira, had just built this fine Georgian home when the Second Continental Congress cut back on British imports, in the aftermath of the gunfire at Concord and Lexington. After Pemberton went bankrupt, the house was razed in 1862, only to be reconstructed a century later. The development of the infant U.S. army and navy is the subject here. The exhibit features continuous showings of a military history of the Revolutionary War, which followed a slow pattern of British advances, defeats, and regroupings to the south. The main theater of battle moved from Boston in 1775 to New York, New Jersey, and Pennsylvania in 1777 and 1778, with a final bottleneck for the British at Chesapeake Bay in 1781. The second floor's highlight is the model gun deck of a frigate, with instructions on maneuvering for a naval battle.

The other side of Chestnut Street is a handsome collection of 19th-century banks and commercial facades, including the 1867 **First National Bank** at no. 315 and the **Philadelphia National Bank** at no. 323. The Chestnut Street entrance to:

6. **Franklin Court** is nestled here (see Chapter 7 for a full description of this wonderful tribute to Benjamin Franklin's final home and spirit).

Walk west along Chestnut Street or back in the gardens, crossing 4th Street until you get to the midblock:

7. **Second Bank of the United States.** Its strong Greek columns have corroded somewhat, but the bank still holds interest. The Second Bank was chartered by Congress in 1816 for a term of 20 years, again at a time when the country felt that it needed reliable circulating money. The building (1819–24), designed like the Merchants Exchange by William Strickland, is adapted from the Parthenon, and the Greeks would have been proud of its capable director, Nicholas Biddle. An elitist to the core, he was the man Andrew Jackson and his supporters had in mind when they complained about private individuals controlling public government. Urged by Henry Clay for reasons of political capital, Biddle asked prematurely for the renewal of the charter, making this the issue of the 1832 presidential election. "Old Hickory" vetoed the charter and won the election; this increased the money supply but ruined Biddle and the bank.

The federal government bought the building in 1844 for about half its original cost of $500,000 and used it as the Customs House until 1934. The National Park Service uses it as a portrait gallery of early Americans. The collection contains many of the oldest "gallery portraits" in the country, painted by Charles Willson

Peale and once displayed in the Long Room of Independence Hall. Sully, Neagle, Stuart, and Allston also are represented.

☕ **TAKE A BREAK**   A **tea garden** in the adjoining holly garden, staffed by the Friends of Independence National Historical Park, provides ice cream and cool drinks from noon to 5pm from mid-May to mid-September.

Just west of the Second Bank lies:

 8. Library Hall, the 1954 reconstruction of Benjamin Franklin's old Library Company, which was the first lending library of its type in the colonies. The Library Company is now at 1314 Locust St. (see "Midtown and the Parkway" stroll below); this graceful Federal building houses the library of the American Philosophical Society based across the street. The collection is entrancing, including Franklin's will, a copy of William Penn's 1701 Charter of Privileges, and Jefferson's own handwritten copy of the Declaration of Independence. The exhibits center on the history of science in America. The library's hours follow the park schedule.

The pull of great government will lead you across 5th Street to:

 9. Independence Square, where on July 8, 1776, John Nixon read the Declaration of Independence to the assembled city. You'll be at the back of the official trio of **Independence Hall, Congress Hall,** and **Old City Hall** on Chestnut Street between 5th and 6th Streets.

On your right is:

10. Philosophical Hall, the home of the American Philosophical Society. The society is a prestigious honor roll of America's outstanding intellects and achievers founded by Ben Franklin. The building's interior is not open to the public, but look for traces of old Georgian springing into new Federal architecture, such as fan-shaped windows, larger windows, and more elaborate doorsteps. In Franklin's day, philosophers were more often than not industrious young men with scientific and learned interests, so the society included mostly intellectually advanced citizens.

To your left is:

11. Independence Hall, grand, graceful, and one of democracy's true shrines (see Chapter 7 for a full description). Ranger-led 35-minute tours depart every 15 minutes or so. The two flanking buildings, **Old City Hall** (Supreme Court Building) and **Congress Hall,** were intended to balance each other, and their fanlighted doors, keystoned windows, and simple lines reward you from any angle. They were used by a combination of federal, state, county, and city governments during a relatively short period (this can get confusing).

12. Congress Hall (1787) held the U.S. Congress for 10 years; Washington departed public life from here. The House of Representatives met downstairs, and the place looks somewhat modern with wall-to-wall carpeting and venetian blinds. It's hard to get mahogany desks and leather armchairs of such workmanship now, though. Washington was inaugurated here in 1793 and John Adams in 1797. Look for the little corners where representatives could smoke, take snuff, and drink sherry during recess. Watching the House and Senate from the balconies became a popular social activity, and if debate was boring one could always admire the ceiling moldings.

13. Old City Hall (1790), at the corner of 5th and Chestnut Streets, contained the only unaccounted-for branch of the federal government, the U.S. Supreme Court under Chief Justice John Jay. (Until the present City Hall anchored Center Square, this was the City Hall from 1800 to 1870.) The park uses the restored courthouse to describe the judiciary's first years.

Across Chestnut Street from this central trio is:

14. The Liberty Bell, once located in Independence Hall and moved for the bicentennial celebration to the special glass pavilion across Chestnut Street (see Chapter 7 for a full description).

Just to the east of the Liberty Bell is:

15. The Bourse, a superb example of late Victorian architecture. It has been renovated as a mall in the form of two arcades surrounding an expansive skylit atrium. The Bourse, built from 1893 to 1895 as a merchants exchange, handsomely combines a brick-and-sandstone exterior with a cool and colorful interior.

☕ **TAKE A BREAK** The Bourse's spacious, cool ground-floor **Food Court** is open Monday, Tuesday, and Thursday from 10am to 6pm; Wednesday, Friday, and Saturday until 8pm; and Sunday from 11am to 6pm.

Now cut through Independence Square to the greenery at the southwest corner. This is Washington Square.

16. Washington Square seems a little unbalanced since Independence National Historical Park opened up the block to the northeast—but it's just as expansive and even more leafy than when it was the town's pasture. In the 1840s, this was the center of fashionable Philadelphia. Many handsome structures have been razed to make room for chunky offices and apartment houses. Only the 1823 southwest corner Federals, the **Meredith-Penrose House** and its neighbors, give you a sense of what was lost. It now holds the Tomb of the Unknown Soldier from the Revolutionary War, complete with eternal flame. The square has also housed Philadelphia publishing for 150 years, with **Lea and Febiger** and **J. B. Lippincott** at no. 227. The massive white building on the north face has been redeveloped, but the Curtis Publishing Co. once sent out the *Saturday Evening Post* and other magazines from here. The **Curtis Center Museum of Norman Rockwell Art** in the corner section pays tribute to the *Post's* frequent illustrator (see Chapter 7 for a fuller description). As you enter, admire that luminous mosaic mural *The Dream Garden:* Tiffany Studios executed a drawing by Maxfield Parrish, and the 1916, 49-foot hand-fired masterpiece must be worth a fortune.

That solid, Italianate Revival brownstone (1845–47) on Washington Square East is the:

17. Athenaeum, a corner of virtually unchanged 19th-century society (see Chapter 7 for a fuller description).

Society Hill wasn't named that because only the upper crust of Philadelphia lived there in colonial times, although they did. The name refers to the Free Society of Traders, a group of businessmen and investors persuaded by William Penn to settle here with their families in 1683. The name applies to the area east of Washington Square between Walnut and Lombard Streets. Most of Philadelphia's white-collar workers, clerics, teachers, importers, and politicos have lived and worked here.

In 1945 nobody would have considered walking through the decrepit and undesirable neighborhood, despite the hundreds of colonial facades. That's all changed now because of a massive urban-renewal project. Many new housing developments fit in discreet courts; they, too, use simple brick facades that blend with the Georgian exteriors superbly.

What's a Trinity? Colonial Homes in Philadelphia

It's a good idea for you to know something about colonial and Federal architecture as you stroll about Society Hill and Queen Village because many homes aren't open to individual tours. Brick is everywhere, since English settlers found clay by the Delaware's banks—but the types and the construction methods have varied over 150 years. Generally, houses built before the 1750s, such as the **Trump House** at 214 Delancey St., have two-and-a-half stories, with two rooms per floor and a dormer window jutting out of a steep gambrel roof. An eave usually separates the simple door and its transom windows from the second level. Careful bricklayers liked to alternate the long and short sides of bricks, called "stretchers" and "headers"; this was named Flemish Bond, and the headers often were glazed to create a checkerboard pattern. Wrought-iron boot scrapers flank the doorsteps.

Houses built in Philadelphia's colonial heyday soared to three or four stories—taller after the Revolution—and adopted heavy Georgian cornices (the underside of a roof overhang) and elaborate doorways. The homes of the truly wealthy, such as the **Powel House** at 244 S. 3rd St. and the **Morris House** at 235 S. 8th St., have fanlights above their arched brick doorways; the **Davis-Lenox House** at 217 Spruce St. has a simple raised pediment. Since the Georgian style demanded symmetry, the parlors often were given imaginary doors and windows to even things out. The less wealthy lived in "trinity" homes—one room on each of three floors, named for faith, hope, and charity. Few town houses stood on individual plots; the **Hill-Physick-Keith House** at 321 S. 4th St. is the exception that proves the rule.

Federal architecture, which blew in from England and New England in the 1790s, is less heavy (no more Flemish Bond for bricks) and more graceful (more glass, with delicate molding instead of wainscoting). Any house such as the **Meredith House** at 700 S. Washington Sq., with a half story of marble stairs leading to a raised mahogany door, was surely constructed after 1800. Greek Revival elements such as rounded dormer windows and oval staircases became the fashion from the 1810s on. Three of the few Victorian brownstones at 260 S. 3rd St. once belonged to Michel Bouvier, Jacqueline Kennedy Onassis's great-great-grandfather.

If you're here in May, don't pass up **Philadelphia Open House** to view the bandbox interiors of dozens of homes (volunteered by proud owners). Call **215/928-1188** for information.

Of course, houses aren't all there is to Society Hill. Georgian and Federal public buildings and churches, from **Head House Square** and **Pennsylvania Hospital** to **St. Peter's** and **St. Paul's,** may make you feel as if you've stumbled onto a movie set. But all of the buildings are used—and the area works as a living community today. Fine restaurants and charming stores cluster south of Lombard, too, especially around Head House Square (1803) at 2nd and Lombard Streets.

Continuing on your tour, leave the Athenaeum and walk west one block on St. James Street, then go north on 5th Street and take a right turn onto Walnut Street for two blocks. As you walk down Walnut to 3rd Street, the restored row houses will catch your eye, with their paneled doors and shutters, bands of brick or stone between floors, and small lozenges of painted metal. These last are fire-insurance markers—all early American cities had terrible fire hazards, and Philadelphia, led by Benjamin Franklin, was the first to do anything about them.

Impression

The vast extent of the streets of small, low, yet snug-looking houses. . . . Philadelphia must contain in comfort the largest number of small householders of any city in the world.

—London Times Reporter William Bussell, *My Diary North and South* (1850)

Groups of citizens formed such companies as the Philadelphia Contributionship, which suggested prevention strategy with leather fire buckets and lightning rods. The plaques of leafy green trees (on the Mutual Assurance Company) or four clasped hands (on the Contributionship) functioned as advertisements but also helped the firemen identify which houses they were responsible for saving. Now the houses belong to park offices and the Pennsylvania Horticultural Association, which maintains an 18th-century formal garden open to the public. At the corner of Fourth and Walnut Streets is the:

18. Todd House (1775). Tours (for 10 at a time) are required, and tickets by advance reservation are available gratis at the Visitors Center. John Todd, Jr., was a young Quaker lawyer of moderate means. His house cannot compare to that of Bishop White, but it is far grander than Betsy Ross's. Todd died in the 1793 epidemic of yellow fever, and his vivacious widow married a Virginia lawyer.named James Madison, the future president. The Todds lived and entertained on the second floor, since Todd used the ground-floor parlor as his law office.

Farther down Walnut toward 3rd Street is the other park-run dwelling, the:

19. Bishop White House, at no. 309. Tours (for 10 at a time) are required; again, free tickets can be obtained at the Visitors Center. This house is on one of the loveliest row-house blocks in the city, giving the park a life-size example of how a pillar of the community lived in Federal America. Bishop White (1748–1836) studied for the Anglican priesthood in England, then returned home to tend Christ Church; he later founded Episcopalianism after the break from the mother country. He traveled abroad with Benjamin West and was Franklin's warm friend, which his upstairs library shows. White stayed out of politics as an expression of his belief in the separation of church and state. Notice the painted cloth floor in the entrance hall—after 20 varnishings, it survived muddy boots remarkably well. And, in case you take the indoor "necessity" for granted, remember that outhouses provided the only relief on most colonial property. The library shows "modern" tastes, with Sir Walter Scott's Waverley novels, the *Encyclopaedia Britannica,* and even the Koran alongside traditional religious texts. The collection has survived intact.

Across the street, the park has purchased property and made a garden that exposes the side of:

20. St. Joseph's Church, the first Roman Catholic church in Philadelphia (see Chapter 7 for a description). It's much more intriguing if you enter through Willing's Alley and walk back to 4th Street and south half a block because an iron gate and archway conceal it well.

Not many tourists know about them, but the headquarters of 18th-century fire-insurance companies are open to the public, in the heart of Society Hill. In a neighborhood that was as moneyed and as crowded as this one, fire was a constant danger. Groups of subscribers pledged to help each other in case of fire—there were no fire departments in those days! Ironically, many companies required a complete inventory of the possessions before they would set premiums, and these inventories have guided modern restorers of run-down town houses. You can see the insurance plaques on the upper facades of many homes. In fact, the:

21. **Philadelphia Contributionship** (1836), 212 S. 4th St. (below Walnut Street), has used the "Hand-in-Hand" mark since 1752. This facade is all Greek Revival—with a gorgeous limestone entrance, columns, and balustrades leading to the front door. Architect Thomas U. Walter also designed the dome and the House and Senate wings on the U.S. Capitol. Entrance to the building is free, and it's open Monday through Friday from 10am to 3pm. The normal exhibition displays old leather fire-fighting equipment, desks with inkwells, and the original policy statement and list of members. If you call **215/627-1752** ahead of time, you'll get to view two meeting rooms and a dining room, with their veined marble fireplaces and rare bird's-eye maple dining-room chairs.

Just below Locust Street on the same block is the:

22. **Episcopal Diocese of Philadelphia,** at no. 240, which combines two splendid row houses built in 1750 and 1826 for the Cadwallader family. Both houses are closed to the public. Just opposite the Diocese is **Bingham Court,** a 1967 adaptation within the Society Hill idiom of brick row houses. A few doors down 4th Street is:

23. **Old St. Mary's Church,** the most important Roman Catholic church during the Revolution (this was the "Sunday" church, as opposed to St. Joseph's weekday chapel). The interior is fairly prosaic, but the paved graveyard is a picturesque spot for a breather, with some interesting headstones and memorials.

The corner of Spruce and 4th Streets is a good place to take a breath, with the town houses of **Girard Row** in front of you. Half a block to the west at 426 Spruce St., Thomas U. Walter, the architect of the Capitol's dome in Washington and a master of Greek Revival, designed a Baptist church in 1830 that has been modified as the **Society Hill Synagogue** (run by Romanian immigrants at the turn of the century and by Conservative Jews more recently).

A half block down 4th Street is the:

24. **Hill-Physick-Keith House,** at no. 321, possibly the nicest residential structure in Society Hill (see Chapter 7 for a fuller description). Take a few steps east on adjoining Cypress Street to reach **Delancey Park,** a delightful playground with sturdy activities and a group of stone bears that are perfect for photo props.

More Georgian and Federal church facades appear at the corners of 4th and Pine Streets. One is Old Pine:

25. **Old Pine Presbyterian,** with its enormous raised facade and forbidding iron fence, didn't always look like a Greek temple, but that's what makes it worth seeing (it's free and open daily from 9am to 5pm). The Penns granted the Presbyterians this land in perpetuity, and the first sanctuary took shape in 1768. The double Corinthian columns, inside and out, were added in 1830, after the occupying British soldiers burned most of the interior. Everything is linear at Old Pine: The portico leads into a rectangle of pews, and slim pillars support a gallery with an elaborately carved rail of flowers and dentils. The altar will surprise you—it's just a dais backed by elaborate columns and entablature. You'll find it hard to believe that this filigree is of wood and not clay or plaster.

Old Pine Community Center on the block south to Lombard Street leads to South Street's funky shopping and nightlife district just beyond. Walk east on Pine Street to:

26. **St. Peter's Episcopal Church** (1761), an example of classic Georgian simplicity (see Chapter 7 for a fuller description).

Farther east, at 301 Pine St., is the:

27. Kosciuszko National Memorial, a double 1775 Georgian that housed this Polish engineer and soldier who turned the tide for American forces at Saratoga. He returned to the United States, exiled from Poland, in search of a pension from Congress and lived here in 1797 while pursuing this.

Now follow Pine Street to 2nd Street, the major north–south route through Philadelphia in colonial days. Open markets were a big part of urban life. In fact, no colonial native would recognize Market Street today without its wooden sheds that covered stalls from Front to 6th Streets and its narrow cart paths on both sides. One place that would be recognized, though, is:

28. Head House Square, built in 1803 in the middle of 2nd Street as a place where fire companies and shoppers could congregate. Head House itself, that brick shed with a cupola that once held a fire bell, trails a simple brick arcade between Pine and South Streets. In those days, market took place on Tuesday and Friday at dawn. Butter and eggs were sold on the west side, meat under the eaves, and herbs and vegetables on the river side. Fish sellers were relegated to the far sidewalks (it isn't hard to imagine why). Now, in summer, craftspeople spread out their goods, especially on weekends.

☕ **TAKE A BREAK   Dickens Inn,** 421 S. 2nd St., and several other Head House Square restaurants make excellent lunch or snack stopovers; Dickens Inn (open from 11:30am daily) has an English afternoon tea, as well as a tempting ground-floor bakery. For great on-street chocolate chip cookies or brownies, go to **Koffmeyer's Bakery** on 2nd near Lombard.

Now head up 2nd Street, perhaps cutting in to Delancey Street between 2nd and 3rd Streets, north on Philip Street's quaint court, and back to 2nd on Spruce Street. Across the street from the 1765 **Abercrombie House** (one of the tallest colonial dwellings in America) is the:

29. Man Full of Trouble Tavern, at 127 Spruce St. This place re-creates a big part of Capt. James Abercrombie's life. The Knauer Foundation has restored the tavern to its original appearance with Delft tiles, a cagelike bar, and tables with Windsor chairs and pewter candlesticks. The 1760 tavern bordered Little Dock Creek then, and sailors and dock workers ate, drank, and roughhoused here nightly. Admission is now by group appointment only.

Just up the hill are **Society Hill Towers** (1964), the I. M. Pei twins that signaled the 20th century and stick out like 30-story sore thumbs today. It's best to walk west back to 3rd Street, then north to a stunning block of row-house mansions including **Bishop Stevens** at no. 232, with its cast-iron balcony; **Atkinson House** at no. 236, which today conceals an indoor pool; and **Penn-Chew House** at no. 242, owned by the grandson of William and the last colonial governor of Pennsylvania. The mansion that you can enter is:

30. Powel House, at 244 S. 3rd St. This home of Philadelphia's last colonial and first U.S. mayor beats the Bishop White House by far (see Chapter 7).

Across the street is:

31. St. Paul's Episcopal Church (1761), at 225 S. 3rd St., founded because of another example of Philadelphia's religious tolerance. Christ Church on Market Street had a young clergyman, William McClenachan, who preached such radical notions as the separation of church and state. Since the High Anglican Church refused to license his speech, St. Paul's was set up as his "bully pulpit," and the money for the Georgian hall was raised through donations and lotteries. Now it houses the headquarters of the denomination's community services, inside beautiful pre-Revolutionary wrought-iron gates and marble-topped enclosing walls. If you head for the second floor (open Monday through Friday from 9am to 5pm), you can still see most of the original chancel.

Standing at the corner of 3rd and Walnut Streets, you can't miss the:

32. Philadelphia Merchants' Exchange (1832), a masterwork by William Strickland (described in Chapter 7). It's not open to the public. Heading toward 2nd Street and the river, you'll cross one of my favorite spaces, a broad area of cobblestones covering Dock Street (Dock Creek in Penn's day) and the Delaware River beyond. The **Ritz 5** movie house on your left offers fine independent fare. Soon you'll approach the reconstructed:

33. City Tavern restaurant and gardens from the rear. This was the most opulent and genteel tavern and social hall in the colonies and the scene of many discussions among the Founding Fathers. Unlike most of the city's pubs, it was built in 1773 with businessmen's subscriptions, to assure its quality. In fact, George Washington met with most delegates to the Constitutional Convention for a farewell dinner here in 1787. The park now operates the City Tavern as a concession, which serves continuously from 11am (see Chapter 6). The back garden seating is shady and cool for a mid-afternoon break.

If you choose to continue toward the Delaware via the pleasant pedestrian extension of Walnut Street and the staircase at its end, you'll pass between the new **Sheraton Society Hill** hotel and the famed **Old Original Bookbinder's** restaurant, winding up more or less in front of the wonderful **Independence Seaport Museum** on the waterfront. Consult the "Penn's Landing" description in Chapter 7 for more details.

2 Old City

Start: Visitors Center, 3rd and Walnut Streets.
Finish: Market Place East, 7th and Market Streets.
Time: 3–5 hours.
Best Time: No later than 3pm, to avoid museum closings. If contemporary art and socializing is your interest, the first Friday of every month brings special late hours for all galleries, all cafés, and many historic attractions.

Old City is an intriguing blend of 18th- and even 17th-century artisan row houses, robust 19th-century commercial structures, and 20th-century rehabs of all of the above featuring artist lofts and galleries. See it now; many property owners would rather demolish than rehab, and classics on 110–112 S. Front St., for example, were destroyed despite public outcry in March 1994. Walk out the south entrance of the **Visitors Center** and along the narrow lane adjoining **City Tavern** to:

1. Welcome Park, the site of the Slate Roof House where William Penn granted the "Charter of Privileges" (now at the Library Hall off Independence Square) in 1701. The pavement bears a massive and whimsical map of Penn's City, with a time line of his life on the walls.

Next door is the **Thomas Bond House,** a restored 1769 Georgian row house that's now a bed-and-breakfast (see Chapter 5 for more information). Walk along the block-long **AMC Olde City 2** cinemas to:

2. Front Street, which actually lapped at the river's edge throughout colonial times. A walk north brings you to **Bonnie's Exceptional Ice Cream** at the corner of Chestnut Street and the possibility of exploring Penn's Landing (see Chapter 7 for a description) via a beautifully terraced park. However, head back to the florid **Corn Exchange Bank** at 2nd and Chestnut Streets, then turn right onto one of the liveliest blocks in the historic area.

☕ **TAKE A BREAK**   The block of "Two Street" between Chestnut and Market contains good restaurants such as **Serrano's, New Mexico Grille, Rib-It** for ribs, and **Sassafras** for burgers (see Chapter 5 for details). My favorite is the quiet, cool seating for 40 at the rear of **Foodtek Market and Café,** with great hot and cold charcuterie. It's open on Monday through Thursday from 7:30am to 1am, on Saturday and Sunday until 2am.

Once you hit the newly widened sidewalks of Market Street (High Street in colonial times), you'll find a different world, where a burst of natural food stores and upgraded bistros like **Brothers** are moving in on sharp discount clothing and wholesale toy stores. The many alleyways between Front and 5th Streets, with names like **Trotter Street, Black Horse Alley, Bank Street,** and **Strawberry Lane,** testify to the activities and preoccupations of colonial residents. A particular favorite facade of mine is that of the:

3. **Norwegian Seaman's Church,** at 22 S. 3rd St. This William Strickland 1837 gem with Corinthian columns and granite steps is now **Jake & Oliver's,** a fine restaurant and club. If you haven't taken the first walking tour, go now to:

4. **Franklin Court,** the final home and reconstructed post office of Benjamin Franklin between 3rd and 4th Streets. Standing on Market Street, you'll find the graceful spire of:

5. **Christ Church,** which is unmissable. Urban renewal removed the unsightly buildings that hid its walls from Market until the 1950s (see Chapter 7 for a fuller description of revolutionary Philadelphia's leading place of worship and its restful benches and adjoining cemetery).

It may be a bit early for another refueling stop, but the block of Church Street directly to the west of the church contains **Old City Coffee** at no. 221, a favorite place for marvelous coffee and light lunches. If by the time you get here the end of the day is approaching, duck underneath the Market Street ramp to I-95 at Front Street to reach **Panorama's** wine bar and bistro.

Walk north along Front Street for four short blocks to get the flavor of 1830s warehouses, such as the **Girard** at 18–30 N. Front St. and **Smythe** at 101 Arch St. If you continued north and east, you would come to the attractive new clubs and restaurants on the water, such as **Meiji-en, Rock Lobster,** and **The Beach Club.** Instead, take a left onto:

6. **Elfreth's Alley** (from 1702), the oldest continuously occupied group of homes in America (see "More Attractions" in Chapter 7 for a full description). The homes are tiny, and you can enter no. 126. Several courts are perfect for wandering.

Back on 2nd Street with its china and restaurant supply stores, you might detour north for a minute to look at **2nd Street Art Building,** housing the Clay Studio and NEXUS galleries, or to visit the:

7. **Fireman's Hall Museum,** at Quarry Street, housed in an 1876 firehouse.

Then head south to Arch Street, turning right onto it to the:

8. **Betsy Ross House,** at no. 239 (see Chapter 7 for full details). It's a short walk through the house, but there's a large garden. Directly opposite are the **Mulberry Market,** an upscale deli with seating in the rear, and **Humphry Flags** if you're feeling patriotic.

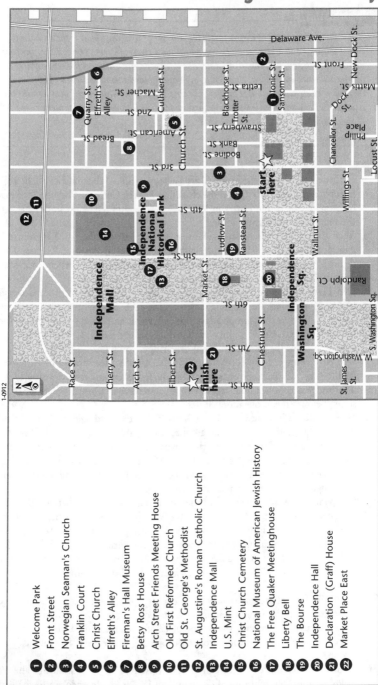

1-0912

Delaware Ave.

start here

finish here

Independence Mall

Independence National Historical Park

Independence Sq.

Washington Sq.

1 Welcome Park
2 Front Street
3 Norwegian Seaman's Church
4 Franklin Court
5 Christ Church
6 Elfreth's Alley
7 Fireman's Hall Museum
8 Betsy Ross House
9 Arch Street Friends Meeting House
10 Old First Reformed Church
11 Old St. George's Methodist
12 St. Augustine's Roman Catholic Church
13 Independence Mall
14 U.S. Mint
15 Christ Church Cemetery
16 National Museum of American Jewish History
17 The Free Quaker Meetinghouse
18 Liberty Bell
19 The Bourse
20 Independence Hall
21 Declaration (Graff) House
22 Market Place East

145

Impression

It is a handsome city, but distractingly regular. After walking about it for an hour or two, I felt that I would have given the world for a crooked street. The collar of my coat appeared to stiffen, and the brim of my hat to expand, beneath its Quakery influence. My hair shrunk into a sleek short crop, my hands folded themselves upon my breast of their own calm accord, and thoughts of taking lodgings in Mark Lane over against the Market Place, and of making a large fortune by speculations in corn, came over me involuntarily.

—Charles Dickens, *American Notes* (1842)

Cross 3rd Street to the **Hoop Skirt Factory** at 309–313 Arch St., a light 1875 factory renovated in 1980, and the charming **Loxley Court** just beyond, designed by carpenter Benjamin Loxley in 1741. It stayed within the family until 1901. On the south side of the street is the:

9. **Arch Street Friends Meeting House,** the largest Quaker meetinghouse in America, a simple 1805 structure with a substantial history (see Chapter 7 for details). You could keep walking straight west one block to Independence Mall, but I recommend that you take a slightly gritty walk north on 4th Street to:

10. **Old First Reformed Church,** at 151 N. 4th St. Built in 1837 for a sect of German Protestants, the building survived a late 19th-century stint as a paint warehouse. Note that this church functions as a small and always full youth hostel during July and August nights (see Chapter 5 for details). Crossing under the gloomy piers of the **Benjamin Franklin Bridge,** you'll see:

11. **Old St. George's Methodist,** at 235 N. 4th St., the cradle of American Methodism and the scene of fanatic religious revival meetings in the early 1770s. The bridge was in fact built farther south to preserve it. On the other side of the street, below Vine, is one more church:

12. **St. Augustine's Roman Catholic Church**. It's another 18th-century building, this one built for German and Irish Catholics who couldn't make it south of Market Street. Villanova University, and the Augustinian presence in the United States, started here. This building is actually an 1844 structure, built to replace the original, which burned down during anti-Catholic riots. Now, keep walking west along the bridge to 5th Street, then head south along:

13. **Independence Mall,** a swath of urban renewal that bit off more than the Historical Park could chew. At the upper end of the Mall (Florist Street) is the bicycle and pedestrian entrance to the Benjamin Franklin Bridge; biking and walking across the bridge make thrilling but time-consuming expeditions. Mayor Ed Rendell is making a major push to site a $20 million new National Constitution Center here by the year 2000. Continuing on, it's best to head down 5th Street, stopping at the:

14. **U.S. Mint,** one of the three places in the country that churns out U.S. coinage (see Chapter 7 for its hours and description). Just south of the U.S. Mint is:

15. **Christ Church Cemetery,** the resting place of Benjamin and Deborah Franklin and other notables (toss a coin through the opening in the brick wall for luck), and also the:

16. **National Museum of American Jewish History,** at 55 N. 5th St. The city of Philadelphia has a history of distinguished Jewish involvement in town affairs almost as long as the life of the town itself. The museum, connected to the city's oldest congregation, commemorates this story (see Chapter 7 for a fuller

description). You'll notice how much lower street level used to be by looking at the statuary outside.

In Independence Mall, a small building across from the Franklin graves is the:

17. **Free Quaker Meetinghouse,** run by the Park Service. These "Fighting Quakers," such as Betsy Ross, were willing to support the Revolutionary War; since this violated the tenets of pure Quakerism, they were read out of Arch Street Friends.

Now, recross Market Street to see the:

18. **Liberty Bell,** if you haven't seen it yet (see Chapter 7 for details). Near the Liberty Bell is:

19. **The Bourse,** a 19th-century exchange that now contains a food court and pleasant urban mall (a "Take a Break" stop described in the "Historic Highlights" tour above). Reenter Independence Mall and you'll be in front of:

20. **Independence Hall,** with its two flanking buildings, **Congress Hall** and **Old City Hall.**

Continue west along Chestnut Street to 7th Street, and turn right onto a historic block containing the **Atwater Kent Museum** of city memorabilia, the **Balch Institute of Ethnic Studies,** and:

21. **Declaration (Graff) House,** a reconstruction of the lodgings where Thomas Jefferson drafted the Declaration of Independence. It is run by the National Park Service, with free daily admission. (All of the above are described more fully in Chapter 7.)

From the old to the new: Right behind Graff House on Market Street is a huge McDonald's designed for children; directly opposite it on Market Street is:

22. **Market Place East,** the converted and rehabilitated former home of Lit Brothers Department Store, a wrought-iron palace that's a block long (see the full description in Chapter 9). The below-ground food area contains an **Au Bon Pain** and **Pagano's** charcuterie.

3 Midtown & the Parkway

Start: Visitors Center, 16th Street and John F. Kennedy Boulevard.
Finish: Logan Circle, intersection of 19th Street, Race Street, and the Benjamin Franklin Parkway.
Time: 6 hours.
Best Time: No later than noon, to avoid museum closings.
Worst Time: Sunday, when many stores are closed, and Monday, when most museums are shuttered.

This tour encompasses the confident heart of 19th-century Philadelphia. If you've already sampled the charm and excitement of historic Philadelphia, the downtown area and southwest of Center City may seem anticlimactic. But there's plenty to see here, too, starting with the massive French Renaissance City Hall. Center Square and its environs were farmland or parkland during the 18th century. But as commercial buildings and loft warehouses began to dominate Old City, old Philadelphia families began to consider Rittenhouse Square to be the fashionable part of town. Individual dwellings, such as Hockley House (1875) at 235 S. 21st St. and the present Art Alliance Building on Rittenhouse Square, coexist with attractive row houses such as those at 18th Street and Delancey Place. Churches, the Academy of Fine Arts (at Broad and Cherry), the Academy of Music (at Broad and Locust), and such private clubs as the Union League (at Broad and Sansom) enhanced the Victorian lifestyle.

The 20th century has added skyscrapers to the business district, notably the international style PSFS Building and such postmodern structures as I. M. Pei's

Commerce Square (41 stories, at Market and 21st Streets) and Helmut Jahn's One and Two Liberty Place (61 and 54 stories, respectively, three blocks east). This is also a wonderful shopping, cultural, and restaurant area, catering to up-to-the-minute tastes.

Start your walking tour at the:

1. **Visitors Center,** run by the Philadelphia Convention and Visitors Bureau at 16th Street and John F. Kennedy Boulevard. The Visitors Center has it all in a shiny wedding cake of a building that's open daily from 9am to 6pm. Half-priced tickets to many evening events are sold here as well.

Passing by Robert Indiana's *LOVE* statue, you'll reach:

2. **City Hall.** You can't help knowing where City Hall is, at the intersection of Broad and Market Streets. This fanciful, exuberant hodgepodge graced with a huge statue of William Penn has free tours and elevators to the viewing area at Penn's feet. Until Liberty Place was built, Penn's hat was by custom the tallest point within city limits. (See Chapter 7 for full details.)

Everyone wonders what that chiseled-looking building just north of City Hall with the single tower is—a church? No, it's the:

3. **Masonic Temple,** one of the world's largest (see Chapter 7 for a full description).

Continue two blocks up North Broad Street to:

4. **Museum of American Art of the Pennsylvania Academy of Fine Arts,** founded in 1804. This 1876 building is now overshadowed by the Philadelphia Museum of Art as *the* museum in town, but it hosts an excellent blend of the best in old and new American art, in a wonderful renovated High Victorian building (see Chapter 7 for details).

Now backtrack to City Hall and head east through:

5. **Hecht's,** now a shadow of its former self as Wanamaker's but still an impressive department store. It features an enormous pipe organ; an atrium; and "the Iggle," a central statue of our national bird that has been a rendezvous for generations of shoppers (see Chapter 9 for details).

Back on Market Street, you'll pass the classic international style **Philadelphia Savings Fund Society (PSFS) Building** skyscraper at 12th Street. Directly opposite that is:

6. **Reading Terminal,** once a commuter terminal but now the facade of the brand-new **Pennsylvania Convention Center** (see Chapter 7 for tour details). The **Reading Terminal Market,** just north of Market Street, is one of the country's great surviving urban food markets (see Chapter 6 for the delicious details).

Three blocks south, Locust and 12th Streets are the center for:

7. **Philadelphia's littlest streets,** a group of wonderfully charming row houses tucked into alleys and courtyards. My favorites are the art clubs of **South Camac Street** between 12th and 13th Streets and between Locust and Spruce Streets, followed by **Manning, Sartain, Quince,** and **Jessup** Streets, between 11th and 12th Streets at the same latitude. If you care to continue two blocks south, you'll find **Antique Row** lining Pine Street with galleries between 9th and 12th Streets.

The 1300 block of Locust Street has two wonderful collections. The finest collection of colonial furniture and art in Center City won't be found at any museum but at the:

8. **Historical Society of Pennsylvania,** 1300 Locust St. (see Chapter 7 for a full description). Alas, exhibits open to the public will cease in July 1997. The modern, connected:

1 Visitors Center
2 City Hall
3 Masonic Temple
4 Pennsylvania Academy of Fine Arts
5 Hecht's
6 Pennsylvania Covention Center/Reading Terminal
7 Philadelphia's littlest streets
8 Historical Society of Pennsylvania
9 Library Company of Philadelphia
10 South Broad Street ("Avenue of the Arts")
11 Academy of Music
12 The Bellevue Hotel
13 Rittenhouse Square area shopping
14 Rittenhouse Square
15 Rosenbach Museum and Library
16 Liberty Place
17 Penn Center (the former Suburban) Station
18 Logan Circle
19 Cathedral-Basilica of Sts. Peter and Paul
20 Academy of Natural Sciences
21 Franklin Institute Science Museum and Futures Center
22 Free Library of Philadelphia
23 Rodin Museum

9. **Library Company of Philadelphia,** at no. 1314, is the current home of Ben Franklin's original lending library. It contains 300,000 volumes, including Lewis and Clark's records of their 1804 expedition. Grand old houses lie across the street at no. 1319 and no. 1321 Locust.

   From here, walk past the Doubletree Hotel Philadelphia to:

10. **South Broad Street,** once the undisputed cultural capital of the city, now picking up steam as a revitalized "Avenue of the Arts." For reasons of safety and convenience, the city is pushing to link this stretch in an unbroken series of theaters and performance halls. So far, the Philadelphia College of Art at Broad and Pine has become the University of the Arts; the Clef Club, Arts Bank, and Wilma Theater buildings are all up and running; and construction of a new home for the Philadelphia Orchestra is pending. The:

11. **Academy of Music** is modeled on La Scala in Milan. It is open for daytime tours or evening performances of the Philadelphia Orchestra, one of the best ensembles in the country (see Chapter 10 for details). Walk one block north (passing Philadelphia's most opulent health club) to:

12. **The Bellevue Hotel,** the current incarnation of a grand 1901 hostelry. Thomas Edison designed the lighting fixtures; it's worth a peek at the former lobby, now the site for the **Shops at the Bellevue** and the below-ground **Food Court** (public restrooms and refueling available). (See Chapters 5 and 6 for full information.)

    Keep walking north to the **Union League** at Broad and Sansom Streets, the most evident of Philadelphia's many private clubs. This one was formed and constructed in the flush of Civil War sentiment for the Republican Party. Then backtrack to Walnut Street and next turn left to:

13. **Rittenhouse Square area shopping**. The blocks between Broad and 18th are dotted with the city's finest independent stores (see Chapter 9 for a full listing). You'll pass the city's (and probably the country's) highest concentration of great restaurants per foot!

    ☕ **TAKE A BREAK**   For a physical and intellectual pick-me-up, the second floor of **Borders,** the city's best bookstore at 1727 Walnut St., has a comfortable espresso bar with racks of newspapers and magazines. It's open Monday through Friday from 7am to 10pm, Saturday from 9am to 9pm, and Sunday from 11am to 7pm. **Starbucks** at 1528 Walnut St. or **New World Coffee** at 1809 Walnut St. both have several blends and excellent muffins and scones.

14. **Rittenhouse Square** functioned as the city's center of social prestige roughly from 1870 through 1930, or until proper Philadelphians discovered that they could live in the Main Line suburbs permanently. Despite the construction of apartment houses to replace such mansions as **McIlhenny House** at the southwest corner, it still adds a touch of elegance to the city, bolstered by the **Curtis School of Music** at Locust Street and the **Rittenhouse Hotel** (though not by the jagged architecture it inherited). The park itself has splendid curving walks around whimsical fountains and decorative pools, with sunlight or winter chill dappling through the trees.

    South and west of Rittenhouse Square are unusual turn-of-the-century town houses ranging from severe Georgian to fanciful neomedieval. A favorite "summary" street of styles is **Delancey Street,** between Spruce and Lombard Streets. If you detour as far west as 20th Street, you'll be rewarded with the interiors and garden of:

15. Rosenbach Museum and Library, at no. 2010, a shrine of book collectors and lovers of literature (see Chapter 7 for a full description).

From Rittenhouse Square, head north on 18th Street to Chestnut Street, taking a right and following a block to:

16. Liberty Place, a tremendously inviting 1991 urban mall and superb family refueling stop at the second-floor food court. (See Chapter 6 for the cuisine and Chapter 9 for the shops.)

Walking east one block, then north one block, you'll see the Visitors Center. Look northwest, and begin your stroll along Benjamin Franklin Parkway. The Parkway connects City Hall with the welcoming arms of the Philadelphia Museum of Art, just over a mile away, swirling through Logan Circle and its fountain en route. The last decade's explosive growth of the new corporate headquarters in town has solidified the many grand cultural institutions built on its edges. If you visit the cultural attractions, you can pick up a "Parkway Passport" offering discounts on most local restaurants—and vice versa.

Walking up from the **Visitors Center** at 16th Street and John F. Kennedy Boulevard, you'll pass:

17. Penn Center (the former Suburban) Station, a compact art-deco terminal whose street level has been transformed into the inviting **Marathon Grill.** An underground concourse linking the station to City Hall also contains dozens of shops, services, and food vendors. A left turn brings you onto the Parkway itself.

Two blocks up, the Parkway intersects with Cherry and 17th Streets. On the Parkway's north side, **Friends Select School,** a leading Quaker-founded preparatory school, occupies new headquarters in the Pennwalt Building, while on the south side, **Marabella's** dishes up Tuscan pastas and antipasti for hungry grazers. One block west on Cherry Street, **Dock Street Brewing Co.** dispenses American bistro fare and beer, freshly brewed on the premises, in a relaxed setting. A block farther, past **TGI Friday's** and the rounded marble tower of the **Embassy Suites Hotel,** lies:

18. Logan Circle. Originally a square, it was converted with the Parkway construction. This most corporate and institutional setting of all of William Penn's original city parks has the lowest buildings surrounding it. The highlight is the 1920 **Swann Fountain,** designed by Alexander S. Calder with evocations of the three waters (Delaware, Schuylkill, Wissahickon) that nourish Philadelphia.

At the eastern end of Logan Circle is the:

19. Cathedral-Basilica of Sts. Peter and Paul. Built in 1846, this sober Roman church with a copper dome made the statement that Catholics would recover and populate a newer part of Center City after the anti-Catholic riots of the early 1840s.

Continue walking clockwise around Logan Circle. The four-story **Four Seasons Hotel** was sensitively designed not to intrude architecturally; furthermore, the hotel renovated the Swann Fountain in the mid-1980s and maintains its hothouse gardens. Afternoon tea at the **Fountain Café** within is a quintessential Philadelphia experience.

Just past 19th Street on Logan Circle is the:

20. Academy of Natural Sciences, displaying flora and fauna from the world over, from dinosaurs to contemporary volcanoes (see Chapter 7 for details).

Next to the academy is **Moore College of Art,** with its street-level exhibition space open to the public. Taking up the whole west side of Logan Circle is the neoclassical facade of the:

21. Franklin Institute Science Museum and Futures Center, a top attraction (see the details in Chapter 7). Don't forget that even without admission you can eat at the entranceway at **Ben's Café.** With a detour two blocks south on 21st Street, you'll come to the **Please Touch Museum** (also see Chapter 7).

To the north side lie both the:

22. Free Library of Philadelphia, with a wonderful Children's Library as well as research and circulating collections and an inexpensive rooftop cafeteria (again, Chapter 7 has the details), and the twin **Municipal Court Building.**

If you continue up toward the **Philadelphia Museum of Art** on the north side of the Parkway from the Free Library, two blocks up you'll come to the ancillary collection of the:

23. Rodin Museum, bequeathed to the city in the 1920s and renovated in 1989. It has a very pleasant outdoor sculpture garden in a leafy atmosphere (see the full description in Chapter 7).

Shopping 9

In colonial days, Philadelphia was one of the most interesting shopping marts in the world. Franklin's *Autobiography* tells of his surprise upon coming to breakfast one morning to find a china bowl and silver spoon: "Luxury will enter families and make a progress in spite of principle." Due to its proximity to New York City, Philadelphia has plenty of goods to help luxury enter your life.

1 The Shopping Scene

The best places to look for high fashion and international wares are the specialty shops around **Liberty Place** and **Rittenhouse Square.** Virtually all of these boutiques are duplicated in one of the enormous malls to the north of the city, in **King of Prussia**—a 450-store behemoth, second only to Minnesota's Mall of America—and at **Franklin Mills,** an outlet mall that draws four times the traffic of the Liberty Bell. For more contemporary items, **Manayunk** is Philadelphia's hippest neighborhood.

The once-funky area on **South Street,** just south of Society Hill, has turned into big business. Because restaurants and nightlife now line South Street from Front to 8th Streets, many of the 180 stores here are open well into the evening and offer goods ranging from the gentrified to the somewhat grotesque. Along with national reps of **The Gap** and **Tower Records,** the stores I recommend are **Queen Village Flowers,** 700 S. 2nd St. (☎ **215/925-0484**); antique and contemporary fashions at **Xog,** 340 South St. (☎ **215/925-0907**); and terrific books and records at **The Book Trader,** 5th and South Streets (☎ **215/925-0219**).

There is no sales tax on clothing; other items are taxed at 7%. Most stores stay open during regular business hours on Monday through Friday, on Saturday, and later on Wednesday evening. Some are also open on Sunday.

OUTLET MALLS & SHOPPING CENTERS

Ⓢ **Franklin Mills.** 1455 Franklin Mills Circle. Follow the signs from I-95 (take Exit 24 north) or from Pa. 276 [take Exit 28 south]. ☎ **215/632-1500.**

About 15 miles northeast of Center City on the edge of Bucks County the former Liberty Bell racetrack opened in mid-1989 as Franklin Mills, the city's largest mall, with 1.8 million square feet devoted to 215 discount and outlet stores. There's parking for more than 9,000 cars in four color-coded zones. More recently, Franklin Mills has become a discount shoppers' landmark, with last-call outlets from Saks Fifth Avenue, Neiman Marcus, Nordstrom, Bally Shoes, Burlington Coat Factory, and Kaspar. For amusement, the **49th Street Galleria** has bowling, roller skating, miniature golf, batting cages, and rides and games. (It's open Monday through Thursday from 10am to 11pm, Friday and Saturday until midnight, and Sunday until 9pm.) If you can't stop there, two ancillary malls are a 61-checkout-lane (that's right, 61 lanes) **Carrefour** supermarket/department store and a 30-store **Home and Design Centre.**

Franklin Mills is open Monday through Saturday from 10am to 9:30pm and Sunday from 11am to 6pm. SEPTA trains go right to the complex.

The Gallery at Market East. 8th to 11th and Market sts. ☎ **215/625-4962.**

The Gallery at Market East, next to the Pennsylvania Convention Center, is built on four levels accommodating more than 170 stores and restaurants around sunken arcades and a glass atrium. The JC Penney department store, at the 10th Street corner of Market Street, has fit in Gimbel's shoes, and Clover in the old Stern's. The **food court** has over 25 snack bars and take-out spots. The **Hardshell Café,** at the street corner of 9th and Market, offers all-you-can-eat specials. Stores offer running shoes, books, pets, cameras, jewelry, fresh produce, toys, and all the clothing that you could ever need. **Strawbridge's** connects over 9th Street with merchandise of slightly higher quality and prices. You can pick up a substantial coupon discount book at the Gallery's Information Center, which also provides city maps and sells SEPTA day passes and PHLASH bus passes. It's open Monday, Tuesday, Thursday, and Saturday from 10am to 7pm, Wednesday and Friday from 10am to 8pm, and Sunday from noon to 5pm.

✪ **King of Prussia Court and Plaza.** Near junction of U.S. 202 and Pa. 363, one-half mile south of I-276; 3 miles south of Valley Forge National Historical Park via Rte. 422. ☎ ~~215~~/ **265-5727.**

People have always been drawn to King of Prussia because of its name, though it is generally referred to as the Court and Plaza. It's now the second largest mall in the country, with 450 establishments in three connected tiers, grouped roughly by price range. The major stores include Bloomingdale's, Hecht's, JC Penney, Lord & Taylor, Neiman Marcus, Nordstrom, Strawbridge's, and Sears. Other top-quality boutiques include Hugo Boss, Williams–Sonoma, Hermes, Guess Home Collection, and Tiffany & Co. Choose from 30 restaurants, but there's no in-house entertainment—just shopping. And with 126 acres of parking, don't forget where you left your car.

Market Place East. 701 Market St., between 7th and 8th sts. ☎ **215/592-8905.**

The century-old Lit Brothers Department Store was a sprawling assembly of wrought-iron facades that introduced hundreds of thousands to their first adult clothes. It has been recently and beautifully resuscitated. The ground floor has attracted tenants including **Ross Dress for Less** and **Dress Barn.** The lower level has a food court with atrium seating. There is garage space nearby.

Market Place East is open from 10am to 6pm on Monday through Thursday and Saturday, and until 8pm on Wednesday. Some stores are open noon to 5pm on Sunday.

Shops at the Bellevue. Broad and Walnut sts. ☎ **215/875-8350.**

The lower floors of the Bellevue Hotel have been turned into a very upscale collection of top names in retailing. Browsing here is quite low-key; you'll feel that the wares are displayed in a private club. **Polo/Ralph Lauren** is the third largest in the world, with three floors of mahogany-and-brass splendor and a private elevator. Other tenants include **Tiffany & Co.,** with its extraordinary jewelry, silver, and accessories; **Hope Chest** for intimates and lingerie; **Rizzoli** for books and gifts; **Suky Rosan** for women's fashion; **Vigant** luggage; and **Neuchatel Chocolates.** Dining is at **Ciboulette** on the mezzanine, the **Palm Restaurant,** or the new lower-level food court.

Shops at the Bellevue is open from 10am to 6pm on Monday through Saturday (until 8pm on Wednesday).

✪ **Shops at Liberty Place.** 1625 Chestnut St. between 16th and 17th sts. ☎ **215/851-9055.**

The Liberty Place development is the real thing: It's the handsome 60-story tower that supplanted City Hall as the city's tallest spire, and it contains 70 stores and stalls that together achieve an ambience and a comfort level that are the finest in the city. It's beautifully designed and signed, with many street exits and entrances that curve and converge on a soaring, glass-domed rotunda with teal-blue andbrass accents. Representative of the retailers are **Rand McNally** for maps and children's games, **Brentano's** for books, **The Coach Store** for luggage, **Country Road Australia** and **Warner Bros. Studio Store** for casual clothes, **Handblock** for high-quality Indian clothes and fabrics, and **Jos. A. Bank** and **J. Crew** for traditional clothes. The second floor is a wonderfully convenient, reasonable court where you can eat on the run, with hundreds of well-kept tables and chairs around quality food stalls. Provident Bank operates an automatic teller machine inside near 17th Street, and the garage directly underneath holds 750 cars. The Shops at Liberty Place are open Monday through Saturday from 9:30am to 7pm and Sunday from noon to 6pm.

2 Shopping A to Z

ANTIQUES

Philadelphia is one big attic that's full of the undervalued heirlooms and cast-offs of previous generations. Pine Street from 9th to 12th Streets boasts about 25 stores, many of which do their own refinishing. Old City stores may select any decade from the 1850s through the 1970s, and Germantown Avenue in Chestnut Hill also has a concentration of shops. As in any antique market, you'll have to bring your expertise to the store and you'll have to trust your dealer. There are usually dozens of antique markets every week in the Delaware Valley. Consult the "Weekend" section of the *Philadelphia Inquirer* for details.

Calderwood Gallery. 1427 Walnut St. ☎ **215/568-7475.**

This is an international resource for French art-nouveau and art-deco furnishings, which are beautifully displayed. The prices are reasonable compared to those in New York City.

First Loyalty Antiques. 1036 Pine St. ☎ **215/592-1670.**

The displays of Victorian and art-deco furnishings and jewelry here are remarkably uncluttered compared to others in the neighborhood.

Freeman Fine Arts. 1808 Chestnut St. ☎ **215/563-9275.**

The dean of the nation's auction houses since 1805, Freeman's stages a full auction every Wednesday (previews on Monday and Tuesday). They specialize in most Americana. Special fully cataloged auctions for jewelry and fine furniture are held here about once a month. Regular auctions include standard home furnishings and some fine silver, rugs, jewelry, and decorative arts.

✪ Gargoyles. 512 S. 3rd St. ☎ **215/629-1700.**

In Society Hill, my personal favorite is Gargoyles, which has everything from toothpick holders to mantels and bars. Although much of the stock is American, there's also a delightful selection of English pub signs, dart boards, and the like. Several large items have been salvaged from 19th-century buildings and businesses.

M. Finkel and Daughter. 936 Pine St. ☎ **215/627-7797.**

Finkel is one of the true anchors of the Pine Street neighborhood. Look here for folk art, furniture, and painting. And if you're looking for antique needlework samplers, this is the place.

Reese's Antiques. 928–930 Pine St. ☎ **215/922-0796.**

This place is not quite as wonderful as the cigar-store Indian out front, and the help can be nearly as somnolent, but Reese's is one of the oldest Pine Street shops, featuring a large selection of china and silver.

✪ W. Graham Arader III Gallery. 1308 Walnut St. ☎ **215/735-5977.**

Arader has become one of the country's leading rare book, map, and print dealers in the past 15 years because of its aggressive purchasing and higher pricing. You'll find a variety of interesting items here.

ART GALLERIES

The line between museums that exhibit studio artists, such as the Pennsylvania Academy of Fine Arts (PAFA), and galleries that promote sales is smaller here than in many cities. The line between art and crafts is fine also (see "Crafts" below for more listings). Many of the less traditional galleries are in the colonial district or on South Street.

AIA Bookstore and Design Center. 117 S. 17th St. ☎ **215/569-3188.**

This recently renovated gallery specializes in architectural renderings, watercolors, and drawings. They've also added custom framing and home furnishings. Connected to it is an excellent bookstore (see below).

The Eyes Gallery. 402 South St. ☎ **215/925-0193.**

Julia Zagar presents a cheerful assortment of Latin American folk art, including Santos and retablos. Also included are one-of-a-kind articles of clothing and jewelry spread over three floors. Open every day of the week.

Gilbert Luber Gallery. 1220 Walnut St. ☎ **215/732-2996.**

Here you can find superb Japanese and Chinese antique and contemporary graphics and art books. The gallery is branching into antique and contemporary Thai and Indonesian objects. Exhibitions change every two months.

Gross-McCleaf Gallery. 127 S. 16th St. ☎ **215/665-8138.**

Now in its 27th year, this gallery features exhibits of regional painters. The focus is on painterly realism, including landscape, still life, and figurative work.

Helen Drutt. 1721 Walnut St. ☎ **215/735-1625.**

Among the private galleries, Helen Drutt has influential shows of crafted objects of fiber, clay, and metal—both beautiful and utilitarian. Winter hours are Wednesday through Saturday from 10am to 5pm; summer hours are Wednesday and Thursday from 11am to 5pm and Friday from 11am to 4pm.

Fleisher. 211 S. 17th St. ☎ **215/545-7562.**

This gallery is known for carrying the finest works by American self-taught artists as well as emerging contemporary artists.

Locks. 600 Washington Sq. South. ☎ **215/629-1000.**

This is another powerhouse gallery for paintings, sculptures, and mixed-media works. Gallery 1 is frequently devoted to group theme shows, and the smaller Gallery 2 usually focuses on a single artist.

Makler. 225 S. 18th St. ☎ **215/735-2540.**

Makler presents the weightiest contemporary artists, such as Louise Nevelson and Jim Dine. By appointment only.

✪ **Newman Galleries.** 1625 Walnut St. ☎ **215/563-1779.**

The oldest gallery in Philadelphia (it was founded in 1865), Newman Galleries provides a very strong representation of Bucks County artists and of American sculptors and painters in general. Custom framing and art conservation are also available.

✪ **Philadelphia Art Alliance.** Rittenhouse Square, 251 S. 18th St. ☎ **215/545-4302.**

The three floors of local talent here are chosen by the alliance's committee of laypersons and artists. Most of the material—pottery, sculpture, and hangings—already has a stamp of approval.

The School Gallery of the Pennsylvania Academy of Fine Arts. 1301 Cherry St. ☎ **215/569-2797.**

The first art school in the country has student and faculty exhibits that change frequently during the year. Housed in a gorgeous rehab near the Convention Center, it's open daily from 9am to 7pm. Admission is free.

✪ **Snyderman Gallery.** 303 Cherry St. ☎ **215/238-9576.**

Snyderman Gallery is one of my favorites. It recently moved from South Street to a 6,000-square-foot space in Old City. The gallery now focuses primarily on painting, sculpture, and studio artists working in wood, clay, and glass.

BOOKSTORES

AIA Bookstore and Design Center. 117 S. 17th St. at Sansom St. ☎ **215/569-3188.**

Boasting some of the finest shelves you'll see anywhere, this bookstore has expanded to include gardening along with architecture and design. It also offers an excellent downstairs gallery of architectural renderings, watercolors, and drawings. A triple "Best of Philly" award winner.

Book Trader. 501 South St. ☎ **215/925-0219.**

If you're on South Street and feel like browsing or just resting, Book Trader has a fine paperback collection and benches, along with a resident cat. It's open until midnight on most nights. You can also find a good selection of out-of-print books, American fiction, and used LPs, tapes, and CDs.

The Bookstore of the University of Pennsylvania. 3729 Locust Walk at 37th St. ☎ **215/898-7595.**

Obviously, you'll find complete course readings for thousands of courses, but you'll also find excellent selections of quality fiction and nonfiction and children's books. The Bookstore carries stationery, gifts, and has a film-developing service as well.

Joseph Fox Bookstore. 1724 Sansom St. ☎ **215/563-4184.**

This bookstore has choice selections in art, graphic design, architecture, photography, current and classic fiction, and books for children.

COLONIAL REPRODUCTIONS

Fried Brothers. 467 N. 7th St. ☎ **800/356-5050** or 215/627-3205.

Near the Edgar Allan Poe National Historical Site, Fried Brothers specializes in hardware suitable for colonial buildings and furnishings. If you admire the doorknobs in Society Hill, you'll see the like here.

CRAFTS

Philadelphia artisanry has always commanded respect. The tradition lingers on, in both small individual workshops and cooperative stores. The Old City section, north of Society Hill, has seen a mushrooming of contemporary crafts and design stores. The Craft Show held every November is one of the top five in the country.

For outdoor crafts vendors, check **Independence Mall** during summer weekends, although flea-market items seem to predominate there. **Head House Square** becomes a bustling bunch of booths all day Saturday and on Sunday afternoon from April through September.

✪ **The Black Cat.** 3424 Sansom St. ☎ **215/386-6664.**

Next door to the White Dog Café, Judy Wicks has set up a charming arts-and-crafts store that's open until 9pm on Monday through Wednesday, 11pm Thursday through Sunday. Living-room knickknacks are displayed in a living room, and so forth. Also, there's a small number of antiques and near antiques.

The Fabric Workshop and Museum. 1315 Cherry St., 5th floor. ☎ **215/922-7303.**

This is the only nonprofit arts organization in the U.S. devoted to creating new work in fabric and other materials. They operate in collaboration with both emerging and recognized artists. Don't miss the bags, scarves, ties, and umbrellas of Venturi and Red Grooms designs. It's close to the new Convention Center.

Moderne. 111 N. 3rd St. ☎ **215/923-8536.**

This Old City stalwart gives a slant to European art-deco furniture. It offers a very good selection of American and French ironworks—furniture and decorative items. They've also added inventory from the 1940s and 1950s, along with vintage pieces by woodworker George Nakashima. Books and fabrics appropriate to 20th-century design are also available.

OLC. 152–154 N. 3rd St. ☎ **215/923-6085.**

OLC, in the Old City, has 6,000 feet of sophisticated lighting and furnishings displayed in a museum-quality setting that's been cited by the American Institute of Architects.

✪ **Thos. Moser Cabinetmakers.** 1401 Walnut St. ☎ **215/569-8848.**

Recently relocated to Rittenhouse Row is one of this country's great craftsmen of wooden furniture—or his store at least, since Tom Moser lives and works out of Maine. The beds, cabinets, desks, and chairs here are inspired by Shaker and other rural American designs, and the execution and finishes are wondrous. Custom furniture inquiries are welcome.

The Works Gallery. 303 Cherry St. ☎ **215/922-7775.**

Recently relocated to Old City, the specialties here are ceramics, glass creations, and furniture transcending the boundary between craft and art. Photography is also tucked in between rooms.

DEPARTMENT STORES

Hecht's. Between Market and Chestnut and 13th and Juniper sts. ☎ **215/422-2000.**

As Wanamaker's, this was one of the first of the great department stores in the country, and a real city institution. Several owners later, it's a subdivision of May Department Stores. The present building (1902–10) fills a city block and is modeled ingeniously on Renaissance motifs, which give its 12 stories proportion and grace.

Ralph Lauren now has a first-floor boutique. The store also contains various snack bars. On the first floor, there's an Adrien Arpel salon, a chiropodist on call at the shoe salon, and an estate-jewelry counter. On the mezzanine, you'll find a service center with a post office, film developer, travel bureau, dry cleaner, and optometrist. The retail area has shrunk from eight to five floors, with three stories of commercial offices on top. A five-story court presents Christmas shows with a massive 30,000-pipe organ; this court also hosts daily organ concerts at 11:15am and 5:15pm.

Strawbridge's. 8th and Market sts. ☎ **215/629-6000.**

Formerly Strawbridge & Clothier, this once family-run store was bought by the May company in July 1996 and reopened as Strawbridge's. It quietly anchors the Market East neighborhood. Now connected to the Gallery Mall, it carries a full line over three stories; its prices and boutiques are moderately scaled, with frequent sales of 20% to 30% off. It contains an underrated but excellent food hall.

DISCOUNT SHOPPING

Daffy's. 17th and Chestnut sts. ☎ **215/963-9996.**

Bonwit Teller occupied this handsome four-story site for decades, and from December 1992 Daffy's has presented excellent value for name and house brands for men, women, and children. Prices are 40% to 75% off regular retail, and men's and women's Italian suits, fine leather items on the third floor, and lingerie are particular bargains. And Kirk Windra does terrific windows.

Eddie Bauer Outlet Store. 1411 Walnut St. ☎ **215/569-9691.**

Better known through its catalog, Eddie Bauer is tucked into an excellent location for superior preppie/outdoor men's and women's clothes. Items are (mostly) overstocks rather than defective, and discounting starts at 30% and goes beyond 50%, although selection is not complete. Women's clothes tend to run large.

Filene's Basement. 1608 Chestnut St. ☎ **215/864-9080.**

This Boston discounter has finally moved into Center City. Lines such as Barneys New York can be seen here, though expect more along the lines of Jones New York. You'll find great accessories here.

House of Bargains. 1939–1943 Juniper St. ☎ **215/465-8841.**

This South Philly institution for children's clothes stocks a remarkable assembly of brand names anywhere from 40% to 80% off retail prices. It's actually located at the intersection of South Broad Street and Passyunk Avenue, where postshopping treats abound.

Night Dressing. 2100 Walnut St. ☎ **215/563-2828.** Also at 724 S. 4th St. (☎ 215/627-5244).

Locations in Rittenhouse Square and Society Hill carry Lily of France, Olga, Warners, and so forth, almost all at half price. New arrivals come in almost daily. There's a big selection of sleepwear and robes.

Ron Friedman Co. 14 S. 3rd St. ☎ **215/922-4877.**

Save 40% to 60% on American and imported leather handbags, wallets, and briefcases.

FASHION

Look for the more conservative styles in the many stores around Rittenhouse Square and in the department stores and the more sharply styled or contemporary fashions on South Street and in the malls. Remember, clothing carries no state sales tax.

Burberrys Limited. 1705 Walnut St. ☎ **215/557-7400.**

Burberrys has all the suits, raincoats, and accessories suitable for gentlemen and ladies.

J. Crew. Liberty Place, 1625 Chestnut St. ☎ **215/977-7335.**

This store offers a nice merging of casual with formal clothes, all brightly colored and softly styled, plus beautiful cable-knit sweaters. It's a meeting place for high-school and college-aged students.

✪ **The Original I. Goldberg.** 902 Chestnut St. ☎ **215/925-9393.**

An army–navy paradise and then some for three generations, I. Goldberg provides at excellent prices the basic goods that you'll need for anything in the outdoors, with styles from the determinedly antifashion to up-to-the-minute. The selection is very large, but the help is harried.

Polo/Ralph Lauren. The Shops at the Bellevue, Broad and Walnut sts. ☎ **215/985-2800.**

The new Polo/Ralph Lauren has its own private elevator and fabulous settings for the plushest suitings in town.

Urban Outfitters. 1801 Walnut St. ☎ **215/564-2313.** Also at 4040 Locust St. (☎ 215/387-0373).

Housed in a turn-of-the-century mansion on the corner of Rittenhouse Square, this store has been branching off from the conservative preppy look. The basement has a terrific greeting card selection, along with an unusual children's, home furnishings, and book selection.

CHILDREN'S FASHION

Born Yesterday. 1901 Walnut St. ☎ **215/568-6556.**

Right on Rittenhouse Square, this store fits babies, boys to size 8, and girls to size 10. The fashions are always current, with a good sense of style and selection of classics. This is a "Best of Philly" store for unique baby gifts, with an attentive staff.

The Children's Boutique. 1717 Walnut St. ☎ **215/563-3881.**

This place features many all-cotton, color-coordinated outfits by local designers and a good selection of top-of-the-line traditional children's clothes. The store also has a large infant department and stocks some toys.

Kamikaze Kids. 527 S. 4th St. ☎ **215/574-9800.**

Aggressively styled fashion wear is sold here. The stock ranges from tights to hair ornaments—everything the urban chic child needs. It also stocks incredible Halloween costumes. The items are not cheap.

K.I.D.S. Children's Shoe Boutique. 56 N. 3rd St. ☎ **215/592-9033.**

Somewhere between a postmodern carnival and a shoe store, this place is very convenient to Franklin Court and other Independence Hall sites.

MEN'S FASHION

Black Tie. 1120 Walnut St. ☎ **215/925-4404.**

If formal wear is a sudden necessity, sales and rentals can be found at Black Tie. It carries Lord West, After Six, Bill Blass, and other suave styles, as well as custom tailoring and accessories and shirts.

✪ **Boyd's.** 1818 Chestnut St. ☎ **215/564-9000.**

Under the Gushner family, Boyd's has moved "uptown" to a beautifully restored blue-and-white commercial palace. It's the largest in the city, with 65 tailors on site, and has European and American lines of all types, as well as alterations for a variety of fine designers such as Ermenegildo Zegna. Boyd's still has its valet and has added a cafe. Sale periods are January and July.

Brooks Brothers. 1500 Chestnut St. ☎ **215/564-4100.**

Brooks Brothers won't steer you wrong on perfectly acceptable items for business and casual wear; slimmer men should head for the Brooksgate section because the regular styles are cut generously.

Wayne Edwards. 1521 Walnut St. ☎ **215/563-6801.**

This stretch of Walnut Street is really the block for fashion. Wayne Edwards sports a slightly larger selection of contemporary styles than nearby Allure.

WOMEN'S FASHION

✪ **Boyd's.** 1818 Chestnut St. ☎ **215/564-9000.**

Boyd's, a superb men's fashion mansion, leapt into the women's wear game in fall 1993 with a third-floor boutique. Look for classic suits, dresses, and casual wear by names such as Yves St. Laurent, Genny, Ungaro, Isaac Mizrahi, and Krizia. They provide free custom alterations and an in-store cafe.

✪ **Knit Wit.** 1721 Walnut St. ☎ **215/564-4760.**

Now in a chic new location, Knit Wit specializes in the latest in contemporary fashions and accessories for women. Sales come in March and September.

Mendelsohn. 229 S. 18th St. ☎ **215/546-6333.**

Offered here are stylish clothes for the mature woman with fashion sense. This place feels like a throwback to an earlier, pleasant era in Rittenhouse Square.

Plage Tahiti. 128 S. 17th St. ☎ **215/569-9139.**

A selective store and a 1995 "Best of Philly" winner, Plage Tahiti has original separates with an artistic slant. As the name suggests, French bathing suits are a constant.

Rodier of Paris. 135 S. 18th St. ☎ **215/496-0447.**

This expensive, fashion-forward retailer is now back in Rittenhouse Square, after an untimely fling at The Bourse. The sophisticated clothing offered is designed and manufactured in France.

Toby Lerner. 117 S. 17th St. ☎ **215/568-5760.**

With an intimate setting for clothes, accessories, and shoes, this spot is in one of the most affluent neighborhoods in town—and the prices reflect this. Selections in-clude Armani, Anne Klein, Calvin Klein, and Moschino, with lower-priced lines from Jenne Maag, Votre Nom, and others.

FOOD

✪ **The Reading Terminal Market** at 12th and Market Streets, with its dozens of individual booths and cafes, has been recommended in Chapter 6. Also, see the "Local Favorites" section at the end of Chapter 6.

Assouline and Ting. 314 Brown St. ☎ **215/627-3000.**

This superb gourmet market 12 blocks north of Market Street requires a special trip north of the Liberty Bell by car, but the prices make a detour worth contemplating. There's a very active schedule of master classes with Philly's best chefs.

✪ **Chef's Market.** 231 South St. ☎ **215/925-8360.**

The premier gourmet store in Society Hill is Chef's Market, with a staggering array of charcuterie, cookbooks, and condiments. Would you believe this place stocks breads and cakes supplied by 20 bakeries?

Italian Market. 9th St. between Christian and Wharton sts.

The Italian Market comes straight out of another era, with about 150 push-carts and open stalls selling fresh goods, produce, and cheese from Tuesday through Saturday (the end of the week is better). Many shops are open until noon on Sunday. Particular favorites are **DiBruno's** at 930 S. 9th St. for cheese, **Sarcone and Sons** at 758 S. 9th St. for bread, and the pound cake at the **Pasticceria** at 9th and Federal Streets. You can always snack on fried dough or pastries along the route, as well as save money or pick up an espresso machine at **Fante's.** The Italian Market is also a great place to pick up cheap clothes; try **Evantash** lingerie or **Irv's** endless racks. In the next couple of years, look for significant upgrading including street lighting, curb cuts, asphalt paving, and new awnings; some vendors will be relocated. To reach the market, head five blocks south of South Street; SEPTA bus 47 goes south on 8th Street from Market.

Michelfelder's Lunchmeats. 1234 Market St. ☎ **215/568-7948.**

Michelfelder's has links of German and domestic wurst, plus lunch sandwiches. There is another store at the Gallery at Market East (☎ **215/627-2288**).

Pagano's Gourmet. 1507 Walnut St. ☎ **215/568-0891.**

Pagano's stocks a large selection of cheeses, deluxe meats, exotic condiments, and breads and crackers. Gift packages and box lunches are prepared from $7.95. There's a Pagano's Gourmet branch in Penn Center Station Concourse, beneath 17th Street and John F. Kennedy Boulevard (☎ **215/557-0423**).

R&W Delicatessen. 19th and Walnut sts. ☎ **215/563-7247.**

The deli nearest to Rittenhouse Square, R&W has plenty of fixings for do-it-yourself lunches, including hearty noodle pudding.

Rago. 258 S. 20th St. ☎ **215/732-0444.**

A small gem of a store just north of Spruce Street, Rago is run by the same family that operates Fratelli Rago, a fine Italian trattoria three blocks away.

GIFTS & SOUVENIRS

Amy & Friends. 2124 Walnut St. ☎ **215/496-1778** or 215/232-3714.

You have to put up with a fair amount of free-flowing disorder to enjoy this place, but there's a truly eclectic assortment of antiques and bric-a-brac, including Classic Writing, a boutique specializing in top-quality fountain pens.

Country Elegance. 269 S. 20th St. ☎ **215/545-2992.**

Unique gifts and home accessories, along with a great selection of fine and antique linens, are sold here.

✪ **Dandelion.** 1718 Sansom St. ☎ **215/972-0999.**

Proprietor Beth Fluke has traveled to see and buy it all, and has a discriminating sense of handcrafted jewelry and gifts from the American Southwest, the Near East, and East Coast artisans. A great place for wedding or birthday gifts—that is, sophisticated pieces at many different price levels. There's a nice selection of blank cards too.

Details. 131 S. 18th St. ☎ **215/977-9559.**

Sumptuous gifts, such as invitation cards, desktop accessories, picture frames, and stationery, are sold in this turn-of-the-century town house.

Touches. 225 S. 15th St. ☎ **215/546-1221.**

This upscale boutique stocks clothing and accessories, leather goods, boxes, perfume bottles, handmade jewelry, frames, and baby gifts.

Urban Outfitters. 1801 Walnut St. ☎ **215/569-3131.**

Urban Outfitters specializes in campus-trendy furniture, clothing, health foods, kitchen equipment, and fabrics such as Marimekko.

Xenos Candy and Gifts. 231 Chestnut St. ☎ **215/922-1445.**

Miniature Liberty Bells? Snow globes of Independence Hall? Tea towels with the Betsy Ross story? All this and much more, just around the corner from the sites themselves.

JEWELRY & SILVER

Philadelphia is known for all types of jewelry—traditional, one-of-a-kind, heirloom, and contemporary. Most of the city's jewelers occupy two city blocks at **Jeweler's Row,** centering on Sansom and 8th Streets.

Bailey, Banks & Biddle. 16th and Chestnut sts. ☎ **215/564-6200.**

Established in 1832, Bailey, Banks & Biddle has extraordinary silverware and stationery as well as jewelry. It's a huge store (or museum, if you're not looking to spend).

I. Switt. 130 S. 8th St. ☎ **215/922-3830.**

Don't let the crotchety help scare you away; the store does beautiful traditional settings at reasonable prices.

Jack Kellmer. 717 Chestnut St. ☎ **215/627-8350.**

With a magnificent marble showroom, Kellmer imports diamonds by the dozen and sells unusual gold and diamond jewelry.

✪ **J. E. Caldwell & Co.** 1339 Chestnut at Juniper St. ☎ **215/864-7800.**

This is another big and traditional store, founded in 1839. It stocks watches and silver as well as jewelry; lines carried include Waterford, Orrefors, Kosta Boda, Lalique, and

Reed and Barton. It also does repairs, and the building has just been magnificently renovated.

✪ **Jeweler's Row.** Between Sansom and Walnut sts. and 7th and 8th sts.

This area contains more than 350 retailers, wholesalers, and craftspeople. Particularly noted is **Sydney Rosen** at 714 Sansom St. (☎ **215/922-3500**). **Robinson Jewelers,** 730 Chestnut St. (☎ **215/627-3066**), specializes in Masonic jewelry and watch repair.

Linde Meyer Gold & Silver. Liberty Place, 1625 Chestnut St. ☎ **215/851-8555.**

This contemporary nook on the ground floor passage to the central atrium presents contemporary designer jewelry in precious metals, along with a unique collection of estate jewelry.

Niederkorn Silver. 2005 Locust St. ☎ **215/567-2606.**

Antique baby items, dressing-table adornments, napkin rings, picture frames, and Judaica are featured here. Also on display is Philadelphia's largest selection of period silver, including works of such fine crafters as Jensen, Tiffany, and Spratling.

Spiros Doulis. 136 S. 11th St. ☎ **215/922-1199.**

Browsing in this small shop is like looking through your grandmother's jewelry and watch collection—there's a combination of unusual and antique settings and new pieces. They will happily customize pieces and repair watches.

✪ **Tiffany & Co**. The Shops at the Bellevue, 1414 Walnut St. ☎ **215/735-1919.**

Tiffany & Co. is an American institution with an international reputation for quality, craftsmanship, and design. Today, the store has an extensive collection of sterling and jewelry, but also china, crystal, timepieces, writing instruments, and fragrance. Though many items are very expensive here, there are plenty of attractive items under $100.

LUGGAGE

Robinson Luggage Company. Broad and Walnut sts. ☎ **215/735-9859.**

Here you'll find a great selection of leather, along with discounted travel accessories and briefcases.

Travel-Wise. 132 S. 18th St. ☎ **215/563-7001.**

This Rittenhouse Square store carries gadgets and gifts as well as luggage.

MUSIC

✪ **HMV.** 1504 Walnut St. ☎ **215/875-5100.**

How they got zoning approval for a gleaming two-story, double-width cube of a building on Rittenhouse Row's best block is best left unasked—but it's huge, with wonderful depth across all genres and price ranges of CDs.

Jacobs Music Co. 1718 Chestnut St. ☎ **215/568-7800.**

Known primarily as a piano store (since 1900), Jacobs is Center City's best source of sheet music for serious and pop musicians alike (in the same building as Theodore Presser).

Third Street Jazz and Rock. 20 N. 3rd St. ☎ **800/486-8745** or 215/627-3366.

With 20 years of experience and 25,000 CDs in stock, Jerry Gordon has one of the finest collections of jazz in the country. Also featured are new wave, Caribbean, and African music.

✪ **Tower Records.** 610 South St. ☎ **215/574-9888.**

The Los Angeles–based Tower Records stocks virtually all current recordings at lower prices, and the Tower Records Classical Annex across the street at no. 537 (☎ **215/925-0422**) has even lower prices.

SHOES

Aldo. 1625 Chestnut St. ☎ **215/564-4630.**

This new women's shoe store in Liberty Place has classics and up-to-date fashions and great service.

Bottino Shoes. 121 S. 18th St. ☎ **215/854-0907.**

Look here for sharper, more avant-garde European (and particularly Italian) men's and women's fashions.

Dan's Shoes. 1733 Chestnut St. ☎ **215/922-6622.**

Fully guaranteed and tremendously discounted designer shoes are found here. It's more like a bazaar than a full-service store, but there are some real finds along with the regular stuff.

Sherman Brothers. 1520 Sansom St. ☎ **215/561-4550.**

Here over 35 years, and recently expanding into the suburbs, Sherman Brothers has the city's best collection of fine men's shoes like Cole Haan, Allen Edmonds, and Bally, as well as difficult sizes. Everything's discounted 10% to 25% every day.

SPORTING GOODS

City Sports. 1608 Walnut St. ☎ **215/985-5860.**

This 1996 full-service and well-designed store has captured the Center City market.

✪ **The Original I. Goldberg.** 902 Chestnut St. ☎ **215/925-9393.**

An army–navy paradise and then some for three generations, I. Goldberg provides at excellent prices the basic goods that you'll need for anything outdoors, with styles from the determinedly antifashion to up-to-the-minute. The selection is very large, but the help is harried.

TOBACCO

Holt's. 1522 Walnut St. ☎ **215/732-8500.**

Holt's is renowned throughout the country for its selection of pipes and tobaccos. There are enough fresh cigars here to fill every humidor on Wall Street, plus an excellent pen selection. The opulent relocation and late hours fit perfectly with the neighborhood.

TOYS

✪ **Einstein Presents of Mind.** 1624 Chestnut St. ☎ **215/665-3622.**

From Russian dolls to origami, from fossils to Babar the Elephant—it's all here for the 1990s family. The expanded space, just across from Library Place, is wonderful, and the staff creates a sense of festival with the constantly changing displays, although the hurdy-gurdy outside can get wearing. There's a new 11,000-square-foot museum upstairs; 80% of the 4,000 items are for sale.

Past Present Future. 24 S. 18th St. ☎ **215/854-0444.**

Past Present Future sells soft sculpture, custom and wooden handmade toys, and puzzles. I've seen plenty of adults whiling away some time in here. There's also a good selection of toys and gifts for adults, including craft jewelry.

WINE & LIQUOR

After the repeal of Prohibition, Pennsylvania decided not to license private liquor retailing but to establish a government monopoly on alcohol sales. You, or any tavern keeper or restaurateur, can find liquor only in state stores (or at a vineyard within the state). They are usually open Monday through Wednesday from 9am to 5pm and Thursday through Saturday until 9pm. The selection has improved greatly in recent years. For chilled beer or champagne, try a delicatessen, distributor, or licensed supermarket.

Near Independence Hall, **Old City Liquor,** 32 S. 2nd St. (☎ **215/625-0906**), looks—and acts—almost like a nonstate store. It's open Monday and Tuesday from 11am to 7pm and Wednesday through Saturday from 9am to 9pm.

Also in the Independence Hall area, try the **Bourse Building,** 5th and Chestnut Streets (☎ **215/560-5504**); 32 S. 2nd Street (☎ **215/625-0906**); or **Society Hill Shopping Center** (☎ **215/922-4224**). In the City Hall area, there are state stores at 1318 Walnut St. (☎ **215/735-8464**) and 265 S. 10th St. (☎ **215/922-6497**). Around Rittenhouse Square, you might try **The Wine Reserve,** at 205 S. 18th St. (☎ **215/560-4529**), a 1990 upscale version of a state store where consumers can browse freely amid mahogany counters and shelves. Bottles of some 800 wines are stacked horizontally—a first in Philadelphia. In University City there's a state store at 4049 Walnut St. (☎ **215/222-3547**).

3 Manayunk Shopping

This neighborhood, 8 miles up the Schuylkill from the Art Museum and Center City, has rocketed to popularity in the last decade, with some of Philadelphia's hippest restaurants and shops (see Chapter 6 for the former). A wonderful hour's stroll can put you in touch with contemporary crafts, clothing, antiques, and galleries. It helps that the geography is so simple; from the Belmont Avenue exit (north, crossing the Schuylkill River) off I-76 or one block south of the Green Lane SEPTA stop, just follow Main Street east alongside the river from the 4400 to 3900 addresses. Also, a cohesive local development group runs a continual series of attractive weekend festivals and events to attract business. Parking is plentiful, and store hours tend to run late to match dinner reservations.

ART, CRAFTS & GIFTS   I like **Xcessories Inc. by Design,** 4319 Main St. (☎ **215/483-9665**) for its elegant candlesticks, updated Tiffany-style lamps, and contemporary frames; the entrance is on Cotton Street. I'm also partial to **Home Grown,** 4321 Main St. (☎ **215/482-1910**), with kitchenware, tabletop accessories, and home furnishings you'd expect to see in a whimsical, cultured country house. **Owen/Patrick Gallery,** 4345 Main St. (☎ **215/482-9395**), has interesting glass and ceramics; they have much bigger furniture and sculptural art, and carry American West/Urbana upholstered pieces from California. **Artistes en Fleurs,** 4363 Main St. (☎ **215/508-9908**), specializes in hand-painted furnishings and uncommon pieces perfect for gardeners. If you're in the market for a modern watch or clock, you should definitely save a purchase for **Timeworks,** 4386 Main St. (☎ **215/482-5959**)—there are hundreds, in every price range.

FASHION   In two years, **Nicole Miller,** 4249 Main St. (☎ **215/930-0307**), has become the high priestess of high fashion, with little black dresses, cool sportswear, and whimsical men's neckties, formal wear, and boxers. The three delightful Boston sisters run **Ma Jolie Atelier,** 4340 Main St. (☎ **215/483-8850**), in a handsome two-story cross between a boutique and mansion. It's primarily aimed at the fashionable woman from elegant to casual wear, but they've added an adorable kids' fashion area and upstairs cappuccino bar also. **Public Image,** 4390 Main St. (☎ **215/482-4008**), has two stories of designer labels such as Product, Vivienne Tam, Diesel, and Freelance; and **Touchables,** 4309 Main St. (☎ **215/487-7988**), has a very extensive selection of lingerie and nightwear, including Swiss cotton and silk loungewear and peignoirs. **Neo Deco,** 4409 Main St. (☎ **215/487-7757**), sounds dated, but is a very well-chosen selection of men's and women's chic fashions at reasonable prices.

FOOD   It is literally impossible to walk in Manayunk without being seduced, storefront by storefront, by tempting baked goods, sandwiches, coffee bars, sweets, and full-scale restaurants. If your aim is only to purchase for future consumption, the center is probably the **Manayunk Farmer's Market,** 4120 Main St. (☎ **215/ 483-0100**), a former factory near the eastern edge of chic, with a wonderful deck overlooking the river. It's got some true farmstand booths, but also elegantly packaged processed goods of all sorts.

10

Philadelphia After Dark

If you ask Philadelphians to name the biggest change in their city over the last 20 years, the explosion of entertainment and nightlife possibilities will rank right up there with the drain of the manufacturing economy and the restaurant renaissance. From sound-and-light shows at Independence Hall to sound-and-light shows at the Columbus Boulevard dance clubs, there's enough pizzazz and activity in this city to fill months of idle evenings.

The city itself seems a little surprised with its newfound vitality, since Philadelphia has always been known for its sedate domestic pleasures. Individual initiatives on the piers along the Delaware River, Old City north of Society Hill, and the northwest quadrant of Center City have joined South Broad Street and Rittenhouse Square as lively areas for cafe- or barhopping and live entertainment.

Philadelphia's city government has a big economic stake in aiding these efforts, particularly in the renovation of street areas around Independence National Historical Park and the cultural heart of Center City. A project to make South Broad Street into "Avenue of the Arts" is picking up steam, with the new **ARTS BANK** and **Wilma Theater** performance spaces, the revitalized **Merriam Theater,** and an impending new home for the Philadelphia Orchestra. The Academy of Music presents a full season of the marvelous Philadelphia Orchestra and the financially struggling but artistically vital Pennsylvania Ballet. Two or three theaters offer road productions and preliminary versions of Broadway shows, and the Walnut Street Theatre has been going strong since 1809.

The best sources for what's current are the "Weekend" supplement of the *Philadelphia Inquirer* (it comes out on Friday) and the free tabloids *City Paper* and *Philadelphia Weekly,* copies of which are distributed throughout Center City. Most hotel lobbies carry them, as does the Visitors Center, which is also an excellent information source. For monthly happenings, consult the front section of *Philadelphia* magazine.

Most cultural attractions will have individual box offices open until curtain time. Check out **Upstages** (☎ 215/893-1145), the city's premier nonprofit box-office service. Locations are at the Visitors Center, 16th Street and John F. Kennedy Boulevard (☎ 215/567-0670); the ARTS BANK, 601 S. Broad St.; Plays and Players Theater, 1714 Delancey St.; and at the top of the escalators at Liberty Place, 1625 Chestnut St. All are open Tuesday through

Saturday from 10am to 5pm; the Liberty Place location also offers half-price tickets on the day of the show. There's a small service charge.

For commercial attractions from theater to pop shows, an advance call to Teletron (☎ **800/233-4050**), Tele-Charge (☎ **800/833-0080**), or TicketMaster (☎ **215/ 336-2000**) is your best bet. Ticket brokers contract with individual presenters; the surcharge for city brokers such as **Philadelphia Ticket Office,** 1500 Locust St. (☎ **215/735-1903**), is supposed to be limited to 25% above face value. Out-of-state brokers have no limit, so while they may have better selections, the prices could be exorbitant.

Senior citizens can receive discounts of about 10% or $5 per ticket or more at many theaters, including the Annenberg Center, American Music Theater Festival, and Wilma Theater. Concert halls generally make rush or last-minute seats available to students at prices under $10; these programs sometimes extend to adults as well. Groups can generally get discounts of 20% to 50% by calling well in advance.

1 The Performing Arts

Music, theater, and dance are presented regularly all over the city. I have restricted the venues below to Center City and West Philadelphia, where you'll be most of the time and where the quality of entertainment tends to be highest. There's really no off-season for the performing arts in Philadelphia; when the regular seasons of the Philadelphia Orchestra or Pennsylvania Ballet end, the outdoor activities that make Philadelphia so pleasant take over.

OPERA

The **Opera Company Of Philadelphia,** 510 Walnut St., Suite 1600 (☎ **215/ 928-2100**), presents full stagings of four operas per year at the Academy of Music. The performances take place on Monday, Tuesday, Thursday, or Friday evenings and there are Sunday matinees; seating preference is given to season subscribers. Such international opera stars as Benita Valente (who lives down the street), Elena Filipova, and Vinson Cole appear in about half of the productions. They have snagged Luciano Pavarotti to judge and host an annual International Voice Competition, with the winner receiving a role in a production the following season. Tickets cost $20 to $130; half-price amphitheater tickets are available on the day of the performance.

CLASSICAL MUSIC

All-Star Forum. 1530 Locust St. ☎ **215/735-7506.** Tickets $15–$45.

Moe Septee, Philadelphia's top concert impresario, brings recital soloists, chamber groups, dance troupes, and occasionally theater groups to the Academy of Music on weekday nights at 8pm or on Sunday at 3pm. The talent is world-class.

The All-Star Forum also presents the **Philadelphia Pops** in four series per year. Bridging the symphonic and the popular under acclaimed pianist Peter Nero, the Pops sells out for most performances.

Concerto Soloists Chamber Orchestra. 338 S. 15th St. ☎ **215/545-5451**, office or 215/ 893-1145, box office through Upstages. Tickets $15–$35.

Marc Mostovoy has assembled a group of excellent New York visitors and home-grown Curtis graduates for full seasons of chamber music. The concerts take place at the **Church of the Holy Trinity** (☎ **215/567-1267**) near Rittenhouse Square at 19th and Walnut Streets and at the **Convention Center Recital Hall,** 11th and Arch Streets.

✪ **Curtis Institute Of Music.** 1726 Locust St. ☎ **215/893-5252.**

Philadelphia has a surfeit of really excellent musicians and programs, many of them springing from the world-famous Curtis Institute, which was led for many years by Rudolf Serkin and is now headed by Gary Graffman. Curtis itself has a small hall that's good for chamber works, just off Rittenhouse Square; call **215/893-5261** for a schedule of the mostly free concerts, operas, and recitals. Student recitals are on Monday, Wednesday, and Friday. The Curtis Opera Theater presents full-scale productions; tickets are $20.

Mann Music Center. George's Hill near 52nd St. and Parkside Ave. ☎ **215/567-0707** office, or ☎ 215/878-7707, box office. Reserved seats $17–$31.50.

The Mann Music Center presentation of the Philadelphia Orchestra in the six-week PNC Bank Summer Concert Series is one of the delights of summer. Seats in the Fairmount Park amphitheater fill up quickly for all 18 concerts, led by Charles Dutoit and featuring celebrated soloists. Special SEPTA buses travel from Center City and there's plenty of parking available in lots around the Mann for a fee. Concerts are on Monday, Wednesday, and Thursday at 8pm. Tickets for reserved, under-cover seats may be purchased at the Box Office there, or by calling ahead.

If you prefer, you can enjoy music under the stars for free by sitting on grassy slopes above the orchestra. Tickets are required for these lawn seats. Send your request along with a self-addressed, stamped envelope to the Department of Recreation, P.O. Box 1000, Philadelphia, PA 19105. Two is the limit, and requests made too far in advance will be returned. And don't forget the blankets and insect repellent.

Philadelphia Chamber Music Society. 135 S. 18th St. ☎ **215/569-8587.** Tickets $17.50.

Celebrating its 12th season in 1997, the PCMS is committed to bringing renowned international soloists, chamber musicians and jazz artists to the city. All 33 concerts are at the Pennsylvania Convention Center's 600-seat hall. Ticket prices for this quality of artist are exceptionally low.

✪ **Philadelphia Orchestra.** Regular season Sept–May at the Academy of Music, Broad and Locust sts. ☎ **215/893-1900,** or 215/893-1999 to charge tickets. Tickets $12–$80; student rush seats are sold for $7 at 7:30pm for all Tues and Thurs concerts. Unreserved amphitheater seats are sold for $4 at 1:30pm on Fri and 7pm on Fri and Sat.

For many people, a visit to Philadelphia isn't complete without hearing a concert given by the smooth, powerful ensemble under Wolfgang Sawallisch. The orchestra achieved renown under Leopold Stokowski, then was led for 44 years by the legendary Eugene Ormandy and for 12 years by Riccardo Muti. The Philadelphia has built a reputation for virtuosity and balance that only a handful of the world's orchestras can match.

The backbone of its year is the subscription schedule at the Academy of Music. The average season includes 102 concerts: 30 on Saturday evenings, 18 each on Tuesday and Thursday evenings and Friday afternoons, 12 on Friday evenings, and 6 on Sunday afternoons. The orchestra also offers nonsubscription and youth programs. In summer it moves to Mann Music Center for 6 weeks of free concerts (see above). More tickets to individual performances are available than in the past, with certain dress rehearsals open and fewer subscriptions sold. Try to buy tickets well in advance of the date for best seats.

Relâche Ensemble. Various venues. Office at 11 S. Strawberry St. ☎ **215/574-8246.** Tickets $10–$25.

This contemporary music group of about a dozen instrumentalists has expanded into copresenting world music or cutting-edge performances at, primarily, the new ARTS BANK on South Broad Street, but also at the Mandell Theatre at the Annenberg Center. Relâche strikes a refreshing balance between interesting and overintellectualized choices, and has a particular affinity for young composers.

THEATER

At any time there will be at least one Broadway show in Philadelphia, on the way into or out of New York. There'll also be student repertory, professional performances by casts connected with the University of Pennsylvania, small-theater offerings in neighborhoods of Center City, and cabaret or dinner theater in the suburbs.

The premier modern theater company in town has to be the ✪ **Wilma Theater,** Broad and Spruce Streets (☎ **215/963-0249;** box office ☎ 215/963-0345), which has grown to receive national acclaim and grants from the National Endowment for the Arts. Recent seasons featured new plays by Athol Fugard, Tom Stoppard, Charles Ludlam, and Tina Howe. They've just left old quarters for a new, state-of-the-art 300-seat theater designed by Hugh Hardy in the heart of the "Avenue of the Arts."

Founded in 1984 by visionary Marjorie Samoff, the **American Music Theater Festival,** 123 S. Broad St., Suite 2515 (☎ **215/893-1570,** or 215/567-0670 for ticket charges), presents music theater in all major forms—opera, musical comedy, cabaret, and experimental. Lee Breuer's *The Gospel at Colonus* and Anthony Davis's *X* are two of nearly 50 productions of national interest. Tickets run between $10 and $40. Currently, performances are mostly held at Plays & Players, 1714 Delancey St. By 1997, it's likely that Samoff will convert the old Midtown movie theater to a two-stage center and lab. American Music Theater also copresents a great cabaret series at Hotel Atop the Bellevue.

One of the city's most popular professional theaters, the **Arden Theatre Company,** 40 N. 2nd St. (☎ **215/922-8900,** or UPSTAGES at 215/893-1145), has recently relocated among the trendy galleries and restaurants of Old City. The Arden performs in an intimate 175-seat space and has mounted 34 diverse productions in 8 years, including 11 world premieres; tickets run $15 to $25.

Founded in 1809, the **Walnut Street Theatre,** 9th and Walnut Streets (☎ **215/ 574-3550**), continues its distinctive role in the history of the American stage. The regional Walnut Street Company as well as numerous local and touring attractions play here. The orchestra pit can seat 50 musicians. In the 1,052-seat theater, the resident company presents five plays from September through June; both subscriptions and single tickets are available. Tickets run $22 to $39, with $5 student rush. Wednesday is singles night, with half-price tickets and reception, and same-day tickets (if available, of course) are sold for half price between 6 and 6:30pm. In 1986 the company began a Studio Theater Season, presenting new and more experimental works in the 75-seat and 90-seat studio spaces at 825 Walnut St., adjoining the theater. Barrymore's Café is a welcome downstairs addition.

Several local companies use the Annenberg Center (see "Multiuse Venues" below) to stage their productions. The **Philadelphia Drama Guild (PDG),** 1617 John F. Kennedy Blvd., Suite 1630 (☎ **215/563-7530;** box office ☎ 215/898-6791), a company of national prominence under former artistic director Mary B. Robinson, puts on five productions annually. A recent season included top-quality productions of Brian Friel, Sean O'Casey, August Wilson, and William Shakespeare. Tickets are available from the subscription director at the above address or at the theater door and cost between $12 and $33.50; discounts are available for students and seniors. The season runs from late October through early April.

The **Philadelphia Festival Theatre for New Plays (PFTNP),** 1515 Locust St., 7th floor (☎ **215/735-1500**), was founded in 1981 to help develop and produce new plays at the highest level; since 1990, they've gotten into new translations, adaptations, commissions, and coproductions. They have 2,100 subscribers for a season of four plays; tickets cost $10 to $25.

There's also the **InterAct Theatre Company,** 2030 Sansom St. (☎ **215/ 568-8077**), which produces three contemporary plays from September to May.

DANCE

Local troupes vie successfully with such distinguished visitors as Alwin Nikolais, Pilobolus, and the Dance Theater of Harlem. Contact the **Philadelphia Dance Alliance,** an organization that appears at WHYY's Forum Theater and includes most of the performing dance companies in the city, at 135 S. 23rd St., Philadelphia, PA 19103 (☎ **215/564-5270**). **Movement Theatre International [MTI],** 3700 Chestnut St. (☎ **215/382-0600**), goes well beyond modern dance to present vaudeville, clown theater, mime, circus acts, and classical dance-drama. Productions are held at a tabernacle temple near the University of Pennsylvania campus; tickets are usually $15. It produces an annual festival, and rents to outside presenters as well.

Founded in 1963, the nationally renowned ✪ **Pennsylvania Ballet,** 1101 S. Broad St. at Washington Ave. (☎ **215/551-7014;** box office at Academy of Music ☎ 215/ 893-1930, at Merriam ☎ 215/875-4829), almost went under in 1991 but was rejuvenated under young director Christopher d'Amboise, son of choreographer Jacques d'Amboise, and later by Roy Kaiser. The company, with current stars Jodie Gates and Cara Oculato, performs at the Academy of Music, the Annenberg Center, and the Merriam Theater during the yearly season. Its Christmas-season performances of Tchaikovsky's *Nutcracker,* with the complete Balanchine choreography, are a new city tradition. Each of the company's dozens of performances from September through June offers something old, something new, maybe something blue, and always something interesting. Tickets cost $15 to $65; *Nutcracker* performances are slightly more at $20 to $80.

MULTIUSE VENUES

In addition to musical performances held at the following major institutions, look for the many concerts presented in churches, especially around Rittenhouse Square; the city suffers from a dearth of medium-size concert halls.

Academy of Music. Broad and Locust sts. ☎ **215/893-1935** for general information, or 215/ 893-1930 for ticket availability.

In the early 19th century constructing an Academy of Music was a proposal much discussed by the cultured movers and shakers in Philadelphia. At the time, opera was the hallmark of culture, and Philadelphia lagged behind New York and Boston in the construction of a music hall equipped for it. The cornerstone was laid in 1852. Modeled on La Scala in Milan, it's grand, ornate, acoustically problematic, and is used some 300 evenings annually. The academy was refurbished in 1986, but it remains a symphony of Victorian crimson and gold, with original gaslights still flaming at the Broad Street entrance. The marble planned for the facade has never been added, and the brick and glass seem to suit Philadelphia far better.

The Philadelphia Orchestra has been a resident since its inception, playing same 100 dates annually; however, they'll be moving within a decade to a brand-new hall one block south. When that happens, look for many more touring orchestras to touch base here. Other days are given over to opera and ballet performances, travel films, and other events.

The box office is open Monday through Saturday from 10am to 5:30pm (until 8:30pm on event dates) and Sunday from 1pm on event dates. Tickets for any one event go on sale four weeks before at the box office; prices vary widely depending on the event. You can write for tickets from one month ahead of curtain time. The address is Academy of Music Box Office, Broad and Locust Streets, Philadelphia, PA 19102; include a self-addressed stamped envelope. Tours of the academy are given for $3; reservations are required (☎ **215/893-1935**).

Actors' Center Theater. The Bourse, 21 S. 5th St. ☎ **215/928-0404.**

A recent start-up, this eclectic and refreshing use of The Bourse near the Liberty Bell offers cabaret and theater, play readings, art exhibitions, and children's theater.

Annenberg Center. 3680 Walnut St. ☎ **215/898-6791.**

Located on the beautiful University of Pennsylvania campus and easily reached by bus or subway, the Annenberg Center presents a wide variety of performances by American and international companies from September through June. Of the two stages, the Harold Prince Theater generally has more intimate productions, and usually the more avant-garde choices. The Zellerbach Theater can handle the most demanding lighting and staging needs.

The Annenberg Center Theatre Series includes touring and regional theater and productions by the Philadelphia Festival Theatre for New Plays, who produce a professional season by both established and emerging playwrights. Dance Celebration, copresented with Dance Affiliates, offers a wide selection of companies. Music events include concerts by major contemporary composers and musicians. For young people, the Annenberg presents Theatre for Children; Young Adult Theatre; and the Philadelphia International Theatre Festival for Children, a 5-day event that attracts a regional audience. The box office is open noon to 6pm on weekdays, with extended hours during performances. TDD phone is **215/898-4939.** Prices vary with performance. Discounts are available for students and seniors.

Arts Bank. 601 S. Broad St. at South St. ☎ **215/545-0590,** or box office 215/567-0670.

One of the cornerstones of the new Avenue of the Arts project, the ARTS BANK is a gift of the William Penn Foundation, which realized that there wasn't enough quality, affordable performance space in Center City. The 230-seat theater is owned and operated by the nearby University of the Arts and serves a large, diverse constituency. The stage has a sprung (that's bouncy) wood floor and state-of-the-art computerized lighting and sound. Relâche, Philadanco, and University of the Arts students are just a few of the performing artists. Prices depend on the event.

The Forrest. 11th and Walnut sts. ☎ **215/923-1515.**

Of the commercial Philadelphia theaters, The Forrest is the best equipped to handle big musicals like *Crazy for You,* and it hosts several during the year, along with other short-running plays and concerts. Performances are usually on Tuesday through Saturday at 8pm (occasionally Sunday night as well) and on Wednesday, Saturday, and Sunday at 2pm. Tickets prices vary depending on the event.

Merriam Theater. Broad and Locust sts. ☎ **215/732-5446.**

The Merriam, belonging to the newly rejuvenated University of the Arts, hosts many of Broadway's top touring shows in addition to popular artists like Patti LaBelle, Barry Manilow, comedians, magicians, and the Pennsylvania Ballet. It's an ornate turn-of-the-century hall, renovated to some degree for uses never foreseen during the vaudeville era. Tickets prices vary depending on the event.

Painted Bride Art Center. 230 Vine St. ☎ **215/925-9914.**

It's hard to know what to call the Painted Bride Art Center, near the entrance to the Benjamin Franklin Bridge. It's an art gallery with contemporary tastes, but it also stays open for business and energy, in various forms—folk, electronic and new music, jazz, dance, and theater. Although its director claims that the room can hold 300, the official seat count for the main hall is 60. Ticket prices vary depending on the event.

2 The Club & Music Scene

The minimum legal drinking age in Pennsylvania is 21. Bars may stay open until 2am; establishments that operate as private clubs can serve until 3am.

NIGHTLIFE CENTERS
✪ DELAWARE WATERFRONT

With huge spaces of fantasyland and night lights shimmering off the water, the unused piers and warehouses of Delaware Avenue (renamed Christopher Columbus Boulevard in 1992, but confusion reigns) both north and south of the Ben Franklin Bridge exploded as a social scene in the early 1990s. Although many waterfront spots serve passable food (I recommend **Meiji-en, Moshulu on Pier 34, Rock Lobster,** and **The Chart House**), they shine most for nightlife.

If you're driving, park at Pier 24 at Callowhill Street, between **Rock Lobster** and **Kat Man Du,** three blocks north of the bridge ($5), or at Pier 34 ($3) well to the south. In the interests of reducing drunk driving, the club owners have subsidized free 26-foot water taxis with surrey tops that run from 9pm to 2am on Friday, Saturday, and Sunday nights. Other nights, they cost $3 per ride or $5 for an all-night pass until 11pm. The water taxis run every 30 minutes to most locations. Most clubs charge admission of $10 to $15 during peak hours and take major credit cards.

The clubs are constantly changing; I've included the current favorites. Start about three blocks north of the intersection of Delaware Avenue and Spring Garden Street and work south to:

Maui. Pier 53, 1143 N. Delaware Ave. ☎ **215/423-8116.**

Lush tropical foliage out of "Gilligan's Island," outdoor beach grill and volleyball court, the city's biggest dance floor, and King Sunny Ade live music at deafening levels. The crowd is in their 20s and 30s.

Bahama Bay at Pier 42. 950 N. Delaware Ave. ☎ **215/829-9799.**

This is the largest outdoor nightclub on the water, and is the premier meeting spot for African-Americans from 25 to 40 who will dance to anything but rap. This outdoor-only beach setting is Atlantic City in a block: the city's biggest sandbox, volleyball games, wonderfully wacky cocktails, beach-stand food, Friday pig roasts, and very casual attire. Wednesday nights bring major live talent.

Eighth Floor. 800 N. Delaware Ave. ☎ **215/922-1000.**

Opened in June 1994, this very upscale spot attracts a style-conscious 30s and 40s crowd. The wraparound waterfront view is terrific, and with 15,000 square feet it's

Sleepless in Philadelphia

Philadelphia has the reputation of rolling up the sidewalks after 10pm. Statistically, this is probably true—but only because there are so many sidewalks, and so many diverse little pockets of late-night activity. The best places to start looking for entertainment after the sun goes down include:

- The Delaware Avenue pier clubs—watch the traffic, because these clubs all hold hundreds of people.
- The area from the waterfront, west along either Spring Garden Street to the north (rehabbed industrial warehouse clubs and restaurants, edging into smaller bistros in Old City to the south) or into South Street's funky to tawdry vibrancy.
- The 1500 block of Walnut, with Circa, Le Bar Lyonnais, and the nearby bars of the Bellevue Hotel, for sophisticated clubbing.
- The fringes of the University of Pennsylvania, west of the Schuylkill.
- South Philly, for those craving cheesesteak or pasta.

usually comfortable, and easier to get a drink than at most of the clubs. Friday happy hour cover is $5 until 8pm, $10 thereafter.

Egypt. 520 N. Delaware Ave. at Spring Garden St. ☎ **215/922-6500.**

On the land side of Delaware Avenue, this bilevel dance floor features concert light and sound systems in a campy "oasis" setting. They make a special effort to woo Asian neighbors from nearby Chinatown on Tuesday.

KatManDu. Pier 25, 417 N. Delaware Ave. ☎ **215/629-1101** or 215/627-5151.

Club Med in Philadelphia, anyone? KatManDu was the first (1988) and remains the most pleasant outdoor island getaway complete with palm trees, white-sand beaches, world dance music, daiquiris, and an island "mall" with travel agency. There's a reasonably priced outdoor pit barbecue, plenty of secluded nooks, and dancing to classic rock. Cover is $5.

Dave & Buster's. Pier 19, 325 N. Delaware Ave. ☎ **215/413-1951.**

Traffic is huge for this urban country club with video arcades, virtual reality headsets, electronic golf, billiards, and blackjack. Burgers are good at the Bridgeside Grill, and there's a murder mystery dinner theater every Saturday night in winter, at $32.95 per person.

Rock Lobster. 221 N. Delaware Ave. ☎ **215/627-7625.**

At the corner of Race Street, just north of Ben Franklin Bridge and on the Marina, is this blend of top nightclub/disco and good restaurant. It serves hundreds of moderately priced lunches and dinners daily, in a 4,000-square-foot tent or al-fresco area designed to look like a Maine yacht club. The crowd is in their 30s, 40s, and 50s. There's no cover until 9pm, then it's usually $5 Monday through Thursday, $7 Friday and Saturday. The cover is higher when national acts appear.

Moshulu, The Port Saloon and Club 34. 735 S. Columbus Blvd. ☎ **215/923-2500.**

This club is set apart from the rest of the waterfront night spots, at Fitzwater Street, just south of the historic ships at **Penn's Landing** and **The Chart House.** The world's largest and only four-masted restaurant sailing ship has been restored in art-nouveau design. Complementing the ship are the Port Saloon, with a painstaking 1904-era look, and Club 34, a casual eatery with a fireplace lounge, pool tables, and dance area. The views are spectacular as it's the longest of all the Delaware piers and somewhat set apart. Danny Fleischmann, from the Ritz-Carlton, will be supervising lunch and dinner daily, with entrees in the $14 to $23 range.

OLD CITY AREA

Spurred by the Delaware riverfront boom, a number of new clubs and bars have opened in the shadow of the Ben Franklin Bridge.

The Bank. 600 Spring Garden St. ☎ **215/351-9404.**

The Bank, now a decade old, was created by the same people who started Chestnut Cabaret. It offers one of the city's largest dance floors, situated in a shabby yet chic renovated 1872 Frank Furness–designed bank. The young but sophisticated crowd is kind of J. Crew meets Seattle. The Thursday open bar and buffet, 9pm to 2am, is a steal at $10. Cover is $10 on Thursday, $7 on Friday, and $5 on Saturday.

Black Banana. 3rd and Race sts. ☎ **215/925-4433.**

Even though this is technically a private club, nonmembers can join for the night. You can dance to cool postmodernism until 3am. Videos are shown on the first floor, and the dance floor is on the second. American Express is accepted. The cover charge is a steep $55.

Middle East. 126 Chestnut St. ☎ **215/922-1003.**

Traditional Lebanese dinners and live belly dancing have always had a home here. The more recent recognition of its own kitschiness has brought the addition of live bands Monday through Saturday. Friday and Saturday are best, with dancers and live Middle Eastern music 7 to 11pm (no cover charge), followed by rock bands. It's not quiet. There's a $10 minimum with shows.

Silk City Lounge. 5th and Spring Garden sts. ☎ **215/592-8838.**

This is what would have been called a dive in the pre-postmodern era, with lava lamps and a young, ultra-hip crowd. Occasional nights are devoted to music of the Sinatra era; live bands play about once a week. It's attached to the American Diner, open throughout the night Friday through Sunday.

Sugar Mom's Church Street Lounge. 225 Church St. ☎ **215/925-8219.**

This basement, next door to Christ Church, draws a diverse and hip 20s to early 30s crowd, with plenty of friendly chatter and a wide-ranging music selection.

SOUTH STREET AREA

Love Lounge. 232 South St., above Knave of Hearts. ☎ **215/922-3956.**

Knave of Hearts has been a long-time South Street standby for its continental menu and art-deco bar. The Love Lounge attracts an artsy, sophisticated crowd in their 40s, with rosy lighting, plush couches, and informal ambience.

Monte Carlo Living Room. 2nd and South sts. ☎ **215/925-2220.**

A brass plaque on the door states that proper attire is required (coats and ties for men, dresses for women). The way to do the Monte Carlo is to dine romantically and, well, then dance the night away at the piano bar and old-style disco upstairs, complete with sentimental artwork and a tinkling fountain illuminated in alternating reds and blues, all reflected in lots of mirrors. The Living Room is open Monday through Saturday from 6pm to 2am. There's dancing to continental crooners after 9:30pm, with a deejay playing Top 40 between sets. Cover is $10, unless you've dined downstairs or are a member.

Xero. 613 S. 4th St., half block south of South St. ☎ **215/629-0565.**

This has been one of the most solid and successful bar/restaurant/clubs in town since the early 1990s. Thursday brings a complete food, drink, and dance package for $5, and alternative deejays set the mood on weekends. Happy hour is 7 to 9pm on Friday and Saturday.

CENTER CITY AREA

Circa. 1518 Walnut St. ☎ **215/545-6800.**

This new club is absolutely the greatest: It tastes like the Mediterranean, looks like Paris, and feels like Manhattan. Thursday through Saturday, following the excellent dinner (see Chapter 6), the main room is cleared to accommodate stylish throngs on a wooden dance floor until 2am. Music is deejay-spun house, pop, and '70s disco. Cover is $5 on Friday and Saturday after 9pm, $8 after 10pm. There's free admission for two if you use valet parking.

CITY LINE/MANAYUNK

Quincy's. City Line Ave. at Monument Rd., at the Adam's Mark. ☎ **215/581-5000.**

The top choice in this flashy suburban-mall area is Quincy's. Clean sounds emanate from good bands, there's lots of wood paneling and old brass, and there are backgammon tables galore. Quincy's also provides one of the best happy hours anywhere, with incredible buffet tables. There's a singles dance on Sunday from 5 to 10pm, with no cover charge. Cover ranges from free to $10.

River Cafe. 4100 Main St., Manayunk. ☎ **215/483-4100.**

This complex overlooks the Schuylkill and mixes a great dance floor with a fine restaurant.

ROCK CLUBS

Two firms now control the presentation of large rock concerts in town, for which advance tickets are almost obligatory. The long-established local firm is **Electric Factory Concerts** (☎ 215/569-9416 or 215/568-3222), which usually books major talent into the CoreStates Spectrum (box office ☎ 215/336-3600), the city's major indoor arena in South Philly. They also present out of their own **The Electric Factory,** 421 N. 7th St., a plain industrial rehab with questionable acoustics, and own the **Tower Theater** at 69th and Market Streets in West Philadelphia, and the **Theater of Living Arts** at 334 South St. (newly bereft of all seating) for smaller shows like Mary Chapin Carpenter. They also book Mann Music Center in Fairmount Park for the summer. Recently, Houston-based **Pace Concerts** has begun muscling in national acts such as Diana Ross, Barry Manilow, and George Benson through their exclusive contract with the spanking new $56 million **Blockbuster-Sony Music Entertainment Centre at the Waterfront** in Camden. Locally, try the box office at **609/365-1300,** or in advance through **Tele-Charge** (☎ 800/833-0800).

Chestnut Cabaret. 38th and Chestnut sts. ☎ **215/382-1201.**

The Chestnut Cabaret, in the heart of University City, is committed to bringing the best in local, regional, and even national acts in rock, pop, jazz, reggae, blues, and rhythm and blues on Tuesday through Saturday nights. It does not serve food. Cover varies, but there's no minimum.

J. C. Dobbs. 304 South St. ☎ **215/925-4053.**

Dobbs features rock bands, both crude and smooth, every night until 2am. The upstairs serves food until 1am, and the air is always leaden. It's a hard-drinking place, with lots of energy when the band is good. Cover is $5 or less.

Khyber Pass Pub. 56 S. 2nd St. ☎ **215/440-9683.**

This is one of the most popular spots to hear jazz, funk, and rock nightly. There's live entertainment from 9:30pm until 1 or 2am, depending on the crowd and the day. Khyber Pass is named after the route the British took to get through Pakistan, and it's somebody's version of what a British overseas officers' club would look like. It does have a certain attic-like charm, nevertheless, and English ales and Irish stout are served. Cover is usually $5.

North Star Bar. 27th and Poplar sts. ☎ **215/235-7827.**

North Star, located near the Philadelphia Museum of Art, has photo exhibits and poetry readings. Rock groups perform five nights a week in a recently glassed-in courtyard. You'll see an older bar as you enter. It's a very comfortable place to drink, and the spicy chicken wings are fine. Cover ranges from $3 to $10.

JAZZ & BLUES

Philadelphia is one of the great American hothouses for jazz, from John Coltrane to the current sax phenomenon Grover Washington, Jr.—who still lives in Mount Airy—and new bassist Christian McBride. The Peco Energy Jazz Festival takes place over Presidents' Day weekend in February and June brings the Mellon PSFS Jazz Festival. The new Philadelphia Clef Club on the "Avenue of the Arts" has given jazz a legitimate performance home. Increasingly, major cultural venues like the Philadelphia Museum of Art are also getting into the act. For specific information, write or call Mill Creek Jazz and Cultural Society, 4624 Lancaster Ave., Philadelphia, PA 19131 (☎ **215/473-2880**).

Blue Moon Jazz Club. 21 S. 5th St. at The Bourse. ☎ **215/413-2272.**

This pub has nightly sets at 9:30pm. Shirley Scott, Mickey Roker, or assorted quartets perform Wednesday through Saturday, with open sessions Sunday through Thursday. There's no cover charge.

Philadelphia Clef Club of Jazz & Performing Arts. 736–738 S. Broad St. ☎ **215/893-9912.**

The first of its kind in the country, the nonprofit Clef Club is dedicated solely to the preservation and promotion of jazz. In its handsome building on the "Avenue of the Arts" it presents jazz workshops and instrumental training as well as concerts in a 250-seat performance hall.

Liberties. 705 N. 2nd St. above Fairmount Ave. ☎ **215/238-0660.**

A carved walnut bar and high-backed booths highlight this pub with a changing schedule of jazz trios. It's a favorite haunt of local artists and musicians. Live music is featured nightly from 8:30pm to 12:30am.

Ortlieb's Jazzhaus. 847 N. 3rd St. at Poplar St. ☎ **215/922-1035.**

The expansion of Delaware riverfront life has caught up with this longtime hangout of quartets headed by Shirley Scott and Mickey Roker. There's a terrific seven-piece house band that performs nightly at 9:30, and no cover charge to enjoy the smoky, downhome ambience.

Warmdaddy's. Front & Market sts. ☎ **215/627-2500.**

Opened in 1995 by the Bynum brothers who made a success of Zanzibar Blue, this wine-colored, sophisticated entrant to the historic district features authentic live blues from Koko Taylor, Murali Coryell, and the like, and excellent traditional Southern cuisine. The stage and sound system are first-rate, and the ambience is simultaneously sexy and familial. A cover of $8 is waived with dinner.

Zanzibar Blue. 305 S. 11th St. ☎ **215/829-0300.**

This place features the best of the city's jazz bands, and increasingly the nation's. The ambience is elegant—Denzel Washington loved it while filming *Philadelphia*—so you may wish to dress up for a visit. Zanzibar is open until 2am nightly; there's also a jazz brunch ($15) on Sunday. Cover is $8 to $10.

FOLK & COUNTRY

Boot N Saddle. 1131 S. Broad St. ☎ **215/336-1742.**

In the heart of South Philly, this cash-only place features live country music every Friday and Saturday night in the back, with seating at tiny tables. There's a large island bar in the front. It's open Monday through Saturday until 2am.

Bronko Bill's. Grant Ave. and Bluegrass Rd., Northeast. ☎ **215/677-8700.**

This unlikely and immense spot, near Route 1 across from the Northeast Airport, highlights its reincarnation as a home for country and western line dancing with foam mountains outside. Inside is a 4,000-square-foot dance floor, crowded with Texas-style boots and genteel five-steps. Once you work up a sweat, repair to the Ranch Lounge or the American Indian area.

Tin Angel Acoustic Cafe. 20 S. 2nd St. ☎ **215/574-2900.**

This very conveniently located club is riding the unplugged wave with artists like John Wesley Harding, Dan Hicks, and Susan Werner. Open Wednesday through Saturday. There's no cover for Wednesday's open-mike evenings; other nights run $8 to $15.

A DANCE CLUB

Jake & Oliver's. 22 S. 3rd St. ☎ **215/627-4825.**

This beautiful 1837 church now features techno, house, and alternative music and a large dance floor, Monday through Saturday nights. The first floor has a fine restaurant with 40 microbrewery products. Cover ranges from $1 to $10, for ages 21 and over. Major credit cards accepted.

BALLROOM DANCING

While there's no live entertainment at the **Social Club,** 2009 Sansom St., 2nd floor (☎ 215/564-2277), the sound system is programmed with mambos, foxtrots, and swing. Most attendees are members, but nonmembers are welcome. Admission is $10.

That's Amore: Italian Crooning in South Philly

There's a tremendous history of Italian crooning in South Philadelphia, as the operatic training got transmitted to American popular singing. The style of Frank Sinatra in the 1940s and 1950s led to other jazz-influenced singers like Vic Damone, and in turn to the smooth harmonics of singers like Frankie Avalon and equivalent groups like The Persuasions. Here are four places where you can get a good handle on this history in rambunctious action.

On Friday and Saturday, Dave Morris and his band bring the otherwise sedate **D'Medici Restaurant,** 824 S. 8th St. (☎ **215/922-3986**), in South Philadelphia, to life with renditions of Sinatra, Mel Tormé, Tony Bennett, and other neighborhood favorites. There's no cover charge.

Michael's, 239 Chestnut St. (☎ **215/829-9126**), couldn't be more convenient to the historic part of town, and the intensity of emotion from live vocal groups performing on the small stage rises as the night progresses.

Deep in the heart of South Philly, **The Saloon,** 7th and Catharine Streets (☎ **215/627-1811**), features Victorian antiques that accent a fine Italian restaurant. If you want to hear mellow music, head upstairs by the glossy mahogany bar. The Saloon bar is open Wednesday through Saturday until 12:30am. The drinks average $2.50 and admission is free.

If you're in search of where Rocky Balboa would go to sing along with the band, go no further than the **Triangle Tavern,** 10th and Reed Streets (☎ **215/467-8683**), which couldn't be cheaper. The help really participates.

COMEDY CLUBS

Comedy Cabaret. 126 Chestnut St. ☎ **215/625-5653.**

This addition to the Middle East complex operates from Wednesday (open stage) to Saturday nights. Shows are on Friday at 8:30 and 11pm and on Saturday at 8 and 11pm. There is a separate $10 admission.

Catch a Rising Star. 211 South St. ☎ **215/440-3131.**

This Abbott Square lounge has writers and performers from Comedy Central, among other breeding grounds. Shows are on Tuesday, Wednesday, and Thursday at 8:30pm, on Friday and Saturday at 8:30 and 11pm, and on Sunday at 8:30pm. Admission is $8 on weeknights and $10 on weekends.

CABARET

Ethel Barrymore Room. Broad and Locust sts., in the Bellevue Hotel. ☎ **215/893-1776.**

In collaboration with the American Musical Theater Festival, major cabaret stars such as Julie Wilson are presented in this classic setting every winter and spring. Old-timers will recognize this room as the Bellevue-Stratford's original home. Cover is $25.

GAY & LESBIAN CLUBS

12th Air Command. 254 S. 12th St. ☎ **215/545-8088.**

The former Hepburn's now caters to a primarily male clientele nightly until 2am. Downstairs there's a lounge bar and game room; Italian cuisine is served Wednesday through Saturday and there's a Sunday brunch. There's another bar and a crowded disco upstairs. No credit cards are accepted. There's a $5 cover for disco only on Friday and Saturday.

247 Bar. 247 S. 17th St. ☎ **215/545-9779.**

Animal heads and pine paneling mark this macho stalwart in the Rittenhouse Square area. There are pool tables and plenty of TVs for sports watching.

Rodz. 1418 Rodman St. ☎ **215/546-1900.**

Rodz has a cute piano bar along with excellent, affordable eclectic American cuisine.

Woody's. 202 S. 13th St. ☎ **215/545-1893.**

Woody's party atmosphere also attracts many straights. The original bar is downstairs, and a sandwich counter has been added alongside. The disco adjoining the upstairs lounge features trompe l'oeil atlases holding up a roof of stars. Free two-step lessons on Tuesday, 5 to 6pm. Cover on Friday and Saturday ranges from $5 to $10.

3 The Bar Scene

BREWERIES & PUBS

Bridgid's. 726 N. 24th St. ☎ **215/232-3232.**

This tiny, very friendly horseshoe-shaped bar near the Philadelphia Museum of Art stocks a superb collection of Belgian beers, including an array of fruit- to hops-originated brews. A tapas menu is also available at the bar.

Dock Street Brewing Co. 18th and Cherry sts., 2 Logan Square. ☎ **215/496-0413.**

This comfortable, moderate place brews and sells only its own beers, nestled into a top corporate corner. Offered at two separate bars are up to six varieties of beer at $2.50 per glass (or a sampler of all six for $3.50), painstakingly brewed within the last month. You can even inspect the spotless fermenting vats to the right of the bar. There's live jazz and Latin music on Friday and Saturday.

Houlihan's Old Place. 18th St. and Rittenhouse Square. ☎ **215/546-5940.**

Houlihan's Old Place isn't exactly old, and the decor is more that of Albert Hall with peppy graffiti than that of an Irish pub. But it's one of Center City's most active pubs, especially among young professionals and older students. The decor and noise level are determinedly eclectic and on the loud side. Mixed drinks start at $2.50. A substantial dining area serves lunch, dinner, and Sunday brunch.

Irish Pub. 1123 Walnut St. ☎ **215/925-3311.** Also at 2007 Walnut St. ☎ 215/568-5603.

With one located across from the Forrest Theatre and the other off Rittenhouse Square, both Irish Pubs pack in hundreds of good-natured professionals, of both genders and all ages. There is Irish and American folk music in the front, but you can get far away and a floor down if you wish. Both are open until 2am nightly.

Samuel Adams Brew House. 1516 Sansom St. ☎ **215/563-2326.**

The brew house was opened in the late 1980s as an offshoot of the Sansom Street Oyster House downstairs. Three beers are regularly brewed right here: a light ale, an amber ale, and a dark porter. The bar of aged wood and etched glass was imported from Great Britain.

Serrano. 20 S. 2nd St. ☎ **215/928-0770.**

Serrano—which now also holds Tin Angel Acoustic Cafe—offers a wonderful collection of brews in an intimate setting. It is also on one of the Historic District's nicest blocks. The old wooden bar has antique stained glass behind it, and the wood fire is spiced. Until you get out to Stoudt's own brew pub in Adamstown (see Chapter 12), try their unpasteurized here ($5.95 per bottle).

PIANO BARS & LOUNGES

Bridget Foy's South Street Grill. 200 South St. ☎ **215/922-1813.**

Newly renovated and with a fine open-style grill at reasonable prices, Bridget Foy's offers a nice, mellow atmosphere with no pressure to socialize if you don't feel like it and the company to keep you entertained if you do. It's open every evening until 1am. Situated at the lower corner of Head House Square, the establishment features a lively sidewalk café in summer.

Cutters. 2005 Market St. ☎ **215/851-6262.**

This is the quintessential 1990s bar: long, high, massively stocked, with businesslike high-tech systems and a friendly and elegant atmosphere. The location, in the IBM building at Commerce Square, makes it a fine postbusiness meeting place.

Downey's. Front and South sts. ☎ **215/625-9500.**

Downey's is a terrific Irish pub with a contemporary flair. Many of the local professional athletes head here after a game to relax upstairs, downstairs, or at the café tables outside. The new upstairs bar has classy skylights set into the original tin-plate ceiling and the obligatory Irish coin nailed to the portal. The music is upstairs on piano and accompaniment nightly from 8pm to 1am on Friday and Saturday. At Sunday brunch (11:30am to 3pm) a strolling string quartet punctuates the atmosphere. A beautiful new wraparound second-floor deck offers waterfront views for dining or cocktails.

Le Bar Lyonnais. 1523 Walnut St. ☎ **215/567-1000.**

Downstairs from the famed Le Bec-Fin Restaurant is this crowded, intimate, smoky bar, a favorite hangout of those with high bank balances, hormones, or hopes.

The Lounge at the Omni. 4th and Chestnut sts. ☎ **215/925-0000.**

This lounge is a very posh spot, with dark woods and Oriental carpets, a crackling fireplace, a piano trio, and large picture windows surveying Independence National Historical Park across the street. It stays open past midnight on weekends.

Melange. 17th and Locust sts., in the Warwick Hotel. ☎ **215/545-4655.**

Open 24 hours, Melange offers plenty of smooth, sophisticated peace and quiet in an ambience aimed at Iberian seductiveness.

Society Hill Hotel. 3rd and Chestnut sts. ☎ **215/925-1919.**

The Society Hill Hotel, a renovated 1832 shell, has a dozen rooms upstairs—but the bar has all of Society Hill excited. It's one of the few modern bars in town that's sophisticated but not glitzy, and the outdoor café makes it even more charming on a summer eve. (Why don't more places follow their lead and screw hooks into the undersides of tables and counters so that women can hang their purses and pocketbooks safely but conveniently?)

TGI Friday's. 18th St. and the Parkway. ☎ **215/665-8443.**

It's hard to believe that a place this obviously corporate in intent and atmosphere could make it—but it has become a favorite of the younger crowd that populates Logan Circle's new office towers. There's standing room only at the outdoor terrace on summer evenings for the happy-hour buffet and socializing.

WINE BARS

Jeannine's Bistro. 10 S. Front St. ☎ **215/925-1126.**

This is a more moderate effort by Jeanne Mermet, situated above her La Truffe. Guitar and violin music are offered on the weekend, though the bistro is open only until 10:30pm (you can shift to Warmdaddy's for blues next door). The ambience of plush pillows, padded bench seats, and candlelight is charming. About 20 wines are available by the glass at $4.50 to $7 each.

Panorama. 14 N. Front St. at Front and Market sts. ☎ **215/922-7800.**

Panorama is at the rear of Penn's View Inn but separate from the moderately priced Italian restaurant. Its curving wine bar features 120 different selections by the glass. Most cost about $5. There's piano entertainment. Panorama is open Monday through Saturday until 1am, Sunday until 10:30pm.

4 More Entertainment

READINGS

Borders Book Shop and Espresso Bar, 1727 Walnut St. (☎ **215/568-7400**), runs one of the country's top series of author readings in an elegant setting that's steps from Rittenhouse Square. In a recent month, authors included Anna Quindlen, Marilyn French, Nancy Lemann, Spalding Grey, Michael Pollan, and Meg Pei. Readings usually are at 7:30pm on weekdays and at 2pm on weekends.

City Book Shop, 1129 Pine St. (☎ **215/592-1992**), features poetry readings every Friday night, in a comfortable setting.

SALONS

Judy Wicks at the **White Dog Café,** 3420 Sansom St. (☎ **215/386-9224**), has instituted salon meals, tapping into local academics, artists, and her own contacts. Issues addressed include domestic and foreign policy, the arts, and social movements. Dinner talks include a three-course dinner for $25 per person, and reservations are recommended. A great singles activity for the intellectually curious.

SPECTACLES

The **Benjamin Franklin Bridge** has been outfitted with special lighting effects by the noted architectural firm Venturi, Rauch and Scott Brown. The lights are triggered into mesmerizing patterns by the auto and train traffic along the span. Some summers **Independence Hall** is the scene of a 9pm show produced by Historic Philadelphia (☎ **800/764-4786** or 215/629-5801) with 1776 as its theme.

MOVIE THEATERS

In the Historic District, **Ritz 5 Movies,** 214 Walnut St. (☎ **215/925-7900/1**), is the single best choice for independent releases. It has five comfortable screening rooms and shows sophisticated—often foreign—fare. The first daily matinee performances cost $4.

The new five-screen **Ritz at the Bourse,** 4th and Ranstead Streets (☎ **215/ 925-7900**), behind The Bourse and the new Omni Hotel, has the advantage of a superb espresso/cappuccino bar replete with long leather sofas before or after screenings.

In Center City, standard studio releases are offered only at **United Artists Sameric,** 1908 Chestnut St. (☎ **215/567-0604**), and **AMC Midtown 2,** Chestnut Street at Broad Street (☎ **215/567-7021**).

In University City, **International House,** 3701 Chestnut St. (☎ **215/387-5125**), presents a fine series of foreign films, political documentaries, and the work of independent filmmakers. Admission is $3.50. **Cinemagic 3 at Penn,** 3925 Walnut St. (☎ **215/222-5555**), screens intelligent releases for the College Crowd from the United States and abroad. The popcorn is outstanding.

Side Trips from Philadelphia

11

The same boats that brought Penn's Quakers also brought the pioneers that fanned out into the Delaware Valley to the south, Bucks County to the north, and what is now Pennsylvania Dutch Country to the west. This chapter covers Bucks and Brandywine counties, while the next chapter guides you through the Amish heartland of Lancaster County.

Much of this area remains lush and unspoiled, although development-versus-environment struggles are becoming pointed. The major attractions of the Bucks and Brandywine countryside are historical: colonial mansions and inns, early American factories or businesses, and battlegrounds of the Revolution and the Civil War.

1 Bucks County & Nearby New Jersey

Bucks County, at most an hour by car from Philadelphia, is bordered by the Delaware River to the east and Montgomery County to the west. Historic estates and sites, along with the antique stores and country inns they've spawned, abound. Many artists and authors, including Oscar Hammerstein II, Pearl Buck, and James Michener, have gained inspiration from the natural beauty, which has survived major development so far. A newer interest is "ecotourism"—the area is great for gentle outdoor activities. Nearby New Jersey offers scenic routes for bicycling and walking as well as fine restaurants.

ESSENTIALS

GETTING THERE   The best automobile route into Bucks County from Center City is I-95 (north). Pa. 32 (which intersects I-95 in Yardley) runs along the Delaware past Washington Crossing State Park to New Hope, which connects to Doylestown by U.S. 202. By train, the R5 SEPTA commuter rail ends at Doylestown, with connections to New Hope and Lahaska.

From New York, take the New Jersey Turnpike to I-78 west; follow to Exit 29 and pick up Route 287 south to Route 202, which crosses the Delaware River at Lambertville straight into New Hope.

VISITOR INFORMATION   To find out more about the hundreds of historic sites, camping facilities, and accommodations here, contact the **Bucks County Tourist Commission,** 152 Swamp Rd.,

Where Washington Crossed the Delaware

A trip along the Delaware via Route 32 through Morrisville and Yardley will bring you to **Washington Crossing State Park,** 500 acres that are open year-round. Most people know that Washington crossed a big river in a small boat on Christmas Eve of 1776. This was the place, although the Durham boats on display in the boat barn used to hold 30. The state park, located at the intersection of Pa. 532 and Pa. 32 (River Road), 3 miles north of I-95 from Exit 31, is divided into an upper and a lower section separated by 3 miles; Washington left from the lower park. You can sip a glass of punch at the low-ceilinged **Old (McKonkey's) Ferry Inn** (1752), where he ate before the assault, and tour the bird sanctuary and the Memorial Building at the point of embarkation. The 30-minute film in the Visitors Center is dated and not worth sitting through; just start exploring on your own.

The **Wild Flower Preserve** in the upper park is really a 100-acre arboretum, flower garden, and shrub preserve rolled into one; it contains 15 different paths, each emphasizing different botanical wonders. The **Thompson-Neely House** was intact when General Washington, Brigadier General Stirling, and Lt. James Monroe decided on the year-end push into New Jersey. Next to the Wild Flower Preserve is the stone **Bowman's Hill Tower;** it will reward you (or the children) with a view of this part of the Delaware Valley, which would probably belong to the British Commonwealth if Washington's troops hadn't routed the Hessians in 1776.

An annual reenactment of the historic crossing takes place here on Christmas. For more information, contact the park at P.O. Box 103, Washington Crossing, PA 18977 (☎ **215/493-4076**).

A combination ticket, including a walking tour, Thompson-Neely House, Bowman's Hill and Tower, costs $4 for adults, $3 for seniors, and $2 for children ages 6 to 12. The buildings are open Monday through Saturday from 9am to 5pm, Sunday noon to 5pm. The grounds are open daily from 9am to 8pm or sunset.

Doylestown, PA 18901 (☎ **800/836-2825** or 215/345-4552). You can also write to or stop by the **New Hope Information Center,** South Main and Mechanic Streets, Box 141, New Hope, PA 18938 (☎ **215/862-5880**); it's open Monday through Friday from 9am to 5pm, Saturday and Sunday from 10am to 6pm.

ATTRACTIONS IN BUCKS COUNTY

✪ **Sesame Place.** 100 Sesame Rd., Langhorne, PA 19047. ☎ **215/752-7070.** Admission $22.95 adults and children 3–13, $20.65 seniors over 55. Second-day tickets at discounted rate with validated first-day ticket. Parking $4 per day. *Note:* Many hotels in the area offer discount tickets in their package rates. May to mid-June, Mon–Fri 10am–5pm, Sat–Sun 10am–7pm; late June–Aug, daily 9am–8pm; Sept–Oct, Sat–Sun 10am–5pm. Junction of Route 1 and I-95.

The nation's only theme park based on the award-winning television show, *Sesame Street,* is located 30 minutes from Center City. My kids and millions of others spend a totally involved day climbing through three stories of sloping, swaying fun on the Nets and Climbs or crawling through tubes and tunnels amid splashing fountains and showers of spray at Mumford's Water Maze. A festive musical parade daily is a fun-filled interactive celebration starring Big Bird, Elmo, Zoe, Bert and Ernie, and the rest. The kids will want their swimsuits for 15 age-safe water rides including Sky Splash, the five-story water adventure in Twiddlebug Land, as well as Rubber Duckie, Runaway Rapids, and Big Bird's Rambling River (locker rooms are provided). All of

Bucks County

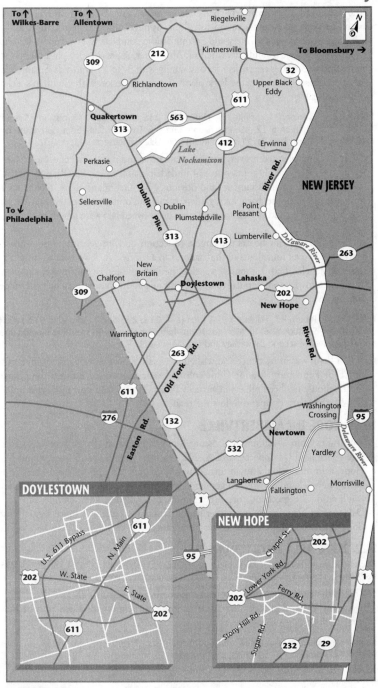

the best-loved "Sesame Street" characters perform in shows at Big Bird Theatre and stroll on Sesame Neighborhood for photo opportunities. Indoors, there are the air-conditioned Games Gallery and Sesame Studio complete with a chroma-key show for young "TV stars" and scientific fun. Altogether, more than 60 physical play stations and water rides are perfect for any family with 3- to 15-year-olds. Sesame Place is an Anheuser-Busch Theme Park planned in conjunction with Children's Television Workshop.

Pennsbury Manor. Morrisville, PA 19067. ☎ **215/946-0400.** Admission $5 adults, $4 seniors, $3 children 6–12, free for children under 6. Tues–Sat 9am–5pm, Sun noon–5pm. Last tour at 3:30pm. Take Pa. 9 (Tyburn Road) from U.S. 1 (intersects I-95) or U.S. 13.

William Penn planned his very English plantation and manor at Pennsbury Manor, along the Delaware, 24 miles north of Philadelphia on Route 32 (River Road). On it, he designed a self-sustaining (and obviously pre-Georgian) estate, replete with a smokehouse, icehouse, barn, herb garden, plantation office, and boathouse. The various dependencies and the manor itself were demolished but were rebuilt to the smallest detail in 1939.

Pennsbury Manor boasts the largest collection of 17th-century antiques in the state, spread over four floors of the manor. On a sunny day, it's a treat to inspect the carefully labeled herb garden, step inside the icehouse for a cool respite, and watch the guinea fowl (more popular than chickens in 1600s) wandering along the golden brick paths.

Fallsington. Tyburn Rd., Fallsington, PA 19054. ☎ **215/295-6567.** Admission $3.50 adults, $2.50 seniors, $1 students 6–18. Mon–Sat 10am–4pm, Sun 1pm–4pm. Special Fallsington open-house days are the second Sat in May and Oct. South off U.S. 1 at Tyburn Road.

When Penn was in residence and wished to worship, he'd go to Fallsington, 6 miles north of Pennsbury Manor. This colonial village grouped around the Quaker meetinghouse has been preserved virtually intact. Take Pa. 13 north to Tyburn Road (Pa. 9), then turn right and follow the road.

NEW HOPE & LAMBERTVILLE

Four miles from Washington Crossing, along River Road (Pa. 32), punctuated by lovely farmland (as opposed to U.S. 202's factory outlets), you'll come upon New Hope, a former colonial town turned artists' colony. It's somewhat commercial by now. The weekend crowds can get fierce, and parking is cramped, but once on foot you'll enjoy the specialty stores, restaurants, and galleries. Lambertville, across the Delaware in New Jersey, has rather pedestrian architecture but more scenic routes along the river and, many say, better restaurants.

NEW HOPE AREA ATTRACTIONS

Bucks County Playhouse. 70 S. Main St. (P.O. Box 313), New Hope, PA 18938. ☎ **215/862-2041.** Tickets $15–$20. Apr–Dec Wed–Sun evenings and Wed and Thurs matinees.

This is the center of New Hope entertainment with summer theater that features Broadway hits and musical revivals. It's a former gristmill with a seating capacity of almost 500.

New Hope Mule Barge. New and South Main sts., New Hope, PA 18938. ☎ **215/862-2842.** Admission $7.50 adults, $6.75 seniors, $5.50 students, $4.75 children under 12. May 1–Oct 15, six launchings daily. Apr and Oct 16–Nov 15, reduced launchings on Wed, Sat, and Sun.

For a while in the early 1800s, canals were thought to be the transport revolution in England and the eastern United States. Coal was floated down this one in the 1830s from mines in the Lehigh Valley, and the barges are still pulled by mules. The barges run April through October and leave from New Street.

Parry Mansion Museum. Main and Ferry sts., New Hope, PA 18938. ☎ **215/862-5652.** Admission $3 adults, 50¢ children under 12. May–Dec, Fri–Sun 1–5pm.

One of the loveliest old homes in town, this mansion was erected in 1784 by the elite of New Hope. The Parry family lived in this 11-room Georgian until 1966, and the rooms are decorated in different period styles of 1775 (whitewash and candles) to 1900 (wallpaper and oil lamps).

Peddler's Village. U.S. 202 and Rte. 263, Lahaska, PA 18931. ☎ **215/794-4000.** Most stores Mon–Thurs 10am–5:30pm, Fri–Sat 10am–9pm, Sun 11am–5pm. Special Strawberry Festival in May.

Five miles south of New Hope, on Route 202, Peddler's Village looks antique, but the appeal to customers is timeless and most of the merchandise is contemporary. It's not a country market; the prices are marked up considerably, but the ambience and convenience are attractive. **Carousel World** can spin the family on a 1926 restored carousel, along with other fine examples of this art (museum admission is $3 for adults, $2.75 for seniors, $2 for children 3 to 13; rides cost $1.25 each). **Jenny's** on Route 202 at Street Road (☎ 215/794-4020) offers elegant continental dining in an atmosphere of brass and stained glass. The specialties of the **Cock 'n' Bull** (☎ 215/794-4010) include a massive buffet on Thursday, an unlimited Sunday brunch, and beef burgundy served in a loaf of bread that's baked in the hearth. The 60 rooms in the **Golden Plough Inn** are scattered throughout the village, all with private baths and complimentary champagne.

COUNTRY WALKING & BICYCLING

Walking or riding along the Delaware River or along the canals built for coal hauling on either side can be the highlight of a summer. The two most convenient routes are the following.

In Stockton, New Jersey, take Route 263 just over the Delaware to Pennsylvania. Then park your car, cross the old bridge on foot or bicycle, and follow the towpath on the Pennsylvania side north toward Lumberville and its cute general store, 3 miles away. The **Lumberville Store Bicycle Rental Co.** (Route 32, Lumberville, PA 18933; ☎ 215/297-5388) has all kinds of bicycles for rent at moderate day rates. It's open April through mid-October daily from 8am to 6pm.

The second route, just south of Lumberville, follows River Road south and west to Cuttalossa Road, which winds past an alpine chalet, creeks, ponds, and sheep grazing and clanking their antique Swiss bells. **Cuttalossa Inn,** Cuttalossa Road, Lumberville, PA 18933 (☎ 215/297-5082), offers high-class cuisine in a spectacular setting.

MORE OUTDOOR ACTIVITIES

Other transport-based attractions of the New Hope area are a **covered-bridges tour** (☎ 215/345-4552 for information about this self-guided free tour); **river tubing** at Point Pleasant Canoe, up the Delaware from New Hope at upper Black Eddy and Riegelsville (☎ 215/297-8181), for two to four hours of relaxing family fun; and a **steam railway** out of New Hope (☎ 215/862-2707).

SHOPPING

Rice's Sale & Country Market. New Hope, PA 18938. ☎ **215/297-5993.** Admission $1 Tues, free on Sat. Tues and Sat, 6am–1pm. One mile north of Peddler's Village on Greenhill Rd., just off Route 263 in Lahaska.

Rice's Market is the real thing—a quality market of country goods and crafts. Amish wares are sold in the main building, along with antiques and collectibles; more than a thousand outdoor stalls have vendors. New features include indoor bathrooms and paved walkways for strollers and wheelchairs. Get there early.

WHERE TO STAY

New Hope and its New Jersey neighbor across the Delaware River, Lambertville, have well-deserved reputations for their country inns and restaurants. All used to require two-day stays and frown on children, but Sesame Place's success is changing this. The listings here only scratch the surface; other choices might include the romantic **Inn at Phillips Mill** in New Hope (☎ 215/862-2984), the newly opened and fashionable **Auldridge Mead** in Tinicum Township (☎ 215/847-5842), or the tranquil **Bucksville House** in Kintnersville (☎ 215/847-8948).

Country Inns

✪ **Centre Bridge Inn.** P.O. Box 74, Rte. 32, New Hope, PA 18938. ☎ **215/862-2048.** 9 rms. A/C. $80–$105 weekday single or double; $110–$135 weekend single or double. Rates include continental breakfast. AE, MC, V.

Situated beside the Delaware River 3¹/₂ miles north of New Hope, the current building is the third since the early 18th century. Many of the elegant guest rooms have canopy, four-poster, or brass beds; wall-high armoires; modern private baths; outside decks; and views of the river or countryside. Five rooms have TVs. The inn also has a pretty restaurant overlooking the river and the adjoining canal (and the mule-drawn barges coasting on it), serving lunch, dinner, and $19.95 prix-fixe Sunday brunch.

Evermay-on-the-Delaware. River Rd., Erwinna, PA 18920. ☎ **610/294-9100.** Fax 610/294-8249. 16 rms, 1 carriage house suite. A/C TEL. $55–$80 single; $85–$170 double; $220 suite. Rates include continental breakfast and 4pm tea. MC, V.

Thirteen miles north of New Hope on River Road in Erwinna lies this gracious historic inn, now under the ownership of William and Danielle Moffley. Combining privacy with a romantic setting overlooking the Delaware, Evermay once hosted the Barrymores for croquet weekends. The inn now offers rooms with luxurious antique furnishings. At a 7:30pm seating on Friday, Saturday, Sunday, and holidays, the formal dining room offers an excellent prix-fixe six-course $52 dinner that's open to the public as well as guests; reserve well in advance.

✪ **Whitehall Inn.** 1370 Pineville Rd., New Hope, PA 18938. ☎ **215/598-7945.** 6 rms (4 with bath). A/C TEL. $140–$210 per night, single or double. Rates include four-course breakfast and 4pm high tea. Two-night minimum. AE, DC, MC, V.

Four miles outside New Hope is this 18th-century manor house on a former horse farm, complete with a pool. Mike and Suella Wass serve magnificent four-course breakfasts, and their "innsmanship" is nationally known, with such touches as fresh fruit bowls, a bottle of mineral water in every room, and afternoon tea concerts.

Hotels & Motels

✪ **Comfort Inn.** 3660 Street Rd., Bensalem, PA 19020. ☎ **800/228-5150** or 215/245-0100. 141 rms. A/C TV TEL. $62–$77 single; $72–$87 double. Rates include good continental breakfast. Children under 18 stay free in parents' room. AE, DC, MC, V.

For moderate lodgings in Bucks County, this is one of the best choices, off I-95 about 20 miles from Washington Crossing and 5 miles from Sesame Place. The inn is a modern, bright, three-story property with two double beds, queen-size bed plus sofa bed, or a king-size bed in each room. There's also an exercise room. There's only one elevator, so get used to the stairs.

✪ **New Hope Motel in the Woods.** 400 W. Bridge St., New Hope, PA 18938. ☎ **215/862-2800.** 28 rms. A/C TV. $59 single; $69 double. DC, DISC, MC, V.

Just a mile west of town is this motel tucked in a peaceful woodland setting off Route 179. For over 30 years, it has offered modern ground-level rooms with private baths and standard motel amenities. Open all year, it has a swimming pool that's open during the summer.

Sheraton Bucks County Hotel. 400 Oxford Valley Rd., Langhorne, PA 19047. ☎ **800/325-3535** or 215/547-4100. 167 rms. A/C TV TEL. $155–$165 single or double. Sesame Street packages $139–$169 include free shuttle and free room and board for children. AE, DC, MC, V.

This festive, modern, 14-story hotel opened right across the street from Sesame Place in 1987. The soundproof guest rooms have oversized beds and quilted fabrics, many with extra sofa beds. Other facilities include a health club, an indoor swimming pool and sauna, and a full-service restaurant.

Where To Dine

Karla's. 5 W. Mechanic St., New Hope, PA 18938. ☎ **215/862-2612.** Reservations recommended for dinner. Main courses $13–$20; lunch $3.95–$7.95. AE, DC, MC, V. Sun–Thurs 11am–10pm, Fri–Sat 11am–4am. INTERNATIONAL.

In the heart of New Hope, next door to the Information Center, this lively and informal restaurant offers three settings: a sunlit conservatory with ceiling fans, stained glass, and plants; a gallery room with local artists' works; and a bistro with marble tabletops. The eclectic menu offers grilled rib-eye steak, veal francese, and chicken breast with Thai ginger sauce. The lunch items are tamer.

✪ **Odette's Fine Country Dining.** S. River Rd. and Route 32, New Hope, PA 18938. ☎ **215/862-3000.** Reservations recommended. Main courses $16–$26; lunch $7–$10. AE, DC, MC, V. Mon–Sat 11:30am–3pm; Mon–Fri 5–10pm, Sat 5–11pm, Sun 3–10pm; Sun brunch 10:30am–2:30pm. INTERNATIONAL.

Surrounded by the river and the canal on the southern edge of town, this elegant restaurant has been an inn since 1794. The previous owner, Odette Myrtil, was a Ziegfeld Follies girl whose memorabilia adorns the place. The menus are seasonal and change thrice annually, providing nice twists on standard bases of steak, seafood, duck, and veal. There is also a weekend cabaret.

DOYLESTOWN

The triangle where U.S. 202 (west of New Hope), Pa. 313 (south of Scranton), and U.S. 611 (that's North Broad Street in Philadelphia) intersect defines Doylestown, the county seat. It's a pleasant town just to walk around, but three interesting collections in town invite you indoors. They were all endowed by the same man, Dr. Henry Chapman Mercer (1856–1930). Mercer was a collector, local archeologist, and master of pottery techniques.

Three Local Museums

✪ **Fonthill Museum.** E. Court St., off Swamp Road (Route 313), Doylestown, PA 18901. ☎ **215/348-9461.** Admission $5 adults, $4.50 seniors, $1.50 children. Mon–Sat 10am–5pm, Sun noon–5pm. Closed Thanksgiving, Christmas, and New Year's Day. Guided tours only; reservations recommended.

Not many people can call their home a castle, but Dr. Mercer could, and the castle was built with reinforced concrete of his own design. The core of the building is a 19th-century farmhouse, but towers, turrets, and tiles have been amassed beyond belief. All the rooms are of different shapes, and each has tiles of Mercer's collection set into the chamber.

Moravian Pottery and Tile Works. Swamp Rd., Doylestown, PA 18901. ☎ **215/ 345-6722.** Admission $3 adults, $1.50 youths, $2.50 seniors. Daily 10am–4:45pm. Tours available every 30 minutes until 4pm. Closed major holidays.

Down the road on Pa. 313, the Moravian Pottery and Tile Works was Dr. Mercer's next big project. It's also made of reinforced concrete. If you go to the State Capitol in Harrisburg, you can see over 400 mosaics from here that illustrate the history of Pennsylvania. The working ceramists at the pottery today turn out tiles and mosaics available through the museum shop; prices range from $5 to $1,800.

✪ **Mercer Museum.** Pine St. at Ashland St., Doylestown, PA 18901. ☎ **215/345-0210.** Admission to the museum and library $5 adults, $4.50 seniors, $1.50 children 6–17, free for children under 6. Mon–Sat 10am–5pm, Sun noon–5pm, Tues 10am–9pm. Spruance Library (Bucks County history), Tues 1–9pm, Wed–Sat 10am–5pm. Closed Thanksgiving, Christmas, and New Year's Day.

Mercer Museum displays thousands of early American tools, vehicles, cooking pieces, looms, and even weather vanes. Mercer had the collecting bug in a big way, and you can't help being impressed with the breadth of the collection and the castle that houses it. It rivals the Shelburne, Vermont, complex—and that's 35 buildings on 100 acres! The open atrium rises five stories, and suspends a Conestoga wagon, chairs, and sleighs as if they were Christmas-tree ornaments. During the summer, a log cabin, schoolhouse, and other large bits of American life are open for inspection. The museum recently added six hands-on stations for children to build a log house, try on period clothes, and drive a buggy.

WHERE TO DINE

✪ **Sign of the Sorrel Horse Country Inn.** 4424 Old Easton Rd., Doylestown, PA 18901. ☎ **215/230-9999.** Reservations required. Jackets recommended for men. Main courses $12– $20; prix-fixe dinners $42 and $62. MC, V. Wed–Sat 5:30–9:30pm; Sun brunch 11:30am–2pm. FRENCH.

Led by the indefatigable team of Jon Atkin and Monique Gaumont, this is the best restaurant in the Doylestown area. Atkin and Gaumont trained at the Cordon Bleu school, and moved to this 200-year-old inn in 1994. I prefer the new Cafe Room to the original low-ceilinged Escoffier Room, but the cuisine remains superb in both. The menu is rich, with smoked sea scallops, lobster, and filet mignon—all served with fresh reductions and mousses. Salads are abundant with their own herbs. The ice cream is homemade with honey, not sugar.

2 Valley Forge

Montgomery County is a region of rivers, hills, fall foliage, and Main Line suburban development. It's best known for Valley Forge, Washington's winter headquarters at the nadir of the Revolutionary War, and the emormous King of Prussia mall, the second largest in the nation.

The **Valley Forge Convention and Visitors Bureau,** 600 W. Germantown Pike, Plymouth Meeting, PA 19462 (☎ **800/345-8112** or 610/834-1550) has particulars on sites, recreation, annual events, and campgrounds.

EXPLORING VALLEY FORGE NATIONAL HISTORICAL PARK

Only 30 minutes from central Philadelphia and a half-day excursion in itself now, Valley Forge was hours of frozen trails away in the winter of 1777 to 1778. The Revolutionary forces had just lost the battles of Brandywine and Germantown. While the British occupied Philadelphia, Washington's forces repaired to winter quarters near an iron forge where the Schuylkill met Valley Creek, 18 miles northwest. A sawmill and gristmill were supposed to help provide basic requirements, but they had been destroyed by the British. Some 12,000 men and boys straggled into the encampment, setting up quarters and lines of defense.

Unfortunately, the winter turned bitter, with 6 inches of snow and iced-up rivers. Critical shortages of food and clothing, along with damp shelters, left nearly 4,000 men diseased and unfit for duty. Almost 2,000 perished, and many others deserted. Congress, which had left Philadelphia hurriedly, couldn't persuade the colonies to give money to alleviate the conditions. Nevertheless, the forces slowly gained strength and confidence, due in part to the Prussian army veteran Baron von Steuben, appointed by Washington to retrain the Continental Army under his revised and distinctly American "Manual of Arms." By springtime the Continentals were an army on which their new allies, the French, could rely. Replicas of their huts, some of the officers' lodgings, and later memorials dot the park today.

Start your visit at the **Visitors Center** (☎ 610/783-1077) at the junction of Pa. 23 and North Gulph Road. If you're driving, access is from Exit 24 of the Pennsylvania Turnpike or Exit 25 of the Schuylkill Expressway (I-76) to Route 363. Follow the signs. From Philadelphia, you can take bus 45 from the Visitors Center at 16th Street and JFK Boulevard to King of Prussia Plaza, then take the hourly 99 bus to the park. A 15-minute film depicting the encampment is shown at the Visitors Center every half hour. Also at the Visitors Center is a museum containing Washington's tent, an extensive collection of Revolutionary War artifacts, and a bookstore.

Highlights within the park include the **National Memorial Arch;** an 1865 covered bridge; the **Isaac Potts House** (1770), which Washington commandeered as his headquarters; and the 1993 Monument to Patriots of African Descent.

If you're here in late April or early May, you'll see the magnificent dogwood blossoms.

That Gothic chapel (1903) houses the **Washington Memorial Chapel** (it's free, with Sunday carillon recitals in the bell tower at 2pm), next to the Valley Forge Historical Society Museum (see below). Like the Memorial Arch, the chapel seems to honor an American hero in a peculiarly European way, with flags and stained-glass medievalism.

Next to the chapel is the **Valley Forge Historical Society Museum** (☎ 610/783-0535). The museum has a large collection of Washingtoniana and the deposits of history. Admission is $1.50 for adults, 50¢ for children ages 6 to 18. It's open Monday through Saturday from 9:30am to 4:30pm, Sunday from 1 to 4:30pm; closed major holidays.

Admission to the park is free, but there's a $2 charge for adults to Washington's headquarters from April through November. An autotape tour costs $8 for two hours; there's also tour bus service from the Visitors Center, which costs $5.50 for adults, $4.50 for ages 5 to 16. The park is open daily from 9am to 5pm, later in summer.

A WILDLIFE SANCTUARY

Mill Grove. Audubon and Pawlings rds., Box 25, Audubon, PA 19407. ☎ **610/666-5593.** Free admission. Museum, Tues–Sun 10am–4pm. Grounds, dawn to dusk. Closed major holidays. Take Audubon Road directly, or Route 422 north to Route 363 north, then a left onto it just over the Schuylkill River.

Situated 2 miles north of Valley Forge, the Audubon Wildlife Sanctuary preserves 170 acres around the home of the young John James Audubon. Now the fieldstone mansion with Georgian touches and a kitchen wing is decorated with 1950s murals of birdlife and Audubon's observance of it. The third-floor attic has been restored to his use of it as a drawing studio and taxidermy workplace. Outside, miles of walks among nature's calls and chirps make it easy to linger here for an afternoon. You're welcome to walk but not to picnic or pick.

SHOPPING

King of Prussia Court and Plaza. Near the junction of U.S. 202 and Pa. 363, a half mile south of I-276; 3 miles south of Valley Forge National Historical Park via Route 422. ☎ **215/265-5727.** Mon–Sat 10am–9:30pm, Sun 11am–5pm.

With 450 establishments in three connected tiers, grouped roughly by price range, this is now the second largest mall in the country. It's a fantastic experience; see Chapter 9 for specific retailers and tips.

WHERE TO STAY

Comfort Inn Valley Forge/King of Prussia. 550 W. DeKalb Pike, King of Prussia, PA 19406. ☎ **800/222-0222** or 610/962-0700. Fax 610/962-0218. 121 rms. A/C MINIBAR TV TEL. $78 single or double on Mon–Thurs; weekend specials from $70. Rates include continental-plus breakfast. AAA and CAA discounts. AE, DC, DISC, MC, V.

This five-floor inn is only a mile from the Valley Forge National Park, which makes it good for families. It's 30% to 40% more reasonable than similar hotels in the area. There's a coin-operated laundry and a fitness center on the premises.

Sheraton Valley Forge Hotel. North Gulph Road and 1st Ave., Valley Forge, PA 19406. ☎ **800/325-3535** or 610/337-2000. Fax 610/768-3222. 327 rms, 72 fantasy suites. A/C MINIBAR TV TEL. $120–$130 single; $130–$140 double; suites from $170. AE, DC, MC, V.

This is a busy highrise complex with rooms, suites, five restaurants, and two lounges, all of primary interest to getaway weekenders. The fantasy suites, ranging from Caveman, Wild West, and pre-Raphaelite to Futurist, are remarkably popular. The health club ($15 additional) is open until 12:30am, with Nautilus machines, racquetball courts, a whirlpool, a tanning bed, and a steam room. There is also an outdoor pool and no-smoking floors.

GOING WEST OF VALLEY FORGE

Ridley Creek State Park

Ridley Creek State Park, on Route 3 (West Chester Pike), is about 15 miles west of Center City, 17 miles from the Valley Forge interchange, and 7 miles north of Media and I-95 via Pa. 352. It has two unusual attractions: the bonafide **Colonial Pennsylvania Plantation,** handed down straight from William Penn's charter; and a **superb park** with miles of picnic areas, playgrounds, and hiking and cycling trails. The plantation is the best example in the area of how a "yeoman," or common, family lived in virtual self-sufficiency on a colonial farm. It's staffed mostly by talented schoolteachers who come summer after summer to build wood fences, garden and grow corn, tend pigs and shear sheep, and weave cloth for clothes. Children love it.

The park (☎ **610/566-4800**) is 3 miles past Newtown Square, Sycamore Mills Road, Media, PA 19063. You can contact the Colonial Pennsylvania Plantation, within the park, at P.O. Box 150, Edgemont, PA 19028 (☎ **610/566-1725**). Park admission is free, and plantation admission is $2.50 for adults, $1.50 for seniors and children ages 4 to 12. The park is open daily from 8am to dusk. The plantation is open April through June and October, Friday to Sunday, from 10am to 5pm; July and August, Thursday to Sunday, from 10am to 5pm.

Skippack Village

Skippack Creek feeds into the Schuylkill near Mill Grove, and entrepreneurs have refurbished about 40 colonial and Federal manses as restaurants and shops. As you'd expect, antiques and collectibles rate high on the popularity list, but you can also pursue casual clothes and international dolls. The restaurants here include the moderately priced **Trolley Stop** (☎ **610/584-4849**). To get here, follow Pa. 363 north to Pa. 73.

WHERE TO DINE

Skippack Roadhouse. 4022 Skippack Pike (Rte. 73), Skippack. ☎ **610/584-4231.** Reservations recommended. Main courses $8–$12 at lunch, $17–$26.50 at dinner. Prix-fixe dinner menu at $25 before 6:15pm. AE, DC, MC, V. Mon–Sat 11:30am–2:30pm; Mon–Thurs 5–9pm, Fri–Sat 5–10pm, Sun 4:30–8:30pm. Jazz on Fri and Sat. AMERICAN.

This elegant, charming country roadhouse with a white tile bar, mirrors, and fresh flowers is composed of six intimate dining rooms. The extensive blackboard specials of seasonal items include game and fresh fish and traditional meals of beef, chicken, and lamb. They've also opened the **4022 Rotisserie** next door for reasonable deli fair.

3 Exploring the Brandywine Valley

The Brandywine Valley is a great one- or two-day excursion into rolling country filled with Americana from colonial days through the Gilded Age.

Many of the farms that kept the Revolutionary troops fed have survived to this day. There are 15 covered bridges and 100 antique stores in Chester County alone, with miles of country roads and horse trails between them. Spring and fall are particularly colorful, and don't forget Delaware's tax-free shopping.

The Brandywine Valley is particularly rich in history. Without the defeat at Brandywine, Washington would never have ended up at Valley Forge, from which he emerged with a competent army. When the Du Pont de Nemours family fled post-Revolutionary France, they wound up owning powder mills on the Brandywine Creek. Every pioneer needed gunpowder and iron, and their business grew astronomically, expanding into chemicals and textiles. The Du Ponts controlled upper Delaware as a virtual fiefdom, building splendid estates and gardens. Most of these, along with the original mills, are open to visitors. Winterthur houses the finest collection of American decorative arts ever assembled, and artists like Pyle and Wyeth left rich collections now on public view.

ESSENTIALS

GETTING THERE   I-95 South from Philadelphia has various exits north of Wilmington marked for specific sites, most of which are off Exit 7 to Pa. 52 North. If you have time, Pa. 100 off Pa. 52 North, linking West Chester to Wilmington, passes through picturesque pastureland, forest, and crops. From New York, take Exit 2 off the New Jersey Turnpike onto Route 322 West over the Commodore Barry Bridge into Pennsylvania, and continue on Route 322 to Route 452; take Route 452 north 4 miles to Route 1, the main artery of the valley.

VISITOR INFORMATION   For more information, call the **Brandywine Valley Tourist Information Center,** just outside the gates of **Longwood Gardens** at **800/ 343-3983** or 610/388-2900. For motorists on I-95, Delaware maintains a Visitors Center just south of Wilmington, between Routes 272 and 896. It operates from 8am to 8pm.

CHADDS FORD

Land where a Native American trail (now U.S. 1) forded the Brandywine Creek was purchased from William Penn by Francis Chadsey, an early Quaker immigrant. The present **Chadds Ford Inn,** at the junction of U.S. 1 and U.S. 100

❓ Did You Know?

- The Brandywine Valley has inspired three generations of Wyeths, America's foremost family of artists.
- Pennsylvania has the largest rural population of any state in the nation at 32%, according to the 1990 census.
- Within a 50-mile radius of Kennett Square are grown almost half of all mushrooms produced in the U.S.—that works out to 330 million pounds of cultivated mushrooms annually.

(☎ 610/388-7361) became one of the village's first requirements, a tavern. Taverns were important to small villages in the middle colonies; they served as mail depots, law courts, election hustings, and occasionally prisons. Before the Battle of Brandywine, Washington's officers stayed at the inn; afterward, British troops slaughtered the cattle before marching on the capital of Philadelphia. A small shopping area augments the premises.

BRANDYWINE BATTLEFIELD STATE PARK

This park, 2 miles east of Chadds Ford on Route 1, has no monuments, since the guides say the actual battle was fought outside park borders, but Washington's and Lafayette's reconstructed headquarters mark the site. The grounds, which are excellent for picnicking and hiking, are open from Memorial Day to Labor Day until 8pm. For information, call **610/459-3342.** Admission is $3.50 for adults, $2.50 for seniors, $1.50 for children ages 6 to 17, free for children under 6. Open Tuesday through Saturday from 9am to 5pm, Sunday from noon to 5pm.

✪ **Brandywine River Museum.** Routes 1 and 100, Chadds Ford, PA 19317. ☎ **610/388-2700.** Admission $5 adults, $2.50 children 6–12, free for children under 6. AAA 2-for-1 discount. Daily 9:30am–4:30pm. A self-service restaurant is open from 11am to 3pm.

Across the road from the Brandywine Battlefield State Park, the museum showcases the Brandywine school and other American painters. A 19th-century gristmill has been restored and joined by a dramatic spiral of brick and glass, and the museum's paintings hang in beamed galleries with pine floors. A more recent wing contains a gallery devoted to paintings by Andrew Wyeth. Howard Pyle, a painter and illustrator of adventure tales in the late 19th century, established a school nearby; his students included N. C. Wyeth, Frank Schoonover, and Harvey Dunn. Three generations of Wyeths, from N. C., Carolyn, and Andrew, to Jamie, have stayed, and the museum is particularly strong in their works. Many of the museum's exhibits display the art of book and magazine illustration at its pretelevision zenith.

✪ LONGWOOD GARDENS

This is simply one of the world's great garden displays. Pierre S. Du Pont devoted his life to horticulture; he bought a 19th-century arboretum and created the ultimate estate garden on 1,050 acres. You should plan a half day here.

Longwood Gardens (☎ **610/388-1000**) are on Route 1, just west of the junction of Pa. 52. A Visitors Center has a multimedia briefing of the gardens.

Most people head to the left, toward the Main Fountain Garden, with special evening shows of fluid fireworks in June through September on Tuesday, Thursday, and Saturday evenings, usually preceded by hour-long garden concerts. Wrought-iron chairs and clipped trees and shrubs overlook the jets of water, which rise up to 130 feet. A topiary garden of closely pruned shrubs surrounds a 37-foot sundial.

If you prefer indoors, 4 acres of massive bronze-and-glass conservatories are among the finest and largest in the United States. Orangery displays are breathtaking. African violets, bonsai trees up to 400 years old, hibiscus, orchids, and tropical plants are among the specialties, but look for anything from Easter lilies to scarlet begonias. Subsections display silver desert plants, plants of the Mediterranean, and roses, among others. The plants are exhibited only at their peak and are replaced with others from the extensive growing houses. A parquet-floor ballroom was later added, along with a 10,000-pipe organ, a magnificent instrument played during the year and on Sunday afternoon in winter.

Ahead and to the right of the Visitors Center, more gardens and fountains await along with the Longwood Heritage Exhibit inside the Peirce-du Pont House, the founder's residence. This exhibit, opened in 1995, shows the history of the property, from 2,000-year-old spear points to du Pont family movies. The restaurant offers cafeteria-style dining year-round and full service dining in mid-April through December, with surprisingly good meals.

Admission is $10 for adults ($6 Tuesday), $6 for ages 16 to 20, $2 for ages 6 to 15, free for children under 6. Note that admissions were lowered in 1996 while extensive conservatory work has closed many attractions; work should be completed by 1997. Open April to October daily from 9am to 6pm (conservatories 10am to 6pm); November to March, daily 9am to 5pm. The grounds and conservatories are frequently open late for special events and holiday displays.

✪ WINTERTHUR MUSEUM, GARDEN AND LIBRARY

The later home of the Du Ponts now provides the setting for America's best native collection of decorative arts. Winterthur (☎ **800/448-3883** or 302/888-4600) is 6 miles northwest of Wilmington, Delaware, on Route 52.

Henry Francis Du Pont, a great-grandson of E. I. Du Pont, was a connoisseur of European antiques. But when he turned his attention to a simple Pennsylvania Dutch chest in 1923, he realized that no study had illustrated how American pieces are related to European ones and how the concepts of beauty and taste differed on the two continents. Du Pont collected furniture, then native decorative objects, then interior woodwork of entire homes built between 1640 and 1840. Finally, he added over 200 rooms to put items on display. Because the museum was first a private home, the rooms have a unique richness and intimacy.

In 1992, Winterthur opened the Galleries, a new building adjacent to the existing period rooms. On the first floor the exhibition *Perspectives on the Decorative Arts in Early America* focuses on the social, functional, and other meanings of objects in everyday lives. The second floor features three areas on various aspects of craftsmanship and changing exhibitions. The Main Museum, open for specific guided tours, displays the bulk of the collection and includes complete interiors from every eastern seaboard colony. Special landmarks include the famous Montmorenci Stair Hall, two Shaker Rooms, fine examples of Pennsylvania Dutch decorative arts, and the Du Pont dining room.

In spring the extensive Winterthur Gardens explode with an abundance of cherry and crabapple blossoms, rhododendrons, Virginia bluebells, and azaleas. The lush, carefully planned gardens are well worth viewing any season. Garden tram rides through the grounds are available when weather permits. There are two superb gift shops selling a selection of licensed reproductions, gifts, books, jewelry, and plants.

The Visitor Pavilion Restaurant cooks breakfast, lunch, brunch, and tea to order and seats 350; the Cappuccino Cafe next to the museum offers lighter fare.

There are four admission options: The **General Admission ticket** ($8 adults, $6 seniors and students, $4 children 5 to 11) available year-round includes the Galleries, a self-guided garden walk, and the garden tram. The **Introduction to Winterthur** tour ($5 in addition to General Admission) adds a guided tour of a selection of 175 period rooms. **Decorative Arts tours** ($9 for one-hour and $13 for two-hour tour in addition to General Admission) offer in-depth guided tours for ages 12 and up; reservations are required. **Guided Garden Walks** are $5 in addition to General Admission. Winterthur is open Monday through Saturday from 9:30am to 5pm, Sunday from noon to 5pm; it's closed major holidays.

☺ HAGLEY MUSEUM: THE STORY OF THE DU PONTS

The northern part of Delaware saw early skirmishes among the Swedes, Dutch, and English, and the Revolution was never far away. Since the early 1800s this has been Du Pont country, and the Hagley Museum shows how and when they got their start. It's a wonderful illustration of early American industrialism and manufacturing. The museum (☎ **302/658-2400**) is located on Route 141 in Wilmington; take Route 52 to Route 100, then go to the junction of Routes 100 and 141, then follow directions on Route 141.

Hagley has three parts: the museum building, the reconstructed grounds, and the Upper Residence. The museum building covers the harnessing of the Brandywine River, originally for flour mills; the Du Ponts, who made their first fortune in gunpowder, needed waterpower and willow charcoal—both were here, and the raw materials a barge ride away. E. Irénée Du Pont, the founder, had experience in France with gunpowder and lived at the Upper Residence (despite explosions, which happened every decade or so) to supervise the delicate production process.

On Blacksmith Hill, part of the workers' community has been restored. A visit through the Gibbons House reveals the lifestyle of a typical family, from foods to furniture. Nearby is the school the children attended, complete with lesson demonstrations. At the base of Blacksmith Hill a restored machine shop of the 1880s offers an exciting picture of change in the workplace. Volunteers demonstrate how the din of power tools with whirring belts and grinding metal replaced the quiet, painstaking hand-tooling of the earlier artisans.

Jitneys traverse the tour of the powder yard, but it's just as easy to walk the part of the 240 acres between private family roads on the Upper Residence and the burbling Brandywine. A restored New Century Power House (1880) generates electricity here. Next to the electrical generator, a waterwheel, steam engine, and water turbine show improvements in power through the decades.

The wisteria-covered Georgian residence of the Du Ponts was renovated by a member of the fourth generation, Mrs. Louis Crowninshield, who lived there until her death in 1958. Empire, Federal, and Victorian periods of furniture are highlighted in various room settings. As with all Du Pont residences, the gardens and espaliered trees are superb, and there are flowers throughout the year.

The Belin House on Blacksmith Hill offers light lunches and drinks.

Admission is $9.75 for adults, $7.50 for seniors and students ages 14 to 20, $3.50 for children 6 to 14, free for children under 6. Open March 15 through December daily from 9:30am to 4:30pm; January through March, Saturday and Sunday, from 9:30am to 4:30pm. The Upper Eleutherian Mills Residence is open seasonally in spring and fall; the last jitney goes at 3:30pm.

WHERE TO STAY

You might want to contact the **All About the Brandywine Valley—B&B,** P.O. Box 562, Valley Forge, PA 19481 (☎ **800/344-0123** or 610/783-7783; open 9am to 9pm); they have dozens of charming rooms at rates from $40.

🅂 **Abbey Green Motor Lodge.** 1036 Wilmington Pike (Route 202), West Chester, PA 19382. ☎ **610/692-3310.** 18 rms. A/C TV TEL. $45 single, $55 double. AE, DC, MC, V.

This excellent budget choice is close to the battlefield site at scenic Routes 52 and 100. The family-run motel is designed with a courtyard with its own picnic tables, gazebo, and outdoor fireplace, all set back from the road. All rooms have double beds and a refrigerator, and six units have individual fireplaces.

✪ **Brandywine River Hotel.** Routes 1 and 100, P.O. Box 1058, Chadds Ford, PA 19317-1058. ☎ **610/388-1200.** Fax 610/388-1200, ext. 301. 40 rms, 4 suites. A/C TV TEL. $125 single or double, $149–$169 suite. Rates include continental breakfast and afternoon tea. Children under 12 stay free in parents' room. AE, DC, MC, V.

Built in 1988 and completely renovated by its new owners in 1995, this hotel blends into a hillside, with a facade of brick and cedar shingle, steps away from Chadds Ford Inn. Several rooms have working fireplaces and Jacuzzis. The lobby has a huge open stone fireplace and friendly service, and guest rooms are decorated with Queen Anne cherry-wood furnishings, brass fixtures, chintz fabrics, and local paintings. Breakfast is served in an attractive hospitality room with a fireplace.

✪ **Hamanasett Bed & Breakfast.** P.O. Box 129, Lima, PA 19037. ☎ **610/459-3000.** 8 rms; private bath on second-floor rooms. TV. $85–$120 double. Children over 14 welcome. MC, V only through reservation service. No smoking in bedrooms.

Built in 1856, this farmhouse now functions as one of the most impressive bed & breakfasts in the state—the house itself has been in the hands of Evelene Dohan's family since 1870. Mrs. Dohan's mother was director of the University of Pennsylvania Museum, and her father was a Philadelphia lawyer. The inn and its 48 acres reflect these ties to world-class travels and achievements of the local "aristocracy." All rooms are beautifully furnished in family antiques; the first floor has a conservatory, 2,000-book library, and magnificent foyer stairway. Breakfast is opulent; afternoon tea and evening coffee are available. Mrs. Dohan has an encyclopedic knowledge of the history and attractions of the county; in her youth she covered it all on horseback.

🅂 **Meadow Spring Farm.** 201 E. Street Rd., Kennett Square, PA 19348. ☎ **215/444-3903.** 6 rms (4 with private bath). A/C TV. $75–$85 single or double. Rates include full country breakfast. $10 per child in parents' room. No credit cards. Two-night minimum on weekends; reservations recommended two months in advance.

Anne Hicks operates this working 1936 farmhouse, situated on 125 acres traversed by walking paths. Rooms come with Amish quilts, and common areas display family antiques and dolls. Families are welcome; children may collect eggs, feed the animals, swim in the outdoor pool, or fish in the pond. There's also a hot tub in the solarium and a game room.

WHERE TO DINE

Of the many inns and restaurants connected to them, try the **Chadds Ford Inn,** Routes 1 and 100, Chadds Ford (☎ **610/388-7361**), with its Wyeth paintings; **Dilworthtown Inn,** Old Wilmington Pike and Brinton's Bridge Road, Dilworthtown (☎ **610/399-1390**), for homegrown vegetables and game birds; and **Longwood Inn,** 815 E. Baltimore Pike (Route 1), Kennett Square (☎ **610/444-3515**), showing off this area's position as the mushroom capital of the world.

12

Lancaster County: The Amish Country

Drive about 50 miles west of Philadelphia along Route 30, and you will come to a quietly beautiful region of rolling hills, winding creeks, neatly cultivated farms, covered bridges, and towns with picturesque names like Paradise and Bird-in-Hand: Amish Country or Pennsylvania Dutch Country is an area of 7,100 square miles centered around Lancaster County in the heart of the state. Out of Lancaster County's 422,000 people, who are the 70,000 Pennsylvania Dutch Amish and Mennonites? And why has this small group become increasingly intriguing to 3 to 4 million visitors annually? The answers involve the way the Amish conduct their lives. These people quietly and steadfastly retain a life of agrarian simplicity centered around religious worship and family cohesiveness. As the economic, social, and technological pressures on their lives mount, the preservation of their world evokes feelings of curiosity, nostalgia, amazement, and respect. Not all of these feelings are legitimate or welcomed by the Pennsylvania Dutch. But they are a rare lantern for us to see in sharp relief the distance that our own "outside" world has come over the last two centuries.

For the visitor, Pennsylvania Dutch Country has many special qualities. The area is relatively small with good roads for motorist and bicyclist alike. The attention on the Amish has spurred lots of interesting facsimile and even some authentic pathways into Amish life, although you have to sift through them if you want to avoid overt religious messages. Tourism has in fact promoted excellence in quiltmaking, antiques, and farm-based crafts. There are historical sites, pretzel and chocolate factories, covered bridges, and wonderful farmer's markets, as well as modern diversions such as movie theaters, amusement parks, and great outlet mall shopping. And, of course, the family-style, smorgasbord, all-you-can-eat, or gourmet Pennsylvania Dutch restaurants are experiences as well as meals.

1 Introducing the Pennsylvania Dutch Country

This land has been a major farming region since German settlers found its limestone-rich soil and rolling hills three centuries ago. The county is the most productive nonirrigated farmland county in the United States, and the country's fifth-largest dairy-producing county.

The ease of getting goods to market in Philadelphia, the natural abundance, and the hard work of its settlers all have preserved major portions of the land for farms, although these intelligent people have also stimulated manufacturing in Lancaster, York, and other towns. Lancaster in its day was a major town and center of culture and politics; it was the largest inland city in the United States from 1760 to 1810, and one-time candidate for the honor of serving as the new nation's capital. (In fact, Lancaster *was* the national capital for one day—September 27, 1777—when Congress fled from Philadelphia.) The balance between factory and farm has been pressured in this century by the development of the automobile and the construction of major roads like the Pennsylvania Turnpike. These have made former fields within commuting distance for suburban workers of Harrisburg and Philadelphia. The buildup of housing developments and attendant schools, services, and strip malls for this exploding population competes with lovely, placid fields dotted with farmhouses, barns, silos, and small creeks crossed by covered bridges.

A LOOK AT THE PAST

Originally peopled by subsections of the Delaware and Iroquois Indians, Lancaster County's first permanent white settlers were a group of Swiss refugees originally from the Palatinate. Word of mouth about the fertile farmland—very much like that back home, but much more abundant—and William Penn's promise of religious freedom drew thousands of German-speaking immigrants in the early 18th century. These were lumped together as Pennsylvania "Dutch"—a corruption of *Deutsch,* the German word for their own language and ethnicity. While the most famous and long-lasting immigrants remain Mennonite sects and particularly the Amish, it should be noted that the colonial period also saw a mixture of Scotch–Irish Presbyterians, French Protestants, English from Maryland, and Jews from Iberia settle the region. Still, you won't see too much variation in ethnic stock between 1796 and 1996 in this part of the country.

The religious sects that make up the Pennsylvania Dutch are part of the Mennonite strand of the Protestant Reformation. The political wars and social atrocities carried out during this period of religious separation from the Catholic Church tore apart the lands of the Holy Roman Empire for 150 years, forcing some groups to seek refuge in the New World. Both the Amish and the Mennonites, as well as the Brethren and Schwenkfelders (another Lancaster County sect), are Anabaptists. A Christian faith that emerged during the 16th century, Anabaptism believes in the literal interpretation of the Bible, in baptism only for people adult enough to volunteer to undergo this rite of transformation, and in remaining separate from larger society. Menno Simons, a Catholic priest from Holland, joined the Anabaptists in 1536 and united the various groups, who became known after him as Mennonites. In 1693, a Mennonite bishop, Jacob Amman, found the Mennonite Church too tolerant of lax sinners and broke with his followers to establish the Old Order Amish.

Both the Amish and the Mennonites faced persecution as heretics by both Catholics and Protestants; many were put to death, and many others fled to the mountains of Switzerland and Germany. In the first third of the 18th century, a substantial number of Amish and Mennonites emigrated to the American colonies to escape persecution. They settled in Pennsylvania, where William Penn's "holy experiment" of religious tolerance promised them a haven.

TOURIST DOLLARS VS. STRIP MALLS: THE AMISH TODAY

Until about 40 years ago, the Amish were not particularly noteworthy as a tourist attraction. However, since the mid-1950s, with rapid development of new technologies in all areas of life, Amish tenacity in maintaining their traditional ways of life and religious convictions have made them both unusual and alluring. For better or worse, in the last several decades, the Amish have become the cornerstone of Lancaster County's tourist industry.

As this process began, most people, including many Amish, saw the increase in tourism as a positive development. Money flowed into the county, and the Amish found a growing market for such goods as quilts, metalwork, crafts, and foodstuffs literally appearing at their doors. For the Amish, however, the less benign consequences of this development are becoming more apparent today. The Amish population is about 20,000 and growing, but as outsiders move to Lancaster County, so is the non-Amish population of 400,000. Their need for affordable housing drives up land prices and attracts strip developers. In past years when Amish families looked for land to buy for their children's farms, they turned to non-Amish farmers quitting the area. Today, those farmers can get better prices from developers. In 1986 and 1987, 15,000 acres were transformed from fields to developments, leaving about 400,000 acres of farmland. As farm prices rise, it is becoming increasingly difficult for parents to purchase land for their children.

This means many Amish are forced to leave their farms and set up nonfarming businesses. The local construction business in Lancaster County ironically includes many Amish workers who travel to Delaware and Maryland on jobs. Women who traditionally worked in the home and the farm are increasingly running businesses such as restaurants and shops or overseeing quilting and craft enterprises. Despite the injuction to remain separate from wider society, many families offer "Amish-style" dinners at their homes, and aggressively exploit the cachet that "Amish-made" gives to foods, craft objects, clothing, hex signs, and other souvenirs and products.

MEET THE AMISH

The three major Anabaptist sects in Lancaster County—Amish, Mennonite, and Brethren—share many beliefs, including those concerning baptism, nonresistance, and basic Bible doctrine. They differ in matters of dress, use or avoidance of technology, literal interpretation of the Bible, and form of worship. For example, the Amish worship in home services, while Mennonites have churches. The Amish do not proselytize, while Mennonites have a strong tradition of missionary work.

Today the Amish live in settlements in 20 states and in Ontario, Canada. In Lancaster County they center around Intercourse, Bird-in-Hand, and Lancaster (city); Mennonites center around Terre Hill and Martindale, a few miles to the northeast within the county. The majority of Amish live and work on farms growing corn, wheat, tobacco (though most will not smoke it, and some won't grow it, for religious reasons), and alfalfa, although an increasing number earn their incomes at other jobs, either as sidelines from their homes related to craft production of quilts or preserves, or in the nonfarm economy of the region. They are a trilingual people, speaking Pennsylvania Dutch (essentially a dialect of German) at home, English at school and with members of the larger society, and High German at worship services.

The family is the most important social unit among the Amish, and large families with 7 or 10 children are the norm. Not surprisingly, the Amish population is growing—it has more than doubled since the 1970s—and more than half the Amish in Lancaster County are under the age of 18. You will see dozens of postboxes marked with Zook, Stoltzfus, and Zinn as testimony to the proliferation of extended families. The Old Testament–sounding practice of "shunning," or of complete excommunication from family relations for Amish who marry outsiders or violate basic tenets, seems to have relaxed in recent decades. Even so, about 80% of Amish children choose to spend their entire lives in the same framework as their upbringing, including birth and death within the home.

Children attend school in one-room schoolhouses, built and maintained by the Amish, through the eighth grade. There are approximately 150 such schools in Lancaster County, and new ones are still being built. Amish schools teach the basics only, and students have special exemptions from standard state curriculum and are allowed to leave school at the age of 16 if they choose. There is no formal religious instruction in school; this is kept within the family.

To the visitor, the two most distinctive characteristics of the Amish are their clothing and their use of horse and buggies rather than cars. Both these features are linked to their religious beliefs. The distinctive clothing worn by about 35,000 "Plain People" in Lancaster County is meant to encourage humility and modesty, as well as separation from larger society. Amish men and boys wear dark-colored suits, straight-cut coats without lapels, broadcloth trousers, suspenders, solid-colored shirts, black socks and shoes, and black or straw broad-brimmed hats. Men wait to grow beards until they are married, and do not grow mustaches. Women and girls wear solid-colored, modest dresses with long sleeves and long full skirts, covered by a cape and an apron. They never cut their hair, but gather it in a bun on the back of the head, concealed by a white prayer covering. Amish women do not wear jewelry or printed fabric. Single women in their teens and 20s wear black prayer coverings for church services. After marriage, a white covering is worn.

The Amish are reluctant to accept technology, which could weaken the family structure. Rather than cars, most Amish drive horse-drawn buggies, which help keep them close to home by limiting distances that can be traveled in a day. However, inline skating is allowed. Most use no electricity or telephone. As new ideas emerge, each district congregation of about 100 families evaluates them and decides what to accept and what to reject. The fundamental criterion is that an innovation not jeopardize the simplicity of their lives and the strength of the family unit.

RECOMMENDED BOOKS & FILMS

There are a number of excellent books on the Amish way of life. The classic is John Hostetler's *Amish Society* (Johns Hopkins, 3rd ed., 1983); a more impassioned if ideological new age approach is *After the Fire: The Destruction of the Lancaster County Amish* (University Press of New England, 1992) by Randy-Michael Testa. Children's books include *Growing Up Amish* by Richard Ammon (Macmillan, 1990), and wonderful color photographs in *Amish Home* by Raymond Bial (Houghton Mifflin, 1993). Since Amish do not permit photography, any film depiction is going to be compromised. In *Witness* (1985), Harrison Ford goes undercover in the region as a Philadelphia cop; his cover is blown when he slugs a local redneck taunting the Amish.

2 Essentials

The heart of Pennsylvania Dutch Country centers on wedges of land to the east and (to a lesser extent) west of county capital Lancaster. It is bordered on the west by the Susquehanna River, and to the south, by the Maryland border and the Mason-Dixon line.

GETTING THERE

Lancaster County is 57 miles and 90 minutes west of Philadelphia, directly on Route 30. From the Northeast, the easiest route is to take I-95 south from New York

City onto the New Jersey Turnpike, then take Exit 6 onto the Pennsylvania Turnpike (I-76), following this to Exit 21 or 20 on either side of Lancaster city. You'll still be about 10 miles north of Lancaster: from exit 21 you'll follow Rout 222 into the city; from exit 20, Route 72. Travel time is 2¼ hours, and tolls amount to $6. From the south, follow I-83 north for 90 minutes from Baltimore, then head east on Route 30 from York into the county. If you're in Brandywine County or Longwood Gardens, you're only minutes from Amish farms in Gap, via Routes 41 and 741.

By train, Amtrak takes 70 minutes from 30th Street Station in Philadelphia to the great old Lancaster station, 10 blocks from Penn Square. The fare is $12, and eight trains run daily. Three buses run daily ($12.35) and take two hours from the Convention Center Trailways Terminal in Philadelphia to the Capitol Trailways Bus Terminal, 22 W. Clay St., in Lancaster (☎ 717/397-4861).

VISITOR INFORMATION

Before you set out you should get in touch with the **Pennsylvania Dutch Convention & Visitors Bureau,** 501 Greenfield Rd., Lancaster, PA 17601 (☎ **800/ PA DUTCH** ext. 2405 or 717/299-8901). The office itself is off the Route 30 bypass east of Lancaster. They provide an excellent detailed map and visitors' guide to the region, along with answers to specific questions and interests. They also have a wealth of brochures, direct telephone links to many local hotels, and a multi-image slide show, "There Is a Season," a good 14-minute overview of the county. The bureau is open Sunday through Thursday from 8am to 6pm and on Friday and Saturday from 8am to 7pm.

The **Mennonite Information Center,** 2209 Millstream Rd., Lancaster (☎ 717/ 299-0954), has a lot of the same information but specializes in linking you with Mennonite guest houses and church worship. On the half hour they show "A Morning Song," a film featuring a Mennonite family at home on their farm. They will also provide Mennonite tour guides who will travel the back roads in your car to farm stands and local crafters and quilters; expect a dose of religious dialogue. The center is open Monday through Saturday from 8am to 5pm.

Many towns such as Intercourse, Strasburg, and Lancaster have local information centers, and the **Exit 21 Tourist Information Center** on Route 272 just south of I-76 is open from 10am to 2pm daily. It's next to **Zinn's Diner** (☎ 717/336-2210), which looks suspect with its statue of "Big Amos," batting cages, and miniature golf, but the menu, portions, and clientele are very typically Pennsylvania Dutch. The diner is open daily from 6am to 11pm.

GETTING AROUND

Lancaster County's principal artery is Route 30, which runs from Philadelphia to York and Gettysburg, but beware: Major roads like Route 30 and Route 222 at Lancaster, and Route 340 from Intercourse to Lancaster, can be crowded, especially in the summer with the onslaught of bus tours. The 25,000 horse-drawn vehicles in the county tend to stick to quieter back roads, but some highways cannot be avoided. Traffic is much lighter in spring and autumn. And please be careful; there have been several horrible rear-end crashes in the 1990s in which tourist autos have destroyed Amish families in buggies. If you're in a jam, you can reach AAA service at **717/ 397-6135.**

Within Lancaster County, Red Rose Transit, 45 Erick St. (☎ 717/397-4246), serves the region, with a base fare of $1.

Lancaster & the Pennsylvania Dutch Country

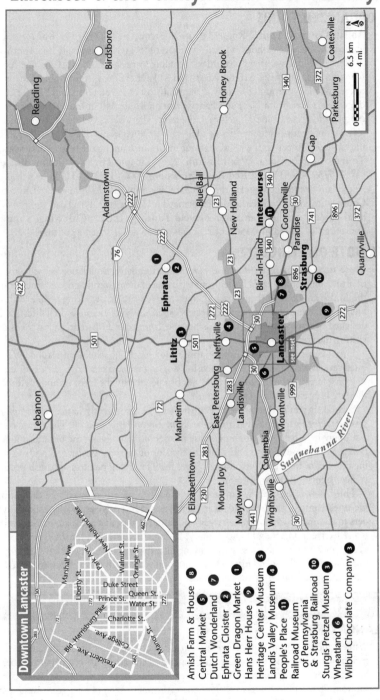

Downtown Lancaster

Amish Farm & House **8**
Central Market **5**
Dutch Wonderland **7**
Ephrata Cloister **2**
Green Dragon Market **1**
Hans Herr House **9**
Heritage Center Museum **5**
Landis Valley Museum **4**
People's Place **11**
Railroad Museum
 of Pennsylvania
 & Strasburg Railroad **10**
Sturgis Pretzel Museum **3**
Wheatland **6**
Wilbur Chocolate Company **3**

ORGANIZED TOURS

Amish Country Tours, Route 340 in Intercourse (☎ **717/392-8622**), offers guided back-road two-hour bus and minivan tours at 10:30am daily and 1pm and 2:30pm on Monday through Saturday, including stops at Amish farms and one-room schoolhouses. The fee is $16 for adults and $11 for children. A four-hour version is offered Monday through Saturday at 9am and costs $25 for adults and $15 for children. Tours leave from Plain and Fancy Farm on Route 340 in Intercourse, and you can procure tickets at local hotels or at the farm. The Visitors Center can recommend several tours with private guides in their vans or in your car. They generally run in the range of $30 per hour with a two-hour minimum. Among the best are **Brunswick Tours,** at the National Wax Museum, 2249 Lincoln Highway, Route 30 East (☎ **717/397-7451**), and **Red Rose Excursions,** (☎ **717/397-3175**), which provides Plain People on Monday through Saturday from 9am to 9pm to any Lancaster County location. The **Mennonite Information Center** (see above) can also provide local guides. Finally, **Lancaster Bicycle Touring, Inc.,** 3 Colt Ridge Lane in Strasburg (☎ **717/396-0456**), offers maps and an active schedule of tours.

A NOTE ON ETIQUETTE

There aren't too many settings in the world where a native population is itself a tourist attraction. Pennsylvania Dutch country is one of them, but that doesn't mean that the Amish are there as theme park characters. They are hardworking people leading busy lives. Your courtesy and respect is especially vital because their lifestyle is designed to remove them as much as possible from your 20th-century fast focus on visiting the area.

First, *do not trespass* onto Amish farms, homesteads, or schools in session. We've listed several settings where you can visit a working farm, take a carriage ride, or even stay on a farm. Although these would not be operated by the most orthodox Amish, they are near enough in letter and spirit.

Second, if you're dealing with Pennsylvania Dutch directly, *don't even think of photographing these people, and ask before taking any photographs at all.* The Amish have a strongly held belief that photographic images of them violate the biblical injunction against graven images and promote the sins of personal vanity and pride. Taking pictures of their land and animals is permissible; taking pictures of Amish people is inconsiderate and disrespectful.

Third, *watch the road.* What passes for moderate suburban speed in a car can be life-threatening in this area. Roads in Lancaster County have especially wide shoulders to accommodate horses, carriages, and farm tractors, and these are marked with red reflective triangles and lights at night. It's much better, even for the sights alone, to slow down to Amish paces; and honking disturbs the horses. If you have the time, this is superb walking and bicycling country, punctuated by farm stands for refreshment and quiet conversations with Amish families.

3 Exploring Amish Country

LANCASTER

While Lancaster (pronounced *lank*-uh-stir) has been the most important city in the region, it hit its peaks in the Colonial era and as an early 20th-century urban beehive, and the architecture and attractions reflect this. The basic street grid layout copied from Philadelphia centers at Penn Square, the intersection of King (east–west) and Queen (north–south) Streets. You won't see too many Plain People venturing into town anymore since they can buy provisions and equipment more easily at regional stores, but they still sell at the **Central Market.** Erected in 1889 just off Penn Square but operating since the 1730s, it's the nation's oldest farmer's market, with more than 80 stalls. You can savor and select regional produce and foods, from sweet bologna and scrapple to breads, cheeses, egg noodles, shoofly pie, and *schnitzel* or dried apple. The market is open Tuesday and Friday from 6am to 4:30pm and Saturday from 6am to 2pm.

Beside the Market is a **Heritage Center Museum** (☎ 717/299-6440) in the old City Hall, with a moderately interesting collection of crafts and historical artifacts of the county. It's open Tuesday through Saturday from 10am to 4pm and is free. On the western edge of town is **Wheatland,** 1120 Marietta Ave. (Route 23; ☎ 717/392-8721), the gracious Federal mansion of the 15th U.S. president, James Buchanan. It features costumed guides and is open daily from 10am to 4:15pm from April to November; admission is $5.50 for adults, $4.50 for seniors, $3.50 for students, and $1.75 for children 6 through 12.

Five miles south of town near Willow Street rests the 1719 **Hans Herr House,** 1849 Hans Herr Dr., off Route 222 (☎ 717/464-4438), the oldest building in the county. It's now owned by the Lancaster Mennonite Historical Society, and restored and furnished to illustrate early Mennonite life, with a historic orchard and outdoor exhibit of agricultural tools. You can visit Monday through Saturday from 9am to 4pm from April through December only; admission is $3.50 for adults and $1 for children 7 to 12.

The eastern side of town peters into a welter of faux Amish attractions and amusements like Dutch Wonderland and Running Pump Mini-Golf, fast-food restaurants, and outlet stores on Route 30 near where Route 340 splits to the north toward Intercourse. The **Amish Farm & House,** 2395 Lincoln Highway (☎ 717/394-6185), offers guided tours of a 10-room Old Order Amish house, with live animals and exhibits including a waterwheel outside. A Dutch Food Pavilion provides local treats. It's open daily from 8:30am to 6pm from June to September and from 8:30am to 4pm from October to May; admission is $5 for adults and $2.50 for children 5 to 11.

INTERCOURSE

Intercourse's suggestive name refers to the intersection of two old highways, the King's Highway (now Route 340 or Old Philadelphia Pike) and Newport Road (now Route 772). The King's Highway was used by the Conestoga wagons invented a few miles south; these unusually broad and deep wagons became famous for transporting homesteaders all the way west to the Pacific.

The town is now ground zero for Amish life, in the midst of the wedge of country east of Lancaster; unfortunately the buildup of commercial attractions, from the schlocky to good quality, about equals places of genuine interest along Route 340. One not to miss is **The People's Place,** 3513 Old Philadelphia Pike (☎ 717/768-7171), an interpretive center with the 30-minute documentary "Who Are the Amish?" as well as an excellent hands-on museum with antique quilts and a bookshop/gallery. It's open Monday through Saturday from 9:30am to 9pm from April to October and from 9:30am to 5pm from November to March; admission is $5 for adults and $2.50 for children. Of the commercial developments, try **Kitchen Kettle Village,** also on the Old Philadelphia Pike (Route 340; ☎ 717/768-8261), 32 stores selling crafts from decoys to fudge grouped around Pat and Bob Burnley's 1954 jam and relish kitchen. Their Lapp Family Farms ice-cream store, with 20 all-natural flavors, is much more convenient than the original farm stand near New Holland.

The Bridges of Lancaster County

Forget about the Midwest and Clint Eastwood—Pennsylvania is the birthplace of covered bridge building, with some 1,500 built between the 1820s and 1900. Today 219 remain, mostly on secondary country roads, and you can actually drive (slowly!) through most of them. Lancaster County has the largest concentration with 28, including one on the way to Paradise, a small village east of Lancaster City. Bridges were covered to protect the trusses from the weather, and more are lost through floods and hurricanes than anything else. The link between good luck and kissing inside one? Well, they're protected from rain, and their one-lane width means a certain amount of privacy—not to mention those evocative wooden planks. The Lancaster County Visitors Bureau map indicates all covered bridge locations; call 800/723-8824, extension 2435, for a copy.

Of the 28 county bridges, the following three are interesting and relatively easy to get to:

- **Hunsecker Bridge:** This is the largest covered bridge in the county, and was built in 1975 to replace the original, which was washed away in Hurricane Agnes. From Lancaster, drive 5 miles north on Route 272. After you pass Landis Valley Farm Museum, turn right on Hunsecker Road and drive 2 miles.
- **Paradise/Leaman Place Bridge:** This bridge is in the midst of Amish cornfields and farms. A truck that couldn't fit through the bridge put it out of commission in the 1980s, but it has been restored. Drive north 1 mile on Belmont Road from Route 30, just east of the center of Paradise.
- **Kauffman's Distillery Bridge:** Drive west on Route 772 from Manheim, and make a left onto West Sunhill Road. The bridge will be in front of you, along with horses grazing nearby.

EPHRATA

Ephrata, near Exit 21 off I-76 northeast of Lancaster, combines a historic 18th-century Moravian religious site with some pleasant country and the area's largest farmer's market and auction center. **Ephrata Cloister,** 632 W. Main St. (☎ 717/733-6600), near the junction of Routes 272 and 322, was one of America's earliest communal societies, known for its fraktur (calligraphied print and pottery in Gothic German), music, and printing. Ten austere wooden 18th-century buildings (no nails, even) remain in a grassy park setting. The cloister is open Monday through Saturday from 9am to 5pm and on Sunday from noon to 5pm; admission is $5 for adults, $4 for seniors, and $3 for children 6 to 17. Saturday evenings in summer bring "Vorspiel" performances that feel like Bach live.

The main street of Ephrata is pleasant for strolling and includes an old rail car where the train line used to run. **Doneckers** (see below) has expanded from a single inn north of town into a farmer's market, gourmet restaurant, and shopping complex. Four miles north of town on North State Street is the wonderful ✪ **Green Dragon Market** (☎ 717/738-1117), open Friday from 6am to 7pm. Two auction houses make up the heart of Green Dragon—one for antiques and bric-a-brac, one for farm animals. It's an amazing sight to see goats and cows changing hands in the most elemental way, and children are allowed total petting access in the process. Summer brings fresh corn, fruit, and melons. Around the auctions a full flea market and arcade has sprung up, with plenty of cotton candy, clams on the half-shell, and fresh corn.

LITITZ

Founded in 1756, this town, 6 miles north of Lancaster on Route 501, is one of the state's most charming. The cottage facades along East Main Street haven't changed much in the past two centuries. One of the most interesting is the **Linden Hall Academy,** founded in 1794 as the first school for girls in the United States and still private; there are several Revolutionary War–era churches and buildings on the grounds. Lititz was once known as "the Pretzel Town," and across the street from Linden Hall is the **Julius Sturgis Pretzel House,** 219 E. Main St. (☎ 717/626-4354). Founded in 1861, it's the oldest such bakery in the country, and offers 20-minute guided tours; at their conclusion you can try your own hand at rolling, twisting, and sprinkling with coarse salt. Summer tours are given Monday through Saturday from 9:30am to 4:30pm and cost $1.50; the store is open Sunday from noon to 5pm as well.

At the junction of Route 501 and Main Street is **Wilbur Chocolate Company's Candy Americana Museum & Store,** 48 N. Broad St. (☎ 717/626-3249). Famous for its Wilbur buds, the factory offers a brief look at the process and history, with samples and sales in a country store atmosphere. Next door is the **Lititz Springs Park,** with a lovely duck-filled brook emanating from the 1756 spring, fields, and playgrounds, and the historic **General Sutter Inn.**

STRASBURG

This little town named by French Huguenots southeast of Lancaster on Route 896 is a haven for rail buffs. Until the invention of the auto, railroads were the major mode of American transport; tracks went even to small towns, and Pennsylvania was a leader in building and servicing thousands of engines. The **Strasburg Rail Road** (☎ 717/687-7522) winds 9 miles of preserved track from Strasburg to Paradise and back, as it has since 1832; wooden coaches and a Victorian parlor car are pulled by an iron steam locomotive. It's on Route 741 east of town and is open daily from April to October and on weekends only from November to March; the fare is $7.50 for adults and $3 for children. Other attractions include the **Railroad Museum of Pennsylvania** (☎ 717/687-8628), with dozens of stationary engines right across the street; the **National Toy Train Museum** (☎ 717/687-8976), on Paradise Lane off Route 741, with five huge push-button operating layouts; and **Choo Choo Barn** (☎ 717/687-7911), a 1,700-square-foot miniature county landscape filled with animated trains, figures, and activities such as parades and circuses. It recently linked up with the inevitable authorized Thomas Trackside Station store.

4 Especially for Kids

With the exception of beaches, Pennsylvania Dutch Country has everything for families, including rainy-day alternatives. In addition to the suggestions below, try the above-mentioned **Julius Sturgis Pretzel Museum** in Lititz, **People's Place** in Intercourse, and the various railroad-related attractions in Strasburg.

BUGGY RIDES

Driving for a couple of miles along a country lane in a horse-drawn carriage not only sounds irresistible but fits right in with the time frame the Amish share. Of the half-dozen outfits, the most reliable are **Abe's Buggy Ride** (☎ 717/664-4888), Route 340, one-half mile east of the Route 896 junction, with 2-mile jaunts, and **Ed's Buggy Rides** (☎ 717/687-0360), on Route 896, 1 1/2 miles south of Route 30 in Strasburg, with 3-mile rides leaving from the Red Caboose Motel. Jack Meyer of Abe's is slightly more expensive ($8 for adults and $4 for children vs. $6.50 and

$3.50); both are open Monday through Saturday until dusk, and both have knowledgeable characters behind the reins. Note that Jack Meyer, his wife Dee Dee, and their six children are River Brethren and are open to inviting guests to their home for dinner; the meal is $15 for adults and $7.50 for children. Call them at **717/664-4888** for reservations or information.

DUTCH WONDERLAND

That ersatz castle (☎ **717/291-1888**) you see heading east on 2249 Lincoln Highway (Route 30) out of Lancaster is the headquarters for a 44-acre amusement park with gardens and shows like high diving. There's a moderately wild roller coaster, but most of the 24 rides are easy to take for young families. Unlimited rides cost $18.50 for adults, $14.50 for children 3 to 5 and seniors; a five-ride ticket is $12. The park is open daily from Memorial Day to Labor Day from 10am to 7pm; it's also open weekends in the spring and fall until November.

HERSHEY

Hershey is technically 30 minutes northwest of Lancaster, outside the county on Route 422, but the assembly of rides, amusements, and natural scenery in a storybook setting makes this the sweetest town on earth. Milton Hershey set up a town that reflected his business and philanthropy, and it has expanded into **Hershey's Chocolate World,** Park Boulevard (☎ **717/534-4900**), a free tour that takes you from cacao beans to wrapped samples, and **Hersheypark,** a huge theme park at the junctions of Routes 743 and 422 (☎ **800/HERSHEY** or 717/534-3090), with more than 50 rides and attractions including water rides, 4 coasters, 5 theaters with periodic music, and 20 kiddie rides. Hersheypark also includes the 11-acre **ZooAmerica,** with over 200 animals native to North America. Hersheypark is open from mid-May to September, and all summer until 10pm on Monday through Thursday and until 11pm on Friday through Sunday. Admission is $27 for adults and $16 for children 3 to 8; you can enter ZooAmerica separately for much less.

The logical place to stay is the **Hershey Lodge,** West Chocolate Avenue and University Drive (☎ **717/534-8600**), with miniature golf, tennis courts, and its own movie theater. And if you're tempted to sneak away without kids, Hershey does have superb gardens, 72 holes of championship golf, and the palace-like **Hotel Hershey** (☎ **717/533-2176**) up the mountain.

LANDIS VALLEY MUSEUM

Following Oregon Pike (Route 272) north from Lancaster for 5 miles, you'll come to Landis Valley, 2451 Kissel Hill Rd. (☎ **717/569-0401**). This is the largest outdoor museum of the distinct Pennsylvania German culture, folk traditions, decorative arts, and language. George and Henry Landis began to collect their ancestors' objects and established a small museum here in the 1920s; this has mushroomed into a "living arts" complex of 21 buildings since the Commonwealth of Pennsylvania acquired it in 1953. The costumed practitioners—clockmakers and clergymen, tavern keepers and tinsmiths, storekeepers, teachers, printers, and weavers, as well as farmers—are expert and also free with samples, which are also for sale in the shop. The museum is open Tuesday through Saturday from 9am to 5pm and on Sunday from noon to 5pm; admission is $6 for adults and $4 for children 6 through 17.

5 Shopping

There are three reasons to keep that credit card handy in Lancaster County. Quilts and other craft products unique to the area are sold in dozens of small stores and out of individual farms. The thrifty character of the Pennsylvania Dutch has translated into 300 years of keeping old furniture and objects in their barns and attics, so antiquing is plentiful here. Fine pieces tend to migrate toward New Hope and Bucks County for resale; you compete directly with dealers at the many fairs and shows. Finally, a dozen outlet centers will provide name-brand items at discounts of 30% to 70%, along Route 30 east of Lancaster and in central Reading.

QUILTS

Quilts occupy a special place in the crafts of the county. German immigrant women took the necessity of reworking strips of used but still usable fabric, and created an ever-expanding series of pleasant designs linked with their folkways. Popular designs include *Wedding Ring*, interlocking sets of four circles; the eight-pointed *Lone Star* radiating out with bursts of colors; *Sunshine and Shadow*, virtuoso displays of diamonded color; and herringboned *Log Cabin* squares with multicolored strips. More contemporary quilters have added free-form picture designs to these traditional patterns. The process is laborious and technically astounding—think of choosing, cutting, and affixing thousands of pieces of fabric, then filling it in with up to 100 hours of intricate needlework designs on the white "ground" that holds the layers of the quilt together! Expect to pay $500 or more for a good-quality quilt, and $25 and up for potholders, bags, and throw pillows.

The People's Place in Intercourse, 3513 Old Philadelphia Pike, is a good place to start looking for quilts; their Old Country Store (☎ 717/768-7171) has a knowledgeable sales staff and excellent inventory. **The Quiltworks at Doneckers,** located at The Artworks complex, 100 N. State St. in Ephrata, has collected more than 100 traditional Amish and contemporary quilts from the area and is open daily. Emma Witmer's mother was one of the first women to hang out a shingle to sell quilts 30 years ago, and she continues with over 100 patterns at **Witmer Quilt Shop,** 1070 W. Main St. in New Holland (☎ 717/656-9526). The shop is open 8am to 6pm on Tuesday through Thursday and Saturday and until 8pm on Monday and Friday.

Most of the county's back roads will have simple signs indicating that quilts are sold; selections tend to be more limited but prices are slightly lower. Rosa Stoltzfus operates **Hand Made Quilts** at 102 N. Ronks Rd. in Ronks (no telephone) out of a room in her Amish home surrounded by cornfields. **Hannah Stoltzfoos** has a similar selection on 216 Witmer Rd. (no telephone), just south of Route 340 near Smoketown.

OTHER CRAFTS

Amish and Mennonites have produced their own baskets, dolls, furniture, pillows, toys, wall hangings, and hex designs for centuries, and tourism has led to a healthy growth in their production. Much of this output is channeled into the stores lining Route 340 in Intercourse and Bird-in-Hand such as the Amish-owned **Country Barn Quilts and Crafts,** 2808 Old Philadelphia Pike (no telephone), **Family Creations,** 3453 Old Philadelphia Pike (☎ 717/768-8651), and **Dutchland Quilt Patch,** 4361 Old Philadelphia Pike (☎ 717/687-0534). The **Weathervane Shop** at Landis Valley Museum (see "Especially for Kids" earlier in the chapter) has a fine collection of what's produced by their own craftspeople, from tin and pottery to caned chairs. On the contemporary side, no one works harder than **The Artworks at Doneckers,** 100 N. State St., Ephrata (☎ 717/738-9503), which combines crafts with designer clothing and contemporary needs.

ANTIQUES

Two miles east of Exit 21 off I-76, Route 272 in Adamstown, just before it crosses into Berks County to the northeast, is the undisputed local center of Sunday fairs, with six or seven competitors within 5 miles. The largest are **Stoudt's Black Angus Antique Mall,** with more than 350 permanent dealers, and **Renninger's Antique and Collectors Market,** with 370 dealers. At Renninger's, check out stall 52^1/$_2$ A for Tiffany glass, 89 for chldren's clothes, or 32A for antique linens and hooked rugs. For weekday stocks, try the 125 dealers at **White Horses Antiques Market,** 973 W. Main St. (Route 230; ☎ **717/653-6338**), in Mount Joy, a pleasant town north of some covered bridges.

FARMER'S MARKETS

Most farmers markets in Lancaster County today are stable shedlike buildings with stalls at which local farmers, butchers, and bakers vend their fruits and vegetables, eggs and cheese, baked goods and pastries, and meat products like turkey sausage and scrapple. Since farmers can only afford to get away once or twice a week (for example, the Amish commute to sell at Germantown and at Reading Terminal in Philadelphia on Thursday through Saturday), the more commercial markets tend to augment the local goods with gourmet stalls selling everything from deerskin to candy, and "hard goods" like souvenirs. A low-ceilinged, air-conditioned space also doesn't carry the same zest as, say, **Central Market** in Lancaster (see "Lancaster" above), with its swirling fans and 1860 tiles and hitching posts, or Friday at **Green Dragon Market** (see "Ephrata" above), North State Street in Ephrata.

A notable contemporary market is the **Bird-in-Hand Farmer's Market** at Route 340 and Maple Avenue (☎ **717/393-9674**). It's open from 8:30am to 5:30pm on Friday and Saturday year-round, as well as Wednesday and Thursday during the summer. They have homemade ice cream and are linked to Good 'n' Plenty Restaurant nearby. I also like **Meadowbrook Farmer's Market** on Route 23 in Leola (☎ **717/656-0944**), open Friday from 8am to 7pm and Saturday from 8am to 5pm, with 180 stands. **Root's Country Market and Auction,** just south of Manheim on Route 72, is a very complete market on Tuesday.

Among the dozens of roadside stands you'll see, try the homemade root beer, breads, and pies at **Countryside Stand,** on Stumptown Road; take a right turn from Route 772 heading west out of Intercourse and follow Stumptown for one-half mile. **Fisher's Produce,** on Route 741 between Strasburg and Gap, sells baked goods along with fresh corn and melons in the summer.

OUTLET CENTERS

With 106 stores, **Rockvale Square Factory Outlet Village,** Route 30 East, is Lancaster's largest. Jonathan Logan, Harvé Bernard, Evan-Picone, Nautica, Izod, Jockey, London Fog, and Bass Shoes are represented, with Oneida, Lenox, Dansk, and Pfaltzgraff for housewares. I prefer the newer **Tanger Outlet Center at Millstream,** 311 Outlet Drive, Route 30 East, for shops like Donna Karan, Ann Taylor, Reebok, J. Crew, Guess?, London Fog, and Brooks Brothers. It's slightly closer to Lancaster and more compact. The project also includes a 125-seat bakery and deli run by Miller's of Miller's Smorgasbord fame. My children love the selection of leggings (and also the movies) at So Fun, Kids! Both complexes are open Monday through Saturday from 9:30am to 9pm, and Sunday from noon to 5pm.

Manufacturers Outlet Mall, at the junction of Exit 22 off the Pennsylvania Turnpike and Route 23 in Morgantown, has more than 50 stores, including Levi Strauss, Munsingweat, and Van Heusen, in an entirely enclosed mall with a food court; a Holiday Inn with indoor recreation rounds out the premises. It's open Monday through Saturday from 10am to 9pm and Sunday from 11am to 5pm.

I don't have the space or the adjectives to detail what's been built up in **Reading** to retool the enormous mills along the Schuylkill as "The Outlet Capital of the

World." But 260 separate centers draw some 6 million shoppers annually, and it's 30 minutes from Lancaster or 75 from Philadelphia, via I-76 to I-176 north to Route 422. The two largest destinations are **Vanity Fair Factory Outlet Complex,** just west of the city in Wyomissing, with nine substantial buildings, and **Reading Outlet Center,** a multistory rehab in the heart of the city.

6 Where to Stay

From campsites and bedrooms in working Amish farms, to exquisite inns and luxury conference resorts, there's a wide variety of places to stay. The higher the price level, the more advance notice is recommended; this also goes for some farms that only have two or three rooms.

HOTELS & RESORTS

✪ **Best Western Eden Resort Inn and Conference Center.** 222 Eden Rd., Rtes. 30 and 272, Lancaster, PA 17601. ☎ **800/528-1234** or 717/569-6444. Fax 717/569-4208. 275 rms; some Club Suites include kitchenette. A/C TV TEL. $119 standard; $185 suite. Up to two children under age 18 stay free in parents' room. 25% AAA/AARP discount. AE, CB, DC, MC, V. Free parking.

The amenities of this hotel are incongruous with the region; that is, they provide comforts you almost forget about, including plush if bland rooms (request poolside) and a tropically landscaped atrium and pool. The resort has two restaurants: Arthur's overlooks the atrium courtyard; Garfield's is a more relaxed family setting. Facilities include two movie theaters, indoor and outdoor pools, tennis and basketball courts, shuffleboard, health club, and Jacuzzi.

✪ **The Inns at Doneckers.** 322 N. State St. (near junction of Rtes. 322 and 222), Ephrata, PA 17522. ☎ **717/738-9502.** Fax 717/738-9554. 41 rms in 4 houses. AC TEL. $59–$95 standard; $185 suite. Rates include full buffet breakfast. Rollaway bed $10; crib charge $8. AE, CB, DC, MC, V. Free parking.

Bill Donecker started building his customer service empire on Ephrata's north side in the early 1960s, beginning with the complex of stores featuring gifts, accessories, fashions, and collectibles. He's since added the fine Restaurant at Doneckers serving all meals (see "Where to Dine" below), the Artworks loft spaces for contemporary artists to work and market their crafts, the Farmer's Market (see above), and four inns, spicing the mixture with frequent events and festivals. Of the four, the 1777 House, built by a clockmaker member of Ephrata Cloister, is the most stately and distinguished; I also like the Gerhart House for its small size and removal from main streets. All rooms have hand stenciling, local antiques and objects, and each site has a parlor with television and library. The staff is outstandingly helpful; five rooms have Jacuzzis.

Willow Valley Family Resort. 2416 Willow St. Pike (3 miles south of Lancaster on Rte. 222), Lancaster, PA 17602. ☎ **800/444-1714** or 717/464-2711. 352 rms. A/C TV TEL. $117 standard; add $17 per person for all-you-can-eat dinner and breakfast smorgasbord. Children under 6 stay free in parents' room; $5 for children above 6. AE, DC, MC, V. Free parking.

This Mennonite-owned resort (no liquor is permitted on premises) started with a farm stand in 1943, and now links modern comforts like a nine-hole golf course, lighted tennis courts, and indoor and outdoor pools with local touches including a bakery specializing in apple dumplings, shoofly pie, and fresh-baked pies. A late 1980s renovation added a skylighted atrium. There are two smorgasbords as well as the Palm Court restaurant in the atrium. Free bus tours of Amish country are offered Monday through Saturday.

INNS

✪ **Cameron Estates Inn & Restaurant.** 1895 Donegal Springs Rd., Mount Joy, PA 17552. ☎ **717/653-1773.** Fax 717/653-9432. 18 rms (16 with private bath). A/C TV TEL. $75–110. Rates include continental breakfast. No children under 12. AE, CB, DISC, MC, V. Free parking.

Simon Cameron was secretary of war for Abraham Lincoln, and this 1805 Federal mansion was his summer house. Proprietors Abe and Betty Groff have restored the estate and its 15 acres into one of Pennsylvania's most elegant country inns, with Oriental rugs, antiques, and period reproductions. On the grounds, a trout-stocked stream flows under an old arched stone bridge. Less expensive rooms utilize dormer windows on the third floor; weekends for all rooms fill up about a month in advance. Facilities include access to tennis courts and pool nearby, as well as lawn games.

The Groffs—also proprietors of Groff's Farm Restaurant 4¹/₂miles south—know cuisine, and the *Travel/Holiday* Fine Dining Award-winning dining room specializes in basic French with absolutely fresh ingredients.

✪ **General Sutter Inn.** 14 E. Main St.-junction of Rtes. 501 and 772), Lititz, PA 17543. ☎ **717/626-2115.** 12 rms, 2 suites. A/C TV TEL. $75–$100 double; $120–$140 suite. Additional guests $3. AE, DISC, MC, V. Free parking.

The General Sutter Inn has operated continuously since 1764 at this charming intersection complete with fountain and marble-topped tables on verandas. While wings have been added, most of the rooms occupy the original building and are decorated in solid Victorian style with folk art touches. There is a coffee shop for breakfast, lunch, and a notable Sunday brunch; the dining room offers a solid continental gourmet menu.

BED & BREAKFASTS

✪ **Alden House.** 62 E. Main St. (Rte. 772), Lititz, PA 17543. ☎ **717/627-3363.** 6 rms, 3 suites. A/C TV TEL. $75–120 double and suite (all with private bath). MC, V. Free parking.

Owned and operated by the Fletchers, this 1850 brick Victorian house is at the center of the town's historic district, and was recently completely renovated, with private baths installed in all rooms. Two suites can be accessed either through the house or an outdoor spiral staircase to the second-floor porch. The morning brings a full breakfast with waffles or cinnamon-chip pancakes served in the dining room or outside overlooking the charming gardens.

Churchtown Inn Bed and Breakfast. Main St. (Rte. 23), Churchtown, PA 17555 ☎ **717/445-7794.** 8 rms. A/C. $75–$125. Children over 12 welcome. Two-night weekend minimum. AE, MC, V. Free parking.

This completely restored 1735 stone inn has evening cocktail hours in the Victorian parlor, and the opulent breakfast is served in a glassed-in porch overlooking the garden. Guest rooms all have private bath. You can arrange for dinner with nearby Mennonite or Amish families. Innkeeper Stuart Smith believes in a lot of camaraderie and good fellowship between guests. The Cornwall iron forge nearby, still functioning as a working historic site, supplied Revolutionary War troops with cannon balls and musket shot.

Smithtown Inn. 900 W. Main St., Ephrata, PA 17522. ☎ **717/733-6094.** 7 rms, 1 suite. A/C TEL. $65–$115 double; $140–$170 suite. Rates include breakfast. Children welcome; under 12, $20 additional; over 12, $35 additional. Two-night minimum on weekends and holidays. AE, MC, V. Free parking.

This inn, near Ephrata Cloister, is a pre–Revolutionary War stagecoach stop whose owners have restored each room with canopy feather beds with collector-quality quilts, working fireplaces, sitting areas, and leather upholstered chairs. Triple-pane windows for quiet, magazines, and fresh flowers are typical thoughtful touches; the grounds have lovely gardens and a gazebo. There is a restaurant on the premises. Smoking is not permitted.

✪ **Strasburg Village Inn.** 1 W. Main St. (Rte. 896), Strasburg, PA 17579. ☎ **800/ 541-1055** or 717/687-0900. 11 rms. A/C TV TEL. $80–140 double. AARP discount. Children $10 extra. AE, CB, DC, MC, V. Free parking.

You couldn't be more central than this vaguely 18th-century inn, yet it's set on 58 acres. Rooms carry the colonial motif forward with poster beds. There's a nice reading room upstairs, and a second-floor porch. A full breakfast is served in the adjacent ice-cream parlor. There is a restaurant on the premises as well as an outdoor pool.

MOTELS

Best Western Revere Motor Inn. Rte. 30, Paradise, PA 17562. ☎ **800/528-1234** or 717/ 687-7683. 29 rms. A/C TV TEL. $76–$84 double. Rates include continental breakfast. Children under 12 stay free in parents' room. AE, MC, V. Free parking.

Eight miles east of Lancaster, this simple motor inn is built off a historic 1740 post house now used as the restaurant and lounge. It's close to the outlet malls and there's an outdoor pool.

Bird-in-Hand Family Inn & Restaurant. Rte. 340, Bird-in-Hand, PA 17505. ☎ **800/ 537-2535.** 100 rms. A/C TEL TV. $83–$88 double. Packages with meals and local attractions up to $135. Children under 16 stay free in parents' room. AE, DC, MC, V. Free parking.

John and Jim Smucker are the third generation to augment their farm with the hospitality business, and this is one of the best situated motels to get you directly into the heart of Amish country. Seventy percent of their guests are repeat customers or have gotten word-of-mouth recommendations. I prefer the back building, with rooms off an indoor hallway, to the front building's motel setup. The simple utilitarian rooms were recently renovated. The restaurant operation is a popular tour stop. The hotel restaurant serves all meals buffet style and is a popular tour stop. Grandma Smucker's Bakery offers wet-bottom shoofly pie and apple dumplings. Facilities include indoor and outdoor pools, two lighted tennis courts, game room, playground, and free two-hour bus tour of country roads.

Harvest Drive Family Motel & Restaurant. Box 498, Intercourse, PA 17534. ☎ **800/ 233-0176** or 717/768-7186. 50 rms. A/C TEL TV. $69–$79 double. Two-night minimum on holiday weekends. $5 for children over 14 in parents' room. AE, MC, V. A/C TEL TV. Free Parking. Take Clearview Rd. south off Route 340 just west of Intercourse, and bear right to 3370 Harvest Drive.

Good farmland was converted to create this family-owned motel, but it's surrounded by corn and alfalfa fields on a quiet back road next to the family farm. The motel building has rooms with one to three double beds and pleasant but utilitarian decor. The simple restaurant features Dutch home cooking all day, and there's a gift shop in the barn.

Mill Stream Motor Lodge. Rte. 896 (between Rtes. 30 and 340), Smoketown, PA 17576. ☎ **800/444-1714** or 717/299-0931. 52 rms. A/C TEL TV. $78–$88 double. Two-night minimum on weekends. Children under 6 stay free in parents' room; additional $5 for ages 6–11. Package including breakfast adds $3 per person. AE, MC, V. Free parking.

Of the dozens of motor lodges in the vicinity, this more modest sister of Willow Valley Resort is one of the most popular, with three floors of simple rooms. The rear rooms are away from the road and overlook a stream. It's owned by Mennonites, and most rooms are nonsmoking. The restaurant serves breakfast and lunch.

FARM VACATION BED & BREAKFASTS

What better way to get the flavor of Amish country than by staying with a farm family? The Pennsylvania Dutch Country Convention & Visitors Bureau (☎ **800/ PA DUTCH**) has a complete listing of about 40 working farms that take guests. Reservations are recommended since most offer only three to five rooms; expect simple lodgings, hall baths, and filling breakfasts, all at less than motel rates. Dinners with the family are sometimes offered at additional charge. You'll be able to chat with the women in the family (the men start and end their days with the sun) and get suggestions on local routes, walks, and crafts producers. One tip: If you have a sensitive nose, stay away from dairy and poultry farms!

Belmont View Bed & Breakfast. 5204 Newport Rd. (Rte. 772, 0.8 miles north of Rte. 30 west of Gap), Gap, PA 17527. ☎ **717/442-5269.** 2 rms. A/C. $59–$69 double; $9 for additional person 8 and up.

Although there are only two rooms, this is an unusually pretty situation, both for the 200-year-old ambience and for the spectacular views of this 117-acre dairy farm and its neighbors. Both rooms have antique beds and modern baths, refrigerator, and microwave, and there's a common living room. No smoking or alcoholic beverages are allowed.

Green Acres Farm. 1382 Pinkerton Rd., Mount Joy, PA 17552. Pinkerton is south of Rte. 772 just west of Mt. Joy town center, and winds past Groff's Farm Restaurant and a creek before the farm. ☎ **717/653-4028.** Fax 717/653-2840. 7 rms. A/C. $60 standard; $6 per additional child. Summer reservations are recommended. MC, V.

Wayne and Yvonne Miller can sleep 26 people in this 150-year farmhouse, with private baths in all rooms. It's a corn and soybean farm but also offers pony cart rides, farm pets, a play house, and swings and trampoline for kids. All rooms have one double or queen-sized bed plus bunk beds. There's no smoking, but alcohol is permitted if you bring your own.

Spahr's Century Farm. 192 Green Acre Rd., Lititz, PA 17543. ☎ **717/627-2185.** 3 rms. A/C. $50–$60 double. MC, V. Green Acre Road is south of Rte. 772, just west of Lititz town center.

This peaceful 70-acre farm has been in Bob and Naomi Spahr's family since 1855, and the countryside is unspoiled. It's closed from November 1 through April 1.

Rayba Acres Farm. 183 Black Horse Rd., Paradise, PA 17562. From Paradise center, south from Rte. 30 onto Black Horse, follow 2 miles. ☎ **717/687-6729.** 6 rms. A/C TEL. $38–$50 double. MC, V.

Ray and Reba Black offer clean, quiet rooms on a working fifth-generation dairy farm; you're welcome to try milking yourself. Rooms are in a modernized 1863 farmhouse with a private entrance, or with private bath and TV in two motel-like units. There's complimentary coffee in your room, but no smoking.

7 Where to Dine

While Ben Franklin might be staggered at the size of a modern Pennsylvania Dutch meal or smorgasbord, he'd recognize everything on it—the baked goods, meat and poultry, and fruits and vegetables have been offered here since Colonial times. The Amish way of life calls for substantial, wholesome, long-cooking dishes, rich in butter and cream. Don't look for crunchy vegetables; if they're not creamed, they're marinated or thoroughly boiled. Even the main courses tend to the sweet, and baked goods are renowned. Shoofly pie, a concoction of molasses and sweet dough (hence its attraction to flies), is probably the most famous. Decor tends to take a back seat to quantity and cost.

Included here are the most representative family-style and smorgasbord dining spots, as well as restaurants that use but update local ingredients and traditions. Family-style means that you'll be part of a group of 10 or 12, ushered to long tables and brought heaping platters of food, course after course. At a smorgasbord, you construct your own plate at central food stations, with unlimited refills. Prices are fixed per person at both.

And when looking for a meal, don't neglect the signs along the road, or "Community Event" listings in the Thursday "Weekend" section of the *Lancaster New Era*, for church or firehouse pancake breakfasts, corn roasts, or barbecue or game suppers. These generally charge a minimal amount for all the food you can eat and all the iced tea or soda you can drink; and they're great chances to meet the locals. You can also catch annual festivals, such as the rhubarb fair in Intercourse, and the Sertoma Club's enormous chicken barbecues at Long's Park in Lancaster, both in May. The Dutch Food and Folk Fair is held in Bird-in-Hand each June.

FAMILY-STYLE/SMORGASBORD

⑤ Good 'N' Plenty Restaurant. Rte. 896 between Rtes. 30 and 340, Smoketown. ☎ **717/394-7111.** Reservations not accepted. Adults $14.50, children $6.50 for ages 4–10, free for children under 4; tax included. MC, V. Mon–Sat 11:30am–8pm. PENNSYLVANIA DUTCH.

They've added the 500-seat Dutch Room to the original 110-seat farmhouse here. The location is very convenient, tables seat 10 to 12, and expect waits at peak dining hours. You can purchase baked goods and other gift items.

⑤ Miller's Smorgasbord/Country Fare Restaurant. Rte. 30 at Ronks Rd., 5 miles east of Lancaster. ☎ **800/669-3568** or 717/687-6621. Reservations accepted. Dinner $18.75 adults, $5.95 for children 3–8, $8.95 for children 9–12; breakfast $8.95 adults, $4.95 for children 3–12; tax included. AE, DC, MC, V. Peak summer hours Sun–Fri 8am–8pm, Sat 8am–9pm; weekend breakfast Nov–April. SMORGASBORD.

In 1929, Anna Miller prepared chicken and waffles for truckers while Enos Miller repaired their vehicles. For millions since then, Miller's has been the definitive Pennsylvania Dutch smorgasbord. Homemade chicken corn soup, slow-roasted carved beef, turkey, and ham, chicken pot pies, and a rich apple pie are just the tip of the iceberg. The breakfast smorgasbord offers made-to-order eggs and omelets, along with local sausage and pastries. The health-conscious diner finds plenty of choices, also.

Plain & Fancy Farm & Dining Room. Rte. 340, 7 miles east of Lancaster, Bird-in-Hand, PA. ☎ **717/768-8281.** Reservations recommended. Adults $14.79, $5.95 for children 4–11; tax included. AE, CB, DC, MC, V. Mon–Sat 11:30am–8pm, Sun noon–7pm in summer. PENNSYLVANIA DUTCH.

This 40-year-old family-style restaurant started as a barn, and the posts still support the front dining room; a back addition gives it a capacity of 260. The complex now includes a village of craft shops and a bakery. Smoking is not permitted.

⑤ Shady Maple. Rte. 23, East Earl, PA (1 mile east of Blue Ball, at intersection with Rte. 897). ☎ **800/238-7365** or 717/354-8222. Reservations not accepted. Dinner $11.50–$13.50; breakfast $7.95. Children 4–10 half-price; 10% discount for seniors. AE, MC, V. Mon–Sat 5am–8pm. SMORGASBORD.

This is somewhat north of many attractions, but does an enormous business, with waits of up to 30 minutes on Saturday for one of the 600 seats. Tourist buses have their own entrance and seating. It features a mind-boggling 140-foot-long buffet of

Pennsylvania Dutch cooking—46 salads, 14 vegetables, 8 meats, 8 breads, 27 desserts, plus a make-your-own-sundae station. Breakfast includes everything you've ever contemplated at that hour. There's a touristy gift shop downstairs. The cheapest days are Monday, Wednesday, and Friday; the dinner price of $11.29 includes tax, tip, and all nonalcoholic beverages. Smoking is not permitted.

MORE DINING CHOICES

Groff's Farm Restaurant. 650 Pinkerton Rd., Mount Joy, PA. ☎ **717/653-2048.** Reservations recommended. Main courses $14–$17; family-style all-inclusive $15–$24.50. AE, CB, DC, MC, V. Tues–Sat 11:30am–1:30pm; dinner seatings Tues–Fri 5pm and 7pm, Sat 5pm and 8pm. AMERICAN/PENNSYLVANIA DUTCH.

At Groff's, the Pennsylvania Dutch cuisine's emphasis on fresh ingredients and ribsticking heartiness has received an injection of the 20th century's lighter touch. Betty Groff—who still greets every guest—was born Mennonite, and she and Abe began cooking reinterpreted meals as a hobby for friends in their 1756 farmhouse overlooking meadows and ponds. Famed food writer James Beard came, tasted, and raved about the results, and the next 20 years have seen expansion of the physical plant and the menu. The appetizer plate still features a famous cracker pudding, celery relish, and a sweet such as chocolate cake. Seafood has been added in the last decade, as have à la carte dishes; most first-timers still prefer the family-style entrée of beef or chicken Stoltzfus, served creamed over little buttered pastry diamonds. All drinks are extremely reasonable, and they push local porters and lagers.

The Restaurant at Doneckers. 333 N. State St., Ephrata. ☎ **717/738-9501.** Reservations recommended. Main courses $17–$27. AE, CB, DC, MC, V. Daily 11am–10pm, Sun brunch 11:30am–3pm. CONTINENTAL.

This restaurant is one of the area's closest to a Center City approach to cuisine, mixing classic French cuisine such as chateaubriand and veal Oscar with American techniques of infused oils, lighter ingredients, and healthier cooking techniques. It's still pure pleasure if you want to enjoy creamy sauces, though. Sorbet is served to cleanse the palate, and breads and desserts are baked on the premises daily. The wine list is extensive.

Stoudt's Black Angus and Brew Pub. Rte. 272, 1 mile north of Exit 21 from I-76, Adamstown, PA. ☎ **717/484-4385.** Reservations recommended. Main courses $12–$24; brew pub $5–$10. AE, CB, DC, MC, V. Mon–Fri 4–11pm, Sat 1–11pm, Sun 11:30am–9pm. STEAKHOUSE/BREW PUB.

Stoudt's Golden Lager, Pilsner, and other German-style varieties are brewed here and make a perfect conclusion to lugging around your finds from the famed adjacent Sunday antique market. The family has added both a steakhouse specializing in aged prime beef, clam and oyster bar, and an agreeable pub with Pennsylvania Dutch ham and chicken dishes augmented by burgers, wursts, and soups and salads. The restaurant has a 1928 Packard in the lobby, and the pub offers country dancing Friday and Saturday.

Index

ACCOMMODATIONS

RESTAURANTS

FROMMER'S COMPLETE TRAVEL GUIDES
(Comprehensive guides to destinations around the world, with selections in all price ranges—from deluxe to budget)

FROMMER'S FRUGAL TRAVELER'S GUIDES
*(The grown-up guides to budget travel, offering dream vacations
at down-to-earth prices)*

Australia from $45 a Day

Berlin from $50 a Day

California from $60 a Day

Caribbean from $60 a Day

Costa Rica & Belize from $35 a Day

Eastern Europe from $30 a Day

England from $50 a Day

Europe from $50 a Day

Florida from $50 a Day

Greece from $45 a Day

Hawaii from $60 a Day

India from $40 a Day

Ireland from $45 a Day

Italy from $50 a Day

Israel from $45 a Day

London from $60 a Day

Mexico from $35 a Day

New York from $70 a Day

New Zealand from $45 a Day

Paris from $65 a Day

Washington, D.C. from $50 a Day

FROMMER'S PORTABLE GUIDES
(Pocket-size guides for travelers who want everything in a nutshell)

Charleston & Savannah

Las Vegas

New Orleans

San Francisco

FROMMER'S IRREVERENT GUIDES
(Wickedly honest guides for sophisticated travelers)

Amsterdam

Chicago

London

Manhattan

Miami

New Orleans

Paris

San Francisco

Santa Fe

U.S. Virgin Islands

Walt Disney World

Washington, D.C.

FROMMER'S AMERICA ON WHEELS
*(Everything you need for a successful road trip, including full-color
road maps and ratings for every hotel)*

California & Nevada

Florida

Mid-Atlantic

Midwest & the Great Lakes

New England & New York

Northwest & Great Plains

South Central &Texas

Southeast

Southwest

FROMMER'S BY NIGHT GUIDES
(The series for those who know that life begins after dark)

Amsterdam

Chicago

Las Vegas

London

Los Angeles

Miami

New Orleans

New York

Paris

San Francisco

WHEREVER YOU TRAVEL, *H*ELP IS NEVER FAR AWAY.

From planning your trip to providing travel assistance along the way, American Express® Travel Service Offices are always there to help.

Philadelphia

American Express Travel Service
2 Penn Center Plaza
S.E. corner 16th & JFK
Philadelphia
215/587-2300

Travel

http://www.americanexpress.com/travel

American Express Travel Service Offices are found in central locations throughout Pennsylvania. For the location nearest you please call 1-800-AXP-3429.